Diffusion of Innovations
in English Language Teaching

Recent Titles in
Contributions to the Study of Education

Diffusion of Innovations in English Language Teaching

The ELEC Effort in Japan, 1956–1968

Lynn Earl Henrichsen

Contributions to the Study of Education, Number 33

Greenwood Press
New York • Westport, Connecticut • London

Library of Congress Cataloging-in-Publication Data

Henrichsen, Lynn Earl.
   Diffusion of innovations in English language teaching: the ELEC
effort in Japan, 1956-1968 / Lynn Earl Henrichsen.
     p.   cm. — (Contributions to the study of education, ISSN
0196-707X ; no. 33)
   Bibliography: p.
   Includes index.
   ISBN 0-313-26617-4 (lib. bdg. : alk. paper)
   1. English language—Study and teaching—Japan. 2. Diffusion of
innovations—Japan. I. Title. II. Series.
PE1068.J3H4 1989
428´.007´052—dc20   89-11906

British Library Cataloguing in Publication Data is available.

Library of Congress Catalog Card Number: 89-11906
ISBN: 0-313-26617-4
ISSN: 0196-707X

First published in 1989

Greenwood Press, Inc.
88 Post Road West, Westport, Connecticut 06881

Printed in the United States of America

The paper used in this book complies with the
Permanent Paper Standard issued by the National
Information Standards Organization (Z39.48-1984).

10 9 8 7 6 5 4 3 2 1

Copyright Acknowledgment

The author and publisher are grateful to the following for granting
the use of their material:

Reprinted with permission of The Free Press, a Division of Macmillan,
Inc. from *Communication of Innovations: A Cross-Cultural Approach*,
Second Edition, by Everett M. Rogers with F. Floyd Shoemaker.
Copyright © 1971 by The Free Press.

Every reasonable effort has been made to trace the owners of copyright
materials in this book, but in some instances this has proven impossible. The
publisher will be glad to receive information leading to more complete
acknowledgments in subsequent printings of the book and in the meantime
extend their apologies for any omissions.

To Terumi

who made it all possible

Contents

Preface

Although this book deals with events that took place years ago, it is more than a historical study. And even though it investigates an effort to change English language teaching (ELT) in Japan, it is not an attempt to prescribe a solution for Japan's ELT "problem." Rather, through an investigation and description of the campaign conducted by the Rockefeller-funded English Language Exploratory Committee (ELEC) to revolutionize ELT practices in Japan, it addresses the much larger question and more universally applicable issue of how internationally oriented reformers of educational systems and practices can go about creating change and dealing with resistances to it.

The thesis on which the study rests is that innovation alone is seldom sufficient to bring about change. Nor is merely communicating the innovation to the target audience adequate. Successfully creating change across cultural boundaries requires both a careful analysis of the target setting, which takes into account the potential barriers to change, and an appropriate implementation strategy to overcome them.

To analyze ELEC's reform campaign, this study develops and employs a hybrid diffusion-of-innovations model that represents both the diffusion/implementation process and the multitude of factors that affect it. This model and the example of the ELEC effort can provide planners of other reform campaigns with an understanding of what these factors are, how they are interrelated, and how to deal with them.

The book is divided into six chapters. The first introduces the study and makes a case for studying the diffusion and implementation of innovations. Chapter two tells the story of the ELEC effort, providing background information and a chronological overview of important events. A chronological account, however, does not lead to the conclusions that can make the ELEC story truly useful. For that, an analysis of the ELEC experience is necessary, and chapter three presents the model that is used as the framework for subsequent chapters that analyze the ELEC effort in Japan. Inasmuch as the first major element in the model is antecedents, chapter four discusses the historical development of various characteristics of the Japanese ELT system. It also illustrates how socio-cultural forces have influenced language teaching in Japan throughout history. Chapter five analyzes the ELEC effort using the process portion of the model. The characteristics of the Oral Approach itself, the ELEC resource system, and the Japanese ELT user system, as well as a number of critical inter-elemental factors are all investigated. The final chapter discusses the consequences of the ELEC effort and draws some general principles from the particulars of this historical case study. It concludes by making recommendations, both for future researchers and for would-be reformers.

Producing a work of this nature inevitably entails incurring enormous debts of gratitude. Throughout the process of researching and writing, I was most fortunate to have the unwavering support of my wife, Terumi, and our children, Cristina, Daniel, Linda, and James. For their sacrifices, support, and patience I will be ever grateful. As I worked on this project, I also enjoyed the benefits of periodic funding and released time for which I am thankful to the administration of Brigham Young University—Hawaii. The Rockefeller Archive Center graciously allowed access to hundreds of original documents, later granting permission to use them in this book, and the highly professional and cooperative staff of the Center made the task of gathering information about John D. Rockefeller 3rd's involvement with ELEC both efficient and pleasant. In like manner, Peter H. Fries willingly provided documents relating to Charles C. Fries' role in the ELEC effort. Without their cooperation the story of ELEC could never have been accurately told. I was also favored with expert assistance from a number of advisors and colleagues, who provided guidance and moral support in the initial stages of the research and/or evaluated versions of the manuscript as the work proceeded. For that help, my thanks go to Edward R. Beauchamp, Jack C. Richards, Richard R. Day, Victor N. Kobayashi, Melvin Ezer, Ted Plaister, Jeris E. Strain, Peter H. Fries, and Robert T. Henderson. In addition, numerous people, both in the United States and Japan, generously volunteered their time and their memories as they were interviewed: Bernard Choseed (Lado International College), Gerald Dykstra (University of Hawaii), Agnes Fries (La Jolla, California), Shigeo Imamura (Himeji Dokkyo University), Hiroyoshi Hatori (Tokyo Gakugei University), Toshikazu Horiguchi (Tokyo Gakugei University), Naomi Kakita (Hiroshima University), Ken Kanatani (Tokyo Gakugei University), Osamu Kimpara (The English Language Education Council), Everett Kleinjans (Hawaii Pacific College), Ikuo Koike (Keio University), Midori Kusube (Tokyo Gakugei University), Robert Lado (Lado International Institute), Yoichi Maeda (The International House of Japan), Shigeharu Matsumoto (The International House of Japan), Mikio Matsumura (Hiroshima University), Tetsuya Noda (Tokyo Gakugei University), William Norris (Georgetown University), Linju Ogasawara (Japanese Ministry of Education), Akira Ota (Sophia University), Mamoru Shimizu (The English Language Education Council), Peter Strevens (The Bell Educational Trust), Genji Takahashi (Obirin University), and Tamotsu Yambe (Toyoko Gakuen Women's Junior College). I would be seriously lacking in gratitude if I did not express my appreciation to all these people and acknowledge their contribution to this work.

Finally, a few words of explanation regarding this book's use of Japanese names, romanization, and professional terminology are necessary.

Since the normal Japanese pattern is to place the family name first, and the English pattern is to place it last, a problem arises when Japanese names are used in English. In this book the Western pattern has been followed. The only exceptions are in direct quotations, where the order used by the original author has been preserved.

When Japanese words are written in roman letters, lengthened vowels are sometimes indicated with a macron, e.g., shōgun, Kyōto, Kyūshū, Dōshisha. Although the difference in vowel length can reflect a significant difference in meaning, such diacritics have not been used in this book for the sake of simplicity and consistency and to preserve the form used in most of the original sources.

Among professionals who work with non-native learners of English, a crucial distinction is often made between English as a *second* language (ESL) and English as a *foreign* language (EFL). When this distinction is not important or desired, however, the most commonly used cover term (in the United States and areas within its sphere of influence) for both ESL and EFL is *English to speakers of other languages* (ESOL). In the United Kingdom (and wherever the influence of the British Council is felt), however, the preferred cover term is *English language teaching* (ELT). In this book, for the sake of stylistic variation and to preserve authors' original words in quotations, all of these terms are used. Starting with the title, however, the term *English language teaching* is used most often. This preference for ELT is due to its worldwide usage and its stylistic superiority, and not to any intention to draw a distinction between it and ESOL, EFL, or ESL.

Acronyms

ACTT	Advisory Committee on the Training of Teachers of Foreign Languages
ADC	Agricultural Development Council
ASTP	Army Specialized Training Program
CCEJ	Committee for Cooperation on English in Japan
CECA	Council on Cultural and Economic Affairs
CI&E	Civil Information and Education
ELEC	English Language Education Council (1963-present)
ELEC	English Language Exploratory Committee (1956-1963)
ELI	English Language Institute
ELT	English Language Teaching
ERIC	Educational Resources Information Center
GARIOA	Government Aid and Relief in Occupied Areas
ICU	International Christian University
IRET	Institute for Research in English Teaching
JACET	Japan Association of College English Teachers
JALT	Japan Association of Language Teachers
JDR 3rd	John D. Rockefeller 3rd
LSA	Linguistic Society of America
NDEA	National Defense Education Act
RD&D	Research, Development, and Diffusion
SCAP	Supreme Commander Allied Powers
SI	Social Interaction
(T)EFL	(Teaching) English as a Foreign Language
(T)ESL	(Teaching) English as a Second language
(T)ESOL	(Teaching/Teachers of) English to Speakers of Other Languages
UNESCO	United Nations Educational, Scientific, and Cultural Organization
USEC	United States Educational Commission (in Japan)

1
Introduction

The assumption is that a much greater development would be found...in the adoption of [an] almost revolutionized system of teaching of English.[1]

My understanding is that the necessary improvement in the [English] teaching system would require almost revolutionary change.[2]

Revolution is a strong word, especially in tradition-bound Japan, particularly at a time when that country had only recently been released from the yoke of the Allied Occupation. Yet, as the lines above reveal, the planners of the first conference of the English Language Exploratory Committee (ELEC) in 1956 spoke of revolutionizing the Japanese English-language-teaching (ELT) system.

Formed in the early 1950s under the impetus of John D. Rockefeller 3rd, ELEC energetically promoted Charles C. Fries' Oral Approach throughout Japan for over a decade. In this effort to reform the teaching of English in Japan, ELEC experts provided training to thousands of Japanese teachers of English and produced and published a special set of Oral Approach textbooks. At ELEC's invitation, between 1956 and 1959, Professor Fries himself made annual visits to Japan, working with the ELEC staff, writing materials, and traveling the length and breadth of the nation on lecture tours.

As it pursued its revolutionary goals, ELEC encountered considerable resistance. It eventually achieved some successes, but after more than ten years of heavy expense and intense effort even Rockefeller's staff recognized that ELEC had "failed to achieve its main objective....ELEC was not able to change the grand strategy of English-language teaching in Japan or to bring overall improvement in teaching methods."[3]

INTENDED OUTCOMES OF THIS STUDY

This investigation and analysis of the English Language Exploratory Committee's attempt to change the methods and materials used for teaching

English in Japan is of more than historical interest. While it brings to light much information about the experiences of John D. Rockefeller 3rd, Charles C. Fries, and their ELEC colleagues in Japan, that is not its major purpose. Neither is its object to prescribe a solution for Japan's ELT "problem." Rather, through an investigation and description of ELEC's campaign to change English-teaching practices in Japan, this book addresses the much larger question of how internationally oriented reformers of educational systems and practices can create change and deal with resistance to their reforms.

The experiences of the ELEC "revolutionaries" were by no means unique. Numerous would-be reformers of the Japanese system for teaching English could tell a similar tale of woe. In fact, most of the conditions that hindered the ELEC campaign are still very prevalent in Japan.[4] Moreover, English-language-teaching reformers in that country have much in common with the experiences of crusading educational reformers—in ELT and other fields—throughout the world.

Of course, some of the elements of the system within which ELEC operated were unique to post-Occupation Japan and therefore restrict the generalizability of this study's findings. Nevertheless, "many of the problems encountered [in Japan] are also found in one form or another almost everywhere that languages are taught."[5] Thus, while caution must be exercised to avoid overgeneralization, it would be far from correct to conclude that generalization from this case to others is invalid. General principles can be drawn from the ELEC case that can be of immense value to those who attempt to create change, not just in ELT and not just in Japan but in other educational endeavors and settings also.

With a greater awareness and more accurate perception of the innovation-implementation process and the constraints within which reformers operate, the leaders of reform campaigns that cross cultural boundaries can plan accordingly and avoid much wasted time, money, and effort.

FUNDAMENTAL CONSIDERATIONS

At the outset, it is best to note a pair of fundamental considerations which will affect points made throughout the remainder of this book.

Types of Change

All change is not of the same type, and different types of change involve different elements and processes. Consequently, the type of change that is attempted in a particular case is an important factor which must be considered when analyzing that case, as well as when any attempt is made to generalize the results of such an analysis.

In this regard, Rogers and Shoemaker provide a useful typology of social change. Their categorization system is based on two factors: the source of the change and the recognition of the need for change (see figure 1).

Figure 1
Paradigm of Types of Social Change

ORIGIN OF THE NEW IDEA

RECOGNITION OF THE NEED FOR CHANGE	INTERNAL to the social system	EXTERNAL to the social system
INTERNAL: Recognition is by members of the social system	**I. Immanent change**	**II. Selective contact change**
EXTERNAL: Recognition may be by change agents outside the social system	**III. Induced immanent change**	**IV. Directed contact change**

Source: Rogers and Shoemaker, 8. (Used by permission.)

Immanent change is perhaps the simplest type, since both source and recognition are internal to the same social system. It occurs when, with little or no outside influence, members of the system develop an innovation that is then disseminated throughout the system. The professional literature on curriculum development deals almost exclusively with this type of change, in which changes are formulated and implemented within the same system.

Induced immanent change is somewhat more complicated but much less common. It takes place when a problem within a social system is noted by outsiders, but the solution is developed by members of the system.

On the other hand, it is not uncommon for change to originate with and even be promoted by outside forces. *Selective contact change* happens when members of a society encounter new ideas or products from a foreign source and then select and adopt them in order to satisfy their needs. In contrast, *directed contact change* occurs when agents from outside a social system purposefully introduce an innovation from an external source in order to achieve goals that they (not the intended users of the innovation) have set.[6]

This final type of change, in which outsiders, equipped with their foreign ideas, make a "conscious, deliberate, and collaborative effort to improve the operations of a human system,"[7] merits serious study for two important reasons. First, directed change campaigns that reach across socio-cultural boundaries are not uncommon in our rapidly shrinking and increasingly interconnected world. Educational practices that seem to work in one setting are frequently transplanted to a foreign context in the hope that they will produce favorable results there also. Especially in modern-day English language teaching, with its worldwide scope, teachers and ideas travel quickly from one country to another. Furthermore, directed contact change that crosses cultural boundaries is the most challenging type to bring about. In a foreign socio-cultural matrix, a variety of factors that are often ignored in immanent change campaigns limited to domestic settings become critical, and the process of implementing an innovation becomes much more complex.

The Insufficiency of Innovation Alone

The belief that improvements naturally catch on and spread is widely held. Traditional faith in the inevitability of progress is epitomized by the American proverb: "Build a better mousetrap, and the world will beat a path to your door."[8]

In contrast, the experiences of many innovators and would-be reformers demonstrate that although change in a desired direction is possible it seldom happens by itself. Innovation is seldom sufficient on its own. Neither is merely communicating the news of an innovation to the appropriate audience enough to bring about change.

In education as well as many other fields, carrying out a revolution involves much more than coming up with a new idea—even if it does seem to be "better." As Miles explains, "Educational innovations are almost never installed on their merits. Characteristics of the local system, of the innovating person or group, and of other relevant groups often outweigh the impact of what the innovation *is*" [italics in original].[9]

THE NEED FOR A
DIFFUSION-OF-INNOVATIONS PERSPECTIVE

Diffusion-of-innovations theories and models draw upon a variety of academic disciplines, such as sociology, psychology, and organizational behavior. Diffusion-of-innovations studies also vary widely in the fields they deal with—business administration, education, agriculture, and public health, to name only a few. Wherever new ideas can benefit practitioners, a diffusion-of-innovations approach can be valuable. Unfortunately, it is seldom employed.

The Need in Formal Education

"Educational reform and the influence of foreign educational models are common, at least to some degree, in all societies."[10] In education today, attempts at reform are certainly widespread, but few of these attempts are based on an adequate foundation of knowledge about how new practices can best be diffused and implemented. "Around the world,...the starting gun has sounded in a race to overhaul education systems, but no one knows quite how to run it."[11] This concern is not merely transient, of course, but has a long history.

History also shows that in spite of large and expensive campaigns, disappointingly few proposed "improvements" catch on. Goodman notes that "throughout the history of education, text books have lagged behind the best knowledge in the fields they represent." He goes on to claim that in reading instruction today that gap is "actually widening."[12] Other researchers concur: "The decision by a school or district to adopt a new educational program by no means guarantees successful implementation, as is amply demonstrated by the failure of many well-intentioned and potentially valuable efforts."[13] Regarding school reforms, Mann estimates that "innovations or revisions in programs have had only about a 20 percent success rate."[14]

Unfortunately, "few educational researchers concern themselves with systematic study of widely accepted diffusion/utilization generalizations within educational settings."[15] Nevertheless, until questions of this sort are addressed and answered, educators are bound to endure consequences that "amount to repeating the mistakes of the past, to inventing the same wheel repeatedly, and to tolerating a myriad of usually well intentioned charlatans who profess, but in fact do not command, know-how essential either to resolve communication problems or to modify current practices meaningfully."[16]   For this reason, Collado exclaimed, "Methods of determining what is useful and accelerating the adoption of proven ideas may well be the greatest need of all in our educational system."[17]

The Need in Foreign Language Teaching

Foreign language teaching is an educational specialty with some distinctive characteristics. Its objective is the building of communication skills that require the rapid and accurate use of a complex set of cognitive and motor skills. All these complexities must be managed by language users almost subconsciously, since to truly communicate they must pay more attention to the message than the medium. For this reason, foreign language teaching employs methods quite different from those used to teach most other school subjects. In addition, successful language learning depends heavily on a number of social and psychological factors that are not of such great concern in most content areas.

In at least one respect, however, foreign language teaching is no different from other branches of education. Attempts to get teachers to change from traditional methods and materials and employ new approaches are common. In fact, foreign language teachers may experience more than the usual share of such attempts. Dostert et al. state: "It is an important and widely recognized characteristic of our culture to be subject to sudden shifts of interest and emphasis. This is certainly true in the realm of education generally. It is particularly true today in our field of foreign language teaching."[18] Of course, wherever there are new ideas, there are corresponding efforts to promote them. For example, the foreword to a recently published book that deals with a variety of innovative methods for foreign language teaching states, "A principal aim of the book is to accelerate change in language teaching."[19]   Nevertheless, the book fails to deal with any of the challenges of diffusing and implementing innovations. Lamentably, it is by no means unusual in this regard.   In contrast to the many new ideas that receive much attention in the professional literature of foreign language teaching, discussions of how to bring about change are virtually nonexistent.

Rather, in foreign-language-teaching circles, the efforts of materials developers and the controversies among methodologists, as well as the supporting research of linguists and psychologists, have typically been aimed at answering the question, "What is better?"   The operating assumption seems to have been "If we can just develop a better science of linguistics, or get a better understanding of how people learn languages, the ideal teaching methods and materials will naturally follow and then be adopted by classroom teachers."

While linguistics, psychology, and the other concerns relative to coming up with a better product are undoubtedly important—even necessary—they are far from sufficient if a language-teaching innovation is to spread and become widely used.   A wide gap exists between what researchers have discovered about successful language learning and actual language-teaching practices.[20]   A sound program is only the beginning and, as Tajima notes, its successful use and spread are often highly dependent on "external conditions."[21]   Likewise, Kelly, in his historical overview of language teaching, points out that "every age...has its rebels whose teaching techniques, though scientifically justifiable, failed to gain acceptance because they did not fit the atmosphere of the time."   He pities "the innovator who takes his stand on scientific proof and is unaware of the social forces which isolate him."[22]

The Need in English Language Teaching

Around the world today the most commonly taught foreign language is English.   In virtually every country, English language teaching is a major educational endeavor.   Estimates of the number of learners and users of English as a second language vary considerably due to the almost universal scope of the undertaking and to difficulties in determining what qualifies one to count as a "learner of English."   After quoting figures ranging from 400 million to 2 billion, Crystal calculates 1 billion to be a "conservative" total.[23]

As in the field of foreign language teaching generally, attempts at reform and change are common in English language teaching. "Methodological innovators abound and they all seem to desire 'instant implementation on a world-wide basis.'"[24]

Nevertheless, among these would-be reformers there has been (and continues to be) a discouraging lack of awareness of diffusion-of-innovation factors and processes.   Innovators commonly promote change in ELT practices around the globe in virtual ignorance of the contexts into which they would introduce change and of the process of change and the factors it involves. Generally speaking, the promoters of new ideas for teaching English as a foreign language seem to rely on the supposed merit of the innovation itself and seldom employ an adequate implementation strategy.

The idea that the successful spread of a method depends heavily on how its promoters deal with a variety of social, cultural, and political factors is rarely considered in ELT circles. In a pioneering article on this subject, Richards points out that "the reasons for the rise and fall of methods are often independent of either the theories behind those methods or their effectiveness in practice."[25] He goes on to explain that an accurate understanding of the rise and fall of methods depends on an awareness of the nature and power of various social, political, and economic forces. Nevertheless, in the ELT profession, there is such a lack of awareness regarding these implementation factors that he labels them the "secret life of methods."

The Need in Japanese English Language Teaching

Because the worldwide scope of English language teaching is so great, this study focuses on ELT reform in only one country—Japan. ELT reform in Japan is a subject of considerable interest and importance as well as promise for many reasons.

One is the large size of Japan's ELT program. The teaching of English as a foreign language is a major educational enterprise in Japan. Throughout the country a tremendous amount of time, money, and energy are devoted to the teaching and studying of English. Children begin working on English in the first year of junior high school, and they continue to study the language for at least the next six years. Although the present-day ELT effort in the People's Republic of China probably surpasses Japan's (at least in number of students), for many years English teaching in Japan ranked "as the largest, single modern foreign language program in the world."[26] In 1971 Brosnahan reported, "The current efforts being made [in Japan] to teach English are the greatest dedicated to a single foreign language by any nation on earth."[27] The number of people involved in this undertaking is truly impressive.

> In 1976, 4,700,000 students in junior high schools, 4,400,000 in senior high schools, 50,000 in technical colleges, 380,000 in junior colleges and 1,840,000 in universities were studying English. To accommodate this large number of students, 58,000 high school teachers and 6,000 university and college professors have been trained and are currently teaching. By now, approximately one eleventh of the Japanese population is engaged in the study of English.[28]

In an enterprise of this magnitude, "success and failure loom large in importance."[29] Unfortunately, the result of the tremendous Japanese investment in English teaching is often disappointing. Harasawa charges, "Of all the countries in the world where English has been taught on a nationwide scale, Japan seems to me about the least successful....The time and energy our students devote to English is mostly wasted....On balance our English teaching...has become a disastrous failure."[30] Reischauer agrees, "The amount of effort put into English language teaching and learning probably produces smaller results in Japan than anywhere else."[31]

As Brosnahan puts it, "For everyone to spend 3 years—and most people 6 years, and many people 10 years—in pursuit of a language and then remain unable to function effectively in it is obviously a situation demanding change."[32] In 1955, when the ELEC movement was just getting under way, Reischauer expressed a similar sentiment. Calling for reform, he labeled the teaching of English in Japan as "the most important problem in all modern Japanese education."[33]

In the course of Japan's history, outsiders have made several attempts to reform language-teaching practices. For instance, thirty years before the ELEC effort, Harold E. Palmer headed up another prominent reform campaign. Nevertheless, few of these reformers have understood the complexities of cross-cultural diffusion and implementation. Not surprisingly, few of their reform movements have met with the success they desired.

POTENTIAL BENEFITS

Understanding the process of creating change and the factors that determine the success of reforms can be of benefit in at least three ways:

• Increasing the likelihood of success in diffusion and utilization campaigns
• Helping to close the gap between knowledge and practice
• Improving educators' understanding of the structures with which they deal

Increased Likelihood of Success in Reform Efforts

The rate of success in educational reform efforts is generally low. After reviewing studies by Berman and McLaughlin; Pincus; House; Leithwood et al.; Smith and Keith; Gross et al.; and Goodlad and Klein, Leithwood concludes, "Substantial evidence has demonstrated that while schools have adopted many curricular innovations in the past two decades, the degree of their actual use in classrooms has been very limited."[34] In discussing "the generally melancholy picture of how little of the reform agenda of the recent past has been achieved," Mann notes, "Most educators realize that the amount and pace of change has fallen far short of initial expectations....Programs were planned, curriculum was developed, teaching/learning units were packaged, teachers were trained, and the results were frustrating, uneven, unexpected, and temporary."[35]

The failure of educational reformers to attend to implementation factors is a significant reason for the lack of real change amid so much attempted change. Sarason contends that those who wish to change the schools generally suffer from "an amazing degree of ignorance about the culture of the school, and (equally as fateful)...seem to have no theory of the change process."[36] In the same vein, Rodgers holds that "failures in program innovation are not as often failures of content as failures of contextual planning."[37]   Parish and Arends agree that "lack of success in implementing programs may be related to a lack of understanding of how schools work as social systems, how political processes influence change efforts, and the many dilemmas facing those who attempt to facilitate school improvement."[38]   In fact, Sarason writes, "Many of those who are aware that intended outcomes have not been achieved have no clear understanding of the factors contributing to failure."[39]

If lack of success comes from lack of understanding, then it follows that greater understanding of the factors involved will lead to more control and increased success.   In fact, after investigating attempts to implement innovations in Japanese ELT, Flenley reported, "Success or failure turned on how well the constraints had been negotiated; if innovations are to succeed they cannot be ignored."[40]   Greater knowledge of the factors that affect the change process will result in an enlarged ability to achieve reforms, a decrease in wasted time, and less disillusionment.

Closing the Knowledge-Practice Gap

Research, while often necessary, is not sufficient to solve most problems.   Before the benefits of research can be realized, its results must be communicated to the appropriate audience and then implemented.[41]   To close the gap between knowledge and practice, an understanding of the process of change and the factors that influence it is also required.

Rogers and Shoemaker point out that this "implementation gap" is a serious concern in many fields:

> Our activities in education, agriculture, medicine, industry, and the like are often without the benefit of the most current research knowledge. The gap between what is known and what is effectively put to use needs to be closed. To bridge this gap we must understand how new ideas spread from their source to potential receivers and understand the factors affecting the adoption of such innovations.[42]

Leithwood makes a similar point: "Many pressing social problems and aspirations could be much more effectively addressed than they are at present by existing, underutilized knowledge, systematically applied."[43]   Roberts-Gray and Gray echo: "The cost of faulty implementation can be counted not only in money wasted on development or acquisition of new knowledge or technology; it also represents lost opportunities to achieve benefits offered by the innovation."[44]

Greater Understanding of the
Structures with Which Educators Deal

A greater understanding of the school system itself is a third benefit of a diffusion-of-innovations perspective.   In reform campaigns, many seemingly simple factors turn out to be amazingly complex as many previously "invisible" aspects become painfully obvious.   Speaking of the public schools, for instance, House explains: "The public schools are composed of substances so common that their study is a bore....Only when we try to change them do we realize that we really do not understand their structure. Suddenly we encounter complexities we never envisioned."[45]

Likewise, a realization of the constraints within which reformers operate can help define the boundaries of a system as well as the forces that surround it. To use an analogy, in order to understand a room, it is necessary to discover not only the furniture it contains but also the location and nature of its walls.

ADVANTAGES OF A CROSS-CULTURAL PERSPECTIVE ON THE DIFFUSION OF INNOVATIONS

Studying directed contact change that crosses socio-cultural boundaries strengthens the promise of the three benefits mentioned in the preceding section and also offers additional advantages.

For one, a cross-cultural perspective highlights social factors that might otherwise be ignored. Change does not take place merely within the school system. As Sarason notes, "the school culture reflects and is a part of a larger society."[46] Yet when study of diffusion and innovation phenomena is restricted to a single culture, powerful social variables that can help or hinder the spread of an innovation may appear to be constants, and consequently may be ignored. A cross-cultural perspective often reveals these factors as variables that must be taken into account in forming an effective implementation strategy. Furthermore, after implementation efforts in various cultures have been studied and compared, those universal factors that transcend cultural boundaries become apparent.

The benefits of a cross-cultural perspective for understanding the diffusion of innovations are similar to several of the values of the comparative study of education in general. In discussing these, Noah explains, "Cross-national work has not only pointed toward improved theoretical models but has also, in fact, prevented overgeneralization on the basis of results derived from a single country." He adds,

> A comparative approach enlarges the framework within which we can view the results obtained in a single country: by providing counterinstances, it challenges us to refine our theories and test their validity against the reality of different societies; and, by providing parallel results, it can yield important confirmation of results obtained elsewhere.[47]

ADVANTAGES OF A HISTORICAL PERSPECTIVE

A historical, case study approach is employed in this examination of ELEC's attempt to reform English teaching in Japan. Yin notes that "the common stereotype of the 'case study' is that this way of doing research: (1) should be used at the exploratory stages, (2) leads only to unconfirmable conclusions, and (3) is really a method of last resort."[48] He goes on to point out, however, that "case studies paradoxically seem to be appearing with increasing frequency" and concludes that "the stereotype is in fact wrong. Although case studies indeed can be used for exploratory purposes, the approach also may be used for either descriptive or explanatory purposes as well."[49]

Yin also holds that "case studies are relevant for studying knowledge utilization, because the topic covers a phenomenon that seems to be inseparable from its context."[50]   Other diffusion-of-innovations researchers agree. For example, Havelock pleads, "We need more case studies which carefully document and report dissemination and utilization events."[51] Miles adds, "In the development of theoretical understanding, there is no substitute for the close examination of concrete, particular situations."[52]

A historical perspective is also valuable for other reasons. A diachronic perspective reveals aspects of elements and processes that a synchronic view often misses. As Claude Lévi-Strauss explains, "By showing institutions in the process of transformation, history alone makes it possible to abstract the structure which underlies the many manifestations and remains permanent throughout a succession of events."[53]

In addition, when a study deals with events that took place several decades earlier, the resulting temporal distance makes it possible to gain access to information that might not be available otherwise. "It is politically naive to expect open discussion of problems of implementation (even when this is invited by sponsors) in most large scale programs."[54] Nevertheless, issues that are "sensitive" during a reform campaign can be discussed freely many years later, and access to once "private" documents becomes possible with the passage of time.

RELATED STUDIES

The subject of ELEC's attempt to promote change in ELT practices in Japan does not fit neatly within any one field. Rather, it calls for the intersection of several: curriculum development, the diffusion of innovations, cross-cultural studies, and English language teaching.

Curriculum Development

Curriculum development is a broad field that includes "activities such as conceptualizing, planning, implementing, field testing, and researching."[55] The professional literature in this area is, in sheer volume, overwhelming. The ERIC (Educational Resources Information Center) database, accessed through Dialog Information Retrieval Service, lists 26,678 items (journal articles, books, conference presentations, etc.) dealing with curriculum development. In the last ten years alone, 11,707 of these have been produced. Only a fraction of them, however, are pertinent to the subtopic of curriculum implementation.

Diffusion of Innovations

The number of diffusion-of-innovations studies that have been conducted is smaller but still formidable. In 1969, Havelock found over four thousand studies "which pertained directly or indirectly to knowledge dissemination and utilization, innovation and technological change....By field, the largest number appear in 'education' (17%), followed by 'agriculture' (13%), and 'communication' (13%)."[56]

When the above-mentioned Dialog search of the ERIC database was narrowed to focus on "program implementation," it produced a total of 3,993 items, a figure close to Havelock's count. Combining this descriptor with "curriculum development" in education, however, reduced the total to 407 items. Findings from many of these studies are discussed in chapter three, where they contribute to the development of the hybrid analytical model used in this study.

Comparative Study of Education

Adding an international, comparative, cross-cultural dimension to the Dialog search reduced the aforementioned numbers dramatically. Of the studies dealing with curriculum development and program implementation, only forty dealt with education in foreign countries. Adding the descriptor "comparative education" reduced the number to only five.

The smallness of this figure attests to Kelly and Altbach's assertion that studies dealing with the nature of the knowledge transfer process "looking at the ways in which knowledge was disseminated, produced, and used" have been "hitherto ignored" in comparative education.[57] Nevertheless, Kelly and Altbach consider such studies to be one of the important challenges of the present and future of the comparative study of education.

Although relatively little comparative education work has been done in "program implementation" in foreign countries, one of the pleasant exceptions is an article by Coleman entitled "Professorial Training and Institution Building in the Third World: Two Rockefeller Foundation Experiences." Coleman identifies "the various factors associated with the success or failure" of efforts "to further the advanced professional education of prospective members of the professoriate" at the National University of Zaire and Mahidol University (Bangkok, Thailand). He also compares "the effects of the sociopolitical-cultural environment and the professional infrastructure" in the two different home countries "on the reception, retention, and professional performance" of indigenous scholars.[58]

Another comparative education study dealing with a diffusion-of-innovations topic was conducted by Lillis. His report, "Processes of Secondary Curriculum Innovation in Kenya," focuses on the period following Kenyan independence (1963-81) and consists of case studies of two curriculum innovations—the Africanization of the literature curriculum and the new School Mathematics of East Africa program. Both of these innovations failed to spread, and Lillis compares the history and major features of each. Most importantly, he notes that "the complex interrelationships among the factors involved, the processes of adoption and development, the nature of the curriculum content, and the nature of the infrastructure are important determinants of the nature of the change process."[59]

On the other side of Africa, Ouedraogo studied the factors affecting curriculum development in Upper Volta and reached the conclusion that proposed reforms in the school system had brought about a number of "opposing and negative reactions against implementing suggested changes." His report, however, does little more than list those factors that hampered change:

> language of instruction, (French vs. Voltaic); concentration on productive instruction (e.g., animal husbandry) [which] gives rise to fears about obstruction for the student who may be socially upwardly mobile; parents' negative attitudes; difficulty in recruiting and training teachers; differences between urban and rural needs and opportunities; and the question of the role the government should play in education."[60]

In Australia, Marsh conducted a study relevant to the diffusion of innovations and comparative education.[61] The implementation effort he investigated promoted immanent change rather than directed contact change, and it did not involve cross-cultural implementation (in fact, it was limited to only one state in Australia). Nevertheless, his findings emphasize the importance of specific contextual factors and their influence on the course of implementation.

Program Implementation in English Language Teaching

ELT professionals generally have paid little attention to program implementation. The Dialog search of the ERIC database bore this out. Starting with the nearly 27,000 documents dealing with curriculum development, and then restricting the focus to those that dealt with program implementation and the teaching of English as a second or foreign language, produced only twelve items.

Foremost among these studies is Richards' "The Secret Life of Methods."[62] Of the few articles on ELT program implementation and change, it is by far the most influential by virtue of its publication in the widely read *TESOL Quarterly*, as well as Richards' delivery of a plenary address with the same title and much the same content at the annual international convention of TESOL (Teachers of English to Speakers of Other Languages) in 1983. Richards' analysis deserves credit as a pioneering effort, but utilizes a simple framework and reflects no awareness of other studies in educational change and diffusion of innovations. Interestingly, Richards uses the case of Charles C. Fries' Oral Approach in the United States as an example of successful implementation.

A recent book for ESOL teachers by Celce-Murcia contains a section on "The Implementation Process." Unfortunately, neither of the two articles in this section deals with directed contact change in English language teaching. One (by Olshtain) addresses a few diffusion-of-innovations factors, but the discussion is limited to immanent change scenarios.[63]

An article by Raimes bears a promising title, "Tradition and Revolution in ESL Teaching," but it deals with revolutions at the theory or "approach" level only.[64]   Drawing heavily on Kuhn's *The Structure of Scientific Revolutions*, Raimes discusses paradigm shifts, but never deals with the challenges of changing actual language-teaching practices in particular situations.

The Determination and Implementation of Language Policy is a noteworthy but unfortunately obscure book (it was not listed in the ERIC database).[65] In their discussion of efforts to determine and then implement an official language policy in the Philippines in the late 1950s and 1960s, the authors (Ramos, Aguilar and Sibayan) discuss the role of research, as well as the training of teachers and production of materials. They urge "careful planning and preparation of both people and materials" and warn against "hasty implementation." The authors also discuss a lengthy list of factors to consider, ranging from funding to public relations to the role of colleges and universities. Lacking, however, is a model to show the interrelationships among these factors. Interestingly, it was a grant from the Rockefeller Foundation that provided funding for the Philippine Center for Language Study, which in turn sponsored not only a considerable amount of research on language teaching in the Philippines but also the publication of this valuable book.

In his discussions of the process of creating change, Freeman stresses the *teacher training* vs. *teacher development* distinction.[66]

> Training deals with building specific teaching skills: how to sequence a lesson or how to teach a dialogue, for instance. Development, on the other hand, focuses on the individual teacher—on the process of reflection, examination, and change which can lead to doing a better job and to personal and professional growth.[67]

Freeman's interest, however, has been restricted to creating change in teachers. He does not deal with the larger issues of curriculum and program change.

In her book, *Beyond Methodology: Second Language Teaching and the Community,* Ashworth warns teachers of English as a foreign language who might entertain visions of reforming teaching practices in a foreign setting of the importance of social context.

> EFL teachers should study the educational system—its values, structure, and goals—and the social and economic systems; and they should consult with local teachers and try to see the situation through their eyes before launching into a program of change which may be both harmful and ineffective. It is better to make haste slowly! What works in the United States, Britain, Canada, and Australia may not work in China, Nigeria, Thailand or Saudi Arabia, and vice versa.[68]

Beyond this general warning, however, she offers little to would-be innovators in the way of a framework for analyzing the target situation or for planning a program of change.

In contrast, Maley, in a paper presented at a Singapore conference on "Trends in Language Syllabus Design," provides a detailed examination of "the problems involved in implementing syllabuses."[69] Based on his experience in the People's Republic of China (although he tries to "avoid the impression that these issues are China specific"), Maley lists over 150 questions that would-be reformers should ask about the target situation. These are grouped according to whether they deal with cultural, educational, organizational/administrative, learner, teacher, or material factors. Although Maley's study lacks a solid theoretical base, it is still valuable, and many of the points he raises that are relevant to the ELEC case are discussed in the appropriate chapters of this book.

At the same Singapore conference, a number of other papers dealt with the topic of curriculum reform. None of the authors, however, went into the detail that Maley did.

Rodgers' paper on "Communicative Syllabus Design and Implementation" provides a useful matrix "for estimating the implementation difficulty of new programs." It takes into consideration factors such as "the educational requirement sought," "renewal activities and resources required," and "the content of the renewal program." Although Rodgers ignores some important implementation factors, his matrix is still useful. With it, reform planners can plot a "difficulty profile" that will help them decide whether to proceed and, if so, where to place emphasis.[70]

In his paper, Hawkey notes that "'Constraints' apply to syllabus *design* as well as implementation." Emphasizing the importance of diffusion and implementation planning at the earliest stages of a project, he comments, "No wonder there is concern when people want to leave constraints till later. Traditional constraints like untrained teachers and book shortages are all connected with the syllabus specification *itself* as a constraint" [italics in original].[71]

Other presenters at the Singaporean syllabus design conference either ignored implementation factors or mentioned them only incidentally.

Pascasio, for instance, presented a case study from the Philippines. Although it notes that "the implementation of the...syllabus has to go hand in hand with the development of the language materials," her paper devotes twelve pages to a description of the syllabus and only one paragraph to implementation. [72]

Thanachanan addressed the problems associated with implementing a new language syllabus but the only solutions she recommends are developing "pertinent teaching materials" and making the new syllabus "as explicit as possible to all teachers, administrators, and educators concerned."[73]

Abu Samah reported on the implementation of a new communicative syllabus for English language teaching in Malaysia and the resistance the movement encountered. Respecting implementation, Abu Samah's report indicates that only a minimal strategy was employed. Resource materials for teachers were duplicated and disseminated to the schools, textbook publishers were briefed, and a group of "pioneer" teachers were selected. This "key-personnel system of teacher-orientation" was intended to have a "multiplier role of ensuring positive snowballing of the new programme."[74]   Although these pioneers "bravely survived" and "persevered," their task would have been much easier had other implementation factors been taken into consideration.

ELT Program Implementation in Japan

When the descriptor "Japan" was added to the previous combination in the Dialog search, the number of relevant studies in the ERIC database dropped even further. In fact, no items were found. Although it is possible that studies of ELT program implementation in Japan have been done, their results have not been reported in a form that makes them widely available.[75] This is a distressing finding in light of the numerous attempts to reform the English teaching system in Japan. If such efforts are to ever succeed, studies of the factors that influence them are needed.

LIMITATIONS TO THE PREVIOUS STUDIES

The most obvious conclusion to be drawn from the preceding review of literature is that, in spite of the need for knowledge about the process of reforming English language teaching in Japan, there is a paucity of studies focusing on this topic.

Given the worldwide nature of English language teaching and the frequency of attempts to bring about reform in this field, the relatively small number of studies dealing with the implementation of change in English-language-teaching practices is equally disturbing. Moreover, the few studies that have been done typically lack a solid theoretical base.

Relative to formal education in general, many more studies dealing with program implementation have been conducted and reported, but most of them still suffer from problems that make them inapplicable to the analysis of cross-cultural campaigns aimed at bringing about directed contact change in educational practices. Much more is said in this respect in chapter three. Here it will only be noted that these studies typically suffer from one or more of the following drawbacks:

- The great majority deal with immanent change only and thus are not relevant to cases involving directed contact change;

- Many are extremely narrow, focusing only on factors within the school system and ignoring the larger social context of education;

- Most are not comparative in nature and thus suffer from mono-cultural blindness and fail to deal with the complexities of cross-cultural change;

- Many reports consist primarily of a description of a situation followed by a list of factors related to the problems of implementation (e.g., Maley) or lessons learned from an implementation experience (e.g., Parish and Arends) and lack a theoretical base or a coherent framework for analysis;

- Even when studies are based on a model of change, it is usually an oversimplistic one. Gordon and Lawton, for instance, base their study on an unsophisticated two-element process.[76] Cochran Slaugh identifies only two barriers to implementing reforms.[77]

This study of ELEC's attempt to change ELT practices in Japan attempts to overcome these difficulties. First of all, it avoids confusing the factors and processes involved in different types of change by focusing on only one type—directed contact change. Also, in contrast to the narrow, mono-cultural studies, it takes a broad, cross-cultural point of view. Furthermore, it benefits from a solid base in diffusion-of-innovations theory. As a result, the hybrid model it proposes and utilizes is complex and includes many factors that others ignore. Nevertheless, such complexity is to be preferred over misleading simplicity.

In the chapters that follow, the ELEC case is studied from two different perspectives—chronological and analytical. To facilitate understanding, each of these perspectives is treated separately. It would be confusing to attempt to analyze the ELEC experience without first explaining the events that constituted it in the order in which they occurred. Conversely, the analysis would quickly become disjointed if it addressed the components of the ELEC experience in chronological order. After the nature of both the ELEC story and the analytical model have been established, however, they can be put together and the analysis of the ELEC experience conducted in a comprehensible and fruitful manner.

NOTES

1. Memorandum, "12th meeting on English Teaching Method."
2. Takagi, 25 April 1956.
3. Smith to Rockefeller, 20 May 1974, 4.
4. For a recent analysis of present-day constraints hindering ELT innovation in Japan, see Flenley, "Innovation in English Language Teaching."
5. Brosnahan and Haynes, 71.
6. Rogers and Shoemaker, 8-9.
7. Bennis, Benne, and Chin, 4.
8. Attributed to Ralph Waldo Emerson, who wrote: "If a man can write a better book, preach a better sermon, or make a better mouse trap than his neighbor, though he builds his house in the woods, the world will make a beaten path to his door." Further illustrating this optimistic attitude, Emerson also wrote: "I trust a good deal to common fame, as we all must. If a man has good corn or wood, or boards, or pigs to sell, or can make better chairs or knives, crucibles or church organs, than anybody else, you will find a broad hard beaten road to his house, though it be in the woods." Cited by Beck, 605.
9. Miles, 635
10. Beauchamp, "Reform Traditions," 1.
11. Lord and Horn, 64.
12. Goodman, 358.
13. Vaughan, Wang, and Dytman, 40.
14. Cited by Parish and Arends, 62.
15. Wolf, 331.
16. Wolf, 334.
17. Committee for Economic Development, 7.
18. Dostert, Eddy, Lehmann, and Marckwardt, 220.
19. Cohen, iii.
20. Wajnryb.
21. Tajima, 152.
22. Kelly, 408.
23. Crystal, 7-9.
24. Richards, "The Secret Life of Methods," *TESOL Quarterly,* 17.
25. Richards, "The Secret Life of Methods," *TESOL Quarterly,* 7.
26. Brownell, 10.

27. Brosnahan and Haynes, 71.
28. Koike et al., iv.
29. Brownell, 13.
30. Harasawa, 71-72.
31. Reischauer, "The English Language and Japan's Role in the World," 19.
32. Brosnahan and Haynes, 77
33. Reischauer to Borton.
34. Leithwood, 341.
35. Mann, xi.
36. Sarason, 2.
37. Rodgers, "Syllabus Design, Curriculum Development and Polity Deliberation," 1.
38. Parish and Arends, 63.
39. Sarason, 46.
40. Flenley, "Innovation in English Language Teaching," 9.
41. Rogers and Shoemaker, 1.
42. Rogers and Shoemaker, 1.
43. Leithwood, 342.
44. Roberts-Gray and Gray, 214.
45. House, 1.
46. Sarason, 1.
47. Noah, 557-558.
48. Yin, 97.
49. Yin, 97-98.
50. Yin, 99.
51. Havelock, *Planning for Innovation*, chap. 11, p. 2.
52. Miles, 47.
53. Lévi-Strauss, 22.
54. Fullan and Pomfret, 389.
55. Houston, 63.
56. Havelock, *Planning,* chap. 11, p. 1.
57. Kelly and Altbach, 96.
58. Coleman, 180.
59. Lillis, 96.
60. Ouedraogo, abstract.
61. Marsh, 37-58.
62. Richards, "The Secret Life of Methods," *TESOL Quarterly,* 7-23.
63. Olshtain, 155-66.
64. Raimes, 535-52.
65. Ramos, Aguilar, and Sibayan.
66. In addition to writing the article cited in the next note, Freeman has presented a number of convention papers dealing with the subject of "The Training/Development Continuum." See bibliography for full references.
67. Freeman, "Observing Teachers," 21.
68. Ashworth, 124.
69. Maley, 90.
70. Rodgers, "Communicative Syllabus Design and Implementation," 41, Appendix B.
71. Hawkey, 130.
72. Pascasio, 229.
73. Thanachanan, 254, 256.
74. Abu Samah, 203.
75. A welcome exception is Flenley's research on innovations in Japanese ELT, the results of which have only recently begun to appear in print.
76. Gordon and Lawton, 217.
77. Cochran Slaugh.

2
Background and Overview of the ELEC Effort

A noteworthy characteristic of the history of foreign language teaching/learning in Japan has been a cyclical pattern of waves of interest. One of the strongest of these waves occurred after World War II as Japanese contacts with Western nations (especially the United States) increased and the need for practical communication skills in English became apparent. Since the traditional approaches employed in Japan's school system did not lead to the ability to communicate in spoken English, many Japanese—especially those in business and financial circles—desired reforms in English-teaching methods and materials. The catalyst that started the action of the English Language Exploratory Committee, however, was an American—John D. Rockefeller 3rd. This chapter, therefore, will begin by examining Mr. Rockefeller's role, and that of the Rockefeller Foundation, in the ELEC effort.

ROCKEFELLER FOUNDATION EFFORTS AROUND THE WORLD AND IN JAPAN

Since its establishment in 1913, the Rockefeller Foundation has funded projects around the world. This international pattern of spending continues today. According to a recent report, the Rockefeller Foundation plans to spend nearly $300 million between 1986 and 1991 on developing nations.[1] Various explanations for this generosity have been advanced, and most of them would seem to apply to the case of Rockefeller support for ELEC in post World War II Japan.

Humanitarian, Philanthropic Interests

The "official" explanation, of course, is that the Rockefeller Foundation was established by John D. Rockefeller, Sr., "with the sole motive of devoting a portion of [his] fortune to the service of [his] fellow men."[2] As the responsibility for the foundation has passed from generation to generation of Rockefellers, they have channeled their efforts "along lines that might mean a step forward in the long struggle of nations to find a way to live peacefully together."[3]

After the destruction of World War II, the promotion of world peace undoubtedly seemed especially appropriate and desirable. Future peace, however, would depend on true communication among nations. Consequently, English language teaching was seen as playing an important role in furthering U.S.-Japanese relations and intercultural understanding. In a 1953 memorandum to John D. Rockefeller 3rd, Donald H. McLean, Jr., Rockefeller's legal advisor, urged:

> If I had additional funds for this purpose, I would undertake a program of English-language teaching in Japan on an extensive scale on the theory that if the Japanese accepted English as a "second language" they would naturally read our literature without the problem of translation and if they learn the language while they are young enough they will have a feeling of understanding toward us which they probably would not have toward any other country.[4]

Furthering U.S. Foreign Policy and Commercial Interests

Others take a less idealistic view of the intentions behind the international activities of the Rockefeller and other U.S. foundations. Berman, for example, argues that "this public rhetoric of disinterested humanitarianism" has been "little more than a facade behind which the economic and strategic interests of the United States have been actively furthered." His thesis is that after World War II, "since overt colonialism was no longer acceptable to world opinion, the United States needed surrogate organizations to protect and further her interests in the developing areas of Asia, Africa, and Latin America" and that U.S. foundations played this role. "The foundations accomplished this primarily by funding programs linking the educational systems of the new African nations to the values, *modus operandi,* and institutions of the United States."[5]

Proponents of the foundations argue back that such interpretations of their purposes are both incorrect and unfounded. A spokesman for the Ford Foundation maintains, "The benefits from trade, investment, or educational exchange do not all flow one way." A more abrupt response comes from a Rockefeller Foundation representative who labels Berman's allegations, "unsubstantiated assertions."[6]

Nevertheless, it seems likely that at least one purpose of the ELEC effort to improve English-teaching methods in Japan was related to U.S. foreign policy. The ELEC campaign began during the years of the cold war, at a time when Communist agitation in Japan was growing. The United States did not want Japan to go over to the Soviet side, so efforts were made to strengthen Japan's ties with the United States. As early as 1953, in a follow-up to the "Dulles Report" of 1951 (written after John D. Rockefeller 3rd toured Japan with U.S. Secretary of State John Foster Dulles), it was recognized that "private agencies" could "improve the relationship between the two countries" and "aid on the Marxism problem," and such efforts were encouraged.[7]   In a memo written shortly before the formation of the Rockefeller-supported Japan Society in 1952, McLean wrote:

> The peace treaty has now been signed by Japan and is awaiting confirmation by the United States Senate.   Since the end of the war there has been a considerable change in the relationship between Japan and the United States and it seems essential that in our own self-interest as a nation we take affirmative steps to further a healthy understanding between the two countries.[8]

Believing that a sound economy was another prerequisite to healthy relationships and hoping to help strengthen Japan's economy after World War II,   John D. Rockefeller 3rd established "a small philanthropic fund called the Council on Economic and Cultural Affairs."[9]   (Most of his later financial support for the ELEC operation was provided through CECA.)

Of course, the economic recovery of Japan, the introduction of American technology into that country, and the establishment of strong economic ties between the United States and Japan were in the commercial interest of many parties in the United States also.[10]   The Rockefellers were no exception.   A 1955 report to the president of the Standard-Vacuum Oil Company concluded with these words:

> I think we should join hands with the most competent Japanese we can find because it will help us to build a more solid business here.   I think that we should actively promote policies which will strengthen the over-all foreign exchange position of Japan because it will broaden the market for our products....We have the chance at this point to take a significant step forward in good corporate citizenship.[11]

Absolving Guilt

Rockefeller's concern for Japan may have also stemmed, at least in part, from feelings of guilt after the great nuclear destruction at Hiroshima and Nagasaki, for "the Foundation contributed heavily to the development of nuclear fission and, unhappily, the atomic bomb."[12]

Interesting though such *ex post facto* analysis may be, it will not be pursued further.   For the purposes of this study, it is sufficient to note that whatever the intention(s) may have been, Rockefeller Foundation interest in and support for reforming English-language-teaching methods in Japan after World War II was strong—especially in the case of John D. Rockefeller 3rd.[13]

JOHN D. ROCKEFELLER 3RD'S INTEREST IN JAPAN AND ENGLISH-LANGUAGE TEACHING

A history of the Rockefeller brothers notes:

> John's greatest postwar interest...has been in the Far East, particularly Japan, and in 1952 he became president of Japan Society, Inc., which has the purpose of helping to bring the people of the United States and of Japan closer together in their appreciation and understanding of each other and each other's way of life.[14]

John D. Rockefeller 3rd's interest in Japan began, however, more than twenty years prior to the formation of the Japan Society. In 1929, after graduating from college, "he took a trip around the world, visiting in Asia, Japan, China and Korea." At that time he became greatly interested in Japan, and visited the country on several occasions prior to World War II.[15] After the war, he returned and "then accompanied the John Foster Dulles mission to Tokyo when the peace treaty was being negotiated. At that time he met with many Japanese in all stations of life and out of those discussions began to emerge a plan for a cultural center that would work for harmony between the two peoples."[16]

This plan was in keeping with his idealistic proposition that "if the people of different nations understood each other better, international problems will be much more capable of solution and the lives of all will be enriched." It was also based on the more realistic thesis that "a peace treaty is only as valid as the relationships between the contracting parties are good."[17]

It was not long before Rockefeller realized the important role that English language teaching would play in his plans. Economic development and cross-cultural understanding required the interchange of scholarship and information. This interchange demanded communication with the outside world, and—since Japanese was rarely used outside of Japan and English was fast becoming the language of international communication— this process depended on the English language ability of the Japanese.

Unfortunately, most Japanese were woefully lacking in English communication skills—especially in listening and speaking. Although both spoken and written English had been widely studied in Japan in the 1800s, the emphasis changed in the the twentieth century, and only the written modality was stressed. Then, prior to and during the war, English came to be seen as "the enemy's language" and its popularity declined dramatically.[18] Consequently, after the war, the level of English proficiency—especially oral proficiency—among the Japanese was very low.

This general lack of proficiency in English created problems for many Japanese when the postwar need for English skills became critical. For instance, when Japanese scholars were sent to the United States under the GARIOA (Government Aid and Relief in Occupied Areas) program (1949-53), it quickly became apparent that to succeed in America these scholars needed better English listening and speaking skills. The Japan Society, which was also funding Japanese scholars in the United States at this time, found that they needed an extra year, just to get their English up to standard, before beginning study in their content area.[19]

In response to this situation, some proposed the establishment of an intensive English course in Japan for those chosen to study in the United States.[20] Another course of action, however, which would benefit many more Japanese, would be to improve the quality of English instruction throughout Japan.[21] As early as 1951, in the "Dulles Report" (which

Rockefeller helped prepare) English language teaching was recognized as "a field of the greatest and most fundamental importance."[22]

Nevertheless, little action was taken to improve Japanese ELT. Four of Rockefeller's colleagues reported:

> Despite the comments of the Dulles Report and the fact that English-language teaching constitutes one of President Cole's four recommendations, very little is being done to improve English-language teaching in Japan. On the contrary, we understand that for budgetary reasons the State Department has abandoned the idea of sending an English-teaching specialist to Japan.[23]

Although Rockefeller's advisors attached importance to the need to improve Japanese ELT practices, they were "not enthusiastic about the establishment of an independent language center in Japan, as suggested in the Dulles Report." Instead, they recommended providing several Japanese universities with "the most modern facilities for the teaching of the English language."[24] An alternative solution was to encourage the spread of modern methods for teaching English through the existing school system. Reporting to Rockefeller in 1953, McLean, Overton, Borton, and Carman suggested, "It is clearly impossible to provide enough English-speaking teachers to change the situation....But it should be possible somehow or other to introduce the newer language teaching methods now in use with such success in American colleges."[25] Still, nothing was done to implement these suggestions.

As time went by, Rockefeller's concern increased. He sensed that, more than ever before, the world needed a common language. He also realized that as Japan recovered from the war it would need to learn to communicate with the world better than it had done in the past.[26] In July 1955, from Tokyo, he wrote of his feelings about the importance of improving English language teaching in Japan:

> As never before I am appreciating on this trip the importance of English language teaching in Japan. The lack of a common foreign language is a barrier which becomes increasingly serious with the development of modern communications. What has particularly struck me on this visit is the fact that it is not only a barrier to the west but also within Asia itself. This all makes me keener than ever to consider the further possibility of whether English language teaching in Japan can be made more effective.[27]

THE EARLY EXPLORATORY PHASE

As his concern grew, Rockefeller suggested that the Japan Society study the problem of ELT practices in Japan and recommend possible solutions. Douglas Overton, executive director of the Japan Society, and Hugh Borton, one of the Society's vice presidents, decided to commission an expert, third-party assessment of the situation. Interestingly, Charles C. Fries, who later played such a significant role in the ELEC campaign, was recommended as one who "would be well qualified to make the survey, especially in Japan and the Philippines."[28] In the end, however, William

Cullen Bryant, Jr., head of the American Language Center (for foreign students) at Columbia University, was selected.

Bryant's Report and Recommendations

William Cullen Bryant, Jr. traveled to Japan in the fall and winter of 1954-55 and did extensive research. During his three months in Japan, he visited "about 50 classes in 20 secondary schools" both public and private, in metropolitan areas, smaller cities, and rural areas. He also "observed classes in teacher training institutions," visited fifteen universities, and "held discussions with English teachers from fifteen more." In addition, he visited a number of private English schools for adults. He even attended "the annual conferences of two professional organizations in the field." and a "festival of English plays, speeches, and songs" put on by lower secondary school students.[29]

Bryant's hefty (ninety-page) report was quite thorough, beginning with "A History of English in Japan," examining "English Teaching Today—The Situation and the Problem," and finally making recommendations.[30] It emphasized the importance of understanding the background of the Japanese ELT situation and going through proper channels in any attempt to modify it.[31] His advice was that it would be a "fatal mistake" not to work with the Ministry of Education and other prestigious, influential organizations.[32] His report also discussed the potential for poisonous interorganization "jealousies" to develop if things were not handled sensitively.[33] In addition, it recognized the power of Japanese university and high school entrance examinations and the difficulty of changing them.[34] The fact that older men who were less interested in change headed the hierarchy of leaders within the Japanese school system was also perceived as a serious obstacle to any attempt to change ELT practices in Japan. Generally, Bryant's message was that "the problem of English teaching improvement is an immense one which is...unlikely to be solved by a single 'pilot project' built around a 'new method,' no matter how carefully planned."[35]

Unfortunately, many of the recommendations in Bryant's report were not taken seriously enough and its warnings were not heeded. In fact, the reaction to the report was rather critical. One commentator, for instance, began, "Haven't read this report very thoroughly, as I am suspicious of its method," and went on, "I don't see why anyone couldn't have turned out this particular version after one course at Teachers' Training and two books on Japan....I don't see why a visit to Japan was necessary to this report given the library facilities of 1955."[36]

Perhaps Bryant's recommendations were criticized and ignored because they were not in keeping with what had already been decided. By late summer of 1955, when his report was submitted, Rockefeller "insiders" had already made plans to establish some sort of "Japan English Center" (as envisioned by JDR 3rd in the 1951 "Dulles Report").

Deliberations on How to Proceed

Nearly a year before the English Language Exploratory Committee was formed, deliberations regarding the proper course of action began. At first, there was only an informal "committee on English teaching method" spearheaded by Shigeharu Matsumoto and involving Takeshi Saito, Yasaka Takagi, and Edwin O. Reischauer.   Matsumoto—a prominent Japanese lawyer and statesman, a graduate of Yale, and a personal friend of John D. Rockefeller 3rd[37]—had been encouraged by Rockefeller "to explore possibilities in this direction."[38] The first meeting of this informal committee was held August 6, 1955, at the International House of Japan.[39] They agreed on the following points (outlined in a subsequent letter to JDR 3rd from Matsumoto, who emphasized their compliance with Rockefeller's wishes):

(1) The sponsoring organization or committee should be organized and operated on Japanese initiatives and Japanese responsibility; this point was one of your basic points, I remember.

(2) The sponsoring body should consist more of laymen than of experts. Experts should form a technical advisory committee under this sponsoring body; this is again in harmony with your thinking I believe.

(3) The sponsoring body should have no special affiliation with any of the existing institutions being interested or to be interested in this program of teaching method; this is [the] last of the points you had in mind I think.

(4) All four of us have agreed that Chairman of the Committee should be either a public-minded businessman or a senior diplomat.

(5) Four of us agreed on the timelyness and pertinency of the project; time is just getting ripe enough to start this kind of project afresh; and also there will not be strong opposition from any quarters concerned if the plan is launched tactfully enough.

(6) As a practical approach, the plan of giving intensive courses to "in service" secondary school teachers is believed to be most effective. Special courses of functional English in the curriculum for college students would be another approach. Both can be carried out simultaneously.

(7) In as much as a certain length of time is necessary to get organized a Japanese committee chiefly due to absence of the most of future participants in the program from town during the summer, the suggested visit of Dr. Bryant to Japan in September would be rather premature and it was agreed to advise you to postpone the arrangement of his trip to some future date.[40] [sic]

The proposed budget for this program (in two phases, over a period of three years) to cover operating, administrative, and research and development costs in both Japan and the United States ranged between $150,000 (minimum) and $300,000 (maximum).[41]

The Temporary Committee on English Teaching Methods was organized in November 1955. Members were Dr. Gordon T. Bowles, Professor at the University of Tokyo; Miss Tano Jodai, President, Japan Women's University; Mr. Shigeharu Matsumoto; Professor Edwin O. Reischauer; Dr. Takeshi Saito; Professor Mamoru Shimizu of International Christian University; Mr. Ryohei Shishido, a curriculum specialist from the Ministry of Education; and Dr. Yasaka Takagi a professor at the University of Tokyo.[42]

The speed with which the movement should proceed was one subject of committee discussion. Reischauer regarded English language teaching as "the most important problem in all modern Japanese education," but recommended a "go-slow policy" lest the attempt to reform ELT methods be "bumbled by inexpert or hasty handling."[43] Donald H. McLean, Jr., Rockefeller's on-site representative, agreed that an effective movement would "take time and a considerable amount of negotiating."[44]

Nevertheless, the events of the next few months proceeded at an almost dizzying pace. The committee recommended that a "conference of technical advisors be held for about a week sometime in late March 1956." It also planned for a three-week "experimental In-Service Training Course scheduled for August 1956."[45] Although this conference and training course did not take place quite as soon as they hoped, the committee did work faithfully over the next few months, holding twelve meetings by April 25, 1956.[46]

In these meetings, Reischauer also emphasized the need for any movement to "grow fundamentally out of a genuine Japanese interest in the problem" and "to have the sympathetic support of influential members of the former group ['old fashioned teachers of English literature and English as a language only to be read']" if it was to have much success.[47] This was in accord with John D. Rockefeller 3rd's wishes that it be "a genuinely indigenous movement in its origin and nature."[48]

Nevertheless, in the same communication, Rockefeller also suggested that "advice and support" come from outside Japan and urged the committee "to consider some responsible group like a University, and preferably in the United States where so much time and thought have been given to the improvement of language teaching methods."[49] Some questioned whether a university should be involved ("Universities do not do these jobs too well...."[50]), but there was never any question that the methodological expertise behind the reform should come from the United States.

As time went by, the plans for the ELEC conference became more definite. Within a short time, a budget (totaling $9,500) for the "Proposed Specialists' Conference" was drawn up. It included expenses for "visiting consultants," two from the United States and one from England.[51] This was in keeping with one of the conference's major purposes—to bring to Japan "some of the outstanding Americans in the field with the thought that as a result of such a conference the views of the Japanese might become more definite and certain not only as to the contribution which Americans could make but also as to the individuals who could make this contribution."[52]

Meanwhile, back in New York, the search began for the right experts and methods to be sent to Japan from the United States. A number of major American universities offered intensive English language courses for foreign students and had faculty with experience and expertise in English language teaching. Michigan and Cornell were recognized as being "foremost," with Michigan being given "the edge."[53] Naturally then, Charles C. Fries, the head of the Michigan English Language Institute and originator of the Oral Approach employed there, was a prime candidate.

Rockefeller's workers also investigated the Ford Foundation's English-language-teaching project in Indonesia, which had begun a few years earlier. They reported that "at the outset, instructors were drawn from Cornell, but it was found that there was a scarcity of trained personnel with the result that Michigan personnel were recruited. The result was that Michigan techniques proved more successful and have since been adopted."[54] This report undoubtedly swayed the committee in favor of inviting Fries to Japan.

With this information, the Conference Preparation Committee met in early May and "agreed unanimously that the middle of October would be the best time for holding this Conference of experts." They also reported: "The first scholar we should like to have among us for this purpose is Prof[essor] Fries. As to another scholar to be invited from the United States, our conclusion was that it would be best to leave that choice to Prof[essor] Fries."[55] So high was their regard for Fries that they not only left the choice of the second scholar up to him, they also rescheduled the conference to September to accommodate his schedule when they learned he could not come in October.[56]

Fries chose Freeman Twaddell, a professor of linguistics and German at Brown University who had done summer teaching at Michigan in 1945, 1947, 1949, and 1956, to be the second American scholar.[57] A. S. Hornby, who had spent nearly twenty years in Japan before the war, represented the British Council. By far the most influential of these three scholars was Fries. He, "more than anyone else," played a major role in establishing ELEC's methodological foundation.[58] ELEC would advocate his Oral Approach "as the most effective way of teaching and learning English"[59] for many years—long after Fries had come and gone.[60]

CHARLES C. FRIES AND HIS ORAL APPROACH

Fries was born in Reading, Pennsylvania in 1887. His death in 1967, at the age of eighty, marked the end of a long and productive life—professionally and otherwise.

Fries earned his first university degrees in Greek and Latin and became a teacher of Greek and rhetoric in the classics department at Bucknell University. In 1915 (to the astonishment of his colleagues) he transferred to the English department. He later went to the University of Michigan, where he completed his Ph.D. in English in 1922 and then joined the faculty. Until he retired as Professor Emeritus in 1958, the University of Michigan served as the base for Fries' wide-ranging academic career.[61]

In the 1930s (with financial support from the Rockefeller-funded General Education Board[62]) Fries did extensive research work on sixteenth- and seventeenth-century English, leading to the production of an *Early Modern English Dictionary.*[63]

Fries also became involved with American applied linguistics in its early stages. He was a founding member of the Linguistic Society of America (LSA) and became its president in 1939. Nevertheless, unlike many linguists of the time, who worked with exotic or at least "foreign" languages, Fries devoted himself to the English language, and his major emphasis was in applying linguistics to pedagogy. In fact, Howatt calls Fries "the first applied linguist in the modern sense."[64]

Fries was active in various professional organizations. In addition to his involvement with the LSA, he served as president of the National Council of Teachers of English (1927-28) and also served on committees of other professional groups, such as the American Council of Learned Societies and the Modern Language Association.[65]

Fries' work covered a wide range of topics—lexicography, the teaching of reading, signals grammar, vocabulary frequency, etc. He published extensively also. By 1956, when he went to Japan, he had authored numerous articles and seven books: *The Teaching of Literature* (1925), *The Teaching of the English Language* (1927), *English Word Lists—A Study of their Adaptability for Instruction* (1940), *Language Study in American Education* (1940), *American English Grammar* (1940), *Teaching and Learning English as a Foreign Language* (1945), and *The Structure of English* (1952).

At the University of Michigan, in 1941, Fries established the first English Language Institute in the United States.[66] Interestingly, this institute was originally funded by a grant from the Rockefeller Foundation.[67] Reports on Fries and his work were favorable. One Rockefeller Foundation worker commented, "I am convinced that Fries is going rapidly in the right direction..."[68] Fifteen years later, as preparations for the first ELEC Specialists Conference were being made, Rockefeller personnel recognized Fries as "a creative pioneer in the language field"[69] and "the outstanding man in the United States on the teaching of English as a foreign language."[70]

Basic Principles of Fries' Oral Approach

In his 1945 book, *Teaching and Learning English as a Foreign Language,* Fries outlined the basic tenets of his Oral Approach.

> "Oral approach" is a name primarily for the *end* [italics in original] to be attained in the first stage of language learning rather than a descriptive limitation of the permissible devices to attain that end. That end is the building up of a set of habits for the oral production of a language and for the receptive understanding of the language when it is spoken.[71]

To this end, the Oral Approach relied on materials that had been carefully prepared utilizing the principles of "modern linguistic science." Fries insisted, "The most efficient materials are those that are based upon a scientific description of the language to be learned, carefully compared with a parallel description of the native language of the learner."[72]

For Fries, the Oral Approach was much broader than a set of classroom procedures, and he never used the term *method* when referring to it. He explained: "The word 'approach' rather than 'method' has been chosen deliberately. It has been chosen in order to stress the fact that we are concerned with a path to a goal....We are concerned with such a path rather than with a method of teaching."[73]

That path was the "oral use of English." Fries emphasized oral language not only because modern linguists viewed language as primarily vocal but also for pedagogical reasons. Oral practice was less time-consuming than practice in written language. Fries declared, "What we have called the 'oral approach' is the most efficient, the most time-saving way to begin the study of English...."[74] The Oral Approach also led to good reading habits because it prevented students from going back and forth to decipher the text (a typical Japanese practice in translation).[75] Of course, this approach contrasted dramatically with the traditional language teaching methods used in Japan, which emphasized the written language and relied on translation.

The goal of the "first stage" in the Oral Approach was also quite different from the typical outcomes of English study in Japan. Fries asserted:

> A person has "learned" a foreign language when he has thus first, *within a limited vocabulary* [italics in original] mastered the sound system (that is, when he can understand the stream of speech and achieve an understandable production of it) and has, second, made the structural devices (that is[,] the basic arrangements of utterances) matters of automatic habit.[76]

Although the "special goal" of the Oral Approach and the "special materials" that it employed were of primary importance to Fries, he also admitted that it also necessitated "certain special principles of method." Most of these were also in stark contrast with traditional Japanese methods for English language teaching. For instance, Fries insisted:

> On the whole the classes using the "oral approach" are thought of and planned in terms of opportunities for pupil practice....Practice exercises to be most effective must proceed through at least three important steps....
>
> Accurate imitation of the pattern in the sentence as presented by the teacher; and then enough repetition of the complete sentence to make the oral production by the pupil easy, smooth, and in a proper English tempo....
>
> Practice by the pupil in choosing the proper item of a contrastive pair...
>
> Automatic unconscious use of the appropriate item or structure, when the attention is centered upon the meaning of the whole utterance and is thus drawn away from the particular necessity of making a selection....
>
> All practice should lead to the stage of learning in which the language forms themselves sink below the threshold of attention and the speaker becomes conscious only of the meaning....
>
> A satisfactory control of a language can not be achieved through a process of memorizing rules and trying to remember and apply them.[77]

Much more could be said about Fries' Oral Approach, but that is not the purpose of this book. However, one final point about Fries and his Oral Approach must be made. The man and his ideas have been the subject of much debate in recent years. Nevertheless, whether one regards them as "classic" or "old fashioned," one indisputable point remains—for his time, Fries was a "radical."[78] He was a pedagogical revolutionary. "Compared with foreign language teaching in the U.S. before 1940,...the innovations established by Fries were a radical departure from previous concepts of language instruction."[79] Moreover, his innovative ideas spread far beyond the University of Michigan campus. Decades later, it was said of him, "Whether one chooses to accept or to reject specific elements of the 'Fries Legacy,' one can neither ignore nor deny the importance of the impact of Charles C. Fries on ESL and on the applied linguistics research underlying it."[80]

The Spread of the Oral Approach

As early as 1939, "in anticipation of increased concern with the teaching of English in Puerto Rico and the Latin American countries" due to President Franklin D. Roosevelt's "Good Neighbor Policy," a conference was held to determine which methodological approach U.S. Department of State operations would follow in teaching English. The choice was between "the Basic English with pictures proposed by I.A. Richards and a linguistically based approach advocated by Fries."[81] After some deliberation, the decision was to support Fries.

A few years later, Fries' English Language Institute (ELI) at Michigan, the first of its kind in the United States, created even greater interest in his methods and materials. "The experimental intensive course was a resounding success and the English Language Institute was established as a permanent part of the university. By 1943, the ELI offered continuous eight-week intensive English courses throughout the entire calendar year....From modest numbers of students during the first few years, enrollments rose steadily."[82] Because of its reputation, the Michigan Institute served as a model for ELI programs set up at numerous other American universities in subsequent years, and the books produced by Fries and his staff for use in the Michigan ELI were adopted throughout the country.

Fries' 1945 book for teachers, *Teaching and Learning English as a Foreign Language,* became a classic. Moreover, an intensive Teacher Education Program was set up on the University of Michigan campus that would eventually train "over 4,000 teachers of English from the United States and from countries around the world."[83]

Michigan started its own journal, *Language Learning,* in 1948. Devoted to "the pedagogical implications of linguistic science," it was unique for its day and found an eager audience.[84] In its early years, most articles were written by Fries' disciples and dealt with their language-teaching principles and programs. In this manner, *Language Learning* lent prestige to Fries' work and aided in disseminating his Oral Approach ideas.

Conditions Encouraging the Spread of Oral Approach Ideas in the U.S.A.

Of course, the spread of Fries' language-teaching methods throughout the United States was also encouraged by favorable conditions.

When the United States entered World War II, the importance of foreign languages soon became apparent. The "frighteningly practical and urgent communication needs of the battlefields, the refugee and prisoner of war camps, and of military intelligence"[85] often demanded personnel who could communicate in non-English languages. Yet, "only one American out of 5,000 could speak passable French or German" and "there were practically no trusted Americans who spoke Japanese, Malay, or Yapese."[86]

To remedy this problem, the U.S. Army set up a special language training program. This Army Specialized Training Program (ASTP) commenced operations in 1943 and soon involved 15,000 trainees at fifty-five American colleges and universities. It is noteworthy that although it used existing campuses, the army did not contract with the universities to provide conventional language courses. Many of the military students had already been through traditional language courses, and they did not lead to the utilitarian command of the spoken language that the military operations required.[87]

The ASTP had a wide-ranging and enduring influence on the teaching of foreign languages in the United States. "Achievement was, on the whole, greatly superior to that in the conventional language courses previously given in schools and colleges."[88] "The results after a few months seemed so impressive that it was believed that the 'Army Method' contained the secret of successful language teaching."[89] Consequently, the program "caused great interest among language teachers generally"[90] and it gained "widespread recognition...both through articles in scholarly journals and...the popular press."[91] Naturally then, after the war, there was a demand for similar courses in American secondary schools and universities,[92] and many institutions attempted to duplicate them.[93]

The method and materials used by the army were based on those used in the relatively obscure Intensive Language Program started in 1941 by the American Council of Learned Societies. The program was originated by and for anthropological linguists (with the aid of two $50,000 grants from the Rockefeller Foundation[94]) and derived from the work of Franz Boas and Edward Sapir, as well as Leonard Bloomfield, the "father" of American structural linguistics.

Fries' Oral Approach, though it developed distinctly at Michigan, also applied the principles of modern linguistics to language pedagogy and benefited from the postwar interest in "scientific language learning." Fries' book for teachers appeared and his English Language Institute successes occurred at a time when the mood for reforming U.S. foreign language courses was strong. As Anthony explains, "the War provided an irresistible force that weakened the previously immovable traditions of grammar-translation....And this change enabled some foreign language teachers to break with tradition and to innovate."[95]

A decade later, the Sputnik panic renewed the emphasis on reforming foreign language teaching in America's schools. The resultant National Defense Education Act (NDEA) gave modern language teaching high priority. Books such as *The National Interest and Foreign Languages* [96] appeared, and U.S. educators lamented "the general ignorance of foreign languages throughout the country."[97] Intended to remedy this situation, the NDEA provided money to "pay for a teacher's attendance at a summer institute where his knowledge of the language he teaches [was] improved and he [was] given an acquaintance with linguistics and the audiolingual method."[98] Large numbers of teachers attended such institutes, and language courses throughout the country were affected.

In sum, a crisis was perceived, and sweeping changes occurred.[99] A "new age" dawned in the history of American foreign language teaching[100] and many of the innovations came from Charles C. Fries.[101] His ideas spread widely, and "in the 1950s, the Michigan approach and the Michigan materials became nothing less than the 'American way,' the orthodox methodology of American English specialists in both the United States and abroad."[102]

The Spread of the Oral Approach
Outside of the United States

The influence of Fries' "Michigan Method" quickly spread to different parts of the world. The first place it was exported was Mexico. "In 1943, the United States for the first time in its history moved through the Department of State to set up an ongoing English-teaching program abroad. It provided a grant to the Michigan Institute to support for eighteen months the English Language Institute at the Benjamin Franklin Library in Mexico City."[103] But Mexico was only the first of many countries to which the ideas developed at Michigan for teaching ESL would be exported. "In the 1940s, 1950s, and 1960s, the ELI was deeply involved in English language instruction on five continents. In total, during the years from 1941 to 1984, the ELI has conducted special programs in language teaching and/or teacher training in Ann Arbor and in over 30 host countries around the world."[104]

Fries was personally involved in many of these ventures. In the early 1940s, his experiences teaching English to Spanish speakers at Michigan led to other projects in Latin America. From 1949 to 1954, he headed up a program to revise the English teaching program in Puerto Rico.[105] One very tangible outcome of his involvement was the *Fries American English Series* textbooks, published in 1952 and promoted as "a pioneer attempt to apply the recent advances of linguistic science to the teaching of English as a second language in elementary and secondary schools."[106] When

Rockefeller personnel inquired about Fries' work in Puerto Rico, the report they received was that it "was well received and that the results have been significant."[107]

In 1954-55, when ELEC was investigating the possibility of having him attend the Specialists' Conference in Tokyo, Fries was lecturing in Germany on a Fulbright award.[108]   While there, he received numerous invitations to lecture in other countries: Singapore, Syria, Hong Kong, Ceylon, Indonesia, Taiwan, the Philippines, and Japan.[109] (The Japanese invitations were to lecture at Meiji Gakuin and International Christian University.[110])

Fries was willing, even eager to visit Japan, having become acquainted with the country through contacts with GARIOA students at Michigan. Unfortunately, due to delays and misunderstandings, he did not make it to Japan in 1955. He expressed his regrets to the United States Educational Commission (USEC) officer in Germany, lamenting, "Japan is the one place in which I could do the most good."[111] To the USEC executive secretary in Japan he apologized: "I am exceedingly sorry, not because of myself for it would have been a strenuous trip, but because of the fact that I did feel that I could have been of some use to your teachers of English. Perhaps the opportunity may arise again for me to give some help to the teachers of your country."[112]

His words were more than just a polite apology. Fries was genuinely interested in Japan, and later that year he investigated a possible Fulbright opening teaching English as a foreign language in Japan.[113] In Ann Arbor there was also discussion of opening a University of Michigan Center in Japan with which Fries would be involved.[114]

Ironically, at the time he was investigating possible opportunities in Japan, Rockefeller representatives were investigating the possibility of involving him in their effort to reform English teaching in that country. Only a few months later he would receive an invitation from the newly formed English Language Exploratory Committee to attend their upcoming Specialists' Conference.

ESTABLISHMENT OF THE
ENGLISH LANGUAGE EXPLORATORY COMMITTEE

The name *English Language Exploratory Committee* was first used in May 1956. The "First Meeting of the Central Committee" of ELEC was not held, however, until July 28 of that year.

The Committee consisted of an elite group of prestigious and powerful Japanese:

Eikichi Araki	Governor, The Bank of Japan
Daishiro Hidaka	Former Vice-Minister of Education; Dean, Institute of Education, International Christian University
Sanki Ichikawa	Director, Institute for Research on Language Teaching; Professor-Emeritus, University of Tokyo
Taizo Ishizaka	President, Federation of Economic Organizations
Tamihei Iwasaki	President, Tokyo University of Foreign Studies

Miss Tano Jodai	President, Japan Women's University
Seiji Kaya	President, Japan Science Council
Nobutane Kiuchi	Managing Director, Institute of World Economy
Shinzo Koizumi	Former President, Keio University
Takashi Kuroda	Professor of English, Tokyo University of Education
Tamon Maeda	President, Japanese National Commission for UNESCO; Former Minister of Education
Tatsuo Morito	President, Hiroshima University; Former Minister of Education
Mrs. Hanako (Keizo) Muraoka	Writer and Social Critic; Member, Japanese National Commission for UNESCO
Fumio Nakajima	Professor of English, University of Tokyo
Nobumoto Ohama	President, Waseda University
Takeshi Saito	Former President, Tokyo Woman's Christian College; Professor-Emeritus, University of Tokyo
Genji Takahashi	President, Federation of English Teachers Unions; Professor of English, Meiji Gakuin University
Yasaka Takagi	Professor-Emeritus, University of Tokyo
Yoshio Tanaka	Vice-Minister of Education
Minoru Toyoda	Former Chancellor, Professor of English, Aoyama Gakuin University
Shigeharu Matsumoto	Managing Director, International House of Japan; Member, Fulbright Commission in Japan
Mamoru Shimizu	Professor of English, International Christian University[115]

Some members of this committee were elected only about a month before the Specialists' Conference and were never deeply involved in ELEC's affairs. Nevertheless, the prestige of this impressive group lent considerable power and credibility to the ELEC cause.

ELEC's "aims and aspirations" were ambitious. Plainly stated, they were "to change English teaching methods in Japan," to reeducate the teachers of English in that country.[116] As early as April 1956, ELEC's intentions to encourage the adoption of an "almost revolutionized system of teaching of English," and "the preparation of entirely new series of textbooks and other teaching materials" [sic] had been discussed privately.[117] In August of that year, ELEC's long-term objectives were explained in a letter sent to "all individuals concerned":

> In spite of all the efforts made by authorities concerned as well as by teachers of English themselves, the present status of the teaching of English in this country still has much room left for improvement. If we can effect fundamental improvement of this situation by training as many young Japanese as possible to speak good practical English, this will undoubtedly be a contribution to the future international activities of our country. This is the reason we organized the English Language Exploratory Committee last July.[118]

In spite of these ambitious plans, the committee was still "exploratory" only, and a careful, "go slow" philosophy prevailed. In a memorandum to Rockefeller, McLean explained, "I think that the situation has developed in a healthy sort of way. We are not committed to anything beyond the conference....In short, it seems better to take one step at a time rather than to try to lay out a grand plan."[119] Whatever advantages this "let things develop as they may" approach had, the lack of a "grand plan" for ELEC also proved to have some serious disadvantages in the long run.

THE ELEC "SPECIALISTS' CONFERENCE"

The immediate concern of the committee was the upcoming "Conference of Specialists." This Specialists' Conference had three major purposes:

1. to stimulate interest in English-teaching methods generally
2. to point out problems with the English-teaching methods commonly used in Japan
3. to spread information about new methods (particularly, the American methods)

The conference was held at International House in Tokyo and lasted six days (from Monday, September 3 to Saturday, September 8, 1956) and was prepared "in such a way that...all of the important problems of English teaching...in Japan [could] be discussed."[120] Session topics included the following:

- "Problems of Teaching English in Japan"
- "Present Situation of English Teaching in the Upper and Lower Secondary Schools: The Standard of Achievement to be Required in the University Entrance Examination"
- "Comparison of Japanese and English"
- "Audio-Visual Aids in the Classroom"
- "Training in Universities of Prospective Teachers of English"[121]

It is worthy of note that the "guest consultants" were originally scheduled to speak on "How to Improve English Teaching in Japan" even though Fries and Twaddell would arrive in the country for the first time only a few days before the conference.[122] Apparently, the planners were willing to accept whatever prescriptions the specialists might give. The assumption seems to have been that what worked in the United States would work equally well in Japan. Wisely, however, the guests spoke on topics with which they were more familiar.[123]

Of course, most of the conference participants were Japanese, and many of the papers were presented by Japanese scholars. Their participation helped prevent the ELEC movement from being perceived as an attempt by foreigners to impose a solution on Japan. To emphasize the point that "the initiative for the present project was taken by Japanese," the conference planners, who had earlier officially added "Nihon" to the committee's Japanese name (*Eigo-Kyoiku Kenkyu Iinkai*), decided to "make no reference to Mr. Rockefeller's interest" and involved the Japanese Ministry of Education as one of the official sponsors of the conference.[124]

The "Conclusions and Recommendations" drawn up at the end of the Specialists' Conference, however, evidenced the strong influence of Fries' Oral Approach ideas. Divided into four general categories, they also outlined the directions ELEC's future activities would take:

1. General Principles of Teaching Methods. Today too many Japanese teachers of English are teaching about English instead of teaching English itself. Often they are not aware of the ultimate aim toward which their efforts should be directed....Few of them know much about modern developments in the field of linguistic science.

They ought to be made aware of the need of applying these theories to their classroom work. If they were, English teaching and learning here, we are firmly convinced, would become more effective....Oral practice with materials prepared according to scientific principles is considered essential at the beginning of language learning.

2. Teaching Materials. Teaching materials to be used for the new approach must be built upon a systematic comparison of the analyzed structural patterns of English and Japanese....In accord with the principles of the new approach, the textbook used must indicate those activities for the students which guide them in the building-up of speech habits as near as possible to those of native speakers of English....Such a textbook must be accompanied by a teachers' guide with complete descriptions of the activities suggested to induce efficient oral practice....In order to make the new textbook most usable, teacher training must go hand in hand with the compilation. Regarding the preparation and completion of the textbook, it is desirable that the Committee should undertake it promptly.

3. General and Specialized Training of English Teachers. To meet the immediate needs a summer training program in 1957 is highly desirable, primarily for lower secondary school teachers and lasting three to six weeks....For continuing needs consideration should be given to the desirability of establishing one or more institutes which might or might not be attached to existing universities. Such institutes should...perform the following tasks: (a) training younger teachers with new methods and new materials, (b) re-training older teachers, (c) supplementing the training of prospective teachers of English in universities.

4. Achievement Tests and University Entrance Examinations. Entrance examinations tend to become a means of selection only....The Specialists' Conference herewith asserts its earnest desire to have the achievement test conducted always as a means of evaluation rather than as a means of selection....In recent years there has been a steady improvement in the quality of the university entrance examinations in English....But there remains the danger of unrealistic entrance examinations, which are neither a reliable test of the applicant's ability to use English in his future studies nor a just evaluation of his achievement in upper secondary schools....The Specialist's Conference recognizes the great difficulties of administering university entrance examinations in English in view of the large numbers of applicants....It suggests the exploration of language testing procedure with a view to improving the quality of the examinations and reducing the expenditure of trained scholars' energies in this task....[125]

Once the Specialists' Conference was over, its sponsors judged it an unqualified success. McLean reported to John D. Rockefeller 3rd:

1. The Conference clearly served the purpose for which it was held in that there now appears to be a firm resolve on the part of the leaders in the English-teaching profession to initiate active steps to improve conditions in this field.

2. The feeling is that the present materials and methods are completely inadequate and that a fresh start must be made. Initially this will probably be at the lower secondary-school level.

3. The current time schedule for the preparation of the proposed materials is indicated in the attached notes on the conference....Indications are that this work will start promptly....

4. A summer teacher-training session is contemplated for 1957. For this they may desire Fries and Twaddell who complement one another beautifully. Fries is about 65 but vigorous. His strength...is linguistics. Twaddell is about 55 and...a really outstanding teacher—tho [sic] a competent linguist as well. They have really done a superb job here!

5.   ...That there has been such unanimity has been a surprise and a source of great satisfaction...It is a great tribute to the consultants.[126]

Fries and Twaddell were much more impressive than Hornby, the British representative, who was "overshadowed completely." McLean confided, "The British and Palmer have, I feel, been reasonably well eliminated as ghosts[,] which greatly simplifies matters and clears the road for progress."[127]

In the euphoria of this success, grand plans for ELEC's future were drawn up. The conference recommended: (1) "that the English Language Exploratory Committee continue as a permanent organization," and (2) that an executive committee be established and authorized to employ a secretariat so that they could carry forward the program.[128] Two major subcommittees were formed—"one for preparing teaching materials, and the other for planning a summer program for 1957."[129]

Thus, the two major prongs of ELEC's attack on the traditional Japanese ELT system were defined: (1) training teachers, and (2) producing Oral Approach materials. Virtually no action was taken in regard to ELEC's third area of concern—university-entrance examinations. Neglecting this aspect of the Japanese ELT system turned out to be a serious error.

Efforts, successes, and problems in each of these areas will be discussed at length in later sections of this book. First, however, the remainder of the story of Charles C. Fries' work with ELEC will be presented. Although Fries did not actively participate in the ELEC campaign after 1959, he helped lay ELEC's ideological foundation, and his ideas and activities continued to affect the campaign for many years.

CHARLES C. FRIES' INVOLVEMENT WITH ELEC

Fries' influence at the Specialists' Conference was substantial. Matsumoto reported to McLean:

I am convinced that what contributed most to the successful results was the presence of Dr. Fries himself. I believe also that what will sustain the concerted efforts of the Japanese specialists hereafter most effectively is our expectation that Dr. Fries is revisiting us next March.[130]

In turn, McLean reported to Rockefeller:

As Matsumoto has already indicated to us in a recent letter, Fries' performance was outstanding and is probably responsible for whatever success may have been achieved in the past. I think he has a very significant role to play in the future along with Professor Twaddell....A strong desire has been expressed by the Japanese for them to return.[131]

Rockefeller himself wrote to Fries:

I could not resist writing you this note not only because of my satisfaction as to the results but also because I realized that they were so largely due to your own participation and leadership in the conference. Also I was most happy to learn that you had agreed to go back to Japan next spring for a period of several weeks. The enthusiasm generated by the conference is liable to diminish as they face the hard facts of the job to be done. The anticipation of your return will give them an incentive which will be I think most important in the launching of their program.[132]

Fries did return to Japan, not only the next spring but a number of other times also, and served as "senior USA consultant to ELEC" for several years. Following the 1956 Specialists' Conference, he remained in Japan for nearly three weeks, traveling throughout the country, visiting many universities and secondary schools, and giving lectures. In March of 1957, on his way back from a UNESCO (United Nations Educational, Scientific, and Cultural Organization) conference on the teaching of modern languages held in Australia, he stopped in Japan and stayed until June 18, working on the preparation of materials. In 1958 (April 10 to June 21) and 1959 (April through May) he was involved in similar ELEC-sponsored activities in Japan.[133] In 1960 and 1961 he returned to Japan again, but this time as a consultant for the Asia Foundation, which was setting up a college-level English course at the Japanese Defense Academy.[134] In 1966, he paid his final visit to Japan, but it was only a short one as he was merely passing through.[135]

During the years of his involvement with ELEC, Fries was involved in three types of activities: lecturing, preparing materials, and planning for ELEC's summer program for teachers.

Lecture Tours

During the first three years, Fries traveled throughout Japan giving lectures on the Oral Approach. He was a powerful, persuasive speaker and was "very popular."[136] There were "great audiences wherever he went."[137] In 1956, after the Specialists' Conference, he traveled as far as Osaka and Fukuoka. On August 21 he also gave a lecture at the prestigious University of Tokyo.[138] In 1957 he toured as far as Yamaguchi-ken. A professor at Yamaguchi National University expressed the feelings of many when he heard that Fries was coming:

> In the Educational Faculty I am teaching on your *principles* and *approaches*, and not only the students but all the teachers of English in junior and senior high schools hereabout are so serious, so earnest studying your Michigan Approaches. And that great news that you are coming is a great stimulus indeed. [sic][italics in original][139]

In 1958, his lectures and discussions took him to Hiroshima and then to the island of Shikoku. Upon returning to Tokyo he spoke with several large groups, including one at the Tokyo University of Education.[140]

Materials and "Corpus" Preparation

One of Charles C. Fries fundamental beliefs was that "only with satisfactory basic materials can one efficiently begin the study of a foreign language. No matter what happens later, the ease and speed of attainment in the early stages of the learning of a language will depend primarily upon the selection and sequence of the materials to be studied."[141]

From the start of his work with ELEC, Fries emphasized the importance of materials. In his preconference contacts with Rockefeller representatives, he stressed "time and time again" the point "that the method is not what is important but that what is important are the materials which are developed through the use of linguistics."[142]

A related, and equally critical point for Fries was that

> "foreign" language teaching is always a matter of teaching a specific "foreign" language with its special structural features to students who have a specific "native" language background with fundamentally different structural features. To be efficient, separate and differing sets of materials for learning English must be used for those of each different linguistic background.[143]

In other words, "a different set of teaching materials must be prepared for each linguistic background."[144]

It was not surprising, then, that one of the recommendations made at the end of the Fries-dominated Specialists' Conference was that a set of Oral Approach textbooks designed especially for Japanese students be prepared. The plan was to make the two parts of ELEC's double emphasis (materials preparation and teacher training) work together by preparing Oral Approach materials for Japan and then using them with the teachers in the summer program. Given his predilection toward materials and the limits on his time in Japan, Fries placed his major emphasis on materials production and left the summer program to Twaddell and others.

Fries' major work was in producing what he called a "corpus," "a detailed outline of English structure, vocabulary, and content" that was "not intended for classroom work but as a basic guide to future textbook writers and publishers."[145] It undergirded the ELEC summer program courses and also became the foundation for the textbooks ELEC produced.

Fries was most involved when the first-year materials were being written. In fact, progress came only after he had personally overcome a number of obstacles. For instance, arriving in Tokyo in March of 1957, he expected to help polish up what the materials production subcommittee had produced, but he found that very little work had been done. He wrote to Twaddell, "Miss O'Connor did everything she could but they didn't even get together until January and then the subcommittee met every 3 weeks to *talk* about it" [italics in original]. As Fries got things going, finding skilled personnel in Japan was a challenge. In the same letter, he wrote, "There is difficulty getting real help on whipping the rough material into shape."[146] Furthermore, in the beginning ELEC had no physical facilities to speak of, so "from 1957 to 1958, the work of compilation was carried on at Dr. Yasaka Takagi's house in Shibuya."[147] Despite these problems, Fries managed to get the materials for the 1957 summer seminar prepared and, according to his optimistic report, the program "succeeded brilliantly."[148]

The following year, 1958, when the second-year materials were produced, better help was secured and success came more easily. In fact, although Fries (who was in Japan for a shorter time period) drafted the materials[149] and "contributed greatly to the project,"[150] the real load was passed to a number of newly recruited ELEC workers—Dr. Ernest Haden (a professor at the University of Texas), Dr. Einar Haugen (a professor at the University of Wisconsin), Dr. Mary Lu Joynes (an instructor at The University of Wisconsin), and Dr. Everett Kleinjans (a recent graduate of Fries' program at Michigan and a faculty member at International Christian University).

In 1958, however, additional challenges also arose. There were some serious disagreements between Fries and Twaddell (discussed in detail under "harmony" in chapter five).[151] This "friction" was—to say the least—discouraging for both men, and although they were eventually able to work around their differences, both Fries and Twaddell nearly abandoned the project at this time.   In addition, after working so strenuously, both men were very tired. The burden weighed especially heavily on the older Fries. In light of these factors, it was concluded "that although the contribution of Professor Fries had been an indispensable one to date, he should not be permitted to be involved in any operational sense in the development of materials lest he hold up progress since he has lost a considerable amount of his vigor in recent months as a result of his advancing years."[152] Fries himself admitted, "I was not in very good shape as I left Japan" and was worried about a possible gall bladder operation in January.[153] He later wrote to ELEC, "Those who have been concerned with my physical welfare [realize] that I must not continue to push myself as vigorously as I have in the past."[154]

Besides these reasons for Fries' diminishing involvement, the Japanese leaders of ELEC[155] as well as the "Japanese junior trainers"[156] were beginning to take on more responsibility. Such being the case, it was agreed that "there would be no ranking American professor."[157]

By this time also, Fries' attention was being drawn to other areas of the world. For example, in October of 1958, he traveled to England and then on to India to conduct "consultations concerning linguistic programs."[158]

Nevertheless, Fries was not yet out of the ELEC picture. When in late 1958 it looked as if he might not travel to Japan in 1959, the ELEC executive committee wrote, "We would like to assure you that your forthcoming visit next spring is vital to ELEC's work and we crave your continued support."[159] He was also asked "to prepare a corpus for the third-year material similar to the corpus prepared for the first and the second year, provided that this could be accomplished by the end of 1958."[160] When he responded (from India) that it would be impossible for him to do the corpus work by that time, the deadline was extended to May 31, 1959.[161]

In the spring of 1959, Fries did return to Japan, but his schedule (and his desire not to overlap with Twaddell) required him to leave by June 1.[162] During this time, Akira Ota and Vernon Brown worked on the third-year materials "with the co-operation of Dr. Fries."[163]

By mutual agreement, 1959 was to be the last year Charles C. Fries would come to Japan under the auspices of ELEC.[164]   After 1959,

Twaddell, who found it "difficult to be away for three consecutive summers," did not continue to work with ELEC either.[165]

In late 1959, the ELEC executive committee expressed their view that the corpus materials, which Fries had produced to provide guidance for those producing the soon-to-be-published ELEC textbooks, should also be published in book form.[166] As Fries himself expressed, "Such a book should provide a guide to writers of textbooks, not only for the first three years of the Japanese secondary schools, but also for those who wish to make materials for teaching the English language to Japanese speakers at other levels...."[167] Fries (and his wife) compiled and polished the work of the previous years into a large corpus, and the book was published by ELEC in 1961 under the title *Foundations for English Teaching: A Corpus of Materials upon Which to Build Textbooks and Teachers' Guides for Teaching English in Japan*. It was the culmination of Fries' years of work in Japan, and ELEC was pleased with it. Shortly after it appeared, Overton reported to Rockefeller, "We are now the proud possessors of a first-rate Fries book."[168] How much this publication influenced ELT in Japan is impossible to determine, but there is no doubt that it added to ELEC's reputation and prestige.

Planning for the ELEC Summer Program for Teachers[169]

Fries never actually taught in the ELEC summer program for training teachers. That aspect of the ELEC effort was left primarily to Twaddell and others, while Fries worked on materials. Nevertheless, Fries played an important role in planning and preparing for the summer program—partly because he usually arrived in Japan several months ahead of Twaddell and partly because the "scripts" for the summer courses were based heavily on his materials and "corpus" work.

This preparatory work was not always pleasant for Fries and those who worked with him. The initial plans for the first ELEC summer program for teachers were made at the close of the Specialists' Conference in 1956. On the basis of these plans and his experience conducting similar training programs in other countries, Fries had definite ideas regarding how it would be handled. When he arrived in Tokyo in March of 1957, however, he found that the plans for the summer program had been made contrary to his expectations. In fact, he felt strongly that if these plans were followed, ELEC's Oral Approach goals would be jeopardized. First of all, as he explained in a letter to Twaddell, the training course was to be held at International Christian University and would be "dominated by ICU personnel," who had been "very vocal and insistent concerning the abundant and completely satisfying virtues of their own program." Furthermore, "lectures on English literature in Japanese" were planned. Finally, the summer program teachers were to consist of "one participant selected from each prefecture, by the prefecture authorities." He confided, "Somehow this didn't strike me as a good training program to [teach] 7th grade teachers to handle successfully the kind of materials I had planned to write."   Since the first summer program would serve as a model for subsequent ELEC teacher institutes, Fries felt it was essential that it be carried out according to his plan. Consequently, he "got to work and had some changes made." In spite of the late date, he announced, "We're *not* going to ICU and we'll have our *own* staff without *ICU* assistance" [italics in original].[170]

In retrospect, it is difficult to decide whether this course of action helped or hindered ELEC. Whatever good it may have accomplished, it also offended important people (both in ELEC and at ICU) and damaged university relationships that would have otherwise been helpful.[171] Nevertheless, at its conclusion, Fries announced that the revised summer program had "succeeded brilliantly," demonstrating that "even in a brief three weeks English teachers with firmly fixed habits could not only learn to understand and use a new approach to their teaching but could greatly improve their own English."[172]

GENERAL ELEC ACTIVITIES

After the Specialists' Conference, ELEC became involved in activities in three general areas: "compiling efficient English textbooks based upon the results of modern linguistic science, sponsoring in-service training seminars for teachers of English every summer, and [later] establishing a permanent English Language Institute."[173]

Textbook Production

The idea of a "new series of textbooks to correct some of the inappropriatenesses [sic] of existing texts" was suggested as early as July 1956, in a planning session for the ELEC Specialists' Conference.[174] After the conference, the production of Oral Approach textbooks for junior high school English classes became one of ELEC's major projects.

Right away, ELEC workers began preparing examples of first-year, oral practice material, which would be used for training the teachers in the summer. It was anticipated that every year thereafter, an additional "year" of textbook material would be produced and tried out. By August 1961, the first three Oral Approach books would be ready to be submitted to the Ministry of Education for approval and subsequent publication.[175]

Surprisingly, the ELEC textbooks were not the first Oral Approach books to be published in Japan. In 1956, before the Specialists' Conference, Tamotsu Yambe—who had studied at Michigan under the GARIOA program, learned about Fries' Oral Approach while there, and returned to Japan in 1953—produced a book entitled *Pattern Practice and Contrast*.[176] It was only a pioneering effort, however, and was never widely used.

The ELEC textbooks were produced by a joint working group of Americans and Japanese. Funds from Rockefeller's Council on Economic and Cultural Affairs made the involvement of the American consultants possible by providing U.S. dollars for their salaries and travel expenses.[177]

As noted above, Charles Fries was the most prominent of these Americans, but Ernest Haden, Einar Haugen, Mary Lu Joynes, Everett Kleinjans, Patricia O'Connor, W. Freeman Twaddell, and Vernon Brown were also involved at one stage or another. The Japanese members of the group included Akira Ota, Katsumasa Ikenaga, Kenzo Ito, and Tsutomu Makino.[178] Professors Takashi Kuroda of the Tokyo University of Education, Fumio Nakajima of the University of Tokyo, and Kotaro Ishibashi of Nihon University also cooperated in the venture.[179]

In 1958, after the texts had been designed and work on them was well under way, the Japanese Ministry of Education published its *Revised Draft of the Course of Study*. Since book inspection and approval were in the hands of ministry officials[180] and books that did not meet ministry standards could not be used in Japanese public schools, some ELEC leaders feared that the new guidelines would necessitate a complete revision of ELEC's work to date.[181] Nevertheless, Fries reassured the committee that "the basic 'corpus' as it was planned...would satisfy the most critical of the Board of Examiners for the Ministry,"[182] and that "practically every one of the five hundred and fifty vocabulary items listed in the Mombusho Tables as required is already in our three corpora."[183]

Another challenge that arose at about this same time was the need to field test the ELEC textbook materials on "actual secondary school pupils in the actual classroom environment" and not just on secondary school teachers in the summer program.[184] Since ELEC had no formal association with any secondary schools at that time, this problem was not resolved.

In 1960, slightly ahead of schedule, the three English textbooks for junior high schools were completed. They were dubbed *New Approach to English*. Nevertheless, before the new ELEC textbooks could be sold they had to first be approved by the Ministry of Education. This approval procedure vexed the ELEC workers—especially the Americans—but all they could do was submit their work and then wait anxiously for the verdict. Their books were new and revolutionary, and no one knew how the examiners would react.

Fortunately, the reaction was not negative, although the ministry officials did suggest some changes. It upset some members of the ELEC production team to have to "compromise" their genuine Oral Approach textbooks, but "they were obliged to conform to the requirements," and the textbooks underwent some modifications—to their "dissatisfaction."[185] Nevertheless, the changes were not major and were quickly accomplished. The *New Approach* textbooks finally appeared in print, published through Taishukan Shoten.

English teachers in Japan had been hearing about the Oral Approach for many years. As early as 1958, the ELEC executive committee had reported, "The Japanese teachers of English are getting more and more interested in the oral approach and the ELEC project, but this enthusiasm will not keep long unless we feed it with new fuel. The best fuel we can supply is the appearance of our textbook everybody is looking forward to."[186] Thus, when they were published, ELEC's *New Approach* books created quite a stir. Many people were interested in them.

Disappointingly, however, relatively few teachers actually used them. At the time there were approximately six million pupils studying English[187] in 13,622 lower secondary schools in Japan.[188] ELEC's books were adopted by only 130 junior high schools[189] in 1961, and sales totaled 76,000 copies—only about one percent of the potential audience. Worse still, sales failed to increase substantially in subsequent years.

Work on revising the textbooks was started in 1962, by Mabell B. Nardin. In 1963, the revision continued, "with the co-operation of Professor Grant E. Taylor, Director of the American Language Institute, New York University."[190] The three revised textbooks were authorized by the Ministry of Education in 1964 and published in 1965 through Gakken Shoseki.

Unfortunately, even the revised *New Approach* books "did not enjoy large circulation."[191] They were adopted by only 101 junior high schools.[192] Nor did the number of adoptions increase with time. Eventually, in 1972, publication of the *New Approach to English* books was discontinued.[193]

This inability to penetrate the Japanese textbook market was undoubtedly a great disappointment to the people at ELEC. But, from an optimistic perspective, it was not necessarily a failure. Although, according to some, the books were "too revolutionary,"[194] "too progressive for that time, and teachers could not follow them,"[195] with the passage of time they had an indirect influence on other books. In fact, some ELEC supporters claim that this "by-product" was very great.[196] As one Japanese ELT expert put it, "The ELEC books did not last, but others were influenced by them."[197] ELEC personnel took solace in the fact that "although [the books] seemed like a failure, they left a permanent impression. They were imitated by other publishers."[198] As one of the more poetic ELEC stalwarts phrased it, "Thus with a dying fall, they quickened a good many others to the new note of Oral Approach."[199]

It should be mentioned also that ELEC's publications were not limited to the *New Approach* texts. ELEC also published the *ELEC Bulletin* and an impressive collection of books and pamphlets including *Addresses and Papers at the Specialists' Conference* (Kenkyusha, 1957); *Lectures by C. C. Fries and W. F. Twaddell* (Kenkyusha, 1958); "On the Oral Approach" [pamphlet] (Taishukan, 1959); *ELEC Publications, Vol III.* (Kenkyusha, 1959); *ELEC Publications, Vol. IV.* (Kenkyusha, 1960); *ELEC Publications, Vol. V.* (Kenkyusha, 1961); and *Foundations for English Teaching* (Kenkyusha, 1961).[200] These publications helped spread the doctrine of the Oral Approach throughout Japan (and the world).

Retraining Teachers

As a nation, the Japanese have studied foreign languages for many centuries, and they began studying English nearly a hundred years before

ELEC's campaign commenced. In the course of this history, powerful pedagogical traditions developed. Such traditions change slowly. In many ways schools are self-duplicating institutions, and the old saying "Teachers teach the way they were taught" rings discouragingly true when it involves the unfortunate "reproduction of a bad tradition."[201]

ELEC's leaders recognized this problem, and their "highest priority" was to retrain teachers, improving their linguistic abilities and teaching methods.[202] This objective was pursued primarily through their ELEC summer programs for teachers. The purpose of this ELEC summer program (and the ones that followed) was best explained by Fries himself:

> Through this course we expect, first, to make these teachers competent to teach the materials of this new approach, both by improving their own practical control of English and by giving them a thorough grasp of the patterns to be taught and the linguistic basis underlying the whole work. We expect, second, to test the teaching materials themselves and to carry on daily revision and supplementation. We hope that this group of teachers will come from this summer of work with considerable competence and real enthusiasm.[203]

The first ELEC summer program was held in 1957 at Toyo Eiwa Jogakuin.[204] Trainees consisted of "young teachers, who were regarded by competent judges as 'promising' on the basis of their performance in the classroom....Their preparation usually included a standard language-and-literature major, and a prescribed complement of courses in Education. They had a fair-to-excellent reading knowledge of English; their writing in English was fair-to-good." Yet, "their oral control of English ranged from poor to fair; they frequently failed to understand and were frequently incomprehensible in conversation." Most importantly, "they were unfamiliar with (and hesitant to attempt) the methods appropriate to an oral-approach beginning classroom, since they rightly distrusted their oral command of English."[205]

The ELEC course consisted of "fifteen days of six hours each."[206] Trainees experienced and participated in "oral presentation and structure drills, pronunciation drills, controlled conversations, lectures on linguistics and teaching methods, practice teaching and other activities," all aimed at giving them the skills and knowledge they needed to implement the Oral Approach in their English classes.[207]

An important feature of these ELEC summer programs was that they utilized "native speakers of English exclusively as instructors for drills in English."[208] This feature, along with the "scientific materials" employed, made ELEC's program "unique in its quality."[209]

After the first summer session, a favorable newspaper article reported:

> The fundamental purpose was to improve the quality and the skill of lower secondary school teachers, and concurrently to try out the teaching materials prepared for the 7th graders by an ELEC committee. Emphasis was laid on intensive drill of the oral approach and the use of Japanese was prohibited throughout the program, even at recreation hour or meals...The three-week intensive course gave the trainees

confidence in teaching and handling their pupils. Their English was remarkably improved....They are really well-trained teachers.[210]

With such success and favorable publicity, ELEC's summer program grew steadily. The number of 1957 trainees (22) was small, but plans were made for a much larger group (of about 80) the following summer.[211] The 1958 ELEC summer seminar, held at Sophia University, featured "a galaxy of scholars of modern linguistic science."[212] Eighty-two trainees "representing prefectures and five major cities all over Japan, ranging from Hokkaido to the north down to the Ryukyus to the south" participated.[213] In 1959, there were 95 trainees, only a few more than in 1958, but in 1960, the number tripled—to 296—with ELEC seminars being held in three locations: Tokyo (International Christian University), Kyoto (Doshisha Women's College), and Sendai.[214] The following year, 1961, the number of ELEC Oral Approach trainees almost doubled again, and the geographical spread of summer program sites also increased. A total of 514 teachers received training at ICU; Doshisha University; Tsurugi, Ishikawa-ken; Shimoda, Shizuoka-ken; Sendai; and Nagoya.[215] In 1962, the ELEC summer program's peak year, participation ballooned. In eight widespread locations—Toyo Eiwa Jogakuin; ICU; Kawatabi, Miyagi-ken; Shizuoka; Nagoya; Niigata; Ebino, Miyazaki-ken; and Asahikawa— 1,169 teachers were trained in the principles and procedures of the Oral Approach.

From this peak, however, the number of trainees in successive years declined—to 844 in 1963, 732 in 1964, and 418 in 1965. From that point on, for the next few years, the number of trainees averaged a mere "400 teachers per year."[216] Equally disappointing was the fact that by 1965 almost all of the seminars were held only in the Tokyo area.[217]

Despite this drop in the number of trainees, the ELEC summer program for English teachers was not abandoned. Unlike the publication of the *New Approach* textbooks, this aspect of the original ELEC purpose continues even today. These summer institutes are small (in 1984, a total of only 187 teachers were enrolled) and generally lose money, but they are subsidized by income from ELEC's year-round English Language Institute program.[218]

Over the years, an impressive number of Japanese teachers have attended these summer seminars. From 1957 to 1965, a total of 5,889 teachers benefited from the ELEC summer program.[219] By 1984, this total had risen to 10,028.[220] Of course, this cumulative total is still only a small fraction of the total number of English teachers in Japan (estimated in 1956 at 62,000 in the junior high schools and 22,500 in the senior high schools).[221]

The ELEC English Language Institute

The third—and least revolutionary—of ELEC's major activities began several years after the start of its summer institutes for teachers and the preparation of its *New Approach* textbooks. Nevertheless, ELEC's English Language Institute proved to be the most popular of its activities.

In March 1961, ELEC set up an "experimental" English Language Institute. Night classes were held at Toyo Eiwa Jogakuin Junior College in Tokyo, and 294 students (teachers of English and others) signed up for the six-month course. The second session enrolled 355 students. All of them paid tuition, for by this time ELEC was working toward "full self-support."[222] The curriculum was designed by Professor Archibald Hill, of the University of Texas at Austin, who had started his teaching career at the University of Michigan. The ELI faculty consisted primarily of "eight young American and Canadian trainers residing in the Tokyo area." From the beginning, this institute was a success and attracted capacity crowds.[223] The biggest problems it encountered were related to its physical facilities. The Toyo Eiwa Jogakuin location was inconvenient for the students, and the rent for the classrooms was expensive. Later, these problems were solved when the ELEC building was constructed. Today, this institute is ELEC's primary activity, and its profits subsidize the summer program for training teachers.

ELEC "AT THE CROSSROADS"

In 1962, Yasaka Takagi wrote that ELEC was "at a crossroads."[224] His words reflected the mixed feelings and questioning attitude toward ELEC held by the trustees of the Council on Economic and Cultural Affairs at that time. Large sums of money had already been spent on the ELEC effort. Nevertheless, realizing the enormity of the task (retraining the nearly 100,000 teachers of English in Japan), the trustees also recognized that the summer seminars could go on "indefinitely." After spending nearly $100,000 annually on ELEC for several years, the CECA board had become more realistic and less willing to fund ELEC. They encouraged consultations to "determine what can be done to broaden ELEC and ELEC's base of support." They advised ELEC to "work out plans for its long-range support...with a view to minimizing ELEC's continuing dependence on the CECA." They even made the point that "teacher training on the scale required in Japan should be a large-scale governmental operation."[225]

CECA had no intention of making "a precipitate withdrawal"of its support, which might bring the ELEC program "to a premature halt."[226] Nevertheless, the Japan Society advisory committee to ELEC (Borton, McLean, and Overton) reported, "The time has come to undertake a full review of the ELEC program, with particular reference to the role of the CECA."[227] This review resulted in a mixed picture of successes and problems.

Successes

"ELEC's specific accomplishments during the past five years" included:

- The completion and publication of the *New Approach* textbooks.
- A series of summer seminars "in various parts of Japan every year since 1957," which provided valuable in-service training for Japanese teachers of English.
- A growing ELEC Institute for English teaching, which provided instruction in oral English to approximately eight hundred Japanese teachers (and others) each year.[228]

Problems/Opposition

These successes, of course, were not unqualified. The textbooks did not sell well. The summer program, although still increasing in size at this point, required a proportionately larger CECA grant to pay for the expensive "foreign trainers," who made it valuable and popular. The English Language Institute required larger facilities, which would require even more CECA funding.

With the expansion of ELEC's activities and the passage of time, the forces in opposition to the ELEC movement had become more pronounced also. For instance, the early appearance of cooperation with the Ministry of Education later gave way—in the case of a few key individuals—to feelings of rivalry and resistance, and—more generally—to a lack of support.

Planning for the Future

After considering these pros and cons, CECA's judgment was that ELEC's successes and promise for the future outweighed the problems. One of Overton's confidants set forth his conclusions on ELEC this way:

> I think everyone is agreed that a good job has been done to date and that a solid 'bridgehead' has been established. It seems to be generally agreed that ELEC has served effectively as a pioneer and as a leader and that those responsible for this are the most influential group ever assembled in Japan in relation to this problem....The results from these influences have been significant and everyone seems to be agreed that ELEC should be encouraged and assisted in its future efforts.[229]

McLean wrote to John D. Rockefeller 3rd,

> I think we all agree that the English Language Exploratory Committee has served as a very effective pioneer and gadfly in relation to the teaching of English in Japan. Not only have they made considerable progress in the publication of materials, but their work has also been responsible for influencing others who were already concerned with the subject. In short, I feel that our investment to date has had consequential results.[230]

Another memo to Rockefeller agreed, "The work of the English Language Exploratory Committee has been effective directly and indirectly in creating a greater awareness of the need to teach English through the oral approach which has resulted in a liberalization of the attitude of the Ministry of Education and improvements in the textbooks of other publishers."[231]

Sensing renewed support, Minoru Toyoda, chair of the ELEC executive committee, urged that ELEC "assume the leadership and forge ahead...on the basis of our own original principles...[and] apply a massive effort to the critically important problem of language teaching." He outlined four major steps required to meet this challenge:

* Reorganization. By this he meant "official incorporation" as well as "adding to our present group new members from the fields of government, radio, television, press, and business."

* Training activities. Although he noted that "to date ELEC's own seminars have been the best," Toyoda proposed that ELEC go beyond its rather limited role and "accept the fact of its leadership in this field." He urged that ELEC assume "the role of a central agency prepared to offer all kinds of training courses to Japanese teachers of English at all levels...[and] of all types."

* Materials and research. Toyoda also proposed not only the revision and republication of the *New Approach* textbooks for junior high school English classes, but also the preparation of a new set of materials for senior high school students. In addition, he insisted that ELEC keep its "hand in research activity in order to refine and improve constantly the quality of English teaching in Japan."

* Promotion. Finally, Toyoda recognized the importance of promoting ELEC's methods and materials through speakers, demonstrators, bulletins, and other promotional literature in order to overcome the "well entrenched" publishers of "the old-line English texts."[232]

THE ENGLISH LANGUAGE EDUCATION COUNCIL, INC.

The English Language Exploratory Committee was a "voluntary organization," but as early as 1958, plans had been made for its incorporation. In fact, funds were reserved to have the necessary capital to do so.[233] Nevertheless, this step was not taken for several years. Finally, in May 1962, Takahashi wrote to Overton: "We are going to take steps at long last to incorporate ELEC as the English Language Education Council."[234]

The English Language Exploratory Committee was officially dissolved at a conference held at International House on December 3, 1962. It was succeeded by another conference that officially established the English Language Education Council, Inc. (abbreviated ELEC, as before). "The application for incorporation was submitted to the authorities concerned on January 14, 1963....On February 26 of the same year the establishment of the corporation was authorized by the Minister of Education." According to its optimistic leaders, "ELEC was thus placed on a legal basis firm enough to promote its activities more powerfully than ever."[235]

Headquarters Building

The ELEC offices in Tokyo lacked both adequacy and permanency for many years. (From 1957 to 1963, they were located in Suzuya Kaikan, Iigura, Minato-ku. Later, in 1963-64, they were moved to the Suzuki Building, Yotsuya, Shinjuku-ku.) Moreover, most of the major ELEC operations, such as the summer program for teachers and the English Language Institute, were conducted in rented or loaned facilities.

In 1960, when the ELEC Institute was just starting at Toyo Eiwa Jogakuin, the idea of constructing and equipping a special ELEC building ("If the experimental institute proves a success") was first proposed to the CECA board.[236] Gaining approval for this proposal was an uphill battle. Merely procuring a favorable site on which to build was a considerable challenge in crowded Tokyo. The 1960 report to CECA noted, "Land is no small item—$100,000, at least, in this instance."[237] That amount was greater than ELEC's total expenditures on all its projects for the year 1959.

A year later, when the success of ELEC's English Language Institute was apparent, Matsumoto wrote to Overton:

> For the past several weeks, our ELEC friends and myself have devoted most of our time to hunting for a good premises as the permanent headquarters of ELEC....Our present institute...is somewhat handicapped in its location. We are now inclined to choose a site or a premises nearer to the center of Tokyo, more accessible to most of [the] prospective trainees, students and young business people. In our thinking the question of location has become of paramount importance.[238]

Matsumoto went on to describe how "urban sites are rising in price" and how "the plight of Japanese economy has become quite bad" [sic] making the idea of raising the money for the purchase of land and construction of the building "taboo." He therefore appealed to CECA for ¥90,000,000 ($250,000), with the balance of costs coming from institute and rental income once the building was finished. Such action, he explained, would "solve the major problems in ELEC's future finance once [and] for all."[239]

Minoru Toyoda also appealed for funding to procure a "central headquarters." He noted problems such as "minimum space for a central office," "no room for a library or study room," the poor location of the Toyo Eiwa site, the inavailability of the Toyo Eiwa facility for ELEC Institute courses during the daytime, and the "exorbitant" rent charged for ELEC's use of the building. Projecting income and expenditures for the next five years, he concluded, "whereas we will always run a deficit for our office, seminars, and publications, the building and the training institute within the building will be money-makers. In fact, from the very beginning the Institute will yield a profit, and by 1964 that profit will amount to some ¥19,000,000, or nearly $60,000."[240]

Nevertheless, in the questioning review period of 1962, CECA determined to "take no action on ELEC's request for help with respect to a permanent building until a further study is made of its exact purposes, location, cost, maintenance, and management."[241]

After several unsuccessful attempts to locate a good site for the desired building, the undaunted ELEC executive committee finally reported exciting news:

> We have...recently located a very good site for the ELEC building. It is a square lot of 202 tsubo (about 800 sq. yd.) located at 3-8 Jimbo-cho, Kanda, Chiyoda-ku, Tokyo just next to Senshu University. It is very conveniently located in terms of transportation, because it is quite near either to Suidobashi Station of the National

Railway or to the streetcar stops—Senshu Daigaku Mae, Kudan Shita and Jimbo-cho. The owner of the lot is Mr. Toko Kaneda. He would like to offer his land for construction of a building on condition that he should continue to own the land and should be allowed to use a part of the building....Since this is really a rare good chance for ELEC to have its own building we would like to solicit the special financial assistance of the CECA.[242]

Excited about this prospect, Takahashi wrote to Overton:

As you know, we are firmly convinced that if the ELEC activities are to be continued, it is urgently needed to make ELEC self-supporting and the only means we could think of to achieve that purpose is to have our own building constructed. We also believe that we should not miss this godsent chance, because it would be almost impossible to find another landowner like Mr. Kaneda in the near future, who would offer his land for the building.[243]

Takahashi went on to note that the Japanese side hoped to be able to raise and borrow ¥205,000,000 and therefore would need only ¥45,000,000 ($125,000) from CECA, half of what had been requested previously.

CECA opinion began to turn in favor of providing money for an ELEC headquarters building. In April of 1962, McLean recommended to Rockefeller that "serious consideration should be given to the strong feeling of the Japanese that they need a permanent headquarters building."[244]

Finally, approval was given and construction commenced. About two years later, on January 5, 1965, the impressive building was completed. It was seven stories high, of ferro-concrete construction, with an auditorium, its own recording studio, two language laboratories, twenty classrooms, two research rooms, one faculty room, one conference room, three office rooms, and even a restaurant.[245]

"The construction costs totaled two hundred forty-nine million yen. Of this amount, approximately one half was paid by a grant-in-aid from the Agricultural Development Council [the successor to CECA] and the other half was paid partly through a bank loan and partly with funds contributed by financial circles in Japan."[246] The ELEC Supporters Association had been established many years before, in 1958,[247] and despite difficulties created by the sagging Japanese economy, ELEC experienced success in its drive to raise funds locally.

The dedication ceremony was held on February 23, 1965, and congratulatory addresses were given by Mr. Kiichi Aichi, Minister of Education; Mr. John D. Rockefeller 3rd (representing the Japan Society); Edwin O Reischauer, then the United States ambassador to Japan; and a number of other prestigious individuals.[248]

The main function of the building was to house the ELEC Institute. In addition, it provided office space for the ELEC staff and the growing ELEC library. It also became the primary site of the ELEC summer program for retraining teachers.

Stability, Losing Momentum, and Becoming Self-Sufficient

With the stability brought about by incorporation and the new headquarters building, ELEC's influence was expected to increase. Surprisingly, the opposite seemed to occur. ELEC's influence on ELT in Japan began to wane. For example, the number of teachers in the summer program dropped off considerably—from 1,169 in 1962 to only 418 in 1965—and it never went back up. "With the exception of 1967...there was a gradual decrease in the number of the ELEC teacher-training programs, until there were no more than two Tokyo seminars held at the ELEC Building from 1969 through 1972. Thus the once far flung front was drawn back to its headquarters alone."[249]

There were cutbacks in the area of publications for teachers also. The *ELEC Bulletin,* once published quarterly, now comes out only twice a year.[250]

The present-day opinion about ELEC is that it "is not strong now."[251] Its ELEC Institute has flourished, regularly enrolling one thousand students in both day and night classes, but most are not teachers but businessmen, who are able to pay the tuition. The 1984 summer institute for teachers enrolled only 187.[252] In brief, ELEC has become little more than "another English school."[253]

One probable reason for ELEC's decline is the fatigue its promoters must have felt after exerting such a strenuous effort to reform English language teaching in Japan. One report was that "The ELEC staff had aged more than five years in the five years they had been in office. They were tired and caught in routine."[254] Furthermore, the revolution they had hoped to bring about was occurring very slowly—if at all—despite the energies they had devoted to it.

The same report noted another problem. "There was no longer any lively interchange with scholars from other countries, and the staff was reluctant to undertake challenging experimental projects of their own."[255] This situation came about for two reasons: First, the problems created by the conflict between Fries and Twaddell soured the ELEC leaders on the desirability of involving high-powered experts in their campaign. Yet without these experts, the spark of new ideas was lost. Secondly, there was a fundamental conflict between the desire, on the part of some of ELEC's Japanese leaders, for stability and continuity , and the desire, on the part of the American funding organizations, for innovation and change.[256] Thus, as ELEC achieved self-sufficiency—in the form of incorporation, a popular English Language Institute, and an impressive building—it became less experimental and innovative and thus lost the support of its American backers. Once this cycle began, it spiraled inevitably downward. Under financial pressure, ELEC (like any business operation) naturally cut or reduced its more expensive, less profitable operations, such as publications and institutes for teachers. The end result was a successful commercial enterprise that had virtually abandoned its original revolutionary goals.

THE RISE OF OTHER ORGANIZATIONS
FOR IMPROVING ELT IN JAPAN

Another possible reason for ELEC's decline was the creation of other organizations in Japan dedicated to similar purposes. The Ministry of Education formed its own Council for the Improvement of English Language Teaching in 1960.[257] Its goal, similar to ELEC's, was to enable teachers to "lead their students to proficiency in oral English." To accomplish this end, the council conducted an "in-service training program to strengthen the hearing and speaking abilities of the teachers of English in the lower and the upper secondary school throughout the nation for five years starting from 1961 fiscal."[258]

Other private foundations also got into the act. The Ford Foundation became interested in improving English-language-teaching practices in Japan and, taking a "top-down" approach, sponsored "a project to establish and strengthen programs for the training of teachers of English and other foreign languages in selected Japanese universities."[259] This Advisory Committee on the Training of Teachers of Foreign Languages (ACTT) ran from 1959 to 1964. Because its purpose overlapped with ELEC's, the latter's continuation became less critical.

The Ford Foundation's increasing involvement with ELT in Japan also led to another development that further contributed to ELEC's decline. In mid-1962, it was recommended to John D. Rockefeller 3rd that CECA and the Ford Foundation "work out some arrangement" for a cooperative effort toward improving English teaching in Japan.[260] Initially, the Ford Foundation contributed to the operation of ELEC, and during ELEC's expensive building construction period this support was very welcome. As time went by, however, in light of the problems that ELEC had encountered, the inclination—of both sides, Ford and Rockefeller—was to start afresh with a new approach. They hoped that a new organization would offer an "effective means of renewing foreign scholars' interest in Japan's language problems, and of using that foreign interest as a means of revitalizing Japanese willingness to consider new approaches."[261]

Consequently, a new organization, the Committee for Cooperation on English in Japan (CCEJ) was formed in October 1967. Its general purpose was "to promote the development of English as a second language in Japan."[262] Funded in equal parts by the Ford Foundation and the John D. Rockefeller 3rd Fund, the CCEJ had twenty-four goals, one of which was "continued close cooperation with ELEC."[263] Unlike ELEC—whose approach of maintaining distance and independence from other organizations led to rivalries—the CCEJ hoped "to work closely with existing organizations."[264]

PHASING OUT SUPPORT FOR ELEC

In 1968, the Ford Foundation, which had joined the Agricultural Development Council in subsidizing ELEC, "decided it did not want to continue its support and the managers of JDR 3rd Fund had already reached the same conclusion."[265] Nevertheless, the Rockefeller side, which had provided the impetus for establishing ELEC, felt "some special obligation—not to continue for much longer but at least to use special consideration in working out the termination of our support."[266]

When the topic of termination was brought up, "the ELEC board and staff were literally horrified at the prospect of what they regarded as a sudden and unexpected end of support."[267] Nevertheless, seeing the handwriting on the wall, they suggested a generous terminal grant of $1,000,000. When told that such an amount "could not even be considered," they submitted a request for $250,000 for the year beginning in 1968. This proposal was approved only after the amount had been reduced to $100,000. "That grant was accompanied by a statement of the possibility of two more grants of $100,000 each, in 1969 and 1970, if such grants should be recommended by the CCEJ, which had just been organized." Unfortunately, for reasons that can only be surmised, "the CCEJ declined to recommend any further general-support grants for ELEC."[268]

Thus, at the end of 1968, twelve years after it started, ELEC was finally on its own financially, and fell back on its own resources to survive. As an institution, ELEC did continue, but never with the same power and revolutionary purpose as before.

WAS ELEC A SUCCESS?

A May 1974 report to John D. Rockefeller 3rd from Datus C. Smith, Jr. marked "a final end of the Fund's (and [JDR 3rd's]) long and interesting involvement in the whole question of English in Japan."[269] Rockefeller's contributions to ELT in Japan (directly and through other organizations) had been substantial. Between 1963 and 1969 alone he had provided $1,112,250. Given the size of this investment, the questions that naturally arose were "Was it all worthwhile? Were [Rockefeller's] goals achieved?"[270]

Whether or not ELEC was a success, however, is not a valid question. Success is not a simple dichotomy; it usually comes in degrees rather than absolutes. Furthermore, it is normal for a campaign to be successful in some areas and not others, and such was certainly the case with the ELEC campaign.

A better question (modeled after Coleman's[271]) is "What factors were associated with the various successes and failures of the ELEC effort?" Along with that question comes another: "What were the obstacles to ELEC's success, and how did ELEC personnel deal with them?"

The answers to these questions are of more than historical interest. They can benefit reform-minded educators of today and tomorrow. The ELEC story has much in common with other reform campaigns—in ELT as well as other fields. Modern-day reformers still confront many of the obstacles the ELEC leaders encountered. Thus, understanding and analyzing the ELEC effort can help reformers of the present and future achieve their goals as they learn from the past and turn hindsight into foresight.

NOTES

1. "Rockefeller Fund to Double Its Spending," 26.
2. Morris, 143.
3. Morris, 3.
4. McLean to Rockefeller, 15 May 1953, 5.
5. Berman, 146.
6. "Responses to Edward H. Berman," 180-84.
7. McLean et al., 1, 20.
8. McLean, 11 Jan. 1952.
9. Untitled draft.
10. Matsumoto, interview.
11. Report to Prioleau, 71.
12. Morris, 153.
13. The strength of the Rockefeller feelings regarding the importance of improving ELT in Japan is evidenced by the fact that at the same time they were providing large sums of money for ELEC they were turning down funding requests for other projects, such as an orphanage in Sasebo (Rockefeller to Dewing) and a library for International Christian University (Rockefeller to Overton).
14. Morris, 246.
15. Untitled draft.
16. Morris, 247.
17. Untitled draft.
18. Ogasawara, "The Educational System and English in Japan," 88.
19. Matsumoto, interview.
20. Overton, 25 June 1953.
21. Matsumoto, interview.
22. McLean, et al., 19.
23. McLean, et al., 20.
24. McLean, et al., 20-21.
25. McLean, et al., (quoting "President Cole"), 20.
26. Kleinjans, interview.
27. Rockefeller to Bryant.
28. Gilpatric.
29. Bryant, "English Language Teaching," 30.
30. Bryant, "English Teaching in Japan."
31. Bryant, "English Teaching in Japan," 76.
32. Bryant, "English Teaching in Japan," 78.
33. Bryant, "English Teaching in Japan," 87.
34. Bryant, "English Teaching in Japan," 84
35. Bryant, "English Teaching in Japan," 81.
36. Lamb, August 1955.
37. Rockefeller wrote to Hadley on 23 Nov. 1953 that Matsumoto had been "very seriously considered by his government as the first post-war Ambassador in Washington and then as Observer of Japan to the United Nations." Health factors kept these plans from materializing.
38. Matsumoto to McLean, 22 Dec. 1955.
39. Muto, 126.
40. Matsumoto to Rockefeller, 16 Aug. 1955.
41. "English Language Teaching in Japan."
42. Muto, 126.
43. Reischauer to Borton.
44. McLean to Rockefeller, 9 Dec. 1955.
45. "Matsumoto's Memorandum," 31 Dec. 1955.

46. "Agenda: 12th Meeting on English Teaching Method," and attachments, 25 April 1956.

47. Reischauer to Borton.

48. Rockefeller to Matsumoto, 11 Jan. 1956.

49. Rockefeller to Matsumoto, 11 Jan. 1956.

50. McLean to Rockefeller, 6 January 1956.

51. "Estimated Expenses for the Proposed Specialists' Conference," 1956.

52. McLean to Rockefeller, 3 Apr. 1956.

53. Bradley to McLean, 1.

54. Bradley to McLean, 2.

55. Toyoda to McLean.

56. McLean to Takagi and Matsumoto.

57. Nakajima, *Addresses and Papers,* 7.

58. Matsumoto, interview.

59. Nakajima, preface to *Foundations for English Teaching*, xi.

60. As recently as Spring 1985, an article in the *ELEC Bulletin* (no. 83, p. 8) reported on a panel discussion about the best way to use the Oral Approach in the classroom.

61. Bailey, 2.

62. Rockefeller Foundation resolution 34037.

63. Fries to Stevens.

64. Howatt, 313.

65. Bailey, 2.

66. "10-Week English Language Center Opens On Campus."

67. Hopkins to Stevens; Reports on grants and appropriations; "English Language Institute" flyer.

68. Stevens.

69. Smith to McLean.

70. Letter to Matsumoto.

71. Fries, *Teaching and Learning English,* 8.

72. Fries, *Teaching and Learning English*, 9.

73. Fries, "On the Oral Approach," 204.

74. Fries, "On the Oral Approach," 204.

75. Ota, "Methods," 49.

76. Fries, *Teaching and Learning English*, 3.

77. Fries, "On the Oral Approach," 211-12.

78. Fries, "Linguistics, Language, and Language Learning," notes from 7 Jul. 1981.

79. Strain, 12.

80. Morley et al., 172.

81. Allen, 1-2.

82. Morley et al., 174.

83. Morley et al., 174.

84. Reed, 1.

85. Anthony, 2.

86. Hughes, 67.

87. Hughes, 68.

88. Hughes, 76.

89. Mackey, 149.

90. Howatt, 267.

91. Bowen, Madsen, and Hilferty, 34.

92. Marckwardt, 3.

93. Mackey, 150.

94. Hughes, 69.

95. Anthony, 2.

96. Parker.

97. Marquardt, 33.

98. Hughes, 77.

99. Meyer, 49.

100. Hughes, 77.

101. Moulton, 3. It should be noted that Moulton's interpretation of Fries' thinking is not universally accepted. For example, Strain ("Issues and Observations," 61-62 in the same volume) contests it, noting significant differences between the ACLS/ASTP Foreign/Modern Language programs and the Michigan EFL language program.
102. Richards, "The Secret Life of Methods," *TESOL Quarterly*, 15.
103. Allen, 2.
104. Morley et al., 175.
105. Nakajima, *Addresses and Papers*, 6.
106. Rojas & staff, v.
107. McLean, 1 Mar. 1956.
108. Espinosa to Fries.
109. Summarized in Fries to Anderson.
110. Kleinjans to Fries.
111. Fries to Roeloffs.
112. Fries to Nishimura.
113. Pierson to Fries.
114. Hall to Hatcher.
115. "Agenda: Specialists' Conference on English Teaching in Japan." (Note: This agenda was drafted in early August of 1956, but the Specialists' Conference did not occur until September 3-7.)
116. Matsumoto, interview.
117. Memorandum, "12th meeting on English Teaching Method."
118. Muto, 127.
119. McLean to Rockefeller, 22 May 1956.
120. Araki, 14.
121. Nakajima, *Addresses and Papers*, v.
122. "Agenda: Specialists' Conference," 9 Aug. 1956.
123. Nakajima, *Addresses and Papers*, v.
124. "English Language Exploratory Committee, Minutes of the First Meeting."
125. "Conclusions and Recommendations, The Specialists' Conference 1956," 291-95.
126. McLean to Rockefeller, 19 Sept. 1956.
127. McLean to Rockefeller, 19 Sept. 1956.
128. "Conclusions and Recommendations," 22 Sept. 1956.
129. Muto, 134.
130. Matsumoto to McLean, 29 Sept. 1956.
131. McLean to Rockefeller, 8 Oct. 1956.
132. Rockefeller to Fries.
133. Fries to Kano.
134. Overton to Rockefeller.
135. Yambe, "C. C. Fries Re-evaluated," 8; Fries, interview.
136. Takahashi, interview.
137. Yambe, interview.
138. Nakajima, *Addresses and Papers*, 11-12.
139. Hayashi to Fries.
140. Fries to McLean, 24 May 1958.
141. Fries, "As We See It," 12.
142. Memorandum on English-language teaching.
143. Fries, "As We See It," 15.
144. Fries, "Preparation of Teaching Materials," 44.
145. Overton, 28 March 1960; Memorandum, 24 Sept. 1958, 1.
146. Fries to Twaddell, 15 May 1957.
147. Muto, 134.
148. Fries, "Brief Report."
149. Nakajima, preface to *Lectures*, iii.
150. Muto, 135.
151. Fries to Twaddell, 4 Jan. 1958.
152. Memorandum, 24 Sept. 1958, 2.
153. Fries to Matsumoto.

154. Fries to ELEC.
155. ELEC executive committee to Fries, 20 Oct. 1958.
156. Brown to Fries.
157. Memorandum, 24 Sept. 1958, 1.
158. Fries to Matsumoto.
159. ELEC executive committee to Fries, 20 Oct. 1958.
160. Memorandum, 24 Sept. 1958, 3.
161. ELEC executive committee to Fries, 20 Oct. 1958.
162. Fries to Overton, 20 Nov. 1958; Fries to Overton, 13 Sept. 1959.
163. Muto, 135.
164. CECA, Japan Society, Joint Committee.
165. ELEC executive committee to Charles C. Fries, 20 Oct. 1958.
166. Fries to Overton, 13 Sept. 1959.
167. Fries to Overton, 5 Aug. 1959.
168. Overton to Rockefeller.
169. ELEC and Rockefeller personnel used various names when referring to this program: "summer course," "summer institute," "summer program," "summer seminar," and "teachers' summer training seminar."
170. Fries to Twaddell, 15 May 1957.
171. Shimizu, interview.
172. Fries, "Brief Report."
173. Muto, 128.
174. "English Language Exploratory Committee: Minutes of the First Meeting."
175. Kuroda, "Plan of Teaching Material Preparation."
176. Yambe, "C. C. Fries Re-evaluated," 6.
177. CECA, Japan Society, Joint Committee.
178. Muto, 134.
179. Muto, 135.
180. Anderson, *Japan: Three Epochs*, 119.
181. ELEC executive committee to Fries, 1 Sept. 1958.
182. Fries to Matsumoto.
183. Fries to Overton, 5 Aug. 1959.
184. ELEC executive committee to Fries, 1 Sept. 1958.
185. Nakajima, preface to *Foundations for English Teaching*, xii.
186. ELEC executive committee to Fries, 1 Sept. 1958.
187. Toyoda, B.2.
188. Anderson, *Japan: Three Epochs*, 216.
189. Muto, 128.
190. Muto, 135.
191. Shimizu, "ELEC Past & Present," 99.
192. Muto, 135.
193. Shimizu, "ELEC Past & Present," 99.
194. Brown to Dr. and Mrs. Fries.
195. Koike, interview.
196. Matsumoto, interview.
197. Koike, interview.
198. Shimizu, interview.
199. Shimizu, "ELEC Past & Present," 100.
200. Toyoda, B.13
201. Kanatani.
202. Overton, 28 Mar. 1960.
203. Fries to McLean, 29 May 1957.
204. Muto, 137.
205. O'Connor and Twaddell, 9.
206. O'Connor and Twaddell, 12.
207. Muto, 136.
208. Muto, 136.
209. Toyoda, Appendix B.

210. "The Oral Method of Teaching English."
211. Fries, "Brief Report."
212. Kano, Takahashi, and Kuroda, 32.
213. Kano, Takahashi, and Kuroda, 32.
214. Apparently, by this time the rift between ELEC and ICU created by Fries' insistence on not holding the 1957 summer seminars at ICU had healed. Also helping to placate matters was the fact that, by the summer of 1959 Fries was no longer involved with ELEC's seminars. In addition, the pattern of the seminars was firmly established by this time, so there was less reason to fear that ELEC's purposes would be compromised by connections with Japanese universities.
215. Muto, 137.
216. Brownell to Smith.
217. Muto, 137.
218. Kimpara.
219. Muto, 136.
220. Kimpara.
221. Bryant, "English Language Teaching," 27-28.
222. Overton to Rockefeller.
223. Toyoda, Appendix B.
224. Takagi to McLean.
225. CECA Resolution E4.
226. CECA Resolution E4.
227. CECA Resolution E4.
228. Toyoda, B.2-B.3.
229. Letter to Overton, 1-2.
230. McLean to Rockefeller, 19 Apr. 1962.
231. Memorandum to Rockefeller.
232. Toyoda to CECA.
233. Overton to trustees of CECA.
234. Takahashi to Overton.
235. Muto, 128.
236. Overton, Report to CECA, 7.
237. Overton, Report to CECA, 7.
238. Matsumoto to Overton.
239. Matsumoto to Overton.
240. Toyoda to CECA. Note: At the exchange rate of 360¥/$1.00 that then prevailed, ¥19,000,000 would actually amount to only $52,778, not "nearly $60,000." Perhaps the exaggeration can be attributed to the ELEC leaders' zeal to persuade CECA to approve the construction of the ELEC building.
241. CECA Resolution E4.
242. Toyoda, B.9.
243. Takahashi to Overton.
244. McLean to Rockefeller, 19 Apr. 1962.
245. Muto, 131.
246. Muto, 131.
247. Muto, 129.
248. Muto, 131.
249. Shimizu, "ELEC Past & Present," 105.
250. Ota, interview.
251. Hatori.
252. Kimpara.
253. Ogasawara, interview.
254. Smith to Rockefeller, 20 May 1974, 13.
255. Smith to Rockefeller, 20 May 1974, 13.
256. Kleinjans, interview.
257. Toyoda, Appendix B.
258. *Guidebook: Seminar for Teachers of English*, i.
259. "Final Report to the Ford Foundation," 1.

260. Memorandum to Rockefeller, 7.
261. Smith to Rockefeller, 20 May 1974, 13.
262. "Announcement of Organization, Committee for Cooperation on English in Japan."
263. "Committee for Cooperation on English in Japan, Annual Report."
264. "Announcement of Organization, Committee for Cooperation on English in Japan."
265. Smith to Rockefeller, 20 May 1974, 6.
266. Smith to Rockefeller, 20 May 1974, 6.
267. Smith to Rockefeller, 20 May 1974, 12.
268. Smith to Rockefeller, 20 May 1974, 6-7.
269. Smith to Rockefeller, 20 May 1974.
270. Smith to Rockefeller 3 Apr. 1969.
271. Coleman, 180.

3

The Hybrid Model

The model developed and explained in this chapter is employed in the next two chapters to analyze the ELEC effort. In addition, it may be profitably applied in other settings—to analyze past campaigns or to plan future ones.

THE IMPORTANCE OF PLANNING FOR IMPLEMENTATION

"*No innovation,* no matter how promising, produces any benefits until it is used" [italics in original].[1] Nevertheless, in contrast to the high hopes of their creators, disappointingly few innovations in education are ever implemented and utilized—often to the detriment of those who would benefit from a particular innovation and to the frustration of those who promote its diffusion and utilization. To diminish this gap between knowledge and practice, "the implementation phase of planned change should receive at least as much careful planning and attention as the research, development, and technology transfer phases which precede it."[2] It is foolish to hope that the great variety of factors involved in the change process will all "fall into place" naturally.

Diffusion-of-innovation researchers generally agree that effective planning is critical if a diffusion/implementation effort is to meet with success. Pratt, Thurber, Hall, and Hord state, "Thinking out the overall design of interventions that will be needed to support a school improvement effort and doing this in advance is critical."[3] Michaletz maintains that "the most important and time consuming phase in bringing about curriculum change is the planning phase....When the planning phase is carried out effectively, both the implementation and evaluation phases will follow more readily. If the planning phase is not dealt with adequately, the other phases could be ineffective."[4]

As Michaletz explains, planning should be deliberative, determinative, collaborative, future-oriented, and structured yet flexible.[5] In other words, the planning ought to involve careful thought, serve to decide or resolve issues beforehand, and involve all interested, affected parties in the planning. Furthermore, the plan should consider the setting for change as it will become, not merely as it presently is. Finally, structure in a plan is critical, but that structure should still be capable of being altered as conditions change. Havelock agrees that structure in planning "strongly affects the utilization process" since "effective dissemination and utilization must take place within a coherent framework." In his experience, "successful utilization activities tend to be *structured* activities, and useful knowledge is *structured* knowledge."[6]

Lamentably, however, "the literature on innovation and planned change is replete with examples of programs heavily invested in research and development without an accompanying plan for implementation."[7]

THE CHALLENGE OF ANALYZING IMPLEMENTATION

There is a singular lack of curiosity about what happened to an innovation between the time it was designed and various people agreed to carry it out, and the time that the consequences became evident. Once an innovation was planned and adopted, interest tended to shift toward the monitoring of outcomes. The assumption appears to have been that the move from the drawing board to the school or classroom was unproblemàtic, that the innovation would be implemented or used more or less as planned, and that the actual use would eventually correspond to planned or intended use. The whole area of implementation…was viewed as a "black box" where innovations entering one side somehow produce the consequences emanating from the other.[8]

Unfortunately, those who have probed inside the "black box" of implementation hoping to find some guiding principles (e.g., Lortie, Miles, Sarason, and Fullan and Pomfret) have found that the process is extremely complex. An understanding of how and why certain implementation strategies succeed is important in order "to close the implementation gap and secure the highest possible return on investments in innovation,"[9], but "successful implementation is much more complex and difficult than one might expect."[10]

This complexity presents a considerable challenge to researchers and planners concerned with the process of implementing educational innovations; "the factors that could plausibly influence it are potentially enormous in number."[11] Fullan and Pomfret counsel, "Implementation is a highly complex process involving relationships between users and managers, and among various groups of users, in a process characterized by inevitable conflict and by anticipated and unanticipated problems that should be prepared for prior to attempting implementation, and continually addressed during it."[12]

Although this complexity makes analysis difficult, it also makes a proper and thorough analysis more important than ever. As Mackey points out: "Problems before being solved must first be analysed. The more complex the problem, the more is its solution dependent on a sound analysis."[13]

THOUGHTS ON CHANGE

Throughout history considerable thought and attention have been devoted to the topic of change, but little agreement has been reached. As early as the fifth century B.C., Heraclitus alleged, "Nothing endures but change."[14]   In the second century A.D., Marcus Aurelius Antoninus maintained, "The universe is change."[15] A millennium and a half later, in the seventeenth century, Honorat de Bueil, Marquis de Racan, reiterated, "Nothing in the world lasts save eternal change,"[16] and in 1647 Abraham Cowley penned, "The world's a scene of changes, and to be constant, in nature were inconstancy."[17]

The opposite point of view, that true change is either rare or nonexistent, has also been widely espoused. For instance, in 1849 Alphonse Karr contended (and many have since repeated), "The more things change, the more they stay the same."[18]

Others have warned about the dangers of change.   Shakespeare penned, "Striving to better, oft we mar what's well,"[19] and in 1776, as the American Revolution was getting under way, John Adams wrote, "All great changes are irksome to the human mind, especially those which are attended with great dangers and uncertain effects."[20]

GENERAL THEORIES OF SOCIAL CHANGE

A variety of theories dealing with social change have developed over the years. These can be grouped into the general categories of equilibrium, evolutionary, conflict theories, rise-and-fall, and diffusion theories.[21]

Equilibrium Theory

Equilibrium theory "emphasizes stability at the expense of change."[22] Society is seen as a highly complex but smooth-running organism that is inherently stable. In other words, society is "homeostatic" and it possesses "mechanisms designed to restore equilibrium once the latter is upset."[23] In this sort of theory, it is only natural that little attention is given to change. In fact, Appelbaum claims that equilibrium theory has "a conservative bias against endogenous structural change,"[24] and concludes that "equilibrium theory can neither explain the occurrence of radical changes in society nor account for the phenomena which accompany them."[25] For these reasons, equilibrium theory has little to offer those who would analyze or plan directed contact change campaigns. It may, however, serve as a possible explanation for the commonly encountered resistance to the implementation of innovations.

Evolutionary Theory

One of the oldest and most widely accepted views of social change is that it takes place naturally, slowly, and inevitably. This continual, smooth process of internal adaptation to the social environment is based on the evolutionary principle originally popularized by Darwin to explain change in living organisms. Of course, over the years, many variations on the classic model of social evolution have been proposed, including "multilinear evolution"[26] and "modernization" theory.[27] These diachronic theories of gradual, unidirectional change have been both widely accepted and widely criticized.

A rather simplistic version of evolutionary theory has been applied to the process of "successful change in ESOL [English to speakers of other languages]" by Smith. He uses the analogy of a sculptor who creates amazingly lifelike figures of elephants by starting with a big rock and chipping away until he has "eliminated everything that doesn't look like an elephant." Smith urges English language teachers not satisfied with the present "state of the art" to "begin chipping away."[28]

For the purposes of this study, however, an evolutionary model is inappropriate for two reasons. First, evolutionary theory presupposes gradual, smooth, and inevitable change,[29] and secondly, it views the change process as instinctive and natural, arising from chance mutations.[30] It is incapable of dealing with radical, sudden, directed change that has a definite guiding force behind it.

Conflict Theory

"Conflict theories conceive of social organization as arising in response to a scarcity of desired resources."[31] Based on Hegel's thesis-antithesis-synthesis idea and Marx's "without conflict no progress" postulate, "conflict theory looks everywhere for sources of instability" and defines change as "the working out of conflict."[32] In other words, change is created by conflict among the polarized groups in society.

Encouraging change among English teachers by producing conflict within them has been proposed. To solve the problem of teachers who do not want to change, who "just want to survive, somehow, until retirement," Thompson and Williams advocate creating "dissonance" among the ranks.

> Supervisors must not assume that teachers want help, that they want to improve, that they want to change to make their instruction more effective....Instead, supervisors need to take another approach....Teachers who are no longer learners must, by whatever means, be led to a point where they recognize that what they are doing in the classroom is not in the best interest of their students or themselves. Until such dissonance is created, any attempt to change them or to teach them something new is likely to fail. It is a paradox, but only when teachers are led to a state of confusion do supervisors have a chance to change teachers' attitudes and restructure, at least in part, the way teachers go about teaching.[33]

Havelock allows that a conflict model has potential for analyzing the diffusion and implementation of innovations.

> Certainly the historical dialectic of Hegel and Marx suggests the rudiments of an alternative perspective on D&U [diffusion and utilization]; we have said little about the *conflict* of opposing innovative and non-innovative social groups as a pattern of movement toward social change, but undoubtedly it is. Such a "conflict" model of D&U seems especially appropriate to our turbulent contemporary scene...[34]

He also notes, however, that "no one has proposed such a perspective in considering D&U phenomena." This factor makes conflict theory a weak base for the current study.

Rise and Fall Theory

Rise and fall theory takes an approach entirely different from that of the three preceding theoretical stances. Instead of concerning itself with the stability of society, it focuses on fluctuations in the direction of change.[35]   Using the analogy of the human organism, it points out the possibility of decline as well as progress and growth. It sees change as being cyclical rather than cumulative.[36] Rise and fall theory is also distinctive in that it is typically "characterized by a grandiose vision" that covers large expanses of time. In addition, it focuses on "cultural systems as well as social systems."[37]

Rise and fall theory, however, says nothing about the process or problems of creating change. Consequently, it has little to offer in terms of the purpose and topic of this study. Merely waiting for the next "wave" of change to arrive could hardly be considered an efficient implementation strategy.

Diffusion Theory

A fifth theory emphasizes "the empirical interrelations among societies and how societies as a consequence 'borrow' from one another."[38] This classic diffusion theory views the process of change in terms of the discovery of an idea, its transmittal from the source to the potential user, and its eventual adoption.

Because it allows for the "dynamic" of change to be an outside force, diffusion theory seems to offer the most appropriate theoretical base for analyzing or planning directed contact change campaigns, such as the ELEC effort. Nevertheless, in its classic form diffusion theory is very general and is minimally concerned with social-system contexts. A more up-to-date, linkage version shows greater promise for analyzing the cross-cultural diffusion/implementation of innovations.

GENERAL PERSPECTIVES ON
THE DIFFUSION OF INNOVATIONS

"Innovation is a species of the genus 'change.'...[It is] a deliberate, novel, specific change, which is thought to be more efficacious in accomplishing the goals of a system." In addition, an innovation is usually "willed and planned for, rather than...occurring haphazardly."[39]

Regarding the diffusion and implementation of innovations, there are a number of differing perspectives. Many of these correspond to social change theories. In line with the evolutionary view, for instance, Francis Bacon wrote, "It were good therefore, that men in their innovations would follow the example of time itself, which indeed innovateth greatly, but

quietly and by degrees scarce to be perceived."[40]   The great physicist Max
Planck expressed a contrasting (but still somewhat evolutionary) opinion on
the subject of innovations: "An important scientific innovation rarely
makes its way by gradually winning over and converting its opponents; it
rarely happens that Saul becomes Paul.   What does happen is that its
opponents gradually die out and that the growing generation is familiarized
with the idea from the beginning."[41]

Others have proposed additional perspectives. Havelock groups ideas
about the diffusion and utilization of knowledge into three major
categories: the research, development, and diffusion perspective; the social
interaction perspective; and the problem solver perspective. He also
proposes a "linkage perspective" that "incorporates important features of
all three."[42]

Research, Development, and Diffusion

In the research, development, and diffusion (RD&D) perspective,
basic research leads to applied research. Following development and
testing of prototypes, the resulting "innovation" is mass produced and
packaged. Mass dissemination activities then take it to the user who accepts
it.

Unfortunately, this model suffers from a number of drawbacks. First,
it is little more than a sequential list of steps. Secondly, it is clearly
oriented toward material innovations and therefore is not suitable for many
nonmaterial educational innovations. Furthermore, it assumes a far-from-
real "passive consumer," and is "over-rational, over-idealized, excessively
research oriented and inadequately user oriented."[43] For these reasons it
fails to consider the "real-world" obstacles to change and is incapable of
explaining many failures in implementation efforts.

Similar to the RD&D perspective is the discovery-transmittal-adoption
view in which discovering or inventing something "better" and then simply
telling others about it is thought to be enough to ensure its adoption.
Nevertheless, this approach suffers from a number of problems, primary
among which is that it frequently does not work. As Roberts-Gray and
Gray explain,

> knowledge creators tend to have great faith in the "Better Mousetrap Theory" which
> contends that "if it works and if it's needed, then it will get used."...If there is some
> problem with utilization, it is most often perceived as a user problem. Knowledge
> creators are reluctant to intervene in the affairs of users (except, of course, to
> convince them that the innovation really will work and really is needed)....The
> evidence, however, argues both against the "Better Mousetrap Theory" and against
> the assumption that users will solve implementation problems on their own.[44]

Those who have studied the process of change in schools usually
conclude that a simple discovery-transmittal-adoption or "delivery of the
curriculum" approach is inadequate.[45] Nevertheless, educators seem
especially prone to subscribe to it. Those who work in schools typically
hold "common and deeply rooted assumptions," such as "people can be

changed" (education is a way of accomplishing this change) and "people are rational" (if they are provided with more information they will modify their behavior accordingly).   Unfortunately, if they are used as the basis for campaigns to implement educational innovations, these beliefs may lead to failure, for "even in an 'educational' mode, change raises fundamental questions of values and power."[46]   Thus, "the peculiar disadvantage of change agents in education lies in applying methods that are largely educational to situations that are fundamentally political."[47]

Social Interaction

Quite different from the research-development-diffusion or discovery-transmittal-adoption views, the social interaction (SI) perspective "is relatively indifferent to the value of the innovation or to the type of scientific and technical know-how that might have gone into its original development and manufacture."   Instead, it focuses on "the pattern of flow [of an innovation through a social system over time] and the effects of social structure and social relationships and groupings on the fate of innovations."   Researchers in the SI tradition focus on the "complex and intricate set of human substructures and processes" that "must be operative before diffusion will succeed."[48]

The SI perspective has several advantages.   Firstly, unlike the RD&D approach, it recognizes the fact that "individual human beings are embedded in and inextricably connected to a social network made up of other individuals."[49]   In addition, it takes into consideration at least one important factor that hinders/facilitates the implementation of innovations—the individual's group identity and group loyalty.

Nevertheless, the SI perspective also has some serious weaknesses. One is that it "ignores psychological processes inside the user-adopter."[50] Another is that most SI research focuses on easily traceable "innovations which appear in a concrete, 'diffusable' form, such as a type of fertilizer or a new prescription drug."[51]   This limits its usefulness, since many educational innovations produce psychological repercussions in their intended users and do not consist of easy-to-identify "stable elements."

Problem Solving

A third perspective on the process of change is that it "begins with a need and ends with the satisfaction of that need."   This problem-solving process consists of six stages involving both a user system and an outside process, consultant, or change agent:

1. Need sensing and articulation
2. Diagnosis and formulation of the need as a problem to be solved
3. Identification and search for resources relevant to the problem
4. Retrieval of potentially feasible solutions and solution-pertinent ideas
5. Translation of this retrieved knowledge into specific solutions
6. Behavioral try-out or application of the solution to the need[52]

If the solution does not satisfy the need, then the cycle begins again.

This problem-solving perspective is based on five "very solid points": "(1) the user is the starting place, (2) diagnosis precedes solution identification, (3) the outside helping role is non-directive, (4) the importance of internal resources, [and] (5) user-initiated change is the strongest."[53]

Nevertheless, it is not without problems. It places excessive strain on the user and minimizes the role of outside resources. For these reasons, it is not appropriate for understanding directed contact change, where an external source applies a preconceived solution to a foreign setting.

Linkage

Linkage theory stresses connections between outside agencies and the intended user of an innovation. Change is planned, coordinated, and pursued through "a series of two-way interaction processes, which connect user systems with various resource systems."[54]   Various linkage models have been proposed. Rogers and Shoemaker present a basic linkage model in their discussion of the role of the change agent, through whom innovations flow from the "change agency" to the "client system." The agent also carries back to the change agency information regarding the client system's needs and the effectiveness of the innovation.[55]   Havelock's more complicated linkage model (see figure 2) begins with the user as a problem solver but "stresses that the user must be meaningfully related to outside resources."[56]

For the purpose of studying directed contact change, a linkage perspective is definitely more advantageous than traditional diffusion theory. In all linkage models, change is viewed as the product of "collaborative interaction" since the linkage relationship between user and resource systems is reciprocal. Each interacts with and affects the other. An additional advantage of a linkage perspective is that, while it allows for research and development of an innovation, it does not assume that RD&D is all that is required for successful implementation of an innovation. Furthermore, a linkage model allows for the "dynamic" of change to be an outside force, making it appropriate for explaining directed contact change—even across cultural boundaries.

CRITERIA FOR AN ADEQUATE MODEL

Just any linkage model, however, will not do. In order to apply to cross-cultural campaigns intended to create reforms in educational practices, a linkage model must satisfy the following five criteria:

Coherent Framework

Reports on reform attempts often conclude with lists of disconnected "implementation lessons," with no reference to a larger framework or

Figure 2
The Linkage Perspective

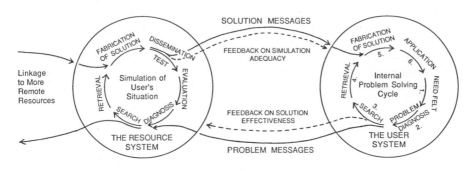

Source: Havelock, *Planning for Innovation,* chap. 11, p. 16. (Used by permission.)

model for analysis. Parish and Arends, for instance, provide only a list of guidelines such as the following: "extend time for training teachers," "develop a two-level school site implementation plan," and "expect, encourage, and assist with adaptations."[57]   A booklet published by The American Psychological Association to guide those who wish to reform psychology courses consists of little more than a lengthy checklist.[58] Somewhat ironically, while calling for the design "of an educational *system* that gives educators the time, protection, encouragement and support they need to improve schools" [italics mine], Corbett and D'Amico propose no *system* for bringing about such change, only a list of suggestions based on experiences.[59] Cavanagh and Styles fall into the same trap. They present "twenty frequently heard objections—and responses to them" and a list of "potential activities" in the implementation process, but no overall framework for understanding, analyzing, or planning the implementation of new curriculum.[60] Likewise, in his examination of the problems of implementing English-language-teaching syllabuses in the People's Republic of China, Maley categorizes a variety of factors into checklists "which syllabus and programme designers can use as a starting point."[61]

A model, however, is more than a mere list of suggestions. A model shows the structure of the thing it represents. It provides a cohesive framework that recognizes that the various individual factors do not exist only as independent elements. A model shows how these factors affect each other, indicating their interrelationships and the direction(s) of influence. An adequate model also shows process. Many of the elements involved in a reform campaign are observable and can be listed, but the change process itself and many of the forces that affect it are intangible and cannot be directly observed. For this reason, the framework of a model must depict not only the forces that affect the change process but also the process itself.

Abstractness

Yet another characteristic of a good model is abstractness, a quality that allows it to represent phenomena in a general (and thus more widely applicable) fashion. Rogers and Kincaid emphasize this characteristic, as they define a model as "a representation of real-world phenomena in more abstract terms," which "can be applied to other cases at other times."[62] While abstractness is not necessarily a unique characteristic of a model, it is still an important one. Without it, a model becomes little more than a description. Abstractness increases its usefulness.

Completeness

To be most useful, a model must also have all the parts necessary to recognize and account for the complexity of the diffusion/implementation process. Unfortunately, many overly simplistic (and therefore misleading) diffusion-of-innovations models exist. Gordon and Lawton, for instance, ignore a multitude of powerful variables when they state that in order for a curriculum innovation initiated by an individual to be successful, the promoter merely "requires access to a wide audience and the ability to express clearly the changes advocated."[63] Pratt, Thurber, Hall, and Hord present an equally simplistic model of the school improvement process, which consists of only three stages: school review, selection/development of a solution, and implementation.[64]

The many factors involved in the implementation process create a complicated picture, but such complexity is to be preferred over misleading simplicity. Pelz reports, "In analyses to date, no single predictors of innovation effectiveness have been found."[65] He later concludes, "Perhaps any single-factor explanation of effectiveness is bound to fall short."[66] What is needed is a multiple-element model that considers a constellation of related factors.

Relevance to Directed Contact Change

Of course, different types of change involve different implementation processes. Consequently, some types of social change are simpler to accomplish than others. Martin and Saif, for instance, propose a "grassroots" approach to curriculum reform, beginning with teachers, not outside curriculum change agents, which may be appropriate for immanent social change.[67] It is hardly applicable, however, to a case of directed contact change, such as the ELEC campaign, which urged a generally reluctant Japanese audience to adopt an American approach to language teaching. Directed contact change inevitably encounters more obstacles than the types of change that emanate from within a system. Therefore, a model for planning/analyzing such efforts must reflect this fact and take into account the strength and capacities of the implementation-promoting resource system as well as the numerous "barriers" to implementation in the intended-user system.

Cross-Cultural Applicability

As directed contact change efforts cross cultural boundaries, the complexity of the diffusion/implementation process increases, requiring an approach that considers a variety of socio-cultural factors. By way of illustration, when Rogers and Shoemaker developed their "cross-cultural approach" to communicating innovations, they found it necessary to break from "traditional diffusion research" (including Rogers' own), which had "always emphasized the 'individual' adopter of innovations," and instead focus on "the informal social group and the formally organized system."[68] Likewise, in his discussion of the challenges associated with providing "aid to English learning in overseas countries," Strevens emphasizes the need to study all the "social, educational, academic and administrative systems which determine how effective the aid can in practice be made."[69] A model adequate for analyzing/planning cross-cultural change campaigns will allow for this increased complexity.

Many of the models found in the diffusion-of-innovations literature fail to include elements that represent pertinent socio-cultural factors, and are therefore suitable for use only in mono-cultural (usually American) contexts. For example, King's research dealing with an urban middle school in the southern United States ignores socio-cultural factors entirely.[70] Likewise, Gee's model attempts to identify factors that explain the process of applying educational research to instructional practice, but it concerns itself only with agencies, forces, and personnel within the school system.[71]

Predictability?

Some models are predictive in an "if...then..." fashion. Nevertheless, in a highly complex system of interdependent variables, the prediction of specific outcomes is virtually impossible. It is only possible to make general predictions based on particular variables. For instance, one might predict that if the promoters of an innovation enjoy powerful and favorable support networks, then their chances of success will increase. If other forces work against the innovation, however, the final outcome may still not be what was desired. No single implementation variable can predict success or failure in the diffusion of an innovation. It is only the cumulative effect of many variable forces, either pro or con, which ultimately determines the outcome.

That realization brings up another question, which is "How many elements/forces must work in favor of an innovation in order for it to catch on and spread?" Here again, it is not possible to give an answer, since the final outcome depends not only on the number of favorable forces but on their weight and power. Since these elements vary in power and importance from one setting to another, those that are critical to implementational success must be determined locally, on a case by case basis, after a thorough investigation of the current and antecedent situations.

STAGES IN THE DIFFUSION/IMPLEMENTATION PROCESS

While it is generally agreed that an adequate diffusion/implementation model shows process and stages, there is much variety of opinion regarding what those stages are. Some conceptualizations are simple, while others exhibit considerable complexity. In one common view, change is seen as a gradual process of natural growth passing through five stages:

1. Awareness (first knowledge of the idea)
2. Interest (gaining further knowledge)
3. Evaluation (gaining a favorable or unfavorable attitude)
4. Small-scale trial
5. Adoption or rejection decision[72]

While this process may occur in some immanent change scenarios, it seems to be based on a social-interaction view of change and is far too simple to apply to cross-cultural directed contact change campaigns.

Michaletz proposes a more complex planning model that consists of seven deliberate and sequential steps:

1. Identification of the change;
2. Formation of a support group
3. Assessment
4. Future awareness
5. Analysis
6. Action plans
7. Evaluation[73]

Reflective of the research, development, and diffusion perspective, these stages bear considerable resemblance to those taken by ELEC. Nevertheless, this unidirectional list of steps is unable to explain the difficulties the ELEC campaign encountered. A robust model with stages where innovators cope with barriers to implementation is called for.

An approach to implementing change that takes into account the intended users of an innovation is proposed by Roberts-Gray and Gray. The first (and the most complex) of their four steps is "fit analysis," in which the "fit" between innovation and user is analyzed and appropriate modifications made. The remaining steps are (deceptively) simple: (2) "identify specific needs for change—i.e.,…set objectives for each of the 'determinants' of implementation," (3) "apply the plan to facilitate change and establish conditions that foster successful implementation," and (4) "obtain feedback."[74]

Havelock outlines a complicated series of steps in the change process that reflect a problem-solving view of change:

1. Building a relationship
2. Diagnosing the problem
3. Acquiring relevant resources
4. Choosing the solution
5. Gaining acceptance
6. Stabilizing the innovation and regenerating self-renewal[75]

Such a plan, however, fails to fit cases of directed change where "choosing the solution" is often the first (not the fourth) step. Also, the fifth step in this sequence, gaining acceptance, is overly simple and thus misrepresents the difficult and challenging process of bringing about change.

Addressing the challenge of directed contact change, Leithwood identifies three main phases and eight steps in the process of implementing curriculum innovations.   In his "Diagnosis" phase, goals for implementation are identified and decisions regarding which ones to pursue are made.   Then, discrepancies between the innovative and the current curricula are identified and certain ones are targeted for reduction. The final step in this phase consists of identifying the obstacles to discrepancy reduction.   In the next phase, "Application," procedures for overcoming lack of knowledge and skill as well as procedures for restructuring incentives and rewards are all designed and carried out.   Then, the necessary material resources and organizational arrangements are provided. The "Evaluation" phase, which consists of both formative and summative evaluation, is ongoing and may result in a return to the diagnostic phase.[76] Regarding obstacles to implementation, however, Leithwood mentions only "inadequate knowledge about the innovation and skill in its implementation," "ineffective organizational control structures," and "lack of material resources and compatible organizational arrangements in the classroom or school."[77] There are many other factors that can impede implementation and which, therefore, must be taken into account.

In contrast, Rogers and Shoemaker outline only four main steps in the diffusion/implementation process:

1. Knowledge
2. Persuasion
3. Decision
4. Confirmation[78]

Although quite simple, this conceptualization is also powerful. It can be profitably applied to cases of directed contact change since it recognizes the potential of external forces as providers of knowledge. It also takes into account the obstacles to change that must be overcome through "persuasion." Nevertheless, it needs to be filled out with more detailed strategies within these general stages.

STRATEGIES FOR BRINGING ABOUT CHANGE

Just as there are many different conceptualizations of the stages in the implementation process, there are many different ideas about the strategies that can/should be used to bring about change.

Some strategies are simplistic. According to House, for instance, "most innovation is dependent on face-to-face personal contacts."[79] Although interpersonal contacts are undoubtedly important, such a strategy is woefully inadequate—especially when directed contact change on a large scale is the goal.

Recognizing that different situations call for different strategies, Roberts-Gray and Gray describe four general strategies to facilitate change:

> *Assistance* strategies provide technical or fiscal support for making organizational arrangements to receive and use the innovation. *Education* strategies provide individuals with information and training needed to use the innovation and integrate it into their routine performances. *Power* strategies are applied to establish rules and sanctions to force the innovation into place and provide organizational control over its use. And *persuasion* strategies shape people's attitudes and values to foster personal commitment to the innovation [italics in original].[80]

Along these same lines, Mann provides a basic typology of five strategies for promoting change, depending on characteristics of the resource and the intended-user systems. *Reinforcing change* is a strategy in which the change agent intensifies or extends the original impetus for change. *Forcing change* can be done (at least attempted) by those who are in positions of power. *Buying change* is a strategy wherein users are given rewards for complying with the desired change. *Persuading change* involves a rational approach that utilizes logic and/or evidence of the superiority of an innovation. *Manipulating change* consists of creating a "new self interest in the other party."[81]

Focusing on change in education, Fullan and Pomfret discuss four strategies: (1) in-service training; (2) resource support (the time and materials needed to implement the innovation); (3) feedback mechanisms (which stimulate interaction and are useful in the identification of problems); and (4) participation (in decision making) "by those who are expected to implement the new program."[82]

A basic and widely used strategy is to work through "opinion leaders" in the system of intended users. In every society there are individuals whom other members look to for both information and counsel. A few of these opinion leaders can influence a large number of people. In a society with a modern orientation they can be very powerful promoters of change if they decide to support an innovation. On the other hand, in a conservatively oriented society, the opinion leaders tend to be conservative themselves and often constitute a powerful barrier to the spread of an innovation.[83]

Communication channels are also important in a diffusion effort, and choosing the most effective channel for communicating information about an innovation to the intended users is a crucial strategic decision. Communication may be accomplished through either mass media or interpersonal channels. Each has its particular advantages. For simply diffusing information about an innovation, especially when the number of potential users is large, mass media channels offer the advantages of speed and efficiency. Nevertheless, if intended users need both information and persuasion (in order to create favorable attitudes toward adopting the innovation) then a more effective (albeit slower) approach is to work through interpersonal channels.[84]

SPECIFIC LINKAGE MODELS OF THE
DIFFUSION/IMPLEMENTATION PROCESS

Elements, stages, and strategies are important, but to form a useful model they must be organized into a coherent whole. A number of models and frameworks which are based on a linkage perspective and attempt to deal with the complexities of creating directed contact change have been proposed. For purposes of illustration and comparison, a few are presented in this section.

Gee's

Gee proposes a model that shows the interaction between various agencies and factors that affect "the process of the application of research on effective instruction."[85] Although it captures the linkage relationships between these different elements rather well, it is concerned with forces, agencies, and personnel only within the school system, such as teacher-education faculty, student teachers, and cooperating teachers. Its narrow range of concern contrasts dramatically with the much broader scope of the hybrid model.

Richards'

One of the few who has gone beyond simple checklists when writing about implementation factors and their effect on methodological innovations in English language teaching is Richards. In fact, the dearth of ELT-oriented research in this area and English language teachers' general lack of awareness when it comes to the influence of implementation factors led Richards to label this aspect of methodology the "secret life of methods."[86] In his analysis, he acknowledges that "methods have a life beyond the classroom, beyond the questions of content, philosophy, and procedure which characterize them." He also points out that success in endeavors to implement a new language-teaching method is highly dependent on a number of factors other than the method itself, such as "the influence of fads and fashions, of profit-seekers and promoters, as well as the forces of the intellectual marketplace."[87]

Although Richards discusses a number of "implementation factors" that apply to language-teaching innovations, he provides no overall model of the change process. Since it was developed outside of the mainstream of diffusion-of-innovations studies, Richards' framework also fails to consider many important diffusion/implementation factors. Nevertheless, because of its focus on ELT, Richards' analysis also contributes new ideas that are particularly valuable in the analysis of change campaigns in language teaching.

Richards considers several ways of "validating" an innovative method. In his original conference address, he grouped implementation concerns into three categories: "the quest for legitimacy, publish or perish, and sanctions from on high."[88] In the published version of this address, the elements in Richards' framework were modified and renamed: "the form a method takes, publish or perish, and support networks."[89]

Under "the quest for legitimacy," Richards discusses the value of "appealing to facts" that come from research. A common alternative to research is authority. There are two types of ELT "authority": current theoretical constructs and recognized experts in the field. Either of these can be a powerful supporter of a methodological innovation.[90]

Although Richards seems to have arrived at them independently, these two implementation factors and their importance have been mentioned by other diffusion-of-innovations researchers. Regarding authority, for example, Havelock explains:

> One of the most important variables that determines whether or not a sender will be able to influence a receiver is the extent to which he is perceived as a reliable and believable source of information....A number of well-known experiments have shown that when a source (a sender) is considered by an audience (receiver) to be prestigeful and trustworthy, there is a strong tendency for the audience to change their attitude in accordance with the attitudes of the source.[91]

Because of their importance, these two factors are integrated into the hybrid model. "Appeals to facts" pertain to relative advantage and observability, while "authorities" are important elements in the resource system's capacity.

Richards' third implementation factor is the form an innovative method takes—whether it results in a publishable textbook or remains merely an instructional philosophy. This "publish or perish" factor is not usually mentioned by experts in the diffusion of educational innovations, yet experience shows that it plays an important role—at least in language teaching. For this reason "form" is included in the hybrid model's section on characteristics of the innovation that hinder or facilitate change.

The fourth—although by no means the least important—of Richards' "secret life" implementation factors was originally called "sanctions from on high," but he later renamed it "support networks." There are various types of support networks: professional teaching organizations, universities, professional journals, and educational agencies, and all would seem to be important for promoters of innovations to consider. Other researchers agree with Richards that support groups, as features of the capacity and structure of the resource system, can be extremely influential. Gordon and Lawton, for instance, discuss the success of "pressure groups" in influencing policy and legislation. Such pressure groups can be either protective, defending a segment of society, or promotional, promoting a cause.[92] "Support networks" are included in the interelemental portion of the hybrid model, and various types of support groups are considered in the analysis of the ELEC effort.

In a more recent discussion of this subject, entitled "The Context of Language Teaching," Richards mentions a number of additional "factors affecting the success of a language program" that "go beyond the mere content and presentation of teaching materials." These are grouped under four headings: "sociocultural factors," "teaching and learning styles," "learner factors," and "program characteristics." Sociocultural factors are related to the role English plays and the status English proficiency has in different societies. The "teaching and learning styles" factor recognizes that "education in different countries reflects culturally specific traditions of teaching and learning that may substantially shape the form and content of much school learning." Learner factors include profiles of talents, interests, learning habits, purposes, print-orientation, tolerance of ambiguity, shyness, etc., which also vary from one setting to another. The most complex group of factors, however, is "program characteristics," which is subdivided into a number of other characteristics: "degree of preparation of teachers," "validity of existing curriculum and testing procedures," "characteristics of the student population," "software and materials," "coordination of resources," and "testing and evaluation procedures."[93] Many of these learner, teacher, and school-system factors are mentioned by other researchers also and are included in the hybrid model.

Rogers and Shoemaker's

Several characteristics of Rogers and Shoemaker's classic paradigm of the "innovation-decision process" (see figure 3) make it particularly appropriate for the purposes of this study. It is applicable to directed contact change efforts and reflects the complexity of the diffusion/implementation process. It can be used with cross-cultural as well as domestic change campaigns. And it offers a coherent framework that shows the relationships among its various elements as well as the process of change.

The paradigm involves two main components. One deals with the process of diffusion and treats it as primarily a communication problem. The other part pictures the forces and factors that influence the innovation-decision process.

Rogers and Shoemaker maintain that diffusion is a special kind of communication.[94] Consequently, they analyze diffusion with a communication process model consisting of five elements: (1) source, (2) message, (3) channel, (4) receiver, and (5) effects. The corresponding elements in the diffusion-of-innovations process are "(1) inventors, scientists, change agents, or opinion leaders, (2) the innovation and its perceived attributes (such as, relative advantage, compatibility, etc.), (3) communication channels (mass media or interpersonal), (4) members of a social system, (5) consequences over time (such as, knowledge, attitude change, behavioral change, etc.)."[95]

The second part of Rogers and Shoemaker's paradigm consists of three main elements: antecedents, process, and consequences. "Antecedents" are given considerable prominence. They consist of receiver variables (such as personality characteristics, social characteristics, and the perceived need for the innovation) and social system variables (social norms, tolerance of deviancy, etc.). The "process" component is complex and attempts to

Figure 3
Rogers and Shoemaker's Paradigm of
the "Innovation-Decision Process"

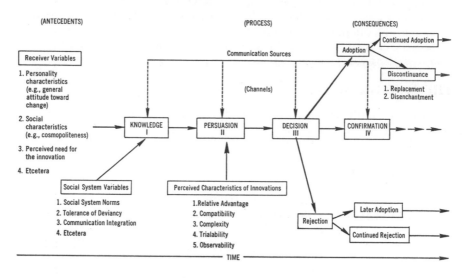

Source: Rogers and Shoemaker, 102. (Used by permission.)

portray the mental process that potential users pass through from the time they first gain knowledge about an innovation to when they decide to adopt or reject it.[96] "Consequences" include adoption or rejection of the innovation, but are not limited to such a simple dichotomy. Additional possibilities, allowing for the passage of time, include confirmation, discontinuance, later adoption, and continued rejection. [97]

INADEQUACIES OF THE FOREGOING MODELS

All these models (or "frameworks," or "paradigms") have strengths, and ideas can be profitably borrowed from them. Nevertheless, none of them meets all the criteria previously established: coherent framework, abstractness, completeness, relevance to directed change, and cross-cultural applicability.

Rogers and Shoemaker's "paradigm of the innovation-decision process" comes closest to satisfying these criteria. It takes into account a variety of important factors that affect the process of implementation. It also goes beyond simply listing stages or factors in the implementation process and shows how these elements relate to each other in a coherent whole. Most of the other models were designed for a single-culture setting (usually the United States) and ignore many of the important socio-cultural factors that a comparative, cross-cultural perspective reveals, but Rogers and Shoemaker's model can also be applied to cross-cultural efforts to implement directed change.

As it stands, however, Rogers and Shoemaker's innovation-decision paradigm is still inadequate and requires supplementation and modification in several ways. For instance, it does not include a number of factors that other researchers have noted and that experience has shown to be critical promoters of (or impediments to) change. Making the necessary changes results in the hybrid model.

THE HYBRID MODEL

Figure 4 illustrates the hybrid model and shows how its various components are arranged and interrelated. The three main elements are antecedents, process, and consequences.

ANTECEDENTS

"There is virtually unanimous agreement that an educational system is essentially an organic outgrowth of a society's unique history and culture...."[98] This history and culture form the background against which reforms are attempted and the foundation upon which change campaigns must build. In the case of school reform efforts, four major antecedent factors exert a strong influence: characteristics of the intended-user system, characteristics of the intended users of the innovation, traditional pedagogical practices, and experiences of previous reformers.

The antecedents section of the hybrid model focuses attention on the historical nature and development of these factors and reminds reformers of the necessity of investigating them as part of the planning process. Inasmuch as these characteristics of the intended-user system continue to affect the course of a reform campaign as it proceeds, many of the same social system and receiver variables also receive attention in the second major element of the model—as factors that facilitate/hinder the diffusion/implementation process. As would-be reformers' understanding of these factors deepens—from both antecedent and concurrent perspectives—their chances of success will increase.

Characteristics of the Intended-User System

Efforts to create change in schools must take into consideration the nature of the school system and of the society in which those schools are found. "The schools...take their shape from the social winds and waters....There is an implicit order in...society basic to all else—the order of the institutions. The schools do not exist freely outside that order; they are an integral part of it. Education can deviate only in the direction and to the extent that society allows."[99]

The structure of society and the schools, especially the power hierarchy among the various elements within these systems, also strongly affects the course of the diffusion/implementation process. Of course, these

Figure 4
The Hybrid Model

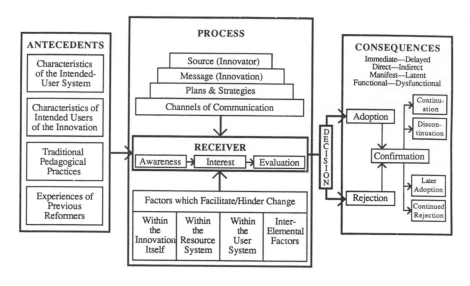

social and school system characteristics do not appear overnight. Each is the product of a long historical development. Reformers cannot afford to overlook these factors nor their historical roots, even though they antedate the change campaign. As Shiori notes, "In order to understand the present we must understand the past."[100]

Characteristics of the Intended Users of the Innovation

The system that reformers wish to change is composed of individuals who share a number of important general characteristics. Intended users' attitudes, values, norms, and abilities strongly influence the course of a diffusion/implementation effort. When intended users are committed to the status quo and their attitudes are staunchly conservative, innovations have little chance of spreading. In cross-cultural change campaigns, intended users' willingness to look beyond their own borders and accept foreign solutions to local problems is equally crucial. Values are "the basic stop-and-go signals for human behavior....Messages which clearly contradict pre-existing values will not get anywhere and those which appeal to them will get far."[101] Likewise, social norms influence intended users' behavior by serving as a standard and defining a range of tolerances beyond which members of a society rarely deviate.[102] When an innovation affects any aspect of the schooling process, its promoters must take into account the intended users' values relative to education as well as local norms regarding school practices The diffusion and implementation of an educational innovation also depend on the target population's ability to use it. In many cases—especially when an innovation from one country is exported to a less developed country—a critical question is whether users possess the requisite level of basic education or literacy.

Of course, these user characteristics do not appear suddenly. Each is the product of a lengthy period of development. Wise reformers will neither ignore the history of these antecedent factors nor expect them to change quickly. Rather, to increase their chances of success, they will understand and deal with them.

Traditional Pedagogical Practices

"Education in different countries reflects culturally specific traditions of teaching and learning that may substantially shape the form and content of much school learning."[103] These traditional practices (which teachers have used for years, decades, and even centuries) must also be taken into account in the planning and/or analysis of any educational change effort—especially in cultures where tradition is highly valued. In support of this thesis (and focusing on English-teaching programs), Hino maintains, "In developing or selecting [a] teaching methodology suitable for any EFL [English as a foreign language] country, it is essential to investigate its indigenous educational tradition."[104]

Experiences of Previous Reformers

Not to be overlooked are the experiences of earlier reform efforts in the same (or a similar) socio-cultural context. A knowledge of how they achieved their successes can provide extremely valuable guidance to subsequent change campaigns. An understanding of the difficulties they encountered can alert later reformers to potentially serious problems, allowing them to take action accordingly.

FACTORS THAT INFLUENCE THE CHANGE PROCESS

In the hybrid model, Rogers and Shoemaker's "perceived characteristics of innovations" section is expanded to include a much greater number and variety of factors that hinder/facilitate the implementation of change. These include several "barrier" factors noted by Havelock (and others) and the "secret life" factors described by Richards.

Attention to these factors is critical in the analysis of change campaigns. A fundamental question underlying studies on the diffusion of innovations is "What factors contribute to the prompt diffusion and rapid adoption of one particular innovation, while another—introduced at the same time into the same social system—is rejected or requires far greater time for its adoption?"[105]

In the development of an implementation strategy, a consideration of these "implementation factors" and how they can work for or against the intended innovation is also important. In fact, it should take precedence over other aspects of planning. "Research suggests that the process of implementation requires careful attention to myriad concerns; the identification of these concerns is necessary *before strategies* for overcoming the concerns can be determined" [italics added].[106] Furthermore, these factors cannot be forgotten once a strategy has been mapped out. They often appear in unexpected, new forms and foil the best laid plan. Williams wisely warns, "Always think about implementation problems, and always worry that others are not thinking about them."[107]

Since these facilitating/inhibiting factors are so varied and important, each of them will be discussed individually in the remainder of this section. They are grouped into four general categories based on their primary location: within the innovation itself, within the resource system, within the user system, or between elements (see figure 5).

Characteristics of the Innovation Itself

Miles insists that "innovations are almost never installed on their merits. Characteristics of the local system, of the innovating person or group, and of other relevant groups often outweigh the impact of what the innovation is."[108]   Nevertheless, the characteristics of the innovation itself are not unimportant. On the contrary, these characteristics—especially as they are perceived by the intended adopters of an innovation—are crucial both in and of themselves and as they interact with other implementation factors.

Originality.   One property that is widely regarded as critical to implementation is an innovation's "originality." Pelz notes that the degree of originality in an innovation determines the nature of the change process—whether it is categorized as *origination* ("the innovation is invented locally without benefit of a prior model"), *adaptation* ("the innovation is modified from external examples"), or *borrowing* ("a standardized model is copied with little change").[109] Others make a similar distinction although the labels vary. Mintzberg, for instance, categorizes solutions as "custom-made," "modified," and "ready-made."[110]

Originality is important for another (and perhaps more crucial) reason also. Particularly in cross-cultural change campaigns, a high degree of originality in the innovation may result in a low degree of compatibility between it and the intended-user system, a problem that can have devastating effects.

Complexity.   The complexity of an innovation is also recognized as an important factor by many who have studied the diffusion/implementation process. It comes first on Dow, Whitehead, and Wright's list of barriers to change. They recommend that implementors carefully consider the amount of change that is expected and how many people will be involved.[111]   Rogers and Shoemaker define complexity from a somewhat different perspective as "the degree to which an innovation is perceived as difficult to understand and use." They agree, however, that it is a crucial determining factor and generalize that innovations which do not

Figure 5
Factors That Hinder/Facilitate Change

Within the Innovation Itself	Within the Resource System	Within the Intended-User System	Inter-Elemental
Originality	Capacity	Geographic Location	Compatibility
Complexity	Structure		Linkage
Explicitness	Openness	Centralization of Power and Administration	Reward
Relative Advantage	Harmony	Size of the Adopting Unit	Proximity
Trialability			Synergism
Observability		Communication Structure	
Status		Group Orientation and Tolerance of Deviancy	
Practicality		Openness	
Flexibility/ Adaptability		Teacher Factors	
Primacy		Learner Factors	
Form		Capacities	
		Educational Philosophy	
		Examinations	

require potential users to spend much time, effort, or money developing the skills and understanding required to use them will be implemented more quickly than new ideas or products which require a large learning investment.[112] Regarding educational innovations, Fullan and Pomfret affirm that "complex changes in teachers' behaviors are usually more difficult to bring about and, therefore, less likely to occur."[113] Pelz is another who devotes considerable attention to the characteristic of "complexity." He reports that among seven studies with appropriate data, "six reported a negative relationship between the complexity of an innovation and its adoption."[114] In simpler words, the greater the complexity of an innovation, the lesser the likelihood of adoption.

Complexity is not a simple concept, however. Pelz notes that "complexity is seen to embrace multiple concepts." These he calls "technical complexity," "organizational complexity," "sophistication or intellectual difficulty," and "radicalness."[115]

Complexity is also related to other factors. For example, it affects explicitness, since the "greater the complexity, the more difficult it is to be explicit about the operational characteristics of the innovation."[116]

Explicitness. The term explicitness refers to more than the clarity with which the innovation is described. It also involves the degree of its development or formulation. In this regard, Dow, Whitehead, and Wright suggest that implementors ask, "Is there a rationale? Is the philosophy apparent? Are the goals and objectives specified?"[117]

In their discussion of "determinants of implementation," explicitness is one of two characteristics of the innovation that Fullan and Pomfret list as being most important (complexity is the other). A low degree of explicitness can lead to user confusion, a lack of clarity regarding what is desired, and frustration among those who receive the innovation.[118] When desired reforms are characterized by generalities and vagueness, "some process of developing greater explicitness or specification" can increase the likelihood of their implementation.[119]

Relative Advantage. This characteristic is defined as "the degree to which an innovation is perceived as better than the idea it supersedes."[120] It may be measured in terms of economics, social prestige, convenience, and/or user satisfaction. Interestingly, "objective" advantage (as measured by an outsider) is not nearly as important as "perceived" advantage (in the eyes of the intended user). In either case, however, as an innovation's objective and/or perceived relative advantage increases, so will its rate of diffusion/implementation.[121]

Trialability. Trialability refers to how easily new users can experiment with an innovation on a limited basis. Small-scale experimentation is less risky for the adopter. Therefore, Rogers and Shoemaker claim, "New ideas which can be tried on the installment plan will generally be adopted more quickly than innovations which are not divisible."[122] Havelock concurs that an innovation should be "'open' in allowing potential users to try out and sample its effects prior to an all-out commitment to adopt."[123]

Of course, some innovations are more difficult to try out than others, and some may not even work on a piecemeal basis. Also, it should be noted that this characteristic decreases in importance with the passage of time. It is most important for early adopters, who have no precedent to follow. Innovation "laggards" need not experiment since they can observe the experiences of their colleagues who have already adopted the innovation.

Observability. Observability is the extent to which an innovation's benefits are visible to potential users. When individuals can easily and clearly see the results of an innovation, they are more likely to accept and use it.[124] Because of this factor, material innovations, which are generally quite observable, catch on more readily than nonmaterial ones do.

Rogers and Shoemaker provide a memorable example of the effect of observability on the spread of an agricultural innovation: A new, very effective weed killer was still slow to catch on among farmers, the reason being that it was sprayed on fields before the plants sprouted and, therefore, potential users did not see any dead weeds.[125]

Status. Status refers to association with a higher social level which can impart legitimacy and attract attention to an innovation.[126] Although it is not the same as "power" to implement, it can be a powerful influencing factor—especially in academic circles.

Practicality. Practicality is an obvious factor that, surprisingly often, is overlooked. It is crucial for implementors to consider whether the demands of an innovation can be met by the intended-user system. Regarding classroom innovations, Dow, Whitehead, and Wright suggest that reformers ask questions such as the following: "Are expectations for students realistic? Are there aids for planning instruction? Is there adequate reference to resource materials? Is the expectation for teachers to cover material realistic? Are the other expectations for teachers realistic?"[127]

Flexibility/Adaptability. Another factor mentioned by Dow, Whitehead, and Wright (and many other implementation researchers) is concerned with whether an innovation is flexible enough to adapt to fit a particular situation. Havelock calls this characteristic "openness," rather than flexibility, but agrees that an innovation should be "adjustable and adaptable to the special circumstances of different users."[128]

Primacy. The relative timing of an innovation is also important. In human affairs, "being first" often carries an inordinate amount of weight. Havelock notes, "We cling to our first resource systems...the longest, and we tend to color our dealings with all later resource systems with our feelings about that first one."[129] Previously adopted practices form a barrier to the promotion of an innovation that is especially difficult to overcome in societies that value tradition and loyalty

Form. A final important characteristic of an innovation is the form that it takes. While most diffusion-of-innovations models ignore this factor, Richards asserts that a crucial determinant of a method's survival is whether it takes the form of a publishable textbook or remains merely an instructional philosophy. "Methods that lead to texts have a much higher adoption and survival rate than those which do not." Since textbook sales create profits for publishing companies, "publishers promote texts at conferences, book exhibits, and through direct visits to schools and institutions, and they finance workshops and lectures by authorities whose names lend credence to the philosophies behind the texts."[130] Discussing the teaching of reading, Miles makes a similar point—that "materials have exerted far more influence on practice...than has the available research."[131] Richards' frank "publish or perish" conclusion is that "anyone who has an innovative instructional philosophy to market had better make it dependent upon the use of a student text."[132]

Characteristics of the Resource System

The resource system that promotes an innovation also has characteristics that affect the course and success of implementation efforts. Although they are fewer in number than those of the innovation itself, these characteristics are still important .

Capacity. The resource system's "capability to retrieve and marshall diverse resources," accounts "for much of the variance in diffusion studies."

> Generally speaking, the more power, prestige and capital possessed by the resource system, the more effective it will be as a resource and as a diffuser. If the resource system collectively possesses a high degree of intelligence, education, power, and wealth, it will then have the ability to summon and invest diverse resources; it will be able to plan and structure its activities on a grand scale over a long time span to produce "high performance products."[133]

This factor also applies to the medium used by the resource system to communicate the innovation. "A 'high capacity' medium...can *convey* a large quantity of information to a user in the shortest possible time." It can also "*store* a large amount of knowledge for the user...in such a way that it is readily retrievable." Furthermore, a high capacity medium also has "a high *power to influence* the potential user, to monopolize his attention, to involve and to captivate" [italics in original].[134]

Structure. The resource system "needs a degree of structure in terms of meaningful *division of labor and coordination* of effort." It also needs to have "a structured and *coherent view of the client system*; it should be able to understand the various subsystems of the client system and how they are interrelated." Finally, the resource system also "should be able to *plan* D&U activities in a structured sequence" [italics in original]. It is also of critical importance to "have a structured program for getting the message across to the user."[135]

Openness. In relation to the innovation itself, openness means flexibility or adaptability. For the resource system, however, openness refers to "a *willingness to help and a willingness to listen* and to be influenced by user needs and aspirations" [italics in original]. In yet another sense, successful resource systems remain "open to the newest developments of science and technology" and thus continuously "renew their skills and their competence."[136]

Harmony. In their discussion of innovation problems in developing countries, Havelock and Huberman mention poor social relations or disharmony within the project.[137]   Harmonious relations among the different people and elements of the resource system would seem to be a crucial factor in all campaigns. Planners/managers of implementation projects who ignore social relations problems until they reach the critical stage may find their efforts crippled by internal disharmony.

Characteristics of the Intended-User System

Various characteristics of the target society/organization can be powerful determinants of success in diffusion/implementation. Havelock's list of inhibiting factors includes the need for stability, fear of malevolence of outsiders, local pride, status differences among organizations, economic condition, and size. Facilitating factors include perception of crisis, awareness, training, capacity, and professionalism.[138] In the same vein, Maley calls cultural characteristics "the most powerful factors in the implementation of any language programme." His examples of things to consider include the following:

> the attitudes of a given society toward the learning process, towards books, towards teachers;...attitudes to authority: whether people naturally conform or diverge from a norm; the degree to which learners cooperate or operate individually; the importance of "face," and whether conflict is solved by confrontation or compromise;...attitudes to effort: whether it is esteemed or disparaged; whether the society is elitist or egalitarian (or whether, professing the one, it is in fact the other!);...whether the society is based on seniority or on merit.[139]

Obviously, user-system factors are both numerous and complicated. Those included in the hybrid model range from the geographic location and size of the target system, to teachers' capabilities and characteristics of students' learning style.

Geographic Location. Among the diffusion/implementation researchers surveyed for this study, only Havelock and Huberman mention geographic barriers to change, and they use the term *geography* to refer to problems such as the slow transport of materials in developing countries.[140] Nevertheless, in directed contact change campaigns that involve widely separated user and resource systems, the location of the intended user system can affect the diffusion/implementation process in numerous ways. For instance, the geographic isolation of some countries not only limits their access to innovations, it also affects people's attitudes toward outsiders.

Centralization of Power and Administration. In some user systems, control is highly centralized, while in others local control is the norm. This variable affects implementation strategies. According to King, "There are many ways of penetrating a decentralized system" (such as the one found in U.S. schools), but in a highly centralized school system like Japan's you get "only one shot," win or lose.[141]

A related variable is whether administration is authoritarian or participatory in nature. When control is exercised by a central, authoritarian body, a critical question is whether the top-level administrators "understand, and are...in sympathy with, the declared objectives" of the innovation-implementation process.[142] When they are not, their opposition constitutes a serious barrier.   Reforms can be effectively blocked by opposition from ruling elites.[143]

When their members are opposed to change and in positions of authority, vested interest groups create "one of the major stumbling blocks in the effective dissemination and utilization of innovations and new knowledge...."[144]   Because both the character of these interest groups and the power they wield varies from country to country, an innovator from outside the intended-user system may not even be aware of key groups, much less understand how to deal with them.   Once the centers of power have been identified, however, there are a number of tactics for dealing with resistance:

> One possibility is presenting the innovation in such a way as not to arouse the vested interests of a powerful group. This sounds simple but unfortunately assumes ignorance on the part of the interest group, which is often not the case.
> A second more commonly used strategy is the inducement of the vested interest groups to accept the innovations in return for some desired resources.
> A strategy that has proven effective in some settings is the involvement of the vested interests in the decision-making process.[145]

Size of the Adopting Unit.   Even though some diffusion-of-innovations researchers (especially those who take a social-interaction view of change) state that size makes little difference,[146] most agree that, generally speaking, the greater the number of individuals in the receiving system, the more difficult it is to create change.   Using Japan as an example, Maeda affirms, "The greatest obstacle to change in English teaching...is the large number of people studying and teaching it."[147]

A related factor is the type of decision to be made.   When "authority decisions" rule, the size of the affected unit makes less difference than when decisions are of the "collective" type.   In the latter case, however, an increase in the number of people involved in making the decision slows the innovation's rate of adoption.[148]   In such cases, the rate of adoption and implementation may be speeded up by altering the type of decision or the size of the "decision-unit."

Communication Structure.   Another social system variable that reformers must attend to is the nature of the communication system(s) within the targeted user system.   This characteristic, along with the size of the adopting unit, determines which strategy (e.g., mass media, interpersonal contacts, etc.) will be most successful in conveying information about the innovation to its intended users.

Group Orientation and Tolerance of Deviancy.   "People tend to adopt and maintain attitudes and behaviors which they perceive as normative for their psychological reference group."[149]   In cultures where individuality is valued and deviancy tolerated, innovators are often encouraged.   On the other hand, in societies where the tendency toward group identity and loyalty is strong, conformity usually prevails and tolerance of deviancy is typically low.   Consequently, promoters of new practices have a difficult time, and early adopters of innovations—who might be seen as leaders in a more individualistic society—feel social pressure to abandon them and conform to the status quo.

Openness. Intended users' willingness to seek and receive new information from outside sources is a vitally important quality. As Havelock explains, "closed systems and closed minds are, by definition, incapable of taking in important new messages from outside; if they cannot take in, then they cannot utilize knowledge for internal change." Openness involves attitudes toward new as well as foreign ideas, but it is always more than "passive receptivity." "Rather it is an active faith that outside resources will be useful and an *active reaching out* for new ideas, new products, and new ways of doing things." In addition, openness refers to a "willingness to take risks and to make an effort to *adapt* innovations to one's own situation" [italics in original].[150]

"There are societies which are essentially outward-looking, and which welcome innovation. And those which look inward, seeking their inspiration from deeply-rooted traditional values."[151] Traditional social systems can be characterized by negative attitudes toward change, social pressure to conform to the status quo, minimal communication between members and outsiders, and lack of ability on the part of members to empathize or imagine themselves in other roles. In contrast, modern social systems are typified by favorable attitudes toward change, acceptance of advancing technology, heavy investments in science and education, "businesslike" social relationships, and cosmopolitan views and social empathy among their members.[152] Where a social system lies on this traditional-to-modern continuum reflects its openness and determines to a considerable extent whether innovation is welcomed or obstructed.

The intended-user society's willingness to accept foreign ideas and practices is also critical in cross-cultural change efforts. The tendency to borrow from outside sources is strong—even traditional—in some cultures. Other societies tend to be xenophobic. This variable must be considered in the early stages of planning a change campaign, for when intended receivers have an unrealistic fear of foreign things, bringing in an outside solution to a local problem is a poor approach.

In the case of language teaching, this aspect of openness takes on an additional dimension. Attitudes toward the foreign language itself are also important.

> In highly ethnocentric societies, the language is usually a powerful cohesive force. There is often a belief in the intrinsic superiority of one's own language over others, and tenacious pride in it as a badge of identity. This is often reflected in an ambivalent attitude to foreigners and to their language. Such attitudes will clearly have profound effects upon the teaching of a foreign language. It may be publicly confessed, but privately regretted, that English is necessary. And this will affect the deep-seated motivations of learners.[153]

Teacher Factors. In most cases of educational innovation, change at the classroom level is implemented by teachers. Since changes in teacher behavior require both commitment and capability, promoters of an innovation must concern themselves with these two types of change: "changes that make the user capable of using the innovation and changes that commit the user to the innovation."[154]   Alone, neither commitment nor capability is enough. "Capability determines what *can* be implemented, and commitment determines what *will* be implemented" [italics in original].[155] "If teachers are not committed to the change, it is unlikely to occur."[156]   Nevertheless, it is impossible for teachers to use an innovation properly—even when inner desires and external pressures are strong—unless they have the capability to do so.

Teacher capability is widely recognized as being crucial to many reforms.   Beeby states that two factors determine the ability of an educational system to move from one stage to another: (1) the level of general education among teachers, and (2) the amount and kind of training teachers have received.[157]   Maley agrees that critical teacher factors include the "training and experience of those who will have to carry out any previously devised program," their "degree of understanding," the "availability of teacher training," and their expectations about the nature of the teaching/learning experience.[158] For this reason, Dow, Whitehead, and Wright remind reformers to ask: "Do teachers...have the skills necessary to implement the guidelines?"   (And, if they don't possess them: "Have adequate workshops and inservice programmes been provided to develop the knowledge and skills necessary for implementation?")[159]

In the case of foreign language teaching, one of the most important capabilities teachers must have is proficiency in the target language. In many cases, however, English teachers around the world do not possess the level of accuracy and fluency in English that is necessary to use new teaching approaches and techniques developed by teachers who are native-speakers of English in nations where it is the primary language. When teachers' English skills are inadequate to handle a new approach, they must be developed, or else the innovation will have to be either heavily adapted or abandoned entirely. Nevertheless, English proficiency can seldom be built up sufficiently in an afternoon in-service meeting or a weekend workshop. Improved proficiency requires a heavy investment of both time and effort.

Unfortunately, teachers typically approach this formidable task "with limited resources."[160]   In most situations—especially those where improvement is most needed—teachers are extremely busy and overburdened, with multiple preparations and large class sizes. They have little time, energy, or motivation to take effective steps toward innovation. "Lack of time and energy, teacher overload, and multiple demands are...frequently cited by teachers...among the major implementation problems they face." In such cases, "reducing the costs of the innovation—the personal time and difficulty in learning new skills—may be one of the most efficient ways of promoting innovation."[161]

Learner Factors. When an educational innovation designed for use in one cultural setting is transplanted to another, the various perceptual, social, cognitive, and affective characteristics of students in the target society that comprise their "learning style" and that differ from those of learners in the innovation's "home" culture   cannot be ignored. Overlooking these factors or assuming that students will accept a foreign innovation unquestioningly and be able to use it comfortably is a serious error.

Capacities.   In educational reform efforts, teachers' and students' capacities "to perform in new ways" are crucial.[162] In addition, however, capacity—which refers to more tangible factors—must not be forgotten. Speaking from experience, Maley warns that unless the physical capacities of the adopting unit are sufficient to support the desired innovation "material factors" can be a serious problem for educational reformers. Unfortunately, despite their obvious nature, these factors are "consistently overlooked." He cites specific examples of

> a major language programme which had to start without hardware, and with very little software either, because orders had not been placed in time; an institution with three language laboratories in crates because the buildings to house them had not yet been constructed; a photocopier rendered unusable because no paper had been provided for it; sets of text-books on listening skills without the cassettes which perform an essential role in their use; video equipment which was incompatible; a language laboratory which caught fire after being used once and which could not be repaired since the nearest qualified technician was in Norway; equipment locked away and unused on the grounds that it was too valuable to use.[163]

Anticipatory consideration of critical capacity factors (from budgetary provisions to servicing of hardware) will help avoid such problems when new programs are implemented.

Educational Philosophy.   A fundamental factor in school-system reforms is the "prevailing educational philosophy."[164] For instance, is schooling provided for primarily egalitarian, or elitist purposes?   Does education serve culturally enriching, or purely practical ends?   Whatever the philosophy may be, an innovation that is not in harmony with it will have little chance of success.   Although this factor is of prime importance, it is often overlooked by reformers who focus their attention on technical aspects of the teaching-learning process.

Examinations.   The role of examinations is typically overlooked by American educational reformers.   Given the decentralized, credit-oriented nature of the U.S. school system, this neglect is only natural.   Nevertheless, in many other nations, this "examination factor" is of critical importance and carries great weight.   Reflecting on experiences in several Asian countries, Maley laments, "Many a good scheme has been drowned in the washback from an intractable examination system."[165] From a historical, British perspective, Gordon and Lawton note that examination pressure can facilitate as well as hinder change.   "Examinations have at times restricted curriculum development, but at other times they have certainly been a progressive influence on the educational system."[166]

Inter-Elemental Factors

A number of factors exist "between" rather than "within" the elements involved in the diffusion and implementation of innovations. Five critical inter-elemental factors are compatibility, linkage, reward, proximity, and synergism.

Compatibility. In directed contact change efforts that cross cultural boundaries, compatibility can be a decisive factor and should not be taken for granted. Two types of compatibility are of primary concern: (1) between the innovation and its intended users, and (2) between the resource system and the intended-user system To avoid or remedy potentially threatening mismatches, experts recommend conducting a preliminary analysis of the "fit" between the systems concerned and then making adjustments based on the findings.

Innovation-user compatibility involves the degree to which potential adopters feel an innovation is "consistent with their existing values and past experiences."[167] An innovation that is not compatible with the prevailing norms of the intended users will not spread as quickly as an innovation that is.[168] In fact, it may not be adopted at all.

When incompatibilities between an innovation and its intended users discourage diffusion and implementation, two different approaches can be used to improve the "fit." "Adaptive implementation" involves modifying or adapting the innovation so that it is more easily assimilated into user practices and values. "Programmed implementation" attempts to "bring about changes in the user so that characteristics of the innovation are accommodated."[169]

Before such steps can be taken, however, incompatibilities must be identified. Very generally, the characteristics of the innovation and the characteristics of the user can be grouped into four categories as follows:

Characteristics of the Innovation	Characteristics of the User
Resource demands	Organizational structures and facilities
Concept of use	Organizational policies and regulations
Task demands	Individual abilities and behavior patterns
Expected benefits	Individual attitudes and values

Regarding the first characteristic, resource demands, "the user organization must have structures to obtain and manage resources to support use of the innovation" or else the process will be hampered. In the second category, "the concept of use for the innovation must be consistent with policies and regulations that control activity within the organization." Relative to task demands, "to acquire the *know-how* to perform with the innovation, individuals must have abilities and behavior patterns that will allow them to integrate the new task requirements into existing routines." And respecting the final set of characteristics, "to obtain *personal commitment* to its use, the innovation must offer benefits that are compatible with attitudes and values held by individual users" [italics in original].[170]

Resource-user compatibility is a particularly important concern in cross-cultural implementation efforts where socio-cultural differences between the resource system and the intended users of the innovation are great. The homophily-heterophily distinction, made by Rogers and Shoemaker, provides terminology and concepts useful in discussing and understanding such problems. They define homophily as "the degree to which pairs of individuals who interact are similar in certain attributes, such as beliefs, values, education, social status, and the like." When resource systems and user systems have freedom to choose each other, they tend to select those that they regard as homophilous. Nevertheless, in directed contact change efforts (especially campaigns that cross cultural boundaries) the resource system and the innovation it promotes are typically heterophilous to the intended user.[171] A wide heterophily gap can result in numerous difficulties in areas such as communication and role expectations.[172] On the other hand, "a perception of shared values will bring resource and user systems together."[173]

Linkage.   In his review of reports on diffusion of innovations, Havelock notes that "certain things seemed to keep coming up, regardless of the area of focus and regardless of the level of analysis." The first of these is linkage, "the number, variety, and mutuality of contacts between the Resource System and the User System." It reflects the "degree of inter-personal or intergroup connection" that exists in a given situation. Generally, "the more linkages there are and the stronger these linkages are, the more effective will be the day-to-day contact and exchange of information, hence the greater will be the mutual utilization of knowledge."[174] In educational reform campaigns, a number of linkage factors play an important role. Regarding the spread of language-teaching innovations, for example, Richards discusses the importance of various types of "support networks": professional teacher organizations, universities, professional journals, and official educational agencies.[175] There is nothing new about the power of such linkages. Nearly a century ago, Sweet mentioned the "good fortune" of any new method that was "taken up by the editor of some popular periodical."[176]

Reward.   Reward refers to "the frequency, immediacy, amount, mutuality of, planning, and structuring of positive reinforcements."[177] Innovations can provide rewards to their users, and resource systems can reward (or reinforce) user systems. These rewards can take various forms—profitability (for commercial systems), recognition by colleagues, satisfaction in creating something that works, or feedback from a satisfied client, to mention only a few.[178] In any case, a clear channel of rewards can create motivation for change.

Unfortunately, in many school systems, the rewards for implementing an innovation are few—if they exist at all. In fact, it is not uncommon for innovation decisions to be *negatively* reinforced. The "teacher's predicament" is that rewards for trying innovations are few, and the personal costs are frequently high.[179] Costs include the energy, time, difficulty, and trauma involved in learning skills. Moreover, teachers are typically expected to go through this process "at their own personal expense."[180]

Proximity. The "nearness in time, place, and context" of the resource and user systems and their "familiarity, similarity, [and] recency" can be a "powerful predictor of utilization."[181] Havelock explains:

> When we live as neighbors, when we bump into one another and have the chance to observe and stimulate one another by reason of being in the same place at the same time, we will inevitably *learn* from one another. Hence, users who have close proximity to resources are more likely to use them. Anything which is "handy," i.e., easily accessible, is more likely to be used.[182]

Of course, in cross-cultural implementation efforts, the distance between resource and user systems may be great, reducing the likelihood of success. Special efforts must be made to overcome this barrier.

Synergism. The term synergism means, literally, a working together. Together, a variety of forces can achieve an effect which, working individually, they would not be capable of. For the purposes of this study, *synergism* refers to "the number, variety, frequency, and persistence of forces that can be mobilized to produce a knowledge utilization effect."[183] Because this final factor is rather nebulous, Havelock mentions it with "reluctance," yet he recognizes that it captures a critical idea or force in the diffusion/implementation process.

CONSEQUENCES

Just as the process of a change campaign is not simple, neither are the decisions and outcomes that it may lead to. The hybrid model provides for this complexity in types of decisions and outcomes

Types of Innovation Decisions

The types of decisions that the intended users of an innovation can make constitute a critical concern of careful implementation planners, who begin with the end in mind. *Optional* decisions are not dependent on other members of society. An individual (or individual group) may choose to implement an innovation regardless of the decision made by others. *Collective* decisions, on the other hand, are made only by consensus agreement among all the parties involved. *Authority* decisions come from "above." They are forced upon individuals by someone in a superordinate power position, perhaps a school administrator or government official. *Contingent* decisions are chained to other, preceding decisions. They are made only after a prior decision and depend on the nature of that decision.[184]

These different types of decisions vary in both the speed with which they can be made and the effectiveness or duration of their outcomes. Generally, authority decisions can be made quickly and produce the fastest rate of diffusion and implementation. Optional decisions take longer to make, although they are usually faster than collective decisions. Authority decisions, however, do not guarantee long-term use of the innovation. In fact, of all the types of decisions, they are the most likely to generate negative reactions among intended users, leading to avoidance, circumvention, and discontinuation of the imposed practice. On the other hand, optional and collective decisions—even though they take more time to arrive at and implement—tend to produce more lasting effects. That is because they involve the users from the start—building on their interest in the innovation, creating a commitment to it, and encouraging adaptation along the way.[185]

Types of Outcomes

The hybrid model also allows for several types of outcomes. The results of a change campaign may be either immediate or delayed—and often both. In addition, consequences may be direct (coming about in response to the innovation itself) or indirect (resulting from other consequences). Consequences may also be manifest or latent. Manifest consequences are those that are not only intended by the resource system but also recognized by members of the receiving system, whereas latent consequences may be neither recognized nor intended. And finally, despite reformers' good intentions, consequences may be both functional and dysfunctional; they may have undesirable as well as desirable effects on the functioning of the user system.[186]

SUMMARY AND PREVIEW

The hybrid linkage model developed in this chapter incorporates ideas from many sources in order to satisfy the criteria of coherent framework, abstractness, completeness, relevance to directed change, and cross-cultural applicability. In the remaining chapters, this model will be applied to a particular case—the ELEC effort in Japan. First, antecedent variables, including the development of pedagogical traditions associated with foreign language teaching in Japan, will be discussed. After that, the process and consequences of the ELEC campaign will be considered. In contrast to chapter two, which outlined the ELEC story in chronological order, these chapters will discuss various aspects of the ELEC experience as they relate to the elements in the hybrid model.

NOTES

1. Roberts-Gray and Gray, 213.
2. Roberts-Gray and Gray, 213.
3. Pratt et al., 67.
4. Michaletz, 2.
5. Michaletz, 2.
6. Havelock, *Planning,* chap. 11, p. 23.
7. Roberts-Gray and Gray, 214.

8. Fullan and Pomfret, 337.
9. Roberts-Gray and Gray, 215.
10. Parish and Arends, 62.
11. Fullan and Pomfret, 367.
12. Fullan and Pomfret, 390.
13. Mackey, v.
14. Heraclitus, from Diogenes Laertius bk IX, Sec. 8, and Plato, *Cratylus,* in Beck, 402.
15. Marcus Aurelius Antoninus, *Meditations* II, 3, in Beck, 141.
16. Honorat de Bueil, Marquis de Racan, *Odes, The Coming of Spring,* in Beck, 318.
17. Abraham Cowley, *Inconstancy,* in Beck, 357.
18. Alphonse Karr, *Les Guêpes,* [Janvier, 1849], in Beck, 627.
19. *King Lear,* I.iv.346.
20. John Adams, Letter to James Warren, [22 April 1776], in Beck, 463.
21. Appelbaum, 123.
22. Appelbaum, 123.
23. Appelbaum, 132.
24. Appelbaum, 167.
25. Appelbaum, 72.
26. Appelbaum, 56.
27. Appelbaum, 36.
28. Smith, 4.
29. Appelbaum, 19.
30. Appelbaum, 16.
31. Appelbaum, 133.
32. Appelbaum, 134.
33. Thompson and Williams, 14.
34. Havelock, *Planning,* chap. 11, p. 19.
35. Appelbaum, 126.
36. Appelbaum, 121.
37. Appelbaum, 134.
38. Appelbaum, 120.
39. Miles, 14.
40. Francis Bacon, *Of Innovations,* in Evans, *Dictionary* , 348.
41. Max Planck, *The Philosophy of Physics,* in Beck, 847
42. Havelock, *Planning,* chap. 11, p. 4.
43. Havelock, *Planning,* chap. 11, p. 7.
44. Roberts-Gray and Gray, 214
45. Sarason, 19
46. Mann, xii.
47. Mann, back cover.
48. Havelock, *Planning,* chap. 11, p. 7.
49. Havelock, *Planning,* chap. 11, p. 7.
50. Havelock, *Planning,* chap. 11, p. 11.
51. Havelock, *Planning,* chap. 11, p. 7.
52. Havelock, *Planning,* chap. 11, p. 11.
53. Havelock, *Planning,* chap. 11, pp. 13-14.
54. Havelock, *Planning,* chap. 11, p. 4.
55. Rogers and Shoemaker, 228.
56. Havelock, *Planning,* chap. 11, p. 15.
57. Parish and Arends, 65.
58. American Psychological Association.
59. Corbett and D'Amico, 70-72.
60. Cavanagh and Styles, 9-15
61. Maley, 90-111.
62. Rogers and Kincaid, 32.
63. Gordon and Lawton, 217.
64. Pratt et al., 67.

65. Pelz, 285.
66. Pelz, 289.
67. Martin and Saif.
68. Havelock, Huber, and Zimmerman, 37
69. Strevens, 1.
70. King, *A Piece of the Dirt.*
71. Gee, 14, 8a.
72. Rogers and Shoemaker, 25.
73. Michaletz, 4.
74. Roberts-Gray and Gray, 224.
75. Havelock, *The Change Agents Guide*, 11.
76. Leithwood, 357.
77. Leithwood, 347.
78. Rogers and Shoemaker, 25.
79. House, 3.
80. Roberts-Gray and Gray, 220.
81. Mann, 288.
82. Fullan and Pomfret, 368, 375.
83. Rogers and Shoemaker, 34-35.
84. Rogers and Shoemaker, 23.
85. Gee, 14.
86. Richards, "The Secret Life of Methods," *TESOL Quarterly,* 7-23.
87. Richards, "The Secret Life of Methods," *TESOL Quarterly,* 13.
88. Richards, "The Secret Life of Methods," plenary address; Richards, "The Secret Life of Methods," *Working Papers*, 11-16.
89. Richards, "The Secret Life of Methods," *TESOL Quarterly,* 13-14.
90. Richards, "The Secret Life of Methods," *Working Papers*, 11-12.
91. Havelock, *Planning*, chap. 5, p. 16.
92. Gordon and Lawton, 205.
93. Richards, "The Context," 11-15.
94. Rogers and Shoemaker, 12.
95. Rogers and Shoemaker, 20.
96. Rogers and Shoemaker, 25
97. Rogers and Shoemaker, 102.
98. Beauchamp, "Reform Traditions," 3.
99. House, 5.
100. Wada and McCarty, 28.
101. Havelock, *Planning*, chap. 11, p. 31.
102. Rogers and Shoemaker, 30-31.
103. Richards, "The Context," 12.
104. Hino, "Yakudoku: The Japanese Approach," 52.
105. Evans, *Resistance to Innovation,* 14.
106. Dow, Whitehead, and Wright.
107. Williams, 566.
108. Miles, 635.
109. Pelz, 262-263.
110. Mintzberg, Raisinghani, and Théorêt, 246-75.
111. Dow, Whitehead, and Wright, 2.
112. Rogers and Shoemaker, 22.
113. Fullan and Pomfret, 371.
114. Pelz, 264.
115. Pelz, 264.
116. Fullan and Pomfret, 371.
117. Dow, Whitehead, and Wright, 3.
118. Fullan and Pomfret, 367.
119. Fullan and Pomfret, 370.
120. Rogers and Shoemaker, 138.
121. Rogers and Shoemaker, 22.

122. Rogers and Shoemaker, 155.
123. Havelock, *Planning*, chap. 11, p. 25.
124. Rogers and Shoemaker, 23
125. Rogers and Shoemaker, 156.
126. Havelock, *Planning*, chap. 11, 31.
127. Dow, Whitehead, and Wright, 3.
128. Havelock, *Planning*, chap. 11, p. 25.
129. Havelock, *Planning*, chap. 11, p. 31.
130. Richards, "The Secret Life of Methods," *TESOL Quarterly,* 14.
131. Miles, 637.
132. Richards, "The Secret Life of Methods," *TESOL Quarterly,* 14.
133. Havelock, *Planning*, chap. 11, p. 25.
134. Havelock, *Planning*, chap. 11, p. 26.
135. Havelock, *Planning*, chap. 11, pp. 23-24
136. Havelock, *Planning*, chap. 11, p. 24.
137. Havelock and Huberman, 241.
138. Havelock, *Planning*, chap. 6, pp. 7-ff.
139. Maley, 91-92.
140. Havelock and Huberman, 222.
141. King, interview.
142. Maley, 92.
143. Havelock and Huberman, 239.
144. Havelock, *Planning*, chap. 5, p. 20.
145. Havelock, *Planning*, chap. 5, p. 21.
146. Havelock, *Planning*, chap. 11, p. 7.
147. Maeda, interview.
148. Rogers and Shoemaker, 159.
149. Havelock, *Planning*, chap. 11, p. 9.
150. Havelock, *Planning*, chap. 11, p. 24.
151. Maley, 91.
152. Rogers and Shoemaker, 32.
153. Maley, 91.
154. Roberts-Gray and Gray, 217.
155. Roberts-Gray and Gray, 219.
156. Dow, Whitehead, and Wright, 4.
157. Beeby, 20.
158. Maley, 96-97.
159. Dow, Whitehead, and Wright, 4.
160. House, 80.
161. Fullan and Pomfret, 388.
162. Fullan and Pomfret, 371.
163. Maley, 97.
164. Maley, 92.
165. Maley, 93.
166. Gordon and Lawton, 179.
167. Evans, *Resistance to Innovation,* 17.
168. Rogers and Shoemaker, 22.
169. Roberts-Gray and Gray, 216.
170. Roberts-Gray and Gray, 223.
171. Rogers and Shoemaker, 14-15.
172. Rogers and Shoemaker, 229.
173. Havelock, *Planning*, chap. 11, p. 31.
174. Havelock, *Planning*, chap. 11, pp. 20-21.
175. Richards, "The Secret Life of Methods," *TESOL Quarterly,* 14-16.
176. Sweet, 2.
177. Havelock, *Planning*, chap. 11, p. 20.
178. Havelock, *Planning*, chap. 11, pp. 26-27.
179. House, 73.

180. House, 97.
181. Havelock, *Planning*, chap. 11, p. 20.
182. Havelock, *Planning*, chap. 11, p. 27.
183. Havelock, *Planning*, chap. 11, p. 20.
184. Rogers and Shoemaker, 37-38.
185. Rogers and Shoemaker, 37
186. Rogers and Shoemaker, 17.

4
Antecedents

Understanding antecedents is a crucial part of the process of analyzing or planning any effort to diffuse and/or implement an educational innovation. They form the historical foundation for the conditions that a change campaign must deal with.

In Japan, the widespread study of English is by no means a purely modern phenomenon; its roots extend far back into Japanese history. Those who wish to reform Japanese English language teaching are well advised to examine "cultural and historical influences."[1] Suzuki explains, "Our lack of proficiency in English may be ascribed to certain national traits developed over a long period of historical and geographical isolation."[2] Similarly, Harasawa maintains that the major challenge of ELT reform in Japan is to "modify a nation's 2,000-year-old mental habit or psychological complex."[3]

Unfortunately, many well-meaning critics and would-be reformers of the Japanese English-teaching system ignore the history of the practices they wish to change. That they confine themselves to the immediate situation only is not entirely surprising. A "minor scandal" in English language teaching is that many degree-holding professionals know virtually nothing about ELT practices before World War II.[4]

In like manner and to a discouraging extent, the ELEC reformers lacked a historical perspective on the system they desired to change. For example, although it was claimed that "all of the important problems of English teaching" in Japan were discussed at the first ELEC conference, the topics were limited to the "present situation."[5] This, of course, was a serious oversight. As they had for many centuries, antecedent factors affected the way foreign languages were taught in Japan in the 1950s, and they influenced the ELEC attempt to change these methods.

FOUR MAJOR TYPES OF ANTECEDENT FACTORS

The antecedents portion of the hybrid model is concerned with four main factors: the development of various characteristics of the intended-user system, the history of a number of characteristics of the intended users of the innovation, traditional pedagogical practices, and the experiences of previous reformers. Accordingly, this chapter traces the history of the Japanese school system and focuses on the development of certain characteristics of the Japanese who (the ELEC reformers hoped) would use the Oral Approach. It also investigates a number of powerful Japanese pedagogical traditions related to English language teaching. In addition, it notes the experiences of prior ELT and educational reform movements in Japan, which set the stage for the ELEC effort.

A brief consideration of the major factors in each of these four areas follows. In the historical overview that makes up the rest of the chapter, these and other related factors are discussed in greater depth.

Characteristics of the Intended-User System

Immediately prior to the ELEC campaign, "democratic" reforms had expanded educational opportunity in Japan, but formal schooling in that country already had a long history—one of the longest in the world. Over a hundred years earlier, prior to the Meiji Restoration, an operating network of schools had been established throughout the country.

> One important respect in which mid-nineteenth century Japan differed from its Asian neighbors...[was that] Japan already had a developed system of formal school education....It was class-ridden, formalistic, backward looking, out-of-date. But it was also intellectually sophisticated, disciplined, occasionally stimulating, and politically relevant,...Nearly every fief had its fief-endowed school and there were hundreds of private schools for samurai.[6]

In any large, complex system, there naturally exists a hierarchy of power among its different elements. From country to country, this "ladder of influence" varies in its nature and in the strength of its constituents. In Japan in the 1950s, the relationships among the different elements in the school system certainly were not the same as those that existed in the United States at that time. For example, just prior to the commencement of the ELEC effort, a recentralization movement had returned a degree of control over local schools to the Japanese Ministry of Education (*Mombusho*) that the United States Office of Education had never possessed. In addition, key Japanese universities and their entrance examinations wielded power significantly greater than that exercised by their counterparts in the United States.

Because of these differences and their failure to recognize them, the American ELEC reformers misunderstood and underestimated the power of various elements in the Japanese system. This failure to understand and work with the hierarchy of the Japanese educational system led to numerous problems.

Characteristics of Intended Users of the Innovation

A number of crucial characteristics of Japanese teachers and students in the 1950s had developed over many centuries. The most important were peoples' attitudes toward education, their level of basic education and literacy, their attitudes toward seeking knowledge from outside sources through the medium of a foreign language, and their enthusiasm for learning that language.

Favorable attitudes toward schooling were a firmly established Japanese tradition dating back to pre-Tokugawa days, and relatively high levels of basic education and literacy—both prerequisites to widespread foreign language study—were reached well over a hundred years before the ELEC effort was conceived.[7]

The development of a national attitude recognizing the need to borrow knowledge from extranational sources and learn through non-Japanese languages was not an isolated post-World War II phenomenon. "Eagerness to learn from others" seems to be part of the Japanese national character, and the "tradition of cultural borrowing is deeply embedded in Japanese history."[8] It dates back at least one thousand years to the time when the Japanese borrowed a large portion of Chinese culture, including the Chinese writing system. The process continued through the years of Portuguese and Dutch influence (when the Japanese were first exposed to European languages and the Roman alphabet). Japanese enthusiasm for Western knowledge culminated in the early Meiji period. One of the major points in the Imperial Charter Oath of 1867 was that "knowledge shall be sought throughout the world."[9] Although this reversal of the Tokugawa policy of national seclusion was dramatic, in the larger historical context it was not at all unusual.

A cyclical pattern of attraction to and rejection of foreign ideas and languages characterizes Japan's history. In the course of this history there has been a clear pattern of strong "swings from nationalism to internationalism."[10] Japan's mood has long alternated "between waves of nationalization and westernization."[11] This pattern has been accompanied by periodic waves of enthusiasm for learning foreign languages. It began with the borrowing of the Chinese writing system. Later came a "craze" for the Portuguese language. This was followed by enthusiasm for Dutch. Finally, during the Meiji period, English became Japan's most widely studied language of wider communication. In the 1950s, enthusiasm for learning English grew strong once again, but that was by no means the first time a wave of "English fever" had swept the country.

Traditional Pedagogical Practices

"The teaching of modern languages has always been somewhat influenced by the teaching of the classical languages."[12] In the Western world, these classical languages were Greek and Latin. The methods used for teaching them in American and European schools were later used for teaching modern languages and became the object of numerous reform efforts in the nineteenth and twentieth centuries.

In Japan also, foreign languages have been studied for many centuries, and a formidable foundation of pedagogical traditions has formed. Most of them are based on a Chinese rather than a Greco-Roman tradition. Like their Western counterparts, these teaching practices have demonstrated a remarkable power to persist. Many of them, such as the "long tradition of learning foreign languages without necessarily being able to converse in them,"[13] started when Japanese scholars studied Chinese in the fourth century. Over a thousand years later, this approach continued with teachers and students of Dutch. It persisted when the switch was made to English and later became one of the major obstacles to the adoption of the Oral Approach. Another Japanese language-teaching tradition that ran counter to the reforms ELEC promoted was a Japanese-style "grammar-translation" approach called *yakudoku,* which originated with the study of Chinese more than a millennium earlier.

Experiences of Previous Reformers

Wise reformers learn from the experiences of their predecessors and thus avoid many implementation problems that those who ignore antecedents often encounter.

With the Meiji Restoration of 1868, a great revolution in Japanese thought and life began. In the first few years of the Meiji period, there was an unprecedented "explosion" of English study, and "English attained a special role...as a tool to facilitate the westernization of the country."[14] From a limited historical perspective, the "swift introduction of foreign language and culture"[15] into Japan in the Meiji days appears to have been accomplished relatively painlessly. This myopic point of view might lead reformers of ELT in Japan to believe that modern-day pedagogical practices can be changed with equal rapidity. In fact, a larger view of the history and development of foreign language teaching practices in Japan reveals quite a different picture.

Harold E. Palmer, a British scholar who traveled to Japan in 1922, was a noteworthy individual reformer. As director of the Institute for Research in English Teaching in Tokyo, Palmer labored for fourteen years trying to improve the teaching of spoken English in Japan. Although he experienced more failures than successes, many of Palmer's disciples remained faithful to his ideas, and this "ghost" haunted ELEC.

The Allied Occupation of Japan (1945-52) came to an end shortly before ELEC's operations began. Although many of its reforms were later reversed, at that point it appeared to have been a stunning success. It is likely that the Occupation's accomplishments encouraged ELEC's leaders and led them to believe that additional reforms could be achieved easily. Without doubt, the Allied Occupation set the stage for the ELEC effort, and its aftermath affected ELEC in many ways.

TRACING THE "ROOTS" OF ELT IN JAPAN

Overcoming challenges involves understanding their roots—especially in tradition-oriented Japan. Tracing these roots reveals that they go back much farther than is commonly thought. Studies of the history of English teaching in Japan typically begin with the Meiji Restoration in 1868, when the study of English became popular. Others maintain that the beginning of English teaching in Japan was marked by the Phaeton Incident of 1808 when a British warship, the HMS *Phaeton*, landed at Nagasaki and created quite a "stir."[16] Nevertheless, incidents equally important to the history of ELT in Japan occurred prior to that time, and the socio-cultural influences that made the rapid expansion of English teaching in nineteenth-century Japan possible had developed over many centuries. To understand these forces, a much larger historical view is required.

As this chapter reviews the forces and developments in Japanese culture and history that provided the foundation on which English language teaching in Japan rested when the ELEC effort began, nine general time frames will be employed. They coincide with events of particular importance in the history of ELT in Japan:

1. Early contacts with China, especially during the Nara period (710-784) and the Heian period (794-1185), when the Japanese first realized the need for a language of wider communication and particular Japanese ways of studying a foreign language developed;

2. Early East-West contacts, from 1543, the year that the first Portuguese ship landed in Japan, to the highly nationalistic and anti-Christian edicts of Hideyoshi in 1587;

3. Repression of Western influences, from 1588 until the end of the Shimabara Rebellion (the Christians' "last stand") in 1638;

4. National seclusion, from 1639, the year after the Shimabara Rebellion, until 1852, the year before the arrival of Commodore Perry's fleet;

5. Official reopening of Japan to Western influences, from 1853, when Commodore Perry first sailed into Edo Bay, until the coup that overthrew the Tokugawa Shogunate in 1867;

6. Meiji period, from 1868 through 1912, and including the following Taisho period (1912-26);

7. Palmer's reform attempts, during his years in Japan (1922-36);

8. Militarism and World War II, beginning in the 1930s and ending with Japan's surrender in 1945;

9. The Allied Occupation and its aftermath, from 1945 to 1952, as well as the "reverse course" years (1952-58) that immediately followed the Occupation and during which the ELEC campaign was officially started.

EARLY CONTACTS WITH CHINA

From early times, the Japanese have looked beyond their own shores for useful information. Whenever they have made contact with the outside world, the Japanese have also realized their need for proficiency in a language of wider communication. As they have pursued this goal, peculiar Japanese methods for studying foreign languages have developed.

In the early days of Japanese history, the "outside world" consisted primarily of China, so naturally, the language that the Japanese learned was Chinese. This contact dates back thousands of years. In fact, as Lombard explains,

it is quite impossible to say when the Chinese language and literature were first known in Japan. As early as the reign of *Kaika* (157-97 B.C.) there is evidence of intercourse with China and, according to Nakano in his *Nihon Kyoikushi*, the latest time to be assigned for the introduction of letters must be the reign of *Sujin* (97-29 B.C.), but at the [sic] date they can have been known only as the forms of a foreign speech understood by a few interpreters, if at all.[17]

Although the Chinese linguistic influence was slight at first, it grew steadily, along with the ascendancy of other aspects of Chinese culture. The introduction of Buddhism to Japan in 552 A.D. marked the beginning of the Asuka epoch in the Age of Reform.[18] There followed more than two centuries of heavy cultural borrowing from China, which did not diminish until Fujiwara rose to power (in A.D. 857) and terminated official relations with China.[19]

During this period of cultural borrowing, a number of Japanese missions journeyed to China. In the years between A.D. 600 and 614, there were four missions to Sui China, and between 630 and 838 there were fifteen missions to T'ang China. "The trip was exceedingly dangerous, and the fact that so many risked it attests to the avidity with which the Japanese of this age sought to acquire the learning and culture of China."[20]

The reforms of A.D. 646 ushered in the Hakuho epoch (645-710) during which the influence of the Chinese language in Japan increased— especially in the limited but growing school system. During this period "there were approximately 800 schools for the training of civil officers and several priest schools....Chinese was acknowledged as the official written language, and it was the only medium of instruction...."[21]

At this time, T'ang China was "the greatest empire in the world," and during the Nara period (710-84) the Japanese continued to be "eager pupils of Chinese civilization." Chinese words were imported to Japan along with the concepts they were associated with. So great was the Japanese dependence on the Chinese written language that "there is no archaeological or other evidence to indicate that the Japanese ever independently attempted to devise a script of their own."[22]

The Japanese court in the early years of the Heian period (794-1185) was "even more enamored of Chinese civilization than its predecessor at Nara a century earlier. Chinese poetry was in particular the rage among Emperor Saga (reigned 809-23) and his intimates...." At least among the nobility, the desire was to make Japan a "miniature model of China."[23]

The imported items, however, were generally "Japanized." For instance, "when Chinese literature was first introduced it was Chinese only in its content...no Chinese word-order or pronunciation was ever introduced."[24]

Despite their interest in China, only a few Japanese, mostly students of Buddhism, actually traveled to that country, and very few Chinese went to Japan. Consequently, the Chinese linguistic influence was limited to the domain of the written language. There was little oral communication between Chinese and Japanese speakers, and Japanese students had neither the need nor the opportunity to use spoken Chinese. In most cases, the ability to read Chinese characters was all that was needed or developed by Japanese scholars.

Over the years, particular Japanese ways of studying and reading Chinese without regard for oral proficiency developed. Due to the differences in the grammatical structure of the two languages, however, this reading process involved more than simply translating each Chinese word into Japanese. Therefore, the Japanese developed a complicated procedure of "reading the characters in a Chinese text by jumping back and forth to make the ideas implied in them compatible with the order of their own ideas...."[25] In this laborious *yakudoku* approach, "the target language [was] first translated word-by-word, and the resulting translation reordered to match Japanese word order."[26]

When the Japanese began studying European languages, *yakudoku* continued to be employed.[27] "This long standing custom of reading foreign literature, inherited from generation to generation for several hundred years, could not be got rid of even when the necessity of oral practice for a foreign language came to be recognized."[28] "In the 18th century it was used for the study of Dutch, and in the 19th century the Japanese produced texts for the study of English in which the *yakudoku* technique was used."[29]

As early as 1727, objections were voiced to this approach to language study. In his book *Gakusoku (Rules of Learning)*, Ogyu wrote: "The traditional method of reading Chinese is a misleading one, which should be avoided. You cannot truly understand Chinese in this way."[30]

In 1911, Okakura published a book on English language teaching in which he voiced his objections to *yakudoku*:

> In the teaching of English in our country, students are taught to translate word-by-word, with forward and regressive eye movement. This is a strongly established convention. I think this comes from our traditional method of reading Chinese, in which Chinese words are reordered to match Japanese word order....This is a wrong method, which treats Chinese not as a foreign language but as a kind of Japanese. We should not use this method in studying English....It is a pity that everyone considers this to be the only way of reading foreign languages.[31]

Modern scholars have also criticized *yakudoku*. Hino laments:

> The *yakudoku* habit clearly is a severe handicap to the Japanese student. It limits the speed at which the student reads, induces fatigue, and reduces the efficiency with which s/he is able to comprehend. The meaning of a text is obtained via Japanese translation, and is only an approximation to the original. *Yakudoku* also has detrimental effects on the other language skills—listening, speaking, writing. Students who have been trained in *yakudoku* reading employ a similar strategy in listening comprehension....As a consequence, they cannot follow speech unless it is delivered very slowly, and they find comprehension a tiring, imprecise, and ineffective process. In speaking and writing, the *yakudoku* process is applied in reverse....The result is seldom idiomatic English sentences, which are produced very slowly.[32]

Despite these criticisms and disadvantages, *yakudoku* has long been widely used by Japanese foreign language learners. In fact, it still prevails in Japanese English classes today.[33] It is a persistent legacy of the early Japanese students of the Chinese language.

EARLY EAST-WEST CONTACTS

The sixteenth century saw the beginning of European influence in Japan. In the cultural interchange that ensued, the Japanese experienced another large influx of foreign products and ideas—including Christianity, Western-style education, European languages, and Western technology. Probably the most desired of these by the feudal lords of Japan was the technology—especially as it pertained to new types of weapons, for the medieval period in Japan's history was characterized by almost continual civil wars. Western languages and learning became important tools in the process of obtaining this technology, and along with them came the "new" Western religion—Christianity.

It is difficult to trace the Western influence back to its beginnings. A reasonable place to start, however, is with the Renaissance in Europe. This period of intellectual and artistic awakening led to great developments in the arts and sciences, and the frontiers of knowledge were extended dramatically. The borders of the leading European nations' spheres of influence and territory were also pushed outward. It was an age of exploration and fierce territorial competition among European nations. But land was not the only thing they argued about. In the 1500s, Europe was "aflame with the fervor of the Counter-Reformation."[34] The Catholic Spanish/Portuguese were at war with Protestant England. Each of these competing powers jealously guarded its own share of the globe. For this reason, the Japanese' early contacts with European powers were limited to the Spanish and Portuguese since Japan fell outside the English sphere of influence. Many years would pass before the Dutch were allowed into Japan, and the British and Americans would arrive last of all.

The small island of Tanegashima, off the coast of Kyushu, was the scene of the first contact between Japanese and Europeans. It was there, when a Portuguese ship landed in 1543, that Japan's relations with Westerners began.

> Japan first awakened to the power of Western science in the form of the cannon. The next importation was Christianity, and the knowledge and culture it brought with it. From 1543, albeit for less than a century, the Japanese were under Portuguese (and Spanish) influence. The learning and the cultural influence of the Portuguese and Spaniards are known as "the culture of the Namban."[35]

Instrumental in the spread of this knowledge were the members of the "recently formed and militantly aggressive Society of Jesus."[36] John III of Portugal asked Loyola, the founder of the Jesuit mission, to send missionaries to the Orient.[37] These early Jesuits viewed science as a missionary tool. "New knowledge came with Christianity, European science being for the missionary a means of spreading the faith."[38] It was, therefore, natural that the Japanese connected Western learning with Western religion.

Francis Xavier (1506-52) was one of the most influential Jesuit "pioneers" in Japan. Arriving in 1549, he and his companions were welcomed by many feudal lords who hoped that Christianity would weaken the influence of the Buddhist priests, who at that time wielded the greatest political power in the empire.[39]   In addition, the Japanese were "keenly interested in foreign trade and, through courtesies extended to the missionaries, sought to lure an ever greater number of Portuguese ships to Japan."[40]

With the rulers' permission and encouragement, Xavier encountered considerable success in his work of propagating Christianity. At first, since he spoke little or no Japanese on arrival, his preaching had to be translated.[41]   Later, however, he and other Jesuits learned to speak the language of the people. Since virtually no one in Japan could understand or speak European languages, the priests needed some proficiency in Japanese in order to fulfill their duties.[42]   After struggling to master this strange foreign tongue, a few of them wrote primitive Japanese grammars and dictionaries to help other Europeans learn it more quickly.[43]

Deviating from this pattern, Alessandro Valegnani (1537?-1606), an Italian padre who arrived in Japan in 1579, set up a college for the study of European languages. This enterprise met with considerable success.

> The students made progress in any subject of studies more rapidly than the foreign teachers had expected. Even in the study of European languages which greatly differed in grammatical structure from their mother tongue, they were proficient enough to read and write well in the course of several months.[44]

The instruction provided in Valegnani's college is the first known instance of the teaching of European languages in Japan, but it was only the beginning. In the decade that followed its establishment, the Japanese' thirst for knowledge of the West became nearly insatiable, and many Japanese studied western languages.

In 1582, the Jesuits in Japan selected four young Japanese to go to Europe and be presented before the Pope. They were gone over eight years and came back so changed by time and their European experiences that they were hardly recognized by their friends. Two were not even recognized by their own mothers! Minakawa notes:

> Imagine how greatly the people at home were surprised to hear about their European experiences! How intoxicated they were in listening to the heavenly music played on the instruments brought home from the opposite side of the world!...The listeners were "spell bound."[45]

Following the return of these young voyagers, the Western "craze" accelerated, and in the mid-1590s it reached its height.

> The most frivolous aspect of the craze for things Western in the 1590s was the aping by Japanese, including Hideyoshi himself, of the Portuguese style of dress and personal adornment. The degree to which these became fashionable can be seen in a letter written by a Jesuit father about this time.[46]
>
> Quambacudono (i.e., the Kwambaku, Toyotomi Hideyoshi) has become so enamored of Portuguese dress and costume that he and his retainers frequently wear this apparel, as do all the other lords of Japan, even the gentiles, with rosaries of driftwood on the breast above all their clothing, and with a crucifix at their side, or hanging from the waist, and sometimes even with kerchiefs in their hands; some of

them are so curious that they learn by rote the litanies of *Pater Noster* and *Ave Maria* and go along praying in the streets.[47]

Of course, the use of Latin in this manner could hardly be labeled true language learning, but neither should its effect on people's attitudes towards European languages be underestimated. Nevertheless, this pro-Western period was to be short-lived.

REPRESSION OF WESTERN INFLUENCES

"In 1587,...Hideyoshi declared the 'nationalization' of Nagasaki and ordered the Jesuit missionaries to leave the country within twenty days."[48] Although the decree was not enforced immediately, it presaged worse times to come in Japan for the Christians, Western influences, and the languages that went with them. In 1597, the ban on Christianity was enforced and twenty-six Christians were burned at the stake on a hill near Nagasaki.[49]

Following Hideyoshi's death in 1598, the ban on Christianity was relaxed as Ieyasu Tokugawa came to power.[50] During his administration, a Jesuit press with movable type was put into operation and "some fifty books in Latin, Portuguese, and Japanese (in both the Romanized and native orthographies)" were printed.[51] The subject matter of these books ranged from *Aesop's Fables* to *The Tale of the Heike*. Some were used as language-learning aids for the missionaries, but it is reasonable to assume that many of them were also used by Japanese learners of Portuguese and/or Latin.

In 1600, William Adams, an English pilot of a Dutch East India Company ship, became the first Englishman in Japan. After a difficult voyage down the Atlantic, through the Straits of Magellan, and across the Pacific, the ship eventually landed at Bungo (near Nagasaki).[52] Only Adams and a few members of the crew survived the trip, and since the ship was no longer fit to sail they had no choice but to remain in Japan. At first forced to rely on an unfriendly Portuguese missionary to translate for him, Adams soon developed some proficiency in Japanese. It was not long until he had gained favor with the Shogun and was taken into Ieyasu's service. In 1611, Adams wrote:

> So in processe of four or five yeeres the Emperour called me, as divers times he had done before. So one time above the rest he would have me to make him a small ship...now beeing in such grace and favour, by reason I learned him some points of *jeometry*, and understanding of the art of *mathematickes*, with other things [sic].[53]

Although Adams undoubtedly used Japanese for teaching the Shogun, it is highly likely that a number of new English technical terms were introduced into Japanese by this process. Beyond that, "no record exists that Adams taught him English."[54] Nevertheless, the realization that there were other advanced "barbarians" besides the Spanish and Portuguese prepared the way for future developments that eventually led to the widespread teaching of English in Japan.

In 1613, an English ship entered Hirado and initiated Anglo-Japanese trade. By this time Adams had learned Japanese quite well and acted as the intermediary between the Japanese ruler and the English captain. The captain carried with him a letter from James I of England, and Adams translated both the letter and Shogun Ieyasu's reply.[55]

During Ieyasu's shogunate, a second mission of Japanese Christians was sent to Europe. This time, 180 Japanese journeyed to Spain by way of Mexico and Cuba. Leaving in 1613, they visited Philip III in Madrid in 1614 and the Pope in Rome in 1615.[56] Upon their return to Japan they must have created quite a stir, with their new knowledge of the Western world.

With Ieyasu's death in 1616, however, things took a decided turn for the worse for Christianity and Namban (Western) learning in Japan. The anti-Christian, anti-Namban feelings of the new rulers intensified, and the persecution of Christians (both European and Japanese) heightened. In the next few years, "wholesale massacres of Christians took place," and "more than 200,000 Christians suffered martyrdom in ways too excruciating for description."[57] The climax came in 1637 when the Shimabara (or Amakusa) Rebellion broke out. Besieged in the Hara Castle, the rebel Christians were finally overcome and eliminated in 1638.

Because of the perceived connection between Western learning and Western religion, when Christianity was proscribed, so were European learning and languages. "With the seclusion policy of the Kan-ei period (1624-44), Namban learning, along with Christianity, was virtually destroyed."[58]

In addition, severe restrictions were applied to all the European powers trading in Japan. Consequently, the English gave up their trading post in 1623. The Spanish were expelled in 1624, and the Portuguese in 1638.[59] Only the Dutch remained, and they were limited to the island of Deshima off Nagasaki, on the western extreme of Kyushu where they were far from the centers of population and where their influence could be strictly limited and controlled. Only one Dutch ship per year was allowed to enter Japanese waters.[60] Naturally, the previous fascination with the Portuguese language died, and the interest of Japanese linguistic scholars shifted towards Dutch. In fact, the interpreters eventually occupied themselves exclusively with Dutch language and science.[61]

During this period, Japanese were not allowed to leave the country. In fact, in 1636, the death penalty was prescribed for any attempt by a Japanese to visit the outside world.[62] Japanese abroad were not allowed to return either. Later, even the "construction of large ships suitable for overseas trade" was prohibited.[63] In sum, the doors to Japan were effectively closed to European influences, and they remained that way for over two centuries.

PROSCRIPTION OF WESTERN INFLUENCES

During the more than two hundred years of the Tokugawa Shogunate, the Japanese followed an official policy of seclusion from the outside world. Nevertheless, this era can not accurately be portrayed as Japan's "dark ages." During the Tokugawa period, important advances were made in consolidating the nation and improving living conditions. In addition, great improvements were made in providing formal education on a widespread basis. Toward the end of the Tokugawa period, even Western learning was again encouraged and the importance of English was recognized.

Expansion of Educational Opportunity

The Japanese system of formal education has a long history. "It was founded on an elaborate basis as early as the eighth century, at the time when Buddhist and Confucian influences were fresh and vigorous....It antedated Charlemagne's Ordinance of Education by nearly a century and the founding of Oxford by nearly two hundred years."[64] Nevertheless, for the most part, this system existed on paper only. It was a "noble idea," which due to numerous difficulties, such as the seemingly unending series of feudal wars that racked Japan in the sixteenth century, was not fully implemented.

It was not until the seventeenth century that the civil strife ceased. The new "national government" brought about by Tokugawa dominance employed a policy of national seclusion to ensure

> a lasting peace that made possible a great upsurge in the domestic economy, especially during the first century of Shogunate rule. Agricultural productivity, for example, was increased markedly in the seventeenth century; transportation and communication facilities were extensively improved; urban populations in the key trading and administrative centers of the country rose dramatically; and commerce, stimulated by a sharp expansion in the use of money, spread at a rate that would have been inconceivable a century earlier.[65]

Under Tokugawa rule, educational opportunity also expanded rapidly. The original impetus for this expansion came from Ieyasu Tokugawa himself in 1615 when he issued the *Buke Shohatto*, a set of instructions for regulating samurai households.

> Article 1 called upon the samurai to devote themselves to both learning and the military arts, learning, it should be noticed, being placed in the first position. The injunction was piously repeated over the succeeding centuries by later Shoguns, and then echoed on down by leading *daimyo* (feudal lords) to their own retainers. In 1629, Shogun Iemitsu repeated the injunction in his revised instructions to the warrior class: "Learning on the left and arms on the right." In 1662, Shogun Ietsuna ordered that samurai "always be concerned with learning and arms." Shoguns Ienobu in 1710 and Yoshimune in 1716 again repeated the same sentiments.[66]

In 1630, the Tokugawa family itself sponsored education for the governing classes with the establishment of the *Shoheiko*, a Confucian academy.[67] Subsequent Shogunal institutions followed the same pattern, as did schools at lower levels of society.

During the Tokugawa period, Japan was divided into about 280 feudal domains (*han*), each of which was ruled by a feudal lord, or *daimyo*. Every *han*, except perhaps the very smallest ones, had at least one *hanko* (school), which generally followed the pattern established by the Shogunal schools. Over the years, about half of these *hanko* extended education to commoners.[68]

Other institutions for commoner education were also established. In fact, during the nineteenth century,

> a great common school movement swept the country. Schools were started by public-spirited citizens either as an expression of their own conviction of the need for public education or in response to growing demand from the urban and rural commoner classes. Shrines, temples, vacant buildings, or private homes were used. As often as not, the teacher simply gathered pupils into his own home for instruction.[69]

The number of schools for commoners snowballed spectacularly. Only 7 *gogaku* (local schools) were established before 1789. Between 1789 and 1867, 104 more were set up. Then, in the next five years, 305 more were started, bringing the total in 1872 to 416.[70]

The bottom rung of the hierarchy of educational institutions of Tokugawa Japan was occupied by the *terakoya,* which became "the most important and widespread institution for commoners' education."[71] The word *terakoya* means "temple-child-house," a clue to the schools' origins.

> In the middle age or before the feudal age children were sometimes taught 3R's at a temple. Therefore a pupil came to be called "Terako" namely temple-child. Afterwards "Terakoya" meant only a school and a layman taught children reading and writing. It was at first a school for the children of merchants or townsmen. As times went on, however, farmers began to send their children to the "terakoya"; they realized the necessity of 3R's through contacts with merchants and their economic ability was now enough to send their children to school.[72]

The *terakoya* typically provided instruction for three or four hours per day for four or five years. The basic core curriculum was reading, writing, and arithmetic.

The number of these lower-level commoners' schools also increased dramatically in the nineteenth century. "558 were established before 1803; then between 1803 and 1843, another 3,050; and between 1844 and 1867, 6,691 more."[73]

Encouragement of Western Learning

In addition to this steady growth in the amount provided, schooling in Japan in the Tokugawa period also experienced "an evolution in its content and purposes."[74] Prior to this time, institutions for studying foreign learning had all operated on a very small scale and had been exclusively for nobility, interpreters, or selected Christian converts. But as educational opportunity eventually reached virtually all classes in Japanese society, the study of European languages and learning also came to be widespread.

The acceptance of Western science in Tokugawa Japan was made possible by the work of Hakuseki Arai, a Confucian scholar and Shogunal advisor, who in 1708 "separated Western science from religion and recognized its practical worth, and as a result opened the way for fresh importations of Western learning!"[75] This conceptual leap opened the way for much learning and borrowing. Later scholars could speak of "the morals of the Orient and the crafts of the Occident" and say, "We shall take the machines and techniques from them, but we have our own ethics and morals."[76]

With the barrier of cultural association (between Christianity and Western learning/languages) out of the way, Japan began, once again, to seek after Dutch learning. In order to gain this knowledge, the Japanese needed the appropriate linguistic tools, so the study of the Dutch language was encouraged also. In this matter, the Shogunate actually took the lead. By 1740, two Japanese retainers of the Shogun were studying the Dutch language under Dutch teachers.[77] Soon after this, there appeared several books for assisting the Japanese in their study of Dutch: Konyo's *Short Treatise on Dutch Writing (Oranda Moji Kyakko)* and *Translating from Dutch (Oranda Bunyaku).* As might have been anticipated, a "Dutch fever" followed during the 1764-89 period. "The taste for things foreign had a considerable following among the merchants, while victims of the *Rampeki*, 'the Dutch craze,' were to be found in the ruling classes."[78]

The curriculum in most schools remained Confucian in nature, focusing on education for character, but toward the end of the era Western studies were added—especially for the students from the lower ranks of society. The prevailing view was that although "it was entirely unsuitable for the realm of wisdom and virtue, and therefore not for the governing classes,...Western learning was quite appropriate to practical matters...."[79] For the Japanese of lower birth, Western learning often served as a key to social mobility. "A good many poor men were able to get themselves a surname and two swords in a daimyo's service simply by virtue of their mastery of some kind of *gakumon*—of Chinese, or of Western, learning."[80]

For this reason, to the basic Confucian curriculum, "some of the *terakoya* added more academic subjects, such as Chinese (*kambun*), history, geography, and composition; and later, occasional Western subjects, such as science, military arts, and in a few cases *even English,...*" [italics added] [81]

The fact that these schools occasionally provided instruction in Western subjects ("even English") is significant. Nevertheless, their major contribution to the later widespread study of English in Japan was to provide basic schooling for people at nearly all levels of society. With a significant portion of its people educated and literate at a basic level and with increasingly favorable attitudes toward Western learning, Japan was ready to take the next step toward Westernization.

Recognition of the Importance of English

By the end of the eighteenth century, the pattern of dominance among the nations of Europe had changed substantially, and the relative status and usefulness of their languages had shifted accordingly. Further complicating matters was the existence of a new power in the West, the United States of America.

Japan's first contact with Americans came in 1798. At this time the Dutch were at war with the English. When the English fleet blockaded Holland, the Dutch were unable to send their yearly ships to resupply their base in Japan, so over the next four years they chartered American ships to carry on their trade with Japan. The arrival of these ships from New England created considerable interest in Japan.[82] Demonstrating how little they knew about the United States, the Japanese were surprised to find that the Americans spoke the same language as the English.[83]

The interest of the Japanese in the English language was further stimulated by the Phaeton Incident in 1808. The H.M.S. *Phaeton*, a British warship, arrived in Japanese waters in search of the annual Dutch ship. After taking two Dutch hostages, "English sailors landed at Nagasaki and rioted throughout the day,...[One of the big problems was that] they could not make themselves understood in English." The ship soon left, but its brief visit was to have far-reaching consequences. "The Tokugawa Government was taken by surprise by this incident and ordered Nagasaki Tsuji (interpreters) to study English in addition to the Dutch, French, and Russian languages."[84]

This was a dramatic reversal of prior policy. Only a few years before, the leading advocates of a plan to open an institute for the teaching of English in Japan "were executed for their pains."[85] Nevertheless, the Phaeton Incident stimulated Japanese interest in Western (especially British) affairs, and the government began seriously considering the need to establish an English-teaching institute.[86]

At Nagasaki, the "first English teacher was Jan Cook Blomhoff of the Dutch factory."[87] He produced two books (in manuscript form) for teaching English, which appeared in 1811. An examination of his *Angeria kokugowage (English Lessons for Beginners)* and *Angeria gorintaisei (English Vocabulary)* reveals that his English was quite limited.[88] Nevertheless, with him English teaching in Japan officially commenced.

As the frequency of contacts with English speakers increased, the Japanese' recognition of their need to be able to communicate in English also grew. In 1818 the English ship *Brothers* entered Uraga, a few years later the English whaler *Saracen* visited the same port, and in 1824 another English whaler landed in Kagoshima. In all these cases, "unhappy incidents"[89] occurred due to the lack of either side's ability to communicate with the other. The climax was reached in 1837 when the American ship *Morrison* came to Uraga on a mission of mercy, trying to return seven shipwrecked Japanese to their homeland. Instead of being rewarded, the *Morrison* was fired on and turned away. Eventually it had to return to America with the seven Japanese still aboard.

In 1844, King William II of Holland wrote a letter to the Shogun in which he cautioned the Japanese leader that continuing the policy of national seclusion was "both unwise and untenable."[90] Although considerable debate on this matter was already taking place in Japan, nothing concrete was done.

Meanwhile, the American presence drew ever closer to Japan. In 1844, the conquest of California extended the United States' boundaries to the west coast. Although Hawaii was still an independent nation, the American influence in the island kingdom was growing also. For Americans, Japan was no longer a distant nation at the end of the earth but almost a neighbor, just across the Pacific. Sooner or later the two nations would have to deal with each other.

In 1848, Ranald MacDonald, an American from Oregon, sought adventure and the chance to play a part in the unfolding of American-Japanese relations by feigning shipwreck on the shores of Hokkaido. He was quickly arrested and sent to Nagasaki where he was imprisoned. During his confinement, the government leaders ordered him to teach English to the interpreters. "Fourteen interpreters of Dutch took lessons in English directly from...MacDonald for seven months from October, 1848, to April of the following year." Although MacDonald was soon returned to the United States, his students remained in Japan, and some of them became "the best scholars of English in the latter part of the Tokugawa Shogunate."[91] In 1851, under orders from the Shogun, a number of them even compiled an English-Japanese dictionary.

The actions of some equally adventurous Japanese demonstrated their growing interest in America. For instance, nineteen-year-old Jo Niishima

> swam out to an American whaler anchored in the harbor of Hakodate, Hokkaido, and asked the crew members to take him to the United States. The captain of the whaler took him to New England, where he studied at Amherst College and Andover Theological Seminary. He came back to Japan, an ordained Congregational minister, to found Doshisha University, the oldest Japanese Christian college, in 1866.[92]

JAPAN'S DOORS REOPEN

Although Japan and the West were coming into contact more and more frequently during the latter years of the Tokugawa Shogunate, the doors of Japan still remained officially closed until 1853, when Commodore Matthew C. Perry paid his first visit to Japan. He delivered a message from the U.S. President, Fillmore, inquiring about the establishment of diplomatic and commercial relations with the Japanese, and then left. Early in 1854, however, Perry returned, and the Japanese, with little real choice in the matter, signed a Treaty of Friendship.

The first American consul, Townsend Harris, arrived in Japan in 1856. Although he eventually met with much success in his diplomatic efforts, in the beginning Harris experienced considerable difficulty dealing with the Japanese because of language problems. Work on the American-Japanese treaty was hindered by language differences and the resultant misunderstandings. For example, his diary entry for Wednesday, June 17, 1857 reads as follows:

> Today we signed the Convention, having been some nine days in setting the wording of the Articles, which by the way is a work of much difficulty, as the Dutch of the Japanese interpreters is that of the ship captains and traders used some two hundred and fifty years ago. They have not been taught a single new word in the interim, so

they are quite ignorant of all the terms used in treaties, conventions, etc., etc. This, joined to their excessive jealousy and fear of being cheated makes it exceedingly difficult to manage such a matter as the present one. They even wanted the words in the Dutch version to stand in the exact order they stood in the Japanese! Owing to the difference of grammatical structure this would have rendered it perfect gibberish.[93]

Progress was made, however, and the government started sending Japanese students abroad, allowed the hiring of foreigners to teach European languages, and encouraged Western studies in various other ways. In quick succession, a Western-style military school was started in 1854, and a naval school in 1857. In 1856, the *Bansho Torishirabe-dokoro* (Institute for the Investigation of Barbarian Writings) was set up to support the growing interest in Western learning. The scholars' linguistic interests quickly broadened, and language research, which had been limited to Dutch, expanded to include English, French, and German. A new term, *yogaku*, (European learning), gained in popularity, often replacing the older *rangaku* (Dutch learning). The new interest in these additional languages and cultures was in part a consequence of the newly opened relations with England, America, France, and Germany. In addition, it resulted from the fact that Dutch and Dutch learning no longer satisfied Japanese scholars. They recognized that English, German, and French science were the sources for most of Dutch science. Consequently, English, German, and French studies flourished, and—of the three languages—English was the most widely studied.[94]

When the treaty opening Japan to the United States was signed, some of the first Americans to enter Japan were English-teaching missionaries. One of the earliest of these was Guido Fridolin Verbeck, an American of Dutch origin, who went to Nagasaki in 1859. There Verbeck taught English courses at the Bureau for European Studies and at an institute sponsored by the Saga clan.[95] He later moved to Tokyo and taught at the government's foreign language school there. This school later developed into the Imperial University of Tokyo.[96]

1859 was also the year that James Curtis Hepburn, another notable ELT missionary, arrived in Japan. A successful New York doctor who had previously served as a medical missionary in China, Hepburn went to Japan as a Presbyterian missionary. However, "since Christians were still proscribed...he and several countrymen...set up a school of foreign languages, principally English, in a rented Buddhist Temple in neighboring Kanagawa. Here they worked with ever-widening influence for eight years."[97] In 1867, Hepburn published his English-Japanese Dictionary, and he later became a founder and the first president of Meiji Gakuin, which grew into a large Tokyo university.

The ELT establishment in Japan grew quickly. Samuel Rollins Brown, one of Hepburn's English-teaching missionary colleagues, opened a private school in Yokohama in 1862. That same year he also published a book entitled *Colloquial Japanese, or Conversational Sentences and Dialogues in English and Japanese* .

In the next few years, many other influential ELT pioneers, such as John Liggins, and William Elliot Griffis, came to Japan and contributed much to the study and teaching of English. Besides teaching, they authored a number of textbooks and dictionaries to help the Japanese learn English.

Foreigners, however, were not the only ones working to support the teaching of English in Japan. For instance, *A Pocket Dictionary of English-Japanese Language (Eiwa Taiyaku Shuchin Jisho)* was compiled and published in Yedo in 1862 "by the order of the Shogunate."[98] The preface to this dictionary reveals the growing importance attached to English study in Japan at that time, as well as the strong Japanese desire to learn from the West:

> As the study of the English language is now rapidly becoming general in our country we have had for some time the desire to publish a "Pocket Dictionary of the English and Japanese Languages" as an assistance to our scholars.
>
> In the meantime we received an order to prepare such a Dictionary as soon as possible having in view how indispensable is the knowledge of a language so universally spoken to become rightly and fully acquainted with the manners, customs and relations of different parts of the world and its daily important occurrences and changes [sic].[99]

At the same time that Americans were arriving in Japan, a growing number of Japanese were going abroad. For instance, on five different occasions during the final years of the Tokugawa period, envoys were sent to America and Europe.[100] The 1860 mission to America returned with two copies of Webster's dictionary. Reports that "those dictionaries were considered so valuable to the students of English that they crowded around them as ants swarming around lumps of sugar" give some idea of the "English fever" that was beginning to sweep the nation in those days.[101]

Curiously, even the "unhappy incidents" during this period lent support to the growing pro-English sentiment. For example, following the "notorious Namamugi Incident" in 1862, "an English squadron bombarded the city of Kagoshima. The overwhelming victory of the English sobered the proud clan and turned it friendly with England."[102]

Of course, the growing popularity and support of Western learning did not go uncontested. During the last years of the Shogunate there was resistance and "anti-barbarian agitation" by some acutely nationalistic Japanese. "There was a strong tendency to look upon *Yogaku* as an arm of 'Kirishitan,' the religion of the devils. Commerce, Christianity, and *Yogaku* were the three arms of the foreign invasion." Equally nationalistic, however, was the government's defense of its English-teaching policy. Nariaki argued that "in order to 'know them' and 'fight them off,' it would be necessary to adopt 'their techniques,'...."[103]

With both the pro-Western and the pro-Japan factions arguing in favor of teaching English, and with a widespread system of schools available to do so, the stage was set for the rapid expansion of ELT in Japan.

THE MEIJI PERIOD

After the coup of 1867, which overthrew the Tokugawa Shogunate and restored the Japanese imperial line in the person of the young Emperor Meiji, dramatic changes took place in Japan. Converting Japan into a strong, modern, capitalist society became a top priority.[104] Since Western knowledge was perceived as the way to strengthen the nation,[105] foreign language study was emphasized, and it expanded dramatically.

The foundation for this rapid and widespread expansion had already been thoroughly laid. The school system was in place and operating; the Japanese possessed basic academic skills; and the idea that in order to progress Japan would need to reach beyond her borders and learn from other nations, through other languages, was almost traditional by this time.

The Growing Influence of the English Language

At the same time that the scope of foreign language study in Japan was expanding, many students switched from Dutch to English. "The more the international positions of Britain and America were generally recognized, the more was Holland, which was on the decline, disregarded." In a surprisingly short time, "English deprived Dutch of the position it had occupied for more than two hundred years as the only medium by which the Japanese imported Western medical art and military science...." As a result, young Japanese students flocked to English language schools. "Even older people who had first studied Dutch sat side by side with them to study English. It was not rare that a man who had once kept a private school for teaching Dutch was, by the change of social conditions, compelled to study English with his former pupils."[106]

In many respects, the story of Yukichi Fukuzawa (1835-1901) typifies many scholars' experiences at this time:

> Fukuzawa was a low-ranking, but personally ambitious and opportunistic, samurai who began the study of Western gunnery and the Dutch language as a youth....Later, when Fukuzawa visited Yokohama shortly after the signing of the Harris treaty in 1858 and observed the newly arrived foreigners at first hand, he learned a sad fact that was to cause anguish for all students of Dutch Studies: Dutch was practically useless as a medium for dealing with most Westerners. Fukuzawa...switched the very next day to the study of English.[107]

The rest of Fukuzawa's story, however, is far from commonplace. Just two years later, in 1860, he was chosen to go to the United States as a member of a Shogunate mission. Later he became the "patriarch of English in Japan and founder of Keio University."[108]

Another powerful promoter of the English language in Japan was Arinori Mori, who, after spending many years in England and the United States, became Japanese minister of education. Mori was also named "Superintendent of Japanese Students in America." In 1871, these young scholars numbered over two hundred, and among them were such future notables as Naibu Kanda, who "believed in the possibilities of the English language as the future universal language of the world."[109] Kanda was to become the "central unifying figure in English teaching in Japan" and later advocated the reform of English teaching by abandoning the traditional method used for the study of Chinese classics.[110]

Mori, however, went even further. At one time he actually advocated that Japanese be abolished and that English become the national language of Japan.[111] He explained, "Our meagre language, which can never be of any use outside of our islands, is doomed to yield to the domination of the English tongue."[112]

Although Japanese was not replaced, English did come to dominate foreign language study in Japan. "In 1874 all foreign language schools outside Tokyo were renamed 'English Language' schools, since about 90 per cent of them taught English, which was also required in public secondary schools."[113] A few years later, in 1880, the study of English was made compulsory in higher elementary schools and also introduced in lower elementary schools.[114]

English as a Medium of Instruction

In Meiji Japan, the thirst for knowledge from the outside world and the lack of textbooks written in Japanese led to the formation of the Bureau of Translation for Foreign Books. Nevertheless, translating and republishing books was a slow process (which required highly proficient translators, who were few in number).

For this reason, English soon became more than a subject to be studied. Early in the Meiji period, it became the medium of instruction in many Japanese institutions of higher education, which "used textbooks imported mainly from the United States (therefore written in English) and employed many foreign teachers (British, American, French, German, etc.)."[115] During the 1870-90 period, "in all the early Christian schools, such as Rikkyo, Doshisha, Aoyama, Meiji, and Tohoku Gakuin, English was the medium of instruction and spoken English was widely taught." Even "in the early Tokyo Imperial University days all lectures were given in English."[116] In fact, it is reported that throughout Japan, "during a decade or two...all higher instruction was imparted in English, French, or German. Even Japanese professors lectured in Western tongues; technical terms had not yet been translated into Japanese."[117]

The Decline of Oral English

Nevertheless, English would not always enjoy such favored status. Powerful forces would eventually "turn Japan back toward its own cultural inheritance." In large part, they were a counter-reaction to the "craze for western ways" which "in the early Meiji years had neared absurdity," threatening to "wipe out the old Japanese culture."[118]

The Meiji Rescript on Education in 1890 marked the beginning of a period of nationalism. During this time, Japanese interest in foreign language learning declined and a large number of the foreign teachers were replaced by native-born Japanese, who were not always highly proficient in

English—especially spoken English. "By the end of the Russo-Japanese War in 1905 Japan had only 41 schools with foreign teachers." Increasingly, in language courses at Japanese universities, emphasis was placed on philology rather than on practical speaking skills, and "English in the universities became a content course."[119]

During the same time period, the Japanese higher education system took on an "increasingly pyramidal structure" with a few universities at the top acquiring great prestige.[120] The keen competition to get into them magnified the power and importance of the examinations used by the universities and high schools to screen applicants.[121] English became a means of sorting students rather than a path to communication. The tests reflected this purpose, and their nature began to affect the way English was taught in the lower schools. "Increasingly, the need to translate complicated passages from English into Japanese and from Japanese into English, to explain abstruse grammatical constructions, and to acquire a large English vocabulary, prevented students from learning to speak or read English with proficiency."[122]

There are several additional reasons for the declining interest in spoken English at this time. One was the fact that as Japan caught up with the Western nations, English was no longer needed so desperately. "As years went by, most textbooks were translated or integrated into textbooks in Japanese. Thus these institutions no longer had to employ many foreign teachers."[123]

Another reason for the decline was the rising spirit of Japanese nationalism and the country's increasing independence.[124] This fit the historical pattern. Throughout Japanese history, "in the Heian, Taisho and present periods, when Japan was strong and self-confident, foreign studies have tended to be criticized as no longer necessary. "[125]

Still another reason given for Japan's diminishing interest in English was the worsening of relations with the United States. The segregation of Japanese children in San Francisco public schools in 1906 and the Japanese exclusion clause in the United States Immigration Act of 1924 "inflicted a wound on Japanese pride, the effect of which it would be difficult to exaggerate."[126]

Furthermore, after the Russo-Japanese War, Japan's attention turned increasingly toward continental Europe and away from the United States and Great Britain. In fact, because of the "popularity of continental European fiction," there was a "revulsion against English among scholars" and a perception that English was a "language for business men." Japanese English teachers responded by stressing the "cultural" and disciplinary aspects of their work and depreciating "the utilitarian value of foreign language study."[127] Nitobe explained:

> For the Japanese,…the advantages of studying foreign languages are of a higher and more intangible nature than are the so-called "practical" benefits. In some ways the most valuable advantage lies in its "unpractical" aspect, namely, in its hidden and unutilitarian effect on the mind.…The age of Chinese classics is gone and with them the severe disciplinarian. His place is taken now by the English grammar, which with manifold rules and exceptions to rules, with its mysterious orthography and

> esoteric idioms, exacts of its neophyte the most strenuous use of his reason and memory, together, as has been hinted before, with unbounded admiration for the people who have mastered its intricacies.[128]

This shift in attitudes led to the decline of conversational English. Nitobe commented that "Japanese teachers make no secret of their utter incompetence in oral intercourse; it is not expected of them. In fact, there is a deplorable propensity to boast of colloquial ignorance."[129]

In this manner, Japanese English language teaching developed "two voices, one saying that cultural enrichment through reading is important in the traditional manner, the other saying that English is needed for international communication."[130] This cultural vs. practical conflict continued to plague Japanese ELT up to and beyond the ELEC era.

PALMER'S ATTEMPT TO REFORM JAPANESE ELT

During the early decades of the Meiji era, "students had read English textbooks in most of their classes, learning '*in* English and *through* English, but never *about* English.' But in the twentieth century, studying from Japanese textbooks and having infrequent contact with native speakers of English, they had reached the stage of learning *about* English in *Japanese*" [italics in original].[131] Of course, this latter approach did not lead to proficiency in speaking English. That was never its intention.

The lack of speaking ability in English, however, sometimes proved embarrassing to Japanese who traveled abroad. After attending the Washington Naval Conference in 1921, Kanda remarked, "We make a poor showing at international conferences when compared with the Chinese."[132] Others "complained that the nation needed at least a few representatives who did not speak pidgin English."[133]

Concerned about the general failure of Japanese students to learn to speak English, a few prominent Japanese took action. In 1920, Dr. Masataro Sawayanagi, president of the Imperial Education Association, who had been sent to Europe by the Japanese Ministry of Education as an educational observer, visited London. He was impressed with the courses given by Harold E. Palmer, an expert in phonetics and language teaching methods. Subsequently, Palmer was invited to become linguistic advisor to the Japanese Ministry of Education.[134] Palmer had long been interested in Japan and "jumped at the opportunity."[135]

Financial support for Palmer's visit came not from the ministry but from a wealthy Japanese citizen, Kojiro Matsukata,[136] who had gone to school in America and France and "considered a working knowledge of English to be an asset" of great worth.[137] Distressed by the "old-fashioned and inefficient" methods used for teaching/learning English in Japan, he was willing to provide financial support for educators like Palmer if they could reform Japanese ELT.[138]

Palmer (1877-1949) was born in England, but his work as a language teacher took him around the globe. As a teenager, he traveled to Boulogne and learned French. Later, in 1902, he began teaching in a Berlitz language school, but soon worked out a method of his own that he called the Oral Method.[139]   He set up his own school of languages and taught English in Belgium, at Verviers and the University of Liége.   As World War I engulfed Europe, however, Palmer fled before the invading German armies and returned to his native England in 1914.   There, he took a post as a lecturer in Spoken English in the Department of Phonetics at University College, London.   Palmer soon "established his reputation as an expert on phonetics and intonation and an authority on linguistic methodology."[140]   In the course of his career, he published over a hundred books, pamphlets, and articles, and lectured widely on the subject of language teaching.   Perhaps the greatest experience of his life, however, began in 1921, when, in response to Sawayanagi's invitation, he traveled to Japan.

Arriving in 1922, Palmer announced that his purpose was reform and that he would emphasize oral English.   In a newspaper interview he declared, "I intend to make the most of the good points and make up for the defects of the current teaching methods.   My basic plan is to teach pronunciation first instead of teaching letters which have been taught first up until now."[141]

In May of 1922, Palmer began his first series of lectures on "English Teaching Methodology" to an audience of five hundred at Tokyo Imperial University.[142]   He later traveled throughout Japan giving lectures on his Oral Method, but he realized that merely lecturing would be insufficient to bring about the desired reforms.

In May of 1923, Palmer was appointed director of the Institute for Research in English Teaching (IRET), which Sawayanagi had recently established.   The IRET had four main aims:

1. the compilation of English language courses
2. the encouragement of reformed methods of language teaching
3. the starting of research and experimental work in linguistic subjects
4. the training of teachers of English by means of lecture courses and demonstration classes[143]

Realizing the power of publications, Palmer also went to work as editor of *The Bulletin*, a professional journal published by the IRET dealing with methodological concerns.   Its first issue came out in June of 1923, and it was published ten times per annum for many years.

In addition, Palmer produced a series of *Standard English Readers*, a full five-year course for middle school students.   He even worked with the Columbia (Nipponphone) Company and produced "educational gramophone" records for English teaching.[144]

Palmer also recognized the importance of professional gatherings, and his institute held "annual conventions to which reports were submitted and at which discussions were held."   These meetings "were an inspiration to the teachers who came to Tokyo from every part of the country."[145]

In 1935, in recognition of his work, Palmer was even awarded an honorary doctorate by Tokyo Imperial University.[146]   Nevertheless, in retrospect, the commonly held conclusion is that his "attempt to initiate reform in methodology was not generally successful."[147] Even those who praise Palmer's efforts agree that their effect on the ELT practices commonly used in Japan was minimal.

A number of critical implementation factors, which Palmer either ignored or could not control, proved to be his undoing. Socio-pedagogical factors comprised one obstacle that Palmer could not overcome. According to Tajima, "the soil of Japan was not well suited to bearing fruits worthy of his great efforts."[148] Others are less poetic in their assessment, saying: "His enthusiasm for oral methods did not always suit the established patterns of relationships in Japanese classrooms."[149] His books were "not welcomed by some Japanese secondary school teachers" who criticized him as "one who is 'fond of novelty and who confuses learners.'"[150]

Furthermore, Palmer's connection with the Ministry of Education was far from strong. In fact, once he arrived in Japan, "the officials did not know quite what to do with him." Furthermore, they were afraid that "reforms imposed, or even proposed, from on high would upset too many important apple carts." The solution was to put him in an advisory position only, hoping that his work with the IRET would keep him busy and thus "prevent anything very drastic from happening."[151] In this way, his role was "simply an advisory one" and his recommendations never became official policy.[152]

Without doubt, unfavorable socio-political conditions also diminished Palmer's influence. Japanese students' lack of motivation to learn to speak English dealt a serious blow to his Oral Method. "His method failed to resuscitate a motivation which had died when students were no longer face to face with foreign teachers and foreign books."[153] Most importantly, the rising nationalism and militarism of the 1930s led to a general abandonment of English study in Japan.

Despite this apparent failure, the spark of Palmer's influence remained alive in Japan long after he left the country. Although his Oral Method and Fries' Oral Approach were similar in many respects,[154] Palmer's had the power of "primacy," and his "ghost" proved to be a hindrance rather than a help to the ELEC reformers.

RISING MILITARISM AND WORLD WAR II

Japanese militarism and nationalism, which became strong in the 1930s and culminated in the war in the Pacific, had a devastating effect on the study of English by the Japanese. During the 1920s and 1930s, "The proportion of Japanese students studying in the United States had progressively decreased...until, with an average of 127 per year going to Germany, only 17 or 18 went to the United States in 1932."[155] In 1937, the Ministry of Education codified the new Japanese nationalism in *Kokutai no Hongi* ("The Cardinal Principles of the National Entity of Japan"). From that time, foreign language study "became optional in secondary schools after the first two years. Formerly, it was required throughout the five years. Then, with the outbreak of World War II, even the study of English was suspected as a sign of disloyalty to the country."[156] At this time, "all but a few of the English speaking missionaries and teachers were repatriated or placed in detention, and as the war proceeded the study of English in secondary schools became suspect, until in 1944 it nearly vanished."[157]

THE ALLIED OCCUPATION

With Japan's surrender in 1945, the decline in the study of English was dramatically reversed. The Allied Occupation of Japan (1945-52) generated great enthusiasm for studying the English language. One commentator noted, "In no other period in the country's history have the Japanese had such direct contact with English-speaking people and shown such keen interest in the study of English."[158] Another exclaimed, "With the beginning of the American Armed Forces occupation, a second Americanization took place rather rapidly with greater intensity in a number of fields and aspects than during the Meiji Restoration."[159]

The Occupation had a number of goals. Those officially spelled out in the Potsdam Proclamation included eliminating the authority and influence of militarists, disarming the military forces, meting out stern justice to all war criminals, removing "all obstacles to the revival and strengthening of democratic tendencies among the Japanese people," establishing "freedom of speech, of religion, and of thought, as well as respect for the fundamental human rights," and maintaining "such industries as will sustain her economy."[160] With the passage of time, these goals—and the means by which they were pursued—became increasingly complex. Nevertheless, it is possible to categorize the Occupation reforms under three headings: demilitarization, democratization, and economic reconstruction.

Reforms in each of these categories involved and affected the Japanese system of formal education and produced conditions that were to influence the ELEC effort to reform Japanese English language teaching. For instance, one step in the demilitarization process was a wide-ranging "purge" of "tainted" personnel. It included former military officers, police, political leaders, and leading businessmen. This purge was extended to the school system by a Supreme Commander Allied Powers (SCAP) directive of October 30, 1945. As a result, over a hundred thousand teachers and administrators either left the school system or were removed from it.[161] The resulting shortage of teachers had long-lasting effects on the system's ability to provide the English instruction desired by both the public and educational administrators.

In contrast to "demilitarization," which was accomplished quite quickly, the "constructive" phase of the Occupation took many years to implement, and was much more involved. Two key events took place in 1946—the First United States Educational Mission to Japan arrived (in March), and the new constitution was passed by the Diet (October 7) and promulgated (November 3). While the constitution provided general, authoritative guidance, the recommendations of the mission served as the source for future SCAP and Civil Information and Education (CI&E) policies regarding education in the "new Japan." The following year, The Fundamental Law of Education and The School Education Law were passed with the intention of cementing some of the reforms in place. Many of these reforms affected the way English would be taught in Japan.

Expansion of Educational Opportunity and Desire to Learn English

Prior to the war, Japanese children were required to attend school for only six years. In the "new Japan," compulsory education was extended to nine years. Occupation reforms also promoted coeducation at all levels of the school system. In a Japan recently devastated by war, this expansion was accomplished only with great difficulty. "Wartime loss, which amounted to 13 per cent of the total school buildings, and also the raising of the school leaving age, which increased the number of children of compulsory attendance age by half, led to a serious shortage of school buildings and facilities, which were hard to supply under the financial constraints of the time."[162]

Not only did large numbers of students flood the school system, but virtually all of them took English classes. In 1956 Bryant reported, "about 7,000,000 Japanese children from 12 to 18 years old are spending five hours a week studying English....In the universities hundreds of thousands more are busy with their seventh, eighth, ninth, or tenth year of English."[163] "More than 76% of junior high and 86% of senior high school students elect to study English." Bryant concluded that, compared to 1929 figures, "nearly *20 times* as many children are now studying a second language as were doing so 25 years ago!" [italics in original].[164]

This "English craze" was, of course, consistent with the traditional Japanese pattern of enthusiasm for the language of foreigners who had demonstrated their superiority in some fashion. This widespread desire to learn English increased the interest in the methods used for teaching the language, and in that manner, supported ELEC's reform effort. Nevertheless, it also created a number of difficulties.

Shortage of Teachers

One of the greatest problems in postwar Japan was a shortage of qualified teachers, and in few areas was the shortage more severe than it was in English teaching. The number of Japanese teachers with any fluency in English contrasted dramatically with the number of students enrolled in English classes. As a result, many poorly qualified individuals were pressed into service teaching English to large groups of pupils. As Bryant lamented, "They are taught by some 85,000 teachers, few of whom have ever heard the language spoken by a native—except, perhaps, over the radio."[165] These teachers' pedagogical skills were also suspect. Bryant noted, "It is a serious fact that only about one-third of the lower secondary school English teachers hold regular English teaching licenses," and "the output of teacher training institutions and university education departments is wholly inadequate."[166]

Teacher Training and Professionalism

Under the reforms of the Occupation, teacher training was raised to the university level (normal school programs were extended to four years and provided both professional and liberal education). Nevertheless, few of the many thousands of practicing English teachers had the opportunity to undertake university-level studies during and/or after the Occupation. Furthermore, university teachers of English in Japan had long demonstrated a tendency to emphasize literary studies, to the detriment of spoken English.

For these reasons, the Occupation authorities established numerous in-service programs for teachers and administrators. These programs were typically short-term institutes dealing with new curricula and methods. They also served as a pattern for later in-service work concerned with improving teachers' English skills. In fact, the ELEC summer institutes for teachers followed this established, Occupation-era pattern.

The Occupation authorities also encouraged the formation of professional societies in various subject-matter areas. Some of these organizations lasted only until the Americans relinquished control, but others flourished and became powerful in post-Occupation Japan. There were several successful organizations of English teachers, and cooperative relationships with them could have helped ELEC.

Decentralization

"One of the major recommendations of the United States Educational Mission called for the decentralization of the Japanese educational system and the dispersal of its control among autonomous popularly elected local bodies."[167] This objective was based on the American view that the centralized Japanese system was "a fundamental cause of the nationalist fervor underlying Japan's military aggression."[168] Accordingly, the Occupation authorities worked vigorously to decentralize the school system. Steps were taken to elect local and prefectural boards of education, and leave the venerable Ministry of Education with only an "advisory and stimulating role."[169]

Nevertheless, once the Occupation ended and the Japanese regained control, decentralization was one of the first reforms to be reversed. As Beauchamp sums it up, "The American efforts to foster decentralization failed, and today Japan once more possesses one of the world's most highly centralized educational systems."[170] ELEC had to deal with this recentralized bureaucracy, which at the time seemed to be "flexing its muscles" in order to demonstrate what it had regained.

Textbook Production

In postwar Japan, "textbooks were no longer written in the Ministry of Education but by private authors to be published through private publishers."[171] This change made it possible for ELEC to publish its own Oral Approach textbooks, although they still had to be approved by the ministry.

Higher Education

The First U.S. Mission report "deplored the early and narrow specialization in the *semmon gakko* which left no room for broad, humanistic studies."[172] Other than that, the mission did not make detailed recommendations regarding higher education in Japan, but CI&E did: All Japanese institutions of higher learning were to be made over into four-year colleges or universities (following the standard American pattern) in spite of the fact that many of these institutions did not have the facilities or faculty for this new purpose. In addition, every prefecture was to have a university (like the state universities in America). American-style graduate programs were also established, and later (as the insistence on four-year colleges abated) a system of junior colleges was set up.

Many of these reforms aroused antagonism and scorn on the part of university personnel. The result of making all Japanese institutions of higher learning into four-year colleges or universities, whether they were truly ready for such a step or not, was a damaging drop in the quality of Japanese higher education. The total number of universities in Japan rose to more than two hundred, and resources were spread extremely thin.[173]

While the number of universities in Japan increased, the number of individuals desiring a university-level education grew even more because of the expansion in educational opportunity at lower levels and the new ideology of "democratic" education. This increase in the number of prospective university students, along with the disparity in the quality of education offered at different universities, led to a greater reliance on entrance examinations to sort out applicants. In this situation, English came to be used not as a means of communication but as a means of discriminating among university hopefuls.

> Since universities have more applicants each year than they can possibly enroll, entrance examinations are highly competitive....Consequently, the influence of entrance examinations upon the education of upper secondary schools is great....Entrance examinations not only influence the selection of subjects of study but also the content and method of teaching such subjects. For example, translation from English to Japanese and grammatical analysis of complicated sentences are the main contents of English courses in upper secondary schools, because these processes constitute the most important part of the entrance examinations.[174]

In sum, the antagonism and defensiveness of university professors toward American "innovations," the stronger-than-ever hierarchical divisions among the many Japanese universities (to compensate for the lack of quality in many of the new ones), and the increased emphasis in English classes on preparing for entrance examinations that did not test communicative skills seriously hindered ELEC's effort to bring about the teaching of oral English in Japan.

Foreign (English) Language Teaching

Although many of the above-mentioned changes directly or indirectly affected English language teaching in Japanese schools, the Occupation reformers "largely ignored the subject of foreign language teaching in Japan."[175] "The occupation authorities were apparently reluctant to seem to be forcing their language on a conquered people, and their decision appears to have been wise." As a consequence, the postwar demand for English "expresse[d] the needs of the Japanese themselves"[176] rather than an American dictum, and it continued to grow even after the Occupation ended. For example, in 1951, as the Occupation drew to a close, the Japanese Ministry of Education (*not* SCAP or CI&E) proclaimed:

> English...can contribute greatly to the development of social competence, by leading to an understanding of the worthwhile elements of the home life and social lives of English-speaking peoples, and to an understanding of the democratic heritage of the peoples of the world, which to an important extent was developed in English-speaking nations.[177]

CONCLUSION

As this chapter has illustrated, the situation that the ELEC reformers faced had a long and complicated history. Widespread teaching of English in Japan would never have been possible without the foundation that had been laid over a period of more than one thousand years. On the other hand, the socio-educational conditions and traditions regarding foreign language study that had developed during that history comprised a formidable obstacle to the accomplishment of ELEC's objectives.

ELEC's willingness and ability to work with and around this constellation of antecedent factors was critical to its success. Nevertheless, the ELEC reformers ignored many of these factors and defied others. The resulting negative interactions explain a number of ELEC's shortcomings.

NOTES

1. Koike et al., 3.
2. Suzuki, 114.
3. Harasawa, 77.
4. Tripp, 28.
5. Araki, 14.
6. Dore, "The Legacy of Tokugawa Education," 99-100.
7. Reischauer, *Japan,* 102-103.
8. Beauchamp, "Reform Traditions," 2.
9. Beasley, 323.
10. Koike, "English Language Teaching Policies in Japan," 9.

11. Koike, "English Language Teaching Policies in Japan," 3.
12. Tripp, 28.
13. Wada and McCarty, 28.
14. Koike, "English Language Teaching Policies in Japan," 3.
15. Koike, "English Language Teaching Policies in Japan," 5.
16. Omura, 91; Ito, 205.
17. Lombard, 23.
18. Varley, 19.
19. Varley, 40.
20. Varley, 16.
21. Kimizuka, *Teaching English to Japanese,* 10.
22. Varley, 22.
23. Varley, 39.
24. Harasawa, 77.
25. Minakawa, 106.
26. Hino, "Yakudoku: Japan's Dominant Tradition," 46.
27. Maeda, interview.
28. Minakawa, 106.
29. Hino, "Yakudoku: The Japanese Approach," 49.
30. Kawazumi, 14-19.
31. Kawazumi, 51.
32. Hino, "Yakudoku: Japan's Dominant Tradition," 48.
33. Hino, "Yakudoku: Japan's Dominant Tradition," 51; Hino, "Yakudoku: The Japanese Approach," 48; Kanatani, interview.
34. Varley, 98.
35. Numata, 231-32.
36. Varley, 98.
37. Minakawa, 13.
38. Numata, 233.
39. Cary, 32.
40. Varley, 99.
41. Minakawa, 13.
42. Minakawa, 118.
43. Minakawa, 35.
44. Minakawa, 26.
45. Minakawa, 28.
46. Varley, 104.
47. Boxer, 207-8.
48. Varley, 99.
49. Minakawa, 29.
50. Minakawa, 39.
51. Varley, 102.
52. Sladen and Lorimer, 210.
53. Sladen and Lorimer, 227.
54. Minakawa, 69.
55. Minakawa, 78.
56. Minakawa, 32-33.
57. Minakawa, 39.
58. Numata, 234.
59. Reischauer, *Japan,* 94.
60. Minakawa, 31.
61. Numata, 234-35.
62. Gibney, *Five Gentlemen,* 70.
63. Reischauer, *Japan,* 95.
64. Nitobe, *The Japanese Nation,* 176.
65. Varley, 115.
66. Passin, 13.
67. Passin, 17.

68. Passin, 18-19.
69. Passin, 28.
70. Passin, 14-15.
71. Passin, 27.
72. Oshiba, 5-6.
73. Passin, 14-15.
74. Dore, "The Legacy," 17.
75. Numata, 235-36.
76. Numata, 241.
77. Passin, 18; Numata, 236.
78. Numata, 237.
79. Passin, 21.
80. Dore, "The Legacy," 19.
81. Passin, 31.
82. Minakawa, 32.
83. Minakawa, 90.
84. Omura, 92.
85. Bryant, "English Teaching in Japan," 4.
86. Minakawa, 90.
87. Omura, 92.
88. Omura, 93.
89. Minakawa, 96.
90. Varley, 159.
91. Minakawa, 98.
92. Gibney, *Five Gentlemen*, 70.
93. Harris, 374-75.
94. Numata, 52.
95. Minakawa, 52.
96. Kikuchi, 42; Kaieda, 878.
97. Bryant, "English Teaching in Japan," 5.
98. Omura, 95.
99. Minakawa, 99-100.
100. Minakawa, 101.
101. Minakawa, 105-6.
102. Minakawa, 103.
103. Numata, 248.
104. Numata, 248.
105. Beauchamp, "Griffis in Japan," 42.
106. Minakawa, 108.
107. Varley, 166.
108. Harasawa, 73.
109. Bryant, "English Teaching in Japan," 12.
110. Bryant, "English Language Teaching in Japanese Schools," 22.
111. Hall, 189.
112. Cited by Bryant, "English Teaching in Japan," 8.
113. Bryant, "English Language Teaching in Japanese Schools," 22.
114. Kimizuka, *Teaching English to Japanese,* 12.
115. Ogasawara, "The Educational System and English," 88.
116. Kanda Memorial Committee, 131.
117. Omura, 93-94.
118. Bryant, "English Teaching in Japan," 13-14.
119. Bryant, "English Language Teaching in Japanese Schools," 23.
120. Bryant, "English Teaching in Japan," 21.
121. Bryant, "English Language Teaching in Japanese Schools," 23.
122. Bryant, "English Teaching in Japan," 22.
123. Ogasawara, "The Educational System and English," 88.
124. Kimizuka, *Teaching English to Japanese,* 12.
125. Wada and McCarty, 28.

126. Bryant, "English Teaching in Japan," 20.
127. Bryant, "English Teaching in Japan," 19.
128. Cited in Bryant, "English Teaching in Japan," 19-20.
129. Nitobe, "The Teaching and Use of Foreign Languages," 338-39.
130. Wada and McCarty, 28.
131. Bryant, "English Language Teaching in Japanese Schools," 25.
132. Quoted by Palmer, "The English Language in Japan," 217.
133. Bryant, "English Language Teaching in Japanese Schools," 23.
134. Bryant, "English Language Teaching in Japanese Schools," 23.
135. Anderson, "Harold E. Palmer," 143.
136. Anderson, "Harold E. Palmer," 146.
137. Yamamoto, 151.
138. Anderson, "Harold E. Palmer," 146-7.
139. Darian, 548.
140. Hornby and Jones, 87-88.
141. Yamamoto, 152.
142. Yamamoto, 152.
143. Hornby and Jones, 88.
144. Anderson, "Harold E. Palmer," 148.
145. Hornby and Jones, 88.
146. Titone, 58-59.
147. Maher, 43.
148. Tajima, 142.
149. Howatt, 233.
150. Yamamoto, 154, 156.
151. Anderson, "Harold E. Palmer," 147.
152. Bryant, "English Language Teaching in Japanese Schools," 25.
153. Bryant, "English Language Teaching in Japanese Schools," 25.
154. Howatt, 268.
155. Bryant, "English Teaching in Japan," 31.
156. Kimizuka, *Teaching English to Japanese,* 13.
157. Bryant, "English Language Teaching in Japanese Schools," 26.
158. Kimizuka, *Teaching English to Japanese,* 22.
159. Ogasawara, "The Educational System and English," 88.
160. Department of State, vol. 2, p. 1281.
161. Kobayashi, "Japan: Under American Occupation," 188.
162. Kobayashi, *Society, Schools, and Progress,* 43.
163. Bryant, "English Language Teaching in Japanese Schools," 21.
164. Bryant, "English Language Teaching in Japanese Schools," 27.
165. Bryant, "English Language Teaching in Japanese Schools," 21.
166. Bryant, "English Language Teaching in Japanese Schools," 32.
167. Kawai, 187.
168. Beauchamp, "Report from Japan," 338.
169. Kobayashi, *Society, Schools, and Progress,* 44.
170. Beauchamp, "Report from Japan," 339.
171. Oshiba and Adams, 14.
172. Kawai, 202.
173. Kawai, 203.
174. Kimizuka, *Teaching English to Japanese,* 14.
175. Bryant, "English Language Teaching in Japanese Schools," 26.
176. Bryant, "English Language Teaching in Japanese Schools," 27.
177. *Suggested Course of Study in English,* vol. 1, p. 9.

5
Process

ELEC's effort to reform English language teaching in Japan met with some successes, but it also encountered numerous difficulties that kept the campaign from achieving its major goals. In retrospect, it is clear that many of these difficulties were due to factors that comprise the process portion of the hybrid model. This chapter employs that portion of the model to analyze how those factors affected the ELEC campaign.

Of course, it is now much easier to look back and discuss what the ELEC reformers should have done than it must have been for them to look forward and decide on an appropriate course of action. The purpose of this study is not to criticize or condemn their actions but rather to learn as much as possible from them. In this way, even ELEC's failures can help create successes for future educational reformers.

THE NATURE AND EXTENT OF ELEC'S PLANNING TO IMPLEMENT THE ORAL APPROACH IN JAPAN

At the 1956 ELEC Specialists' Conference, the remarks made by ELEC Chairman Eikichi Araki in his opening address reflected the importance of implementation. He warned those who would work together in planning ELEC's "revolution" that "the most important thing is the putting into practice of these plans when they are made."[1] Unfortunately, although a large amount of time was spent developing the methods and materials that ELEC would advocate, relatively little went into planning how they would be implemented.

In the Rockefeller camp, the feeling was "It seems better to take one step at a time rather than to try to lay out a grand plan,"[2] bringing to mind the "Let's get started, and we'll find out just what we're doing as we go along" approach against which Sarason warns would-be innovators.[3]

In Japan also, ELEC's planning for diffusion/implementation was minimal. Evidence indicates that the little that did take place was casual and haphazard. For instance, an organizational chart in which ELEC's central committee was pictured as receiving support from U.S. and Japanese sources, interacting with U.S. and British experts, and then initiating projects in cooperation with "existing universities, institutes, and societies" was simply scrawled on the back of an agenda page.[4] (The agenda itself was devoted to other concerns.) Further indicating the lack of serious attention given to careful implementation-oriented planning, this chart did not take into account any potential obstacles to the ELEC campaign.

Fries himself seems to have taken a rather idealistic view of the change process. While acknowledging the complexity of the ELT situation in Japan, its history, and the natural resistance to change which could be expected, he expressed the simple hope that these obstacles could be overcome by bringing "our experiences from various aspects of this problem together."[5]

Although subsequent events demonstrated that this laissez-faire communication of innovations approach was insufficient, ELEC personnel did not become seriously involved in careful planning for implementation until the campaign had been going for five or six years. Unfortunately, by then it was too late. Now, thirty years later, it is possible to see that ELEC's outcomes would have more closely approached its objectives if, at the outset, the diffusion/implementation aspects of the campaign had been planned more carefully, taking into consideration the variety of factors the hybrid model itemizes.

The Challenges of Creating Directed Contact Change

The type of change being pursued is a fundamental consideration in planning. For example, the tactics employed in an immanent change effort will be quite different from (and considerably less complicated than) those necessary for accomplishing directed contact change. Consequently, in the more complex directed contact change efforts, the hybrid model can be especially helpful since it specifies a variety of influential factors that reformers might otherwise ignore. In ELEC's case, lack of awareness of many of these factors led to a number of serious problems.

One problem common to directed contact change campaigns is that resistance is virtually inevitable if they are perceived as being of foreign origin. In such cases, it is wise for the foreign source to establish linkage with and work through locally based organizations. To their credit, ELEC's leading figures were aware of and tried to avoid this potential problem. John D. Rockefeller 3rd, himself, operated discreetly "behind" ELEC. For instance, when Matsumoto made arrangements for a press release concerning the ELEC Specialists' Conference, he assured Rockefeller, "Utmost caution will be taken not to give any publicity to your own name."[6] Reischauer also advised that "the American side, despite Mr. Rockefeller's great service in sparking the movement, should seem to be simply a response to Japanese proposals."[7] From his experience in Puerto Rico, Charles C. Fries had also learned the importance of involving local colleagues in directed change enterprises in order to transform such movements into more indigenous, immanent change efforts. Therefore, in

Japan he wisely insisted on involving the Japanese. When this approach was questioned, his defense was lengthy and showed a considerable awareness of the setting in which ELEC was operating.

> We, I believe, must remember that Japan was an "occupied" country and had a "foreign" educational reform imposed upon it by the US as conquerors. They have not been happy with many of these "reforms" and have gradually been able to nullify or eliminate some of them. Others still annoy them and are a constant reminder of certain "democratic" arrangements *imposed* on them....Many Americans have not realized that there is always such opposition to be dealt with....I have felt that "the part of the Japanese colleagues" must be a fundamental consideration....The textbooks and the teachers guides must, I believe, be convincingly the work of the Japanese specialists themselves, in cooperation with the native speakers of English as consultants....I believe the Japanese collaborators must constantly contribute their full measure and they must really *know* the texts with the familiarity that comes from their own creation. They must know them so thoroughly that they can confidently and enthusiastically meet all *opposers* as well as the hosts of teachers who want to understand the new materials thoroughly in order that they may use them. I needn't tell you that every new textbook for teaching English in a foreign country will meet opposition—often very bitter opposition as it displaces one or more texts out of which someone is making a living. If the new textbooks, no matter how good they are, are *believed* to be the creation of *outsiders*, they are especially vulnerable to attack [italics in original].[8]

In some respects, these attempts to make the ELEC movement more immanent in nature (as well as in appearance) by enlisting the support of Japanese who also wished to reform English language teaching in Japan were successful. The involvement of the Japanese proved to be not just advantageous but essential. Nevertheless, ELEC still was not always able to avoid being perceived as a U.S.-based attempt to impose American teaching methods on Japan. In such instances, it encountered opposition.

Strategies for Bringing About Change

Two fundamental approaches to bringing about change are "from the top down" and "from the bottom up." Unfortunately, the top-down approach, used successfully by Fries in Puerto Rico, was not possible in Japan because ELEC had no power over Japanese teachers of English and failed to establish linkage with those institutions that did. Unfortunately, the opposite, bottom-up approach was not feasible either. ELEC had little grass roots support. Such an approach probably would not have been practical in the hierarchical, centralized Japanese system anyway. The experience of other reform attempts has shown that in Japan, "if you start at the grass roots, you don't get anywhere at all. You have to start at the top."[9]

In this situation, ELEC had little choice but to utilize a less effective, (horizontal) communication approach, and even in this respect it was slow to begin. Of course, Fries traveled throughout Japan on lecture tours as early as 1956, and there were newspaper articles about ELEC conferences from the first, but it was not until 1962 that wide-scale promotion of ELEC materials began in earnest, with speakers, demonstrations, reports of research, and other bulletins.[10] Later that year, strategies for bringing about change were discussed. Herbert Passin wrote to McLean, suggesting a plan that took into account the different ELT interest groups in Japan, how these groups divided up along conservative-progressive lines, what the "key pressure points" (e.g., entrance exams) were, and how the progressive interests could be "harnessed" to put pressure on the conservative interests. Passin's plan included working with business, leading Japanese universities, and educational radio and television, as well as studying the experiences of other countries in reforming their ELT programs.[11] Unfortunately, by this time, ELEC's influence was already waning, and the realization that such a "massive effort" would be required came too late.

In the earlier stages, ELEC's leaders had planned the simple steps they would need to go through to become organized and operable, namely:

1. Organization of Central Committee
2. Central Committee organizes technical group
3. Central Committee establishes relationship...with Cooperating Group in the U.S. (probably Rockefeller Foundation)
4. Technical group holds conferences (with invited American and British experts) to Decide on General Program
5. Institution of Specific Projects[12]

This planning, however, was very general, did not consider how ELEC might deal with opposition to its reform effort, and stopped short of providing for any specific action beyond ELEC's initial Specialists' Conference.

In sum, ELEC's leaders had lofty goals but when it came to implementation they did little more than hope that Japanese teachers of English would see the advantages of the Oral Approach and then— naturally—adopt it. By the time they realized that achieving their goals would require more than communicating the news of a "better mousetrap," it was too late to remedy the error. They had failed to consider the factors that affect diffusion and implementation, and their effort fell victim to many barriers. A discussion of this array of factors will comprise most of the remainder of this chapter. Following the lower portion of the process element in the hybrid model, this discussion of factors that facilitate/hinder change will be divided into four main sections: characteristics of the innovation (the Oral Approach) itself, characteristics of the ELEC resource system, characteristics of the Japanese ELT user system, and inter-elemental factors.

CHARACTERISTICS OF THE ORAL APPROACH ITSELF

Many characteristics of the Oral Approach impeded its spread in Japan, while a few others facilitated its adoption.

Originality

The Oral Approach was, without question, of American origin. Its creators and most prominent promoters were professors at U.S.

universities, and its all-important linguistic foundation came from the American structural school. In this sense, the Oral Approach was a ready-made (in America) solution that was exported to Japan.   Although its American backers kept out of the spotlight and ELEC was portrayed as a Japanese campaign, there was no disguising the American origins of the approach it promoted.

The Oral Approach presented a dramatic contrast to the traditional language-teaching methods that had developed in Japan. In this respect it was highly foreign to Japanese teachers.   In conservative Japan, however, ELEC might have enjoyed greater success in reforming ELT had it focused more on modifying existing practices and less on creating a full-scale pedagogical revolution. As Rogers advises, "Teacher re-training needs to focus more on extending and re-defining the familiar rather than attacking it."[13]

The foreign-ness and American-ness of the Oral Approach inevitably led to opposition from many tradition-oriented Japanese educators— especially in the reactionary "reverse course" years following the Occupation. Even among Japanese teachers who wanted to reform ELT in Japan, the foreign, borrowed nature of the Oral Approach created opposition. For example, one key Ministry of Education official never supported ELEC's campaign because he felt that a new, but particularly Japanese approach to ELT needed to be developed.[14]

Interestingly, opposition to the ELEC campaign also came from those who saw it as less than original. In the eyes of some who remembered Palmer's prewar campaign to reform ELT in Japan, Fries' Oral Approach was merely an American version of Palmer's Oral Method. Palmer still had many disciples in Japan, and they often resisted this American "usurper." At the same time, many of those who had investigated Palmer's approach years before and found fault with it objected to the Oral Approach on the same grounds, without even examining it.

Complexity

As noted in chapter three, simple innovations that require little additional learning investment from receivers will generally be adopted more rapidly than complex innovations that require adopters to develop new skills and understandings.   Unfortunately, adoption of the Oral Approach required a great deal of investment on the part of Japanese teachers of English. To use the Oral Approach they needed to increase their skills in spoken English as well as develop their understanding of new ideas about teaching and learning. Realizing this, ELEC started its summer institutes for teachers, which focused on the development of these capabilities. Language, however, is one of the most complex of human phenomena, and good speaking proficiency is not easy to acquire. Developing linguistic awareness (the conscious knowledge of how language works) and an understanding of how people learn language takes even more time. Furthermore, the large number of teachers of English in Japan who needed to improve both their speaking skills as well as their understanding of language and language teaching far exceeded ELEC's limited resources for providing the training these teachers needed.

Explicitness

Because Fries' Oral Approach consisted of a set of principles rather than a collection of classroom techniques and procedures, it was relatively abstract and difficult to describe with precision. In other words, it suffered from a low degree of explicitness, and that led to confusion, misapplication, and frustration among intended users.

Fries' descriptions of the Oral Approach usually remained at the level of generalizations and were frequently misunderstood. In his later years, he spent considerable time and effort clarifying earlier statements, which his followers had misinterpreted. In fact, one of his original purposes in going to Japan was to correct what he felt were misperceptions about the Oral Approach.[15]   Unfortunately, many Japanese teachers still misunderstood his ideas or comprehended them only partially.

Relative Advantage

Methodological innovators in language teaching usually employ some sort of relative advantage argument to promote their ideas. New methods are touted as being more effective, less stressful, more interesting for students, easier for teachers to use, etc. In short, promoters of innovative methods invariably claim that their adoption will produce some sort of improvement in language learning.[16]

Relative advantage of this sort can be established in various ways. One of the most common is to conduct research to establish the superior effectiveness of a method. Discussing such "appeals to facts," Richards also notes that "facts" can come from research or "pseudo-research." Regarding acceptable (not "pseudo") research, Richards sets a standard that is seldom met—that it employ a true experimental design. Discouragingly, however, in his 1983 address, Richards stated, "There is not a single serious piece of research published to demonstrate precisely what learners learn from...[the] methods which countless journal articles advocate with such enthusiasm."[17]   In 1984, when a revised version of Richards' speech was published, the picture he painted was only a little brighter. He cited one study that satisfied the criterion of using a true experimental design,[18] but he also noted that such studies were "all too rare in the vast promotional literature on methods." He pronounced the majority of reported findings on the effectiveness of methods "largely anecdotal and poorly researched."[19]

Such a charge could be leveled at Fries' Oral Approach. Even its supporters acknowledge that there was no experimental evidence for its effectiveness. Fries and his ELEC colleagues did not randomly assign students to groups, use the Oral Approach with one group and another method with the other, and then compare learners' test results.

It should be noted, however, that it is not really fair to expect such an experimental approach to have been used with the Oral Approach. "The tenor of the times did not require empirical investigations of the type which we have become accustomed to in recent work in applied linguistics."[20] According to Robert Lado, one of Fries' foremost disciples, in the 1940s, 1950s, and early 1960s, a lot of "research" was done, but the use of empirico-statistical methods was unheard of in the field of linguistics, or applied linguistics.[21] At that time, a different paradigm reigned; therefore, while much linguistic research was done at Michigan, it was descriptive rather than experimental in nature.

In Japan, at ELEC, "research" was also conducted. In fact, Tamotsu Yambe's "experiments" with the Oral Approach began even before ELEC started and continued for the next twenty years. In the early 1950s, Yambe had gone to Michigan where he met Charles Fries. When he returned home, he tried some of what he had seen in the English Language Institute in Ann Arbor—pattern practice and contrastive studies—with his classes in Japan, and he liked the way it worked. Of course, this approach was far from being a true experiment. It did, however, convince Yambe, and he became a staunch advocate of Fries' Oral Approach and a key member of the ELEC staff.

Once the ELEC effort began, "research" evidence was used to promote it. For instance, a 1957 newspaper article on "The Oral Method of Teaching English" proclaimed that "Tests conducted over the past year and a half for the teaching of English through the oral rather than visual method have been so successful that the English Language Exploratory Committee (ELEC) has decided to launch a five-year program."[22] Apparently, this report referred to the progress made by the teachers who participated in the first ELEC summer seminar. Obviously, however, biasing factors, such as the carefully selected subjects, prevented this "research" from measuring up to a "true experimental" standard. Still, such reports must have aroused considerable interest among the general public and English-language educators in Japan.

In 1962, when ELEC found itself "at the crossroads" and facing several serious challenges, its leaders began to recognize the need for large-scale promotion, and research was seen as a valuable tool in this effort. They proposed "experimental work on the effectiveness of our materials in the classroom and on the effectiveness of teaching methods."[23] Dr. Shiro Hattori, a "distinguished linguist," was named to head ELEC's "research department," and plans were made to compare "the progress of pupils using ELEC materials and that of pupils using ordinary materials."[24] A Rockefeller communique of this time "agreed that testing [the newly completed ELEC materials] on students against other materials might help to provide solid evidence of the superiority of the materials" but cautioned against letting "the research side get too elaborate beyond this point for the present."[25]

The promotional rather than investigative nature of this research is worth noting. The "experiment" was not intended to discover which approach to ELT in Japan was best or whether the Oral Approach really lived up to its promoters' claims. Rather, its purpose was to demonstrate that the decision already made (to implement the Oral Approach) was correct and should be supported.

In 1962, the junior high school attached to the Japan Women's University became the first of ELEC's "experimental schools," existing schools where the ELEC materials were used on an experimental basis.[26] In 1969, Yambe reported data from a total of six "ELEC associated schools." Four of these had been "associated with ELEC for at least three years": Mitsukaido Junior High School (Mitsukaido City, Ibaraki Prefecture); Horobetsu Junior High School (Noboribetsu Town, Horobetsu County, Hokkaido); Asano Junior High School (private), Yokohama; and the junior high school attached to the education department of Saga University (Saga Prefecture). Nevertheless the data on the effectiveness of the Oral Approach, convincing though it may have been, was far from conclusive. Consisting primarily of "the percentages of the students graded A to E in each month,"[27] it was rather subjective and did not allow for true comparison. It did show that in Oral Approach classes students' grades (assigned by their teachers) gradually improved, but that was not real proof of the Oral Approach's effectiveness.

Later, another Oral Approach "experiment" was conducted at a school in Toyonekko, and in 1979 ELEC published an entire book about it. It was titled *Toyonekko's Class*, and describes the use of the Oral Approach in classes.[28] The length of the report is impressive, and it even includes tables of statistics showing favorable results, but the research design was still not adequate to overcome threats to the study's validity. The students' improvement might have been due to Hawthorne effect or any number of intervening variables. Nevertheless, an entire book of "research" on the Oral Approach still had promotional value. It helped convince people of the Oral Approach's validity and encouraged its spread in Japan.

Trialability

The Oral Approach did not lend itself to easy trial in Japan. The widespread inability of teachers to speak English fluently made it impractical for them to try out the Oral Approach on even a small-scale basis. Developing the necessary proficiency, as the existence and nature of the ELEC summer seminars acknowledged, was no simple task. Other factors, such as heavy teaching loads, and/or pressure to teach students what they needed to know to pass the English portion of the entrance examinations, further reduced Japanese teachers' opportunities for trying out the approach ELEC advocated.

Observability

Observability is greatest when the innovation and its consequences are tangible objects, such as fertilizer and crop yields. In the case of ELEC, however, the innovation was a set of principles for language teaching, and the expected results were proficiency in spoken English. Since speaking ability in English was not measured on the high school and university entrance examinations, oral proficiency did not improve students' test scores. This lack of observable results certainly did not encourage the spread and adoption of the Oral Approach in Japan.

Status

Initially, when the ELEC campaign was just beginning, Fries' Oral Approach enjoyed considerable status. Although his ideas were not always understood and had been tried only on an extremely limited basis in Japan, their preeminence in American language teaching was widely known and gave them status.

Nevertheless, in the 1960s, many of the Oral Approach's undergirding ideas—such as structural linguistics and contrastive analysis—and the audio-lingual method, with which the Oral Approach was associated, came under fire in the United States.[29] "Chomsky's attacks on the Oral Approach's foundation came at the time when the Oral Approach was just beginning to catch on in Japan."[30] Thus, with its supporting pillars knocked out from under it, the Oral Approach lost status in the eyes of many Japanese teachers.[31]

Practicality

The demands that the Oral Approach placed on Japanese teachers were heavy given their lack of training and limited English proficiency in the 1950s and 1960s. Furthermore, suffering under heavy work loads, teachers had very little time or inclination to meet the demands of implementing a new, orally based teaching method in their classrooms. In these respects, the use of the Oral Approach in Japan's schools would have been decidedly unpractical.

ELEC tried to remedy this all-too-obvious problem by providing summer seminars designed to retrain English teachers and build their English proficiency so that they could use the Oral Approach. Nevertheless, given the large number of English teachers in Japan this retraining effort was also far from practical.

Flexibility/Adaptability

In one sense, because it consisted of broad principles rather than particular applications, the Oral Approach could be considered quite adaptable. In 1958, this flexibility was put to the test when the Ministry of Education announced new guidelines for English textbooks. Although ELEC's books were to be published privately, like all textbooks in Japan they still had to be approved by the ministry and, therefore, would have to satisfy the new requirements in order to be authorized for use in secondary schools.[32] Fearing the worst, ELEC's Japanese leaders notified Fries of the new guidelines. They were afraid that the "corpus" which he had been preparing (and upon which the ELEC textbooks would be based) would have to be redone and the project started afresh. To their relief Fries replied,

> I have gone over the revised syllabus from the Ministry and have been rather pleased with the content there given in detail. I believe the basic "corpus" as it was planned will cover quite satisfactorily the materials which are suggested and the reading selections which were planned...would satisfy the most critical of the Board of Examiners for the Ministry.[33]

In another, linguistic sense, the Oral Approach also demonstrated adaptability. Fries and his colleagues believed strongly that a special set of "separate and differing" materials had to be developed for each audience of English learners with a different native-language background.[34] Thus, in Michigan they produced one textbook series for Spanish speakers learning English and another set of books for Chinese speakers. In Japan, the textbooks they produced were designed particularly for Japanese speakers.

Within the limits established by its principles, the Oral Approach was quite flexible, but any attempt to modify the basic principles of the Oral Approach met with stiff resistance. Fries insisted that these principles were not flexible and were not to be compromised. For example, when attempts were made to modify the approach's heavy dependence on oral practice to make it more compatible with Japanese students' goals in studying (written) English, Fries reiterated:

> The final goal of the learner may be the full control of English for speaking and understanding spoken English in meetings, or in college and university classes. Or the learner's final goal may be the limited one of reading scientific books and articles. Or his final goal may be the reading of English literature with real understanding. Or his final goal may be merely the passing of an examination for a university,—an examination in which translation is the only requirement. No matter what the final goal of the person who starts to learn English, I believe we can now demonstrate that what we have called the "oral approach" is the most efficient, the most time-saving way to begin the study of English.[35]

Primacy

Primacy seems to have been especially influential throughout the history of tradition-bound, conservative Japan. Even today, Japanese teachers of foreign languages cling to methods developed over one thousand years ago for studying Chinese as a foreign language. When Harold Palmer went to Japan early in the twentieth century, he found such pedagogical traditions to be major obstacles. Nevertheless, relative to Fries and ELEC, Palmer also enjoyed the advantage of primacy. Thus, Fries was often perceived to be an "imitator" rather than an original. In fact, despite the similarities in the two approaches, followers of Palmer's Oral Method came to constitute an obstacle to the implementation of Fries' Oral Approach in Japan.

At the close of the first ELEC Specialists' Conference, when the ELEC campaign was just getting started, McLean rejoiced, "Fries and

Twaddell so impressed the Japanese that Palmer and Hornby were overshadowed completely. In the process the British and Palmer have, I feel, been reasonably well eliminated as ghosts, which greatly simplifies matters and clears the road for progress."[36] Nevertheless, as later events evidenced, his joy was premature. Yambe, for one, found that as he tried to spread the Oral Approach, "there was a strong tendency among the conservative school of teachers either to stick to the old grammar-translation method or to be loyal to and defend Palmer's oral method against the oral approach."[37]

Form

In support of his contention that the "form of the method proposal" is a decisive factor in determining its spread, Richards mentions the failures of The Silent Way and the Direct Method, instructional philosophies that do not utilize textbooks. In contrast, to exemplify success, he uses the case of Fries' Oral Approach in the United States.[38]

Fries himself always emphasized the preeminence of materials. Time and again, he stressed the point that, to ensure effective language learning, methods were not as important as the use of materials developed through the application of linguistic science.[39] Consequently, the "Michigan method" was highly dependent on the carefully prepared "Michigan materials." Books authored by Fries and Lado and published by the University of Michigan were widely circulated (and imitated by others), helping to spread the doctrine of the Oral Approach throughout the United States.

Robinett, one of Fries' graduate students at Michigan and an instructor in the early English Language Institute there, notes that the program consisted of much more than the textbook materials. "It was clear to Fries that learning a language was not just something that happened in the classroom; the learning process had to go beyond the classroom into the use of language in *real-life communicative situations*" [italics in original].[40] Consequently, he set up an "English House," and the experiences ELI students at the University of Michigan had there were very important to their learning and the institute's success. Nevertheless, evidencing the importance of form to diffusion, in most cases only what appeared in print was exported and adopted at other institutions.

In Japan, the story was quite different. Some of Fries' early disciples tried to use the Michigan books, but they soon found that they didn't work too well. Nevertheless, they reasoned that their problems resulted from the fact that the books had been designed for speakers of Spanish. The popular contrastive analysis hypothesis called for English books designed specifically for Japanese speakers. Therefore, years of work went into producing a series of special Oral Approach books for teaching English to the Japanese. If things were really as simple as "publish or perish," then the publication of these books would have ensured the spread of the Oral

Approach in Japan. Nevertheless, another factor, which will be discussed below under "structure" (of the resource system), complicated matters.

CHARACTERISTICS OF THE ELEC RESOURCE SYSTEM

Besides the characteristics of the innovation itself, various characteristics of the ELEC resource system were also of critical importance.

Capacity

With Rockefeller funding, the English Language Exploratory Committee had the capacity to do things that few other ELT-oriented organizations in Japan could accomplish in the 1950s. For instance, early in the ELEC campaign, its leaders recognized that "there were not in Japan enough trained technical people able to carry as much of the load as had been originally anticipated."[41] With its resources in U.S. dollars, however, ELEC was able to recruit and bring to Japan many Americans who were native-speakers of English. Many of them taught in ELEC's summer program and later in its year-round English Language Institute. Most notable among these expatriates were the authoritative experts ELEC brought to Japan—people like Fries and Twaddell. Their authority and ideas were another important aspect of ELEC's capacity and played a significant role in the ELEC campaign.

Appealing to authority in this manner is a common alternative to showing relative advantage through research. Two types of authorities can be useful in promoting change: popular theoretical constructs and recognized authorities in the field. Although it encountered difficulties in many other respects, ELEC's reform effort enjoyed considerable capacity in both of these areas.

Popular Theoretical Constructs. Regarding the first type of authority, Richards explains, "Methods are promoted and justified through reference to intuitively appealing assertions and theories."[42] The Oral Approach rested on three of these: structural linguistics, behaviorism, and efficiency.

One of the foundations of the Oral Approach was structural linguistics, the new, "scientific study of language." At the time of ELEC's campaign, "scientific" was generally a very appealing label. Of course, this scientific foundation was not merely concocted for promotional purposes. The Oral Approach materials were indeed based on a careful, analytical, scholarly study of language.

Another theoretical construct that promoted the Oral Approach was its compliance with the learning theory *zeitgeist* of the day, behaviorism. Fries frequently mentioned the building of automatic habits,[43] though a careful reading reveals that he was not nearly as mechanistic as many scholars in his day were.[44] Still, the Oral Approach's conformity with the then popular theories of learning promoted its spread and adoption. Later, however, as learning theories changed and behaviorism fell into disfavor among language teachers, the Oral Approach's association with it became a liability.

Another important aspect of the Oral Approach was its efficiency, a widely attractive idea. As Fries and his colleagues in the United States promoted the Oral Approach, they referred to this quality. Lado calculated:

> In pattern practice, the student produces a sentence after each cue at normal conversational speed. A class may produce 20 to 30 different sentences per minute following as many cues supplied by the teacher. This represents 1,000 to 1,500 recitations in a fifty-minute class. Compare this with a grammar-translation class where each student takes one minute to give his part of the translation. This gives only 50 recitations compared with 1,000. With group recitation in pattern practice, the number of student responses in a class of 10 students would be 10 times 1,000 or 10,000.[45]

In postwar Japan, a nation trying to rebuild its industries and businesses, efficiency was also a popular concept. In this environment, Fries and his supporters wisely emphasized the efficiency of the Oral Approach. Fries frequently called the Oral Approach "the most efficient, the most time-saving way to begin the study of English."[46] In his efforts to promote pattern practice, Yambe asserted that it provided "a maximum amount of oral practice within a minimum of time"[47] and was, therefore, "the most efficient teaching technique that has ever been devised."[48]

Recognized Authorities.   Besides referring to *what* is professionally popular, promoters also frequently refer to *who* is professionally popular. A well-known authority's support for a new approach can be its lifeblood. In fact, with backing from powerful people, assertions often "assume the status of dogma."[49]

In this respect also, the Oral Approach did very well in Japan. The Japanese members of ELEC were powerful and important people whose authority lent credibility to the ELEC campaign. The foreign experts served a similar purpose. It was anticipated that the weight of all these prominent figures would help ELEC achieve its goal of revolutionizing ELT in Japan. One major purpose of the first ELEC Specialists' Conference was to gain the support of prestigious authorities. In his post conference report to John D. Rockefeller 3rd, McLean triumphantly noted: "The Japanese participants in the conference included the outstanding men in the field in this country. It also had a representative from the Ministry of Education....Fries and Twaddell were enthusiastically received by *all* as men of professional distinction" [italics in original].[50] Among English teachers in Japan, these men were regarded as "giants" and "kings."[51] Their involvement in ELEC's activities was widely publicized and lent weight and credibility to its campaign.[52] Given his professional reputation, Fries could also function as the validating authority for his Oral Approach. As he traveled the length and breadth of Japan, teachers in all parts of the country flocked to his lectures. Although in the course of the ELEC campaign many errors were made, the use of "authority figures" to bolster the reform effort was definitely something that ELEC did right.

ELEC continued to use authority-based implementation strategies for many years. In the early 1960s, when the obstacles that ELEC faced had become unmistakably formidable, John D. Rockefeller 3rd, himself, employed an authority-oriented strategy in a final attempt to overcome them. As if the authorities ELEC had relied on to this point had not been powerful enough to counter the opposing forces, Rockefeller went straight to the top and contacted Prime Minister Mayato Ikeda, hoping to gain his support for the ELEC movement. In a follow-up note to Ikeda, Rockefeller wrote, "As to the English language matter which we discussed (ELEC),...it would be most helpful to us to know if the program has the backing of yourself and your Government."[53] A record of the prime minister's response, if there was one, is not available. However, this interchange demonstrates: (1) the extent to which Rockefeller was personally concerned with ELEC's campaign, (2) his reliance on authority-based strategies, and (3) the lengths to which he was willing to go in order to use this strategy in support of ELEC.

The problems that continued to plague ELEC, in spite of its use of powerful authorities, also demonstrate that this factor alone is not sufficient to bring about change.

Structure

ELEC was organized rather loosely as a committee, and it was never absolutely clear whether the head was in Japan or in the United States. Officially, of course, it was a Japanese organization, but it relied heavily on U.S. financial support and thus took its cues from the American directors of the (Rockefeller supported) Japan Society, Council on Economic and Cultural Affairs, Agricultural Development Council (which replaced CECA), and John D. Rockefeller 3rd Fund.

The ELEC campaign also suffered from a lack of structure in its plans for reforming Japanese ELT. Its leaders seem to have believed that providing a "better mouse trap" would be sufficient. There is no evidence that strategies for implementing the Oral Approach were planned until more than five years after the campaign commenced.

ELEC's textbook-publishing experience teaches another important lesson regarding structure: In the "secret life" of a method, to publish or not to publish a textbook is not the only question. A very important additional consideration is *who* publishes it. The publishing house becomes part of the resource system, and the structure and strength of its diffusion network is a critical implementation factor.

Although a great deal of time and attention was dedicated to the preparation of ELEC's *New Approach* textbooks, the choice of a publisher doesn't seem to have been a concern of any of the high-level ELEC leaders. Who actually made the arrangements regarding the publisher of the *New Approach* textbooks remains a mystery. Unfortunately, whoever it was

"did not know that the choice of publisher was so important."[54] Reflecting
the simple "better mousetrap" philosophy that prevailed in ELEC circles,
Matsumoto reported, "We thought better textbooks would sell better."[55]
Unfortunately, that naïve assumption was too simple, and ELEC's effort
was later handicapped by weaknesses in the structural network of the
publisher.

Because of his previous experience with textbook publication, Fries
very realistically foresaw opposition to ELEC's *New Approach* books
when they entered the market. He warned:

> All new materials for teaching English as a foreign language will meet opposition—
> opposition that is most likely to be very bitter and to stimulate many detractions and
> criticisms, some published and many whispered, that are unfair and false. Every
> adoption of a new text displaces one or more texts out of which someone is making a
> living, often one who needs this increment to support his family. At the very least, it
> takes away the potential market for another's textbooks.[56]

Nevertheless, Fries did not grasp the complete nature of the situation in
Japan. His advice was that "to be successful against the inevitable
opposition in Japan the textbooks built up must be *convincingly the work of
the Japanese*" [italics in original].[57] Although this advice was good, it was
insufficient. The textbooks that the American and Japanese team produced
for ELEC still failed to penetrate the Japanese market.

Those who worked on the production and publication of ELEC's
textbooks later acknowledged, "We made a mistake in selecting the
publisher."[58] During and after the Occupation, textbook publishing had
become a "lucrative enterprise."[59] By the time the ELEC books appeared
in print, publishers of the old texts were "well entrenched" and went to
great lengths to maintain strong relationships with teachers and the other
people in charge of choosing textbooks.[60] "At textbook selection time, the
publishers would send their representatives around the country, inviting
teachers to parties, and getting them obligated. Then they would 'choose'
the textbooks."[61] The sad lesson, which the idealistic ELEC reformers
learned the hard way, was that the sale of textbooks depends not only on
the quality of the books themselves but also to a large extent on a
"publisher's connections and influence." For a textbook to sell well, the
"publisher must have sales agents all over Japan" and "these agents must
have good relationships with the people who choose textbooks for the
various prefectures and city wards."[62]

Unfortunately, the original publisher of ELEC's textbooks
(Taishukan) specialized in linguistics, not secondary school English, and
thus didn't have the proper connections.[63] As one experienced Japanese
professor put it, "The publisher of the ELEC books didn't have such good
salesmen."[64] Regarding the parties publishers put on for the educators who
selected textbooks, Kleinjans noted, "Taishukan didn't have the resources to
do that."[65] In sum, ELEC's publisher was not successful in making inroads
against the major textbook publishers who had already established the right
connections. ELEC's switch to another publisher (Gakken) did not remedy
the problem because it came too late and other difficulties created

additional obstacles to the books' acceptance. If the importance of the structural capacities of publishers had been recognized sooner, however, this episode in the ELEC story could have had a happier ending.

Openness

There can be little question about ELEC's willingness to help bring about more effective teaching of oral English in Japan. The second aspect of openness, however, willingness to listen, was a characteristic of ELEC only during the first stages of its campaign. Prior to the 1956 Specialists' Conference, ELEC personnel contacted experts (both Japanese and American) for advice on how to proceed. In fact, one purpose of the conference was to provide a forum where experts could present and discuss openly their views on the problems of English teaching in Japan before ELEC arrived at a solution. After the conference, however, ELEC's course became set. The "Conclusions and Recommendations" arrived at during the conference formed the rigid "backbone" of ELEC's campaign, and the Oral Approach became *the* ELEC method for years to come.

It is also worth noting that the input provided to ELEC regarding the solution to Japanese problems in ELT came primarily from high-level experts. Had the ELEC leaders consulted with regular classroom teachers of English regarding their needs and ideas instead of (or in addition to) conducting a conference of and for specialists, they might have arrived at a more comprehensive understanding of the problems Japanese English teachers faced, and they might have even pursued a different "solution."

It would not be correct, however, to conclude that ELEC was completely closed or inflexible. User needs and aspirations were taken into account by at least some individuals. Yambe, for instance, noted that "mere imitation of the type of classes given at the [English Language] Institute [at the University of Michigan] does not necessarily work in Japanese schools" and he made suggestions for adapting the Oral Approach to be more consistent with a Japanese style of learning.[66]

Harmony

In any project that involves various individuals working together it is normal for minor differences and disagreements to occur, requiring negotiation and compromise. ELEC was no exception. There were occasional disagreements among the teachers, their trainers, and the materials producers about how Oral Approach principles should be applied at the level of classroom techniques and procedures.

Unfortunately, in one important case, disharmony went considerably beyond this normal level. Serious "conflicts" developed between Fries and Twaddell, and their disagreements became so severe as to threaten to destroy the ELEC campaign. As Fries' wife put it, "It got nasty at the end."[67]

Twaddell was a professor at Brown University, but he and Fries worked together at Michigan for several summers prior to becoming involved in ELEC. Evidence that they worked together well comes from the fact that Fries himself recommended Twaddell to be the second American expert at the 1956 Specialists' Conference.

In the course of the year 1957, however, conflicts between the two men started and grew increasingly worse. Nevertheless, by dividing up the work so that each could operate in his separate domain (Fries headed up the materials production work and Twaddell conducted the summer seminars), the two men managed to work together reasonably successfully.

As time went by, however, the disharmony between Fries and Twaddell increased, and by 1958 their disagreement had reached crisis proportions. In early January, McLean arranged a special meeting between Fries and Twaddell at Dearborn, Michigan, but it failed to defuse the situation. In his correspondence with others, Twaddell's remarks about Fries became insulting,[68] and Fries' communications with Twaddell, although always gentlemanly, grew increasingly icy.[69]

Apparently resentful of Fries' attempts to control the entire ELEC effort, Twaddell accused him of various faults, from a "Michigan über alles" fixation to a lack of awareness of how the ELEC work was really being done or who was actually doing it for him.[70] Fries responded imperiously, "Please remember that we have at the ELI been producing and revising materials for the teaching of English as a foreign language for a number of very different linguistic and cultural backgrounds for 17 years."[71]

The possible reasons for this conflict between Fries and Twaddell were many. First of all, there were fundamental differences in their teaching principles. Fries emphasized the importance of materials, while Twaddell considered methods to be primary. Furthermore, Fries and Twaddell came from different schools of linguistics. Kleinjans explained, "The Twaddell-Fries conflict was not merely a conflict of personalities but of paradigms."[72] In addition, both men seemed to be dangerously over-extended in their work (in the United States, in Japan, and elsewhere around the globe) and after working feverishly to meet ELEC deadlines, both were becoming over-tired and irritable. Also, on the part of each of the two experts, there seemed to be a fear that the other was trying to control him, and that led to defensiveness and resentment. In addition, as the ELEC operation developed it became apparent that Fries and Twaddell differed on a basic point—the extent to which ELEC operations should involve the Japanese.

This last reason was the one most often given by Fries to explain the schism. To McLean, he explained, "The conflicts which presently exist between Professor Twaddell and me seem to me to stem from fundamentally different beliefs concerning the kind of consideration to be given the native professors and teachers."[73] Fries had always insisted that a dominant role be reserved for the Japanese. He accused Twaddell of making increasing demands for greater American involvement in the summer seminars, up to "three full professors and at least three juniors."

Fries insisted that the Americans should work only "as technical consultants and co-workers."[74]

Nevertheless, Fries considered himself to be the exception to this rule. He even complained that although it had been announced that he was "chairman" and "in charge" his proposals had been "brushed aside" as "something irrelevant."[75] Fries also charged Twaddell with violating clearly marked channels of communication,[76] failing to complete assignments given to him, and with encouraging others to ignore Fries' directions.[77]

All of this was personally upsetting to Fries and counter-productive in terms of ELEC's progress. To other ELEC workers, he confessed: "This break has grieved me more than anyone can ever know."[78] "Never in my life have I faced anything like the suspicion and insinuations concerning motives that have increasingly characterized Freeman's conduct toward me."[79] "I have struggled hard against such a break and, during the last four months, have devoted much of my working time (and many of the hours I should have been sleeping) to efforts to understand the causes of the attitude which he was developing, and to discover some way of relieving the tension."[80]

In light of these problems, Fries finally concluded, "I believe that for Freeman and me both to go to Japan to work together on this project would be most unwise. I believe that a blow-up there of some sort would be inevitable and that that would be the worst possible thing for the whole project."[81] Regarding the materials development work, his decision was

> either the Japanese are to do the textbooks, with us as technical consultants and co-workers in that capacity or we shall be doing them and handing them over completed for their use. I myself can have no part in the latter procedure for it will not only jeopardize this enterprise but it will endanger the advisory work I've been doing in several other countries.[82]

He closed on a noble note: "I have not and do not intend to develop on my part a corresponding attitude of hostility. The important matter in all of this is the ultimate success of the project as a whole."[83]

A few days later, calling the task "one of the hardest things I've had to do in my life," Fries wrote directly to Twaddell, explaining that his efforts to "push the plans and activities in a direction entirely contrary to [Fries'] fundamental beliefs concerning international cooperation" made "a break" necessary. Fries pointed out that his and Twaddell's approaches were "irreconcilable" and then, hoping that "the separation [could] be accomplished without personal animus and without any damage to any person or to the project as a whole," delivered the ultimatum: "If I am to continue I must ask you to withdraw."[84]

When the news of the break between Fries and Twaddell reached ELEC headquarters in Japan, the effect was devastating. After they got over the shock, the ELEC leaders responded that Twaddell's resignation would create great difficulties for the program and refused to accept it. Of course, they wanted Fries to continue also. In a telegram, they insisted that *both* "Professors Fries and Twaddell must participate ELEC activities in

Japan this spring and summer as already nationally publicized or else ELEC future substantially jeopardized [sic]."[85]   Nevertheless, they also feared the inevitability of an open confrontation between the two and the damage that it could cause.   "In order to assure ELEC's future," they proposed a solution in which Fries and Twaddell could make "separate but complementary" contributions at different times.[86] This arrangement proved to be workable. Fries left for Japan on April 21 and worked on the materials until June 10, leaving just before Twaddell arrived to conduct the 1958 summer seminar.[87]   In this way, the 1958 program met with success.[88]

The ELEC leaders had skillfully managed to avoid a disastrous, open confrontation between Fries and Twaddell, while maintaining the continuity of the project. Unwilling to trust their luck a second time around, however, they began reducing ELEC's dependence on both Fries and Twaddell. As they made plans for the future,

> it was agreed that Professor Fries would have no hand in…these ventures but that he would be asked to prepare a corpus for the third-year material…provided this could be accomplished by the end of 1958. It was also agreed that in the future there would be no ranking American professor but that the American professors would be serving as consultants.[89]

Fries had already expressed his intention to withdraw after June, but he agreed to work on the materials as requested, although he did not complete them until 1959, the last year he would travel to Japan under the auspices of ELEC.[90]

"Professor Twaddell expressed doubt as to whether it would be possible for him to be available next summer and fall. He said this would depend upon circumstances at Brown after he returned having been away at Princeton for a year."[91] He was "extremely tired," but it was hoped that he might be persuaded to rejoin the ELEC effort later. Nevertheless, this hope never materialized.

ELEC had weathered the storm of disharmony, but not without damage. Two of its key authority figures had been lost, and without their vision ELEC began to slide from its revolutionary role toward becoming a more conventional English language school.

Aside from the Twaddell-Fries conflict and other, minor methodological quarrels, there were other sources of disharmony within the ELEC resource system. Although they were not so serious as to threaten ELEC's immediate future, in the long run they contributed to ELEC's decline as a force for reforming English teaching in Japan.

At first, the hope that ELEC would play a revolutionary role in Japanese ELT was shared by virtually all ELEC workers, Japanese and American. Nevertheless, with the passage of time, other concerns grew in importance and divided ELEC's managers.

The American funding agencies continued to be interested in research, innovation, and reform. In addition, most of the American teachers had only a short-term commitment to ELEC and never saw their work in Japan as a lifelong career. Following the American pattern, most of them would eventually use their ELEC experience as a stepping stone to a better position somewhere else.

In contrast, but in accordance with the typical Japanese management and employment pattern, the Japanese leaders of ELEC took a long-range view. Afraid that, following the historical pattern, the Americans would soon depart and leave the Japanese "holding the bag," some of ELEC's Japanese leaders began worrying about long-term stability. Yambe, for one, became anxious about how ELEC would assure continuity for its employees.[92] He and others with similar concerns pressed for incorporation, an ELEC building, and a year-round, money-making English Language Institute.

The fears that American funding would eventually be withdrawn turned out to be justified. After 1968, ELEC received no funds from the Rockefeller or Ford Foundations. Nevertheless, from another point of view, the Japanese leaders' apprehensions had been self-fulfilling prophecies. As ELEC moved more and more toward stability, it became less and less the kind of innovative, revolutionary organization that the American foundations were interested in funding, so its U.S. benefactors saw no reason to continue their support.

CHARACTERISTICS OF THE JAPANESE ELT USER SYSTEM

"The dynamic ecology of another cultural situation" is always complex.[93] Nevertheless, an understanding of the target culture's political, social, economic, philosophical, and geographic dimensions is crucial to any attempt to bring about directed contact change across cultural boundaries. Because these many inter-related elements can vary dramatically from one setting to another, "what worked back home" may not produce the same effect in another cultural setting.

Various characteristics of the intended users of the Oral Approach were of critical importance to ELEC's campaign. The norms, values, capacities, and motivations of Japanese teachers and students of English helped determine many of its eventual successes and failures. Nevertheless, in many cases the ELEC leaders were unaware of or ignored these factors. As a result, the campaign suffered accordingly.

It is probably not fair, however, to fault the ELEC personnel for not paying attention to many of these factors. Although those in charge of planning ELEC's reform movement could have (and should have) been aware of some of the characteristics of the Japanese socio-cultural-educational system, many other characteristics did not come to the attention of experts on Japanese society until long after the ELEC campaign commenced.

Ignorance is no protection, of course, and whether or not the people in charge were aware of them, these factors influenced ELEC's efforts to reform ELT in Japan. As the following sections will illustrate, many of these factors are understood much better today.

Antecedents

All of chapter four is devoted to a discussion of the historical development of the socio-cultural, political, and educational situation that the ELEC effort encountered in Japan in 1956. These factors continued to affect ELEC throughout the course of its campaign. Antecedent factors, however, were generally ignored by the ELEC reformers—in spite of Bryant's emphasis on them in his 1955, pre-ELEC report to the Japan Society. This is not to say that ELEC personnel never made reference to the historical antecedents of the situation they were trying to reform. At the Specialists' Conference, for instance, Sanki Ichikawa spoke of the "tradition and influence of Chinese studies" in Japan.[94] Nevertheless, such an awareness was apparently not very widespread among the ELEC workers—especially the American ones—and any influence it may have had on the ELEC materials was not noticeable.   If the ELEC "revolutionaries" took antecedent factors into account at all, they viewed them primarily as "enemies" to be defeated rather than as characteristics of the Japanese setting that might require some adaptation in the Oral Approach doctrine ELEC promoted, or as forces with and through which ELEC might operate.

Geographic Location

An island nation with strong natural boundaries, just off the far edge of Asia (from Europe's perspective) and an ocean away from America, Japan has had relatively few contacts with Westerners in the course of its history. Japan was the last nation the Portuguese explorers discovered in their ventures around Africa and throughout southern and eastern Asia. Furthermore, even after contact with the Western world was made, the Tokugawa rulers officially closed Japan to foreigners for hundreds of years.

This long isolation had a strong effect on the country. Respecting language, for instance, Japan has been "thoroughly monolingual from time immemorial."[95]   Even today it remains one of the most ethnically, culturally, and linguistically homogeneous countries in the world. As a consequence of this insularity and linguistic homogeneity, the Japanese have always needed to learn foreign languages in order to communicate with the rest of the world. In modern times, as Suzuki explains, "Our insularity has made it almost imperative for us to study English in order to communicate with other nations."[96]   Nevertheless, since face-to-face contact with speakers of languages other than Japanese has been rare, foreign language study has been confined to the classroom and the emphasis has been on developing reading rather than speaking skills. As Ichikawa explained at the ELEC Specialists' Conference,

> a university graduate, after taking up employment, *does* find it necessary to *read* English, but seldom has an opportunity of associating with foreigners. So if he has had lessons at school in *speaking* English, his English will soon get rusty, since no opportunity arises after his graduation to speak it. Thus the opinion gains ground that

to drill the students in speaking and writing English at school is but a waste of energy and that we ought rather to encourage the reading of books instead [italics in original].[97]

Fries and others blasted away at this argument, repeatedly stating that even if a reading knowledge were the only goal of language learning the Oral Approach would still be the best way to arrive at it. Nevertheless, they were never able to overcome the resistance to speaking English that stemmed, at least in part, from Japan's insularity.

Centralization of Power and Administration

In spite of American attempts to decentralize control in the Japanese school system during the Occupation, the administration was rapidly recentralized once control reverted to the Japanese. Although the post-Occupation Ministry of Education never regained all of the power it exercised earlier in the century, it still remained an important force to be reckoned with. It controlled educational policy and educational budgets, subsidized budgets for nongovernment schools and colleges, determined the content of courses of study, and authorized textbooks for schools.[98] In this situation, ELEC could have benefited from Maley's modern-day warning to educational reformers: When control is exercised by a central, authoritarian body, a critical implementation factor is whether the top-level administrators "understand, and are...in sympathy with, the declared objectives" of the innovation-implementation process.[99] As King explains, "there are many ways of penetrating a decentralized system" (such as the one found in U.S. schools), but in a highly centralized school system like Japan's you get "only one shot," win or lose.[100]

In short, because of the centralized nature of school-system authority and administration in Japan, the support of the Ministry of Education was essential to ELEC's reform campaign. Citing the example of "earlier struggles to introduce innovations without regard to proper channels," William Cullen Bryant II noted how important it was to make "just the right approach" to the ministry. For instance, in spite of the fact that Harold Palmer was invited to go to Japan by prominent individuals and spent fourteen years there attempting to change ELT practices, even his disciples recognized that his "failure to influence official policies was due to his being brought to Japan by private individuals without sufficient groundwork having first been laid in the Ministry of Education."[101] Therefore, in his report to the Japan Society regarding the challenges and possibilities of reforming ELT practices in Japan, Bryant repeated and emphasized the advice of Japanese experts whom he met on his tour of Japan—that "it would be a fatal mistake not to work through the Ministry of Education."[102]

The founders of ELEC recognized the importance of ministry support and attempted to involve ministry officials in ELEC's activities and to court their favor whenever they could. Tamon Maeda and Tatsuo Morito, both former ministers of education, and Yoshio Tanaka, vice-minister of education, accepted invitations to be members of ELEC's original central committee although their involvement was primarily ceremonial.[103] In addition, at the 1956 Specialists' Conference, Ryohei Shishido, an administrative official in charge of the Secondary Education Section of the Elementary and Secondary Education Bureau of the Ministry of Education was an invited observer.[104]

Going through official channels, however, was not without risks. Primary among them was the possibility that any reform attempt would be stifled or compromised as it passed through the bureaucracy. Other ELEC workers expressed "fear of centering any program in government agencies" because local or prefectural boards of education, as well as private schools and colleges, were jealous of their autonomy and suspicious of Mombusho (Ministry of Education) initiatives.[105] In addition, it was reported that the ministry had a new method of its own that emphasized "ability in hearing and speaking."[106]

Faced with this situation, ELEC chose to go it alone, attempting to circumvent the Ministry of Education and avoid the bureaucracy with all its "red tape."[107] In the United States, such an "end-run" approach might have worked, but given the power of the Ministry of Education in Japan this tactical error virtually doomed ELEC to failure. Contrary to intentions, instead of speeding up the process of implementing the Oral Approach in Japan, it led to serious problems.

Rodgers could have been talking about ELEC and the Japanese Ministry of Education when he warned, "External agencies need to be informed about and, perhaps, directly involved in discussion of syllabus changes....Feelings of being left out or uninformed create the adversary stance that representatives of such agencies often take with regard to new programs."[108] By most accounts, this is what happened in the case of ELEC. A rivalry developed between ELEC and the Mombusho. As one ELEC worker recalled, "At the beginning, ELEC and Mombusho fought."[109] Another noted, "The worst enemy of ELEC was the Mombusho."[110] ELEC got the worst of the fight, and in the end, "the Mombusho won."[111] Even Yambe, the one who fought most staunchly for the Oral Approach admitted that "ELEC did not succeed in overcoming Mombusho resistance."[112] Another ELEC insider, reminiscing about the battle, concluded, "That was a tragedy—for ELEC."[113]

Others claim that the ministry was more neutral. While it was "not too sympathetic,"[114] the "Mombusho was fair" (except for one key individual).[115] According to policy, even today, "The Ministry officially refuses commitment to any particular methodology and forbids its imposition."[116] In ELEC's time, "teachers were expected to examine the merits and disadvantages of each method and decide which one would be optimal for their classrooms."[117] Admittedly, this was difficult for them to do considering how poorly most English teachers of the time had been trained. It can also be argued that the ministry's failure to approve innovative methods gave tacit approval to the traditional ones. Nevertheless, the ministry officials could still claim that in not promoting the Oral Approach and/or ELEC's reform movement, they were merely following the standard procedure of not endorsing any particular teaching method.

At least one ministry official, however, seems to have opposed ELEC and hindered its effort. Because of his position as head of secondary-school English language teaching, Ryohei Shishido was able to block many of ELEC's advances.[118] The reasons for his actions are not clear. Some say that he was a disciple of Palmer, and for this reason he faithfully and staunchly defended Palmer's method, and was "antagonistic toward ELEC."[119] Others (within the Ministry of Education) argue that Shishido was "neutral, and not necessarily a follower of Palmer."[120] Yet another point of view is that this key ministry official was a valiant defender of the nation, guarding against American pedagogical imperialism. He "believed that there should be a Japanese way of teaching English."[121] Whatever the nature of the quarrel or the reasons for it, the most important and unarguable point is that one individual in a key position in the hierarchical and centralized Japanese Ministry of Education was able to thwart ELEC's progress. The ministry failed to support ELEC in any official or meaningful way, and virtually everyone who worked with ELEC agreed that this lack of support was a heavy blow to its reform campaign.

The ministry personnel were in an extremely powerful position— controlling budget appropriations and officially "giving advice to all the junior high school teachers."[122] In contrast, ELEC was innovative and well endowed, but it had no real power over Japanese teachers except the power of persuasion. In the face of ministry resistance and/or neglect, that was not enough.

One cannot help but wonder what might have happened in Japan if ELEC had somehow been able to work through the ministry, or at least had received its support. The only thing that can be concluded without resorting to conjecture, however, is that ELEC's failure to operate through official channels proved to be a major handicap. In his final report on "JDR 3rd and the English Language in Japan," Datus C. Smith, Jr. placed the blame for ELEC's failure to achieve its main objective at the doorstep of the Ministry of Education. Smith wrote:

> No doubt many factors played a part in [ELEC's failure], but I am inclined to accept the judgment of those who say the failure resulted from the opposition of vested interests—chiefly people in the Ministry of Education and in the teaching profession who were scared of new methods which would render their own professional training obsolete.[123]

Yambe, the ELEC stalwart who did battle with the ministry most often, was even more direct in his accusation. Contending that the ministry first misunderstood and then misrepresented the Oral Approach, he concluded, "This is the greatest damage done to the development of the Oral Approach in Japan, and, moreover, the damage was done by none other than the Ministry of Education itself which is supposed to help the education [sic] in Japan."[124]

Size of the Adopting Unit

A major obstacle faced by those who would reform English language teaching in Japan is the sheer immensity of the program. At least one experienced Japanese educator asserts, "The greatest obstacle to change in English teaching in Japan is the large number of people studying and teaching it."[125] After World War II, more Japanese than ever before entered educational institutions, and virtually all of them wanted to take English classes. By the time the ELEC effort began, millions of Japanese pupils (virtually every student in junior and senior high school) were studying English, and around 65,000 teachers, qualified or not, had been drafted to teach the subject. In 1967, Brownell noted, "Perhaps no other country in the world has a program involving as high a percentage of its youth...for as many years in a foreign language."[126]

The American ideal of "democratic" education (education for all) implanted in Japan after World War II was one reason for this explosion. The popularity of English at this time was also in harmony with the traditional Japanese pattern of ardent interest in the language of foreigners who have convincingly demonstrated their superior force or technology. Yet another reason was Japan's very real need to communicate with the outside world. English was the natural vehicle for this purpose since it became the unquestioned international language in the years following the war.

As a result of this postwar English "fever," Japan's English-teaching resources were spread very thin. Since the number of classrooms and teachers was limited, the flood of English learners made large classes the norm. For effective language learning, however, as Otani notes, the ideal class size is less than twenty. Nevertheless, since the end of the war, the average size of a public school English class in Japan has ranged from forty to sixty, and sometimes beyond one hundred.[127] This teacher-student ratio necessitates severe compromises in the teaching of oral English.

A related problem created by the sudden flood of English students during and after the Occupation was a lack of qualified English teachers. As Brosnahan notes, "Where could or can Japan find within itself—and it seems determined to find them within the country—the 65,000 teachers competent to teach the English language?"[128] In reality, most teachers' English skills were weak (especially when it came to speaking the language), and their training in language-teaching methods was minimal.

Training (or retraining) the large number of poorly prepared teachers in the Japanese ELT system was a truly formidable task. As Kleinjans noted, "If ELEC had taught a hundred teachers a month [more than its peak rate], it still would have taken 75 years to get through all of them."[129] The natural result of these conditions was mediocrity in teaching and the continuation of a pedagogical tradition that emphasized analysis rather than communication.

Some feel that it is unrealistic to expect anything more than poor quality from such a mass-education system. Harasawa contends: "It has been absurd trying to teach English to the whole population, as we have so far been doing. If this ceases, I shall be more optimistic about the prospects of English in this country."[130] Others are not so pessimistic, but they are not optimistic about changing such a large system either— especially in a short time and with limited resources. In his report, Bryant noted that English teaching in Japan constituted an "immense problem," and it was "unlikely that a single project [would] solve it."[131] His words seem to have been prophetic. ELEC's campaign reached only a small percentage of the English teachers in Japan.

Communication Structure

Communicating the news of the Oral Approach to English teachers in Japan was difficult—not only because of the large number of teachers but also because ELEC lacked authority over them and had weak connections with those organizations that did. Consequently, it was unable to employ a "top down" strategy for communicating the news of the Oral Approach and its advantages.   For this reason, ELEC resorted to a horizontal communication strategy employing mass media such as newspapers. Articles about ELEC's conferences and visiting dignitaries regularly appeared in at least some Japanese newspapers.[132] In addition, ELEC sent Fries and other visiting authorities on lecture tours throughout Japan. So as to increase their effect, the activities of these traveling scholars were nationally publicized.[133]

ELEC also employed an "opinion leader" approach to communicate information about the Oral Approach throughout Japan. The participants in the ELEC summer program were carefully selected to represent a variety of prefectures. The intent was that after they had received training in oral English and the Oral Approach, these teachers would return to their homes where they would influence their colleagues.   Unfortunately, although the participants in ELEC's summer program could tell their colleagues about the Oral Approach, the requisite level of proficiency in spoken English, which they had developed over the summer, was not so easily transferred.

In an attempt to communicate directly to English teachers in Japan, ELEC published its own professional periodical, the *ELEC Bulletin*. This journal (also discussed below under "support networks") was useful in promoting ELEC's purposes, but due to the size of Japan's ELT program, it failed to reach a significant portion of the large number of Japanese teachers of English.

Group Orientation and Tolerance of Deviancy

In Japan, both ethnic identity and group loyalty are especially strong. Noting that "Japan remains parochial and insular in important respects," Jansen claims, "The unique quality of Japanese culture combines with the limiting nature of the Japanese language to enfold the Japanese in a consciousness of social nationality that may have no parallel elsewhere."[134]

In fact, it is claimed that many Japanese "consider Japan to be the only real country and Japanese the only real language."[135]   While all commentators on Japanese society do not take such an extreme view, scholars generally agree that the Japanese are very group minded and group dependent.[136]   In contrast with American society, which is characterized by "competitive individualism,"[137] Japanese society values harmony and group-orientation. In Japan, "the individual functions only as a member of and in concert with a group....Individual autonomy is suppressed, and loyalty is emphasized."[138]   "Dare he flee to the domain of a maverick, ostracism will immobilize the self-willed soul...and thus coerce him back to the fold where a life of conformity awaits him."[139]   In this setting, tolerance of deviancy is low. "Japanese who do not 'behave like Japanese' are thought deplorable; overseas Japanese such as Japanese-Americans are not easily trusted and may be ridiculed because of their apparent ambiguity of identity in terms of belongingness."[140]

In language behavior, pronunciation is a strong indicator of group identity and loyalty. Sociolinguists have hypothesized that "pronunciation reflects the permanent social group with which the speaker identifies."[141] In many interethnic situations, "the use of an outgroup language, but with a distinctive ethnic accent, does not detract from the speakers' perceived ethnicity."[142] On the other hand, individuals who adopt the speech markers of the dominant group as a "tactic of social mobility are often considered cultural traitors by other members of the ingroup and uncomplimentary labels are often attached to them."[143]

In Japan, the strong emphasis on group loyalty makes such sociolinguistic forces especially powerful. The Japanese have "a traditional contempt for the bilingual person as probably a fool and certainly untrustworthy."[144] Those Japanese who have lived abroad and acquired fluency in English may "arouse suspicion."[145] Unfortunately, Japanese returning from overseas are not the only ones who suffer because of fluency in English. Even those who never leave the country seem to fear becoming "too good" in English. Thus, in spite of the time and effort expended on English study in Japan, there is an undeniable counter-current which implies that "good" Japanese are not supposed to learn English "too well." Paul McLean quotes a senior Finance Ministry official as saying, "It doesn't do to be too proficient in English. If you are thought to be too 'international,' that is a mark against you in government offices and in some big companies too."[146] Teachers of English in Japan often complain, "The educational system as a whole suppresses communicative skills in language because those who learn to communicate tend to become dangerous, 'rocking the boat' rather than making good bureaucrats.[147]

Feelings of identity affect the process of learning a foreign language in another way also. Research has indicated that one of "the primary attitudinal contributions to predicting English acquisition [is] low national consciousness."[148] To make progress most effectively, "second language learners should have the desire to identify with the target group whose language they are learning."[149] It seems to be a language-learning fact that fluency requires a psychological reorientation to new ways of thinking. Furthermore, those who are disenchanted with their own culture are often the best foreign language learners.

For the Japanese, such a psychological reorientation is not only difficult but also undesirable. There is a strong "Japanese sense of being somehow a separate people—of being unique. The line between the 'we' of the Japanese as a national group and the 'they' of the rest of mankind seems to be sharper for them than for most peoples who participate much in international life."[150]   As Harasawa notes, of all people in the world, "the Japanese are unduly addicted to or intoxicated by their own language—so much so that neither English nor any other foreign language can ever succeed in invading their linguistic subconsciousness."[151]   In other words, Japanese students' strong sense of native-language identity and native-group loyalty may help explain why they are such poor language learners.

Another, related problem for English teaching in Japan is the widespread fear of losing one's "Japaneseness." Many Japanese believe that "the acquisition of a foreign language will endanger one's native language and his native culture, which are generally viewed as very fragile and vulnerable."[152]   The result is a resistance to learning English by effective methods. McLean explains:

> In spite of all the talk of learning English in order to become more internationally-minded most Japanese are still obsessed by the fear of somehow losing their "ethnic uniqueness," their *Yamato Damashii* or Japanese spirit. English, then, cannot be allowed to threaten this mental parochialism, and so it is taught in a very special way.[153]

An illustration of this point comes from a response to a letter on English teaching in *The Japan Times,* in which an experienced English teacher wrote:

> What really hit me was Mr. Miyazawa's fear of "losing a 'Japanese' personality" if English is studied at too young an age....Such a limited and narrow view smacks of racism. It seems unnecessarily protectionist, almost culturally paranoic. It also reinforces something I have suspected from time to time with some of my students in the past 3-1/2 years in Japan—namely, that some Japanese put up psychological blocks to foreign language learning because they feel it is dangerous to their very "Japaneseness."[154]

At least some of the ELEC personnel became aware of language-learning problems due to Japanese learners' strong feelings of group identity and loyalty. Kleinjans, for instance, recounts the story of two promising students who dropped out of an English class at ICU because their friends called them "different." After many years of experience with Japanese learners of English, he concluded, "The problem is that they're so afraid of losing their Japaneseness."[155] This fear of losing one's "cultural identity or soul" by becoming too Americanized[156] must have been especially strong in the first years of ELEC's operation immediately following the Occupation.

The strong group orientation and low tolerance of deviancy that prevail in Japan also discourage teachers from using innovative approaches in their classrooms. The saying "The nail that sticks up gets hammered down" definitely applies in such cases. Flenley, for example, reports how a Japanese teacher of English employed a teaching innovation, which worked successfully, but soon abandoned it because of fears that she would be perceived as being too different.[157] In this case, social pressure to conform to the status quo overpowered pedagogical effectiveness.

Openness

Generally speaking, the implementation of innovations seems to be accomplished more easily in social systems that are open to new ideas (i.e., those with a "modern" orientation). Unfortunately for ELEC, the conservative tradition in Japanese education created an organizational climate in the school system that was far from conducive to innovation. In Japan's conservative, patriarchal society, the young are dominated by the old, making tradition especially valued and strong.[158] For this reason, Reischauer cautioned that the ELEC movement simply had to have "the sympathetic support of influential members" of the "old-fashioned" professors of English in Japan.[159] The fact that this support was often withheld hindered the ELEC effort considerably.

In cases involving directed contact change, the intended-user system's openness to foreign ideas is another critical predictor of success. Unfortunately, ELEC's campaign to promote the teaching of spoken English in Japan came at a time when anti-American feelings were on the rise and the forces favoring a return to more traditional Japanese ways were especially powerful. The Japanese had just been through seven years of occupation, during which many reforms—educational and otherwise— had been imposed on them. In the mid-1950s, the sentiment among most Japanese educators was that they had had enough of American ideas. It was time to return to more traditional Japanese ways of doing things. As a result, ELEC fought an uphill battle.

Interestingly, the spirit encountered in the "reverse course" years was nothing new. It had a number of parallels in Japanese history. For instance, in the nineteenth century, following the dramatic reforms of the early Meiji years, there was a counter-reaction to the previous "craze" for modernization and Westernization. The decades following 1890 were a period of traditionalism and growing nationalism during which interest in foreign languages—especially in gaining speaking proficiency in a foreign language—declined. An awareness of this historical pattern of attraction followed by rejection might have alerted the ELEC reformers to the resistance they were apt to encounter in their implementation efforts.   In retrospect, at least, it is clear that they should have entertained no illusions about riding a wave of popular sentiment for reforming English language teaching in Japan, at least not along the lines of an American methodology.

Teacher Factors

Teachers, as front-line users of an innovation, are key figures in the change process. Frequently, they are also targets when accusations about "failures" in education are being hurled. English teachers in Japan are no exception to this rule. Regarding the reform of Japanese ELT, one oft-mentioned obstacle is the many native Japanese teachers of English who demonstrate a traditional "suspicion about innovation in learning and teaching."[160] Dillon and Dillon list a number of other teacher-related reasons why most Japanese do not attain proficiency in English: "a lack of trained native-speaker instructors," "a chronic unwillingness to weed out incompetent teachers," and "a traditional student-teacher relationship which is not conducive to the development of oral skills in a living language."[161] Primary among the obstacles, however, is the fact that "not many of the teachers themselves can really speak English."[162]

For a long time, the limited ability of most teachers of English to speak the language fluently has been viewed as a handicap to the implementation of any sort of oral approach in Japan. During the days when Palmer was trying to get Japanese teachers to utilize his Oral Method, one of the major barriers was that "teachers could not pronounce correctly."[163] Even today, the fact that many Japanese teachers of English "lack a communicative ability themselves" is viewed as a serious handicap by those who would reform the Japanese ELT system.[164]

Such was certainly the case in the early 1950s when the ELEC effort was getting under way. In a "Report on Japanese-American Cultural Relations" prepared for Mr. Rockefeller in 1953, which contained a section on the possibility of starting an English-language teaching program in Japan, it was noted, "Inquiry as to the Japanese inability to speak English even after six or eight years of study including 'conversation' usually elicited the reply that the teachers of English commonly could not themselves speak English with any real facility."[165] Later, in 1956, this same observation was made—"that in Japan very little conversational English is taught since so few Japanese teachers are qualified to teach it."[166]

In the years before and during World War II, most Japanese had stopped studying English. Consequently, the number of English users and their proficiency declined. Also, during the war, many English teachers went to the battlefield and never returned. Then, after the war, there was suddenly a great need for English teachers because of the expansion of educational opportunity and the increased demand for English during the Occupation. At this time, however, the few Japanese who could speak English accurately and fluently were needed as translators and interpreters, and consequently were not available for the classroom. In sum, those who remained to teach English were generally the oldest and the least proficient in the language.[167]

At this same time, many college graduates who had majored in some subject *other than English* but had received passing marks in their English classes (which emphasized English literature rather than practical speaking proficiency in the language) were put into English-teaching positions in order to fill the teacher gap. Later, when more qualified teachers became available, these "stop-gap" individuals could not simply be discarded. As Ichikawa explained in the mid-1950s,

> more than half of the *chugakko* teachers of English, who are said to number roughly 20,000, are those who have majored in other subjects than English, and though they know themselves they are unfit for teaching English, they cannot and will not move to other places, on account of the difficulty of getting other jobs, with the result that they thus shut the door to younger and abler teachers.[168]

This shortage of teachers who could speak English with proficiency was a serious obstacle to Rockefeller's plans to reform English teaching in Japan in a way that would promote the teaching of spoken English. Given the large and growing size of the Japanese ELT program, importing adequate numbers of native speakers of English was out of the question. A report to Mr. Rockefeller emphasized, "It is clearly impossible to provide enough English-speaking teachers to change the situation."[169] (Even today, it is reported that there is an "acute shortage of qualified native speakers of English in Japanese schools."[170]) The only alternative was to provide a program to train new (and retrain old) Japanese teachers of English. As a result, ELEC sponsored its long-running series of summer seminars. In addition to teaching teachers about the Oral Approach, a major purpose of the ELEC summer seminars was to build their oral proficiency. Unfortunately, because of the large numbers of students and teachers of English in Japan, ELEC's retraining effort fell woefully short of being sufficient.

Even if ELEC had possessed capacity adequate to retrain the many thousands of Japanese teachers of English, other teacher factors might have restrained such a movement. For instance, an educational philosophy that favored "cultural" aims made many Japanese teachers of English shun anything that appeared too "practical." Around the turn of the century, negative attitudes toward the teaching of speaking skills had developed. Moreover, because of Japanese teachers' tendency toward "academic scrupulosity" they typically showed an "excessive fondness for hair-splitting discussions of grammatical details," which also precluded fluency in speaking.[171]

Consequently, in trying to promote the Oral Approach, ELEC faced a situation where teachers who lacked speaking proficiency in English were unable (and unwilling) to do what was necessary to learn and/or teach oral English. As Ichikawa lamented, "Our teachers cannot put into effect what they know it is best to do."[172] Merely informing them about the Oral Approach was far from sufficient.

Learner Factors

Traditionally, approaches to language teaching have focused on individuals as mere "perceptual beings" whose emotions, experiences, and desires were irrelevant. In recent years, however, educators have come to realize that learners must be viewed as emotional, dynamic, active, and social beings.[173]   In other words, various characteristics of learners—linguistic, perceptual, social, cognitive, affective, etc.—affect their efforts to learn a foreign language. Japanese students are no exception to this rule. Ogasawara exhorts, "We should remember that along with universal problems of foreign language teaching and learning, Japanese learners of English have their own unique problems. Researchers should be geared to these problems and more flexible and effective methods should be developed to meet the unique problems of English learning in Japan."[174]

Following contrastive analysis procedures, ELEC's linguistically oriented experts paid special attention to the difficulties experienced by Japanese students of English that were attributable to the structural, phonological, and lexical differences between the two languages. Nevertheless, at the time of the ELEC campaign many other important factors, such as learning-style differences, were poorly understood. In fact, only recently have a number of these characteristics been recognized or named.

Of course, although few experts were aware of them thirty years ago, these factors still existed and influenced Japanese learners of English. Consequently, they affected ELEC's effort to promote the Oral Approach. Since then, research and experience have revealed the nature and power of a number of these factors, and it is now possible to see more clearly their effect on Japanese learners of English and on the ELEC campaign.

Interlingual Interference. A widely recognized factor in language learning is interlingual interference. Very simply, *interference* means that when students are learning a second language their first language "gets in the way." Common sense dictates that where the learners' native language and the target language are different, interference will be greatest and learning will be most difficult.

As experts have noted, the linguistic differences between Japanese and English are considerable, resulting in numerous difficulties for Japanese learners of English. "As a matter of basic linguistic structure, Japanese is related to no modern language, except Korean....[For Japanese students of English] there is almost no common ground to begin with as there is, say, for an American studying French or German."[175] "Japanese does not belong to the Indo-European family of languages...and...this fact makes learning English more difficult....English syntax differs radically from Japanese and therefore the construction of thought differs. Compared with English, Japanese has a simple phonetic system."[176]

These arguments, however, ignore the fact that English and Japanese do have a rather extensive "common ground" in the large number of English words that have been borrowed into Japanese over the years. In fact, "it is estimated that 8 per cent of Japanese vocabulary is English-based."[177] Much of this borrowing took place during the Meiji years, but another wave of English linguistic influence engulfed Japan after World War II and thousands of English words made their way into Japanese. Nevertheless, this lexical overlap is still relatively small. Furthermore, it does not reduce interference in the areas of syntax and phonology. In fact, some argue that it has resulted in a type of "*katakana* English" (reflecting the sounds represented by the *katakana* syllabary, which is used for writing foreign words in Japanese) that creates additional pronunciation problems for Japanese learners.[178]

Despite the "common sense" logic behind the idea of interlingual interference, the extent and the nature of interference is still a topic of debate—especially as it applies to grammar and vocabulary. Whitman and Jackson, for example, found little evidence of interference in the errors made by Japanese learners of English.[179] After examining the results of various studies, Taylor claimed that interference errors occur more frequently among language learners at the beginning level and that other processes are more responsible for errors at later stages.[180]   Much research in this area still remains to be done before this debate will be settled.

Even if interlingual influence is strong, it does not explain why Japanese pupils seem to have more difficulty learning English than do students from other language backgrounds (Samoan, Arabic, etc.) which are also radically different from English. Nor does it account for the fact that ELEC's *New Approach* textbooks, which were designed specifically for Japanese learners of English after a careful linguistic analysis and comparison had been done, still were not widely adopted in Japan. Other learner factors—especially learning style differences— are also important.

Learning Style Differences.   Learning style encompasses a number of dimensions—perceptual, social, cognitive, and affective. Each of these includes several factors. For example, learners' perceptual styles may be visual, auditory, tactile, or kinesthetic. In terms of their cognitive operations, learners may be divergent or convergent, serial or holistic, impulsive or reflective, etc. It would require an entire book to discuss all these factors. Therefore, this section will limit its focus to a few learning style factors that are particularly relevant to Japanese students of foreign languages.

Perceptual—Reliance on Visual Signals. An important feature of Japanese students' language learning style is their tendency to rely on visual, rather than aural, signals and to consider the written form the only "true" language. Many blame this Japanese learning pattern on the tradition of Chinese studies and the many hours Japanese pupils spend learning *kanji* (Chinese characters used in writing Japanese). For instance, as the ELEC effort was just beginning, Ichikawa warned, "Born and bred in such [a] peculiar linguistic environment, it is but natural that the Japanese become a visual-type people rather than an auditory-type, and in learning a foreign language fall into the habit of relying on the eye and not on the ear."[181]   This tendency was diametrically opposed to the beliefs held by Fries and his American colleagues at ELEC, who emphasized oral practice and stressed that speech is the primary form of any language, but they had little success in overcoming the tradition. In fact, it is still strong today. That "Japanese people are letter-oriented"[182] continues to be one of the obstacles to the widespread teaching of spoken English in Japan.

Social. A variety of social factors, such as group dominance, integration strategies, enclosure, congruence, cohesiveness, and size have been noted as affecting language learning.[183]   In Japan enclosure and isolation have been especially influential. First of all, the fact that Japan is "an isolated and inward-turning nation" is often given as an explanation for Japanese "ethnocentrism and xenophobia."[184]   Furthermore, the high enclosure and isolation of the Japanese people has created a situation where Japanese people have little contact with foreigners, so with few exceptions, Japanese students are exposed to English only in the classroom.

Within the Japanese classroom, social-communication factors, such as students' preferences for different types of linguistic interaction and learning activities, also play an important role. Generally speaking, "Japanese students are self-conscious, shy, reserved, afraid to make mistakes, [and] reluctant to speak out/up...."[185] This section will focus on three factors underlying these characteristics: the value accorded to silence, the degree of comfort with personal disclosure, and language shock.

Value Accorded to Silence.   In his discussion of Japanese communicative style, Ishii explains what he calls *enryo-sasshi* communication: "The Japanese have traditionally placed a high value on silence, believing that a person of few words is thoughtful, trustworthy, and respectable."[186]   Ishii's views are corroborated by others, who have noted, "In Japan silence is golden, and a talkative person is regarded as superficial."[187]

This cultural norm created problems for ELEC's reform effort since the rapid and frequent oral responses that students were expected to produce in an Oral Approach classroom required behavior that was incompatible with it. Even today, a problem in getting Japanese students to speak in the English classroom is the "high value placed on silence, particularly in the dignified male."[188]

Degree of Comfort with Personal Disclosure. Japanese and American communicative styles contrast in other important ways also. Barnlund investigated the amount of personal disclosure that American and Japanese speakers felt comfortable with and found that the Japanese "prefer an interpersonal style in which the self made accessible to others, that is, the 'public self,' is relatively small, while the proportion of the self that is not revealed, the 'private self,' is relatively large."[189] This was the opposite of the pattern found in Americans. Barnlund concluded that "Americans should, since threat is proportional to the extent of self-concealment, be defensive with fewer persons and in fewer topical areas. When threatened they should favor active-aggressive over passive-withdrawal techniques."[190] Not unexpectedly, he found the reverse pattern among Japanese. The implications for language-teaching methods, such as the Oral Approach, where overt, oral responses are expected, are obvious. Most Japanese students feel extremely uncomfortable in a class where such an approach is employed.

Language Shock. Those who deal with intercultural differences and adjustment are generally familiar with the concept of culture shock and how it can disrupt the normal functioning of an individual. Language shock has a similar potential for interfering with the language-learning process.

> In discussing what can be called language shock, Stengal (1937) points out that when learners attempt to speak a second language they often fear that they will appear comic. He compares the use of a second language with wearing fancy clothes. The adult learner may want to wear his fancy clothes, but he also fears criticism and ridicule. The child, however, sees language as a method of play and finds communication a source of pleasure. Thus, he doesn't fear his fancy clothes; he enjoys wearing them. Stengal states, "The adult will learn the new language more easily, the more of these infantile characteristics he has preserved."[191]

Narrowing the scope of concern to foreign language pronunciation, Fries himself declared that language learners must "throw off all restraint and self-consciousness as far as the making of strange sounds is concerned."[192]   Nevertheless, throwing off inhibitions is easier recommended than done. The fear of being ridiculed is a strong force in the minds of many adolescent and adult foreign language learners, especially in Japan.

To make matters worse, a learner may be subjected to embarrassment not only for incorrect pronunciation but for a "too correct" pronunciation as well. Stevick recounts how members of a Hebrew class had difficulty with the "hard h" (voiceless velar fricative) sound—even though they could pronounce it "with a high degree of accuracy." The problem occurred because it was a strange, "embarrassing" sound. "With each voicing of the phrase, there was uneasy laughter, bordering on the hilarious. One person said, 'When I pronounce it right, I get tingly all over.' Others joked about the need to get a drink of water. One person was gently kidded about how good his pronunciation was." Stevick concludes his account by referring to "the emotional price that some...students had to pay for sounding foreign."[193]   This price may be especially high when students are particularly sensitive to rejection, as most Japanese are.

Other experts agree. Noting the possibility that a learner's performance—good or bad—will bring on negative reactions from the teacher or the other students, Schumann warns that the learner who is sensitive to the negative reinforcing behavior of others would be made particularly anxious in such situations.[194] Likewise, Carroll explains:

> Willingness to try using the language, and to make errors, is somewhat connected with the learner's personality—not necessarily with what is commonly called "extroversion," but with a kind of self-control and confidence whereby the learner can attempt self-expression without feeling self-conscious or threatened by making errors and being corrected.[195]

Carroll concludes with the reminder that "in some cultures classroom errors are extremely embarrassing." He could very possibly have been thinking of the Japanese, who live in "an astonishingly shame-conscious society,"[196] and are generally "extremely sensitive to and concerned about social interaction and relationships."[197] In Japan, group support is important to an individual's security.[198] Consequently, Japanese "are characteristically hypersensitive about making mistakes in public, calling undue attention to themselves, or committing themselves prematurely to a position which may be wrong."[199]

As a result of these forces, Japanese students in foreign language classes typically "elect to remain silent rather than use the language and experience the embarrassment of making mistakes."[200] Harker provides examples, from an English conversation class for female Japanese, of how language shock (which he calls "cultural reserve") can have a detrimental effect.

> Even if students do have ideas that they might be prepared to express in class, the fact that in a class they are always part of a group can be a formidable barrier....The individual tends not to feel free to make a statement without getting group approval. For one student to show that she knows the answer to a question or has an idea of her own to offer seems to mean that she is showing herself to be better than those who do not have anything to say.
>
> Many times one sees a person who wants to volunteer first look around or even confer briefly with those nearby before venturing to speak out. The person who might want to speak up when others are silent fears that this might gain the disapproval of others....
>
> This group-mindedness has another aspect. From childhood, one of the chief sanctions used in disciplining children is laughter....The fear of making a mistake and being laughed at can create a paralysing state of mind that can inhibit the best of students.[201]

English teachers in Japan today generally agree that language shock is a difficult but important barrier to overcome, and some take specific steps to do so. For instance, the author of a recent English textbook designed specifically to help Japanese students overcome this socio-cultural obstacle writes:

> A festival is a marvelous opportunity for us, as human beings, to interact. We let down our hair. We relax. We forget our inhibitions. We don't worry about making fools of ourselves....Herein, I believe, lies the answer to helping the Japanese speak English better. This is a culture of reticence. For that reason, the Japanese are held in respect as perhaps the most polite and courteous people in the world. This reticence is also, unfortunately, an obstacle in speaking foreign languages. Instead of playing it safe by studying grammar until he is so worried about making mistakes that he can't speak anymore, the Japanese speaker, I believe, would be far better off "getting out" and talking.[202]

Unfortunately, the promoters of the Oral Approach in Japan apparently never considered this challenge or how to overcome it.

Cognitive. A wide variety of cognitive factors that affect learning have been identified by researchers. This section, however, will focus only on the most obvious and probably the most influential of these—

Japanese students' normal reliance on studial, analytic (as opposed to experiential, holistic) learning.

The typical Japanese approach to English study stresses conscious knowledge of grammar rules and memorization of long lists of vocabulary items. Edamatsu explains:

> One of the causes of the difficulty the Japanese have in learning English is that they are too bookish; they try to learn English the way they learned other subjects in school such as history, by reading about it, by memorizing facts, by poring over rules of grammar and pronunciation in textbooks (the way dead languages like Latin are studied), instead of using "live" practice the way a living language should be learned.[203]

Language learning experts agree that such an approach to learning English will not lead to fluency.[204]

Following a similar line of thinking, Krashen has argued that learners develop language proficiency in two ways: The first is through "acquisition," a subconscious process similar to first language acquisition, brought about by exposure to and communicative interaction in the target language. The second way is through "learning," an outcome of conscious study that gives the learner knowledge about the target language. According to Krashen, "acquisition" plays the central role in the development of language proficiency and in speech production, while "learned" knowledge has only one function—to act as an editor or "monitor" of linguistic "output." "Monitoring" occurs when learners use their conscious ("learned") knowledge of language rules to check and correct their performance in the foreign language. Monitoring, however, can take place only when learners have time to consciously access and use the rules they have learned. It also requires the language user to focus on the correctness of grammatical forms rather than on the message being communicated. For these reasons, monitoring may be possible when a person is writing, but it seriously impairs the process of speaking.[205] Consequently, "monitoring is most likely to occur on grammar tests and is least likely to occur in free conversation."[206]

Following Krashen's line of thinking, one might conclude that the reason Japanese learners experience problems in using English for communication is because what they have learned in their English classes in school consists of only a conscious knowledge of the rules of English. While this "learned" knowledge may be useful for monitoring, its value in the production of language is very limited. Also, inasmuch as monitoring requires processing time and focus on form, students who possess only learned knowledge about the target language will find it next to impossible to communicate in the oral modality since it requires them to speak at a rapid pace and concentrate on content. In sum, the studial cognitive style of most Japanese students and their reliance on formal classroom learning makes them monitor "over-users" "whose overconcern with conscious rules prevents them from speaking with any fluency at all."[207]

Affective. Perceptual, social, and cognitive aspects of learning style are all important, but students' feelings about the task of learning—its general objectives as well as specific learning activities—are equally critical. In the case of Japanese learners of English, factors such as their academic orientation, attitudes, motivation, and language ego seem to be especially influential. Unfortunately, the methodological approach that ELEC promoted paid little attention to these factors.

Academic Orientation. One advantage English teachers in Japan have enjoyed for at least a century is their students' favorable orientation toward schooling and good academic preparation. In contrast to many of the world's nations, Japan has a long history of schooling. Consequently, as Japan tried to rebuild its economy and its school system after the devastation of war, it could count on an "accumulated expertise" in things academic.[208] Dillon and Dillon explain further:

> Japan's is a highly literate society that places great value on learning and achievement....[The typical student of English] has grown up in a world of books and facts, of language used both for artistic and communicative purposes....The rigorous Japanese educational system and constant contact with the written word have left [the Japanese student] better prepared than students from many other countries to succeed in an academic program of English studies.[209]

Nevertheless, strong academic orientation is only one learner factor. Other characteristics of Japanese learners, which may not be so conducive to students' success, are of equal or greater importance and take on special significance when the object of study is a foreign language.

Attitudes and Motivation. Students' attitudes toward the subject of study are important in any course, and language learning is no exception. "As early as 1949, W. R. Jones demonstrated that attainment of proficiency in Welsh as a second language was correlated with attitudes toward the study of Welsh."[210] Research has also determined that students' attitudes toward various groups and individuals, such as their teachers, peers, and parents, determine how much and what kind of learning takes place in the classroom.[211] In addition, the attitudes that pupils hold toward the target language group are particularly crucial, for they strongly influence motivation. "Negative, prejudiced attitudes and stereotypes about another ethnolinguistic group, quite independent of language learning abilities or verbal intelligence, can upset and disturb the motivation needed to learn the other group's language.[212]

Gardner and Lambert, a pair of leading researchers in this area, have posited two different motivational orientations for language learning—integrative and instrumental. A learner who is integratively oriented desires to learn a language for purposes of meeting with, talking to, finding out about, and perhaps even becoming like its speakers, whom the learner admires and values. On the other hand, a learner with an instrumental orientation has little interest in the speakers of the target language. His reasons for learning it are more utilitarian, such as occupational advancement or recognition from members of his own native language group.   Reasoning "that some process like identification, extended to a whole ethnolinguistic community and coupled with an inquisitiveness and sincere interest in the other group, must underlie the long-term motivation needed to master a second language," Gardner and Lambert favor integrative motivation as being most conducive to effective language learning.[213]   They hypothesize that "the student's attitudinal orientation toward [the target language] group...will influence his progress and efficiency in adopting these novel and strange linguistic habits into his own repertoire, "[214] and argue further "that second-language achievement might be facilitated by a favorable and accepting orientation toward ethnolinguistic groups different from one's own."[215]   Spolsky, after conducting considerable research on language attitudes, concludes similarly, that "a person learns a language better when he wants to be a member of the group speaking that language."[216]

This view—that integrative motivation is more powerful than instrumental—has been widely accepted.   Subsequent research, however, has revealed that the motivational orientation associated with the successful development of target language proficiency varies depending on the setting. In settings where acquiring the second language is neither necessary nor commonplace, integratively motivated learners generally achieve greater proficiency.   In other social situations, however, an anti-integrative motivation correlates with proficiency in the target language. In sum, Gardner and Lamberts' two simple categories are actually complex constructs that interact with a variety of social and psychological variables.[217]

In the Japanese context, things become even more complicated.   It is generally agreed that most high school students study English in order to pass the entrance examinations, but beyond that point, it becomes quite difficult to determine what the Japanese motivations for learning English and their attitudes toward English speakers really are.   Throughout Japanese history, it has been common to classify Europeans (and later, Americans) as *gaijin* (foreigners) and "barbarians."   Yet, Japan has also had a long-term love affair with the West.   The modern-day social craze for things Western (and for merchandise with conspicuous, though often incorrect, English words as part of the decoration) is nothing new.   This pattern dates back at least as far as 1590, shortly after the Portuguese first made contact with Japan.   Following a cyclical pattern, the Japanese love-hate relationship for foreign things has continued to the present.   Since the end of World War II, "English and all things American" have enjoyed a "characteristically exalted status,"[218] which would appear to encourage the learning of English by the Japanese.   Yet, as history demonstrates, it is really a "vacillating, ambivalent feeling that often is only superficial."[219] There is little question about where the true loyalties of the Japanese lie. When Japanese adults enrolled in English classes in Osaka were surveyed regarding their motivation for learning English, the reasons that received the highest ratings were primarily instrumental in nature (to visit another country; to be an educated person; interest in the language, literature, and culture; to fulfill a school requirement). The most integrative of reasons (to have English-speaking friends) received the lowest rating.[220] Thus, a paradox emerges. On the surface, the Japanese appear to be imitating English-speakers, but on the other hand they definitely do not want to become Americans. At least within some individuals, if not in Japanese society generally, these conflicting feelings must create tension that can inhibit English learning.

Language Ego. Another, related affective phenomenon is language ego, a notion that explains the ability of some people to acquire native-like pronunciation in a foreign language.

> In the course of general ego development the child acquires body ego by which he becomes aware of the limits of his physical being and learns to distinguish himself from the object world around him. In a similar fashion...the child acquires a sense of the boundaries of his language....In the early stages of development, language ego boundaries are permeable, but later they become fixed and rigid.[221]

> Language ego...refers to self-representation with physical outlines and firm boundaries: "Grammar and syntax are the solid structure on which speech hangs, lexis the flesh that gives it body, and pronunciation its very core. Pronunciation is the most salient aspect of the language ego, the hardest to penetrate (to acquire in a new language), the most difficult to lose (in one's own)."[222]

Given their high degree of group mindedness, it is likely that the language ego of Japanese students is typically very rigid and affects their pronunciation ability in English. Commenting on this idea, one observer of English teaching in Japan recently wrote:

> It is interesting that women, who tend to be less hungup [sic] on their Japaneseness and asserting themselves, tend to be better at language acquisition than their male counterparts. Could it be that the biggest obstacle to English learning (following the education system itself) is that Japanese, while admittedly not eager to assert themselves aloud, actually house extraordinarily large egos which make it difficult to let go and absorb a foreign language on its own terms?[223]

In a well-known experiment designed to determine the effect of "language ego," Guiora et al. reasoned that if language learners' levels of inhibition were lowered, ego rigidity would be reduced and ego permeability enhanced. To test this hypothesis, they gave subjects varying amounts of alcohol and then tested the subjects' pronunciation in a foreign language. They found that subjects who ingested a small amount of alcohol (one and one-half ounces) had pronunciation that was better than that of either the no alcohol or more alcohol (two or three ounces) groups. Of course, serving drinks in all foreign language classrooms is not a feasible solution. Nevertheless, the discovery that inhibitions and language ego boundaries can be lowered and, in the process, pronunciation improved, is important. Other ways of lowering students' language inhibitions should be explored. Stevick expresses the opinion that "intelligent awareness of factors such as these will do more to improve the teaching of pronunciation than all the charts, diagrams and mechanical devices that we have often depended on in the past."[224]

To summarize, a variety of learning style factors—perceptual, social, cognitive, and affective—exert considerable influence on the process of teaching/learning a foreign language. Because of these factors, most instructional situations "are almost impossible to change for the better simply by improving instruction[al] methods and other external conditions."[225] On the other hand, careful consideration of these learning style differences when plans concerning teaching methods and materials are made, can help teachers avoid, remove, or overcome these blocks to learning. In fact, "a form of learning close to their social milieu could provide Japanese students a supportive learning experience...."[226] In other words, "equipped with a better understanding of the basic cultural patterns that make Japanese students behave in ways they do, the EFL teacher can guide them toward successful learning experiences."[227] Unfortunately, this realization came many years too late to help ELEC achieve its goal of reforming English language teaching in Japan.

Physiological Differences. A traditionally popular explanation for the difficulties experienced by Japanese learners of English and other foreign languages is the physiological differences between Japanese and Occidentals. For example, in a letter to the *Japan Times* one reader referred to the "well known fact" that Japanese are incapable of acquiring perfect English pronunciation due to "the difference in physical constitution between Occidentals and Japanese."[228] While other readers were quick to reply that this "fact" can be easily shown to be false "since second-generation Japanese Americans have no such difficulties,"[229] the idea still enjoys widespread acceptance in Japan.

In the past few years, a new twist on this classic explanation for Japanese learners' difficulties with English has gained considerable popularity in Japan. It is the hypothesis advanced by Tadanobu Tsunoda, a Japanese scientist, in his book *Nihonjin no No* (The Japanese Brain),[230] that "Japanese brains function differently from other people's."[231]

> Such fundamental physiological differences, Tsunoda argues, make it particularly difficult for Japanese to learn English. He further claims that foreign language acquisition may be detrimental to the development of creativity. Japanese who manage to achieve fluency in English are said to run the risk of developing warped personalities.[232]

Since Tsunoda claims that the differences in the way the Japanese brain functions occur "not because of inheritance or conditioning but because of the peculiarities of the Japanese language," his argument cannot be disproven by reference to second-generation Japanese who have grown up speaking English.[233] In fact, he has conducted laboratory experiments that he claims prove that this difference exists. Nevertheless, their validity and replicability are questionable. One investigator of this work concludes that "new research into neurological systems may allow us to discard the theory totally. Until then, however, researchers need to be skeptical of the implications of Tsunoda's research."[234]

Perhaps the most impressive thing about these theories is the popularity they enjoy among the Japanese, in spite of their shallow, if not patently false nature. "While discreet skepticism about Tsunoda's research methods appears among some of his colleagues, the overall framework of his ideas is tolerated and even welcomed."[235] In fact, *Nihonjin no No* has been a best-seller in Japan. It belongs to a "genre of popular and semi-academic writings known as *Nihonjin-ron,* which may be loosely translated as 'Theorizing about the Japanese people.'"[236]

Although such physiologically based explanations for language learning difficulties may be spurious, they are still taken seriously by many Japanese. Therefore, while the actual physiological differences and their effects, if any, may be negligible, the attitudes toward foreign language learning that these ideas create are very real and powerful. In sum, even though Tsunoda's hypothesis may be dismissed, this "intense preoccupation on the part of the Japanese with their own ethnicity" should not be overlooked.[237]

Capacities

In Japan in the 1950s, educational facilities were in short supply. Occupation reforms encouraged more Japanese to go to school and for more years, but many school buildings had been destroyed during the war resulting in a shortage of classrooms. After the war, even though schools were built as quickly as possible, this construction required large amounts of both time and money. Thus, for many years—including the years during which ELEC was trying to reform Japanese ELT—schools in Japan were extremely overcrowded, classes were large, and physical facilities were spartan. Most English teachers could only dream of language laboratories like those that were being installed in many U.S. schools during these years. The cost of creative new textbooks was often prohibitive, while supplementary materials for teaching English were virtually nonexistent. Under these conditions, the likelihood of English teachers' changing to the Oral Approach was low.

Educational Philosophy

Another important factor to consider in any innovation-implementation campaign is the educational philosophy that intended users adhere to. In Japan today, teachers generally divide into two camps regarding the purpose of English teaching, just as they did in the days of ELEC's campaign. Many teachers, administrators, and even students feel that the proper aim of English study is cultural, and they "despise anything practical."[238] In this philosophy, the purposes of studying a second language are for students to develop their intelligence, to understand their own native language grammar and culture, and to read literature in the target language—even if they never actually speak it. Others argue that the proper aim of English study is practical, providing students with the language skills they need to communicate in real-life situations. In this case, speaking skills are paramount, and an oral orientation is most appropriate.

Unfortunately for ELEC, the cultural side predominated in the 1950s and 1960s. At the Specialists' Conference, Ichikawa reported, "The prevailing idea among the teachers of English, and especially among university professors, is that we teach and study English in order to elevate our culture."[239]

According to a recent survey conducted by the Japan Association of College English Teachers (JACET), however, the practical side now seems to be gaining—even at the university level.

> The major purpose of TEFL [teaching English as a foreign language] according to 60.1% of the students is international communication....40.4% of the students feel that gaining knowledge of Western culture is the most important purpose...29.1% of the students also believe that TEFL is important for cultural and intellectual training in order to become international minded....These figures suggest that the students seem to regard TEFL as training for communicative ability in English in order to be ready to undertake international activities. They are not so interested in TEFL training for polishing an intellectual mind.[240]

Although many Japanese professors of English do not seem to be as interested in practical English for communication as their students are, the percentage is growing. In the same JACET survey, 47 percent of the teachers felt that the major purpose of learning English is international communication. "A comparison of the teachers' surveys in 1968 and 1983 shows a stronger inclination [in 1983] to emphasize communicative skills."[241] Encouraging though they may be, these attitudinal/philosophical changes are taking place several decades too late to have helped ELEC's campaign.

Examinations

In most instructional settings, examinations not only reflect but also determine what aspects of the teaching/learning process receive attention. This influence is particularly strong in Japan, where high school and university entrance examinations are of critical importance In fact, according to some, preparing for these exams is "the whole 'purpose' of Japanese primary and secondary education."[242] High scores are the key to acceptance at the best possible school. Later, when college graduates are ready to begin their careers, they are chosen by prospective employers primarily on the basis of the prestige of the university they attended. "Hence the one chance of 'success' in life depends on the entrance exams...."[243]

Even though English is officially an elective for secondary school students, the fact that it is a compulsory part of these examinations explains why virtually all Japanese teenagers study English.[244] Nevertheless, the power of these examinations results in more than high enrollment. This situation, in which "the greatest motivation for [Japanese high school students'] study of English is to pass the final [university] entrance examination,"[245] also generates pressure for teachers and students to focus on those things that will lead to success on the examinations. In other words, examination "backwash" is powerful in Japan. The nature of the exam determines both what teachers teach and what students study. For this reason, nowadays as well as in 1956, "the university entrance examination rules over the upper secondary English teaching."[246]

Sadly, for those who wish that the development of spoken English skills could be encouraged more, these powerful examinations do not test proficiency in spoken English. Rather, they focus on fine points of grammar, low frequency vocabulary, and translation skills. The nature of these examinations is regarded as "the worst obstacle" to the teaching of spoken English.[247] Some go so far as to claim that the tests "are designed to actually stifle oral ESL work."[248] Whether or not that is true, there is general agreement that "a junior or senior high school teacher who spends time on oral English would actually be doing a disservice to his students."[249] This state of affairs, of course, spells trouble for the diffusion and implementation in Japan of a language-teaching approach whose orientation is predominantly oral.

Laments about the problems created by the nature of these English examinations are by no means new. As long ago as 1914, the chairman of a Conference of Experts on the Teaching of English in Japan placed the blame for the lack of oral English skills among Japanese students squarely on the examination system:

> Middle school graduates cannot grasp by an [sic] ear the general meaning of even simple sentences. It is true that pupils could not express their ideas in English and neglected the study of the coloqual [sic]. But for that the higher schools were responsible. It would be easy to remedy that defect if only the higher schools would have oral tests bearing on hearing and speaking besides the written examination.[250]

Many have suggested reforms to these examinations. Harasawa, for instance, considers it "all important" that the English portion of these exams be "made to attach 50 per cent weight to the oral-aural skills, thereby ceasing to distort the teaching of English at the junior- and senior-high-school level."[251] He neatly summarizes the entire examination-reform issue with the following statement:

> I consider this [the changing of the examinations to give equal weight to oral-aural skills in English] the only categorical imperative, the minimum that must be required of the policy-makers for English language teaching in this country, for I am convinced that other necessary reforms would naturally follow. For example, high-school teachers would come to be trained or would retrain themselves well enough in a matter of years, because otherwise they would be unable to perform their professional duties effectively; they would willingly ask the authorities to provide them with opportunities for in-service training, even during their vacations.[252]

Of course, even if one accepts Harasawa's argument, the question of how to change the examinations remains. Some well intentioned but misguided reformers, "urge the ministry to take the initiative to change them," not realizing that "basically the responsibility lies with each university."[253] Persuading thousands of conservative, entrenched professors at hundreds of universities to change the nature of the examinations that they have used for years is no simple task.

As early as 1955, before ELEC was officially formed, Bryant had recommended, "An early objective should be the modification of university and senior high school entrance examinations…, but the examiners must first be convinced of the value of such revision and shown how it can be effected without lowering educational standards."[254] The next year, as the ELEC campaign was just getting under way, Takagi also proposed that efforts be directed toward reforming the English examinations. He noted:

> The kind of questions asked in entrance examinations has a tremendous bearing upon teaching methods and the attitude of the students towards learning English in secondary schools. It is very desirable that these examination questions, while serving as a good means of testing the ability of the candidates, also encourage the adoption of salutary methods of learning English in secondary schools.[255]

A few months later, in July of 1956, as the agenda for the Specialists' Conference was planned, university entrance examination questions were again a topic of discussion. At the conference itself, several speakers addressed this issue and pointed out that the "sole objective" of the examinations appeared to be "the determination of some simple methods of sorting and elimination."[256] The ELEC reformers asserted their "earnest desire to have the achievement test conducted always as a means of evaluation rather than as a means of selection," and reform of university entrance examinations was one of the four major conclusions and recommendations reached at the end of the Specialists' Conference.[257]

Nevertheless, it was not enough merely to recognize the problem and discuss it. Action was called for. Unfortunately, ELEC never took such action. In the following years, great effort was expended on accomplishing the first three recommendations of the Specialists' Conference. Committees were set up to develop materials and train teachers and much work was done. No one, however, dealt with the examination system. This fourth recommendation, that the nature of the exams be changed, was largely ignored.

Given the fact that ELEC had no linkage with Japanese universities, maybe there was nothing that it could do. Of course, ELEC might have tried to work with the Japanese universities, but this would have been extremely difficult. During the Occupation, Japanese university professors had been most resistant to (and most alienated by) American attempts at reforming Japanese education. Moreover, ELEC had pledged to remain an independent force, without compromising ties to any universities, Japanese or American.

Besides, ELEC's leaders—especially the American ones—seemed to think that the superiority of their new methods and materials would be enough to overcome any obstacles placed in their way. Fries, for example, "did not concern himself with 'problems' such as the exam system."[258] Eventually, however, he did realize the necessity of addressing this concern. Nevertheless, he still relied on a "better mousetrap" argument and still underestimated the power of examination backwash in Japan (note his use of "merely" below). Speaking of the goals of a typical Japanese learner, he said:

> Or his final goal may be *merely the passing of an examination for a university*—an examination in which *translation is the only requirement* [italics added]. No matter what the final goal of the person who starts to learn English, I believe...that what we have called the "oral approach" is the most efficient, the most time-saving way to begin the study of English.[259]

Nevertheless, Japanese teachers of English did not take the examinations so lightly, and grammar-translation backwash constituted a serious obstacle to the spread of the Oral Approach. For instance, although he called the effect of the entrance examinations "the most pitiable thing,"[260] one ELEC veteran's final conclusion was that "for the present, until the exams change, grammar-translation teaching is 'a necessary evil.'"[261]

Even today, many English teachers in Japan are still trying to overcome this obstacle to the teaching of oral English skills.[262]   At the same time, many of the factors that prevented ELEC from changing the examination system also persist.   In fact, although there are many complaints about the nature of the examinations, there are also reasons for not changing them.

The relationship between the size of Japan's ELT program and the type of examination questions is strong. Administering oral tests to the hordes of Japanese students who take the entrance exams every year would be next to impossible. Speaking tests cannot be given *en masse*, as written exams are, and a serious personnel shortage would result.[263] This situation challenged ELEC also. As early as 1956, Ichikawa noted that "more than 10,000 apply for entrance to the University of Tokyo" every year. "Since it is impossible to test such large numbers in *hearing* and *speaking*, questions are limited to translations...and other tests requiring *writing*. The scope of tests in entrance examinations being thus limited, it is natural that applicants should prepare in such a way as to meet these requirements" [italics in original].[264]

But the difficulty of testing the English speaking ability of large numbers of Japanese students in a short period of time is not the only reason for not changing the English portion of the examinations for university entrance.   The debate between those who advocate the "practical" objectives of oral English study and those who defend the traditional "cultural" purpose of language study, which is more closely allied with the nature of the exams, is a long standing one and has not yet been resolved. A related factor militating against changing the university entrance exams is the training and professional predilections of most university-level English professors in Japan, who continue a tradition of favoring the more "academically respectable" literary aspects of English to the detriment of speaking skills. A less frequently mentioned but very pragmatic argument is that the primary function of the English examinations is not to determine examinees' proficiency in English but rather to sort them. In other words the purpose of the tests is to measure students' intelligence and/or their diligence in studying more than their actual proficiency in the language.   The English portion of the traditional exams performs this sorting function very well.   In support of this argument, in a recent discussion about why English is taught to junior and senior high school students in Japan and why the exams test such difficult, obscure, and useless points of English grammar, one teacher concluded that the purpose of English teaching in Japanese schools was "to stratify, not to educate—i.e., to separate the smart from the stupid, the diligent from the lazy.   Content, thus, is not important; having students memorize the telephone book would be just as useful."[265]

In sum, proposing that the examinations be changed is easy, and many have done it.   On the other hand, overcoming the barriers to change and actually modifying the exams is a far more difficult task, one that has not yet been accomplished.   Nor is the prospect for change very bright.   As C. P. Snow once said of a similarly entrenched examination system in Great Britain: "Academic patterns change more slowly than any others....I used to think that it would be about as hard to change say, the Oxford and Cambridge scholarship examination as to conduct a major revolution.   I now believe that I was over-optimistic."[266]   In Japan, although favorable backwash from modified examinations could have done a great deal to encourage the changes ELEC sought, the campaign was never in a position to create such modifications and never benefited from them.

For modern-day reformers desirous of encouraging the spread of oral English in Japan, a glimmer of hope is on the horizon.   Tape-recorded listening comprehension sections, which can be delivered *en masse* and encourage the development of oral English skills, have appeared on a number of examinations in recent years.   "About 30 prefectural boards of education and 36 universities now use tapes."[267]   These changes are undoubtedly the result of many forces.   Nevertheless, some ELEC workers find solace in the thought that "ELEC may have contributed a little—in the impetus."[268]

INTER-ELEMENTAL FACTORS

Of course, the user system, the resource system, and the innovation do not exist independently—in separate spheres.   Rather, these   different systems are linked together and need to harmonize with each other if the innovation-implementation effort is to be successful.   Inter-elemental factors that inhibit or facilitate the implementation of an innovation across cultural boundaries include compatibility, linkage, reward, proximity, and synergism.

Compatibility

Compatibility considerations are important in reform efforts concerned with language teaching, as Richards points out:

> The successful implementation of a language program may depend on how well it matches the expectations, learning styles, and values of the learners.   Many

contemporary methods of language teaching make culturally based demands on teachers and learners. It is not a cultural universal, for example, that students should be talkative and communicative in classrooms.[269]

Of course, perfect matches are seldom found—especially when directed contact change campaigns cross cultural boundaries. Regarding the teaching of English to the Japanese, Otani notes, "The European and American cultural system behind English, which is utterly foreign to ours, also aggravates our difficulty in learning English."[270] He goes on to claim that "the linguistic and cultural barriers to efficient learning of English are more formidable [in Japan] than in almost any other country in the world."[271] In a case such as ELEC's, therefore, planning and adaptation to increase compatibility would seem to be particularly crucial

Unfortunately, concerns with compatibility were minimal at ELEC—especially in its early years. The decision to promote Fries' Oral Approach seems to have been based more on his prestige in America and his persuasiveness at the Specialists' Conference than on the Oral Approach's compatibility with the Japanese situation. In fact, because of the revolutionary ideals held by key ELEC supporters, it seems probable that Fries' approach was chosen because it was so different from traditional Japanese practices for teaching foreign languages. ELEC's "end-run" approach to bringing about change was also incompatible with the Japanese school system in many ways.

The result, as has been discussed in various sections of this chapter, was frequently some type of conflict that reduced ELEC's successes. More concern with compatibility and planning to reduce or at least deal with incompatibilities might have eliminated many of these problems.

Linkage

Richards points out a number of special types of linkage relationships that seem to be especially crucial in the spread of language-teaching innovations: professional teaching organizations, universities, professional journals, and official educational agencies.[272] Unfortunately, in almost every one of these areas, ELEC had trouble. Part of the problem was that it was never clearly decided whether or not ELEC would establish relationships with other institutions. There were conflicting opinions in this regard.

On the one hand, it was recognized that to be successful ELEC needed the support of established Japanese institutions. In 1956 McLean advised Rockefeller, "If this idea is worth doing, it must have the support of some established Japanese institution or institutions. It should not be something apart."[273] Another idea was to place ELEC under some kind of American umbrella. After consulting with Fries and Twaddell, McLean recommended that ELEC "try to get a committee concerned with this project under either the American Council on Education or the American Council of Learned Societies."[274] Still another recommendation was to "discover who does the teaching and what organizations they have formed" and then work through them as opinion leaders.[275] Later, as the ELEC campaign got under way, its Japanese leaders hoped that "universities, institutes, and societies" would "cooperate harmoniously under the over-all-plan of the Central Committee."[276]

On the other hand, over the years English teaching in Japan had developed a variety of "cleavages." Antagonism, to a greater or lesser degree, existed

> between rival scholars of the same and different generations, governmental and private institutions, academic and business circles, rival organizations in the English language field, language and literature professors, lower and upper secondary teachers, American and British trained scholars, Japanese and foreign teachers resident in Japan, and between Japanese who have studied abroad and those who have not.[277]

Not wanting to become tied to any "school of thought" or get embroiled in any existing interinstitutional feuds, some leaders jealously guarded ELEC's independence.[278]

In the end, this latter sentiment prevailed, and ELEC established linkage with few (if any) other organizations. In 1960, Overton proudly noted that this was one of ELEC's "unique characteristics": "While it endorses the 'oral approach' in the teaching of English, it is bound to no particular school of linguistics. It has no special ties to any interested groups, foreign or Japanese. It operates independently of the Japanese Ministry of Education."[279] In retrospect, this approach seems to have been a serious mistake. Many of ELEC's problems might have been avoided, or at least been easier to overcome, if ELEC had enjoyed the benefit of appropriate Japanese support networks.

Professional Teaching Organizations. As early as 1955, Bryant recommended that "a realistic, long-range effort to improve English must...first consider which groups are most interested in its improvement and which would be most influential, and then try to insure their cooperation by offering them participation in the effort."[280]

Today there are many organizations of English teachers dedicated to improving the teaching of English in Japan. There were not so many in the 1950s. The Japan Association of Language Teachers (JALT) did not exist at that time. In fact, neither did JALT's parent organization, TESOL (a U.S.-based international association of Teachers of English to Speakers of Other Languages, founded in 1966). JACET, the Japan Association of College English Teachers, started in 1961, long before JALT but still well after Fries' initial visits and the founding of ELEC. Therefore, it was not available for ELEC to establish linkage with. Besides, because of American meddling in Japanese higher education during the Occupation, most university professors could probably not have been counted on to support a reform campaign promoting an American method.

Other Japanese English-teacher organizations, however, did exist at the time ELEC was formed. There was the *Nihon Eibun Gakkai* (an association of college teachers of English literature and linguistics). Founded in 1916, it was a very powerful organization. Nevertheless, it was also very traditional. As far as can be determined, ELEC wisely established no contact with this association. Besides consisting of college professors (generally resistant to American innovations) the *Nihon Eibun Gakkai* was also radically different from ELEC in both its interests and purposes. Conflict with ELEC, rather than support, might have been inevitable.

The Institute for Research on English Teaching (IRET), established by Harold Palmer in the 1920s and revived after the war, proudly claimed to be "the oldest progressive organization in the field." Nevertheless, it did not seem to be a likely candidate to provide support for ELEC either. In fact, Sanki Ichikawa, the institute's director, argued that it "should be the sponsor of any new program."[281] Despite this initial jealousy, Ichikawa accepted an invitation to be a member of ELEC's central committee and even spoke at the ELEC Specialists' Conference. This connection was about as close as ELEC ever got to establishing linkage with any professional organization in Japan.

The National Federation of Prefectural English Teachers' Organizations, *Zen-Ei-Ren*, a very widespread organization of junior and senior high school English teachers in Japan, with a membership of 60,000 in 1966, was founded in 1951, only a few years before ELEC.[282] One of the founders of *Zen-Ei-Ren*. was Genji Takahashi, who was also a member ELEC. Given that connection, and because of ELEC's focus on reforming Japanese ELT beginning at the lower secondary level, a connection between *Zen-Ei-Ren* and ELEC would have been both natural and beneficial— especially to ELEC.

The possibility of cooperation with *Zen-Ei-Ren* and with the IRET was discussed by ELEC leaders as early as 1956.[283] However, with the exception of personal contacts (in which individual IRET and *Zen-Ei-Ren* leaders worked with ELEC), ELEC established no official relationships with any Japanese teacher organizations in its early years.[284] The failure to establish this type of support network seriously damaged ELEC's chances of making a significant impact on English language teaching in Japan.

Years later, ELEC seemed to have learned its lesson and began

> cooperating with other groups concerned with English teaching such as IRLT (Institute for Research in Language Teaching) [sic], *Zen-eiren* (National Federation of English Teachers' Organizations) [sic], JACET (Japan Association of College English Teachers), COLTD (Council on Language Teaching Development), etc., by participating in conferences of joint sponsorship or by offering facilities for their activities.[285]

If ELEC had started such cooperative efforts earlier, the success of its campaign to revolutionize ELT in Japan might have been greater.

Universities. In the United States, Fries and the Oral Approach were associated with the then highly prestigious University of Michigan program. In fact, the Oral Approach became known as the "Michigan method." This connection encouraged the spread of the Oral Approach in America.

In post-war World War II Japan, in large part because of reforms attempted by Occupation authorities, university prestige was extremely important. For this reason, in his 1955 report Bryant recommended that ELEC establish relationships with and work through prestigious Japanese universities.

> The government's Tokyo University of Education (*Kyoiku Daigakku*), as the former higher normal school of greatest prestige in the country, should probably be the locus of a pilot program, as perhaps should Hiroshima University, which has merged with the second ranking normal school.... I was politely warned that such new institutions as International Christian University, no matter how admirable their English teaching programs, are foreign in origin and have not proved their academic excellence in other fields; and that it would be unwise to make them central in an English teaching project.[286]

Nevertheless, Bryant's recommendation was apparently ignored. ELEC did not establish relations with any important Japanese universities; nor did any Japanese university officially support the Oral Approach. A few private university campuses (not nearly as important in Japan as the large national universities) were occasionally used as sites for ELEC's summer seminars, but even they didn't have any official connection with ELEC.

Things might have been different. The first ELEC summer program was scheduled to be held at International Christian University, and "the ICU people were enthusiastic to cooperate with ELEC."[287] Nevertheless, Fries himself refused to go to ICU. His ultimatum, "We're *not* going to ICU and we'll have our *own* staff without *ICU* assistance [italics in original]," foreshadowed both immediate and long-term problems relative to ELEC's relations with Japanese universities.[288] As a result of Fries' resistance, the summer seminar was held at *Toyoeiwa Jogakuin*, a junior high school near International House, not nearly as powerful or prestigious as even a young, private university. Later, perhaps seeing the need for university support after all, Fries tried to court the favor of Japanese university professors. There is little information on how he did this, but according to one ELEC leader, he tried to do too much too fast. "He tried to convert them all at once," and it was "all in vain." As might have been expected in the "reverse course" years, "the universities were very adamant and independent."[289]

In 1959, when he was no longer working with ELEC, Fries clearly recognized the crucial nature of university support for any reform effort. He penned, "It has always been my belief that if this kind of work is to succeed finally in Japan and be a permanent contribution it must be supported by the colleges and universities through which the future teachers of Japan must go."[290]   It is a pity that ELEC's leaders did not come to this realization earlier. Without doubt, linkages with key Japanese universities would have made the story of ELEC substantially different.

On the other hand, even if ELEC had tried to establish contacts with Japanese universities in order to gain support for its revolutionary reform campaign, the attempt might have been to no avail. For many years, the universities—especially the most prestigious universities—continued to be "the real centers of conservatism both in their entrance exams and in their classes."[291]

Professional Journals.   In the United States, the University of Michigan had its own journal, *Language Learning*.   It spread the news of Fries' successes across the nation and lent prestige, power, and credibility to his Oral Approach.

In Japan, ELEC also had a publication, the *ELEC Bulletin*.   Although it was a decent periodical, it never approached becoming as influential as *Language Learning*.   Instead of enjoying the prestige that might have come had it been associated with an important university, it seemed more like a commercial, house organ.   As a result, the Oral Approach was not so well supported in Japan as it had been in the United States, but at least the *ELEC Bulletin* provided some outreach to Japanese teachers of English

Official Educational Agencies.   To illustrate the value of support from official educational agencies, Richards gives the example of the Direct Method, which in 1902—with the official endorsement of the minister of education—became the sole approved method for foreign language teaching in France (and later, by the same process, in Germany).[292]   Such authoritative endorsements are undoubtedly very powerful, especially in countries where the school system is highly centralized.

In Japan, the Ministry of Education, which had been decentralized during the Occupation but had quickly regained most of its former powers in the post-Occupation years, wielded great influence during the time of the ELEC campaign.   The support it could have provided would have been extremely valuable.   Nevertheless, as noted in the section on authority and administration, the Ministry of Education was, at best, neutral, and in the eyes of many, even antagonistic toward ELEC.   Whatever the case may have been, ELEC never enjoyed the benefits that such a powerful, supporting linkage could have provided.

In summary, ELEC failed to establish valuable linkages with professional teaching organizations, universities, and official educational agencies.   ELEC's American sponsors finally realized their error in attempting to keep ELEC "independent," but that realization came too late to help ELEC.   The Ford and Rockefeller Foundation representatives found it easier to start over than to backtrack.   Therefore, in 1967, as ELEC support was being phased out, they formed the Committee for Cooperation on English in Japan (CCEJ), which hoped "to work closely with existing organizations."[293]

Reward

Given the large size of Japan's ELT program as well as ELEC's lack of power over teachers in the Japanese school system, ELEC could not function as a reward system.   It was hoped, however, that the "relative advantage" of the Oral Approach would be reward enough to encourage teachers to adopt the Oral Approach.   Unfortunately, because of factors such as the nature of the English sections of the university entrance examinations, few teachers felt that using the Oral Approach would be to their advantage.

In fact, because of cultural and school system factors, Japanese teachers' potential rewards for trying the Oral Approach were few, and the personal costs were high. To learn how to use the Oral Approach, they would have had to invest their own time, energy, and money—all three of which were preciously scarce for teachers. Furthermore, trying out the Oral Approach in class would have made those teachers whose English speaking skills were deficient (that is, most of them) "run the risk of making mistakes" in front of their pupils.[294] In sum, the classic "teacher's predicament" regarding innovation was especially bad for Japanese teachers during the time of the ELEC campaign.

On the other hand, teachers who did not try to change ran no risks. As one veteran teacher/administrator later put it, "Why should they change? They are paid."[295] In other words, teachers' salaries remained the same regardless of the method they used. In 1955, when Bryant did his survey of ELT in Japan, he noted the same fact.

> Under the present secondary school system, young teachers have no real incentive to improve their ability, for both promotion and salary increases depend on seniority and the number of children a teacher has, while opportunities for appointment as leading teacher or principal depend on the applicant's having graduated from a good higher school.[296]

Thus, there was no real motivation for most Japanese teachers of English to implement the Oral Approach, and there were some powerful reasons for their not doing so. It was only natural that they would prefer to continue using traditional methods. In fact, it would have been truly surprising if many teachers had spent extra time and effort to learn and use the new, unfamiliar, and hence more difficult Oral Approach.

Proximity

To the detriment of the ELEC campaign, the only type of proximity its resource and user systems enjoyed was temporal. The physical distance between Japan and the United States was great and created a number of problems. Although most of the ELEC workers lived in Japan, several of the key figures, such as Fries and Twaddell, seldom spent more than a few months per year there. Although these leaders worked on the materials and summer programs during the rest of the year, the distance between them and their colleagues in Japan created difficulties in communication. When problems arose, correspondence was a poor substitute for conversation. It took valuable time to write letters, and even by air mail they took many days to travel between Japan and the United States. In addition, with written communication the potential for misinterpretation was especially great, particularly when the correspondents had different linguistic and cultural backgrounds. Even when the Americans were in Japan, the great cultural distance between the Japanese and the Americans created difficulties. Because of their experience with students from other nations, ELT educators like Fries were more aware and tolerant of cultural differences, but the American experts' lack of familiarity with Japanese cultural factors still proved to be a common problem, as several sections in this chapter (e.g., learning style factors, educational philosophy, etc.) have pointed out.

Synergism

Synergistic power depends on the number, variety, frequency, and persistence of forces associated with the implementation of the innovation, as well as on the amount of cooperation and communication among them. Lamentably, there is little evidence of synergism in ELEC's case, probably because there was not much opportunity for it. The number and variety of forces working in favor of the changes that ELEC's leaders desired were limited. In its campaign, ELEC encountered many problems and obstacles but experienced only a few successes. Furthermore, lack of planning meant little coordination among these few supportive forces.

CONCLUSION

This chapter has noted many problems—including a variety of historical, political, economic, social, cultural, and school-system forces— that militated against change in Japanese ELT during the time ELEC was trying to bring it about. In conclusion, however, it should be noted that the ELEC campaign was an extremely idealistic one, and even under the best of circumstances change of the magnitude envisioned by ELEC's founders might have been impossible.[297]

Nevertheless, had ELEC's leaders been aware of the many factors discussed in this chapter and the preceding one, it is probably safe to conclude that their successes would have been greater and their failures and difficulties reduced. In the sense that "the past is prologue," perhaps other educational reform movements can benefit from this retrospective analysis of ELEC's experience.

NOTES

1. Nakajima, Addresses and Papers, 14.
2. McLean to Rockefeller, 22 May 1956.
3. Lauter, 236.
4. "Agenda: 12th Meeting on English Teaching Method."
5. Nakajima, Addresses and Papers, 15.
6. Matsumoto to Rockefeller, 12 Aug. 1956, 2.
7. Reischauer to Borton.
8. Fries to Hayden.
9. Lado, interview.
10. Toyoda to CECA, 7.
11. Passin to McLean, 4-5.

12. "Agenda for 2nd Mtg. in Tokyo," 1, attached to "Agenda: 12th Meeting on English Teaching Method."

13. Rodgers, "Communicative Syllabus Design," 41.

14. Ogasawara, interview.

15. Fries, interview.

16. Richards, "The Secret Life of Methods," *TESOL Quarterly,* 18.

17. Richards, "The Secret Life of Methods," *Working Papers,* 11.

18. Wagner and Tilney.

19. Richards, "The Secret Life of Methods," *TESOL Quarterly,* 18.

20. Morley et al., 182.

21. Lado, interview.

22. "The Oral Method of Teaching English."

23. Paper "for Mr. McLane," 12.

24. Toyoda to CECA, 7.

25. Letter to Overton, 2.

26. Toyoda to Overton.

27. Yambe, "The Oral Approach in Japan."

28. Yamaura.

29. Stern, 463.

30. Ota, interview.

31. Koike, interview.

32. Kano, et al. to Fries, 1.

33. Fries to Matsumoto, 2.

34. Fries, "As We See It," 15.

35. Fries, "On the Oral Approach," 204.

36. McLean to Rockefeller, 19 Sept. 1956, 1.

37. Yambe, "C. C. Fries Re-evaluated," 7.

38. Richards, "The Secret Life of Methods," *TESOL Quarterly,* 14.

39. Memorandum on English Language Teaching.

40. Morley et al., 191.

41. Memorandum, 24 Sept. 1958, 1.

42. Richards, "The Secret Life of Methods," *TESOL Quarterly,* 19.

43. For instance, see Fries, *Teaching and Learning,* 3.

44. Peter H. Fries has defended his father's "non-mechanical" view of human behavior in "Fries' Views on Psychology," 11-20.

45. Lado, *Language Teaching,* 105.

46. Fries, "On the Oral Approach," 204.

47. Yambe, "C. C. Fries Re-evaluated," 6.

48. Yambe, "C. C. Fries Re-evaluated," 23.

49. Richards, "The Secret Life of Methods," *TESOL Quarterly,* 19.

50. McLean to Rockefeller, 19 Sept. 1956.

51. Takahashi, interview.

52. For examples, see "The Oral Method of Teaching English," and "Course to Train Teachers of English Opens in Tokyo."

53. Rockefeller to Ikeda.

54. Ota, interview.

55. Matsumoto, interview.

56. Fries to McLean, 15 Feb. 1958, 3.

57. Fries to Mclean, 15 Feb. 1958, 2.

58. Ota, interview.

59. Ichikawa, 22.

60. Toyoda to CECA, 7.

61. Kleinjans, interview.

62. Ota, interview.

63. Ota, interview.

64. Hatori, interview.

65. Kleinjans, interview.

66. Yambe, "Creating a Japanese Type of the Oral Approach," 2.

67. Fries, interview.
68. It is not in the interest of either party to report the exact wording here. For an example, see Twaddell to McLean.
69. For instance, in one letter, Fries scolded, "Please do *not* [italics in original] take the point of view that unless I 'object' immediately to a suggestion you make, it is to be assumed that I approve." Fries to Twaddell, 4 Jan. 1958, 1.
70. Twaddell to McLean.
71. Fries to Twaddell, 4 Jan. 1958, 2.
72. Kleinjans, interview.
73. Fries to McLean, 15 Feb. 1958, 3.
74. Fries to McLean, 15 Feb. 1958, 2-3.
75. Fries to McLean, 15 Feb. 1958, 3-4.
76. Fries to Freeman and Helen Twaddell, 1.
77. Fries to McLean, 15 Feb. 1958, 5.
78. Fries to Haugen, 1.
79. Fries to Hayden, 4.
80. Fries to Takagi and Matsumoto, 1.
81. Fries to McLean, 15 Feb. 1958, 5.
82. Fries to McLean, 15 Feb. 1958, 3.
83. Fries to McLean, 15 Feb. 1958, 6.
84. Fries to Twaddell, 18 Feb. 1958.
85. Telegram to Fries.
86. Telegram to Fries.
87. Fries to McLean, 21 Apr. 1958, 1.
88. Kano, et al. to Fries, 1.
89. Memorandum, 24 Sept. 1958, 3.
90. Fries to McLean, 5 Apr. 1958, 3.
91. Memorandum, 24 Sept. 1958, 3.
92. Kleinjans, interview.
93. King, "Students, Teachers, and Researchers," 34.
94. Ichikawa, 23.
95. Harasawa, 76.
96. Suzuki, 114.
97. Ichikawa, 20.
98. Ogasawara, "The Educational System and English," 88.
99. Maley, 92.
100. King, interview.
101. Bryant, "English Teaching in Japan," 76.
102. Bryant, "English Teaching in Japan, 78.
103. "Agenda: Specialists' Conference."
104. Nakajima, *Addresses and Papers,* 5.
105. Bryant, "English Teaching in Japan," 77.
106. Takagi, "Memorandum."
107. Shimizu, interview.
108. Rodgers, "Communicative Syllabus Design," 41.
109. Kimpara, interview.
110. Yambe, interview.
111. Shimizu, interview.
112. Yambe, interview.
113. Shimizu, interview.
114. Matsumoto, interview.
115. Takahashi, interview.
116. Brosnahan and Haynes, 75.
117. Ogasawara, "The Educational System and English," 88.
118. Shimizu, interview.
119. Ota, interview.
120. Ogasawara, interview.
121. Ogasawara, interview.

122. Shimizu, interview.
123. Smith to Rockefeller, 20 May 1974, 4.
124. Yambe, "C. C. Fries Re-evaluated," 8.
125. Maeda, interview.
126. Brownell, 10.
127. Otani, 120
128. Brosnahan and Haynes, 74.
129. Kleinjans, interview.
130. Harasawa, 78-79.
131. Bryant, "English Teaching in Japan," 81.
132. For examples, see "The Oral Method of Teaching English," and "Course to Train Teachers of English Opens in Tokyo."
133. Telegram to Fries.
134. Jansen, 97-98.
135. Harasawa, 76.
136. Doi.
137. Burstyn and McDade, 36.
138. Nakane, cited by Edamatsu, "The Japanese Psycho-Social Barrier," 6.
139. Moloney, cited by Edamatsu, "The Japanese Psycho-Social Barrier," 6.
140. Lebra, 24-25.
141. Hudson, 48.
142. Giles, 257.
143. Giles, 269.
144. Brosnahan and Haynes, 76.
145. Dore, speech.
146. McLean, "English Language Teaching in Japan," 25.
147. Matthews, 33.
148. Fishman, Cooper, and Conrad, 164.
149. Snow with Shapira, 4.
150. Reischauer, *The Japanese,* 401.
151. Harasawa, 76.
152. Brosnahan and Haynes, 76.
153. Mclean, "English Language Teaching in Japan," 22.
154. Fernstermaker.
155. Kleinjans, interview.
156. Reischauer, *Japan,* 26.
157. Flenley, "A Model."
158. Bryant, "English Teaching in Japan," 80.
159. Reischauer to Borton.
160. Brosnahan and Haynes, 76.
161. Dillon and Dillon, 16.
162. Reischauer, *Japan*, 29.
163. Kimizuka, interview.
164. "Dr. Krashen Interviewed," B5.
165. McLean et al., 19-20.
166. Smith to McLean, 2.
167. Koike, interview.
168. Ichikawa, 22.
169. McLean, et al., 20.
170. Otani, 120.
171. Harasawa, 76.
172. Ichikawa, 20.
173. Yoshikawa, 391-94.
174. Ogasawara, "The Educational System and English," 55-56.
175. Gibney, *Japan: The Fragile Superpower*, 146.
176. Reischauer, "The English Language and Japan's Role."
177. Nelson, 10.
178. Teweles.

179. Whitman and Jackson, 30.
180. Taylor, 391-99.
181. Ichikawa, 24.
182. Sasaki, 18.
183. Schumann, 163-77.
184. Brosnahan and Haynes, 76.
185. Kimizuka, "Teaching English to Japanese Speakers," 8.
186. Ishii, 49.
187. Tajima, 150.
188. Brosnahan and Haynes, 76.
189. Barnlund, 429.
190. Barnlund, 433.
191. Schumann, 166-67.
192. Fries, *Teaching and Learning English,* 5.
193. Stevick, "Toward a Practical Philosophy of Pronunciation," 147-48.
194. Schumann, 170.
195. Carroll, 6.
196. Suzuki, 109.
197. Lebra, 2.
198. Wagatsuma, 6.
199. Gibney, *Japan: The Fragile Superpower,* 146.
200. Sasaki, 18.
201. Harker, 12.
202. Barbieri, preface.
203. Edamatsu, "Back to the Barrier," 14.
204. Carroll, 5.
205. Krashen, "The 'Fundamental Pedagogical Principle,'" 50-52. Also, see Krashen, "Formal and Informal Linguistic Environments," 157-68.
206. Schumann, 173.
207. Krashen, "The Monitor Model," 158.
208. Dore, speech.
209. Dillon and Dillon, 9.
210. Oller, Hudson, and Liu, 2.
211. Spolsky, 273.
212. Lambert, 2.
213. Gardner and Lambert, 12.
214. Gardner and Lambert, 14.
215. Gardner and Lambert, 13.
216. Spolsky, 281.
217. Schumann, 167-68.
218. Dillon and Dillon, 15.
219. Condon and Kurata, 106.
220. Chihara and Oller, 58.
221. Schumann, 168.
222. Guiora, et al., 421-22.
223. Gill.
224. Stevick, *Memory, Meaning and Method*, 56.
225. Tajima, 150.
226. LaForge, 221.
227. Shimazu, 19.
228. Miyazawa.
229. Gill.
230. Tsunoda.
231. Sibatani, 24.
232. DeWolf, 297-98.
233. Sibatani, 24.
234. Thompson, 76.
235. DeWolf, 298.

236. DeWolf, 296-97.
237. DeWolf, 295.
238. Harasawa, 75.
239. Ichikawa, 20.
240. Koike, et al., 158.
241. Koike, et al., 158.
242. "Notes from an International 'Rap' Session," 8.
243. Flenley, "Innovation in English Language Teaching," 9.
244. Ichikawa, 21.
245. Harasawa, 72.
246. "Conclusions and Recommendations," 22 Sept. 1956, sec. IV.
247. Goto, 25.
248. "Notes from an International 'Rap' Session," 8.
249. "Notes from an International 'Rap' Session," 8.
250. "Report of Conference of Experts," 52, cited by Brownell, 51.
251. Harasawa, 78.
252. Harasawa, 78.
253. LoCastro, "Interview with Minoru Wada of the Ministry of Education," 9.
254. Bryant, "English Teaching in Japan," 84.
255. Takagi, "A Section of the Prospectus (Part I)," 2.
256. "Minutes of the First Meeting of the General Committee."
257. "Conclusions and Recommendations," 22 Sept. 1956, sec. IV.
258. Matsumoto, interview.
259. Fries, "On the Oral Approach," 204.
260. Takahashi, interview.
261. Takahashi, interview.
262. For instance, see Pearson.
263. Takahashi, interview.
264. Ichikawa, 21.
265. Matthews, 32.
266. Snow, 1.
267. Koike, interview.
268. Shimizu, interview.
269. Richards, "The Context," 14.
270. Otani, 117.
271. Otani, 117.
272. Richards, "The Secret Life of Methods," *TESOL Quarterly*.
273. McLean to Rockefeller, 3 Apr. 1956, 5.
274. McLean to Rockefeller, 19 Sept. 1956, 3.
275. Lamb, 1.
276. "Agenda for 2nd Mtg. in Tokyo," 3, attached to "Agenda: 12th Meeting on English Teaching Method."
277. Bryant, "English Teaching in Japan," 78.
278. McLean to Rockefeller, 19 Sept. 1956, 3.
279. Overton to CECA, 28 Mar. 1960, 3.
280. Bryant, "English Teaching in Japan," 79.
281. Bryant, "English Teaching in Japan," 79.
282. Glicksberg, 22.
283. "Agenda for 2nd Mtg. in Tokyo," 3, attached to "Agenda: 12th Meeting on English Teaching Method."
284. Hatori, interview.
285. Shimizu, "ELEC Past and Present," 100-101.
286. Bryant, "English Teaching in Japan," 78.
287. Shimizu, "ELEC Past and Present," 102.
288. Fries to Twaddell, 15 May 1957, 2.
289. Matsumoto, interview.
290. Fries to Overton, 13 Sept. 1959, 2.
291. Glicksberg, 23.

292. Richards, "The Secret Life of Methods," *TESOL Quarterly*, 15.
293. Announcement of Organization, CCEJ.
294. Noda, interview.
295. Takahashi, interview.
296. Bryant, "English Teaching in Japan," 80.
297. Kleinjans, interview.

6
Consequences and Conclusions

The final portion of the hybrid model is devoted to the possible outcomes of a decision to accept or reject an innovation. Accordingly, this chapter deals with the consequences of the ELEC campaign. It also arrives at several conclusions and makes a number of recommendations regarding the diffusion and implementation of innovations that will benefit future reformers.

DECISIONS

Authority decisions, the quickest and most powerful type, were not a possibility for ELEC (as they had been for SCAP during the Occupation). Although ELEC's board consisted of a variety of important individuals in the business and academic communities, ELEC itself had no authority over teachers in the Japanese school system. Furthermore, it failed to establish linkage with those institutions that did. Consequently, ELEC's campaign was limited to persuasive, informative strategies that proved to be more costly and less effective than its founders had hoped. Further frustrating their ambitions, the cooperative nature of Japanese society and the recentralized school system discouraged individual action and decision making. In this situation, consensus-type decisions seemed to be the only alternative, but of course, arriving at them required much time and discussion. Moreover, after considering the pros and cons of changing, most Japanese teachers chose to continue with tradition and not adopt the Oral Approach. Despite these setbacks, however, ELEC's campaign still had various consequences.

CONSEQUENCES

Respecting the Rockefeller brothers' various projects, Morris notes:

They have, despite excellent coaching, rung up at least the normal number of errors in the box score. They have occasionally thrown the ball to the wrong base and they have sometimes struck out, swinging. They have never quit trying, however, and even the casual observer can see a pattern emerging from their sometimes fumbling, sometimes idealistic but always grimly determined efforts.[1]

"Idealistic" and "grimly determined" both characterize the Rockefeller-supported ELEC effort. In retrospect, it is also apparent that the ELEC campaign was far from error-free. The analysis of its outcomes, however, is certainly not as simple as "three strikes and you're out" or deciding whether or not the ball was thrown to the right base. As shown in the hybrid model, consequences may be of various types—immediate or delayed, direct or indirect, manifest or latent, and functional or dysfunctional.

For the purpose of analyzing the outcomes of the ELEC campaign, the direct and indirect dichotomy is most useful. Within this general framework, other types of consequences will be noted as appropriate.

Direct Consequences

The ELEC seminars certainly helped numerous individuals directly (and immediately) by improving their English language and teaching skills. In 1985, reflecting back on "ELEC's early days," a panel of individuals commented on how ELEC had revolutionized their professional lives. One noted, "Twenty-five years ago I had a chance to attend the first ELEC seminar held here and that has changed my way of teaching English a great deal."[2] Another remembered his experience after attending an ELEC seminar: "I saw a movie and surprising to say I could understand English. I could understand English dialogue. That was a great joy."[3]

ELEC's "ultimate goal," however, stated as early as 1955 and as late as 1962, was "the transformation of English language teaching methods in schools and universities throughout Japan."[4] Respecting this grand objective of revolutionizing English language teaching in Japan and ultimately producing a new generation of Japanese who could speak English fluently, ELEC would have to be classified as a failure. As Smith admitted to John D. Rockefeller 3rd: "It must be said frankly that ELEC failed to achieve its main objective....ELEC was not able to change the grand strategy of English-language teaching in Japan or to bring overall improvement in teaching methods."[5] Others agree with Smith's assessment. Robert Lado, Fries' foremost disciple and a participant in the ACTT program, commented, "ELEC was defeated. They were sidetracked."[6] Even Yambe, probably Fries' staunchest supporter in Japan and a long-time member of the ELEC staff, admitted, "I don't think ELEC succeeded in overcoming Mombusho resistance."[7]

In the long run, relatively few Japanese teachers adopted the Oral Approach in their classrooms. In 1974, nearly twenty years after ELEC's oral English "revolution" began, Reischauer reported that "teaching methods have remained antiquated and inefficient." He also noted that "extremely few Japanese...can attempt even a simple conversation in English."[8] His opinion was supported by an empirical study conducted a few years later that obtained self-ratings of 123 Japanese students of

English regarding their skill in the language. Despite having studied English for an average of 8.41 years, the highest rating these students gave themselves (on a scale on which 1 = not at all, and 5 = like a native speaker of English) was a far-from-fluent 2.48 in reading. Writing was next with 2.14, and understanding and speaking were near the bottom of the scale with ratings of 1.96 and 1.80 respectively.[9] Even today, "antiquated and inappropriate teaching methods" continue to be used in Japanese schools.[10] A recent report on foreign language teaching around the world noted that "teachers in Japan lack experience speaking English; many read Shakespeare aloud in an incomprehensible accent."[11] From these reports it is apparent that the "lamentable situation"[12] of English language teaching in Japan persists even today.

Indirect Consequences

Despite ELEC's failure to achieve its primary goal, its reform effort was certainly not without consequences. The campaign produced a number of outcomes that were more indirect than direct and more latent than manifest in nature but that were, nonetheless, important. In this respect, as a "pacesetter" or "leaven in the whole mass," ELEC enjoyed many successes.[13] As Smith reassured Rockefeller in 1974, it would be wrong to conclude that "ELEC was a boondoggle or not useful....Everyone I have consulted seems to agree that there were many incidental benefits from which Japan continues to profit."[14]

In fact, those not familiar with ELEC's grand revolutionary goals often judged the campaign to have been highly successful. Glicksberg reported that it had been

> of incalculable aid in the up-grading process. It has brought prominent American linguists to Japan and has produced texts and accompanying audio-visual materials for the three years of junior high school English....In addition, ELEC has a large-scale program of adult English classes at its Tokyo school where much of the teaching is of truly exceptional caliber. ELEC also has a very active summer seminar program which, since its inception, has involved several thousand Japanese English teachers.[15]

In terms of what ELEC's founders originally intended, of course, each of these activities fell short of its goal. The number of teachers retrained by ELEC each year reached a peak of 1,169 (which was still only a small proportion of the total potential audience) in 1962, and then declined considerably. The *New Approach* textbooks were adopted by only about one percent of Japanese lower secondary schools and were in print for only a few years. Perhaps most importantly, ELEC never made any headway in dealing with the powerful effects of backwash from the university entrance examinations.

While acknowledging that ELEC failed to revolutionize Japanese ELT, many who worked with the reform campaign were heartened by relatively small changes that took place years after ELEC ceased to actively promote change. For instance, a number of universities now include sections in their entrance examinations that require students to comprehend spoken English. ELEC's efforts may have helped encourage these modifications. In addition, although the *New Approach* textbooks quickly went out of print, it is reported that they "certainly influenced the development and revision of many of the others."[16] Likewise, changes in the Ministry of Education guidelines regarding English-teaching materials a few years after the ELEC campaign began were "a great encouragement to ELEC" since they were "completely in line with the objectives ELEC had been making great efforts to accomplish."[17] Even today, it is not uncommon for those who wish to encourage more modern methods for language teaching to blame ELEC for the prevalence of audiolingual-like techniques in Japan.[18]

Of course, because they are indirect, it is impossible to say with any certainty whether these purported secondary outcomes of the ELEC effort actually resulted from the ELEC campaign or were due to other forces. It is most likely that they were caused by a variety of factors, only one of which was ELEC. Nevertheless, it is also impossible to rule out ELEC as a force that helped change ELT in Japan—at least in a delayed, latent, and indirect way.

CONCLUSIONS

Larudee acknowledges, "A historical study may not always suggest solutions but it usually contributes to a better understanding of the problems under consideration."[19] This historical study has accomplished that objective through its retrospective analysis of the challenges the ELEC effort encountered. Nevertheless, this final section will also venture to make some suggestions that may help future reformers successfully arrive at solutions to the problems they face. These conclusions will take the form of general principles based on the particulars of the Japanese ELT situation and ELEC's attempt to revolutionize it.

The Importance of Implementation Factors

The successful spread of an educational innovation requires more than relative advantage. A "better mousetrap" alone is not enough. "Good curricula do not diffuse themselves."[20]

Such a conclusion is not new; others have reached it also. Nearly twenty years ago, for instance, Kelly concluded his historical overview of twenty-five centuries of language teaching with these words: "Every age, in fact, has its rebels whose teaching techniques, though scientifically justifiable, fail to gain acceptance because they did not fit the atmosphere of the time."[21] In the same vein, but more recently, Richards has emphasized, "Planning a successful language program involves consideration of factors that go beyond the mere content and presentation of teaching materials."[22]

Unfortunately, this counsel is often ignored by promoters of language-teaching innovations, who regularly propagate their ideas as widely as possible without due regard for the unique characteristics of different socio-cultural settings. That their efforts meet with such little success should come as no surprise.

A related conclusion, of interest not just to reformers but to all methodologists, deals with the nature of language-teaching methods themselves and the forces that shape them. Larudee's historical overview of language teaching methods in the Western world was undertaken in order to "discover what major forces influenced language teaching in each period of history." Likewise, the present study of ELEC's attempt to reform English language teaching in Japan has revealed the influence of a multitude of factors that determine the form and the spread of methods. Larudee attempted to disclose "how methods of language teaching are conceived, and why; how they are nurtured, and by what sources; how and why they die out; and why and how they are revived."[23] His findings demonstrate that "in the course of history, language teaching has been affected by philosophical, theological, political, social, scientific, economic, national, and international as well as pedagogical and linguistic factors."[24] The present study has reached a similar conclusion—in contrast to the widely held belief that methods result from a simple combination of linguistics, psychology, and pedagogy.[25]

The Complexity of Implementation Factors

The numerous factors that influence the diffusion and implementation of an innovation in a given situation form an extremely complicated network. The complexity of this ecosystem of interdependent forces makes bringing about change difficult. Ogasawara, for instance, holds that before English language teaching in Japan changes, many other elements in the Japanese system will need to change first.[26]

The complexities of creating change and the potential barriers to it can be intimidating. Realizing how challenging the process is may even give some would-be reformers second thoughts about their plans. Nevertheless, a careful consideration of the various implementation factors in a particular situation can also comprise the beginning of an understanding that may eventually lead to greater success. As Parish and Arends remind reformers, "We can learn from our efforts...if we view our failures not as resulting from stubborn resistance or bad intentions but instead as ingrained in the complex relationships found in schools."[27] Once they have become aware of these factors, reformers can work with or around them and perhaps even make them work in favor of change.

The Need for Planning and Power

Trusting in a "better mousetrap" and good luck is not an effective change strategy. Especially in directed contact change campaigns, reformers need the advantages that come from planning for diffusion/implementation and the power to carry out those plans. Of course, even planning and power cannot always guarantee success—there may be no way of overcoming some obstacles—but they do maximize reformers' chances of succeeding.

Unfortunately, ELEC's leaders seemed to operate with virtually no diffusion/implementation strategy other than communicating the news of the Oral Approach innovation to Japanese teachers. Apparently, they trusted that a new, improved teaching methodology would catch on automatically once teachers saw its advantages. A great amount of time and effort was spent in planning the linguistic aspects of ELEC's products (e.g., Japanese-English contrastive analysis, "corpus" preparation, and textbook design), but next to nothing went into plotting strategies for overcoming or working around (or with) the numerous barriers to implementing the Oral Approach in Japan. This failure to plan and execute a diffusion/implementation strategy was probably ELEC's greatest shortcoming.

Of course, a reform effort's plans must be not only thorough but also realistic. Wise reformers avoid becoming overambitious. ELEC's campaign, in contrast, was extremely idealistic from the start, attempting to revolutionize the entire system for teaching English in Japanese schools. It might have achieved greater success if it had started with less grandiose expectations and developed specific plans aimed at narrower target objectives.

As an American-inspired effort in the 1950s with no power over Japanese teachers of English and a philosophy of remaining neutral relative to those institutions that did, ELEC naturally employed a "democratic," horizontal, communication approach in its reform effort. Nevertheless, in retrospect it is clear that such an approach was ineffective. It would have been much better for ELEC to gain power by establishing linkages with influential people and institutions and then take a vertical, elitist approach, starting at the top of the hierarchy in the Japanese school system and working down to the classroom teachers.[28]   ELEC's leaders eventually came to this realization, but by then it was too late to save their campaign. Learning from this experience, subsequent Ford and Rockefeller Foundation efforts to change ELT in Japan attempted to start at the top.

The Need for a Special Linkage Model

Linkage between the intended-user group and the resource system is crucial to the success of efforts to bring about selective or directed contact change. Therefore, of the various branches of diffusion theory, a linkage perspective is most appropriate for planning and analyzing campaigns such as the ELEC effort. Nevertheless, not all linkage models are adequate for this purpose. Many models that have been proposed to explain diffusion-of-innovations phenomena in education take into account only a few school-related variables and ignore a variety of important factors outside the school system itself. Such an approach may be adequate when a reform effort is restricted to a single-culture setting, but it ignores social, psychological, political, economic, and historical factors that strongly affect change campaigns that cross cultural boundaries. As the ELEC experience shows, nescience of these factors offers no protection against their effects, and success in a few areas may not be enough to balance failure in others that are neglected.

Since even the more complex linkage models do not allow for the variety of implementation factors that this study identified, it was necessary to combine components from various sources into a hybrid linkage model in order to satisfy the criteria of coherent framework, abstractness, completeness, relevance to directed contact change, and cross-cultural applicability. This model represents both the diffusion/implementation process and the multitude of factors which affect that process. It can remind planners of factors that they might otherwise ignore and give them an understanding of what those factors are, how they are inter-related, and how to deal with them.

While this model is especially applicable to the case of English language teaching in Japan, it is abstract and general enough that it can be used for analyzing other cases of cross-cultural, directed contact change elsewhere. As Palmer and Redman, whose experiences attempting to reform ELT were by no means limited to Japan, once remarked, "In all countries and circumstances...we have encountered identical resistances, expressed though they have been in diverse ways."[29]

Caveat: The Dangers of Over-Planning and Inflexibility

Planning for implementation is essential, and this study has focused on the problems related to ELEC's failure to plan adequately. Nevertheless, it is also appropriate to point out that taking this emphasis on planning to an extreme can result in a different set of problems.

One potential danger arises from the difficulty of distinguishing between adequate planning and over-planning. Taken too far, the desire to plan things carefully may lead to an undesirable result—planning that goes on endlessly. In such cases, the reform movement may become paralyzed, never arriving at the action stage.

Another possible danger of careful preplanning is that it may lead to inflexibility. Because of the complexity of the process of implementing an innovation, it is impossible to plan for all possible contingencies ahead of time. Even the most carefully laid plans will require adjustments. Nevertheless, after much time and money have been invested in detailed planning, reformers may be unwilling to change those plans and make necessary adjustments as the campaign proceeds. This tendency can be resisted by building formative evaluation into the plan and emphasizing, from the very first stages, the need for adaptability. As critical as the need for planning may be, few aspects of the implementation process are as certain as the need for flexibility. Successful implementers will strike a harmonious balance between these requirements.

The Need for Time to Bring About Change

The complexity of a change effort, the need for careful planning, and the many other challenges of diffusing and implementing an innovation all mean that change requires time. Based on his experience, Williams wisely warns enthusiastic reformers, "Do not expect major improvements to come quickly."[30]

Even when reformers are patient, however, they often experience pressure from funding agencies to produce tangible, demonstrable results within a limited period of time. Yet, as the ELEC experience demonstrates, products such as textbooks do not guarantee real or lasting reform. Unfortunately, as the ELEC experience also illustrates, support may be withdrawn before a reform movement has been given adequate time to succeed. Perhaps an awareness of the impressively complex process illustrated in the hybrid model will also encourage those who provide the backing for change efforts to exercise greater forbearance.

Satisfaction with Influences Instead of Revolutions

An understanding of the challenging process of creating change and of the intimidating complex of implementation factors that confront reformers can help leaders of change campaigns understand what kind of change is possible and/or desirable in a particular setting. Even with its considerable resources, ELEC failed to achieve its grand objective of revolutionizing Japanese ELT. The successes it did enjoy took the form of influences on the Ministry of Education guidelines, on other textbook publishers, and on English teaching in Japan in general. Learning from this experience, other reformers may scale down their hopes to a realistic level.

In many situations, gradual, instead of radical change is the only practical possibility, and influences are all that reformers can expect to exert. In such cases, those who desire to bring about change should be satisfied to work within the system and aim at influencing teachers, administrators, and examiners to make meaningful but gradual changes, rather than attempting to revolutionize the entire system overnight.

In the years since ELEC ceased to push for a revolution in the methods and materials used for teaching English in Japan, numerous proposals have been made to reform Japanese ELT in ways similar to what John D. Rockefeller 3rd and other ELEC leaders originally desired. For example, one call for change declared: "A drastic reform should be adopted. Greater emphasis should be placed on oral communication. Training methods involving speaking should be conducted more effectively. The most urgent business is to get really proficient teachers. Every Japanese teacher should be required to have adequate oral proficiency."[31]

Although such proposals may seem discouragingly familiar, an important difference offers a ray of hope. This critical difference is that to an increasing extent, those who are making such proposals are prominent

Japanese educators, not visiting Americans. As Suzuki urges, "It is we Japanese teachers of English who must take the lead in bringing forth these necessary changes. For we alone can understand the vast complexities of the Japanese educational system."[32] As Japanese teachers take the initiative in bringing about change, the character of the reform shifts favorably— from directed contact change to immanent change. Immanent change campaigns generally experience a higher rate of success than directed contact change efforts do. Perhaps these Japanese reformers will achieve the goals that have eluded foreign change agents. Non-Japanese who wish to see reforms take place in Japanese ELT would do well to join and support these indigenous movements rather than confuse the scene with their own independent efforts.

The Value of a Historical Perspective

The Roman god Janus was typically pictured as having two faces, so that he had eyes in front and behind and could look forward and backward at the same time. Promoters of innovations can also benefit from such a dual perspective. By looking back into history and learning from the experiences of others at the same time that they look forward and make plans for their own implementation efforts, they can avoid many problems that plagued previous campaigns. Knowledge about earlier reform attempts can also help would-be reformers set goals more realistically. For instance, Tripp recommends that the story of Harold Palmer's devoted but defeated effort to improve English language teaching in Japan "be required reading for any foreigners new to Japan who imagine they are going to reform language teaching."[33]

The Need for Additional Studies on the Diffusion of Innovations in ELT

It is common for studies to conclude with a plea for more research on the same topic. This book ends on a similar note because there truly is a need for additional studies dealing with attempts to reform English language teaching practices around the world. Few studies of this type have been done. Nevertheless, only when more of them have been conducted will truly useful, generalizable patterns begin to emerge.

A number of individual area studies on this topic will allow for a full-scale, comparative view, and from such a perspective it will be possible to see which approach to creating change in language-teaching practices works best, most often, and under which sets of circumstances. That broader understanding will be more useful than merely knowing what did or did not work (and which alternatives might have worked) in a particular case. For example, educators in Egypt are reportedly making an attempt to reform English language teaching in that country. Apparently, the approach they are taking is to begin at the top, by reforming the school-leaving examinations.[34] Since this approach is similar to what many have said would be the key to reforming ELT in Japan, it will be most interesting to see how it works in Egypt. Of course, Egypt is not Japan, but as Noah affirms, phenomena do not need to be perfectly parallel to be usefully compared. After a "careful analysis of the conditions" that surround a particular case, it is still possible to learn valuable lessons from one case and apply them to another.[35]

A variety of studies focusing on ELT reform attempts that all take place in the same country but at different times would make enlightening diachronic comparisons possible also. For example, a triple comparison of the reform efforts of Palmer in Japan before World War II, ELEC after World War II, and present-day reformers of Japanese ELT, could be extremely revealing.

In sum, this book, which has reported and analyzed the case of ELEC's effort to reform English language teaching in Japan, should by no means be the only such study. Rather, it is hoped that it will encourage similar studies and constitute the beginning of an enlightening series of complementary reports on the subject of the diffusion and implementation of innovations in English language teaching. The important task of gaining the understanding necessary to overcome the intellectual and practical challenges of converting knowledge into practice is far from finished.

NOTES

1. Morris, 3.
2. Nagao, 32.
3. Honda, 32.
4. Paper "for Mr. McLane."
5. Smith to Rockefeller, 20 May 1974, 4.
6. Lado, interview.
7. Yambe, interview.
8. Reischauer, *Japan,* 299.
9. Chihara and Oller, 60.
10. Dillon and Dillon, 16.
11. "Who's at the Head of the Class?," 61.
12. Otani, 122.
13. Toyoda, Appendix B.
14. Smith to Rockefeller, 20 May 1974, 4.
15. Glicksberg, 22.
16. Glicksberg, 22.
17. Muto, 130.
18. Choseed, interview.
19. Larudee, 2
20. Shive, 6.
21. Kelly, 408.
22. Richards, "The Context," 11.
23. Larudee, v.
24. Larudee, iv.
25. For statements to this effect, see Prator, 7; Wardaugh, 80; or Robinett, 160-161.
26. Ogasawara, interview.
27. Parish and Arends, 62.
28. Maeda, interview.
29. Palmer and Redman, 5.
30. Williams, 566.

31. Suzuki, 107.
32. Suzuki, 111.
33. Tripp, 30.
34. Salama, 5.
35. Noah, 552, 558.

Bibliography

The Rockefeller Archive Center (Pocantico Hills, North Tarrytown, New York) is the depository for many of the documents listed in this bibliography. As indicated, they are located in various collections, such as the John D. Rockefeller 3rd (abbreviated JDR 3rd) series and Office of the Messrs. Rockefeller (abbreviated OMR) files in the Rockefeller Family Archives, the John D. Rockefeller 3rd Fund (abbreviated JDR 3rd Fund) records in Special Collections, and the Rockefeller Foundation Archives.

Other documents come from the Charles C. Fries Japan correspondence file (abbreviated CCF Japan), which is part of the personal papers of Charles C. Fries, now in the possession of his son Peter H. Fries of Mount Pleasant, Michigan.

Abu Samah, Asiah. "The English Language (Communicational) Curriculum for Upper Secondary Schools in Malaysia: Rationale, Design and Implementation." In *Trends in Language Syllabus Design*, edited by John A. S. Read. Singapore: SEAMEO Regional Language Centre, 1984.

"Agenda: 12th Meeting on English Teaching Method" and attachments. 25 Apr. 1956. Rockefeller Family Archives. JDR 3rd. Box 38. English Language Teaching Envelope.

"Agenda: Specialists' Conference on English Teaching in Japan." 9 Aug. 1956. Rockefeller Family Archives. JDR 3rd. Box 39. English Language Teaching Envelope No. 2.

Allen, Harold B. *The Teaching of English as a Second Language and U.S. Foreign Policy.* Washington, D.C.: TESOL, 1978.

American Psychological Association. *Checklist for a New Course in Psychology.* 1985. Alexandria, Va.: ERIC Document Reproduction Service, ED 257 755, 1985.

Anderson, Dorothée. "Harold E. Palmer: A Biographical Essay." In *This Language Learning Business,* edited by Harold E. Palmer and H. Vere Redman. George G. Harrap and Co., 1932. Reprint. London: Oxford University Press, 1969.

Anderson, Ronald S. *Japan: Three Epochs of Modern Education.* Washington, D.C.: U.S. Department of Health, Education, and Welfare, Office of Education, 1959.

"Announcement of Organization, Committee for Cooperation on English in Japan." [1967.] Special Collections. JDR 3rd Fund. Box 64. Series 8. Folder 523.

Anthony, Edward M. "The Work of Charles Fries within the Changing Contexts of Language Teacher Education." Paper presented at the First International Seminar on Language Teacher Education, Institute of Language in Education, Hong Kong, 17 Dec. 1985.

Appelbaum, Richard P. *Theories of Social Change.* Boston: Houghton Mifflin, 1970.

Araki, Eikichi. "Opening Address." In *Addresses and Papers at the Specialists' Conference, September 3-7, 1956, English Language Exploratory Committee,* edited by Fumio Nakajima. Tokyo: Kenkyusha, 1957.

Ashworth, Mary. *Beyond Methodology: Second Language Teaching and the Community.* Cambridge, Eng.: Cambridge University Press, 1985.

Bailey, Richard W. "Charles C. Fries: The Life of a Linguist." In *Toward an Understanding of Language: Charles Carpenter Fries in Perspective,* edited by Peter Howard Fries. Amsterdam: John Benjamins, 1985.

Barbieri, Philip. *Fool's Dance: A Communicative Text for Japanese Students.* Aomori-shi, Japan: Mikuni, 1984.

Barnlund, Dean C. "Communicative Styles in Two Cultures: Japan and the United States." In *Organization of Behavior in Face to Face Interaction,* edited by A. Kendon, R. M. Harris, and M. R. Key. The Hague, Paris: Mouton, 1975.

Beasley, William G. *The Meiji Restoration.* Stanford, Calif.: Stanford University Press, 1972.

Beauchamp, Edward R. "Griffis in Japan: The Fukui Interlude, 1871." In his *Learning to be Japanese.* Hamden, Conn.: Linnet Books. 1978.

Beauchamp, Edward R. "Reform Traditions in the United States and Japan." In *Educational Policies in Crisis: Japanese and American Perspectives,* edited by William K. Cummings, Edward R. Beauchamp, Shogo Ichikawa, Victor N. Kobayashi, and Morikazu Ushiogi. New York: Praeger, 1986.

Beauchamp, Edward R. "Report from Japan 1976." In his *Learning to be Japanese.* Hamden. Conn.: Linnet Books, 1978.

Beck, Emily Morison, ed. *Bartlett's Familiar Quotations,* 14th rev. ed. Boston: Little, Brown and Co., 1968.

Beeby, C. E. *The Quality of Education in Developing Countries.* Cambridge, Mass.: Harvard University Press, 1966.

Bennis, Warren G., Kenneth D. Benne, and Robert Chin, eds. *The Planning of Change,* 4th rev. ed. New York: Holt, Rinehart, and Winston, 1985.

Berman, Edward H. "Foundations, United States Foreign Policy, and African Education, 1945-1975." *Harvard Educational Review* 49, no. 2 (1979): 145-179.

Bowen, J. Donald, Harold Madsen, and Ann Hilferty. *TESOL: Techniques and Procedures*. Cambridge, Mass.: Newbury House, 1985.

Boxer, C. R. *The Christian Century in Japan 1549-1650*. Berkeley: University of California Press, 1951.

Bradley, Montgomery S. to Donald H. McLean, Jr. 19 Oct. 1955. Rockefeller Family Archives. JDR 3rd. Box 38. English Language Teaching Envelope.

Brosnahan, Leger, and Charles Haynes. "English Language Teaching in Japan: Two Views." *Exchange* 6, no. 4 (1971): 71.

Brown, Vernon to Charles C. Fries. 10 Nov. 1958. CCF Japan.

Brown, Vernon to Dr. and Mrs. Fries. 11 Aug. 1961. CCF Japan.

Brownell, John A. *Japan's Second Language*. Champaign, Ill.: National Council of Teachers of English, 1967.

Brownell, John A. to Datus Smith. 30 Apr. 1969. Special Collections. JDR 3rd Fund. Box 64. Series 8: English Language Teaching in Japan. Folder 523.

Bryant, William Cullen, II. "English Language Teaching in Japanese Schools." *PMLA* 71, no. 4, part 2 (1956): 21-48.

Bryant, William Cullen, II. "English Teaching in Japan: A Survey with Recommendations." 1955. Rockefeller Family Archives. JDR 3rd. Box 38. English Language Teaching Envelope.

Burstyn, Joan N., and Laurie McDade. "Education, Industry, and the Military: The Legacy of Individual Development." *Issues in Education* 2, no. 1 (1984): 36-43.

Carrol, John B. "Characteristics of Successful Language Learners." In *Viewpoints on English as a Second Language,* edited by Marina Burt, Heidi Dulay, and Mary Finocchiaro. New York: Regents, 1977.

Cary, Otis. *A History of Christianity in Japan: Roman Catholic, Greek Orthodox, and Protestant Missions*. Two volumes in one. Rutland, Vt. and Tokyo, Japan: Charles E. Tuttle Co., 1976. (First edition, 1909, by Fleming H. Revell Co., New York.)

Cavanagh, Gray, and Ken Styles. "The Implementation of New Curriculum Guidelines and Policies." *Education Canada* 23, no. 1 (1983): 9-15.

CECA, Japan Society, Joint Committee on English Language Teaching in Japan, Minutes of Meeting. 14 Nov. 1958. Rockefeller Family Archives. JDR 3rd. Box 39. English Language Teaching Envelope No. 2.

CECA Resolution E4. English Language Exploratory Committee, Japan. [1962.] Rockefeller Family Archives. JDR 3rd. Box 39. English Language Teaching Envelope No. 2.

Chihara, Tetsuro, and John W. Oller, Jr. "Attitudes and Attained Proficiency in EFL: A Sociolinguistic Study of Adult Japanese Speakers." *Language Learning* 28, no. 1 (1978): 55-68.

Choseed, Bernard. Interview with author. Kaneohe, Hawaii, 18 Feb. 1989

Cochran Slaugh, Linda Ann. *Perceived Barriers to Implementing Florida's Competency Based Business Education Curriculum.* Alexandria, Va.: ERIC Document Reproduction Service, ED 253 706, 1984.

Cohen, Andrew D. Foreword to *Innovative Approaches to Language Teaching*, edited by Robert W. Blair. Rowley, Mass.: Newbury House, 1982.

Coleman, James S. "Professorial Training and Institution Building in the Third World: Two Rockefeller Foundation Experiences." *Comparative Education Review* 28, no. 2 (1984): 180-202.

"Committee for Cooperation on English in Japan. Annual Report." Jan. 1968-Jan.1969. Special Collections. JDR 3rd Fund. Box 64. Series 8: English Language Teaching in Japan. Folder 523.

Committee for Economic Development. *Innovation in Education: New Directions for the American School.* New York: Committee for Economic Development, 1968.

"Conclusions and Recommendations." 22 Sept. 1956. Rockefeller Family Archives. JDR 3rd. Box 39. English Language Teaching Envelope No. 2.

"Conclusions and Recomendations, The Specialists' Conference 1956." In *Applied Linguistics and the Teaching of English*, edited by Tamotsu Yambe. Tokyo: ELEC, 1970.

Condon, John, and Keisuke Kurata. *In Search of What's Japanese about Japan.* Tokyo: Shufunotomo, 1974.

Corbett, H. Dickson, and Joseph J. D'Amico. "No More Heroes: Creating Systems to Support Change." *Educational Leadership* 44, no. 1 (1986): 70-72.

"Course to Train Teachers of English Opens in Tokyo." *The Japan Times,* 6 Aug. 1957. CCF Japan.

Crystal, David. "How Many Millions? The Statistics of English Today." *English Today*, Jan. 1985, 7-9.

Darian, Steven. "Backgrounds of Modern Language Teaching: Sweet. Jespersen. and Palmer." *Modern Language Journal* 53, no. 9 (1969): 545-50.

Deasy, Richard J. "Education in Japan: Surprising Lessons." *Educational Leadership* 44, no. 1 (1986): 38-43.

Department of State. *Foreign Relations of the United States, Diplomatic Papers, The Conference of Berlin (The Potsdam Conference) 1945.* 2 vols. Washington, D.C.: U.S. Government Printing Office, 1960.

DeWolf, Charles M. Review of *Japan's Modern Myth: The Language and Beyond* by Roy Andrew Miller. *Papers in Linguistics* 18, no. 2 (1985): 295-316.

Dillon, Drew, and Debbie Dillon. "'The Psycho-Social Barrier' Revisited." *TESL Reporter* 12, no. 2 (1979): 9, 15-16.

Doi, Takeo. *The Anatomy of Dependence.* Tokyo: Kodansha International, 1973.

Dore, Ronald P. "The Legacy." In *Learning to be Japanese*, edited by Edward R. Beauchamp. Hamden, Conn.: Linnet Books, 1978.

Dore, Ronald P. "The Legacy of Tokugawa Education." In *Changing Japanese Attitudes Toward Modernization*, edited by Marius B. Jansen. Princeton, N.J.: Princeton University Press, 1965.

Dore, Ronald P. Speech at the University of Hawaii. 30 Mar. 1983.

Dostert, L. E., Frederick D. Eddy, W. P. Lehmann, and Albert H. Marckwardt. "Tradition and Innovation in Language Teaching." *The Modern Language Journal* 44 (1960): 220-26.

Dow, Ian I., Ruth V. Whitehead, and Ruth L. Wright. *Curriculum Implementation: A Framework for Action*. Alexandria, Va.: ERIC Document Reproduction Service, ED 256 715, 1984.

"Dr. Krashen Interviewed." *Mainichi Daily News,* 23 Nov. 1984, B5.

Edamatsu, Fred J. "Back to the Barrier." *TESL Reporter* 13, no. 1 (1979): 14-16.

Edamatsu, Fred J. "The Japanese Psycho-Social Barrier in Learning English." *TESL Reporter* 12, no. 1 (1978): 4-6, 17-19.

ELEC executive committee to Charles C. Fries. 1 Sept. 1958. CCF Japan.

ELEC executive committee to Charles C. Fries. 20 Oct. 1958. CCF Japan.

"English Language Exploratory Committee, Minutes of the First Meeting of the General Committee." 28 Jul. 1956. Rockefeller Family Archives. JDR 3rd. Box 39. English Language Teaching Envelope No. 2.

"English Language Institute" flyer. University of Michigan. 23 Nov. 1948. Rockefeller Foundation Archives. R.G. 1.1. Series 200. Box 286. Folder 3415.

"English Language Teaching in Japan: Working Paper—Tentative Estimate of Costs." 1955. Rockefeller Family Archives. JDR 3rd. Box 38. English Language Teaching Envelope.

Espinosa, J. Manuel, Department of State, International Educational Exchange Service, to Charles C. Fries. 29 Jul. 1954. CCF Japan.

"Estimated Expenses for the Proposed Specialists' Conference on English Teaching." 1956. Rockefeller Family Archives. JDR 3rd. Box 38. English Language Teaching Envelope.

Evans, Bergen, ed. *Dictionary of Quotations*. New York: Delacorte Press, 1968

Evans, Richard I. *Resistance to Innovation in Higher Education*. San Francisco, Calif.: Jossey-Bass, 1968.

Fernstermaker, R. J. "Readers in Council." *The Japan Times,* 18 Apr. 1983.

"Final Report to the Ford Foundation: A Project to Establish and Strengthen Programs for the Training of Teachers of English and Other Foreign Languages in Selected Japanese Universities, 1959-1964." English Language Institute. The University of Michigan. Xerox. n.d. [Obtained from William Norris, Georgetown University, Washington, D.C.]

Fishman, Joshua A., Robert L. Cooper, and Andrew W. Conrad. *The Spread of English: The Sociology of English as an Additional Language*. Rowley. Mass.: Newbury House, 1977.

Flenley, Anthony. "Innovation in English Language Teaching in Japan." *Teacher Education Newsletter* 4, no. 2 (1988): 8-10.

Flenley, Anthony. "A Model for the Diffusion and Implementation of Innovations in Japanese Schools." Paper presented at the annual meeting of Teachers of English to Speakers of Other Languages, San Antonio, Texas, 11 Mar. 1989.

Freeman, Donald. "Observing Teachers: Three Approaches to In-Service Training and Development." *TESOL Quarterly* 16, no. 1 (1982): 21-28.

Freeman, Donald. "The Training/Development Continuum: A Framework for Analyzing and Working on Teaching." Paper presented at the annual convention of the Japan Association of Language Teachers, Kyoto, Japan, 15 Sept. 1985.

Freeman, Donald. "The Training/Development Continuum: A Framework for Analyzing Teaching." Paper presented at the ABC Colloquium at Teachers College, Columbia University, New York, 6 Jul. 1984.

Fries, Agnes C. Interview with author. La Jolla, Calif., 5 Mar. 1986.

Fries, Charles C. "As We See It." *Language Learning* 1, no. 1 (1948): 12-16.

Fries, Charles C. "Brief Report to ELEC Concerning the Progress of the Work from September 1956 to September 1957 and Recommendations for the Program of the Year 1957-1958." Special Collections. JDR 3rd Fund. Box 61. Folder 506.

Fries, Charles C. "On the Oral Approach." In *Applied Linguistics and the Teaching of English*, edited by Tamotsu Yambe. Tokyo: ELEC, 1970.

Fries, Charles C. "Preparation of Teaching Materials, Practical Grammars, and Dictionaries, Especially for Foreign Languages." *Language Learning* 10, nos. 1-2 (1959): 43-50.

Fries, Charles C. *Teaching and Learning English as a Foreign Language*. Ann Arbor: University of Michigan Press, 1945.

Fries, Charles C. to David H. Stevens. 21 Mar. 1934. Rockefeller Foundation Archives. R.G. 1.1. Series 200. Box 286. Folder 3420.

Fries, Charles C. to Don [McLean]. 24 May 1958. CCF Japan.

Fries, Charles C. to Don McLean. 5 Apr. 1958. CCF Japan.

Fries, Charles C. to Don McLean. 15 Feb. 1958. CCF Japan.

Fries, Charles C. to Donald McLean. 21 Apr. 1958. CCF Japan.

Fries, Charles C. to Donald McLean. 29 May 1957. CCF Japan.

Fries, Charles C. to Douglas Overton. 5 Aug. 1959. CCF Japan.

Fries, Charles C. to Douglas Overton. 13 Sept. 1959. CCF Japan.

Fries, Charles C. to Douglas Overton. 20 Nov. 1958. CCF Japan.

Fries, Charles C. to Einar [Haugen]. 10 Mar. 1958. CCF Japan.

Fries, Charles C. to ELEC. 23 Nov. 1958. CCF Japan.

Fries, Charles C. to Ernest [Hayden]. 13 Mar. 1958. CCF Japan.

Fries, Charles C. to Gilbert Anderson, International Educational Exchange Service, Department of State. 4 Feb. 1955. CCF Japan.

Fries, Charles C. to Hisaakira Kano. 13 Feb 1958. CCF Japan.

Fries, Charles C. to Iwao Nishimura, United States Educational Commission in Japan. 27 May 1955. CCF Japan.

Fries, Charles C. to Karl Roeloffs, United States Educational Commission. 21 Apr. 1955. CCF Japan.

Fries, Charles C. to Shigeharu Matsumoto. 24 Sept. 1958. CCF Japan.

Fries, Charles C. to W. Freeman Twaddell. 4 Jan. 1958. Special Collections. JDR 3rd Fund. Box 61. Folder 507.

Fries, Charles C. to W. Freeman Twaddell. 15 May 1957. CCF Japan.

Fries, Charles C. to [W.] Freeman Twaddell. 18 Feb. 1958. CCF Japan.

Fries, Charles C. to [W.] Freeman and Helen [Twaddell]. 1 Mar. 1958. CCF Japan.

Fries, Charles C. to Yasaka Takagi and Shigeharu Matsumoto. 23 Mar. 1958. CCF Japan.

Fries, Charles C., and Agnes C. Fries. *Foundations for English Teaching*. Tokyo Kenkyusha, 1961.

Fries, Peter H. "Fries' Views on Psychology: His Nonmechanical View of Human Behavior." In *Charles Carpenter Fries: His 'Oral Approach' for Teaching and Learning Foreign Languages*, edited by William E. Norris and Jeris E. Strain. Washington, D. C.: Georgetown University Press, 1989.

Fries, Peter H. "Linguistics, Language, and Language Learning: C. C. Fries in Perspective." Course taught at 1981 TESOL Summer Institute, Teachers College, Columbia University.

Fullan, Michael, and Alan Pomfret. "Research on Curriculum and Instruction Implementation." *Review of Educational Research* 47, no. 2 (1977): 335-93.

Gardner, Robert C., and Wallace E. Lambert. *Attitudes and Motivation in Second-Language Learning*. Rowley, Mass.: Newbury House, 1972.

Gee, Elsie W. *Applying Effective Instruction Research Findings in Teacher Education: Six Influencing Factors*. Alexandria, Va.: ERIC Document Reproduction Service, ED 246 037, 1984.

Gibney, Frank. *Five Gentlemen of Japan*. New York: Farrar, Straus, and Young, 1953.

Gibney, Frank. *Japan: The Fragile Superpower*. New York: Norton, 1975.

Giles, Howard. "Ethnicity Markers in Speech." In *Social Markers in Speech*, edited by Klaus R. Scherer and Howard Giles. Cambridge, Eng.: Cambridge University Press, 1979.

Gill, Robin. "Readers in Council." *The Japan Times,* 15 Apr. 1983.

Gilpatric, Chadbourne, Associate Director of The Rockefeller Foundation. Diary excerpt during trip to Ann Arbor and Chicago. 29, 30, 31 Jul. and 1 Aug. 1955. Rockefeller Family Archives. R.G. 2-1955. Series 200. Box 39. Folder 254.

Glicksberg, Daniel. "English Teaching in Japan." In *On Teaching English to Speakers of Other Languages,* edited by Betty Wallace Robinett. Washington, D.C.: TESOL, 1967.

Goodman, Kenneth S. "Basal Readers: A Call for Action." *Language Arts* 63, no. 4 (1986): 358-63.

Gordon, Peter, and Denis Lawton. *Curriculum Change in the Nineteenth & Twentieth Centuries.* London: Hodder and Stoughton, 1978.

Goto, Shoji. "How to Improve Entrance Examinations on English in Japan." *The Language Teacher* 10, no. 4 (1986): 25.

Guidebook: Seminar for Teachers of English. Tokyo: Japanese Ministry of Education, 1961.

Guiora, Alexander Z., Benjamin Beit-Hallahmi, Robert C. L. Brannon, Cecelia Y. Dull, and Thomas Scovel. "The Effects of Experimentally Induced Changes in Ego States on Pronunciation Ability in a Second Language: An Exploratory Study." *Comprehensive Psychology* 13, no. 5 (1972): 421-28.

Hall, Ivan. *Mori Arinori.* Cambridge, Mass.: Harvard University Press, 1973.

Hall, John W. to President Harlan Hatcher, University of Michigan. 22 Dec. 1955. CCF Japan.

Harasawa, Masayoshi. "A Critical Survey of English Language Teaching in Japan: A Personal View." *English Language Teaching Journal* 29, no. 1 (1974): 71-79.

Harker, Rowland. "A Case Study in Dealing with Cultural Reserve as an Impediment to Language Learning." *Cross Currents* 9, no. 1 (1982): 9-20.

Harris, Townsend. *The Complete Journal of Townsend Harris: First American Consul and Minister to Japan,* 2d rev. ed. Rutland, Vt. and Tokyo, Japan: Charles E. Tuttle Co., 1959.

Hatori, Hiroyoshi. Interview with author. Tokyo, Japan, 3 Sept. 1985.

Havelock, Ronald G. *The Change Agent's Guide to Innovation in Education.* Englewood Cliffs, N.J.: Educational Technology Publications, 1973 .

Havelock, Ronald G. *Planning for Innovation Through Dissemination and Utilization of Knowledge.* Ann Arbor, Mich.: Center for Research on Utilization of Scientific Knowledge, Institute for Social Research, The University of Michigan, 1969.

Havelock, Ronald G., and A. M. Huberman. *Solving Educational Problems: The Theory and Reality of Innovation in Developing Countries.* New York: Praeger, 1978.

Havelock, Ronald G., Janet C. Huber, and Shaindel Zimmerman. *Major Works on Change in Education: An Annotated Bibliography with Author and Subject Indices.* Ann Arbor, Mich.: Center for Research on Utilization of Scientific Knowledge, Institute for Social Research, The University of Michigan, 1969.

Hawkey, Roger. "From Needs to Materials via Constraints: Some General Considerations and Zimbabwean Experience." In *Trends in Language Syllabus Design,* edited by John A. S. Read. Singapore: SEAMEO Regional Language Centre, 1984.

Hayashi, Satoshi to Charles C. Fries. 30 May 1957. CCF Japan.

Hino, Nobuyuki. "Yakudoku: Japan's Dominant Tradition in Foreign Language Learning." *JALT Journal* 10, nos. 1 & 2 (1988): 45-55.

Hino, Nobuyuki. "Yakudoku: The Japanese Approach to Foreign Language Study." *Working Papers* (Department of English as a Second Language, University of Hawaii at Manoa) 1, no. 2 (1982): 45-53.

Honda, Takehisa. "Fond Memories of ELEC's Early Days." *ELEC Bulletin* 79 (1983): 32.

Hopkins, Louis A., Director of University of Michigan Summer Session, to David H. Stevens, Director, The Humanities, The Rockefeller Foundation. 16 Oct. 1940. Rockefeller Foundation Archives. R.G. 1.1. Series 200. Box 286. Folder 3412.

Hornby, A. S., and Daniel Jones. "H. E. Palmer." *English Language Teaching* 4, no. 4 (1950): 87-92.

House, Ernest R. *The Politics of Educational Innovation.* Berkeley, Calif.: McCutchan, 1974.

Houston, James E., ed. *Thesaurus of ERIC Descriptors,* 10th rev. ed. Phoenix, Arizona: Oryx Press, 1984.

Howatt, A.P.R. *A History of English Language Teaching.* Oxford, Eng.: Oxford University Press, 1984.

Hudson, R. A. *Sociolinguistics.* Cambridge, Eng.: Cambridge University Press, 1980.

Hughes, John P. *Linguistics and Language Teaching.* New York: Random House, 1968.

Ichikawa, Sanki. "Problems of Teaching English in Japan." In *Addresses and Papers at the Specialists' Conference, September 3-7, 1956, English Language Exploratory Committee,* edited by Fumio Nakajima. Tokyo: Kenkyusha, 1957.

Ishii, Satoshi. "*Enryo-Sasshi* Communication: A Key to Understanding Japanese Interpersonal Relations." *Cross Currents* 11, no. 1 (1984): 49-58.

Ito, Kaichi. "Traditional Methods and New Methods: A Study on the Methods Suited for the Japanese." In *The Teaching of English in Japan,* edited by Ikuo Koike, Masao Matsuyama, Yasuo Igarashi, and Koji Suzuki. Tokyo: Eichosha, 1978.

Jansen, Marius B. *Japan and Its World: Two Centuries of Change.* Princeton, N.J.: Princeton University Press, 1980.

Kaieda, Susumu. "Teaching Other Foreign Languages in Japan." In *The Teaching of English in Japan,* edited by Ikuo Koike, Masao Matsuyama, Yasuo Igarashi, and Koji Suzuki. Tokyo: Eichosha, 1978.

Kanatani, Ken. Interview with author. Tokyo, Japan, 3 Sept. 1985.

Kanda Memorial Committee, ed. *Memorials of Naibu Kanda.* Tokyo: Toko-Shoin, 1927.

Kano, Hisaakira, Genji Takahashi, and Takashi Kuroda. "Report on the 1958 ELEC Summer Program." *ELEC Publications, Vol III.* Tokyo: Kenkyusha, 1959.

Kano, Hisaakira, Minoru Toyoda, Genji Takahashi, Fumio Nakajima, and Shigeharu Matsumoto to Charles C. Fries. 1 Sept. 1958. CCF Japan.

Kawai, Kazuo. *Japan's American Interlude.* Chicago: University of Chicago Press, 1960.

Kawazumi, Tetsuo. "Yakudoku no rekishi." *The English Teacher's Magazine,* Jul. 1975.

Kelly, Gail P., and Philip G. Altbach. "Comparative Education: Challenge and Response." *Comparative Education Review* 30, no. 1 (1986): 89-107.

Kelly, Louis G. *25 Centuries of Language Teaching.* Rowley. Mass.: Newbury House, 1969.

Kikuchi, Baron Dairoku. *Japanese Education: Lectures Delivered in the University of London.* London: John Murray, 1909.

Kimizuka, Sumako. Interview with author. Laie, Hawaii, 15 Mar. 1985.

Kimizuka, Sumako. *Teaching English to Japanese.* Los Angeles: Anchor Enterprises, 1968.

Kimizuka, Sumako. "Teaching English to Japanese Speakers." In *Collected Reviews from the LIOJ Workshop for Japanese English Teachers,* edited by Joyce Yukawa and Howard Gutow. Odawara, Japan: Language Institute of Japan, 1979.

Kimpara, Osamu. Interview with author. Tokyo, Japan, 6 Sept. 1985.

King, Arthur R. Interview with author. Honolulu, Hawaii, 9 Oct. 1986.

King, Edmund J. "Students, Teachers, and Researchers in Comparative Education." *Comparative Education Review* 3, no. 1 (1959): 33-36.

King, Jean A. *'A Piece of the Dirt': Curriculum Change at Boynton Middle School, August 1983-February 1984.* Alexandria, Va.: ERIC Document Reproduction Service, ED 248 616, 1984.

Kleinjans, Everett. Interview with author. Honolulu, Hawaii, 14 Apr. 1987.

Kleinjans, Everett to Charles C. Fries. 26 Feb. 1955. CCF Japan.

Kobayashi, Tetsuya. *Society, Schools, and Progress in Japan.* Oxford, Eng.: Pergamon Press, 1976.

Kobayashi, Victor N. "Japan: Under American Occupation." In *Learning to be Japanese,* edited by Edward R. Beauchamp. Hamden, Conn.: Linnet Books, 1978.

Koike, Ikuo. "English Language Teaching Policies in Japan: Past, Present, and Future." In *The Teaching of English in Japan,* edited by Ikuo Koike, Masao Matsuyama, Yasuo Igarashi, and Koji Suzuki. Tokyo: Eichosha, 1978.

Koike, Ikuo. Interview with author. Tokyo, Japan, 6 Sept. 1985.

Koike, Ikuo, Masao Matsuyama, Yasuo Igarashi, and Koji Suzuki, eds. *The Teaching of English in Japan.* Tokyo: Eichosha, 1978.

Krashen, Stephen. "Formal and Informal Linguistic Environments in Language Acquisition and Language Learning." *TESOL Quarterly* 10, no. 2 (1976): 157-68.

Krashen, Stephen. "The 'Fundamental Pedagogical Principle' in Second Language Teaching." *Studia Linguistica* 35, nos. 1-2 (1981): 50-52.

Krashen, Stephen. "The Monitor Model for Adult Second Language Performance." In *Viewpoints on English as a Second Language*, edited by Marina K. Burt, Heidi Dulay, and Mary Finocchiaro. New York: Regents, 1977.

Kuroda, Takashi. "Plan of Teaching Material Preparation." 19 Sept. 1956. Rockefeller Family Archives. JDR 3rd. Box 39. English Language Teaching Envelope No. 2.

Lado, Robert. Interview with author. Washington, D.C., 26 Nov. 1985.

Lado, Robert. *Language Teaching: A Scientific Approach*. New York: McGraw-Hill, 1964.

LaForge, Paul. "Community Language Learning: The Japanese Case." In *Language in Japanese Society*, edited by Fred C. C. Peng. Tokyo: University of Tokyo Press, 1975.

Lamb, Sidney. Aug. 1955. Rockefeller Family Archives. JDR 3rd. Box 38. English Language Teaching Envelope.

Lambert, Wallace E. "The Social Psychology of Language: A Perspective for the 1980's." *Focus: Thought-Provoking Papers on Bilingual Education,* No. 5. (Rosslyn, Va.: National Clearinghouse for Bilingual Education, 1981), 1-8.

Larudee, Faze. "Language Teaching in Historical Perspective." Ph.D. diss., University of Michigan, 1964.

Lauter, P. "The Short, Happy Life of the Adams-Morgan Community School Project." *Harvard Educational Review* 38, no. 2 (1968): 235-262.

Lebra, Takie Sugiyama. *Japanese Patterns of Behavior*. Honolulu: University Press of Hawaii, 1976.

Leithwood, K. A. "Managing the Implementation of Curriculum Innovations." *Knowledge: Creation, Diffusion, Utilization* 2, no. 3 (1981): 341-59.

Letter to Douglas Overton (unsigned). 6 Feb. 1962. Special Collections. JDR 3rd Fund. Box 62. Folder 512.

Letter to Shigeharu Matsumoto [from McLean?]. 26 Jul. 1956. Rockefeller Family Archives. JDR 3rd. Box 39. English Language Teaching Envelope No. 2.

Lévi-Strauss, Claude. *Structural Anthropology*. Garden City, N.Y.: Doubleday, 1967.

Lillis, Kevin M. "Processes of Secondary Curriculum Innovation in Kenya." *Comparative Education Review* 29, no. 1 (1985): 80-96.

LoCastro, Virginia. "Interview with Minoru Wada of the Ministry of Education." *The Language Teacher* 12, no. 9 (1988): 5-7, 9.

Lombard, Frank Alanson. *Pre-Meiji Education in Japan.* Tokyo: Kyobunkan, 1916.

Lord, Lewis J., and Miriam Horn. "The Brain Battle." *U.S. News and World Report,* 19 Jan. 1987, 58-64.

Mackey, W. F. *Language Teaching Analysis.* Bloomington and London: Indiana University Press, 1965.

Maeda, Yoichi. Interview with author. Tokyo, Japan, 6 Sept 1985.

Maher, John C. "English Language Education in Japan: Historical and Macro Issues in the Teaching of English in Schools." *Language Learning and Communication* 3, no. 1 (1984): 41-50.

Maley, Alan. "Constraints-based Syllabuses." In *Trends in Language Syllabus Design,* edited by John A. S. Read. Singapore: SEAMEO Regional Language Centre, 1984.

Mann, Dale, ed. *Making Change Happen?* New York: Teachers College Press, 1978.

Marckwardt, Albert H. "Motives for the Study of Modern Languages." *Language Learning* 1, no. 1 (1948): 3-11.

Marquardt, William F. "The Gift of Tongues: A National Challenge." *Language Learning* 10, nos. 1-2 (1960): 33-40.

Marsh, Colin J. "Implementation of a Curriculum Innovation in Australian Schools." *Knowledge: Creation, Diffusion, Utilization* 6, no. 1 (1984): 37-58.

Martin, David S., and Philip J. Saif. *Curriculum Change from the Grass Roots.* Alexandria, Va.: ERIC Document Reproduction Service, ED 254 913, 1984.

Matsumoto, Shigeharu to Donald H. McLean, Jr. 29 Sept. 1956. Rockefeller Family Archives. JDR 3rd. Box 39. English Language Teaching Envelope No. 2.

Matsumoto, Shigeharu to Donald McLean. 22 Dec. 1955. Rockefeller Family Archives. JDR 3rd. Box 38. English Language Teaching Envelope.

Matsumoto, Shigeharu to Douglas Overton. 12 Dec. 1961. Rockefeller Family Archives. JDR 3rd. Box 39. English Language Teaching Envelope No. 2.

Matsumoto, Shigeharu to John D. Rockefeller 3rd. 16 Aug. 1955. Rockefeller Family Archives. JDR 3rd. Box 38. English Language Teaching Envelope.

Matsumoto, Shigeharu to John D. Rockefeller 3rd. 12 Aug. 1956. Rockefeller Family Archives. JDR 3rd. Box 39. English Language Teaching Envelope No. 2.

Matsumoto, Shigeharu. Interview with author. Tokyo, Japan, 5 Sept. 1985.

"Matsumoto's Memorandum on the Progress of the Temporary Committee." 31 Dec. 1955. Rockefeller Family Archives. JDR 3rd. Box 38. English Language Teaching Envelope.

Matthews, Gordon. "Why Teach English? Why Learn English?" *The Language Teacher* 11, no. 2 (1987): 32-33.

McLean, Donald. Memorandum. 11 Jan 1952. Rockefeller Family Archives. R.G. 2. OMR-Cultural Interests. Folder 169J Japan Society.

McLean, Donald H., Jr. Memorandum on "English-Language Teaching in Japan." 1 Mar. 1956. Rockefeller Family Archives. JDR 3rd. Box 38. English Language Teaching Envelope.

McLean, Don H., Jr. to John D. Rockefeller 3rd. 15 May 1953. Rockefeller Family Archives. JDR 3rd. Box 38. Japan—Economic Situation Folder.

McLean, Donald H. to John D. Rockefeller 3rd. 8 Oct. 1956. Rockefeller Family Archives. JDR 3rd. Box 39. English Language Teaching Envelope No. 2.

McLean, Donald H., Jr. to John D. Rockefeller 3rd. 9 Dec. 1955. Rockefeller Family Archives. JDR 3rd. Box 38. English Language Teaching Envelope.

McLean, Donald to John D. Rockefeller 3rd. 22 May 1956. Rockefeller Family Archives. JDR 3rd. Box 38. English Language Teaching Envelope.

McLean, Donald H., Jr. to John D. Rockefeller 3rd. 19 Apr. 1962. Special Collections. JDR 3rd Fund. Box 62. Folder 512.

McLean, Donald H., Jr. to John D. Rockefeller 3rd. Memorandum on "English-Language Teaching in Japan." 19 Sept. 1956. Rockefeller Family Archives. JDR 3rd. Box 39. English Language Teaching Envelope No. 2.

McLean, Donald H., Jr. to John D. Rockefeller 3rd. Memorandum on "English-LanguageTeaching in Japan." 6 Jan. 1956. Rockefeller Family Archives. JDR 3rd. Box 38. English Language Teaching Envelope.

McLean, Donald H. to John D. Rockefeller 3rd. "Thoughts on English-Language Teaching." 3 Apr. 1956. Rockefeller Family Archives. JDR 3rd. Box 38. English Language Teaching Folder.

McLean, Donald H., Jr. to Yasaka Takagi and Shigeharu Matsumoto. 17 May 1956. Rockefeller Family Archives. JDR 3rd. Box 38. English Language Teaching Envelope.

McLean, [Donald, Jr.], [Douglas] Overton, [Hugh] Borton, and Carman. Report on Japanese-American Cultural Relations. 27 Jul. 1953. Rockefeller Family Archives. Box 39. JDR 3rd Personal.

McLean, Paul. "English Language Teaching in Japan: A Paradox." *East-West Education* 5, no. 1 (1984): 21-26.

Memorandum. 24 Sept. 1958. Rockefeller Family Archives. JDR 3rd. Box 39. English Language Teaching Envelope No. 2.

Memorandum attached to the agenda of the "12th meeting on English Teaching Method" of the ELEC conference planning committee. 25 Apr. 1956. Tokyo. Rockefeller Family Archives. JDR 3rd. Box 38. English Language Teaching Envelope.

Memorandum on English-Language Teaching. 5 Apr. 1956. Rockefeller Family Archives. JDR 3rd. Box 39. English Language Teaching Envelope No. 2.

Memorandum to John D. Rockefeller 3rd. 19 Jun. 1962. Special Collections. JDR 3rd Fund. Box 62. Folder 512.

Meyer, John W. "The Politics of Educational Crises in the United States," In *Educational Policies in Crisis: Japanese and American Perspectives*, edited by William K. Cummings, Edward R. Beauchamp, Shogo Ichikawa, Victor N. Kobayashi, and Morikazu Ushiogi. New York: Praeger, 1986.

Michaletz, James E. *An Effective Approach to Curriculum Change: Planning, Implementation, and Evaluation.* Alexandria, Va.: ERIC Document Reproduction Service, ED 259 466, 1985.

Miles, Matthew B., ed. *Innovation in Education.* New York: Teachers College, 1964.

Minakawa, Saburo. *Christian Education and English Teaching in Early Japan.* Yokohama: n.p., 1953.

Mintzberg, Henry, Duru Raisinghani, and Andre Théorêt. "The Structure of 'Unstructured' Decision Processes." *Administrative Science Quarterly* 21, no. 2 (1976): 246-75.

"Minutes of the First Meeting of the General Committee." 28 Jul. 1956. Rockefeller Family Archives. JDR 3rd. Box 39. English Language Teaching Envelope No. 2.

Miyazawa, T. "Readers in Council." *The Japan Times,* 4 Apr. 1983.

Moloney, James Clark. *Understanding the Japanese Mind.* Tokyo: Charles E. Tuttle, 1954.

Morley, Joan, Betty Wallace Robinett, Larry Selinker, and Devon Woods. "ESL Theory and the Fries Legacy." *JALT Journal* 6, no. 2 (1984): 171-207.

Morris, Joe Alex. *Those Rockefeller Brothers.* New York: Harper & Brothers, 1953.

Moulton, William G. "Foreign Language Teaching in America in the 20's and 30's." In *Charles Carpenter Fries: His 'Oral Approach' for Teaching and Learning Foreign Languages*, edited by William E. Norris and Jeris E. Strain. Washington, D. C.: Georgetown University Press, 1989.

[Muto, Yoshio]. "ELEC Past and Present, 1956-1966." Reprinted from *ELEC Publications, Vol. VIII.* Tokyo: Kenkyusha, 1967.

Nagao, Koji. "Fond Memories of ELEC's Early Days." *ELEC Bulletin* 79 (1983): 32.

Nakajima, Fumio, ed. *Addresses and Papers at the Specialists' Conference, September 3-7, 1956, English Language Exploratory Committee.* Tokyo: Kenkyusha, 1957.

Nakajima, Fumio. Preface to *Foundations for English Teaching,* by Charles C. Fries and Agnes C. Fries. Tokyo: Kenkyusha, 1961.

Nakajima, Fumio. Preface to *Lectures,* by Charles C. Fries and W. Freeman Twaddell. Tokyo: ELEC, 1958.

Nakane, Chie. *Japanese Society.* Harmondsworth, Middlesex, Eng.: Penguin, 1973.

Nelson, Cecil L. "English as a Decorative Pattern." *EFL Gazette* [London], Aug. 1987, 10.

Nitobe, Inazo. *The Japanese Nation: Its Land, Its People, and Its Life.* Wilmington, Del.: Scholarly Resources, 1973.

Nitobe, Inazo. "The Teaching and Use of Foreign Languages in Japan." *Sewanee Review* 31 (1923): 338-339.

Noah, Harold J. "The Use and Abuse of Comparative Education." *Comparative Education Review* 28, no. 4 (1984): 550-62.

Noda, Tetsuo. Interview with author. Tokyo, Japan, 3 Sept. 1985.

Norris, William E., and Jeris E. Strain, eds. *Charles Carpenter Fries: His 'Oral Approach' for Teaching and Learning Foreign Languages.* Washington, D. C.: Georgetown University Press, 1989.

"Notes from an International 'Rap' Session." *Teaching English Abroad Newsletter* 3, no. 3 (1982): 8.

Numata, Jiro. "Acceptance and Rejection of Elements of European Culture in Japan." *Cahiers d'Histoire Mondiale (Journal of World History)* 3, no. 1 (1956): 231-53.

O'Connor, Patricia, and W. F. Twaddell. "Intensive Training for an Oral Approach in Language Teaching." *The Modern Language Journal* 44, no. 2, part 2 (1960): 1-42.

Ogasawara, Linju. "The Educational System and English in Japan—A Background." *ELEC Bulletin* 55-56 (1976): 87-94.

Ogasawara, Linju. Interview with author. Tokyo, Japan, 5 Sept. 1985.

Oller, John W., Jr., Alan J. Hudson, and Phyllis Fei Liu. "Attitudes and Attained Proficiency in ESL: A Sociolinguistic Study of Native Speakers of Chinese in the U.S." *Language Learning* 27, no. 1 (1979): 1-27.

Olshtain, Elite. "Language Policy and the Classroom Teacher." In *Beyond Basics: Issues and Research in TESOL,* edited by Marianne Celce-Murcia. Rowley, Mass.: Newbury House, 1985.

Omura, Kiyoshi. "Prewar (before 1945): From the Phaeton Incident up to the Pacific War." In *The Teaching of English in Japan,* edited by Ikuo Koike, Masao Matsuyama, Yasuo Igarashi, and Koji Suzuki. Tokyo: Eichosha, 1978.

"The Oral Method of Teaching English." *Asahi Evening News,* 2 Dec. 1957.

Oshiba, Mamoru. "Education in Japan before and after the Meiji Restoration." In his *Four Articles on Japanese Education.* n.p. [Tokyo?]: n.p. [International Christian University?] [Distributed by Maruzen Kabushi Kaisha, Kobe], 1963.

Oshiba, Mamoru, and Don Adams. "Japanese Education—After the Americans Left." In *Four Articles on Japanese Education*, edited by Mamoru Oshiba. n.p.[Tokyo?]: n.p. [International Christian University?] [Distributed by Maruzen Kabushi Kaisha, Kobe], 1963.

Ota, Akira. Interview with author. Tokyo, Japan, 5 Sept. 1985.

Ota, Akira. "Methods." *ELEC Bulletin* 55-56 (1976): 48-58.

Otani, Yasuteru. "College and University: What are the Barriers to Efficient English Teaching?" In *The Teaching of English in Japan*, edited by Ikuo Koike, Masao Matsuyama, Yasuo Igarashi, and Koji Suzuki. Tokyo: Eichosha, 1978.

Ouedraogo, Mathieu R. *An Analysis of Some Factors that Affect Curriculum Implementation in Upper Volta*. Alexandria, Va.: ERIC Document Reproduction Service, ED 255 475, 1983.

Overton, Douglas. "English Language Teaching in Japan." 28 Mar. 1960. Memorandum. 24 Sept. 1958. Rockefeller Family Archives. JDR 3rd. Box 39. English Language Teaching Envelope No. 2.

Overton, Douglas. Report to CECA on English Language Teaching in Japan. 28 Mar. 1960. Rockefeller Family Archives. JDR 3rd. Box 39. English Language Teaching Envelope No. 2.

Overton, Douglas to John D. Rockefeller 3rd. 17 Feb. 1961. Rockefeller Family Archives. JDR 3rd. Box 39. English Language Teaching Envelope No. 2.

Overton, Douglas, Executive Director of Japan Society, to Trustees of CECA. 10 Dec. 1958. Rockefeller Family Archives. JDR 3rd. Box 39. English Language Teaching Envelope No. 2.

Overton, Douglas W. "U.S. Government Program in Japan." 25 Jun. 1953. Rockefeller Family Archives. JDR 3rd. Box 38. Japan—Economic Situation Folder. Envelope No. 2. Mr. R. 3rd.

Palmer, Harold E. "The English Language in Japan." *Empire Review*, no. 447, Apr. 1938.

Palmer, Harold E. *The Principles of Language Study*. Yonkers-on-Hudson, N.Y.: World Book Co., 1926.

Palmer, Harold E., and H. Vere Redman. *This Language-Learning Business*. George G. Harrap & Co., 1932. Reprint. London: Oxford University Press, 1969.

Paper, "for Mr. McLane" [McLean]. 22 Jul. 1962. Special Collections. JDR 3rd Fund. Box 62. Folder 512.

Parish, Ralph, and Richard Arends. "Why Innovative Programs are Discontinued." *Educational Leadership* 40, no. 4 (1983): 62-65.

Parker, William Riley. *The National Interest and Foreign Languages*. Washington, D.C.: U. S. Department of State, 1957.

Pascasio, Emy M. "An English Communicative Syllabus in Practice: A Case Study from the Philippines." In *Trends in Language Syllabus Design*, edited by John A. S. Read. Singapore: SEAMEO Regional Language Centre, 1984.

Passin, Herbert. *Society and Education in Japan.* New York: Teachers College Press, 1965.

Passin, Herbert to Donald McLean. 6 Jun. 1962. Special Collections. JDR 3rd Fund. Box 62. Folder 512.

Pearson, Eloise. "Oral Interactive Testing at a Japanese University." *Cross Currents* 11, no. 2 (1984): 1-12.

Pelz, Donald C. "Innovation Complexity and the Sequence of Innovating Stages." *Knowledge: Creation, Diffusion, Utilization* 6, no. 3 (1985): 261-91.

Pierson, Harry H., The Asia Foundation, to Charles Fries. 26 Sept. 1955. CCF Japan.

Prator, Clifford H. "The Cornerstones of Method." In *Teaching English as a Second or Foreign Language,* edited by Marianne Celce-Murcia and Lois McIntosh. Rowley, Mass.: Newbury House, 1979.

Pratt, Harold, John C. Thurber, Gene E. Hall, and Shirley M. Hord. *Case Studies of School Improvement: A Concerns Based Approach.* Alexandria, Va.: ERIC Document Reproduction Service, ED 251 491, 1982.

Raimes, Ann. "Tradition and Revolution in ESL Teaching." *TESOL Quarterly* 17, no. 4 (1983): 535-52.

Ramos, Maximo, Jose V. Aguilar, and Bonifacio P. Sibayan. *The Determination and Implementation of Language Policy.* Quezon City, Philippines: Alemar Phoenix, 1967.

Reed, David W. "Editorial." *Language Learning* 1, no. 1 (1948): 1.

Reischauer, Edwin O. "The English Language and Japan's Role in the World." *Conference of the National Federation of Prefectural English Teachers' Organizations.* Tokyo: The Federation, 1961.

Reischauer, Edwin O. *The Japanese.* Tokyo: Charles E. Tuttle, 1977.

Reischauer, Edwin O. *Japan: The Story of a Nation.* Tokyo: Charles E. Tuttle, 1974.

Reischauer, Edwin O. to Hugh Borton. 17 Nov. 1955. Rockefeller Family Archives. JDR 3rd. Box 38. English Language Teaching Folder.

"Report of Conference of Experts on the Teaching of English in Japan." Cited by Brownell, *Japan's Second Language,* 51.

Reports on grants and appropriations to the University of Michigan. 19 Feb 1941 and 16 Sept. 1941. Rockefeller Foundation Archives. R.G. 1.1. Series 200. Box 286. Folder 3412.

Report to Mr. H. F. Prioleau. 28 Aug. 1955. Rockefeller Family Archives. JDR 3rd. Box 38.

"Responses to Edward H. Berman." *Harvard Educational Review* 49, no. 2 (1979): 180-84.

Richards, Jack C. "The Context of Language Teaching." In his *The Context of Language Teaching.* Cambridge, Eng.: Cambridge University Press, 1985.

Richards, Jack C. "The Secret Life of Methods." Plenary address delivered at the annual meeting of Teachers of English to Speakers of Other Languages, Toronto, Canada, 19 Mar. 1983.

Richards, Jack C. "The Secret Life of Methods." *TESOL Quarterly* 18, no. 1 (1984): 7-23.

Richards, Jack C. "The Secret Life of Methods." *Working Papers* (Department of English as a Second Language, University of Hawaii at Manoa) 2, no. 2 (1983): 1-21.

Roberts-Gray, Cynthia, and Thomas Gray. "Implementing Innovations." *Knowledge: Creation, Diffusion, Utilization* 5, no. 2 (1983): 213-32.

Robinett, Betty Wallace. *Teaching English to Speakers of Other Languages.* New York: McGraw-Hill, 1978.

Rockefeller Foundation Resolution 34037. 11 Apr. 1934. Rockefeller Foundation Archives. R.G. 1.1. Series 200R. Box 286. Folder 3420.

"Rockefeller Fund to Double Its Spending on Developing Nations." *The Chronicle of Higher Education,* 7 May 1986, 26.

Rockefeller, John D., 3rd to Charles C. Fries. 15 Oct. 1956. Rockefeller Family Archives. JDR 3rd. Box 39. English Language Teaching Envelope No. 2.

Rockefeller, John D., 3rd to Douglas Overton. 13 Sept. 1956. Rockefeller Family Archives. R.G. 2 OMR-Cultural Interests. Box 81. Japan Society Envelope No. 5. 169J.

Rockefeller, John D., 3rd to His Excellency Mayato Ikeda. 26 Feb. 1962. Rockefeller Family Archives. JDR 3rd Fund. Box 62. Folder 512.

Rockefeller, John D., 3rd to Mrs. Morris Hadley. 23 Nov. 1953. Rockefeller Family Archives. JDR 3rd. Box 41. Japan Interests— Matsumoto, Shigeharu Folder.

Rockefeller, John D., 3rd to Mrs. Philip Dewing. 8 May 1959. Rockefeller Family Archives. JDR 3rd. Box 41. Japan Interests—G.I. Baby Problem Folder.

Rockefeller, John D., 3rd to Shigeharu Matsumoto. 11 Jan. 1956. Rockefeller Family Archives. JDR 3rd. Box 38. English Language Teaching Envelope.

Rockefeller, John D., 3rd to William Cullen Bryant, Jr. 11 Jul. 1955. Rockefeller Family Archives. JDR 3rd. Box 38. English Language Teaching Envelope.

Rodgers, Ted [Theodore S.]. "Syllabus Design, Curriculum Development and Polity Deliberation." Xerox, n.d., 1. [Obtained from author at University of Hawaii at Manoa, Honolulu, Hawaii.]

Rodgers, Theodore S. "Communicative Syllabus Design and Implementation: Reflection on a Decade of Experience." In *Trends in Language Syllabus Design*, edited by John A. S. Read. Singapore: SEAMEO Regional Language Centre, 1984.

Rogers, Everett M., and D. Lawrence Kincaid. *Communication Networks: Toward a New Paradigm for Research.* New York: Free Press, 1981.

Rogers, Everett M., and F. Floyd Shoemaker. *Communication of Innovations: A Cross-Cultural Approach.* 2d ed. New York: The Free Press, 1971.

Rojas, Pauline M. and staff (C. C. Fries, consultant). *Fries American English Series: For the Study of English as a Second Language.* Boston: D. C. Heath, 1952.

Salama, Adel Moh. "Applied Linguistics in Egypt." *TESOL Applied Linguistics Interest Section Newsletter* 8, no. 1 (1986): 5.

Sarason, Seymour B. *The Culture of the School and the Problem of Change.* Boston: Allyn and Bacon, 1971.

Sasaki, Juro. Review of "Cultural Interference in Japanese English Language Education," (Address delivered at 14 Nov. 1982 meeting of JALT-East Kansai) by Linju Ogasawara. *JALT Newsletter* 7, no. 3 (1983): 18.

Schumann, John H. "Social and Psychological Factors in Second Language Acquisition." In *Understanding Second and Foreign Language Learning: Issues and Approaches,* edited by Jack C. Richards. Rowley, Mass.: Newbury House, 1978.

Shimazu, Mitsu. "Japanese Students in EFL/ESL Classrooms." *TESOL Newsletter* 18, no. 2 (1984): 19.

Shimizu, Mamoru. "ELEC Past & Present: 1956-1976." *ELEC Bulletin* 55-56 (1976): 99-105.

Shimizu, Mamoru. Interview with author. Tokyo, Japan, 6 Sept. 1985.

Shive, Glen. "The National Diffusion Network: A Three Legged Strategy to Disseminate Curricula Innovations in American Schools." Paper presented at the Symposium on Curriculum Development and Continuing Teacher Education, Guangzhou, China, 6-13 Dec. 1988.

Sibatani, Atuhiro. "The Japanese Brain." *Science 80* 1, no. 8 (1980): 22-27.

Sladen, Douglas, and Norma Lorimer. *More Queer Things About Japan.* New York: Dodge Publishing Co., n.d.[1905?].

Smith, Datus C., Jr. to John D. Rockefeller 3rd. 3 Apr. 1969. Special Collections. JDR 3rd Fund. Box 64. Series 8: English Language Teaching in Japan. Folder 523.

Smith, Datus C., Jr. to John D. Rockefeller 3rd. "JDR 3rd & the English Language in Japan." 20 May 1974. Special Collections. JDR 3rd Fund. Box 64. Folder 527.

Smith, Larry E. "The Art of Change in ESOL or How to Create an Elephant." *TESL Reporter* 9, no. 1 (1975): 4-5.

Smith, Robert S., Program Assistant, The Asia Foundation, to Donald McLean. 28 Mar. 1956. Rockefeller Family Archives. JDR 3rd. Box 38. English Language Teaching Envelope.

Snow, C. P. "Miasma, Darkness and Torpidity." *New Statesman* 42 (1961): 1587.

Snow, Marguerite Ann, with Rina G. Shapira. "The Role of Social-Psychological Factors in Second Language Learning." In *Beyond Basics: Issues and Research in TESOL*, edited by Marianne Celce-Murcia. Rowley, Mass.: Newbury House, 1985.

Spolsky, Bernard. "Attitudinal Aspects of Second Language Learning." *Language Learning* 19, nos. 3-4 (1969): 271-85.

Stern, H. H. *Fundamental Concepts of Language Teaching*. Oxford, Eng.: Oxford University Press, 1983.

[Stevens], DHS [David H.]. inter-office Correspondence. Rockefeller Foundation Archives. R.G. 1.1. Series 200. Box 286. Folder 3412.

Stevick, Earl W. *Memory, Meaning & Method*. Rowley, Mass.: Newbury House, 1976.

Stevick, Earl W. "Toward a Practical Philosophy of Pronunciation: Another View." *TESOL Quarterly* 12, no. 2 (1978): 145-50.

Strain, Jeris E. "C. C. Fries/Michigan Oral Approach Revisited." Paper presented at the annual meeting of the International Association of Teachers of English as a Foreign Language, Brighton, Eng., 2 Apr. 1986.

Strevens, Peter. "Teacher Training and the Curriculum." Paper presented at the British Council Seminar at Dunford House, Eng., 20 July 1982.

Suggested Course of Study in English for Lower and Upper Secondary Schools, rev. ed. Tokyo: Ministry of Education, 1951.

Suzuki, Koji. "Some Recommendations for Improving English Education in Japan." *Workpapers in Teaching English as a Second Language* (University of California at Los Angeles) 7 (1973): 107-15.

Sweet, Henry. *The Practical Study of Languages*. J. M. Dent & Sons, Ltd., 1899. Reprint. London: Oxford University Press, 1964.

Tajima, Kiyoshi. "English Teaching in Japan." *Workpapers in Teaching English as a Second Language* (University of California at Los Angeles) 10 (1976): 141-55.

Takagi, Y[asaka]. Memorandum drafted for the "12th meeting on English Teaching Method" of the ELEC conference planning committee, 25 Apr. 1956, Tokyo. Rockefeller Family Archives. JDR 3rd. Box 38. English Language Teaching Envelope.

Takagi, Y[asaka]. "A Section of the Prospectus (Part I)." 25 Apr. 1956. Rockefeller Family Archives. JDR 3rd. Box 38. English Language Teaching Folder.

[Takagi], Yasaka to [Donald] McLean. 14 Jun. 1962. Special Collections. JDR 3rd Fund. Box 62. Folder 512.

Takahashi, Genji. Interview with author. Tokyo, Japan, 4 Sept. 1985.

Takahashi, Genji to Douglas W. Overton. 18 May 1962. Special Collections. JDR 3rd Fund. Box 62. Folder 512.

Taylor, Barry P. "Adult Language Learning Strategies and Their Pedagogical Implications." *TESOL Quarterly* 9, no. 4 (1975): 391-99.

Telegram to Charles Fries. Sent 28 Mar. 1958. CCF Japan.

"10-Week English Language Center Opens On Campus." The Ann Arbor News, 23 Jun. 1941. Rockefeller Foundation Archives. R.G. 1.1. Series 200. Box 286. Folder 3412.

Teweles, William Jeffrey. "*Katakana Eigo*—An English Teacher's Friend of Foe?" *Cross Currents* 8, no. 1 (1981): 43-58.

Thanachanan, Pranee. "A Self-Appraising English Syllabus in an EFL Country." In *Trends in Language Syllabus Design*, edited by John A. S. Read. Singapore: SEAMEO Regional Language Centre, 1984.

Thompson, Edgar H., and Leon F. Williams. "Creating Confusion to Encourage Change." *English Education* 17, no. 1 (1985): 14-17.

Thompson, Gregory J. "About the Japanese Brain: Evaluating the Tsunoda Method." *JALT Journal* 3 (1981): 63-77.

Titone, Renzo. *Teaching Foreign Languages: An Historical Sketch.* Washington, D.C.: Georgetown University Press, 1968.

Toyoda, Minoru. 29 Nov. 1961. Appendix B to CECA Resolution E4. English Language Exploratory Committee, Japan, [1962]. Rockefeller Family Archives. JDR 3rd. Box 39. English Language Teaching Envelope No. 2.

Toyoda, Minoru to CECA. 30 Mar. 1962. Special Collections. JDR 3rd Fund. Box 62. Folder 512.

Toyoda, Minoru to Donald H. McLean, Jr. 12 May 1956. Rockefeller Family Archives. JDR 3rd. Box 38. English Language Teaching Envelope.

Toyoda, Minoru to Douglas W. Overton. 27 Mar. 1962. Rockefeller Family Archives. JDR 3rd Fund. Box 62. Folder 512.

Tripp, Steven D. Review of *A History of English Language Teaching,* by A. P. R. Howatt. *The Language Teacher* 9, no. 2 (1985): 28, 30, 32.

Tsunoda, Tadanobu. *Nihonjin no No* (The Japanese Brain). Tokyo: Taishukan Shoten, 1978.

Twaddell, W. Freeman to Don[ald McLean, Jr.]. 9 Jan. 1958. Rockefeller Family Archives. JDR 3rd Fund. Box 61. Folder 507.

Untitled draft. 25 Aug. 1958. Rockefeller Family Archives. JDR 3rd. Box 38. Japan—Economic Situation Folder.

Varley, H. Paul. *Japanese Culture: A Short History.* New York: Praeger Publishers, 1973.

Vaughn, Eva D., Margaret C. Wang, and Joan A. Dytman. "Implementing an Innovative Program: Staff Development and Teacher Classroom Performance." *Journal of Teacher Education* 38, no. 6 (1987): 40-47.

Wada, Akiko, and Steve McCarty. Review of "The History of Foreign Language Education in Japan" (Presentation by a panel of Matsuyama teachers and professors). *The Language Teacher* 8, no. 5 (1984): 28-29.

Wagatsuma, Hiroshi. As quoted by Emilyn Almagro. "Japanese Into Groups. Prof. Says." *Ka Leo O Hawaii*, 9 Feb. 1983, 6.

Wagner, Michael J., and Germaine Tilney. "The Effect of 'Superlearning Techniques' on the Vocabulary Acquisition and Alpha Brainwave Production of Language Learners." *TESOL Quarterly* 17, no. 1 (1983): 5-19.

Wajnryb, Ruth. "Why Teachers are Conservative." *TEA News* (Australia) 3, no. 1 (1985).

Wardaugh, Ronald. "Linguistics, Psychology, and Pedagogy: Trinity or Unity?" *TESOL Quarterly* 2, no. 2 (1968): 80-87.

Whitman, Randal L., and Kenneth L. Jackson. "The Unpredictability of Contrastive Analysis." *Language Learning* 22, no. 1 (1972): 29-41.

"Who's at the Head of the Class?" *U. S. News and World Report,* 19 Jan. 1987, 61.

Williams, W. "Implementation, Analysis, and Assessments." *Policy Analysis* 1, no. 3 (1975): 531-66.

Wolf, W. C., Jr. "Selected Knowledge Diffusion/Utilization Know-How." *Knowledge: Creation, Diffusion, Utilization* 2, no. 3 (1981): 331-40.

Yamamoto, Norman Y. "The Oral Method: Harold E. Palmer and the Reformation of the Teaching of the English Language in Japan." *English Language Teaching Journal* 32, no. 2 (1978): 151-58.

Yamaura, Akio. *Toyonekko's Class.* Tokyo: ELEC, 1979.

Yambe, Tamotsu. "C. C. Fries Re-evaluated: His Contributions to the Teaching of English in Japan." *Bulletin of Toyoko Women's Junior College* 18 (1982): 1-26.

Yambe, Tamotsu. "Creating a Japanese Type of the Oral Approach." Xerox. n.d. [post 1956]. CCF Japan.

Yambe, Tamotsu. Interview with author. Tokyo, Japan, 3 Sept. 1985.

Yambe, Tamotsu. "The Oral Approach in Japan." Feb. 1969. Xerox. CCF Japan.

Yin, Robert K. "The Case Study as a Serious Research Strategy." *Knowledge: Creation, Diffusion, Utilization* 3, no. 1 (1981): 97-114.

Yoshikawa, Muneo. "Language Teaching Methodologies and the Nature of the Individual: A New Definition." *Modern Language Journal* 66, no. 4 (1982): 391-95.

Index

Matsumoto, Shigeharu: biography, 34, 55
n.37: ELEC committees, 25, 34;
correspondence, 37, 50, 134;
textbooks, 147
McLean, Donald H., Jr.: correspondence,
20, 136; Japan, 21; Japan Society, 47;
JDR 3rd's representative in Japan, 26;
meeting with Fries & Twaddell, 149;
reports to JDR 3rd, 36, 37, 48, 51,
142, 145, 180
Meiji Gakuin, 33, 117, 120
Meiji period, 119; counter-reaction, 161;
English language, 105, 120, 164;
Western language and culture, 104, 119
Meiji Rescript on Education, 120
Memorization, 169
Mental benefits of studying English, 121
Methods: factors that determine form and
spread, 197; nature, 197; interest in,
35; for teaching English in Japan, 26,
194; variation according to culture, 76
Mexico, Oral Approach exported to, 32
Militarism in Japan, 105, 124
Minister of Education, 119, 154
Ministry of Education, Japanese: approval
of textbooks, 42, 43, 128, 141; attitude
liberalized by ELEC, 48; ELEC's
attempt to circumvent, 155, 181;
guidelines for textbooks, 43, 141-42;
initiatives for improving ELT, 53, 129,
155; influenced by ELEC, 196; lack of
support for ELEC, 48, 137; neutrality,
155-56; Palmer's connection, 122,
124, 154; power, 24, 43, 102, 127,
184, 154, 156; rivalry with ELEC, 48,
155, 156, 194; support for ELEC, 35,
145
Mission of Japanese Christians to Europe,
111
Missionaries, in Japan, 108, 117, 125;
English-teaching, 117
Mitsukaido Junior High School, 140
Model: complexity, 70; criteria, 69; cross
cultural applicability, 71; Gee's, 75;
hybrid, 17, 61, 79; lacking, 14, 16;
overly simplistic, 16, 70; predictive,
71; relevance to directed contact
change, 95, 199; Richards', 75; Rogers
and Shoemaker's, 77
Modern Language Association, 28
Mombusho. See Ministry of Education
Monitoring, 169
Mori, Arinori, 119, 120
Morito, Tatsuo, 34, 154
Motivation: integrative/instrumental, 170-
171; for Japanese teachers to implement
the Oral Approach, 185; for Japanese to
learn English, 171

Nagasaki: Christians burned, 110; Dutch
restricted to, 111; English sailors riot,
115; MacDonald teaches English, 116;
Verbeck's school, 117
Nagoya, 46
"The nail that sticks up," 161
Nakajima, Fumio, 34, 43
Namamugi Incident, 118
Nardin, Mabell B., 44
National Council of Teachers of English
(NCTE), 28
National Defense Education Act (NDEA),
32
National Federation of Prefectural English
Teachers' Organizations (*Zen-Ei-Ren*),
182
National consciousness and language
acquisition, 159
Nationalism in Japan, 118, 120, 121, 124,
127, 161
Native speakers of English, employed by
ELEC, 45, 144
Need sensing, 67
Need to study diffusion/implementation of
innovations: English language teaching,
6; foreign language teaching, 5; formal
education, 4; Japanese ELT, 7. *See also*
Diffusion-of-innovations studies
New Approach textbooks: contrastive
analysis, 165; discontinued, 44; indirect
influence on others, 44; not widely
adopted, 44, 195; production and
publication, 42-43, 48; revision and
republication, 49
New York University, 44
Newspaper publicity about ELEC, 135,
139, 158
Nihon Eibun Gakkai, 181
Nihon University, 43
Nihonjin-ron, 174
Niigata, 46
Niishima, Jo, 116
Noah, Harold, 10, 202

O'Connor, Patricia, 39, 43
Observability, 83, 84; of Oral Approach
results, 140
Obstacles: to attempts to change ELT in
Japan, 24; to directed contact change,
70; to ELEC's campaign, 39, 48, 54,
104, 134,
Occupation of Japan (1945-52), 105, 125;
successes, 104; decentralization, 127
(*see also* Centralization); expansion of
ELT, 126 (*see also* English language
teaching in Japan); goals, 125;
reversals, 154; shortage of qualified
English teachers, 126, 157 (*see also*
Teachers of English in Japan); teacher

About the Author

LYNN EARL HENRICHSEN is Associate Professor and TESOL Program Director at Brigham Young University, Hawaii. He wrote *Sentence Construction,
Sentence Combination,* and *Popular English for Communication,* and has contributed chapters to several other books devoted to the teaching of English
to speakers of other languages.

Presented to

_____

Gifted by

_____

Baby's Due Date

_____

A Note for the Mom-to-Be

CELEBRATION OF *LIFE*

Everyday Encouragement for Expectant Moms

365 Daily Devotions and Baby Record section to document pregnancy milestones.

The quoted ideas expressed in this book (but not Scripture verses) are not, in all cases, exact quotations, as some have been edited for clarity and brevity. In all cases, the author has attempted to maintain the speaker's original intent. In some cases, quoted material for this book was obtained from secondary sources, primarily print media. While every effort was made to ensure the accuracy of these sources, the accuracy cannot be guaranteed. For additions, deletions, corrections, or clarifications in future editions of this text, please write Freeman-Smith.

Scripture quotations are taken from:

The Holy Bible, King James Version (KJV)

The Holy Bible, New International Version (NIV) Copyright © 1973, 1978, 1984, by International Bible Society. Used by permission of Zondervan Publishing House. All rights reserved.

The Holy Bible, New King James Version (NKJV) Copyright © 1982 by Thomas Nelson, Inc. Used by permission.

Holy Bible, New Living Translation, (NLT) copyright © 1996. Used by permission of Tyndale House Publishers, Inc., Wheaton, Illinois 60189. All rights reserved.

The Message (MSG)- This edition issued by contractual arrangement with NavPress, a division of The Navigators, U.S.A. Originally published by NavPress in English as THE MESSAGE: The Bible in Contemporary Language copyright 2002-2003 by Eugene Peterson. All rights reserved.

New Century Version®. (NCV) Copyright © 1987, 1988, 1991 by Word Publishing, a division of Thomas Nelson, Inc. All rights reserved. Used by permission.

The Holy Bible, The Living Bible (TLB), Copyright © 1971 owned by assignment by Illinois Regional Bank N.A. (as trustee). Used by permission of Tyndale House Publishers, Inc., Wheaton, Illinois 60189. All rights reserved.

The New American Standard Bible®, (NASB) Copyright © 1960, 1962, 1963, 1968, 1971, 1972, 1973, 1975, 1977, 1995 by The Lockman Foundation. Used by permission.

The Holman Christian Standard Bible™ (HCSB) Copyright © 1999, 2000, 2001 by Holman Bible Publishers. Used by permission.

Cover Design by Scott Williams/ Richmond & Williams
Page Layout by Bart Dawson

ISBN 978-1-60587-373-2

1 2 3 4 5—SBI—16 15 14 13 12

Printed in the United States of America

CELEBRATION OF *LIFE*

Everyday
Encouragement
for Expectant
Moms

*365 Daily Devotions
and Baby Record
section to document
pregnancy
milestones.*

INTRODUCTION

As a mother comforts her child, so will I comfort you . . .
—Isaiah 66:13 NIV

Because you've picked up this book, it's safe to assume that congratulations are in order: you're expecting a baby. This collection of devotions is intended to remind you that God will accompany you and your baby throughout your pregnancy, during the birth, and throughout eternity.

The fabric of daily life is woven together with the threads of habit, and no habit is more important than that of consistent prayer and daily devotion to the Creator. And this book is intended to help. This text contains 365 chapters, one for each day of the year. The first 200 devotions in this text are intended for expectant moms, and the final 165 devotions are written for mothers of newborns. On each page is a Pregnancy Milestone area to record short thoughts, prayers, questions, events, or special moments that you want to jot down that day.

During the next 12 months, please try this experiment: read a chapter each day. If you're already committed to a daily worship time, this book will enrich that experience. If you are not, the simple act of giving God a few minutes each morning will change the direction and the quality of your life.

Hannah Whitall Smith observed, "How changed our lives would be if we could only fly through the days on wings of surrender and trust!" During the exciting days ahead, will you surrender yourself to the Creator? Will you entrust Him to guide you, to protect you, and to lead you through, and then beyond your pregnancy? Make certain that the answer to these questions is a resounding "yes." Then, take comfort in the fact that the Creator of the universe stands ready to protect you and your baby today, tomorrow, and forever.

CELEBRATING LIFE

This is the day the Lord has made; let us rejoice and be glad in it.
—Psalm 118:24 HCSB

You're having a baby. Congratulations! The coming weeks and months are destined to be exciting and memorable. The ideas on these pages are intended to remind you that your pregnancy can, and should, be a glorious journey made with family, with friends, and with God.

Elisabeth Elliot noted that, "Joy is the keynote of the Christian life. It is not something that happens. It is a gift, given to us in the coming of Christ."

Today, accept the gift of Christ's joy. And, celebrate the life within you. This day, like every day, is God's creation, a one-of-a-kind opportunity for you, as a mom-to-be, to praise Him, to serve Him, and to rejoice.

A Quote for Today

Not every day of our lives
is overflowing with joy and
celebration. But there are moments
when our hearts nearly burst
within us for the sheer joy of
being alive. The first sight of
our newborn babies, the warmth
of love in another's eyes,
the fresh scent of rain on a hot
summer's eve—moments like
these renew in us
a heartfelt appreciation for life.
—Gwen Ellis

Pregnancy Milestone for Today

_____

_____

_____

_____

_____

THANKING HIM FOR THE GIFT OF LIFE

Thanks be to God for His indescribable gift.
—2 Corinthians 9:15 HCSB

Because you're expecting, so much is expected from you. After all, your normal obligations have not disappeared; you're still doing your work, caring for your family, taking care of yourself, and planning for the new arrival you'll soon be welcoming into your family.

As you continue to meet the obligations of daily life and the challenges of pregnancy, please don't forget the most important obligation of all: your sacred duty to praise the Creator for His incredible gifts.

So many of God's gifts are of the unseen variety, and so it is with your unborn child. Your new baby is a gift you haven't yet met face-to-face, but a gift that you cherish nonetheless.

Today, as you celebrate the precious present and wait patiently for a glorious future that only God can see, please praise Him often. His gifts are, indeed, indescribable. And so, by the way, is His love for you and your baby.

Pregnancy Milestone for Today

_____

_____

_____

_____

_____

_____

A Quote for Today

The life of faith is a daily exploration of the constant and countless ways in which God's grace and love are experienced.

—Eugene Peterson

WHEN YOU WORRY

Be anxious for nothing, but in everything by prayer and supplication,
with thanksgiving, let your requests be made known to God.
—Philippians 4:6 NKJV

Because you're an expectant mom, you worry. From time to time, you worry about your baby, about your family, about your future, and about a host of other things, great and small.

You know that you should trust God in all matters, and you know that all things work together for the good of those who love Him (Romans 8:28). But despite your faith, and despite the certainty of God's promises, you may still find yourself being attacked by anxiety when you least expect it. It simply goes with the territory.

So what should you do when you find yourself fretting about an uncertain future that you cannot see and certainly cannot control? You should take your concerns to God . . . and leave them there.

God loves you; He loves your baby; and He has a beautiful plan for both of you. So trust Him. Trust Him to care for you and your family during this pregnancy. Trust Him to care for you during and after the birth. And, trust Him to care for you throughout eternity.

You can talk to God about your worries. He's always available, always ready to listen, always ready to touch your heart and calm your nerves. So today, pray about everything—including your pregnancy—and then, when you've finished praying, turn everything over God. He's strong enough to meet every need, including yours.

Pregnancy Milestone for Today

_____

_____

_____

_____

_____

PRAYING FOR YOUR UNBORN CHILD

*The earnest prayer of a righteous person has
great power and wonderful results.*
—James 5:16 NLT

What's the best thing—and the most important thing—you can do for your unborn child? Eat well? Of course, that's important. Get plenty of rest? That's smart, too. Establish clear communications with your doctor? Certainly, that's essential. But none of these things, as important as they may be, are as important—or, for that matter, as powerful—as prayer.

Prayer changes things, and it changes you. So, instead of turning things over in your mind, turn them over to God. Instead of worrying about the uncertainties of your pregnancy, ask God for protection, and then leave the rest up to Him. Instead of focusing on the unknowable future, focus, instead, on God's unfathomable love.

Today, be sure to spend quiet moments in prayer. Don't limit your prayers to meals or to bedtime. Pray constantly about your new baby, about your life, and about the great opportunities that lie ahead for your growing family. God can see those opportunities, and He'll bring them to you hour by hour, day by day, year by year. In fact, He may be speaking softly to you right now, and His message may be something you desperately need to hear. So pray!

Pregnancy Milestone for Today

_____

_____

_____

_____

_____

_____

FINDING TIME FOR GOD

Every morning he wakes me. He teaches me to listen like a student.
The Lord God helps me learn . . .
—Isaiah 50:4-5 NCV

Each new day is a gift from God, and wise moms-to-be spend a few quiet moments each morning thanking the Giver. Daily life is woven together with the threads of habit, and no habit is more important to our spiritual health than the discipline of daily prayer and devotion to the Creator.

When we begin each day with heads bowed and hearts lifted, we remind ourselves of God's love, His protection, and His commandments. And if we are wise, we align our priorities for the coming day with the teachings and commandments that God has given us through His Holy Word.

Would you like to improve the condition of your spiritual, physical, or emotional health? If so, ask for God's help . . . and ask for it many times each day . . . starting with your morning devotional.

A Quote for Today

Our devotion to God is strengthened when we offer Him a fresh commitment each day.
—Elizabeth George

A Question to Think On

Are you spending enough high-quality time with God each day?

Pregnancy Milestone for Today

_____

_____

_____

_____

_____

_____

CLAIM THE INNER PEACE

I leave you peace; my peace I give you.
I do not give it to you as the world does.
So don't let your hearts be troubled or afraid.
—John 14:27 NCV

Are you at peace with the direction of your life? Or are you still rushing after the illusion of "peace and happiness" that our world promises but cannot deliver? The answer to this simple question will determine, to a surprising extent, the direction and the quality of your day and your life.

Joyce Meyer observes, "We need to be at peace with our past, content with our present, and sure about our future, knowing they are all in God's hands."

Today, as a gift to yourself, to your unborn child, to your family, and to your friends, claim the inner peace that is your spiritual birthright. It is offered freely; it is yours for the asking. So ask. And then share.

Pregnancy Milestone for Today

_____

_____

_____

_____

_____

_____

A Quote for Today

The peace that Jesus gives is never engineered by circumstances on the outside.
—Oswald Chambers

FOCUS ON HEALTH

Didn't you realize that your body is a sacred place, the place of the Holy Spirit? Don't you see that you can't live however you please, squandering what God paid such a high price for? The physical part of you is not some piece of property belonging to the spiritual part of you.

—1 Corinthians 6:19 MSG

These are vitally important days in the life of your unborn baby, and your decision to focus on health is a profound expression of your love for the child God has entrusted to your care.

During the days and weeks ahead, you'll have many opportunities to indulge in unhealthy habits. Please resist those temptations with all your might. Ask God for the strength to make wise choices. And remember: when it comes to your health, you're not just choosing for yourself. You're also making life-altering choices for your baby.

A Quote for Today

When the law of God is written on our hearts, our duty will be our delight.

—Matthew Henry

A Timely Tip

As a mom-to-be, you have a profound responsibility to care for the health of your unborn child. Don't smoke; don't drink alcohol; and don't take any drugs that are not prescribed by your doctor.

Pregnancy Milestone for Today

_____

_____

_____

_____

_____

_____

FAITH FOR THE FUTURE

For we walk by faith, not by sight.
—2 Corinthians 5:7 NKJV

The first element of a successful life is faith: faith in God, faith in His Son, and faith in His promises. If we place our lives in God's hands, our faith is rewarded in ways that we—as human beings with clouded vision and limited understanding—can scarcely comprehend. But, if we seek to rely solely upon our own resources, or if we seek earthly success outside the boundaries of God's commandments, we reap a bitter harvest for ourselves and for our loved ones.

Do you desire the abundance and success that God has promised? Then trust Him today and every day that you live. Trust Him with every aspect of your life. Trust Him with your future and with your pregnancy. Trust His promises, and trust in the saving grace of His only begotten Son. Then, when you have entrusted your future to the Giver of all things good, rest assured that your future is secure, not only for today but also for all eternity.

Pregnancy Milestone for Today

_____

_____

_____

_____

_____

_____

A Quote for Today

How changed our lives would be if we could only fly through the days on wings of surrender and trust!
—Hannah Whitall Smith

As the World Grows Louder

Be silent before the Lord and wait expectantly for Him.
—Psalm 37:7 HCSB

The world seems to grow louder day by day, and our senses seem to be invaded at every turn. If we allow the distractions of a clamorous society to separate us from God's peace, we do ourselves a profound disservice. Our task, as dutiful believers, is to carve out moments of silence in a world filled with noise.

If we are to maintain righteous minds and compassionate hearts, we must take time each day for prayer and for meditation. We must make ourselves still in the presence of our Creator. We must quiet our minds and our hearts so that we might sense God's will and His love.

Has the hectic pace of life as an expectant mom robbed you of God's peace? If so, it's time to reorder your priorities and your life. Nothing is more important than the time you spend with your Heavenly Father. So be still and claim the genuine peace that is found in the silent moments you spend with God.

A Quote for Today

It is in that stillness that the Voice
will be heard, the only voice
in all the universe that speaks peace
to the deepest part of us.
—Elisabeth Elliot

Pregnancy Milestone for Today

_____

_____

_____

_____

_____

_____

BE OPTIMISTIC

Make me to hear joy and gladness.
—Psalm 51:8 KJV

Are you an optimistic, hopeful, enthusiastic Christian? You should be. After all, as a believer, you have every reason to be optimistic about life here on earth and life eternal. As C. H. Spurgeon observed, "Our hope in Christ for the future is the mainstream of our joy." But sometimes, you may find yourself pulled down by the inevitable demands and worries of life-here-on-earth. If you find yourself discouraged, exhausted, or both, then it's time to take your concerns to God. When you do, He will lift your spirits and renew your strength.

Today, make this promise to yourself and keep it: vow to be a hope-filled Christian. Think optimistically about your pregnancy, your profession, your family, and your future. Trust your hopes, not your fears. Take time to celebrate God's glorious creation. And then, when you've filled your heart with hope and gladness, share your optimism with others. They'll be better for it, and so will you.

Pregnancy Milestone for Today

_____

_____

_____

_____

_____

A Quote for Today

Lovely, complicated wrappings
Sheath the gift of one-day-more;
Breathless, I untie the package—
Never lived this day before!

—Gloria Gaither

WHEN THE SEAS AREN'T CALM

He replied, "You of little faith, why are you so afraid?"
Then he got up and rebuked the winds and the waves,
and it was completely calm.

—Matthew 8:26 NIV

As every expectant mother knows, some days are just plain difficult. You face days when you're sick, when you're concerned, when the laundry is piled high and the bills are piled even higher.

When we find ourselves overtaken by the inevitable frustrations of life, we must catch ourselves, take a deep breath, and lift our thoughts upward. Although we are here on earth struggling to rise above the distractions of the day, we need never struggle alone. God is here—eternal and faithful—and, if we reach out to Him, He will restore perspective and peace to our souls.

Sometimes even the most devout Christians can become discouraged, and you are no exception. After all, you live in a world where expectations can be high and demands can be even higher.

If you find yourself enduring difficult circumstances, remember that God remains in His heaven. If you become discouraged with the direction of your day or your life, take a moment to offer your thoughts and prayers to Him. He is a God of possibility, not negativity. He will guide you through your difficulties and beyond them.

Pregnancy Milestone for Today

_____

_____

_____

_____

_____

_____

YOUR GREAT EXPECTATIONS

When dreams come true, there is life and joy.
—Proverbs 13:12 NLT

Do you expect a bright future for you and your baby? Are you willing to dream king-sized dreams . . . and are you willing to work diligently to make those dreams happen? Hopefully so—after all, God promises that we can do "all things" through Him. Yet most of us, even the most devout among us, live far below our potential. We take half measures; we dream small dreams; we waste precious time and energy on the distractions of the world. But God has other plans for us.

Our Creator intends that we live faithfully, hopefully, courageously, and abundantly. He knows that we are capable of so much more; and He wants us to do the things we're capable of doing; and He wants us to begin doing those things today.

Pregnancy Milestone for Today

_____

_____

_____

_____

_____

_____

A Quote for Today

May your day be fashioned
with joy, sprinkled with dreams,
and touched by the miracle of love.

—Barbara Johnson

GOD FIRST

Honor GOD with everything you own; give him the first and the best.
Your barns will burst, your wine vats will brim over.
—Proverbs 3:9-10 MSG

As you think about the nature of your relationship with God, remember this: you will always have some type of relationship with Him—it is inevitable that your life must be lived in relationship to God. The question is not if you will have a relationship with Him; the burning question is whether or not that relationship will be one that seeks to honor Him . . . or not.

Are you willing to place God first in your life? And, are you willing to welcome God's Son into your heart? Unless you can honestly answer these questions with a resounding "yes," then your relationship with God isn't what it could be or should be. Thankfully, God is always available, He's always ready to forgive, and He's waiting to hear from you now. The rest, of course, is up to you.

A Quote for Today

Jesus challenges you and me to
keep our focus daily on the cross of
His will if we want to be
His disciples.
—Anne Graham Lotz

Pregnancy Milestone for Today

_____

_____

_____

_____

_____

_____

KEEP THANKING HIM

*In everything give thanks; for this is the will of God
in Christ Jesus for you.*
—1 Thessalonians 5:18 NKJV

The words of 1 Thessalonians 5:18 remind us to give thanks in every circumstance of life. But sometimes, when our lives seem to be spinning out of control, we don't feel much like celebrating. Yet God's Word is clear: In all circumstances, our Father offers us His love, His strength, and His grace. And, in all circumstances, we must thank Him.

Have you thanked God today for blessings that are too numerous to count? Have you offered Him your heartfelt prayers and your wholehearted praise? Have you thanked Him for your life, your faith, and your pregnancy? If not, it's time to slow down and offer a prayer of thanksgiving to the One who has given you life on earth and life eternal.

If you are a thoughtful Christian, you will be a thankful Christian. No matter your circumstances, you owe God so much more than you can ever repay, and you owe Him your heartfelt thanks. So thank Him . . . and keep thanking Him, today, tomorrow, and forever.

Pregnancy Milestone for Today

_____

_____

_____

_____

_____

_____

A Quote for Today

No duty is more urgent than
that of returning thanks.
—St. Ambrose

OVERCOMING STRESS

The Lord hears his people when they call to him for help.
He rescues them from all their troubles.
—Psalm 34:17 NLT

Pregnancy puts stress on your body and stress on your mind, but not necessarily in that order. So, how can you overcome the pressure? By turning your days and your life over to God.

Elisabeth Elliot writes, "If my life is surrendered to God, all is well. Let me not grab it back, as though it were in peril in His hand but would be safer in mine!"

Do you feel overwhelmed by the stresses of daily life? Turn your concerns and your prayers over to God. Trust Him. Trust Him completely. Trust Him today. Trust Him always. When it comes to the inevitable challenges of this day, hand them over to God completely and without reservation. He knows your needs and will meet those needs in His own way and in His own time if you let Him.

A Quote for Today

Don't be overwhelmed. Take it one day and one prayer at a time.
—Stormie Omartian

A Timely Tip

Take control of your appointment calendar, and don't hesitate to cut back on visitors, especially the ones who tend to cause you stress.

Pregnancy Milestone for Today

_____

_____

_____

_____

_____

_____

BEYOND DOUBT

Now if any of you lacks wisdom, he should ask God,
who gives to all generously and without criticizing,
and it will be given to him. But let him ask in faith
without doubting. For the doubter is like the surging sea,
driven and tossed by the wind.
—James 1:5-6 HCSB

If you've never had any doubts about your faith, then you can stop reading this page now and skip to the next. But if you've ever been plagued by doubts about your faith or your God, keep reading.

Even some of the most faithful mothers-to-be are, at times, beset by occasional bouts of discouragement and doubt. But even when you feel far removed from God, God is never far removed from you. He is always with you, always willing to calm the storms of life—always willing to replace our doubts with comfort and assurance.

Whenever you're plagued by doubts, that's precisely the moment you should seek God's presence by genuinely seeking to establish a deeper, more meaningful relationship with His Son. Then you may rest assured that in time, God will calm your fears, answer your prayers, and restore your confidence.

Pregnancy Milestone for Today

_____

_____

_____

_____

_____

_____

A Quote for Today

We must lay our questions,
frustrations, anxieties,
and impotence at the feet of God
and wait for His answer.
And then receiving it,
we must live by faith.
—Kay Arthur

GOD'S TIMING

Wait for the Lord; be courageous and let your heart be strong.
Wait for the Lord.
—Psalm 27:14 HCSB

As an expectant mom, you're understandably eager for the big day: the birth of your child. In fact, you might like to give birth to a healthy baby right now. But, wait you must.

God has created a world that unfolds according to His own timetable, not ours . . . thank goodness! We mortals might make a terrible mess of things. God does not. God's plan does not always happen in the way that we would like or at the time of our own choosing. Our task is to wait patiently and trust Him completely.

In the words of Elisabeth Elliot, "We must learn to move according to the timetable of the Timeless One, and to be at peace." That's advice worth following today, tomorrow, and every day until that glorious moment when you meet your newborn face-to-face.

A Quote for Today

Waiting on God brings us
to the journey's end quicker
than our feet.
—Mrs. Charles E. Cowman

Pregnancy Milestone for Today

_____

_____

_____

_____

_____

_____

STILLNESS

Be still, and know that I am God. . . .
—Psalm 46:10 KJV

Are you so busy that you rush through the day with scarcely a single moment for quiet contemplation and prayer? If so, it's time to reorder your priorities.

We live in a noisy world, a world filled with distractions, frustrations, and complications. But if we allow the distractions of a clamorous world to separate us from God's peace, we do ourselves a profound disservice. If we are to maintain righteous minds and compassionate hearts, we must take time each day for prayer and for meditation. We must make ourselves still in the presence of our Creator. We must quiet our minds and our hearts so that we might sense God's will, God's love, and God's Son.

Nothing is more important than the time you spend with your Savior. So be still and claim the inner peace that is your spiritual birthright: the peace of Jesus Christ. It is offered freely; it has been paid for in full; it is yours for the asking. So ask.

Pregnancy Milestone for Today

_____

_____

_____

_____

_____

_____

A Quote for Today

How motivating it has been for me to view my early morning devotions as time of retreat alone with Jesus, Who desires that I "come with Him by myself to a quiet place" in order to pray, read His Word, listen for His voice, and be renewed in my spirit.

—Anne Graham Lotz

FOCUSING YOUR THOUGHTS

This hope we have as an anchor of the soul, both sure and steadfast,
and which enters the Presence behind the veil.
—Hebrews 6:19 NKJV

Paul Valéry observed, "We hope vaguely but dread precisely." How true (especially for expectant moms!). All too often, we allow the worries of everyday life to overwhelm our thoughts and cloud our vision. What's needed is clearer perspective, renewed faith, and a different focus.

When we focus on the discomforts of today or the uncertainties of tomorrow, we rob ourselves of peace in the present moment. But, when we focus on God's grace, and when we trust in the ultimate wisdom of God's plan for our lives, our worries no longer tyrannize us.

Today, remember that God is infinitely greater than the challenges that you face. Remember also that your thoughts are profoundly powerful, so guard them accordingly.

A Quote for Today

The mind is like a clock that is
constantly running down.
It has to be wound up daily
with good thoughts.
—Fulton J. Sheen

Pregnancy Milestone for Today

_____

_____

_____

_____

_____

How Has He Blessed You?

For surely, O LORD, you bless the righteous;
you surround them with your favor as with a shield.
—Psalm 5:12 NIV

Have you counted your blessings lately? If you sincerely wish to follow in Christ's footsteps, you should make thanksgiving a habit, a regular part of your daily routine.

How has God blessed you? First and foremost, He has given you the gift of eternal life through the sacrifice of His only begotten Son, but the blessings don't stop there. He has also blessed you with an unborn child, a precious, miraculous life brimming with eternal possibilities.

Today, take a few moments to list a few of God's gifts: your family, your faith, your opportunities, and your baby, for starters. And then, when you've spent sufficient time listing your blessings, offer a prayer of gratitude to the Giver of all things good . . . and, to the best of your ability, use your gifts for the glory of His kingdom.

Pregnancy Milestone for Today

_____

_____

_____

_____

_____

_____

A Quote for Today

We do not need to beg Him to bless us; He simply cannot help it.
—Hannah Whitall Smith

YOUR DAILY JOURNEY

*Then He said to them all, "If anyone wants to come with Me,
he must deny himself, take up his cross daily, and follow Me."*
—Luke 9:23 HCSB

Because you're expecting, you will, from time to time, find yourself running on empty. The inevitable challenges of everyday life—not to mention the demands of pregnancy—can drain your strength and sap your resources. Thankfully, God stands ready to renew your strength, even on the gloomiest of days.

Are you almost too weary to lift your head? Then bow it—in prayer. Offer your concerns and your needs to your Father in heaven. He is always at your side, offering His love and His strength.

Your search to discover God's plan for your life is not a destination; it is a journey that unfolds day by day. And, that's exactly how often you should seek direction from your Creator: one day at a time, each day followed by the next, without exception.

A Quote for Today

We are meddling with God's business when we let all manner of imaginings loose, predicting disaster, contemplating possibilities instead of following, one day at a time, God's plain and simple pathway.

—Elisabeth Elliot

Pregnancy Milestone for Today

_____

_____

_____

_____

_____

HOLINESS BEFORE HAPPINESS

If they serve Him obediently,
they will end their days in prosperity
and their years in happiness.
—Job 36:11 HCSB

Because you are an imperfect human being, you are not "perfectly" happy—and that's perfectly okay with God. He is far less concerned with your happiness than He is with your holiness.

God continuously reveals Himself in everyday life, but He does not do so in order to make you contented; He does so in order to lead you to His Son. So, as you think about the highs and lows of pregnancy, don't be overly concerned with your current level of happiness: it will change. Be more concerned with the current state of your relationship with Christ: He does not change. And because your Savior transcends time and space, you can be comforted in the knowledge that in the end, His joy will become your joy . . . for all eternity.

Pregnancy Milestone for Today

_____

_____

_____

_____

_____

_____

A Quote for Today

I think God wants us to be whole, too. But maybe sometimes the only way he can make us whole is to teach us things we can learn only by not being whole.

—Madeleine L'Engle

WHEN YOUR COURAGE IS TESTED

Be strong and courageous, all you who put your hope in the Lord.
—Psalm 31:24 HCSB

Even the most dedicated mother-to-be may find her courage tested by the inevitable distractions and discomforts of pregnancy. Old Man Trouble, it seems, is never too far from the front door, and he doesn't make exceptions for expectant moms.

When you focus upon your fears and your doubts, you may find many reasons to lie awake at night and fret about the uncertainties of the coming day. A better strategy, of course, is to focus not upon your fears but instead upon your Creator.

God is as near as your next breath, and He is in control. He offers salvation to all His children, including you. God is your shield and your strength; you are His forever. So don't focus your thoughts upon the fears of the day. Instead, trust God's plan and His eternal love for you. And remember: whatever the size of your challenge, God is bigger.

A Quote for Today

I have found the perfect antidote for fear. Whenever it sticks up its ugly face, I clobber it with prayer.
—Dale Evans Rogers

Pregnancy Milestone for Today

_____

_____

_____

_____

_____

HEALTHY HABITS

And so, dear brothers and sisters, I plead with you to give
your bodies to God. Let them be a living and holy sacrifice—
the kind he will accept. When you think of what
he has done for you, is this too much to ask?
—Romans 12:1 NLT

It's an old saying and a true one: First, you make your habits, and then your habits make you. Some habits will inevitably bring you closer to God; other habits will lead you away from the path He has chosen for you. If you sincerely desire to improve your spiritual health, you must honestly examine the habits that make up the fabric of your day. And you must abandon those habits that are displeasing to God.

If you trust God, and if you keep asking for His help, He can transform your life. If you sincerely ask Him to help you, the same God who created the universe will help you defeat any habits that might be harmful to your unborn baby or to yourself. So, you're trying to change a harmful habit, and if at first you don't succeed, keep praying. God is listening, and He's ready to help you become a better person if you ask Him . . . so ask today.

Pregnancy Milestone for Today

_____

_____

_____

_____

_____

_____

A Quote for Today

Prayer is a habit. Worship is
a habit. Kindness is a habit.
And if you want to please God,
you'd better make sure that these
habits are your habits.
—Marie T. Freeman

BEYOND THE COMFORT ZONE

Be not afraid, only believe.
—Mark 5:36 KJV

Having a baby can be a daunting, fear-provoking adventure, a nine-month journey that takes you far beyond your comfort zone, in more ways than one. As you experience the inevitable joys and the unavoidable apprehensions of pregnancy, please remember that God is always with you.

God is a never-ending source of support and courage for those of us who call upon Him. When we are weary, He gives us strength. When we see no hope, God reminds us of His promises.

Throughout your pregnancy, God will hold your hand and walk with you every day of your life if you let Him. So even if your circumstances are difficult, trust the Father. His love is eternal and His goodness endures forever.

A Timely Tip

As a mom-to-be, you're destined to experience quite a few challenges during the coming months.
Your job is to believe in yourself, to trust your doctors, to take care of yourself, and to trust your Heavenly Father.

Pregnancy Milestone for Today

_____

_____

_____

_____

_____

ACCEPTING HIS GIFTS

*These things have I spoken unto you, that my joy might remain in you,
and that your joy might be full.*
—John 15:11 KJV

God sent His Son so that mankind might enjoy the abundant life that Jesus describes in the familiar words of John 10:10. But, God's gifts are not guaranteed; His gifts must be claimed by those who choose to follow Christ.

Do you sincerely seek the riches that our Savior offers to those who give themselves to Him? Then follow Him completely and obey Him without reservation. When you do, you will receive the love and the abundance that He has promised. Seek first the salvation that is available through a personal, passionate relationship with Christ, and then claim the joy, the peace, and the spiritual abundance that the Shepherd offers His sheep.

Today, as you organize your day and care for your family, accept God's promise of spiritual abundance . . . you may be certain that when you do your part, God will do His part.

Pregnancy Milestone for Today

_____

_____

_____

_____

_____

_____

A Quote for Today

God is the giver, and we are
the receivers. And His richest gifts
are bestowed not upon those who
do the greatest things, but
upon those who accept
His abundance and His grace.

—Hannah Whitall Smith

THE POWER OF ENCOURAGEMENT

He comes alongside us when we go through hard times,
and before you know it, he brings us alongside someone else
who is going through hard times so that we can be there
for that person just as God was there for us.
—2 Corinthians 1:4 MSG

Because you're going through so many changes now, and because you're sure to experience even more changes in the future, you need encouragement. You need encouragement from your husband, from your family, and from your friends. But please don't expect these people to be encouraging all the time. On occasion, even the most thoughtful friends or family members may say things that upset your sensibilities. If an offhanded remark from a well-meaning friend hurts your feelings, please don't let it hurt your feelings for long. Instead of fretting over a thoughtless comment, consider it an opportunity to forgive, to forget, and to move on. Your life is too short to let it be ruined by a casual comment.

And, the same can be said for your pregnancy.

A Timely Tip

If you're a first-time mother-to-be, please don't underestimate the importance of a strong support system. Your body and spirit are going through many changes. So, spend lots of time with women who've been there, done that, and have baby pictures to prove it.

Pregnancy Milestone for Today

_____

_____

_____

_____

_____

_____

WHAT TO DO?

The lines of purpose in your lives never grow slack,
tightly tied as they are to your future in heaven, kept taut by hope.
—Colossians 1:5 MSG

"What on earth does God intend for me to do with my life after this baby arrives?" It's an easy question to ask but, for many expectant moms, a difficult question to answer.

If you have questions about the future that you simply cannot answer, perhaps you'll find comfort in the knowledge that motherhood always requires a leap of faith. Thankfully, when you leap, God will inevitably be right beside you, ready to catch you if you stumble.

During some seasons of life, God's intentions will be clear to you; other times, God's plan will seem uncertain at best. But even on those difficult days when you are unsure which way to turn, you must never lose sight of these overriding facts: God created you for a reason; He has given you your baby for a reason; He has important work for you to do; and He will reveal His plans for you at a time and place of His choosing. Your task is to trust His plans even when you don't fully understand them.

Pregnancy Milestone for Today

_____

_____

_____

_____

_____

_____

A Quote for Today

I want my life to be a faith-filled leap into his arms, knowing he will be there—not that everything will go as I want, but that he will be there and that this will be enough.

—Sheila Walsh

FINDING CONTENTMENT

I know what it is to be in need, and I know what it is to have plenty.
I have learned the secret of being content in any and every situation,
whether well fed or hungry, whether living in plenty or in want.
I can do everything through him who gives me strength.

—Philippians 4:12-13 NIV

The preoccupation with happiness and contentment is an ever-present theme in the modern world. We are bombarded with messages that tell us where to find peace and pleasure in a world that worships materialism and wealth. But, lasting contentment is not found in material possessions; genuine contentment is a spiritual gift from God to those who trust in Him and follow His commandments.

Where do we find contentment? If we don't find it in God, we will never find it anywhere else. But, if we put our faith and our trust in Him, we will be blessed with an inner peace that is beyond human understanding. When God dwells at the center of our lives, peace and contentment will belong to us just as surely as we belong to God.

A Quote for Today

I believe that in every time and place it is within our power to acquiesce in the will of God—and what peace it brings to do so!

—Elisabeth Elliot

Pregnancy Milestone for Today

_____

_____

_____

_____

_____

MAKING SACRIFICES FOR YOUR BABY

Whatever you do, do everything for God's glory.
—1 Corinthians 10:31 HCSB

Pregnancy is no picnic. As a mom-to-be, you must make many sacrifices for your baby. Consider these sacrifices to be investments in a future that only God can see.

Life is like a garden. Every day, God gives us opportunities to plant seeds for the future. When we plant wisely and trust God completely, the harvest is bountiful.

Are you willing to place your future in the hands of a loving and all-knowing God? Do you trust in the ultimate goodness of His plan for your life? And, will you face today's challenges with optimism, hope, and determination? You should. After all, God created you for a very important reason: His reason. And you have important work to do: His work.

So today, as you live in the present and look to the future, remember that God has a very important plan for you. And while you still have time, it's up to you to act—and to believe—accordingly.

Pregnancy Milestone for Today

_____

_____

_____

_____

_____

_____

A Timely Tip

Consider your healthy lifestyle
a form of worship and a priceless gift
to your unborn baby.

HOW WILL YOU WORSHIP?

*For it is written, "You shall worship the Lord your God,
and Him only you shall serve."*
—Matthew 4:10 NKJV

As a mother-to-be, you have many reasons to praise God. Today, as one way of worshipping Him, make every aspect of your life a cause for celebration and praise. Praise God for your baby; praise Him for His love; honor Him for His faithfulness; and thank Him for the sacrifice of His only begotten Son.

The beautiful words found in the 5th chapter of 1 Thessalonians offer clear instructions: "Rejoice evermore. Pray without ceasing. In every thing give thanks: for this is the will of God in Christ Jesus concerning you" (vv. 16-18 KJV).

God deserves your worship, your prayers, your praise, and your thanks. And you deserve the joy that is yours when you worship Him with your prayers, with your deeds, and with your life.

A Quote for Today

God asks that we worship Him with
our concentrated minds as well as
with our wills and emotions.
A divided and scattered mind
is not effective.
—Catherine Marshall

Pregnancy Milestone
for Today

_____

_____

_____

_____

_____

FAITH ABOVE FEELINGS

The righteous will live by his faith.
—Habakkuk 2:4 NIV

Hebrews 10:38 teaches that we should live by faith. Yet sometimes, despite our best intentions, negative feelings can rob us of the peace and abundance that would otherwise be ours through Christ. When anger or anxiety separates us from the spiritual blessings that God has in store, we must rethink our priorities and renew our faith. And we must place faith above feelings. Human emotions are highly variable, decidedly unpredictable, and often unreliable. Our emotions are like the weather, only far more fickle. So we must learn to live by faith, not by the ups and downs of our own emotional roller coasters.

Sometime during this day, you will probably be gripped by a strong negative emotion. Distrust it. Reign it in. Test it. And turn it over to God. Your emotions will inevitably change; God will not. So trust Him completely as you watch your feelings slowly evaporate into thin air—which, of course, they will.

Pregnancy Milestone for Today

_____

_____

_____

_____

_____

_____

A Quote for Today

Our feelings do not affect
God's facts. They may blow up,
like clouds, and cover the eternal
things that we do most truly believe.
We may not see the shining of the
promises—but they still shine!
His strength is not for one moment
less because of our human weakness.

—Amy Carmichael

EMBRACED BY HIM

That is, in Christ, he chose us before the world was made so that we
would be his holy people—people without blame before him.
Because of his love, God had already decided to make us
his own children through Jesus Christ.
That was what he wanted and what pleased him.
—Ephesians 1:4-5 NCV

Have you formed the habit of accepting and sharing God's love? Hopefully so. After all, God's love for you is bigger and better than you can imagine. In fact, God's love is far too big to comprehend (in this lifetime). But this much we do know: God loves you so much that He sent His Son, Jesus, to come to this earth and to die for you.

Lisa Whelchel had this advice: "Believing that you are loved will set you free to be who God created you to be. So rest in His love and just be yourself."

Let these words serve as a powerful reminder: you are a marvelous, glorious being, created by a loving God who wants you to become—completely and without reservation—the woman He created you to be.

A Quote for Today

When once we are assured
that God is good, then there can be
nothing left to fear.
—Hannah Whitall Smith

Pregnancy Milestone for Today

_____

_____

_____

_____

_____

_____

EXPECTING THE BEST

Let us hold fast the confession of our hope without wavering,
for He who promised is faithful.
—Hebrews 10:23 NKJV

What do you expect from the day ahead? Are you expecting God to do wonderful things, or are you living beneath a cloud of apprehension and doubt? Are you determined to celebrate God's gifts? And will you praise His Son for His sacrifices and His love?

Christ came to this earth to give us abundant life and eternal salvation. We give thanks to our Maker when we treasure each day and use it to the fullest.

As a soon-to-be mom, you're blessed beyond measure. So, today, give thanks for the gift of life and for the One who created it. And then, use this day—a precious gift from the Father above—to serve your Savior faithfully, courageously, and joyfully.

Pregnancy Milestone for Today

_____

_____

_____

_____

_____

_____

A Quote for Today

Every day we live is a priceless gift
of God, loaded with possibilities
to learn something new,
to gain fresh insights.
—Dale Evans Rogers

SERENITY

Should we accept only good from God and not adversity?
—Job 2:10 HCSB

As an expectant mom, you're destined to endure moments of discomfort . . . perhaps many moments of discomfort. When you encounter unfortunate circumstances that are beyond your power to control, here's a proven way to retain your sanity: accept those circumstances (no matter how unpleasant), and trust God.

The American theologian Reinhold Niebuhr composed a profoundly simple verse that came to be known as the Serenity Prayer: "God, grant me the serenity to accept the things I cannot change, the courage to change the things I can, and the wisdom to know the difference." Niebuhr's words are far easier to recite than they are to live by. Why? Because most of us want life to unfold in accordance with our own wishes and timetables. But sometimes God has other plans.

When you trust God, you can be comforted in the knowledge that your Creator is both loving and wise, and that He understands His plans perfectly, even when you do not.

A Quote for Today

Acceptance says: True, this is
my situation at the moment.
I'll look unblinkingly at the reality
of it. But, I'll also open my hands
to accept willingly whatever
a loving Father sends me.
—Catherine Marshall

Pregnancy Milestone for Today

_____

_____

_____

_____

_____

A BOOK UNLIKE ANY OTHER

Your word is a lamp for my feet and a light on my path.
—Psalm 119:105 HCSB

As you prepare for the birth of your child, you need the strength, the comfort, and the assurance that comes from God's Word. The Bible is unlike any other book. The words of Matthew 4:4 remind us that, "Man shall not live by bread alone but by every word that proceedeth out of the mouth of God" (KJV). As believers, we are instructed to study the Bible and meditate upon its meaning for our lives, yet far too many Bibles are laid aside by well-intentioned believers who would like to study the Bible if they could "just find the time."

Warren Wiersbe observed, "When the child of God looks into the Word of God, he sees the Son of God. And he is transformed by the Spirit of God to share in the glory of God." God's Holy Word is, indeed, a transforming, life-changing, one-of-a-kind treasure. And it's up to you—and only you—to use it that way.

Pregnancy Milestone for Today

_____

_____

_____

_____

_____

_____

A Quote for Today

Study the Bible and observe how the persons behaved and how God dealt with them. There is explicit teaching on every condition of life.

—Corrie ten Boom

ASKING FOR HIS GUIDANCE

Ask and it shall be given to you; seek and you shall find; knock and it shall be opened to you. For every one who asks receives, and he who seeks finds, and to him who knocks it shall be opened.
—Matthew 7:7-8 NASB

Have you fervently asked God to guide your steps and guard your heart during the exciting (and challenging) days of your pregnancy? If so, then you're continually inviting your Creator to reveal Himself in a variety of ways.

Jesus made it clear to His disciples: they should pray always. So should we. Genuine, heartfelt prayer produces powerful changes in us and in our world. When we lift our hearts to God, we open ourselves to a never-ending source of divine wisdom and infinite love.

Do you have questions about your future that you simply can't answer? Ask for the guidance of your Heavenly Father. Do you sincerely seek to know God's purpose for your life? Then ask Him for direction—and keep asking Him every day that you live. Are you anxious, or fearful, or disheartened? Ask God to renew your courage and your strength. Whatever your need, no matter how great or small, pray about it and never lose hope. God is not just near; He is here, and He's ready to talk with you. Now!

A Quote for Today

I have acted like I'm all alone, but the truth is that I never will be. When my prayers are weak, God is listening. When my words are rote, God is listening. When my heart is dry, amazingly God is still listening.

—Angela Thomas

Pregnancy Milestone for Today

_____

_____

_____

_____

_____

THANK HIM NOW

Our prayers for you are always spilling over into thanksgivings. We can't quit thanking God our Father and Jesus our Messiah for you!
—Colossians 1:3 MSG

The life of a soon-to-be mom can be complicated, demanding, daunting, uncomfortable, and busy. And, if the demands of life leave you rushing from place to place with scarcely a moment to spare, you may not slow down long enough to thank God for His blessings. That's an unfortunate—but easily correctable—mistake.

Today, even if you're busily engaged in life, pause long enough to make a partial inventory of your blessings. You most certainly will not be able to count them all, but take a few moments to jot down as many blessings as you can. Then, give thanks to the Giver of all good things: God. His love for you is eternal, as are His gifts. And it's never too soon—or too late—to offer Him thanks.

Pregnancy Milestone for Today

_____

_____

_____

_____

_____

_____

A Quote for Today

It is only with gratitude that life becomes rich.

—Dietrich Bonhoeffer

TALK TO YOUR DOCTOR

If you become wise, you will be the one to benefit. If you scorn wisdom,
you will be the one to suffer.
—Proverbs 9:12 NLT

Your doctor can be an invaluable guide and a source of encouragement. But, it's up to you to make certain that the lines of communication between you and your physician are clearly established.

If you have questions or concerns about your pregnancy, don't delay: contact the appropriate health professional immediately. Not next week, not tomorrow, not at the next scheduled office visit—if you have health concerns for you or your baby, contact your health provider today.

Are you determined to lead a healthy lifestyle? If so, your baby will be blessed and you'll be blessed, too. So today, and every day hereafter, focus on your health. Your baby deserves it, and so, for that matter, do you.

A Quote for Today

God helps the sick in two ways, through the science of medicine and through the science of faith and prayer.
—Norman Vincent Peale

A Timely Tip

As you make choices throughout the day, slow down and ask yourself this question: Is this how God wants me to take care of my body and my unborn child?

Pregnancy Milestone for Today

_____

_____

_____

_____

_____

WHOM DO YOU TRUST?

The one who understands a matter finds success,
and the one who trusts in the Lord will be happy.
—Proverbs 16:20 HCSB

Where will you place your trust today? Will you trust in the ways of the world, or will you trust in the Word and the will of your Creator? If you aspire to do great things for God's kingdom, you will trust Him completely.

Trusting God means trusting Him in every aspect of your life. You must trust Him with your pregnancy. You must trust Him with your physical and spiritual health. You must follow His commandments and pray for His guidance. Then, you can wait patiently for God's revelations and for His blessings.

When you trust your Heavenly Father without reservation, you can rest assured: in His own fashion and in His own time, God will bless you in ways that you never could have imagined. So trust Him, and then prepare yourself for the abundance and joy that will most certainly be yours through Him.

Pregnancy Milestone for Today

_____

_____

_____

_____

_____

_____

A Quote for Today

Faith is taking God at His Word. No matter how you feel, no matter how you read the circumstances, no matter what anyone else tells you about the truthfulness of what God says. God is truthful.

—Kay Arthur

MANAGING CHANGE

The wise see danger ahead and avoid it,
but fools keep going and get into trouble.
—Proverbs 27:12 NCV

Because you're a soon-to-be mom, nobody needs to tell you that your world is changing constantly, and so is your body. So today's question is this: How will you manage all those changes? Will you do your best and trust God with the rest, or will you spend fruitless hours worrying about things you can't control? The answer to these two simple questions will help determine the direction and quality of your life and the way that you experience your pregnancy.

The best way to confront change is head-on . . . and with God by your side. The same God who created the universe will protect you if you ask Him, so ask Him—and then serve Him with willing hands and a trusting heart. When you do, you may rest assured that while the world changes moment by moment, so does your body, God's love endures—unfathomable and unchanging—forever.

A Quote for Today

Live for today, but hold your hands open to tomorrow. Anticipate the future and its changes with joy. There is a seed of God's love in every event, every circumstance, every unpleasant situation in which you may find yourself.

—Barbara Johnson

Pregnancy Milestone for Today

_____

_____

_____

_____

_____

PRAY FOR YOUR HUSBAND

Don't fret or worry. Instead of worrying, pray. Let petitions and praises
shape your worries into prayers, letting God know your concerns.
Before you know it, a sense of God's wholeness, everything coming
together for good, will come and settle you down. It's wonderful what
happens when Christ displaces worry at the center of your life.
—Philippians 4:6-7 MSG

Pregnancy can be a stressful time for moms-to-be like you. But your pregnancy may also be a stressful time for your husband. He may have unspoken worries, vague concerns, or fears that he hasn't admitted, even to himself.

The old saying is familiar and true: "The couple that prays together stays together." Is prayer an integral part of your married life, or is it a hit-or-miss habit? Do you and your husband "pray without ceasing," or is prayer usually an afterthought? Do you regularly pray together, or do you save it for Sunday morning services? The answers to these questions determine the quality of your prayer life and, to a surprising extent, the spiritual strength of your marriage.

Today, take time to pray with your husband and for your husband. He needs that experience . . . and so do you.

Pregnancy Milestone for Today

_____

_____

_____

_____

_____

_____

A Quote for Today

The institution of marriage has been a sacred bond of fidelity between a man and a woman in every culture throughout recorded history. The pledge of loyalty and mutual support represented by marriage vows is a promise of commitment that extends to every aspect of life.

—James Dobson

LESSONS OF A LIFETIME

No discipline seems pleasant at the time, but painful.
Later on, however, it produces a harvest of righteousness and
peace for those who have been trained by it.
—Hebrews 12:11 NIV

God is always trying to get His messages through. When you listen carefully, there's so much to learn.

During difficult days, you can learn lessons that are impossible to learn during sunny, happier times. Times of testing can—and should—be times of intense spiritual and personal growth. But God will not force you to learn the lessons of adversity. You must learn them for yourself.

As an expectant mom, you experience a wide range of emotions and a wide range of experiences. Sometimes, you'll experience pure joy as you anticipate the arrival of your precious baby. On other occasions, you may endure bouts of discouragement or doubt. In either case, please remember that God is trying to teach you some very important lessons today. Your job, if you choose to accept it, is to learn those lessons as quickly, and as thoroughly, as possible.

A Quote for Today

If you lack knowledge, go to school.
If you lack wisdom,
get on your knees.
—Vance Havner

A Question to Think On

What lesson is God trying
to teach you today?

Pregnancy Milestone for Today

_____

_____

_____

_____

_____

_____

It Pays to Be Patient

Wait on the Lord, and He will rescue you.
—Proverbs 20:22 HCSB

Pregnancy teaches patience. As a mom-to-be, you'll find yourself waiting, and waiting, and waiting some more. You'll be waiting in doctor's offices (those "waiting rooms" are well-named), waiting for your energy to return (you may be in for a long wait), and waiting for the Big Day to arrive.

The next time you find your patience tested to the limit, remember that God is as near as your next breath, and remember that He offers strength and comfort to His children. He is your shield and your strength; He is your protector and your deliverer. Call upon Him, and then be comforted. Whatever your challenge, whatever your trouble, God can help you patiently persevere. And that's precisely what He'll do if you ask Him.

Pregnancy Milestone for Today

_____

_____

_____

_____

_____

_____

A Quote for Today

God has a designated time when His promise will be fulfilled and the prayer will be answered.

—Jim Cymbala

YOUR ETERNAL JOURNEY

For God so loved the world that He gave His only begotten Son,
that whoever believes in Him should not perish but have everlasting life.
—John 3:16 NKJV

Eternal life is not an event that begins when you die. Eternal life begins when you invite Jesus into your heart right here on earth. So it's important to remember that God's plans for you are not limited to the ups and downs of everyday life. If you've allowed Jesus to reign over your heart, you've already begun your eternal journey.

As mere mortals, our vision for the future, like our lives here on earth, is limited. God's vision is not burdened by such limitations: His plans extend throughout all eternity.

Let us praise the Creator for His priceless gift, and let us share the Good News with all who cross our paths. We return our Father's love by accepting His grace and by sharing His message and His love. When we do, we are blessed here on earth and throughout all eternity.

A Quote for Today

O Sovereign God! You have humbled yourself in order to exalt us. You became poor so that we might become rich. You came to us so that we can come to you. You took upon yourself our humanity in order to raise us up into eternal life. All this comes through your grace, free and unmerited; all this through your beloved Son, our Lord and Savior, Jesus Christ.

—Karl Barth

Pregnancy Milestone for Today

_____

_____

_____

_____

_____

_____

TWO TEMPLES

With God's power working in us, God can do much, much more
than anything we can ask or imagine.
—Ephesians 3:20 NCV

The Bible's instructions are clear: you are to treat your body like a temple. But now that you're pregnant, you have two temples to care for: your own body and the body of your precious unborn baby.

How will you treat the two temples that God has entrusted to your care? Will you summon the discipline to make the healthy choices that are so important to your unborn baby's future? Of course you should, and with God's help, you will.

Today, pray about your health. Ask God how He wants you to treat your body. And while you're at it, ask Him for the strength and the discipline to make the sensible choices that are best for yourself and for your baby.

Pregnancy Milestone for Today

_____

_____

_____

_____

_____

A Quote for Today

A Christian should no more defile his body than a Jew would defile the temple.

—Warren Wiersbe

A Timely Tip

Many women benefit from nutritional supplements. If you haven't already done so, ask your doctor to recommend vitamins or supplements that are right for you.

TIME TO CELEBRATE

Rejoice in the Lord always. I will say it again: Rejoice!
—Philippians 4:4 HCSB

Are you living a life of agitation or celebration? If you're a believer, it should most certainly be the latter. With Christ as your Savior, every day should be a time of celebration.

Today, celebrate the life that God has given you and the life you are carrying inside. Today, put a smile on your face, kind words on your lips, and a song in your heart. Be generous with your praise and free with your encouragement. And then, when you have celebrated life to the full, invite your family and friends to do likewise. After all, this is God's day, and He has given us clear instructions for its use. We are commanded to rejoice and be glad. So, with no further ado, let the celebration begin . . .

A Quote for Today

The highest and most desirable state of the soul is to praise God in celebration for being alive.

—Luci Swindoll

Pregnancy Milestone for Today

_____

_____

_____

_____

_____

_____

THAT PRECIOUS LIFE

*So each generation can set its hope anew on God,
remembering his glorious miracles and obeying his commands.*
—Psalm 78:7 NLT

The gift of life is cause for celebration and praise. Today, as you contemplate your pregnancy and your baby's future, take time to thank God for His miraculous gifts.

Your unborn child is a precious treasure from the Creator. But your blessings most certainly don't end there. When you stop to think about it, God has given you more gifts and more opportunities than you can ever count. So the question of the day is this: will you thank your Heavenly Father . . . or will you spend your time and energy doing other things?

God is always listening—are you willing to say thanks? It's up to you, and the next move is yours.

Pregnancy Milestone for Today

_____

_____

_____

_____

_____

_____

A Quote for Today

The Bible instructs—and experience teaches—that praising God results in our burdens being lifted and our joys being multiplied.
—Jim Gallery

A Timely Tip

God deserves your praise today . . . and you deserve the experience of praising Him.

SLOW DOWN

I wait quietly before God, for my salvation comes from him.
—Psalm 62:1 NLT

As your pregnancy progresses, don't be afraid to slow down your pace and simplify your life. After all, you already have a prime responsibility: caring for the baby inside.

You live in a world where simplicity is in short supply. Think for a moment about the complexity of your everyday life and compare it to the lives of your ancestors. Certainly, you are the beneficiary of many technological innovations, but those innovations have a price: in all likelihood, your world is highly complex.

Unless you take firm control of your time and your life, you may be overwhelmed by an ever-increasing tidal wave of complexity that threatens your happiness. So do yourself a favor: keep your life as simple as possible. Simplicity is, indeed, genius. By simplifying your life, you are destined to improve it.

A Timely Tip

As a mom-to-be, you have many responsibilities. Do first things first, and keep your focus on high-priority tasks. And remember this: your highest priority should be your relationship with God and His Son.

Pregnancy Milestone for Today

_____

_____

_____

_____

_____

_____

BEING PATIENT

Rejoice in hope; be patient in affliction; be persistent in prayer.
—Romans 12:12 HCSB

For most of us, patience is a hard thing to master. Why? Because we have lots of things we want, and we know precisely when we want them: NOW (if not sooner). But our Father in heaven has other ideas; the Bible teaches that we must learn to wait patiently for the things that God has in store for us, even when waiting is difficult.

Psalm 37:7 commands us to "rest in the Lord, and wait patiently for Him" (NKJV). But, for most of us, waiting patiently for Him is hard. We are fallible human beings who seek solutions to our problems today, not tomorrow. Still, God instructs us to wait patiently for His plans to unfold, and that's exactly what we should do.

Sometimes, patience is the price we pay for being responsible adults, and that's as it should be. After all, think how patient our Heavenly Father has been with us.

So the next time you find yourself drumming your fingers as you wait for a quick resolution to the inevitable challenges of being an expectant mom, take a deep breath and ask God for patience. Be still before your Heavenly Father and trust His timetable: it's the peaceful way to live.

Pregnancy Milestone for Today

_____

_____

_____

_____

_____

_____

A Quote for Today

No matter what we are going through, no matter how long the waiting for answers, of one thing we may be sure. God is faithful. He keeps His promises. What He starts, He finishes, including His perfect work in us.

—Gloria Gaither

LISTENING TO GOD

The one who is from God listens to God's words. This is why you don't
listen, because you are not from God.
—John 8:47 HCSB

Sometimes God speaks loudly and clearly. More often, He speaks in a quiet voice—and if you are wise, you will be listening carefully when He does. To do so, you must carve out quiet moments each day to study His Word and sense His direction.

Can you quiet yourself long enough to listen to your conscience? Are you attuned to the subtle guidance of your intuition? Are you willing to pray sincerely and then to wait quietly for God's response? Hopefully so. Usually God refrains from sending His messages on stone tablets or city billboards. More often, He communicates in subtler ways. If you sincerely desire to hear His voice, you must listen carefully, and you must do so in the silent corners of your quiet, willing heart.

A Quote for Today

When we come to Jesus stripped
of pretensions, with a needy spirit,
ready to listen, He meets us
at the point of need.
—Catherine Marshall

Pregnancy Milestone for Today

_____

_____

_____

_____

_____

_____

COUNTLESS BLESSINGS

The Lord bless you and keep you;
the Lord make His face shine upon you, and be gracious to you.
—Numbers 6:24-25 NKJV

Because you are an expectant mother, you have been specially blessed by the Creator. God has given you blessings that are, in truth, simply too numerous to count. Your blessings include your life, your baby, your family, your friends, your talents, and your opportunities, for starters. But, your greatest blessing—a priceless treasure that is yours for the asking—is God's gift of salvation through Christ Jesus.

The gifts you receive from God are multiplied when you share them with others. Today, give thanks to God for your blessings, and demonstrate your gratitude by sharing those blessings with your family, with your friends, and with the world.

Pregnancy Milestone for Today

_____

_____

_____

_____

_____

_____

A Quote for Today

Do we not continually pass by blessings innumerable without notice, and instead fix our eyes on what we feel to be our trials and our losses, and think and talk about these until our whole horizon is filled with them, and we almost begin to think we have no blessings at all?
—Hannah Whitall Smith

TALK TO ENCOURAGING MOMS

*Don't you realize that all of you together are the temple of God
and that the Spirit of God lives in you?*
—1 Corinthians 3:16 NLT

If this is your first pregnancy, you have quite a few surprises in store. As your baby grows and your body changes, you'll probably have a laundry-list of questions. Your doctor will provide many answers, but you'll also benefit from the accumulated wisdom of family and friends. And you'll receive special insights from moms who have gone through some of the same experiences that you're going through now.

Today, as you consider the many blessings that God has given you, remember to thank Him for the family and friends He has chosen to place along your path. Seek their guidance and trust the guidance they give. Consider your friends and mentors to be God's gift to you . . . because that's precisely what they are.

A Quote for Today

Christians are like coals of a fire.
Together they glow—apart
they grow cold.
—Anonymous

A Question to Think On

Who's the most encouraging friend
you can talk to today?

Pregnancy Milestone for Today

_____

_____

_____

_____

_____

_____

FEELING BLUE?

I have heard your prayer, I have seen your tears; surely I will heal you.
—2 Kings 20:5 NKJV

Sometimes, we're sad, and we don't know why. But, in time, that sadness runs its course and gradually abates. Depression, on the other hand, goes far beyond those occasional bouts of "the blues." Depression is a physical and emotional condition that is highly treatable.

If you find yourself feeling "blue," perhaps it's a logical reaction to the ups and downs of your pregnancy or to the rigors of daily life. But if you (or someone close to you) become dangerously depressed, it's time to seek professional help.

Some days are light and happy, and some days are not. When we face the inevitable dark days of life, we must choose how we will respond. Will we allow ourselves to sink even more deeply into our own sadness, or will we do the difficult work of pulling ourselves out? We bring light to the dark days of life by turning first to God and then to trusted family members, friends, and medical professionals. When we do, the clouds will eventually part and the sun will shine once more upon our souls.

Pregnancy Milestone for Today

_____

_____

_____

_____

_____

_____

A Quote for Today

Feelings of uselessness and hopelessness are not from God, but from the evil one, the devil, who wants to discourage you and thwart your effectiveness for the Lord.
—Bill Bright

IT PAYS TO PRAISE

So through Jesus let us always offer to God our sacrifice of praise,
coming from lips that speak his name.
—Hebrews 13:15 NCV

The Bible makes it clear: it pays to praise God. But sometimes, we allow ourselves to become so preoccupied with the demands of everyday life that we forget to say "thank You" to the Giver of all good gifts.

Worship and praise should be a part of everything we do. Otherwise, we quickly lose perspective as we fall prey to the demands of the moment.

Do you sincerely desire to be a worthy servant of the One who has given you everything, including that precious unborn child you already love so dearly? Then praise Him for who He is and for what He has done for you. And don't just praise Him on Sunday morning. Praise Him all day long, every day, for as long as you live . . . and then for all eternity.

A Quote for Today

What happens when we praise
the Father? We reestablish
the proper chain of command.
—Max Lucado

Pregnancy Milestone
for Today

_____

_____

_____

_____

_____

_____

KINDNESS IN ACTION

*Yes indeed, it is good when you truly obey our Lord's royal command
found in the Scriptures: "Love your neighbor as yourself."*
—James 2:8 NLT

Kindness is a choice. Sometimes, when we feel happy or prosperous, we find it easy to be kind. Other times, when we are discouraged, or uncomfortable, or simply exhausted, we can scarcely summon the energy to utter a single kind word. But, God's commandment is clear: we must observe the Golden Rule in everything. God intends that we make the conscious choice to treat others with kindness and respect, no matter our circumstances, no matter our emotions. Kindness, therefore, is a choice that we, as Christians, must make many times each day.

When we weave the thread of kindness into the very fabric of our lives, we give a priceless gift to others, and we give glory to the One who gave His life for us. As believers, we must do no less.

Pregnancy Milestone for Today

_____

_____

_____

_____

_____

_____

A Quote for Today

When we do little acts of kindness that make life more bearable for someone else, we are walking in love as the Bible commands us.

—Barbara Johnson

THESE PRECIOUS DAYS

But let all who take refuge in You rejoice..
—Psalm 5:11 HCSB

As a mom-to-be, you know that some days can be difficult. But even on those days when you're overworked, overstressed, and woefully short of energy, don't forget to give thanks for the gift of life: yours and your baby's.

God's Word makes it clear: a wise heart is a thankful heart. Period. We are to worship God, in part, by the genuine gratitude we feel in our hearts for the marvelous blessings that our Creator has bestowed upon us. Yet even the most saintly among us must endure periods of bitterness, fear, doubt, and regret. Why? Because we are imperfect human beings who are incapable of perfect gratitude. Still, even on life's darker days, we must seek to cleanse our hearts of negative emotions and fill them, instead, with praise, with love, with hope, and with thanksgiving. To do otherwise is to be unfair to ourselves, to our loved ones, and to our God.

A Timely Tip

Every day of your life—and every day of your pregnancy—is a gift from God. Treat it that way.

Pregnancy Milestone for Today

_____

_____

_____

_____

_____

FOCUSING ON GOD

*Give your entire attention to what God is doing right now,
and don't get worked up about what may or may not happen tomorrow.
God will help you deal with whatever hard things come up
when the time comes.*
—Matthew 6:34 MSG

All of us may find our courage tested by the inevitable challenges of everyday life. After all, ours is a world filled with uncertainty, hardship, sickness, and danger. Trouble, it seems, is never too far from the front door.

When we focus upon our fears and our doubts, we may find many reasons to lie awake at night and fret about the uncertainties of the coming day. A better strategy, of course, is to focus not upon our fears but instead upon our God.

As you think about your life and your pregnancy, remember that God is as near as your next breath, and He is in control. He offers salvation to all His children, including you. God is your shield and your strength; you are His forever. So don't focus your thoughts upon the fears of the day. Instead, trust God's plan and His eternal love for you. And remember: God is good, and He has the last word.

Pregnancy Milestone for Today

_____

_____

_____

_____

_____

_____

A Quote for Today

His hand on me is a father's hand,
gently guiding and encouraging.
His hand lets me know he is
with me, so I am not afraid.
—Mary Morrison Suggs

HIS GIFT, FREELY GIVEN

For all have sinned, and fall short of the glory of God, being justified freely by His grace through the redemption that is in Christ Jesus.
—Romans 3:23-24 NKJV

Romans 3:23 reminds us that all of us fall short of the glory of God. Yet despite our imperfections and despite our shortcomings, God sent His Son so that we might be redeemed from our sins. In doing so, our Heavenly Father demonstrated His infinite mercy and His infinite love.

We have received countless gifts from God, but none can compare with the gift of salvation. God's grace is the ultimate gift, and we owe Him the ultimate in thanksgiving. Let us praise the Creator for His priceless gift, and let us share the Good News with our families, with our friends, and with the world.

Christ sacrificed His life on the cross so that we might have eternal life. This gift, freely given from God's only begotten Son, is the priceless possession of everyone who accepts Him as Lord and Savior. We return our Savior's love by welcoming Him into our hearts and sharing His message and His love.

A Quote for Today

The gift of God is eternal life, spiritual life, abundant life through faith in Jesus Christ, the Living Word of God.
—Anne Graham Lotz

Pregnancy Milestone for Today

_____

_____

_____

_____

_____

_____

YOUR REASONS TO REJOICE

Keep your eyes focused on what is right,
and look straight ahead to what is good.
—Proverbs 4:25 NCV

As a Christian mother-to-be, you have every reason to rejoice. God is in His heaven; Christ has risen; and dawn has broken on another day of life. But, when the demands of life seem great, you may find yourself feeling exhausted, discouraged, or both. That's when you need a fresh supply of hope . . . and God is ready, willing, and able to supply it.

The advice contained in Proverbs 4:25 is clear-cut: "Keep your eyes focused on what is right, and look straight ahead to what is good" (NCV). That's why you strive to maintain a positive, can-do attitude—an attitude that pleases God.

As you face the inevitable challenges of pregnancy, use God's Word as a tool for directing your thoughts. When you do, your attitude will be pleasing to God, pleasing to your family, pleasing to your friends, and pleasing to yourself.

Pregnancy Milestone for Today

_____

_____

_____

_____

_____

_____

A Quote for Today

Developing a positive attitude
means working continually
to find what is uplifting
and encouraging.

—Barbara Johnson

Day 61 • Today's Date _____

START PLANNING

My child, don't lose sight of good planning and insight. Hang on to them,
for they fill you with life and bring you honor and respect.
—Proverbs 3:21-22 NLT

The big day, that glorious day your baby will be born, may seem far away. But, it's not too early to begin planning for the big arrival: preparing the baby's room, accumulating baby clothes, gathering diapers, wipes, a car seat, and other baby gadgets, for starters.

As you make plans and establish priorities, remember this: you're not the only one working on your behalf. God, too, is at work. And with Him as your partner, your ultimate success is guaranteed.

Would you like a planning strategy that never fails? Here it is: Include God in every aspect of your life's journey, including your pregnancy. If you allow the world to establish your priorities, you will eventually become discouraged, or disappointed, or both. But if you genuinely seek God's will for every important decision that you make, your loving Heavenly Father will guide your steps and enrich your life. So as you plan your work, your pregnancy, and your future, remember that every good plan should start with God, including yours.

A Timely Tip

As you're making plans, consult God early (in the morning) and often (throughout the day).

Pregnancy Milestone for Today

_____

_____

_____

_____

_____

THE WISDOM OF MODERATION

Moderation is better than muscle,
self-control better than political power.
—Proverbs 16:32 MSG

Moderation and wisdom are traveling companions. If we are wise, we must learn to temper our appetites, our desires, and our impulses. When we do, we are blessed, in part, because God has created a world in which temperance is rewarded and intemperance is inevitably punished.

Would you like to improve your life and make your pregnancy a little easier? Then harness your appetites and restrain your impulses. Moderation is difficult, of course; it is especially difficult in a prosperous society such as ours. But the rewards of moderation are numerous and long-lasting. Claim those rewards today.

Pregnancy Milestone for Today

_____

_____

_____

_____

_____

_____

A Quote for Today

Virtue—even attempted virtue—brings light; indulgence brings fog.
—C. S. Lewis

A Timely Tip

Establishing sensible eating habits will pay big dividends for you and your baby. So eat plenty of fruits and vegetables along with moderate portions of other healthy, natural foods.

INFINITE POSSIBILITIES

We know that all things work together for the good of those who love God: those who are called according to His purpose.
—Romans 8:28 HCSB

Ours is a God of infinite possibilities. But sometimes, because of limited faith and limited understanding, we wrongly assume that God cannot or will not intervene in the affairs of mankind. Such assumptions are simply wrong.

Are you afraid to ask God to do big things in your life? And, are you hesitant to ask Him to protect your unborn child? If so, it's time to abandon your doubts and reclaim your faith in God's promises.

God's Holy Word makes it clear: absolutely nothing is impossible for the Lord. And since the Bible means what it says, you can be comforted in the knowledge that the Creator of the universe can do miraculous things in your own life and in the lives of your loved ones. Your challenge, as a believer, is to take God at His word and to expect the miraculous.

A Quote for Today

If you believe in a God who controls the big things, you have to believe in a God who controls the little things. It is we, of course, to whom things look "little" or "big."
—Elisabeth Elliot

Pregnancy Milestone for Today

_____

_____

_____

_____

_____

HOPE NOW

Without wavering, let us hold tightly to the hope we say we have,
for God can be trusted to keep his promise.
—Hebrews 10:23 NLT

Are you a hope-filled soon-to-be mom? You should be. After all, God is good; His love endures; and He has offered you the priceless gift of eternal life. And, of course, God has blessed you with a loving family. But sometimes, in life's darker moments, you may lose sight of those blessings, and when you do, it's easy to lose hope.

When a suffering woman sought healing by touching the hem of His cloak, Jesus replied, "Daughter, be of good comfort; thy faith hath made thee whole" (Matthew 9:22 KJV). The message to believers is clear: if we are to be made whole by God, we must live by faith.

If you find yourself falling into the spiritual traps of worry and discouragement, seek the healing touch of Jesus and the encouraging words of fellow Christians. This world can be a place of trials and tribulations, but as believers, we are secure. Our hope is in God; He has promised us peace, joy, and eternal life. And, of course, God keeps His promises today, tomorrow, and forever, amen!

Pregnancy Milestone for Today

_____

_____

_____

_____

_____

_____

A Quote for Today

Easter comes each year to remind us of a truth that is eternal and universal. The empty tomb of Easter morning says to you and me, "Of course you'll encounter trouble. But behold a God of power who can take any evil and turn it into a door of hope."
—Catherine Marshall

PRAYER CHANGES THINGS AND YOU

And everything—whatever you ask in prayer, believing—you will receive.
—Matthew 21:22 HCSB

Is prayer an integral part of your daily life, or is it a hit-or-miss habit? Do you "pray without ceasing," or is your prayer life an afterthought? As you consider the role that prayer currently plays in your life—and the role that you think it should play—remember that the quality of your spiritual life is inevitably related to the quality of your prayer life.

Prayer changes things and it changes you. So today, instead of turning things over in your mind, turn them over to God in prayer. Instead of worrying about your pregnancy, pray about it. Instead of focusing on the challenges and complications of everyday life, thank God for His infinite blessings. The Creator is listening . . . and He wants to hear from you. Now.

A Quote for Today

Just as omitting an essential vitamin from our diet will make us physically weak, so a lack of prayer will make us spiritually anemic.

—Billy Graham

Pregnancy Milestone for Today

_____

_____

_____

_____

_____

ALL THE THINGS YOU USED TO DO (BUT CAN'T DO NOW)

I wait for the Lord, my soul waits, and in His word I do hope. My soul waits for the Lord more than those who watch for the morning— yes, more than those who watch for the morning.

—Psalm 130:5-6 NKJV

As a mom-to-be, nobody needs to tell you that, as your pregnancy progresses, some of life's simplest tasks become progressively harder, and finally, almost impossible. You can't lift the things you used to lift (doctor's orders), you can't move as quickly as you used to move, and simple tasks that used to be a breeze may now leave you exhausted.

During your pregnancy, please be patient with everybody, including yourself. Don't become discouraged if you need more rest. And, don't be frustrated if you're feeling uncomfortable. Instead of complaining to your family, to your friends, or to yourself, just slow down long enough to catch your breath. And then ask God for the wisdom to celebrate your pregnancy, even when it's hard.

Pregnancy Milestone for Today

_____

_____

_____

_____

_____

A Quote for Today

All things pass.
Patience attains all it strives for.

—St. Teresa of Avila

THE MIRACLE OF LIFE

Depend on the Lord and his strength; always go to him for help.
Remember the miracles he has done;
remember his wonders and his decisions.
—Psalm 105:4-5 NCV

Your unborn child is a miracle, a gift from the Creator, a precious treasure unique in all the universe. And, it's always the right moment to praise God for that miracle.

As children, we are taught to say "please" and "thank you." And, as adults, we should approach God in the same way. We should offer up our needs to Him in prayer ("Please, Dear Lord . . ."), and we should graciously give thanks for the gifts He has given us. Let us praise God and thank Him. He is the Giver of all things good.

A Quote for Today

Gratitude unlocks the fullness of life. It turns what we have into enough, and more. It turns denial into acceptance, chaos to order, confusion to clarity. It can turn a meal into a feast, a house into a home, a stranger into a friend. Gratitude makes sense of our past, brings peace for today, and creates a vision for tomorrow.

—Melody Beattie

Pregnancy Milestone for Today

_____

_____

_____

_____

_____

WATCH WHAT YOU WATCH

*Put on the full armor of God so that you can stand
against the tactics of the Devil.*
—Ephesians 6:11 HCSB

As a mom-to-be, you need rest, you need time to recharge your batteries, and you need peace. And, if you can't seem to find peace amid the chaos of modern-day life, it may be the result of too much popular media.

In the pursuit of profits, the media glamorizes violence, exploits suffering, and sensationalizes sex. So here's a question for you and your family: Will you control what appears on your TV screen, or will you be controlled by it? If you're willing to take complete control over the images that appear inside the four walls of your home, you'll be doing yourselves a king-sized favor.

If you'd like a more peaceful home, forget the media hype, and pay attention to God. Stand up for Him and be counted, not just in church where it's easy to be a Christian but also when you're deciding what to watch. You owe it to your Creator and to yourselves.

Pregnancy Milestone for Today

_____

_____

_____

_____

_____

A Timely Tip

Compare the amount of time you spend watching TV to the time you spend studying God's Word. If you don't like the results of that comparison, it's time to think long and hard about the difference between the media's priorities and God's priorities.

OUR GREATEST REFUGE

For you have need of endurance, so that when you have done
the will of God, you may receive what was promised.
—Hebrews 10:36 NASB

God is our greatest refuge. When every earthly support system fails, God remains steadfast, and His love remains unchanged. When we encounter life's inevitable disappointments and setbacks, God remains faithful. When we suffer losses that leave us breathless, God is always with us, always ready to respond to our prayers, always working in us and through us to turn tragedy into triumph.

Author and speaker Patsy Clairmont observed, "If you are walking toward Jesus to the best of your ability, he will see you through life's unpredictable waters—but you must risk launching the boat." And that's sound advice because even during life's most difficult days, God stands by us. Our job, of course, is to return the favor and stand by Him.

A Quote for Today

Whether our fear is absolutely
realistic or out of proportion
in our minds, our greatest refuge
is Jesus Christ.
—Luci Swindoll

Pregnancy Milestone for Today

_____

_____

_____

_____

_____

STAYING ORGANIZED

God hasn't invited us into a disorderly, unkempt life but into
something holy and beautiful—as beautiful on the inside as the outside.
—1 Thessalonians 4:7 MSG

If your energy is decreasing, then it's only natural that the clutter inside your home may be increasing. After all, it takes energy to keep your life and your house organized. Unfortunately, houses are not like ovens; they aren't self-cleaning. So, if you want a tidier home, you'll probably have to manage the cleanup yourself, which is perfectly okay with God.

When we study God's Word, we are confronted again and again with God's intention that His children lead disciplined lives. God doesn't reward sloppiness. To the contrary, He expects believers to be diligent, energetic, disciplined, and orderly. God's message is clear: we must do our work first, and then we can expect a bountiful harvest. But we should never expect the harvest to precede the labor.

So, if you'd like a simple formula for uplifting your spirits and improving your life, here it is: clean up the clutter. Today.

Pregnancy Milestone for Today

_____

_____

_____

_____

_____

_____

A Timely Tip

If your home is brimming with clutter, it's time for you and your husband to regain order. So, dedicate an entire Saturday to an initial clean-up operation. This major commitment to clutter-free living will get you started on the right foot.

HE RENEWS

Finally, be strengthened by the Lord and by His vast strength.
—Ephesians 6:10 HCSB

God's Word is clear: When we genuinely lift our hearts and prayers to Him, He renews our strength. Are you almost too weary to lift your head? Then bow it. Offer your concerns and your fears to your Father in heaven. He is always at your side, offering His love and His strength.

Your pregnancy will, at times, leave you exhausted. When you're tired or worried, talk to friends and family members. And, whatever you do, don't forget to talk to God. Your Creator will never let you down. To the contrary, He will lift you up when you ask Him to do so. All you must do is ask.

A Quote for Today

Be still, and in the quiet moments, listen to the voice of your heavenly Father. His words can renew your spirit—no one knows you and your needs like He does.

—Janet L. Weaver Smith

Pregnancy Milestone for Today

_____

_____

_____

_____

_____

_____

THE JOY OF SERVING GOD

Shepherd God's flock, for whom you are responsible.
Watch over them because you want to, not because you are forced.
That is how God wants it. Do it because you are happy to serve.
—1 Peter 5:2 NCV

Martha and Mary both loved Jesus, but they showed their love in different ways. Mary sat at the Master's feet, taking in every word. Martha, meanwhile, busied herself with preparations for the meal to come. When Martha asked Jesus if He was concerned about Mary's failure to help, Jesus replied, "Mary has chosen better" (Luke 10:42 NIV). The implication is clear: as believers, we must spend time with Jesus before we spend time for him. But, once we have placed Christ where He belongs—at the center of our hearts—we must go about the business of serving the One who has saved us.

How can we serve Christ? By sharing His message and by serving those in need. As followers of Jesus, we must make ourselves humble servants to our families, to our neighbors, and to the world. We must help the helpless, love the unloved, protect the vulnerable, and care for the infirm. When we do, our lives will be blessed by the One who sacrificed His life for us.

Pregnancy Milestone for Today

_____

_____

_____

_____

_____

_____

A Quote for Today

That's what I love about serving God. In His eyes, there are no little people . . . because there are no big people. We are all on the same playing field.
—Joni Eareckson Tada

LISTENING CAREFULLY TO YOUR CONSCIENCE

*Let us come near to God with a sincere heart and a sure faith,
because we have been made free from a guilty conscience,
and our bodies have been washed with pure water.*
—Hebrews 10:22 NCV

God gave you a conscience for a very good reason: to make your path conform to His will. Billy Graham correctly observed, "Most of us follow our conscience as we follow a wheelbarrow. We push it in front of us in the direction we want to go." To do so, of course, is a profound mistake. Yet all of us, on occasion, have failed to listen to the voice that God planted in our hearts, and all of us have suffered the consequences.

Wise believers make it a practice to listen carefully to that quiet internal voice. Count yourself among that number. When your conscience speaks, listen and learn. In all likelihood, God is trying to get His message through. And in all likelihood, it is a message that you desperately need to hear.

A Quote for Today

God desires that we become spiritually healthy enough through faith to have a conscience that rightly interprets the work of the Holy Spirit.
—Beth Moore

Pregnancy Milestone for Today

_____

_____

_____

_____

_____

GIVING THANKS TO THE CREATOR

And whatever you do, in word or in deed, do everything in the name of the Lord Jesus, giving thanks to God the Father through Him.
—Colossians 3:17 HCSB

As Christians, we are blessed beyond measure. God sent His only Son to die for our sins. And, God has given us the priceless gifts of eternal love and eternal life. We, in turn, are instructed to approach our Heavenly Father with reverence and thanksgiving. But, as busy mothers caught up in the inevitable demands of everyday life, we sometimes fail to pause and thank our Creator for the countless blessings He has bestowed upon us.

When we slow down and express our gratitude to the One who made us, we enrich our own lives and the lives of our loved ones. Thanksgiving should become a habit, a regular part of our daily routines. Yes, God has blessed us beyond measure, and we owe Him everything, including our eternal praise.

Pregnancy Milestone for Today

_____

_____

_____

_____

_____

_____

A Quote for Today

God is in control, and therefore in everything I can give thanks, not because of the situation, but because of the One who directs and rules over it.
—Kay Arthur

MOVING PAST THE PAST

One thing I do, forgetting those things which are behind and reaching forward to those things which are ahead, I press toward the goal for the prize of the upward call of God in Christ Jesus.
—Philippians 3:13-14 NKJV

Man-made plans are fallible; God's plans are not. Yet whenever life takes an unexpected turn, we are tempted to fall into the spiritual traps of worry, self-pity, or bitterness. God intends that we do otherwise.

The old saying is familiar: "Forgive and forget." But when we have been hurt badly, forgiveness is often difficult and forgetting is downright impossible. Since we can't forget yesterday's troubles, we should learn from them. Yesterday has much to teach us about tomorrow. We may learn from the past, but we should never live in the past.

So if you're trying to forget the past, don't waste your time. Instead, try a different approach: learn to accept the past and live in the present. Then, you can focus your thoughts and your energies, not on the struggles of yesterday but instead on the profound opportunities that God has placed before you today.

A Quote for Today

We need to be at peace with our past, content with our present, and sure about our future, knowing they are all in God's hands.

—Joyce Meyer

Pregnancy Milestone for Today

_____

_____

_____

_____

_____

ABUNDANCE, NOT ANXIETY

Therefore don't worry about tomorrow, because tomorrow will worry about itself. Each day has enough trouble of its own.
—Matthew 6:34 HCSB

We live in a world that often breeds anxiety and fear. When we come face-to-face with new experiences, we may fall prey to discouragement, doubt, or depression. But our Father in heaven has other plans. God has promised that we may lead lives of abundance, not anxiety. In fact, His Word instructs us to "be anxious for nothing." But how can we put our fears to rest? By taking those fears to God and leaving them there.

As you face the inevitable challenges of pregnancy, do you find yourself becoming anxious, troubled, discouraged, or fearful? If so, turn every one of your concerns over to your Heavenly Father. The same God who created the universe will comfort you if you ask Him . . . so ask Him and trust Him. And then watch in amazement as your anxieties melt into the warmth of His loving hands.

Pregnancy Milestone for Today

_____

_____

_____

_____

_____

_____

A Quote for Today

Worry is a cycle of inefficient thoughts whirling around a center of fear.

—Corrie ten Boom

PRAYING ABOUT YOUR PREGNANCY

Ask in my name, according to my will, and he'll most certainly give it to you. Your joy will be a river overflowing its banks!
—John 16:24 MSG

Have you asked God to guide you throughout your pregnancy? Have you asked Him to strengthen your faith and protect your unborn baby? Have you taken time throughout the day to praise Him for the priceless gift you're carrying inside? If so, congratulations; if not, it's time to reorder your priorities and rearrange your day.

No task is more important than prayer. God promises that the prayers of righteous men and women can accomplish great things. So pray. Start praying before the sun comes up and keep praying until you fall off to sleep at night. And rest assured: God is always listening and He always wants to hear from you.

A Quote for Today

Prayer accomplishes more
than anything else.
—Bill Bright

A Question to Think On

Do you have a written prayer list
that you look at every day?

Pregnancy Milestone for Today

_____

_____

_____

_____

_____

_____

God Is in Control

I wait quietly before God, for my hope is in him.
—Psalm 62:5 NLT

As a thoughtful mom-to-be, you have understandable concerns about your pregnancy. But of this you can be certain: God is in control. The Creator is not absent; He is not a distant power, far removed from His creation. To the contrary, He is everywhere you've ever been and everywhere you'll ever be.

Your Heavenly Father has a plan for you and a plan for your unborn baby. During your pregnancy, you'll need to trust His plans, even if you don't understand them. Ruth Bell Graham once said, "When I am dealing with an all-powerful, all-knowing God, I, as a mere mortal, must offer my petitions not only with persistence, but also with patience. Someday I'll know why." So, even when you can't understand what God is doing, you must trust Him and never lose faith. He always keeps His promises.

Pregnancy Milestone for Today

_____

_____

_____

_____

_____

_____

A Quote for Today

When you live a surrendered life, God is willing and able to provide for your every need.
—Corrie ten Boom

GOD'S COMFORT

Praise be to the God and Father of our Lord Jesus Christ.
God is the Father who is full of mercy and all comfort.
He comforts us every time we have trouble, so when others have trouble,
we can comfort them with the same comfort God gives us.
—2 Corinthians 1:3-4 NCV

We live in a world that is, at times, a frightening place. We live in a world that is, at times, a discouraging place. We live in a world where life-changing losses can be so painful and so profound that it seems we will never recover. But with God's help, and with the help of encouraging family members and friends, we can recover.

When we are worried or discouraged, we are wise to remember that God is with us always and that He offers us comfort, assurance, and peace—our task, of course, is to accept these gifts.

When we trust in God's promises, the world becomes a less frightening place. With God's comfort and His love in our hearts, we can tackle our problems with courage, determination, and faith.

A Quote for Today

Put your hand into the hand of God.
He gives the calmness and
serenity of heart and soul.
—Mrs. Charles E. Cowman

Pregnancy Milestone for Today

_____

_____

_____

_____

_____

SWAMPED BY YOUR POSSESSIONS?

Don't be obsessed with getting more material things.
Be relaxed with what you have.
—Hebrews 13:5 MSG

Do you sometimes feel swamped by your possessions? Do you seem to be spending more and more time keeping track of the things you own while making mental notes of the things you intend to buy? If so, here's a word of warning: your fondness for material possessions is getting in the way of your relationships—your relationships with the people around you and your relationship with God.

Society teaches us to honor possessions . . . God teaches us to honor people. And if we seek to be worthy followers of Christ, we must never invest too much energy in the acquisition of material possessions. Earthly riches are here today and all too soon gone. Our real riches, of course, are in heaven, and that's where we should focus our thoughts and our energy.

Pregnancy Milestone for Today

_____

_____

_____

_____

_____

_____

A Quote for Today

It's sobering to contemplate how much time, effort, sacrifice, compromise, and attention we give to acquiring and increasing our supply of something that is totally insignificant in eternity.
—Anne Graham Lotz

Expecting and Exhausted

*He gives power to the weak, and to those who have
no might He increases strength.*
—Isaiah 40:29 NKJV

Because you're expecting, you're undoubtedly beset by occasional bouts of exhaustion. If you're almost too exhausted to raise your head, bow it. And ask God to give you the strength to persevere and the wisdom to slow down.

Thankfully, on those cloudy days when your strength is sapped and your faith is shaken, there exists a source from which you can draw courage and wisdom. That source, of course, is God. Whenever you seek to form a more intimate and dynamic relationship with your Creator, He renews your spirits and restores your soul.

God's promise is made clear in Isaiah 40:31: "But those who wait on the Lord shall renew their strength; they shall mount up with wings like eagles, they shall run and not be weary, they shall walk and not faint" (NKJV). Upon this promise you can—and should—depend.

A Quote for Today

Just as courage is faith in good,
so discouragement is faith in evil,
and, while courage opens the door
to good, discouragement
opens it to evil.
—Hannah Whitall Smith

Pregnancy Milestone for Today

_____

_____

_____

_____

_____

_____

FEWER COMPLAINTS

When you are angry, do not sin, and be sure to stop being angry before the end of the day. Do not give the devil a way to defeat you.
—Ephesians 4:26-27 NCV

Perhaps God gave each of us one mouth and two ears in order that we might listen twice as much as we speak. Unfortunately, many of us do otherwise, especially when we become angry.

Being a mom-to-be isn't easy, so during your pregnancy, you'll have many opportunities to become frustrated. When those frustrations arise, please keep them in perspective. Turn away from anger, and turn instead to God.

The next time you are tempted to lose your temper over the minor inconveniences of everyday life or the major inconveniences of your pregnancy, slow down, catch your breath, and start counting your blessings. When you do, you'll have the comfort of knowing that you're following God's instructions, and you'll be giving yourself a priceless gift . . . the gift of peace.

Pregnancy Milestone for Today

_____

_____

_____

_____

_____

_____

A Quote for Today

Anger unresolved will only bring you woe.
—Kay Arthur

WALKING WITH GOD

How happy is everyone who fears the Lord, who walks in His ways!
—Psalm 128:1 HCSB

Are you tired? Discouraged? Fearful? Be comforted. Take a walk with God. Jesus called upon believers to walk with Him, and He promised them that He would teach them how to live freely and lightly (Matthew 11:28-30).

Do you have concerns about your pregnancy? Be confident in God's power. He will never desert you. Do you have worries about your future? Be courageous and call upon God. He will protect you and then use you according to His purposes. Are you hurting? Know that God hears your prayers. He will comfort you and, in time, He will dry your tears. Are you confused? Listen to the quiet voice of your Heavenly Father. He is not a God of confusion. Talk with Him; listen to Him; follow His commandments. He is steadfast, and He is your protector . . . forever.

A Quote for Today

The person who walks with God
always gets to his destination.
—Henrietta Mears

Pregnancy Milestone for Today

_____

_____

_____

_____

_____

_____

A Spiritual Sickness

*But if you harbor bitter envy and selfish ambition in your hearts,
do not boast about it or deny the truth. Such "wisdom" does not come
down from heaven but is earthly, unspiritual, of the devil.*
—James 3:14-16 NIV

Bitterness is a spiritual sickness. It will consume your soul; it is dangerous to your emotional health. It can destroy you if you let it . . . so don't let it!

If you are caught up in intense feelings of anger or resentment, you know all too well the destructive power of these emotions. How can you rid yourself of these feelings? First, you must prayerfully ask God to cleanse your heart. Then, you must learn to catch yourself whenever thoughts of bitterness or hatred begin to attack you. Your challenge is this: You must learn to resist negative thoughts before they hijack your emotions.

Matthew 5:22 teaches us that if we judge our brothers and sisters, we, too, will be subject to judgement. Let us refrain, then, from judging our neighbors. Instead, let us forgive them and love them, while leaving their judgement to a far more capable authority: the One who sits on His throne in heaven.

Pregnancy Milestone for Today

_____

_____

_____

_____

_____

A Quote for Today

Bitterness is a spiritual cancer, a rapidly growing malignancy that can consume your life. Bitterness cannot be ignored but must be healed at the very core, and only Christ can heal bitterness.

—Beth Moore

EMBRACED BY GOD

The unfailing love of the Lord never ends!
—Lamentations 3:22 NLT

Every day of your life—indeed, every moment of your life—you and your baby are embraced by God. He is always with you, and His love for both of you is deeper and more profound than you can imagine. God's love transcends space and time. It reaches beyond the heavens, and it touches the darkest, smallest corner of every human heart. When we become passionate in our devotion to the Father, when we sincerely open our minds and hearts to Him, His love does not arrive "some day"—it arrives immediately.

The words of Romans 8 make this promise: "For I am persuaded that neither death nor life, nor angels nor principalities nor powers, nor things present nor things to come, nor height nor depth, nor any other created thing, shall be able to separate us from the love of God which is in Christ Jesus our Lord" (vv. 38-39 NKJV).

Today, take God at His word and welcome His Son into your heart. When you do, God's transcendent love will surround you and transform you, now and forever.

A Quote for Today

God will never let you be shaken or
moved from your place
near His heart.
—Joni Eareckson Tada

Pregnancy Milestone
for Today

_____

_____

_____

_____

_____

_____

WISDOM AND HOPE

Know that wisdom is sweet to your soul; if you find it, there is a future hope for you, and your hope will not be cut off.
—Proverbs 24:14 NIV

Wisdom and hope are traveling companions. Wise women learn to think optimistically about their lives, their futures, and their faith. The pessimists, however, are not so fortunate; they choose instead to focus their thoughts and energies on fault finding, criticizing, and complaining, with precious little to show for their efforts.

To become wise, we must seek God's wisdom—the wisdom of hope—and we must live according to God's Word. To become wise, we must seek God's guidance with consistency and purpose. To become wise, we must not only learn the lessons of life, we must live by them.

Do you seek wisdom for yourself and for your family? Then remember this: The ultimate source of wisdom is the Word of God. When you study God's Word and live according to His commandments, you will grow wise, you will remain hopeful, and you will be a blessing to your family and to the world.

Pregnancy Milestone for Today

_____

_____

_____

_____

_____

_____

A Quote for Today

Teach us to set our hopes on
heaven, to hold firmly to
the promise of eternal life,
so that we can withstand the
struggles and storms of this world.
—Max Lucado

LOOK FOR THE JOY

You will show me the way of life, granting me the joy of your presence
and the pleasures of living with you forever.
—Psalm 16:11 NLT

Barbara Johnson could have been speaking directly to expectant moms when she said, "You have to look for the joy. Look for the light of God that is hitting your life, and you will find sparkles you didn't know were there."

Have you experienced that kind of joy lately? Hopefully so, because it's not enough to hear someone else talk about being joyful—you must actually experience that kind of joy in order to understand it.

Should you expect to be a joy-filled woman 24 hours a day, seven days a week, from this moment on? No. But you can (and should) experience pockets of joy frequently—that's the kind of joy-filled life that a woman like you deserves to live.

A Quote for Today

Joy is the serious business of heaven.
—C. S. Lewis

Pregnancy Milestone for Today

_____

_____

_____

_____

_____

_____

SPIRITUAL RICHES

In everything I did, I showed you that by this kind of hard work we must
help the weak, remembering the words the Lord Jesus himself said:
"It is more blessed to give than to receive."
—Acts 20:35 NIV

The Bible makes it clear that Christ came to this earth so that His followers might enjoy His abundance (John 10:10). But what, exactly, did Jesus mean when He promised "life . . . more abundantly"? Was He referring to material possessions or financial wealth? Hardly. Jesus offers a different kind of abundance: a spiritual richness that extends beyond the temporal boundaries of this world.

Today, as you contemplate God's plan for you and your unborn baby, be grateful. And, accept the abundance and peace that God offers to His children.

A Quote for Today

Knowing God involves an intimate, personal relationship that is developed over time through prayer and getting answers to prayer, through Bible study and applying its teaching to our lives, through obedience and experiencing the power of God, through moment-by-moment submission to Him that results in a moment-by-moment filling of the Holy Spirit.

—Anne Graham Lotz

Pregnancy Milestone
for Today

_____

_____

_____

_____

_____

_____

WAITING FOR "THE BIG DAY"

He has made everything beautiful in its time.
—Ecclesiastes 3:11 NKJV

It's only natural: you're anxiously awaiting the Big Day. But wait, you must. As your pregnancy progresses, you may become impatient, or discouraged, or both.

We human beings are so impatient. We know what we want, and we know exactly when we want it: RIGHT NOW! But, God knows better. He has created a world that unfolds according to His own timetable, not ours.

As a faithful mom-to-be, please do your best to be patient. Instead of worrying about your future, pray about it. And while you're waiting for that Big Day, don't forget to give thanks to the One who has given you more blessings than you can count.

A Quote for Today

Your times are in His hands.
He's in charge of the timetable,
so wait patiently.
—Kay Arthur

A Timely Tip

You don't know precisely what you need—or when you need it—but God does. So trust His timing.

Pregnancy Milestone for Today

_____

_____

_____

_____

_____

_____

HIS SURPRISING PLANS

*But as it is written in the Scriptures: "No one has ever seen this,
and no one has ever heard about it. No one has ever imagined
what God has prepared for those who love him."*
—1 Corinthians 2:9 NCV

God has big plans for you and your unborn baby, wonderful, surprising plans that only He can see. Your challenge, as an expectant mom, is to pray for guidance, to walk in faith, and to put your trust in God.

Today, as you think about your faith, your family, and your future, remember that God intends to use you in wonderful, unexpected ways if you let Him. Your challenge, of course, is to let Him. When you do, you'll be thoroughly surprised by the creativity and the beauty of His plans.

A Quote for Today

The home you've always wanted,
the home you continue to long for
with all your heart, is the home God
is preparing for you!
—Anne Graham Lotz

A Timely Tip

Pray for guidance. When you seek it,
He will give it. (Luke 11:9)

Pregnancy Milestone for Today

_____

_____

_____

_____

_____

_____

THE PROBLEMS OF PREGNANCY

Let not your heart be troubled.
—John 14:1 KJV

No pregnancy is totally problem-free. And for some moms-to-be, pregnancy is an endurance-testing exercise in problem-solving.

Hidden beneath every problem is the seed of a solution—God's solution. Your challenge, as a faithful believer, is to trust God's providence and seek His solutions. When you do, you will eventually discover that God does nothing without a very good reason: His reason.

Are you willing to faithfully trust God on good days and bad ones? Hopefully so, because an important part of walking with God is finding His purpose in the midst of your problems.

A Quote for Today

God is bigger than your problems. Whatever worries press upon you today, put them in God's hands and leave them there.
—Billy Graham

A Timely Tip

The life of a mom-to-be can be stressful and, at times, exhausting. Be alert for signs of fatigue, and don't be afraid to ask family or friends for help if you need it.

Pregnancy Milestone for Today

_____

_____

_____

_____

_____

_____

THE GLORIOUS GIFT OF LIFE

Seek the Lord, and ye shall live . . .
—Amos 5:6 KJV

Life is a glorious gift from God. Treat it that way.

This day, like every other, is filled to the brim with opportunities, challenges, and choices. But, no choice that you make is more important than the choice you make concerning God. Today, you will either place Him at the center of your life—or not—and the consequences of that choice have implications that are both temporal and eternal.

Sometimes, without our even realizing it, we gradually drift away from the One we need most. Thankfully, God never drifts away from us. He remains always present, always steadfast, always loving.

As you begin this day—and as you ponder the love you feel for your precious unborn child—place God and His Son where they belong: in your head, in your prayers, on your lips, and in your heart.

A Quote for Today

You have a glorious future in Christ!
Live every moment in
His power and love.

—Vonette Bright

Pregnancy Milestone for Today

_____

_____

_____

_____

_____

IF YOU BECOME DISCOURAGED

Do not be afraid or discouraged, for the LORD is the one who goes before you. He will be with you; he will neither fail you nor forsake you.
—Deuteronomy 31:8 NLT

Even the most optimistic moms-to-be are overcome by occasional bouts of fear and doubt. You are no different. When you feel that your faith is being tested to its limits, seek the comfort and assurance of the One who sent His Son as a sacrifice for you.

Have you recently felt your faith in God slipping away? If so, you are not alone. Every life—including yours—is a series of successes and failures, celebrations and disappointments, joys and sorrows, hopes and doubts. But even when we feel very distant from God, God is never distant from us. When we sincerely seek His presence, He will touch our hearts and restore our souls.

A Quote for Today

If I am asked how we are to get rid of discouragements, I can only say, as I have had to say of so many other wrong spiritual habits, we must give them up. It is never worthwhile to argue against discouragement. There is only one argument that can meet it, and that is the argument of God.
—Hannah Whitall Smith

Pregnancy Milestone for Today

_____

_____

_____

_____

_____

_____

YOUR GROWING FAITH

*I want you woven into a tapestry of love, in touch with everything
there is to know of God. Then you will have minds confident and at rest,
focused on Christ, God's great mystery.*
—Colossians 2:2 MSG

Your relationship with God is ongoing; it unfolds day by day, and it offers countless opportunities to grow closer to Him . . . or not. As each new day unfolds, you are confronted with a wide range of decisions: how you will behave, where you will direct your thoughts, with whom you will associate, and what you will choose to worship. These choices, along with many others like them, are yours and yours alone. How you choose determines how your relationship with God will unfold.

Are you continuing to grow in your love and knowledge of the Lord, or are you "satisfied" with the current state of your spiritual health? Hopefully, you're determined to make yourself a growing Christian. Your Savior deserves no less, and neither, by the way, do you.

Pregnancy Milestone
for Today

_____

_____

_____

_____

_____

A Quote for Today

Growing in any area of
the Christian life takes time,
and the key is daily sitting at
the feet of Jesus.
—Cynthia Heald

A LITTLE RESENTFUL?

Be hospitable to one another without complaining.
—1 Peter 4:9 HCSB

Pregnancy is a miraculous experience and spiritual journey. But from time to time, pregnancy can also be a major inconvenience. The next time you're tempted to complain about the major hassles or the minor inconveniences of your pregnancy, slow down, catch your breath, and ask God to help you regain proper perspective.

Today, promise yourself that you'll do whatever it takes to focus your thoughts and energy on the major blessings you've received (not the minor inconveniences you must occasionally endure). And, the next time you're tempted to complain about the inevitable frustrations of pregnancy, don't do it. Make it a practice to count your blessings, not your hardships. It's the truly decent way to live.

A Quote for Today

I am to praise God for all things, regardless of where they seem to originate. Doing this is the key to receiving the blessings of God. Praise will wash away my resentments.
—Catherine Marshall

Pregnancy Milestone for Today

_____

_____

_____

_____

_____

GOD HAS A PLAN

In thee, O Lord, do I put my trust.
—Psalm 31:1 KJV

God has a plan for your life, a plan for your pregnancy, and a plan for your unborn child. As you prepare for the Big Day ahead, you cannot fully understand God's plans, but you must trust them.

During difficult days, you can learn something important about God: He is not required, nor does He intend, to explain Himself in ways that we, as mere mortals, might prefer. God is not in the business of answering all our questions now, but He has promised to answer them someday in heaven. Until that wonderful day arrives, we must learn to trust the Creator even though we cannot understand Him.

So, if you're being assaulted by unexpected challenges, unwelcome discomforts, or unwanted inconveniences, don't abandon hope and don't abandon God. Instead, trust the Creator . . . and guard your heart by turning it over to Him.

Pregnancy Milestone
for Today

_____

_____

_____

_____

_____

A Quote for Today

Ours is an intentional God,
brimming over with motive and
mission. He never does things
capriciously or decides with
the flip of a coin.
—Joni Eareckson Tada

FORGIVENESS IS LIBERATING

Those who show mercy to others are happy,
because God will show mercy to them.
—Matthew 5:7 NCV

Bitterness is a form of self-punishment; forgiveness is a means of self-liberation. Bitterness focuses on the injustices of the past; forgiveness focuses on the blessings of the present and the opportunities of the future. Bitterness is an emotion that destroys you; forgiveness is a decision that empowers you. Bitterness is folly; forgiveness is wisdom.

Sometimes, amid the demands of daily life, we lose perspective. Life seems out of balance, and the pressures of everyday living seem overwhelming. What's needed is a fresh perspective, a restored sense of balance . . . and God's wisdom.

If we call upon the Lord and seek to see the world through His eyes, He will give us guidance, wisdom, and perspective. When we make God's priorities our priorities, He will lead us according to His plan and according to His commandments. When we study God's Word, we are reminded that God's reality is the ultimate reality. May we live—and forgive—accordingly.

A Quote for Today

Forgiveness is the key that unlocks the door of resentment and the handcuffs of hate. It is a power that breaks the chains of bitterness and the shackles of selfishness.

—Corrie ten Boom

Pregnancy Milestone for Today

_____

_____

_____

_____

_____

_____

FEELING SICK?

I am the Lord who heals you.
—Exodus 15:26 NCV

Because you're expecting, you're probably experiencing a variety of unfamiliar (and unwelcome) symptoms, some of which are minor, and some of which are not. Your first concern, of course, is for your baby. And you also have understandable concerns about your own health, too.

Whenever you experience symptoms that you don't understand, contact your doctor immediately and follow her instructions to the letter. But, don't stop there. In addition to a medical prescription, seek out a spiritual one. Ask God for protection—protection for you and for your unborn baby. And while you're at it, ask Him to comfort you.

There's no doubt about it: pregnancy is a long journey and, at times, a difficult one. But with your doctor's medical help, and with God's spiritual guidance, you can face those inevitable challenges with determination and hope.

Pregnancy Milestone for Today

_____

_____

_____

_____

_____

A Timely Tip

Establish clear communications with your doctor and with your doctor's office staff. When you have questions, concerns, or mysterious symptoms, they'll have answers.

HEAVEN IS HOME

Let not your heart be troubled: ye believe in God, believe also in me.
In my Father's house are many mansions: if it were not so, I would have
told you. I go to prepare a place for you. And if I go and prepare
a place for you, I will come again, and receive you unto myself;
that where I am, there ye may be also.

—John 14:1-3 KJV

Sometimes the troubles of this old world are easier to tolerate when we remind ourselves that heaven is our true home. An old hymn contains the words, "This world is not my home; I'm just passing through." Thank goodness!

This crazy world can be a place of trouble and danger. Thankfully, God has offered you a permanent home in heaven, a place of unimaginable glory, a place that your Heavenly Father has already prepared for you,

In John 16:33, Jesus tells us He has overcome the troubles of this world. We should trust Him, and we should obey His commandments. When we do, we can withstand any problem, knowing that our troubles are temporary, but that heaven is not.

A Quote for Today

One of these days, our Father will
scoop us up in His strong arms and
we will hear Him say those
sweet and comforting words,
"Come on, child.
We're going home."

—Gloria Gaither

Pregnancy Milestone for Today

_____

_____

_____

_____

_____

_____

HE IS WITH US ALWAYS

I am not alone, because the Father is with Me.
—John 16:32 HCSB

Where is God? God is eternally with us. He is omnipresent. He is, quite literally, everywhere you have ever been and everywhere you will ever go. He is with you and your unborn child night and day; He knows your every thought; He hears your every heartbeat, and He hears every beat of your baby's heart, too.

Sometimes, in the crush of your daily duties, God may seem far away. Or sometimes, when the challenges of your pregnancy leave you exhausted, God may seem distant, but He is not. When you earnestly seek the Father, you will find Him because He is here, waiting patiently for you to reach out to Him . . . right here . . . right now.

A Quote for Today

What God promises is that He always, always comes. He always shows up. He always saves. He always rescues. His timing is not ours. His methods are usually unconventional. But what we can know, what we can settle in our soul, is that He is faithful to come when we call.

—Angela Thomas

Pregnancy Milestone for Today

_____

_____

_____

_____

_____

_____

STRENGTH FOR TODAY

Those who hope in the LORD will renew their strength.
They will soar on wings like eagles; they will run and not grow weary,
they will walk and not be faint.

—Isaiah 40:31 NIV

Where do you go to find strength? The health food store? The espresso bar? One of those little energy drinks? There's a better source of strength, of course, and that source is God. He is a never-ending source of strength and courage if you call upon Him.

Are you an energized Christian mom-to-be? You should be. But if you're not, you must seek strength and renewal from the source that will never fail: that source, of course, is your Heavenly Father. And rest assured—when you sincerely petition Him, He will give you all the strength you need to live victoriously for Him. And while you're at it, don't forget that, when it comes to strength, God is the Ultimate Source.

A Quote for Today

Worry does not empty tomorrow of
its sorrow; it empties today
of its strength.

—Corrie ten Boom

Pregnancy Milestone
for Today

_____

_____

_____

_____

_____

_____

KINDNESS NOW

God has chosen you and made you his holy people. He loves you.
So always do these things: Show mercy to others, be kind,
humble, gentle, and patient.
—Colossians 3:12 NCV

Christ showed His love for us by willingly sacrificing His own life so that we might have eternal life: "But God demonstrates his own love for us in this: While we were still sinners, Christ died for us" (Romans 5:8 NIV). We, as Christ's followers, are challenged to share His love with kind words on our lips and praise in our hearts.

Just as Christ has been—and will always be—the ultimate friend to His flock, so should we be Christlike in the kindness and generosity that we show toward others, especially those who are most in need.

When we walk each day with Jesus—and obey the commandments found in God's Holy Word—we become worthy ambassadors for Christ. When we share the love of Christ, we share a priceless gift with the world. As His servants, we must do no less.

Pregnancy Milestone for Today

_____

_____

_____

_____

_____

_____

A Quote for Today

Hope looks for the good in people,
opens doors for people, discovers
what can be done to help, lights
a candle, does not yield to cynicism.
Hope sets people free.

—Barbara Johnson

WHEN SOLUTIONS AREN'T EASY

For God has not given us a spirit of fearfulness,
but one of power, love, and sound judgment.
—2 Timothy 1:7 HCSB

As an expectant mom, you'll face numerous challenges and countless decisions. If you find yourself facing a difficult decision, here's a simple formula for making the right choice: let God decide. Instead of fretting about your future, pray about it.

When you consult your Heavenly Father early and often, you'll soon discover that the quiet moments you spend with God can be very helpful. Many times, God will quietly lead you along a path of His choosing, a path that is right for you.

So the next time you arrive at one of life's inevitable crossroads, take a moment or two to bow your head and have a chat with the Ultimate Advisor. When you do, you'll never stay lost for long.

A Quote for Today

The Reference Point for the Christian is the Bible. All values, judgments, and attitudes must be gauged in relationship to this Reference Point.

—Ruth Bell Graham

Pregnancy Milestone for Today

_____

_____

_____

_____

_____

_____

THE JOY HE HAS PROMISED

*Now I am coming to You, and I speak these things in the world
so that they may have My joy completed in them.*
—John 17:13 HCSB

Christ wants you to share His joy. Yet sometimes, amid the inevitable hustle and bustle of life here on earth, you may forfeit—albeit temporarily—the joy of Christ as you wrestle with the challenges of pregnancy or with the demands of everyday life.

Corrie ten Boom correctly observed, "Jesus did not promise to change the circumstances around us. He promised great peace and pure joy to those who would learn to believe that God actually controls all things." So here's a prescription for better spiritual health: Learn to trust God, and open the door of your soul to Christ. When you do, He will most certainly give you the peace and pure joy He has promised.

Pregnancy Milestone for Today

_____

_____

_____

_____

_____

_____

A Quote for Today

He is ever faithful and gives us
the song in the night to soothe
our spirits and fresh joy each
morning to lift our souls.
What a marvelous Lord!

—Bill Bright

BEAUTY ACCORDING TO GOD

Lord, I give myself to you; my God, I trust you.
—Psalm 25:1-2 NCV

Your body is changing, and perhaps you're not totally thrilled by those changes. If so, it's time to pause long enough to ponder the importance—or more accurately, the unimportance—of appearance.

Today, remind yourself that your outward appearance doesn't matter to God. He's concerned, not with the shape of your body, but with the condition of your heart. Try to spend less time pleasing the world and more time pleasing your Father in heaven. Put God first, and don't worry too much about trying to impress the folks you happen to pass on the street. It takes too much energy—and too much life—to keep up appearances. So don't waste your energy or your life.

A Quote for Today

The Bible is a remarkable
commentary on perspective.
Through its divine message,
we are brought face to face with
issues and tests in daily living and
how, by the power of the Holy
Spirit, we are enabled to respond
positively to them.
—Luci Swindoll

A Timely Tip

You have a choice: you can celebrate
your changing body, or you can
grumble about it. The best choice
is to celebrate your appearance,
yourself, and your unborn child.

Pregnancy Milestone for Today

_____

_____

_____

_____

_____

_____

WE BELONG TO HIM

Now return to the LORD your God, for He is gracious and compassionate, slow to anger, abounding in lovingkindness.
—Joel 2:13 NASB

The line from the children's song is reassuring and familiar: "Little ones to Him belong. We are weak but He is strong." That message applies to kids of all ages: we are all indeed weak, but we worship a mighty God who meets our needs and answers our prayers.

If your pregnancy has left you feeling exhausted, or discouraged, or both, turn to God for strength. The Bible promises that you can do all things through the power of our risen Savior, Jesus Christ. Your challenge, then, is clear: you must place Christ where He belongs—at the very center of your life. When you do, you will discover that, yes, Jesus loves you and that, yes, He will give you direction and strength if you ask it in His name.

Pregnancy Milestone for Today

_____

_____

_____

_____

_____

_____

A Quote for Today

If you come to Christ, you will always have the option of an ever-present friend. You don't have to dial long-distance. He'll be with you every step of the way.

—Bill Hybels

ASKING HIM FOR STRENGTH

Keep asking, and it will be given to you. Keep searching,
and you will find. Keep knocking, and the door will be opened to you.
For everyone who asks receives, and the one who searches finds,
and to the one who knocks, the door will be opened.
—Matthew 7:7-8 HCSB

Are you an expectant mom in need of renewal? Ask God to strengthen you. Are you troubled? Take your concerns to Him in prayer. Are you uncomfortable, or frustrated, or discouraged? Seek the comfort of God's promises. Do you feel that you or your family members are living under a cloud of uncertainty? Ask God where He wants you to go, and then go there.

In all matters, ask for God's guidance and avail yourself of God's power. You may be certain that He hears your prayers . . . and you may be certain that He will answer.

A Timely Tip

If you want more from life, ask more from God. If you're searching for peace and abundance, ask for God's help—and keep asking— until He answers your prayers. If you sincerely want to rise above the inevitable stresses and demands of pregnancy, ask for God's help many times each day.

Pregnancy Milestone for Today

_____

_____

_____

_____

_____

WORSHIP HIM

But an hour is coming, and is now here, when the true worshipers will worship the Father in spirit and truth. Yes, the Father wants such people to worship Him. God is Spirit, and those who worship Him must worship in spirit and truth.

—John 4:23-24 HCSB

Where do we worship? In our hearts or in our church? The answer is both. As Christians who have been saved by a loving, compassionate Creator, we are compelled not only to worship the Creator in our hearts but also to worship Him in the presence of fellow believers.

We live in a world that is teeming with temptations and distractions—a world where good and evil struggle in a constant battle to win our hearts and souls. Our challenge, of course, is to ensure that we cast our lot on the side of God. One way to ensure that we do so is by the practice of regular, purposeful worship with our families. When we worship God faithfully and fervently, we are blessed.

Pregnancy Milestone for Today

_____

_____

_____

_____

_____

_____

A Quote for Today

Worship is about rekindling an ashen heart into a blazing fire.

—Liz Curtis Higgs

WHEN IT'S HARD TO BE CHEERFUL

Be cheerful. Keep things in good repair. Keep your spirits up.
Think in harmony. Be agreeable. Do all that,
and the God of love and peace will be with you for sure.
—2 Corinthians 13:11 MSG

Some days, as every expectant mom knows, it's hard to be cheerful. Sometimes, as the demands of pregnancy increase and the supply of energy sags, you may feel less like "cheering up" and more like "tearing up." But even when you're almost too tired, or too discouraged, to bow your head in prayer, you can still turn to God, and He will comfort you.

Mrs. Charles E. Cowman, the author of the classic devotional text *Streams in the Desert*, advised, "Put your hand into the hand of God. He gives the calmness and serenity of heart and soul." And, the noted American pastor Bill Hybels said, "Pour out your heart to God and tell Him how you feel. Be real, be honest, and when you get it all out, you'll start to feel the gradual covering of God's comforting presence."

So, the next time you find yourself being attacked by negative emotions, slow down and take time to have a little talk with your Creator. When you do, you'll soon discover that God can change anything, including your mood.

Pregnancy Milestone for Today

_____

_____

_____

_____

_____

MARVELING AT HIS MIRACLES

The heavens declare the glory of God;
and the firmament shows His handiwork.
—Psalm 19:1 NKJV

When we consider the birth of a child, we marvel. Every baby is a precious gift from God, an integral part of His infinite creation.

Today, as you ponder the precious baby that is growing inside you, and as you fulfill the continuing demands of everyday life, pause to consider the majesty of God's creation: the heavens, the earth, and the miracle of birth.

The psalmist reminds us that the heavens are a declaration of God's glory. May we never cease to praise the Father for a universe that stands as an awesome testimony to His presence and to His power. But, as we gaze at the heavens, let us not forget to praise the Father for wonders that are much closer to home, but just as miraculous.

Pregnancy Milestone for Today

_____

_____

_____

_____

_____

_____

A Quote for Today

Heaven and earth and all that is
in the universe cry out to me
from all directions that I,
O God, must love You.

—St. Augustine

FACING DIFFICULT DAYS

We are pressured in every way but not crushed;
we are perplexed but not in despair.
—2 Corinthians 4:8 HCSB

Every expectant mother faces difficult days. Sometimes, even the most optimistic moms-to-be can become discouraged, and you are no exception.

If you find yourself feeling blue, or if you've come face-to-face with difficult circumstances, don't despair. Remember that God remains in His heaven, and that He will protect you today, tomorrow, and forever.

Billy Graham could have been speaking to expectant moms when he said, "The Christian life is not a constant high." But even if your emotions change from day to day, or from moment to moment, God never changes. So, if you become discouraged with the direction of your day or your life, turn your thoughts and prayers to Him. He's waiting for you to call upon Him. And when you call, He will answer.

A Quote for Today

Trials are not enemies of faith but
opportunities to reveal
God's faithfulness.

—Barbara Johnson

Pregnancy Milestone for Today

_____

_____

_____

_____

_____

_____

THOSE PESKY COMPLAINTS

Do everything without complaining or arguing.
Then you will be innocent and without any wrong.
—Philippians 2:14-15 NCV

Because we are imperfect human beings, we often lose sight of our blessings. Ironically, most of us have more blessings than we can count, but we may still find reasons to complain about the minor frustrations of everyday life. To do so, of course, is not only wrong; it is also the pinnacle of shortsightedness and a serious roadblock on the path to spiritual abundance.

Are you tempted to complain about the inevitable discomforts of pregnancy or the minor frustrations of everyday living? Don't do it! Today and every day, make sure to count your blessings, not your challenges. After all, as a mom-to-be, you're blessed beyond measure. Praise God for that blessing, and be thankful.

Pregnancy Milestone for Today

_____

_____

_____

_____

_____

A Quote for Today

Thanksgiving or complaining—these words express two contrastive attitudes of the souls of God's children in regard to His dealings with them. The soul that gives thanks can find comfort in everything; the soul that complains can find comfort in nothing.

—Hannah Whitall Smith

THE WORLD . . . AND YOU

Don't copy the behavior and customs of this world,
but let God transform you into a new person by
changing the way you think.
—Romans 12:2 NLT

We live in the world, but we must not worship it. Our duty is to place God first and everything else second. But because we are fallible beings with imperfect faith, placing God in His rightful place is often difficult. In fact, at every turn, or so it seems, we are tempted to do otherwise.

The 21st-century world is a noisy, distracting place filled with countless opportunities to stray from God's will. The world seems to cry, "Worship me with your time, your money, your energy, and your thoughts!" But God commands otherwise: He commands us to worship Him and Him alone; everything else must be secondary.

As an expectant mom, you need the rest, the peace, and the assurance that only God can provide. So today, spend less time focusing on the world and more time focusing on the Creator. When you do, you'll improve every aspect of your life. And, God will demonstrate His approval as He showers you with more spiritual blessings than you can count.

A Quote for Today

The more we stuff ourselves with material pleasures, the less we seem to appreciate life.
—Barbara Johnson

Pregnancy Milestone for Today

_____

_____

_____

_____

_____

_____

CELEBRATING YOUR PREGNANCY

You were taught to leave your old self—to stop living the evil way you lived before. That old self becomes worse, because people are fooled by the evil things they want to do. But you were taught to be made new in your hearts, to become a new person. That new person is made to be like God—made to be truly good and holy.

—Ephesians 4:22-24 NCV

Have you made your pregnancy an exciting adventure, or have you allowed the distractions and discomforts of impending motherhood to rob you of the peace and joy that should be yours during this special time in your life?

As a believer, you have every reason to celebrate. And, as a mom-to-be, you have a glorious future ahead of you. So if you find yourself feeling as if you're stuck in a rut, or if you become discouraged by the inevitable demands of pregnancy, slow down, find a quiet place, and have a little chat with your Heavenly Father. In God's glorious kingdom, there should be no place for disciples who are dejected, discouraged, or disheartened. God has a far better plan than that, and so should you.

Pregnancy Milestone for Today

_____

_____

_____

_____

_____

_____

A Quote for Today

When we get rid of inner conflicts and wrong attitudes toward life, we will almost automatically burst into joy.

—E. Stanley Jones

GOD'S ATTENTIVENESS

*For the eyes of the Lord range throughout the earth to show Himself
strong for those whose hearts are completely His.*
—2 Chronicles 16:9 HCSB

God is not distant, and He is not disinterested. To the contrary, your Heavenly Father is attentive to your needs. In fact, God knows precisely what you need and when you need it. But, He still wants to talk with you, and if you're a faithful believer, you should want to talk to Him, too.

Do you have questions that you simply can't answer? Ask for the guidance of your Creator. Do you sincerely seek the gift of everlasting love and eternal life? Accept the grace of God's only begotten Son. Are you concerned for the well-being of your unborn child? Pray for your baby and trust the Giver of all good gifts. Whatever your need, no matter how great or small, pray about it. And remember: God is not just near; He is here, and He's ready to talk with you. Now!

A Quote for Today

Our future may look fearfully
intimidating, yet we can look up
to the Engineer of the Universe,
confident that nothing escapes His
attention or slips out of the control
of those strong hands.
—Elisabeth Elliot

Pregnancy Milestone for Today

_____

_____

_____

_____

_____

THE FUTILITY OF WORRY

Worry is a heavy load . . .
—Proverbs 12:25 NCV

If you are like most expectant mothers, you can always find something to worry about, beginning with the health of your unborn baby. But worry is a heavy load, a load that you should never try to carry by yourself. So, today, if you find yourself fretting about anything, bow your head and talk to the Father about whatever is bothering you. Take your troubles to Him, and your fears, and your doubts, and your sorrows.

Barbara Johnson correctly observed, "Worry is the senseless process of cluttering up tomorrow's opportunities with leftover problems from today." So if you'd like to make the most out of this day (and every one hereafter), turn your worries over to a Power greater than yourself . . . and spend your valuable time and energy solving the problems you can fix . . . while trusting God to do the rest.

Pregnancy Milestone for Today

_____

_____

_____

_____

_____

_____

A Quote for Today

Worship and worry cannot live
in the same heart;
they are mutually exclusive.

—Ruth Bell Graham

GOD REWARDS DISCIPLINE

Apply your heart to discipline and your ears to words of knowledge.
—Proverbs 23:12 NASB

God's Word reminds us again and again that our Creator expects us to lead disciplined lives. God instructs us to behave responsibly . . . and with good, old-fashioned common sense.

As an expectant mom, you're now responsible for two lives. You probably don't need to be reminded that you're eating, drinking, sleeping, and exercising for two. And by now, you know first-hand that pregnancy is, at times, emotionally draining and physically exhausting. So here's today's message: Being a responsible mom-to-be is hard work, but you can do it. And God is ready to help.

Life's greatest rewards require effort, which is perfectly fine with God. After all, He knows that you're up to the task. So, stay the course and be disciplined. And while you're at it, remember that your Heavenly Father has big plans for you and your baby. Very big plans.

A Quote for Today

Simply stated, self-discipline is obedience to God's Word and willingness to submit everything in life to His will, for His ultimate glory.
—John MacArthur

Pregnancy Milestone for Today

_____

_____

_____

_____

_____

_____

PROTECTED BY THE HAND OF GOD

For whatever is born of God overcomes the world.
And this is the victory that has overcome the world—our faith.
—1 John 5:4 NKJV

Have you ever faced challenges that seemed too big to handle? Have you ever faced big problems that, despite your best efforts, simply could not be solved? If so, you know how uncomfortable it is to feel helpless in the face of difficult circumstances. Thankfully, even when there's nowhere else to turn, you can turn your thoughts and prayers to God, and He will respond.

God's hand uplifts those who turn their hearts and prayers to Him. Count yourself among that number. When you do, you can live courageously and joyfully, knowing that "this too will pass"—but that God's love for you will not. As a faith-filled mother-to-be, you can draw strength from the knowledge that both you and your baby are marvelous creations, loved, protected, and uplifted by the ever-present hand of your loving Father.

Pregnancy Milestone for Today

_____

_____

_____

_____

_____

_____

A Quote for Today

Worries carry responsibilities that belong to God, not to you. Worry does not enable us to escape evil; it makes us unfit to cope with it when it comes.

—Corrie ten Boom

THE NEED TO ENDURE

Patient endurance is what you need now, so you will continue
to do God's will. Then you will receive all that he has promised.
—Hebrews 10:36 NLT

Pregnancy can be thought of as a nine-month endurance contest, a test of a woman's patience, perseverance, discipline, and faith.

Has your pregnancy sapped your energy and tested your powers of endurance? If so, you're not alone. Mothers-to-be of every generation have struggled through—and beyond—the inevitable hardships of pregnancy, and so, too, will you.

When you encounter the inevitable difficulties of life, God stands ready to protect you. And, while you're waiting for God's plans to unfold, you can be comforted in the knowledge that your Creator can overcome any obstacle, even if you cannot.

A Quote for Today

We are all on our way somewhere.
We'll get there if we just keep going.

—Barbara Johnson

Pregnancy Milestone for Today

_____

_____

_____

_____

_____

_____

TALKING TO YOURSELF

I said to myself, "Relax and rest.
God has showered you with blessings."
—Psalm 116:7 MSG

Do you spend much time talking to yourself? If so, you're certainly not crazy. To the contrary, you may be very wise indeed, especially if you've learned how to talk to yourself properly.

Do you remind yourself each day of God's blessings? Do you advise the person in the mirror to be thankful, thoughtful, patient, and kind? And do you remind yourself to trust God's Word and to follow His path? If you can answer these questions with a resounding "yes," you are both wise and blessed.

In Psalm 116, the psalmist reminds himself of God's blessings. You should, too. So today, talk to yourself about the Father's love, about His gifts, and about His teachings. Focus on the Father and enjoy a peace like no other: His.

Pregnancy Milestone for Today

_____

_____

_____

_____

_____

A Quote for Today

Human worth does not depend on beauty or intelligence or accomplishments. We are all more valuable than the possessions of the entire world simply because God gave us that value.

—James Dobson

COUNTLESS OPPORTUNITIES

I will instruct you and teach you in the way you should go;
I will counsel you and watch over you.
—Psalm 32:8 NIV

Each waking moment holds the potential to think a creative thought or offer a heartfelt prayer. So even if you're an expectant mom with too many demands and too few hours in which to meet them, don't panic. Instead, be comforted in the knowledge that when you sincerely seek to discover God's priorities for your life, He will provide answers in marvelous and surprising ways.

Remember: This is the day that God has made and He has filled it with countless opportunities to love, to serve, and to seek His guidance. Seize those opportunities. And as a gift to yourself, to your family, and to the world, slow down and establish clear priorities that are pleasing to God.

A Quote for Today

Jesus' life was a constant demonstration that there are only two things that matter in this life: God and people. They are the only things that last forever.
—Rebecca Manley Pippert

Pregnancy Milestone for Today

_____

_____

_____

_____

_____

_____

DISCOVERING PURPOSE DAILY

Yet Lord, You are our Father; we are the clay,
and You are our potter; we all are the work of Your hands.
—Isaiah 64:8 HCSB

Each morning, as the sun rises in the east, you welcome a new day, one that is filled to the brim with opportunities, with possibilities, and with God. As you contemplate God's blessings in your own life, you should prayerfully seek His guidance for the day ahead.

As an expectant mom, you may have many questions about your future. And, you may have unspoken fears about the direction your life will take after your baby arrives. If so, remember that in every season of life, God is willing—and perfectly able—to lead you along a path of His choosing. Your job is to pray often, to watch for His signs, and to follow as closely as you can in the footsteps of His Son.

Discovering God's unfolding purpose for your life is a daily journey, a journey guided by the teachings of God's Holy Word. As you reflect upon God's promises and upon the meaning that those promises hold for you, ask God to lead you throughout the coming day. Let your Heavenly Father direct your steps; concentrate on what God wants you to do now and leave the distant future in hands that are far more capable than your own: His hands.

Pregnancy Milestone for Today

_____

_____

_____

_____

_____

_____

A Quote for Today

The Creator has made us each one of a kind. There is nobody else exactly like us, and there never will be. Each of us is his special creation and is alive for a distinctive purpose.
—Luci Swindoll

YOUR OWN WORST CRITIC?

A devout life does bring wealth,
but it's the rich simplicity of being yourself before God.
—1 Timothy 6:6 MSG

Nobody needs to tell you that your body is changing: as your baby continues to grow, so do you. So, how do you feel about the new you? Are you your own worst critic? If so, it's time to become a little more understanding of the woman you see whenever you look into the mirror.

Millions of words have been written about various ways to improve self-image and increase self-esteem. Yet, maintaining a healthy self-image is, to a surprising extent, a matter of doing three things: 1.) behaving yourself, 2.) thinking healthy thoughts, 3.) finding a purpose for your life that pleases your Creator and yourself.

The Bible affirms the importance of self-acceptance by teaching Christians to love others as they love themselves (Matthew 22:37-40). God accepts us just as we are. And, if He accepts us—faults and all—then who are we to believe otherwise?

A Quote for Today

Being loved by Him whose opinion matters most gives us the security to risk loving, too—even loving ourselves.

—Gloria Gaither

Pregnancy Milestone for Today

_____

_____

_____

_____

_____

LIVING ON PURPOSE

It is God who works in you to will and to act
according to his good purpose.
—Philippians 2:13 NIV

Life is best lived on purpose. And purpose, like everything else in the universe, begins with God. Whether you realize it or not, God has a plan for your life, a divine calling, a direction in which He is leading you. When you welcome God into your heart and establish a genuine relationship with Him, He will begin, in time, to make His purposes known.

Sometimes, God's intentions will be clear to you; other times, God's plan will seem uncertain at best. But even on those difficult days when you are unsure which way to turn, you must never lose sight of these overriding facts: God created you for a reason; He has important work for you to do; and He's waiting patiently for you to do it.

And the next step is up to you.

Pregnancy Milestone for Today

_____

_____

_____

_____

_____

A Quote for Today

There is a path before you that you alone can walk. There is a purpose that you alone can fulfill.

—Karla Dornacher

THE REWARDS WILL COME

But as for you, be strong and do not give up,
for your work will be rewarded.
—2 Chronicles 15:7 NIV

As you anxiously await the arrival of your baby, you may become impatient. You may long for the day when you can resume a more "normal" existence, and you may ache for the moment when you can hold your precious child.

During those times when you become impatient, please remember that God's timing is best. And remember that every sacrifice you make for your unborn baby today is a special gift that you, and only you, can give.

A Quote for Today

Determination and faithfulness are the nails used to build
the house of God's dreams.
—Barbara Johnson

A Timely Tip

God can make all things new, including you. When you are weak or worried, God can renew your spirit. Your task is to let Him.

Pregnancy Milestone for Today

_____

_____

_____

_____

_____

COMFORT COUNTS

Discretion will watch over you, and understanding will guard you.
—Proverbs 2:11 HCSB

As an expectant mom, you're acutely aware that you're now responsible for two human beings. Whenever you're caring for yourself, you're also caring for your unborn baby.

During the next few months, do the wise thing for yourself and for your child: make yourself as comfortable as possible. Wear comfortable clothes; find comfortable shoes; eat sensible portions of healthy foods; get plenty or rest; pray often; and steer clear of those disturbing media images that can be harmful to your spirit. Don't worry too much about fashion; instead, focus on your physical, emotional, and spiritual health. Relax whenever you can and be comfortable. You deserve it . . . and so does your baby.

A Timely Tip

It's important to get seven or eight
hours of sleep every night,
especially during your pregnancy.
So, if you find yourself staying up
late, do the right thing:
Turn off the TV, power down
the smart phone, turn off
the lights, and go to sleep.

Pregnancy Milestone for Today

_____

_____

_____

_____

_____

_____

BEYOND THE WORLD'S WISDOM

For the wisdom of this world is foolishness in God's sight.
—1 Corinthians 3:19 NIV

The world has its own brand of wisdom, a brand of wisdom that is often wrong and sometimes dangerous. God, on the other hand, has a different brand of wisdom, a wisdom that will never lead you astray. Where will you place your trust today? Will you trust in the wisdom of fallible men and women, or will you place your faith in God's perfect wisdom? The answer to this question will determine the direction of your day and the quality of your decisions.

Are you tired? Discouraged about your pregnancy? Fearful of the future? Be comforted and trust God. Are you worried about your health or anxious about your finances? Be confident in God's power. Are you confused? Listen to the quiet voice of your Heavenly Father—He is not a God of confusion. Talk with Him; listen to Him; trust Him. His wisdom, unlike the "wisdom" of the world, will never let you down.

A Quote for Today

Knowledge can be found in books
or in school. Wisdom, on the other
hand, starts with God . . .
and ends there.
—Marie T. Freeman

Pregnancy Milestone for Today

_____

_____

_____

_____

_____

Pregnancy Is Not a Dress Rehearsal

Happy is the person who finds wisdom and gains understanding.
—Proverbs 3:13 NLT

Pregnancy isn't pretend. And, the role of mom-to-be isn't a dress rehearsal; it's a real role, a demanding role that requires tons of patience, plenty of perseverance, and clear vision. But, sometimes, amid the pressures of pregnancy and the concerns of everyday life, you may lose perspective. Life may seem out of balance as you confront an array of stresses that can sap your strength and cloud your thoughts. What's needed is a renewed faith, a fresh perspective, and God's wisdom.

Here in the 21st century, commentary is commonplace and information is everywhere. But the ultimate source of wisdom, the kind of timeless wisdom that God willingly shares with His children, is still available from a single unique source: the Holy Bible.

The wisdom of the world changes with the ever-shifting sands of public opinion. God's wisdom does not. His wisdom is eternal. It never changes. And it most certainly is the wisdom that you must use to plan your pregnancy, your life, and your eternal destiny.

Pregnancy Milestone for Today

_____

_____

_____

_____

_____

_____

A Quote for Today

Live near to God, and so all things will appear to you little in comparison with eternal realities.
—Robert Murray McCheyne

PERFECT PEACE AND FULL CONFIDENCE

May the God of hope fill you with all joy and peace as you trust in him,
so that you may overflow with hope by the power of the Holy Spirit.
—Romans 15:13 NIV

Sometimes, peace can be a scarce commodity for busy mothers-to-be. How, then, can you find "the peace that passes all understanding"? By slowing down, by keeping problems in perspective, by counting your blessings, and by trusting God.

Dorothy Harrison Pentecost writes, "Peace is full confidence that God is who He says He is and that He will keep every promise in His Word."

And Beth Moore advises, "Prayer guards hearts and minds and causes God to bring peace out of chaos."

So today, as you journey out into the chaos of the world, bring God's peace with you. And remember: the chaos is temporary, but God's peace is not.

A Quote for Today

To know God as He really is—
in His essential nature and
character—is to arrive at a citadel of
peace that circumstances may storm,
but can never capture.
—Catherine Marshall

Pregnancy Milestone for Today

_____

_____

_____

_____

_____

Faith-filled Christianity

Commit your works to the Lord, and your thoughts will be established.
—Proverbs 16:3 NKJV

As you ponder your pregnancy, you should do so with feelings of hope and anticipation. After all, as a Christian, you have every reason to be optimistic about life. As John Calvin observed, "There is not one blade of grass, there is no color in this world that is not intended to make us rejoice." But, sometimes, rejoicing may be the last thing on your mind. Sometimes, because you're a soon-to-be mom, and because you care deeply for your unborn baby, you may fall prey to worry, fear, anxiety, or doubt. What's needed is plenty of rest, a large dose of perspective, and God's healing touch, but not necessarily in that order.

A. W. Tozer writes, "Attitude is all-important. Let the soul take a quiet attitude of faith and love toward God, and from there on, the responsibility is God's. He will make good on His commitments." These words remind us that even when the challenges of the day seem daunting, God remains steadfast. And, so must we.

Pregnancy Milestone for Today

_____

_____

_____

_____

_____

A Quote for Today

The Christian lifestyle is not one of legalistic do's and don'ts, but one that is positive, attractive, and joyful.

—Vonette Bright

THE IMPORTANCE OF WORDS

*Watch the way you talk. Let nothing foul or dirty come out
of your mouth. Say only what helps, each word a gift.*
—Ephesians 4:29 MSG

How important are the words we speak? More important than we may realize. Our words have echoes that extend beyond place or time. If our words are encouraging, we can lift others up; if our words are hurtful, we can hold others back.

Do you seek to be a source of encouragement to others? And, do you seek to be a worthy ambassador for Christ? If so, you must speak words that are worthy of your Savior. So avoid angry outbursts. Refrain from impulsive outpourings. Terminate tantrums. Instead, speak words of encouragement and hope to your family and friends, who, by the way, most certainly need all the hope and encouragement they can find.

A Quote for Today

Every word we speak, every action we take, has an effect on the totality of humanity. No one can escape that privilege—or that responsibility.

—Laurie Beth Jones

Pregnancy Milestone for Today

_____

_____

_____

_____

_____

_____

SERVING GOD . . . WITH HUMILITY

The greatest among you must be a servant.
But those who exalt themselves will be humbled,
and those who humble themselves will be exalted.
—Matthew 23:11-12 NLT

If you genuinely seek to discover God's unfolding purpose for your life, you must ask yourself this question: "How does God want me to serve others?"

Whatever your path, whatever your calling, you may be certain of this: service to others is an integral part of God's plan for your life. Christ was the ultimate servant, the Savior who gave His life for mankind. As His followers, we, too, must become humble servants.

Every single day of your life, including this one, God will give you opportunities to serve Him by serving His children. Welcome those opportunities with open arms. They are God's gift to you, His way of allowing you to achieve greatness in His kingdom.

Pregnancy Milestone for Today

_____

_____

_____

_____

_____

A Quote for Today

God wants us to serve Him with a willing spirit, one that would choose no other way.
—Beth Moore

HE WANTS YOUR ATTENTION

Let us lay aside every weight and the sin that so easily ensnares us,
and run with endurance the race that lies before us,
keeping our eyes on Jesus, the source and perfecter of our faith.
—Hebrews 12:1-2 HCSB

I s yours a life of moderation or accumulation? The answers to this
question will determine the direction of your day and, in time, the
direction of your life.

Ours is a highly complicated society, a place where people and
corporations vie for your attention, for your time, and for your dollars. Don't let them succeed in complicating your life! Keep your eyes
focused instead upon God.

If your material possessions are somehow distancing you from
God, discard them. If your outside interests leave you too little time
for your family or your Creator, slow down the merry-go-round, or
better yet, get off the merry-go-round completely. Remember: God
wants your full attention, and He wants it today, so don't let anybody
or anything get in His way.

A Quote for Today

Prescription for a happier and
healthier life: resolve to slow down
your pace; learn to say no gracefully;
resist the temptation to chase after
more pleasure, more hobbies, and
more social entanglements.

—James Dobson

Pregnancy Milestone for Today

_____

_____

_____

_____

_____

EACH DAY A GIFT

*Teach us to number our days carefully
so that we may develop wisdom in our hearts.*
—Psalm 90:12 HCSB

This day is a gift from God. How will you use it? Will you celebrate God's gifts and obey His commandments? Will you share words of encouragement and hope with all who cross your path? Will you share the Good News of the risen Christ? Will you trust in the Father and praise His glorious handiwork? The answer to these questions will determine, to a surprising extent, the direction and the quality of your day.

The familiar words of Psalm 118:24 remind us of a profound yet simple truth: "This is the day which the LORD hath made; we will rejoice and be glad in it" (KJV). For Christian believers, every day begins and ends with God and His Son. Christ came to this earth to give us abundant life and eternal salvation. We give thanks to our Maker when we treasure each day and use it to the fullest.

As an expectant mom, you have every reason to be grateful. Give thanks for this day and for the One who created it.

Pregnancy Milestone for Today

_____

_____

_____

_____

_____

_____

A Quote for Today

Live today fully, expressing gratitude for all you have been, all you are right now, and all you are becoming.
—Melodie Beattie

LIGHT OF THE WORLD

*I have come as a light into the world, so that everyone
who believes in Me would not remain in darkness.*
—John 12:46 HCSB

The Bible says that you are "the light that gives light to the world." The Bible also says that you should live in a way that lets other people understand what it means to be a follower of Jesus.

What kind of light have you been giving off? Hopefully, you've been a good example for everybody to see. Why? Because the world needs all the light it can get, and that includes your light, too!

The familiar hymn begins, "What a friend we have in Jesus . . . ." No truer words were ever penned. Jesus is the sovereign Friend and ultimate Savior of mankind. Christ showed enduring love for you by willingly sacrificing His own life so that you might have eternal life. As a response to His sacrifice, you should love Him, praise Him, and share His message of salvation with your neighbors and with the world.

Do you seek to be an extreme follower of Christ? Then you must let your light shine . . . today and every day.

A Quote for Today

His life is our light—our purpose and meaning and reason for living.
—Anne Graham Lotz

Pregnancy Milestone for Today

_____

_____

_____

_____

_____

God's Gift to You

Everything God made is good,
and nothing should be refused if it is accepted with thanks.
—1 Timothy 4:4 NCV

Life is God's gift to you, and He intends that you celebrate His glorious gift. If you're a woman who treasures each day, you will be blessed by your Father in heaven. Life is also God's gift to your unborn baby, and the Father intends that you celebrate that gift, too.

For wise Christians, every day begins and ends with God and His Son. Jesus came to this earth to give us abundant life and eternal salvation. Our task is to accept Christ's grace with joy in our hearts and praise on our lips. Believers who fashion their days around Jesus are transformed: They see the world differently, they act differently, and they feel differently about themselves and their neighbors.

So whatever this day holds for you, begin it and end it with God as your partner and Christ as your Savior. And throughout the day, give thanks to the One who gave life to you and to your baby. God's love for you is infinite. Accept it joyously and be thankful.

Pregnancy Milestone for Today

_____

_____

_____

_____

_____

A Quote for Today

Shout the shout of faith. Nothing can withstand the triumphant faith that links itself to omnipotence. For "this is the victory that overcometh the world." The secret of all successful living lies in this shout of faith.
—Hannah Whitall Smith

PRAISING THE SAVIOR

At the name of Jesus every knee should bow, of those in heaven,
and of those on earth, and of those under the earth, and that every tongue
should confess that Jesus Christ is Lord, to the glory of God the Father.
—Philippians 2:10-11 NKJV

The words by Fanny Crosby are familiar: "This is my story, this is my song, praising my Savior, all the day long." As believers who have been saved by the blood of a risen Christ, we must do exactly as the song instructs: We must praise our Savior time and time again throughout the day. Worship and praise should be a part of everything we do. Otherwise, we quickly lose perspective as we fall prey to the demands of everyday life.

Do you sincerely desire to be a worthy servant of the One who has given you eternal love and eternal life? And, do you want to honor the One who is constantly watching over you and your unborn child? Then praise your Heavenly Father for who He is and for what He has done for you. And don't just praise Him on Sunday morning. Praise Him all day long, every day, for as long as you live . . . and then for all eternity.

A Quote for Today

The time for universal praise is sure
to come some day. Let us begin
to do our part now.
—Hannah Whitall Smith

Pregnancy Milestone for Today

_____

_____

_____

_____

_____

HIS COMFORTING HAND

When I am filled with cares, Your comfort brings me joy.
—Psalm 94:19 HCSB

As Christians, we can be assured of this fact: Whether we find ourselves on the pinnacle of the mountain or in the darkest depths of the valley, God is there.

If you have been touched by the transforming hand of Jesus, then you have every reason to live courageously. After all, Christ has already won the ultimate battle—and He won it for you—on the cross at Calvary.

So the next time you find your courage tested to the limit, lean upon God's promises. Trust His Son. Remember that God is always near and that He is your protector and your deliverer. When you are worried, anxious, or afraid, call upon Him and accept the touch of His comforting hand. Remember that God rules both mountaintops and valleys—with limitless wisdom and love—now and forever.

Pregnancy Milestone for Today

_____

_____

_____

_____

_____

_____

A Quote for Today

When God allows extraordinary trials for His people, He prepares extraordinary comforts for them.

—Corrie ten Boom

CHOICES MATTER

And we pray this in order that you may live a life worthy of the Lord and may please him in every way: bearing fruit in every good work, growing in the knowledge of God.
—Colossians 1:10 NIV

Life is a series of choices. Each day, we make countless decisions that can bring us closer to God . . . or not. When we live according to God's commandments, we earn for ourselves the abundance and peace that He intends for us to experience. But, when we allow bad habits or poor choices to distance us from the Creator, we suffer.

As a mom-to-be, you're now making choices for two people: yourself and your baby. Please choose carefully. When you're faced with a difficult choice or a powerful temptation, be sure to place your baby's needs above your own, and be sure to seek the Father's guidance. Pray your way through your pregnancy, and trust the counsel God gives. Invite Him into your heart and live according to His commandments. When you do, you and your baby will be blessed today, and tomorrow, and forever.

A Quote for Today

There may be no trumpet sound or loud applause when we make a right decision, just a calm sense of resolution and peace.
—Gloria Gaither

Pregnancy Milestone for Today

_____

_____

_____

_____

_____

BEYOND DISCOURAGEMENT

The Lord is my light and my salvation; whom shall I fear?
The Lord is the strength of my life; of whom shall I be afraid?
—Psalm 27:1 NKJV

The life of a soon-to-be mom can be difficult and discouraging at times. During these darker moments, we can depend upon our friends and family, and upon God. When we do, we find the courage to face the future with hopeful hearts and willing hands.

Eleanor Roosevelt advised, "You gain strength, courage, and confidence by every great experience in which you really stop to look fear in the face. You are able to say to yourself, 'I lived through this. I can take the next thing that comes along.' You must do the thing you think you cannot do."

So the next time you find your courage tested to the limit, remember that you're probably stronger than you think. And remember—with you, your friends, your family, and your God all working together, you have nothing to fear.

Pregnancy Milestone for Today

_____

_____

_____

_____

_____

_____

A Quote for Today

If a person fears God, he or she has no reason to fear anything else. On the other hand, if a person does not fear God, then fear becomes a way of life.

—Beth Moore

THE CHANGES ARE BEAUTIFUL

You made all the delicate, inner parts of my body and knit me together in my mother's womb. Thank you for making me so wonderfully complex! Your workmanship is marvelous—and how well I know it.

—Psalm 139:13-14 NLT

Your body is changing day by day, and the changes are beautiful. Celebrate those changes and thank God for your pregnancy.

When God created you, He made a one-of-a-kind woman with unique opportunities and skills. And now, God has given you another unique being, a priceless treasure with a glorious future that only He can see. Yes, God's plan is beautiful—and so is your unborn baby. And so, for that matter, are you.

A Quote for Today

If you want to know true beauty, ask for grace,
not learning, and ask God, not man.

—St. Bonaventure

A Question to Think On

Have you thanked God today for
the miraculous changes
that are happening to you and
to your unborn child?

Pregnancy Milestone
for Today

_____

_____

_____

_____

_____

_____

SELF-PITY DOESN'T PAY

Obsession with self in these matters is a dead end; attention to God leads us out into the open, into a spacious, free life. Focusing on the self is the opposite of focusing on God. Anyone completely absorbed in self ignores God, ends up thinking more about self than God. That person ignores who God is and what he is doing. And God isn't pleased at being ignored.

—Romans 8:6-8 MSG

Charles Swindoll advises, "When you're on the verge of throwing a pity party thanks to your despairing thoughts, go back to the Word of God." How true. Self-pity is not only an unproductive way to think, it is also an affront to your Father in heaven. God's Word promises that His children can receive abundance, peace, love, and eternal life. These gifts are not earned; they are an outpouring from God, a manifestation of His grace. With these rich blessings, how can we, as believers, feel sorry for ourselves? Self-pity and peace cannot coexist in the same mind. Bitterness and joy cannot coexist in the same heart. Thanksgiving and despair are mutually exclusive. So, if your unreliable thoughts are allowing the discomforts of pregnancy to dominate your day or your life, train yourself to think less about your troubles and more about God's blessings. When you stop to think about it, hasn't He given you enough blessings to occupy your thoughts all day, every day, from now on? Of course He has! So focus your mind on Him, and let your worries fend for themselves.

Pregnancy Milestone for Today

_____

_____

_____

_____

_____

_____

HE DOES NOT FAIL

The LORD is my strength and my song; he has become my victory.
He is my God, and I will praise him.
—Exodus 15:2 NLT

On those cloudy days when our strength is sapped and our faith is shaken, there exists God from whom we can draw courage and wisdom.

The words of Isaiah 40:31 teach us that, "Those who wait on the Lord shall renew their strength; they shall mount up with wings like eagles, they shall run and not be weary, they shall walk and not faint" (NKJV).

So if you're feeling defeated or discouraged, think again. And while you're thinking, consider the following advice from Mrs. Charles E. Cowman: "Never yield to gloomy anticipation. Place your hope and confidence in God. He has no record of failure."

A Quote for Today

The most profane word we use is "hopeless." When you say a situation or person is hopeless, you are slamming the door in the face of God.

—Kathy Troccoli

Pregnancy Milestone for Today

_____

_____

_____

_____

_____

Very Big Dreams

Have faith in the Lord your God, and you will stand strong.
Have faith in his prophets, and you will succeed.
—2 Chronicles 20:20 NCV

Do you expect the future to be bright for yourself and for your soon-to-be-born child? Are you willing to dream king-sized dreams for yourself and your baby . . . and are you willing to work diligently to make those dreams happen? Hopefully so—after all, God promises that we can do "all things" through Him (Philippians 4:13). Yet most of us live far below our potential. We take half measures; we dream small dreams; we waste precious time and energy on the distractions of the world. But God has other plans for us.

You and your loved ones possess great potential, potential that you must use or forfeit. And, the time to begin fulfilling that potential is now. So, don't be afraid to dream big dreams for yourself or for your family. And, don't be afraid to begin the work that will, with God's help, transform those dreams into reality.

Pregnancy Milestone for Today

_____

_____

_____

_____

_____

_____

A Quote for Today

God created us with an overwhelming desire to soar. He designed us to be tremendously productive and "to mount up with wings like eagles," realistically dreaming of what He can do with our potential.

—Carol Kent

THE ROCK

The Lord is my rock, my fortress, and my deliverer.
—Psalm 18:2 HCSB

God is the Creator of life, the Sustainer of life, and the Rock upon which righteous lives are built. God is a never-ending source of support for those who trust Him, and He is a never-ending source of wisdom for those who study His Holy Word.

Is God the Rock upon which you've constructed your own life? If so, then you have chosen wisely. Your faith will give you the inner strength you need to rise above the inevitable demands and struggles of life.

Do the demands of your pregnancy seem overwhelming? If so, you must rely not only upon your own resources but more importantly upon the Rock that cannot be shaken. God will hold your hand and walk with you today and every day if you let Him. Even if your circumstances are difficult, trust the Father. His promises remain true; His love is eternal; and His goodness endures. And because He is the One who can never be moved, you can stand firm in the knowledge that you are protected by Him now and forever.

A Quote for Today

The Rock of Ages is the great sheltering encirclement.
—Oswald Chambers

Pregnancy Milestone for Today

_____

_____

_____

_____

_____

_____

HOW MUCH DOES GOD LOVE YOU AND YOUR BABY?

For God loved the world in this way: He gave His only Son, so that everyone who believes in Him will not perish but have eternal life.
—John 3:16 HCSB

How much does God love you and your baby? To answer that question, you need only to look at the cross. God's love for you is so great that He sent His only Son to this earth to die for you, for your family, and for all of humanity.

Sometimes, in the crush of your daily duties, God may seem far away, but He is not. God is everywhere you have ever been and everywhere you will ever go. He is with you night and day; He knows your thoughts and your prayers. And, when you earnestly seek Him, you will find Him because He is here, waiting patiently for you to reach out to Him.

St. Augustine observed, "God loves each of us as if there were only one of us." Do you believe those words? Do you seek to have an intimate, one-on-one relationship with your Heavenly Father, or are you satisfied to keep Him at a "safe" distance?

God's love is bigger and more powerful than anybody can imagine, but His love is very real. So do yourself a favor right now: accept God's love with open arms and welcome His Son, Jesus, into your heart. When you do, your sense of self-worth—and your life—will be forever changed.

Pregnancy Milestone for Today

_____

_____

_____

_____

_____

_____

THE POWER OF A POSITIVE PREGNANCY

*Dear friend, guard Clear Thinking and Common Sense with your life;
don't for a minute lose sight of them.*
—Proverbs 3:21 MSG

Have you established the habit of thinking positively about your life, your future, and your pregnancy? Or are you occasionally beset by feelings that are more negative than that? If you've allowed a negative attitude to hijack your thoughts, perhaps it's time to reconsider your situation and recount your blessings.

We Christians have many reasons to celebrate. God is in His heaven; Christ has risen; and we are the sheep of His flock. We worship a God of possibility not negativity.

So today, as you manage your life and your pregnancy, count your blessings instead of your hardships. And then, give thanks to the Giver of all things good for gifts that are simply too numerous to count.

A Quote for Today

If you can't tell whether your glass is half-empty or half-full, you don't need another glass; what you need is better eyesight . . . and a more thankful heart.

—Marie T. Freeman

Pregnancy Milestone for Today

_____

_____

_____

_____

_____

_____

HE OVERCOMES THE WORLD

*God decided to let his people know this rich and glorious secret
which he has for all people. This secret is Christ himself,
who is in you. He is our only hope for glory.*
—Colossians 1:27 NCV

There are few sadder sights on earth than the sight of a person who has lost all hope. In difficult times, hope can be elusive, but Christians need never lose it. After all, God is good; His love endures; He has promised His children the gift of eternal life.

If you find yourself falling into the spiritual traps of worry and discouragement, consider the words of Jesus. It was Christ who promised, "In the world you will have tribulation; but be of good cheer, I have overcome the world" (John 16:33 NKJV). This world is, indeed, a place of trials and tribulations, but as believers, we are secure. God has promised us peace, joy, and eternal life. And, of course, God always keeps His promises.

Pregnancy Milestone for Today

_____

_____

_____

_____

_____

A Quote for Today

I can still hardly believe it.
I, with shriveled, bent fingers,
atrophied muscles, gnarled knees,
and no feeling from the shoulders
down, will one day have
a new body—light, bright
and clothed in righteousness—
powerful and dazzling.

—Joni Eareckson Tada

HIS STRENGTH

The Lord is the strength of my life.
—Psalm 27:1 KJV

Have you made God the cornerstone of your life, or is He relegated to a few hours on Sunday morning? Have you genuinely allowed God to reign over every corner of your heart, or have you attempted to place Him in a spiritual compartment? The answer to these questions will determine the direction of your day and the condition of your heart.

God loves you, and He loves your unborn baby. The Creator of the universe hears every heartbeat just as surely as He hears every prayer. Praise Him, and allow Him to rule your heart. And then, accept the peace, and the strength, and the protection, and the abundance that only God can give.

A Quote for Today

He goes before us, follows behind us,
and hems us safe inside the realm
of His protection.
—Beth Moore

**Pregnancy Milestone
for Today**

_____

_____

_____

_____

_____

Walking in the Light

*I have come as a light into the world, that whoever believes
in Me should not abide in darkness.*
—John 12:46 NKJV

Jesus walks with you. Are you walking with Him? Hopefully, you will choose to walk with Him today and every day of your life. And hopefully, you will encourage your family to do the same.

God's Word is clear: When we genuinely invite Christ to reign over our hearts, and when we accept His transforming love, we are forever changed. When we welcome Christ into our hearts, an old life ends and a new way of living—along with a completely new way of viewing the world—begins.

Each morning offers a fresh opportunity to invite Christ, yet once again, to rule over our hearts and our days. Each morning presents yet another opportunity to take up His cross and follow in His footsteps. Today, let us rejoice in the new life that is ours through Christ, and let us follow Him, step by step, on the path that He first walked.

Pregnancy Milestone for Today

_____

_____

_____

_____

_____

A Quote for Today

If we do not radiate the light of Christ around us, the sense of the darkness that prevails in the world will increase.

—Mother Teresa

HEALTHIER HABITS

Are there those among you who are truly wise and understanding?
Then they should show it by living right and doing good things with
a gentleness that comes from wisdom.
—James 3:13 NCV

Perhaps you've tried, on more than one occasion, to become a more disciplined person. So, what should you do if you keep falling back into your old habits? If you desire better health—for yourself and for your unborn baby—today is the perfect day to begin.

If you trust God, and if you keep asking Him to help you change unhealthy behaviors, He will answer your prayers. When you establish healthier habits, you will transform your life, one day at a time.

So, if at first you don't succeed, keep praying. Don't lose hope, and don't give up. Every new day provides a fresh opportunity to establish healthier habits.

A Timely Tip

Life is a gift from God, but health must be earned. We earn good health by cultivating healthy habits. Perhaps, during these important days of your pregnancy, it's the right time for you to commit yourself to a sensible lifestyle. And, the only way that you'll revolutionize your physical health is to revolutionize your habits.

Pregnancy Milestone for Today

_____

_____

_____

_____

_____

_____

BEYOND THE CRISES

But the wisdom that is from above is first pure, then peaceable,
gentle, willing to yield, full of mercy and good fruits,
without partiality and without hypocrisy.
—James 3:17 NKJV

Your decision to seek a deeper relationship with God will not remove all problems from your life; to the contrary, it will bring about a series of personal crises as you constantly seek to say "yes" to God although the world encourages you to do otherwise. You live in a world that seeks to snare your attention and lead you away from God. Each time you are tempted to distance yourself from the Creator, you will face a spiritual crisis. A few of these crises may be monumental in scope, but most will be the small, everyday decisions of life. In fact, life here on earth can be seen as one test after another—and with each crisis comes yet another opportunity to grow closer to God . . . or to distance yourself from His plan for your life.

Today, you will face many opportunities to say "yes" to your Creator—and you will also encounter many opportunities to say "no" to Him. Your answers will determine the quality of your day and the direction of your life, so answer carefully . . . very carefully.

Pregnancy Milestone for Today

_____

_____

_____

_____

_____

_____

A Quote for Today

Crisis brings us face to face with our inadequacy and our inadequacy in turn leads us to the inexhaustible sufficiency of God.
—Catherine Marshall

RENEWAL AND CELEBRATION

And He who sits on the throne said,
"Behold, I am making all things new."
—Revelation 21:5 NASB

Each new day offers countless opportunities to celebrate life and to serve God's children. But each day also offers countless opportunities to fall prey to the countless everyday distractions of our difficult age.

Gigi Graham Tchividjian spoke for women everywhere when she observed, "How much of our lives are, well, so daily. How often our hours are filled with the mundane, seemingly unimportant things that have to be done, whether at home or work. These very 'daily' tasks could—and should—become a celebration."

Make your life a celebration. After all, your family is unique, your talents are unique, and your opportunities are, too. And, the best time to really live—and to really celebrate—is now.

A Quote for Today

God specializes in things fresh and firsthand. His plans for you this year may outshine those of the past. He's prepared to fill your days with reasons to give Him praise.

—Joni Eareckson Tada

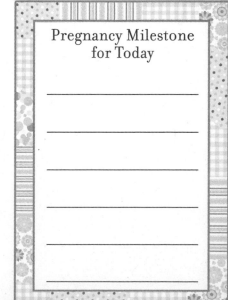

Pregnancy Milestone for Today

_____

_____

_____

_____

_____

DEMONSTRATING OUR LOVE

For this is the love of God, that we keep His commandments. And His commandments are not burdensome.
—1 John 5:3 NKJV

How can we demonstrate our love for God? By accepting His Son as our personal Savior and by placing Christ squarely at the center of our lives and our hearts. Jesus said that if we are to love Him, we must obey His commandments (John 14:15). Thus, our obedience to the Master is an expression of our love for Him.

In Ephesians 2:10 we read, "For we are His workmanship, created in Christ Jesus for good works" (NKJV). These words are instructive: We are not saved by good works, but for good works. Good works are not the root but rather the fruit of our salvation.

Today, let the fruits of your stewardship be a clear demonstration of your love for Christ. When you do, your good heart will bring forth many good things for yourself and for God. Christ has given you spiritual abundance and eternal life. You, in turn, owe Him good treasure from a single obedient heart: yours.

Pregnancy Milestone for Today

_____

_____

_____

_____

_____

_____

A Quote for Today

A wholehearted love for God looks to Him through His Word and prayer, always watching and waiting, ever ready to do all that He says, prepared to act on His expressed desires.

—Elizabeth George

Depending upon God

Search for the Lord and for His strength; seek His face always.
—Psalm 105:4-5 HCSB

God's love and support never changes. From the cradle to the grave, God has promised to give you the strength to meet any challenge. God has promised to lift you up and guide your steps if you let Him. God has promised that when you entrust your life to Him completely and without reservation, He will give you the courage to face any trial and the wisdom to live in His righteousness.

God responds to those who turn their hearts and prayers to Him. Will you count yourself among that number? Will you accept God's peace and wear God's armor against the distractions of your world and inconveniences of your pregnancy? If you do, you can live courageously and optimistically, knowing that you have been forever touched during this glorious season of your life by the loving, unfailing, uplifting hand of God.

A Quote for Today

When we reach the end of our strength, wisdom, and personal resources, we enter into the beginning of His glorious provisions.

—Patsy Clairmont

Pregnancy Milestone for Today

_____

_____

_____

_____

_____

COURTESY MATTERS

Be hospitable to one another without grumbling.
—1 Peter 4:9 NKJV

Did Christ instruct us in matters of etiquette and courtesy? Of course He did. Christ's instructions are clear: "In everything, therefore, treat people the same way you want them to treat you, for this is the Law and the Prophets" (Matthew 7:12 NASB). Jesus did not say, "In some things, treat people as you wish to be treated." And, He did not say, "From time to time, treat others with kindness." Christ said that we should treat others as we wish to be treated in every aspect of our daily lives. This, of course, is a tall order indeed, but as Christians, we are commanded to do our best.

Today, you'll have hundreds of chances to become frustrated. Resist those temptations. And, as an expectant mom, you'll have more than your fair share of discomforts and responsibilities. Instead of falling prey to the frustrations of pregnancy, try a different approach: be a little kinder than necessary to family members, friends, and total strangers. And, as you consider all the things that Christ has done in your life, honor Him with your words and with your deeds. He expects no less, and He deserves no less.

Pregnancy Milestone for Today

_____

_____

_____

_____

_____

_____

A Quote for Today

Be so preoccupied with good will that you haven't room for ill will.
—E. Stanley Jones

GOD PROTECTS

He got up, rebuked the wind, and said to the sea, "Silence! Be still!"
The wind ceased, and there was a great calm. Then He said to them,
"Why are you fearful? Do you still have no faith?"
—Mark 4:39-40 HCSB

God is willing to protect us. We, in turn, must open ourselves to His protection and His love. This point is illustrated by the familiar story found in the 4th chapter of Mark: When a terrible storm rose quickly on the Sea of Galilee, the disciples were afraid. Although they had witnessed many miracles, the disciples feared for their lives, so they turned to Jesus, and He calmed the waters and the wind.

Sometimes, we, like the disciples, feel threatened by the storms of life. And when we are fearful, we, too, can turn to Christ for comfort and for courage. The next time you find yourself fretting about your pregnancy—or fretting about anything else, for that matter—remember that the One who calmed the wind and the waves is also your personal Savior. Then ask yourself which is stronger: your faith or your fear. The answer, friends, should be obvious: Whatever your challenge, God can handle it. Let Him.

A Quote for Today

Only believe, don't fear. Our Master, Jesus, always watches over us, and no matter what the persecution, Jesus will surely overcome it.

—Lottie Moon

Pregnancy Milestone for Today

_____

_____

_____

_____

_____

BIG AND GETTING BIGGER

For You formed my inward parts; You covered me in my mother's womb.
I will praise You, for I am fearfully and wonderfully made;
marvelous are Your works.
—Psalm 139:13-14 NKJV

Even if your family and friends keep telling you how beautiful you look, you may not feel beautiful. To the contrary, you (like many other moms-to-be) may feel downright unattractive. If you've fallen prey to self-consciousness, or self-doubt, or self-criticism, God wants to have a little chat with you.

When God created you, He made a one-of-a-kind being, a woman with special gifts and unique opportunities. And now, because you are an expectant mom, you have been given a special responsibility from the Creator.

Of this you can be sure: You and your child are beautiful to God. And if He believes you're beautiful, shouldn't you believe it, too?

Pregnancy Milestone for Today

_____

_____

_____

_____

_____

_____

A Question to Think On

Have you taken time today to celebrate the miraculous body that God has entrusted to you?

THE TAPESTRY OF LIFE

Let not your heart be troubled; you believe in God, believe also in Me.
In My Father's house are many mansions; if it were not so,
I would have told you. I go to prepare a place for you.
And if I go and prepare a place for you, I will come again and receive you
to Myself; that where I am, there you may be also.

—John 14:1-3 NKJV

Our circumstances change, and our world continues to change. But, God does not change, and His love remains constant. He remains ready to comfort us and strengthen us whenever we turn to Him.

Psalm 145 promises, "The Lord is near to all who call on him, to all who call on him in truth. He fulfills the desires of those who fear him; he hears their cry and saves them" (vv. 18-20 NIV).

The life of a mom-to-be is often challenging, sometimes discouraging, occasionally daunting. But, because you are protected by the Creator of the universe, you should not be afraid.

God loves you and your baby. And, He has promised to care for both of you. So, when the challenges of pregnancy seem overwhelming, don't despair. Instead, build your day and your life on God's promises. His promises never fail, and His love endures forever.

A Quote for Today

When the train goes through a tunnel and the world becomes dark, do you jump out? Of course not. You sit still and trust the engineer to get you through.

—Corrie ten Boom

Pregnancy Milestone for Today

_____

_____

_____

_____

_____

_____

WHERE TO TAKE YOUR ANXIETIES

*Be anxious for nothing, but in everything by prayer and supplication
with thanksgiving let your requests be made known to God.*
—Philippians 4:6 NASB

Sometimes, the world seems to shift beneath our feet. From time to time, all of us face adversity, discouragement, or disappointment. And, throughout life, we must all endure life-changing personal losses that leave us anxiously struggling for breath. When we do, God stands ready to protect us.

The Bible instructs us to, "Be strong and courageous, and do the work. Don't be afraid or discouraged, for the Lord God, my God, is with you. He won't leave you or forsake you" (1 Chronicles 28:20 HCSB). When we are troubled, we must call upon God, and in time He will heal us.

Are you anxious about the concerns of today or the uncertainties of tomorrow? Take those anxieties to God. Are you troubled? Take your troubles to Him. Do you find yourself worrying about your baby's health . . . or your own? Place your trust in the One who is forever faithful. God is trustworthy today, tomorrow, and forever.

Pregnancy Milestone for Today

_____

_____

_____

_____

_____

A Quote for Today

Look around you and you'll be distressed; look within yourself and you'll be depressed; look at Jesus, and you'll be at rest!
—Corrie ten Boom

LAUGHING WITH LIFE

Laugh with your happy friends when they're happy . . .
—Romans 12:15 MSG

Barbara Johnson observes, "In our tense, uptight society where folks are rushing to make appointments they have already missed, a good laugh can be as refreshing as a cup of cold water in the desert." And she's right. Laughter is, indeed, God's gift, and He intends that we enjoy it. Yet sometimes, because of the inevitable stresses of everyday life, laughter seems only a distant memory.

As Christians we have every reason to be cheerful and to be thankful. Our blessings from God are beyond measure, starting, of course, with a gift that is ours for the asking, God's gift of salvation through Christ Jesus.

Few things in life are more absurd than the sight of a grumpy Christian. So today, as you go about your daily activities—and as you confront the inevitable discomforts of pregnancy—approach life with a grin and a chuckle. After all, God created laughter for a reason . . . to use it. So laugh!

A Quote for Today

A keen sense of humor helps us
to overlook the unbecoming,
understand the unconventional,
tolerate the unpleasant, overcome
the unexpected, and outlast
the unbearable.
—Billy Graham

Pregnancy Milestone
for Today

_____

_____

_____

_____

_____

FINDING ENCOURAGEMENT

A word spoken at the right time is like golden apples on a silver tray.
—Proverbs 25:11 HCSB

Because you're an expectant mom, you need heaping helpings of encouragement. If you associate with hope-filled, enthusiastic people, their enthusiasm will have a tendency to lift your spirits. But if you find yourself spending too much time in the company of naysayers, pessimists, or cynics, your thoughts, like theirs, will tend to be negative.

Are you making the effort to spend time with people who make you feel better, not worse? If so, then you're availing yourself of a priceless gift: the encouragement of fellow believers. But, if you find yourself focusing on the negative aspects of life, perhaps it is time to find a few new friends.

As a faithful Christian, you have every reason to be hopeful. So today, look for reasons to celebrate God's endless blessings. And while you're at it, look for people who will join with you in the celebration. You'll be better for their company, and they'll be better for yours.

Pregnancy Milestone for Today

_____

_____

_____

_____

_____

_____

A Quote for Today

Always stay connected to people and seek out things that bring you joy. Dream with abandon.
Pray confidently.

—Barbara Johnson

CONTENTED?

But godliness with contentment is a great gain.
—1 Timothy 6:6 HCSB

Can you honestly say that you're a contented mom-to-be? Are you satisfied with the direction of your life, the course of your pregnancy, and the strength of your faith? If so, you've learned the wisdom of turning everything over to God. If not, you're probably still trying to accomplish everything by yourself . . . and it's probably time to make some changes.

God is steadfast in His willingness to protect us. We, in turn, must be steadfast in our willingness to be protected!

So, the next time you're bothered by the inevitable distractions of everyday life or by the interminable demands of pregnancy, remember that God is your ultimate Protector. When you ask Him to comfort you, He will respond with a love that defies human understanding. When you turn everything over to Him in prayer, you will experience the peace and the contentment that only God can provide.

A Quote for Today

Those who are God's without reserve are, in every sense, content.
—Hannah Whitall Smith

Pregnancy Milestone for Today

_____

_____

_____

_____

_____

THE SOURCE OF STRENGTH

Have you not known? Have you not heard? The everlasting God,
the Lord, the Creator of the ends of the earth, neither faints nor is weary.
His understanding is unsearchable. He gives power to the weak,
and to those who have no might He increases strength.
—Isaiah 40:28-29 NKJV

God is a never-ending source of strength and courage if we call upon Him. When we are weary, He gives us strength. When we see no hope, God reminds us of His promises. When we grieve, God wipes away our tears.

Do you feel overwhelmed by today's responsibilities? Do you feel pressured by the inevitable demands and inconveniences of pregnancy? Are you fearful of an uncertain future? Then turn your concerns and your prayers over to God. He knows your needs, and He has promised to meet those needs. Whatever your circumstances, God will protect you and care for you . . . if you let Him. Invite Him into your heart and allow Him to renew your spirits. When you trust Him and Him alone, He will never fail you.

Pregnancy Milestone for Today

_____

_____

_____

_____

_____

_____

A Quote for Today

The pathway of obedience
can sometimes be difficult, but it
always leads to a strengthening of
our inner woman.
—Vonette Bright

SPIRITUAL TRAPS

Why are you cast down, O my soul? And why are you disquieted
within me? Hope in God; for I shall yet praise Him,
the help of my countenance and my God.
—Psalm 42:11 NKJV

Pessimism and Christianity don't mix. Why? Because Christians have every reason to be optimistic about life here on earth and life eternal.

Sometimes, despite our trust in God, we may fall into the spiritual traps of worry, frustration, anxiety, or sheer exhaustion, and our hearts become heavy. What's needed is plenty of rest, a large dose of perspective, and God's healing touch, but not necessarily in that order.

Today, make this promise to yourself and keep it: vow to be a hope-filled Christian mom. Think optimistically about your life, your baby, your career, your family, and your future. Trust your hopes, not your fears. Take time to celebrate God's glorious creation. And then, when you've filled your heart with hope and gladness, share your optimism with others. They'll be better for it, and so will you. But not necessarily in that order.

A Quote for Today

We never get anywhere—nor do
our conditions and circumstances
change—when we look
at the dark side of life.
—Mrs. Charles E. Cowman

Pregnancy Milestone for Today

_____

_____

_____

_____

_____

ACCEPTANCE TODAY

I have learned to be content whatever the circumstances.
—Philippians 4:11 NIV

Is there something in your past that has left you bitter or resentful? Are you still struggling to overcome a disappointment or injustice from years ago? If so, it's time to accept the unchangeable past and to have faith in the promise of tomorrow. It's time to trust God completely—and it's time to reclaim the peace—His peace—that can and should be yours.

God doesn't explain Himself in ways that we, as mortals with limited insight and clouded vision, can comprehend. So, instead of understanding every aspect of God's unfolding plan for our lives and our universe, we must be satisfied to trust Him completely. We cannot know God's motivations, nor can we understand His actions. We can, however, trust Him, and we must.

A Quote for Today

Faith is the willingness to receive whatever He wants to give, or the willingness not to have what He does not want to give.
—Elisabeth Elliot

Pregnancy Milestone for Today

_____

_____

_____

_____

_____

_____

RESPECT YOURSELF

It is God's desire that by doing good you should stop foolish people from saying stupid things about you. Live as free people, but do not use your freedom as an excuse to do evil. Live as servants of God.
—1 Peter 2:15-16 NCV

Sometimes it's hard to have self-respect, especially if you pay much attention to all those messages the media keeps pumping out. Those messages, which seem to pop up just about everywhere, try to tell you how you and your family should look, how you should behave, and what you should buy.

The media isn't interested in making you feel better about yourself—far from it. The media is interested in selling you products. And one of the best ways that marketers can find to sell you things is by making you feel dissatisfied with your current situation. That's why the media works 24/7 to rearrange your priorities.

So here's a word of warning: Don't fall prey to the media's messages. You are wonderful just as you are . . . don't let anyone tell you otherwise.

A Quote for Today

As I have grown in faith and confidence, I have known more and more that my worth is based on the love of God.
—Leslie Williams

Pregnancy Milestone for Today

_____

_____

_____

_____

_____

THINK ABOUT THE JOY

I have spoken these things to you so that
My joy may be in you and your joy may be complete.
—John 15:11 HCSB

Think, for a moment, about the joy you will experience after your baby is born. Think about the elation you will feel when you first gaze into the eyes of your precious child. Think about the bliss you'll experience when the pain is gone and the miracle of birth is complete.

As an expectant mom, you're probably enduring a wide assortment of aches, pains, discomforts, inconveniences, and minor humiliations. But when your baby is born, all the petty problems of pregnancy will be forgotten, and the joy of motherhood will begin. Think about that today, and be grateful. Someday, in the not-too-distant future, your joy will be complete.

Pregnancy Milestone for Today

_____

_____

_____

_____

_____

_____

A Quote for Today

Joy in life is not the absence of sorrow. The fact that Jesus could have joy in the midst of sorrow is proof that we can experience this too.

—Warren Wiersbe

FREELY GIVE

If you give, you will receive. Your gift will return to you in full measure,
pressed down, shaken together to make room for more, and running over.
Whatever measure you use in giving—large or small—
it will be used to measure what is given back to you.

—Luke 6:38 NLT

The words are familiar to those who study God's Word: "Freely you have received, freely give" (Matthew 10:8 NKJV). As followers of Christ, we have been given so much by God. In return, we must give freely of our time, our possessions, our testimonies, and our love.

Your salvation was earned at a terrible price: Christ gave His life for you on the cross at Calvary. Christ's gift is priceless, yet when you accept Jesus as your personal Savior, His gift of eternal life costs you nothing. From those to whom much has been given, much is required. And because you have received the gift of salvation, you are now called by God to be a cheerful, generous steward of the gifts He has placed under your care.

Today and every day, let Christ's words be your guide and let His eternal love fill your heart. When you do, your stewardship will be a reflection of your love for Him, and that's exactly as it should be. After all, He loved you first.

A Quote for Today

The measure of a life, after all, is not its duration but its donation.

—Corrie ten Boom

Pregnancy Milestone for Today

_____

_____

_____

_____

_____

SELF-ACCEPTANCE

You're blessed when you're content with just who you are—
no more, no less. That's the moment you find yourselves proud
owners of everything that can't be bought.
—Matthew 5:5 MSG

Being patient with other people can be difficult. But sometimes, we find it even more difficult to be patient with ourselves. We want things to be "perfect," but perfection proves impossible to achieve. We want to accomplish things now, not later. And, of course, we want our lives to unfold according to our own timetables, not God's.

Throughout the Bible, we are instructed that patience is the companion of wisdom. Proverbs 16:32 teaches us that "Patience is better than strength" (NCV). And, in 1 Peter 5:6, we are told to "humble yourselves under the mighty hand of God, that He may exalt you in due time" (NKJV).

God's message, then, is clear: we must be patient with all people, beginning with that particular person who stares back at us each time we gaze into the mirror. Offer God a prayer of thanks for making you uniquely you.

Pregnancy Milestone
for Today

_____

_____

_____

_____

_____

_____

A Quote for Today

The great freedom Jesus gives us is to be ourselves, defined by His love and our inner qualities and gifts rather than by any kind of show we put on for the world.
—Leslie Williams

GOD'S LOVE, GOD'S POWER

The Lord your God in your midst, The Mighty One, will save;
He will rejoice over you with gladness, He will quiet you with His love,
He will rejoice over you with singing.
—Zephaniah 3:17 NKJV

God's power is not burdened by boundaries or by limitations—and neither, for that matter, is His love. The love that flows from the heart of God is infinite—and today offers yet another opportunity to celebrate that love.

God's love for you is deeper and more profound than you can fathom. In times of trouble, He will comfort you; in times of sorrow, He will dry your tears. When you are weak or sorrowful, God is as near as your next breath. He stands at the door of your heart and waits. Welcome Him in and allow Him to rule. And then, accept the peace, and the power, and the protection, and the abundance that only God can give.

A Quote for Today

No part of our prayers creates a greater feeling of joy than when we praise God for who He is. He is our Master Creator, our Father, our source of all love.

—Shirley Dobson

Pregnancy Milestone for Today

_____

_____

_____

_____

_____

_____

TRUSTING HIS ANSWERS

Trust in the LORD with all your heart;
do not depend on your own understanding.
—Proverbs 3:5 NLT

God answers our prayers. What God does not do is this: He does not always answer our prayers as soon as we might like, and He does not always answer our prayers by saying "yes." God isn't an order-taker, and He's not some sort of cosmic vending machine. Sometimes—even when we want something very badly—our loving Heavenly Father responds to our requests by saying "no," and we must accept His answer, even if we don't understand it.

God answers prayers not only according to our wishes but also according to His master plan. We cannot know that plan, but we can know the Planner . . . and we must trust His wisdom, His righteousness, and His love. Always.

Pregnancy Milestone for Today

_____

_____

_____

_____

_____

_____

A Quote for Today

Let's never forget that some of God's greatest mercies are His refusals. He says no in order that He may, in some way we cannot imagine, say yes. All His ways with us are merciful. His meaning is always love.

—Elisabeth Elliot

SEEKING HIS WILL

Teach me to do Your will, for You are my God; Your Spirit is good.
Lead me in the land of uprightness.
—Psalm 143:10 NKJV

The Book of Judges tells the story of Deborah, the fearless woman who helped lead the army of Israel to victory over the Canaanites. Deborah was a judge and a prophetess, a woman called by God to lead her people. And when she answered God's call, she was rewarded with one of the great victories of Old Testament times.

Like Deborah, all of us are called to serve our Creator. And, like Deborah, we may sometimes find ourselves facing trials that can bring trembling to the very depths of our souls. As believers, we must seek God's will and follow it. When we do, we are reward with victories, some great and some small. When we entrust our lives to Him completely and without reservation, He gives us the strength to meet any challenge, the courage to face any trial, and the wisdom to live in His righteousness and in His peace.

A Quote for Today

Only God's chosen task for you will ultimately satisfy. Do not wait until it is too late to realize the privilege of serving Him in His chosen position for you.

—Beth Moore

Pregnancy Milestone for Today

_____

_____

_____

_____

_____

_____

LIFE TRIUMPHANT

Shout triumphantly to the Lord, all the earth.
Serve the Lord with gladness; come before Him with joyful songs.
—Psalm 100:1-2 HCSB

A re you living the triumphant life that God has promised? Or are you, instead, a spiritual shrinking violet? As you ponder that question, consider this: God does not intend that you live a life that is commonplace or mediocre. And He doesn't want you to hide your light "under a basket." Instead, He wants you to "Let your light so shine before men, that they may see your good works and glorify your Father in heaven" (Matthew 5:16 NKJV). In short, God wants you to live a triumphant life so that others might know precisely what it means to be a believer.

The Christian life should be a triumphal celebration, a daily exercise in thanksgiving and praise. Join that celebration today. And while you're at it, make sure that you let others know that you've joined.

Pregnancy Milestone for Today

_____

_____

_____

_____

_____

_____

A Quote for Today

When we invite Jesus into our lives,
we experience life in the fullest,
most vital sense.

—Catherine Marshall

PRIORITIES FOR MARRIAGE AND FAMILY

Let love and faithfulness never leave you . . .
write them on the tablet of your heart.
—Proverbs 3:3 NIV

It takes time to build a strong marriage . . . lots of time. Yet we live in a world where time seems to be an ever-shrinking commodity as we rush from place to place with seldom a moment to spare.

Has the busy pace of life—or the inevitable demands of your pregnancy—robbed you of sufficient time with your husband? If so, it's time to adjust your priorities. And God can help.

When you allow God to help you organize your day, you'll soon discover that there is ample time for your husband . . . but there may not be enough time to do everything else. When choosing between your marriage and "everything else," do the wise thing: choose your marriage.

A Quote for Today

A marriage can't survive forever on leftovers. It needs to be fed continually, or it will eventually starve.

—John Maxwell

Pregnancy Milestone for Today

_____

_____

_____

_____

_____

_____

Pray Always

Watch therefore, and pray always that you may be counted worthy . . .
—Luke 21:36 NKJV

Jesus made it clear to His disciples: they should pray always. And so should we. Genuine, heartfelt prayer changes the world and it changes us. When we lift our hearts to our Father in heaven, we open ourselves to a never-ending source of divine wisdom and infinite love.

Do you have questions that you simply can't answer? Ask for the guidance of your Father in heaven. Do you have concerns about your unborn baby, or about your future? Ask God for courage, and wisdom, and faith. Do you sincerely seek the gift of everlasting love and eternal life? Accept the grace of God's only begotten Son. Whatever your need, pray about it. Follow the instruction of your Savior: pray always and never lose heart. And remember: God is not just near; He is here, and He's ready to talk with you. Are you ready to talk to Him?

Pregnancy Milestone for Today

_____

_____

_____

_____

_____

_____

A Quote for Today

Prayer moves the arm that moves the world.

—Annie Armstrong

Making Peace with the Past

Do not remember the past events, pay no attention to things of old.
Look, I am about to do something new; even now it is coming.
Do you not see it? Indeed, I will make a way
in the wilderness, rivers in the desert.
—Isaiah 43:18-19 HCSB

Have you made peace with your past? If so, congratulations. But, if you are mired in the quicksand of regret, it's time to plan your escape. How can you do so? By accepting what has been and by trusting God for what will be.

Because you are human, you may be slow to forget yesterday's disappointments; if so you are not alone. But if you sincerely seek to focus your hopes and energies on the future, then you must find ways to accept the past, no matter how difficult it may be to do so.

If you have not yet made peace with the past, today is the day to declare an end to all hostilities. When you do, you can then turn your thoughts to wondrous promises of God and to the glorious future that He has in store for you.

A Quote for Today

Shake the dust from your past,
and move forward in His promises.
—Kay Arthur

Pregnancy Milestone for Today

_____

_____

_____

_____

_____

_____

PERSEVERANCE WINS THE RACE

*Let us not become weary in doing good, for at the proper time
we will reap a harvest if we do not give up.*
—Galatians 6:9 NIV

As your pregnancy progresses, you will undoubtedly experience your fair share of discomforts, apprehensions, and anxieties. When you do, don't become discouraged: God is with you, and He's with your unborn baby, too. He knows your every need, and He hears every heartbeat.

The old saying is as true today as it was when it was first spoken: "Life is a marathon, not a sprint." That's why wise travelers select a traveling companion who never tires and never falters. That partner, of course, is your Heavenly Father.

Are you just plain tired of being pregnant? Ask God for perspective and for strength. Are you discouraged? Believe in His promises. Are you worried about an uncertain future? Pray as if everything depended upon God, and work as if everything depended upon you. And finally, have faith that you and your baby play important roles in God's great plan for mankind—because you do.

Pregnancy Milestone for Today

_____

_____

_____

_____

_____

A Quote for Today

If things are tough, remember that every flower that ever bloomed had to go through a whole lot of dirt to get there.

—Barbara Johnson

DON'T BE WORRIED . . .
YOU ARE PROTECTED

But seek first his kingdom and his righteousness, and all these things
will be given to you as well. Therefore do not worry about tomorrow,
for tomorrow will worry about itself.
Each day has enough trouble of its own.
—Matthew 6:33-34 NIV

Because we are fallible human beings, we worry. Even though we, as Christians, have the assurance of salvation—even though we, as Christians, have the promise of God's love and protection—we find ourselves fretting over the countless details of everyday life.

If you are like most expectant moms, you may, on occasion, find yourself worrying about your baby, about your health, about finances, about safety, about relationships, about family, and about countless other challenges of life, some great and some small. Where is the best place to take your worries? Take them to God. Take your troubles to Him, and your fears, and your sorrows. And remember: God is trustworthy . . . and you are protected.

A Quote for Today

Today is mine. Tomorrow is none of my business. If I peer anxiously into the fog of the future, I will strain my spiritual eyes so that I will not see clearly what is required of me now.

—Elisabeth Elliott

Pregnancy Milestone
for Today

_____

_____

_____

_____

_____

_____

PRAY WITHOUT CEASING

Anyone who is having troubles should pray.
—James 5:13 NCV

In his first letter to the Thessalonians, Paul advised members of the new church to "pray without ceasing" (5:16-18). His advice applies to Christians of every generation. When we consult God on an hourly basis, we avail ourselves of His wisdom, His strength, and His love. As Corrie ten Boom observed, "Any concern that is too small to be turned into a prayer is too small to be made into a burden."

Today, as you pray for your unborn baby, trust the Father. Ask God for His guidance and His protection, and then leave the rest up to Him. He is big enough, wise enough, and strong enough to manage your life. Your job is to let Him.

A Quote for Today

We must pray literally without ceasing, in every occurrence and employment of our lives. You know I mean that prayer of the heart which is independent of place or situation, or which is, rather, a habit of lifting up the heart to God, as in a constant communication with Him.

—Elizabeth Ann Seton

Pregnancy Milestone for Today

_____

_____

_____

_____

_____

_____

GOD'S INFINITE LOVE

Praise the Lord, all nations! Glorify Him, all peoples!
For great is His faithful love to us;
the Lord's faithfulness endures forever. Hallelujah!
—Psalm 117 HCSB

Because God's power is limitless, it is far beyond the comprehension of mortal minds. But even though we cannot fully understand the heart of God, we can be open to God's love.

God's ability to love is not burdened by temporal boundaries or by earthly limitations. The love that flows from the heart of God is infinite—and today presents yet another opportunity to celebrate that love.

You are a glorious creation, a unique individual, a beautiful example of God's handiwork. God's love for you, like His love for your baby, is limitless. Accept that love, acknowledge it, and be grateful.

A Quote for Today

Though our feelings come
and go, His love for us does not.
It is not wearied by our sins, or our
indifference; and, therefore,
it is quite relentless in its
determination that we shall be
cured of those sins, at whatever cost
to us, at whatever cost to Him.
—C. S. Lewis

Pregnancy Milestone for Today

_____

_____

_____

_____

_____

YOU AND GOD CAN DO IT!

Be of good courage, and he shall strengthen your heart,
all ye that hope in the LORD.
—Psalm 31:24 KJV

Make no mistake about it: God is your ultimate source of security. The world offers no safety nets, but God does. He sent His only begotten Son to offer you the priceless gift of eternal life. And now you are challenged to return God's love by obeying His commandments and honoring His Son.

Being a mom-to-be is a demanding job, especially as the Big Day draws near. But don't worry: you can do it. As you think about the impending birth of your baby, have faith in your Creator, faith in your doctors, and faith in yourself.

During the exciting days ahead, you'll have plenty of opportunities to worry. Turn those worries over to God. Don't be fearful; be faithful. And remember this: you and God, working together, can tackle any challenge you face today and every day after.

Pregnancy Milestone for Today

_____

_____

_____

_____

_____

_____

A Quote for Today

If our hearts have been attuned
to God through an abiding faith
in Christ, the result will be joyous
optimism and good cheer.
—Billy Graham

A Timely Tip

Take time today and every day
to share your optimism with family
and friends. They need
your encouragement,
and you need theirs.

YOUR SPIRITUAL JOURNEY

*Dear brothers and sisters, whenever trouble comes your way,
let it be an opportunity for joy. For when your faith is tested,
your endurance has a chance to grow. So let it grow, for when
your endurance is fully developed, you will be strong in
character and ready for anything.*

—James 1:2-4 NLT

The journey toward spiritual maturity lasts a lifetime. As Christians, we can and should continue to grow in the love and the knowledge of our Savior as long as we live. Norman Vincent Peale had the following advice for believers of all ages: "Ask the God who made you to keep remaking you." That advice, of course, is perfectly sound, but often ignored.

When we cease to grow, either emotionally or spiritually, we do ourselves a profound disservice. But, if we study God's Word, if we obey His commandments, and if we live in the center of His will, we will not be "stagnant" believers; we will, instead, be growing Christians, striving each day to follow in the footsteps of God's Son.

So today, as you think about the impending birth of your baby, ask your Heavenly Father to keep remaking you. And then, take the next step of your spiritual journey secure in the knowledge that this day, like every other, will offer fresh opportunities to serve, to trust, and to grow.

A Quote for Today

You are either becoming more like Christ every day or you're becoming less like Him. There is no neutral position in the Lord.

—Stormie Omartian

Pregnancy Milestone for Today

_____

_____

_____

_____

_____

_____

HIS HEALING TOUCH

"I will give peace, real peace, to those far and near,
and I will heal them," says the Lord.
—Isaiah 57:19 NCV

As an expectant mom, you're vitally concerned with your own health, but you are even more concerned with the health of your baby. So, you're doing your best to eat healthy foods, to get enough rest, and to provide the best possible resources for your unborn child.

God is vitally concerned about every aspect of your life, including your health. And, when you face concerns of any sort—including pregnancy-related health challenges—God is with you.

So trust your medical doctors to do their part, and turn to your family and friends for moral, physical, and spiritual support. But don't be afraid to place your ultimate trust in your benevolent Heavenly Father. His healing touch, like His love, endures forever.

Pregnancy Milestone for Today

_____

_____

_____

_____

_____

_____

A Quote for Today

If you desire to improve your physical well-being and your emotional outlook, increasing your faith can help you.

—John Maxwell

THE COMMANDMENT
TO FORGIVE

Be merciful, just as your Father also is merciful.
—Luke 6:36 HCSB

Life would be much simpler if you could forgive people "once and for all" and be done with it. Yet forgiveness is seldom that easy. Usually, the decision to forgive is straightforward, but the process of forgiving is more difficult. Forgiveness is a journey that requires effort, time, perseverance, and prayer.

God instructs you to treat other people exactly as you wish to be treated. And since you want to be forgiven for the mistakes that you make, you must be willing to extend forgiveness to other people for the mistakes that they have made. If you can't seem to forgive someone, you should keep asking God to help you until you do. And you can be sure of this: if you keep asking for God's help, He will give it.

A Quote for Today

Forgiveness is rarely easy,
but it is always right.
—Cynthia Heald

Pregnancy Milestone
for Today

_____

_____

_____

_____

_____

_____

TAKING CARE OF YOURSELF

In thee, O Lord, do I put my trust; let me never be put into confusion.
—Psalm 71:1 KJV

As you prepare for the upcoming birth of your child, please take care of yourself. Pay careful attention to your physical health, to your emotional health, and to your spiritual health. Get enough rest. Spend more time with encouraging people and less time watching the discouraging mainstream media. Pray early and often. And, trust God to care for you and for your unborn child.

In a few days, you'll have a new baby and many new responsibilities. Until then, slow down if you can. You'll have plenty of work to do after the baby arrives.

A Quote for Today

Some of us would do more for the Lord if we did less.

—Vance Havner

Pregnancy Milestone for Today

_____

_____

_____

_____

_____

A Timely Tip

Oftentimes, feelings of frustration and fear are nothing more than exhaustion in disguise.
So when in doubt, get at least eight hours of sleep each night.

PICKING AND CHOOSING

It is the LORD your God you must follow, and him you must revere.
Keep his commands and obey him; serve him and hold fast to him.
—Deuteronomy 13:4 NIV

We are sorely tempted to pick and choose which of God's commandments we will obey and which of His commandments we will discard. But the Bible clearly instructs us to do otherwise.

God's Word commands us to obey all of His laws, not just the ones that are easy or convenient. When we do, we are blessed by a loving Heavenly Father.

John Calvin had this advice to believers of every generation, "Let us remember therefore this lesson: That to worship our God sincerely we must evermore begin by hearkening to His voice, and by giving ear to what He commands us. For if every person goes after his own way, we shall wander. We may well run, but we shall never be a whit nearer to the right way, but rather farther away from it." Enough said!

A Quote for Today

We cannot be led by our emotions
and still be led by the Holy Spirit,
so we have to make a choice.

—Joyce Meyer

Pregnancy Milestone for Today

_____

_____

_____

_____

_____

_____

SMILE

Jacob said, "For what a relief it is to see your friendly smile.
It is like seeing the smile of God!"
—Genesis 33:10 NLT

A smile is nourishment for the heart, and laughter is medicine for the soul—but sometimes, amid the stresses of the day, we forget to take our medicine. Instead of viewing our world with a mixture of optimism and humor, we allow worries and distractions to rob us of the joy that God intends for our lives.

As an expectant mom, you have so much to be thankful for. But, you may also have a wide array of aches, pains, twinges, throbs, and discomforts . . . along with countless opportunities to complain.

The next time you find yourself dwelling upon the negatives of your pregnancy, refocus your attention to things positive. The next time you find yourself falling prey to the blight of pessimism, stop yourself and turn your thoughts around. With God as your protector and Christ as your Savior, you're blessed now and forever. So smile!

Pregnancy Milestone for Today

_____

_____

_____

_____

_____

_____

A Timely Tip

There is usually some humor in every situation. Look for it.

A GIFT BEYOND COMPREHENSION

Therefore, since we are receiving a kingdom that cannot be shaken,
let us hold on to grace. By it, we may serve God acceptably,
with reverence and awe.
—Hebrews 12:28 HCSB

The grace of God overflows from His heart. And if we open our hearts to Him, we receive His grace, and we are blessed with joy, abundance, peace, and eternal life.

The familiar words of Ephesians 2:8 make God's promise perfectly clear: "For by grace you have been saved through faith, and that not of yourselves; it is the gift of God" (NKJV). We are saved, not by our actions but by God's mercy. We are saved, not because of our good deeds but because of our faith in Christ.

God's grace is the ultimate gift, a gift beyond comprehension and beyond compare. And because it is the ultimate gift, we owe God the ultimate in thanksgiving.

God's grace is indeed a gift from the heart—God's heart. And as believers, we must accept God's precious gift thankfully, humbly, and immediately—today is never too soon because tomorrow may be too late.

A Quote for Today

The Christian life is motivated,
not by a list of do's and don'ts,
but by the gracious outpouring of
God's love and blessing.
—Anne Graham Lotz

Pregnancy Milestone for Today

_____

_____

_____

_____

_____

_____

FINDING HAPPINESS AND ABUNDANCE

Praise the Lord! Happy are those who respect the Lord,
who want what he commands.
—Psalm 112:1 NCV

Do you seek happiness, abundance, and contentment? If so, here are some things you should do: Love God and His Son; depend upon God for strength; try, to the best of your abilities, to follow God's will; and strive to obey His Holy Word. When you do these things, you'll discover that happiness goes hand-in-hand with righteousness. The happiest people are not those who rebel against God; the happiest people are those who love God and obey His commandments.

What does life have in store for you and your unborn child? A world full of possibilities (of course it's up to you to seize them), and God's promise of abundance (of course it's up to you to accept it). So, as you embark upon the next phase of your journey—and as you prepare for the birth of your baby—remember to celebrate the life that God has given you. Your Creator has blessed you beyond measure. Honor Him with your prayers, your words, your deeds, and your joy.

Pregnancy Milestone for Today

_____

_____

_____

_____

_____

_____

A Quote for Today

Christ is the secret, the source, the substance, the center, and the circumference of all true and lasting gladness.
—Mrs. Charles E. Cowman

THE ULTIMATE GIFT

Thanks be to God for his indescribable gift!
—2 Corinthians 9:15 NIV

Christ died on the cross so that we might have eternal life. This gift, freely given from God's only Son, is the priceless possession of everyone who accepts Him as Lord and Savior.

Thankfully, God's grace is not an earthly reward for righteous behavior; it is, instead, a blessed spiritual gift. When we accept Christ into our hearts, we are saved by His grace. The familiar words from the book of Ephesians make God's promise perfectly clear: "For it is by grace you have been saved, through faith—and this not from yourselves, it is the gift of God—not by works, so that no one can boast" (2:8-9 NIV).

God's grace is the ultimate gift, and we owe Him our eternal gratitude. Our Heavenly Father is waiting patiently for each of us to accept His Son and receive His grace. Let us accept that gift today so that we might enjoy God's presence now and throughout all eternity.

A Quote for Today

If you are a believer, your judgment will not determine your eternal destiny. Christ's finished work on Calvary was applied to you the moment you accepted Christ as Savior.

—Beth Moore

Pregnancy Milestone for Today

_____

_____

_____

_____

_____

GOD'S GUIDEBOOK

All Scripture is given by inspiration of God, and is profitable for doctrine,
for reproof, for correction, for instruction in righteousness, that the man
of God may be complete, thoroughly equipped for every good work.
—2 Timothy 3:16-17 NKJV

God has given us a guidebook for righteous living called the Holy Bible. It contains thorough instructions which, if followed, lead to fulfillment, righteousness, and salvation. But, if we choose to ignore God's commandments, the results are as predictable as they are tragic.

God has given us the Bible for the purpose of knowing His promises, His power, His commandments, His wisdom, His love, and His Son. As we study God's teachings and apply them to our lives, we live by the Word that shall never pass away.

Today, let us follow God's commandments, and let us conduct our lives in such a way that we might be shining examples to our students, to our families, and, most importantly, to those who have not yet found Christ.

Pregnancy Milestone for Today

_____

_____

_____

_____

_____

_____

A Quote for Today

The balance of affirmation and discipline, freedom and restraint, encouragement and warning is different for each child and season and generation, yet the absolutes of God's Word are necessary and trustworthy no matter how mercuric the time.
—Gloria Gaither

THE PLAN FOR YOUR LIFE

The plans of hard-working people earn a profit,
but those who act too quickly become poor.
—Proverbs 21:5 NCV

Perhaps you have a clearly defined plan for the future, but even if you don't, rest assured that God does. God's has a definite plan for every aspect of your life. Your challenge is straightforward: to sincerely pray for God's guidance, and to obediently follow the guidance you receive.

If you're burdened by the demands of everyday life here in the 21st century, you are not alone. Life is difficult at times, and uncertain. But of this you can be sure: God has a plan for you and yours. He will communicate His plans using the Holy Spirit, His Holy Word, and your own conscience. So listen to God's voice and be watchful for His signs: He will send you messages every day of your life, including this one. Your job is to listen, to learn, to trust, and to act.

A Quote for Today

The only way you can experience
abundant life is to surrender
your plans to Him.
—Charles Stanley

Pregnancy Milestone for Today

_____

_____

_____

_____

_____

_____

GOD'S TO-DO LIST

Be energetic in your life of salvation, reverent and sensitive before God.
That energy is God's energy, an energy deep within you, God himself
willing and working at what will give him the most pleasure.
—Philippians 2:12-13 MSG

As the expectant mother of a newborn, with too many demands and too few hours in which to meet them, you'll be tempted to complain. And, you'll be tempted to feel sorry for yourself. And, you'll be tempted to respond to your family with a little more anger—and a little less compassion—than usual. Please resist those temptations. After all, motherhood is not only one of the world's most demanding jobs; it is, when done right, the world's most rewarding job.

So, instead of focusing on the expected challenges of motherhood, focus upon God's unending love for you and for your baby. Then, ask Him for the strength you need to fulfill your responsibilities. God will give you the energy to do the most important things on today's to-do list if you ask Him. So ask Him.

Pregnancy Milestone for Today

_____

_____

_____

_____

_____

_____

A Quote for Today

When the dream of our heart is
one that God has planted there,
a strange happiness flows into us.
At that moment, all of the spiritual
resources of the universe are released
to help us. Our praying is then
at one with the will of God and
becomes a channel for the Creator's
purposes for us and our world.

—Catherine Marshall

PRAYING FOR THE "PERFECT" BABY

Our Father which art in heaven, hallowed be thy name.
Thy kingdom come, thy will be done in earth, as it is in heaven.
—Matthew 6:9-10 KJV

Like all mothers, you want your baby to be happy, healthy, and perfect in every way. And of this you can be sure: your baby will, indeed, be perfect in the eyes of God.

Today, trust God in every aspect of your life, and trust that His plans are perfect for you and for your unborn baby. Don't worry about the things you cannot control—leave them up to God. Don't concern yourself with the unknowable future—entrust it to the Father. Don't fret about the inevitable ups and downs of everyday life—remember that God is in control. And, remember that His plans, like your baby, are perfect.

A Quote for Today

There is an active practice of holiness as we carry out, for the glory of God, the ordinary duties of each day, faithfully fulfilling the responsibilities given us. The passive practice consists in loving acceptance of the unexpected, be it welcome or unwelcome, remembering that we have a wise and sovereign Lord who works in mysterious ways and is never taken by surprise.

—Elisabeth Elliot

Pregnancy Milestone for Today

_____

_____

_____

_____

_____

KEEPING COSTS IN PERSPECTIVE

*For the love of money is a root of all kinds of evil, and by craving it,
some have wandered away from the faith and pierced
themselves with many pains.*

—1 Timothy 6:10 HCSB

Having a baby can be expensive. Very expensive. But, as a Christian, you understand that money should be used, but not worshipped. Popular opinion to the contrary, money cannot buy happiness, period.

Money, in and of itself, is not evil; but the worship of money inevitably leads to trouble. So today, as you prioritize matters of importance for you and yours (and as you contemplate the high costs of health care), remember that God is almighty, but the dollar is not.

A Quote for Today

Have you prayed about your resources lately? Find out how God wants you to use your time and your money. No matter what it costs, forsake all that is not of God.

—Kay Arthur

Pregnancy Milestone for Today

_____

_____

_____

_____

_____

_____

CALMING YOUR NERVES, ALLAYING YOUR FEARS

I sought the Lord, and He answered me and delivered me
from all my fears.
—Psalm 34:4 HCSB

As the Big Day draws near, your nerves may begin to fray and your supply of patience may begin to dwindle. If you find yourself caught up in a web of worry, it's time to slow down and find a quiet place where you can talk to God.

Prayer has a way of quieting your soul. When you share your concerns with the Creator, and when you listen carefully for His response, you will be comforted. When you take the time to thank God for His incalculable gifts, you'll soon realize that your problems are temporary, but His love is eternal.

So, the next time you become discouraged by the inevitable demands of pregnancy, have a little chat with God. He's always available, always ready to listen, always ready to help.

A Quote for Today

Do not build up obstacles in your imagination. Difficulties must be studied and dealt with, but they must not be magnified by fear.

—Norman Vincent Peale

Pregnancy Milestone for Today

_____

_____

_____

_____

_____

_____

WHAT NOW, LORD?

For we are His making, created in Christ Jesus for good works, which
God prepared ahead of time so that we should walk in them.
—Ephesians 2:10 HCSB

God has things He wants you to do and places He wants you to go. The most important decision of your life is, of course, your commitment to accept Jesus Christ as your personal Lord and Savior. And, once your eternal destiny is secured, you will undoubtedly ask yourself the question "What now, Lord?" If you earnestly seek God's will for your life, you will find it . . . in time.

Because you are an expectant mother, you have special responsibilities. As you prayerfully consider God's path for your life, you should study His Word and be ever watchful for His signs. You should associate with fellow believers who will encourage your spiritual growth, and you should listen to that inner voice that speaks to you in the quiet moments of your daily devotionals.

Rest assured: God is here, and He intends to use you in wonderful, unexpected ways. He desires to lead you—and your unborn child—along a path of His choosing. Your challenge is to watch, to listen . . . and to follow.

Pregnancy Milestone for Today

_____

_____

_____

_____

_____

_____

A Quote for Today

It is God to whom and with whom
we travel, while He is the End
of our journey, He is also at
every stopping place.
—Elisabeth Elliot

INFINITE POSSIBILITIES

All things are possible for the one who believes.
—Mark 9:23 NCV

We live in a world of infinite possibilities. But sometimes, because of limited faith and limited understanding, we wrongly assume that God cannot or will not intervene in the affairs of mankind. Such assumptions are simply wrong.

Are you afraid to ask God to do big things for you or for your baby? As you've invested so much energy during your pregnancy, have you become discouraged about your future or your faith? If so, it's time to abandon your doubts and reclaim your faith—faith in yourself, faith in your abilities, faith in your family, faith in your future, and faith in your Heavenly Father.

Catherine Marshall notes that, "God specializes in things thought impossible." And make no mistake: God can help you do things you never dreamed possible . . . your job is to let Him.

A Quote for Today

There is Someone who makes possible what seems completely impossible.
—Catherine Marshall

Pregnancy Milestone for Today

_____

_____

_____

_____

_____

WORSHIPPING THE CHRIST CHILD

For there is born to you this day in the city of David a Savior,
who is Christ the Lord. And this will be the sign to you: You will find
a Babe wrapped in swaddling cloths, lying in a manger.
—Luke 2:11-12 NKJV

As you contemplate the birth of your own child, think for a moment about the birth of the Christ child. God sent His Son to transform the world and to save it. Jesus was born in the most humble of circumstances: in a nondescript village, to parents of simple means, far from the seats of earthly power.

God sent His Son, not as a conqueror or a king, but as an innocent babe. Jesus came, not to be served, but to serve. Jesus did not preach a message of retribution or revenge; He spoke words of compassion and forgiveness. We must do our best to imitate Him.

In the second chapter of Luke, we read about shepherds who were tending their flocks on the night Christ was born. May we, like those shepherds of old, leave our fields—wherever they may be—and pause to worship God's priceless gift: His only begotten Son.

Pregnancy Milestone for Today

_____

_____

_____

_____

_____

_____

A Quote for Today

Christ, the Son of God, the complete embodiment of God's Word, came among us. He looked on humanity's losing battle with sin and pitched His divine tent in the middle of the camp so that He could dwell among us.

—Beth Moore

WELCOMING YOUR NEW BABY

He put a child in the middle of the room. Then, cradling the little one in his arms, he said, "Whoever embraces one of these children as I do embraces me, and far more than me—God who sent me."
—Mark 9:36-37 MSG

As you look upon your baby's face for the first time, and as feelings of joy flood over you, it's time to praise God for the miracle of birth and for the miracle of His love. How precious are God's gifts, and how great are His blessings!

You know the profound love that you hold in your heart for your new baby. But, you can scarcely imagine the infinite love that your heavenly Father holds in His heart for you and your child. God's love is boundless and eternal.

Today, while you're celebrating the birth of your baby, take time to praise the Creator for more blessings than you can count and for a love that endures forever.

A Quote for Today

There is no more influential or powerful role on earth than a mother's.
—Charles Swindoll

A Timely Tip

You and your baby are protected by God . . . now and always. God is in control of our world . . . and your world.

Mommy Milestone for Today

_____

_____

_____

_____

_____

Praying for Your New Baby

Let the words of my mouth and the meditation of my heart
be acceptable in Your sight, O Lord, my strength and my Redeemer.
—Psalm 19:14 NKJV

As the mother of a newborn, you have many things to pray for: wisdom, strength, and patience, for starters. But first and foremost, you'll be praying for your baby.

When your baby was born, God presented you with an incredible gift and a profound responsibility. And God also promises to give you everything you'll need to fulfill your responsibilities if you ask Him.

Today, ask God to protect your baby and guide your steps. When you ask, He will respond. And, when the Creator of the universe responds, both you and your child will be blessed.

A Quote for Today

A person who has a praying mother
has a most cherished possession.

—Billy Graham

Mommy Milestone
for Today

_____

_____

_____

_____

_____

_____

PRAYING FOR YOUR FAMILY

Unless the Lord builds the house, they labor in vain who build it;
unless the Lord guards the city, the watchman stays awake in vain.
—Psalm 127:1 NKJV

Your most prized earthly possession is not your home, your car, or your savings account. Your most prized earthly possession is, of course, your family.

Your family is a priceless gift from God. Treasure it, protect it, and dedicate it to Him. When you place God at the center of your clan, He will bless you and yours forever.

Today, take a few extra minutes to pray for every member of your immediate family. Ask God to bless them and keep them in the palm of His hand. And then, after you've finished your prayers, expect the Creator of the universe to answer them in His own way and in His own time.

A Quote for Today

Praying for our children is a noble task. If what we are doing, in this fast-paced society, is taking away from our prayer time for our children, we're doing too much.
—Max Lucado

Mommy Milestone for Today

_____

_____

_____

_____

_____

THANKING GOD FOR YOUR BABY

Our prayers for you are always spilling over into thanksgivings.
We can't quit thanking God our Father and Jesus our Messiah for you!
—Colossians 1:3 MSG

As the mother of a newborn, you have every reason to praise God for the priceless gift He has entrusted to your care. And what a glorious gift it is!

Every good gift comes from God, and we owe Him our unending thanksgiving. Yet sometimes, when the demands of everyday life seem overwhelming, we may not pause long enough to thank our Creator for His countless blessings.

As Christians whose salvation has been purchased on the cross, we are blessed beyond measure. So we should constantly praise the Father for gifts that are simply too wonderful to fully comprehend. Yes, we owe God everything, including our eternal praise . . . starting now.

Mommy Milestone for Today

_____

_____

_____

_____

_____

A Quote for Today

It is always possible to be thankful for what is given rather than to complain about what is not given. One or the other becomes a habit of life.

—Elisabeth Elliot

The Rock That Cannot Be Shaken

Give your burdens to the Lord, and he will take care of you.
He will not permit the godly to slip and fall.
—Psalm 55:22 NLT

As the mother of a newborn, you have responsibilities that don't stop. Your baby has urgent needs from dawn until dusk and from dusk until dawn. And it's up to you to provide those needs. Sometimes, the responsibilities seem overwhelming. But, with God's help, you can meet the challenges of motherhood and still have energy to spare.

God's Word instructs us to give our burdens to Him. When we do, He steadies our steps and prevents us from stumbling. So, when you are troubled, or weak, or discouraged, remember that God is as near as your next breath. Build your life and your family on the rock that cannot be shaken: trust in God. He has promised to lift life's burdens from your shoulders, and He always keeps His promises.

A Quote for Today

When we reach the end of our abilities, God's possibilities are just beginning.

—Emilie Barnes

Mommy Milestone for Today

_____

_____

_____

_____

_____

MESSAGES TO YOURSELF

Happy is the person who finds wisdom, the one who gets understanding.
—Proverbs 3:13 NCV

Hey Mom, what are you telling yourself about yourself? When you look in the mirror, are you staring back at your biggest booster or your harshest critic?

If you can learn to give yourself the benefit of the doubt—if you can learn how to have constructive conversations with the person you see in the mirror—then your self-respect will tend to take care of itself. But, if you're constantly berating yourself—if you're constantly telling yourself that you can't measure up—then you'll find that self-respect is always in short supply.

If you've acquired the habit of thinking constructively about yourself and your circumstances, congratulations. But if you're mired in the mental quicksand of overly self-critical thoughts, it's time to change your thoughts . . . and your life.

Mommy Milestone for Today

_____

_____

_____

_____

_____

_____

A Timely Tip

God loves you for who you are, not because of the things you've done. So open your heart to God's love . . . when you do, you'll feel better about everything, including yourself.

BUSY WITH OUR THOUGHTS

People's thoughts can be like a deep well,
but someone with understanding can find the wisdom there.
—Proverbs 20:5 NCV

Because we are human, we are always busy with our thoughts. We simply can't help ourselves. Our brains never shut off, and even while we're sleeping, we mull things over in our minds. The question is not if we will think; the question is how will we think and what will we think about.

Today, focus your thoughts on God and His will. And if you've been plagued by pessimism and doubt, stop thinking like that! Place your faith in God and give thanks for His blessings. Think optimistically about your world, your life, your future, and your baby. It's the wise way to use your mind. And besides, since you will always be busy with your thoughts, you might as well make those thoughts pleasing (to God) and helpful (to you and yours).

A Quote for Today

Occupy your minds with good thoughts, or the enemy will fill them with bad ones. Unoccupied, they cannot be.

—St. Thomas More

Mommy Milestone for Today

_____

_____

_____

_____

_____

_____

ETERNAL LIFE: GOD'S PRICELESS GIFT

Jesus said, "Everyone who drinks from this water will get thirsty again. But whoever drinks from the water that I will give him will never get thirsty again—ever! In fact, the water I will give him will become a well of water springing up within him for eternal life."
—John 4:13-14 HCSB

Your ability to envision the future, like your life here on earth, is limited. God's vision, however, is not burdened by any such limitations. He sees all things, He knows all things, and His plans for you and your family endure for all time.

God's plans are not limited to the events of life here on earth. Your Heavenly Father has bigger things in mind for you and your loved ones . . . much bigger things. So praise the Creator for the gift of eternal life and share the Good News with all who cross your path. You have given your heart to the Son, so you belong to the Father—today, tomorrow, and for all eternity.

Mommy Milestone for Today

_____

_____

_____

_____

_____

_____

A Quote for Today

Jesus came down from heaven, revealing exactly what God is like, offering eternal life and a personal relationship with God, on the condition of our rebirth—a rebirth made possible through His own death on the cross.

—Anne Graham Lotz

AROUND-THE-CLOCK RESPONSIBILITIES

Be strong and brave, and do the work. Don't be afraid or discouraged,
because the Lord God, my God, is with you.
He will not fail you or leave you.
—1 Chronicles 28:20 NCV

Caring for a newborn baby is not a nine-to-five job. It's an around-the-clock marathon that can sap your strength and cloud your thoughts.

Are you having trouble adjusting to your baby's schedule? If so, perhaps you're relying too much on your own resources and not enough on God's resources. After all, God has promised to give you the things you need if you ask for them (Matthew 7:7-8). But, it's your duty to ask.

Hannah Whitall Smith observed, "God will help us become the people we are meant to be, if only we will ask Him." Today, be quick to ask the Father for the things you need. He's listening carefully, and He wants to hear from you right now.

A Quote for Today

People who say they sleep like
a baby usually don't have one.

—Anonymous

Mommy Milestone for Today

_____

_____

_____

_____

_____

YOUR JOURNEY CONTINUES

I've told you these things for a purpose: that my joy might be your joy,
and your joy wholly mature.
—John 15:11 MSG

Complete spiritual maturity is never achieved in a day, or in a year, or even in a lifetime. The journey toward spiritual maturity is an ongoing process that continues, day by day, throughout every stage of life. Every stage of life has its opportunities and its challenges, and if we're wise, we continue to seek God's guidance as each new chapter of life unfolds.

As the mother of a newborn, you have a profound responsibility to care for your child and to care for yourself. Sometimes, you'll spend so much time on the former that you'll have precious little time for the latter. But, even if you're the busiest mom on the planet, you should still carve out a few moments each day for Bible-reading and for reflection.

If you focus your thoughts—and attune your heart—to the will of God, you can make each day another stage in your spiritual journey . . . and that's precisely what God intends for you to do.

Mommy Milestone
for Today

_____

_____

_____

_____

_____

_____

A Quote for Today

We look at our burdens and heavy loads, and we shrink from them. But, if we lift them and bind them about our hearts, they become wings, and on them we can rise and soar toward God.
—Mrs. Charles E. Cowman

HE IS LOVE

God is love, and the one who remains in love remains in God,
and God remains in him.

—1 John 4:16 HCSB

God is love. It's a sweeping statement, a profoundly important description of what God is and how God works. God's love is perfect. When we open our hearts to His perfect love, we are touched by the Creator's hand, and we are transformed.

Barbara Johnson observed, "We cannot protect ourselves from trouble, but we can dance through the puddles of life with a rainbow smile, twirling the only umbrella we need—the umbrella of God's love."

And the English mystical writer Juliana of Norwich noted, "We are so preciously loved by God that we cannot even comprehend it. No created being can ever know how much and how sweetly and tenderly God loves them."

So today, even if you can only carve out a few quiet moments, offer sincere prayers of thanksgiving to your Father. Thank Him for His blessings and His love.

A Quote for Today

Love has its source in God, for love
is the very essence of His being.

—Kay Arthur

Mommy Milestone
for Today

_____

_____

_____

_____

_____

THE PATH HE WALKED

Therefore as you have received Christ Jesus the Lord, walk in Him.
—Colossians 2:6 HCSB

Today, you will take one more step on your life's journey. Today offers one more opportunity to seek God's will and to follow it. Today has the potential to be a time of praise, a time of thanksgiving, and a time of spiritual abundance. The coming day is a canvas upon which you can compose a beautiful work of art as you care for your baby.

If you choose to follow in the footsteps of the One from Galilee, you will continue to mature every day of your life. If you choose to walk along the path that was first walked by Jesus, your life will become a masterpiece, a powerful work of art, and a tribute to your Savior. So today, as a gift to yourself, to your baby, to your loved ones, and to your God, walk the path that Jesus walked.

A Quote for Today

The Christian faith is meant to be lived moment by moment. It isn't some broad, general outline—it's a long walk with a real Person. Details count: passing thoughts, small sacrifices, a few encouraging words, little acts of kindness, brief victories over nagging sins.

—Joni Eareckson Tada

Mommy Milestone for Today

_____

_____

_____

_____

_____

_____

OUR MERCIFUL FATHER

You know the Lord is full of mercy and is kind.
—James 5:11 NCV

God's hand offers forgiveness and salvation. God's mercy, like His love, is infinite and everlasting—it knows no boundaries. As a demonstration of His mercy, God sent His only Son to die for our sins, and we must praise our Creator for that priceless gift.

Romans 3:23 reminds us of a universal truth: "All have sinned, and come short of the glory of God" (KJV). All of us, even the most righteous among us, are sinners. But despite our imperfections, our merciful Father in heaven offers us salvation through the person of His Son.

As Christians, we have been blessed by a merciful, loving God. May we accept His mercy. And may we, in turn, show love and mercy to our friends, to our families, and to all whom He chooses to place along our paths.

A Quote for Today

Our forgiveness toward others
should flow from a realization
and appreciation of
God's forgiveness toward us.
—Franklin Graham

Mommy Milestone for Today

_____

_____

_____

_____

_____

HELPFUL WORDS

Careful words make for a careful life;
careless talk may ruin everything.
—Proverbs 13:3 MSG

This world can be a difficult place, a place where many of our friends and family members are troubled by the inevitable challenges of everyday life. And since we can never be certain who needs our help, we should be careful to speak helpful words to everybody who crosses our paths.

In the book of Ephesians, Paul writes, "Do not let any unwholesome talk come out of your mouths, but only what is helpful for building others up according to their needs, that it may benefit those who listen" (4:29 NIV). Paul reminds us that when we choose our words carefully, we can have a powerful impact on those around us.

Today, let's share kind words, smiles, encouragement, and hugs with family, with friends, and with the world.

Mommy Milestone for Today

_____

_____

_____

_____

_____

_____

A Quote for Today

When you talk, choose the very same words that you would use if Jesus were looking over your shoulder. Because He is.

—Marie T. Freeman

BE TRANSFORMED

*And do not be conformed to this world, but be transformed by
the renewing of your mind, that you may prove what is that good and
acceptable and perfect will of God.*
—Romans 12:2 NKJV

Moms who fashion their days around Jesus are transformed: They see the world differently; they act differently, and they feel differently about themselves, their babies, and their neighbors.

The Christian faith is an optimistic faith. So, thoughtful believers face the inevitable challenges and disappointments of each day armed with the joy of Christ and the promise of salvation.

Whatever this day holds for you, begin it and end it with God as your partner and Christ as your guide. And throughout the day, give thanks to the One who, in His infinite wisdom, gave you a priceless gift: your new baby. God's love for you and your child is infinite. Praise Him, and be thankful.

A Quote for Today

For God is, indeed, a wonderful
Father who longs to pour out His
mercy upon us, and whose majesty is
so great that He can transform
us from deep within.
—St. Teresa of Avila

Mommy Milestone
for Today

_____

_____

_____

_____

_____

DEFINING SUCCESS

If you do not stand firm in your faith, then you will not stand at all.
—Isaiah 7:9 HCSB

How do you define success? Do you define it as the accumulation of material possessions or the adulation of your neighbors? If so, you need to reorder your priorities. Genuine success has little to do with fame or fortune; it has everything to do with God's gift of love and His promise of salvation.

If you have accepted Christ as your personal Savior, you are already a towering success in the eyes of God, but there is still more that you can do. Your task—as a new mom who has been touched by the Creator's grace—is to accept the spiritual abundance and peace that He offers through the person of His Son. Then, you can share the healing message of God's love and His abundance with a world that desperately needs both. When you do, you have reached the pinnacle of success.

Mommy Milestone for Today

_____

_____

_____

_____

_____

_____

A Quote for Today

Nothing I can do will make me special. No awards I can earn will make me a better person.
The taproot of my being grows in the rich soil of the being of Christ instead of in the shifting sands of worldly accomplishment.
—Leslie Williams

SOLVING LIFE'S RIDDLES

But the wisdom from above is first pure, then peace-loving, gentle,
compliant, full of mercy and good fruits, without favoritism and hypocrisy.
—James 3:17 HCSB

Life presents each of us with countless questions, conundrums, doubts, and problems. Thankfully, the riddles of everyday living are not too difficult to solve if we look for answers in the right places. When we have questions, we should consult God's Word, we should seek the guidance of the Holy Spirit, and we should trust the counsel of God-fearing friends and family members.

Motherhood is an adventure in decision-making. Are you facing one of those difficult decisions? Take your concerns to God and avail yourself of the messages and mentors that He has placed along your path. When you do, God will speak to you in His own way and in His own time, and when He does, you can most certainly trust the answers that He gives.

A Quote for Today

Choices can change our lives profoundly. The choice to mend a broken relationship, to say "yes" to a difficult assignment, to lay aside some important work to play with a child, to visit some forgotten person—these small choices may affect many lives eternally.
—Gloria Gaither

A Question to Think On

Do you make it a habit to pray about big decisions?

Mommy Milestone for Today

_____

_____

_____

_____

_____

HE TAUGHT US TO BE GENEROUS

I have shown you in every way, by laboring like this,
that you must support the weak. And remember the words
of the Lord Jesus, that He said,
"It is more blessed to give than to receive."
—Acts 20:35 NKJV

The thread of generosity is woven—completely and inextricably—into the very fabric of Christ's teachings. As He sent His disciples out to heal the sick and spread God's message of salvation, Jesus offered this guiding principle: "Freely you have received, freely give" (Matthew 10:8 NIV). The principle still applies. If we are to be disciples of Christ, we must give freely of our time, our possessions, and our love. All of us have been blessed, and all of us are called to share those blessings without reservation.

Today, Mom, make this pledge and keep it: Be a cheerful, generous, courageous giver. The world needs your help, and you need the spiritual rewards that will be yours when you share your possessions, your talents, and your time.

Mommy Milestone for Today

_____

_____

_____

_____

_____

A Quote for Today

What is your focus today?
Joy comes when it is Jesus first,
others second . . . then you.

—Kay Arthur

THE BREAD OF LIFE

Then Jesus declared, "I am the bread of life.
He who comes to me will never go hungry,
and he who believes in me will never be thirsty."
—John 6:35 NIV

Who's the best friend this world has ever had? Jesus, of course. And when you form a life-altering relationship with Him, He will be your best friend, too.

Jesus was born into humble circumstances. He walked this earth, not as a ruler of men but as the Savior of mankind. His crucifixion, a torturous punishment that was intended to end His life and His reign, instead became the pivotal event in the history of all humanity.

Jesus is the bread of life. Accept His grace. Share His love with your new baby and with the world. And then follow in His footsteps today, tomorrow, and forever.

A Quote for Today

When we are in a situation where Jesus is all we have, we soon discover he is all we really need.
—Gigi Graham Tchividjian

A Timely Tip

Jesus is the light of the world. Make sure that you are capturing and reflecting His light.

Mommy Milestone for Today

_____

_____

_____

_____

_____

MOUNTAIN-MOVING FAITH

I assure you: If anyone says to this mountain,
"Be lifted up and thrown into the sea," and does not doubt in his heart,
but believes that what he says will happen, it will be done for him.
—Mark 11:23 HCSB

Are you a mother whose faith is evident for all to see? Do you trust God's promises without reservation, or do you question His promises without hesitation?

Every life—including yours—is a series of successes and failures, celebrations and disappointments, joys and sorrows. Every step of the way, through every triumph and tragedy, God will stand by your side and strengthen you . . . if you have faith in Him.

Jesus taught His disciples that if they had faith, they could move mountains. You can, too, and so can your family. But you must have faith. So today and every day, trust your Heavenly Father, praise the sacrifice of His Son . . . and then let the mountain-moving begin.

Mommy Milestone for Today

_____

_____

_____

_____

_____

_____

A Quote for Today

Faith is deliberate confidence in the character of God, whose ways you cannot understand at the time.
—Oswald Chambers

HONORING GOD

Honor the Lord with your possessions, and with the firstfruits
of all your increase; so your barns will be filled with plenty.
—Proverbs 3:9-10 NKJV

Whom will you choose to honor today? If you honor God and place Him at the center of your life, every day is a cause for celebration. But if you fail to honor your Heavenly Father, you're asking for trouble, and lots of it.

As the mother of a newborn, your life is probably hectic, demanding, and complicated. When the demands of motherhood leave you rushing from place to place with scarcely a moment to spare, you may fail to pause and thank your Creator for the blessings He has bestowed upon you. But that's a big mistake.

Do you sincerely seek to be a worthy servant of the One who has given you eternal love and eternal life? Then honor Him for who He is and for what He has done for you. And don't just honor Him on Sunday morning. Praise Him all day long, every day, for as long as you live . . . and then for all eternity.

A Quote for Today

The greatest honor you can give
Almighty God is to live gladly
and joyfully because of
the knowledge of His love.
—Juliana of Norwich

Mommy Milestone
for Today

_____

_____

_____

_____

_____

_____

HE DOES NOT CHANGE

One Lord, one faith, one baptism, one God and Father of all,
who is above all and through all and in all.
—Ephesians 4:5-6 HCSB

We live in a world that is always changing, but we worship a God that never changes—thank goodness! As believers, we can be comforted in the knowledge that our Heavenly Father is the rock that simply cannot be moved: "I am the Lord, I do not change" (Malachi 3:6 NKJV).

Because you're a new mom, your life has been transformed by a miraculous gift from God: your baby. But, caring for that gift can be exhausting. Please remember that caring for your child is a temporary assignment from God, but that the rewards of motherhood last a lifetime, and beyond.

So, instead of worrying about today's inevitable challenges, put your faith in the Father and His only begotten Son: "Jesus Christ is the same yesterday, today, and forever" (Hebrews 13:8 HCSB). And rest assured: It is precisely because your Savior does not change that you can face your challenges with courage for this day and hope for the future.

Mommy Milestone for Today

_____

_____

_____

_____

_____

_____

A Quote for Today

Let nothing disturb you, nothing frighten you; all things are passing; God never changes.

—St. Teresa of Avila

FIRST, PLEASE GOD

*Everything that goes into a life of pleasing God has been miraculously
given to us by getting to know, personally and intimately,
the One who invited us to God. The best invitation we ever received!*
—2 Peter 1:3 MSG

When God created you, He equipped you with an assortment of talents and abilities that are uniquely yours. It's up to you to discover those talents and to use them, but the world may encourage you to do otherwise. At times, society will attempt to pigeonhole you, to standardize you, to distract you, and to make you fit into a particular, preformed mold. Perhaps God has other plans.

At times, because you're an imperfect human being, you may become so wrapped up in meeting society's expectations that you fail to focus on God's expectations.

Who will you try to please today: God or society? Your primary obligation is not to please imperfect men, women, children, or babies. Your obligation is to strive diligently to meet the expectations of your perfect Heavenly Father. So today and every day, put God first. When you do, everything else has a way of falling into place.

A Quote for Today

If you are receiving your affirmation,
love, self-worth, joy, strength and
acceptance from anywhere but God,
He will shake it.
—Lisa Bevere

Mommy Milestone for Today

_____

_____

_____

_____

_____

ACCEPTING HIS ABUNDANCE

*Live in me. Make your home in me just as I do in you. In the same way
that a branch can't bear grapes by itself but only by being joined to
the vine, you can't bear fruit unless you are joined with me.
I am the Vine, you are the branches. When you're joined with me
and I with you, the relation intimate and organic,
the harvest is sure to be abundant.*

—John 15:4-5 MSG

Are you the kind of woman who accepts God's spiritual abundance without reservation? If so, you are availing yourself of the peace and the joy that He has promised. Do you sincerely seek the riches that our Savior offers to those who give themselves to Him? Then follow Him. When you do, you will receive the love and the abundance that Jesus offers to those who follow Him.

Seek first the salvation that is available through a personal, passionate relationship with Christ, and then claim the joy, the peace, and the spiritual abundance that the Shepherd offers His sheep.

Mommy Milestone for Today

_____

_____

_____

_____

_____

_____

A Quote for Today

God loves you and wants you
to experience peace and life—
abundant and eternal.

—Billy Graham

THE MERRY-GO-ROUND

I will give you a new heart and put a new spirit within you.
—Ezekiel 36:26 HCSB

God intends that His children lead joyous lives filled with abundance and peace. But sometimes, as all mothers can attest, abundance and peace seem very far away. It is then that we must turn to God for renewal, and when we do, He will restore us.

As the mother of a new baby, you need energy, and lots of it. Have you "tapped in" to the power of God, or are you muddling along under your own power? If you are weary, worried, fretful, or fearful, then it is time to turn to a strength much greater than your own.

The Bible tells us that we can do all things through the power of our risen Savior, Jesus Christ. Our challenge, then, is clear: we must place Christ where He belongs—at the very center of our lives.

Are you tired or troubled? Turn your heart toward God in prayer. Are you weak or worried? Make the time to delve deeply into God's Holy Word. When you do, you'll discover that the Creator of the universe stands ready and able to create a new sense of wonderment and joy in you.

A Quote for Today

In those desperate times when we feel like we don't have an ounce of strength, He will gently pick up our heads so that our eyes can behold something—something that will keep His hope alive in us.
—Kathy Troccoli

Mommy Milestone for Today

_____

_____

_____

_____

_____

AND THE GREATEST OF THESE

*Love is patient, love is kind and is not jealous; love does not brag and is
not arrogant, does not act unbecomingly; it does not seek its own,
is not provoked, does not take into account a wrong suffered, does not
rejoice in unrighteousness, but rejoices with the truth; bears all things,
believes all things, hopes all things, endures all things.*

—1 Corinthians 13:4-7 NASB

Corrie ten Boom advised, "Live your lives in love, the same sort of love which Christ gives us, and which He perfectly expressed when He gave Himself as a sacrifice to God." And, Vonette Bright correctly observed that, "Living life with a consistent spiritual walk deeply influences those we love most." Today, as you contemplate next steps in your own spiritual walk, remember the the beautiful words of 1st Corinthians 13: "But now abide faith, hope, love, these three; but the greatest of these is love" (v. 13 NASB). Faith is important, of course. So, too, is hope. But, love is more important still. Christ showed His love for us on the cross, and, as Christians, we are called upon to return Christ's love by sharing it. Today, let us spread Christ's love to our families, to our friends, and to the strangers we meet along the way.

Mommy Milestone for Today

_____

_____

_____

_____

_____

_____

A Quote for Today

You can be sure you are abiding in
Christ if you are able to have
a Christlike love toward the people
that irritate you the most.

—Vonette Bright

REAL CHRISTIANITY

But now in Christ Jesus you who formerly were far off have been brought near by the blood of Christ. For He Himself is our peace.
—Ephesians 2:13-14 NASB

What is "real" Christianity? Think of it as an ongoing relationship—an all-encompassing relationship with God and with His Son, Jesus. It is inevitable that your life must be lived in relationship to God. The question is not if you will have a relationship with Him; the burning question is whether or not that relationship will be one that seeks to honor Him or one that seeks to ignore Him.

We live in a world that discourages heartfelt devotion and obedience to God. Everywhere we turn, or so it seems, we are confronted by a mind-numbing assortment of distractions, temptations, obligations, and frustrations. Yet even on our busiest days, God beckons us to slow down and consult Him. When we do, we avail ourselves of the peace and abundance that only He can give.

A Quote for Today

Commitment to His lordship on Easter, at revivals, or even every Sunday is not enough. We must choose this day—and every day—whom we will serve. This deliberate act of the will is the inevitable choice between habitual fellowship and habitual failure.
—Beth Moore

Mommy Milestone for Today

_____

_____

_____

_____

_____

_____

SOLVING PROBLEMS

People who do what is right may have many problems,
but the Lord will solve them all.
—Psalm 34:19 NCV

Motherhood is an exercise in problem-solving. The question is not whether you will encounter challenges; the real question is how you will choose to address them.

When we face the inevitable challenges of everyday life, we have two choices: we can either face them head-on and solve them now, or we can procrastinate. Unfortunately, most problems are not self-solving; in fact, the opposite is true. The more we put things off, the harder they are to solve.

Today, make it a point to tackle your problems sooner rather than later. When you do, you'll be rewarded for your efforts . . . sooner rather than later.

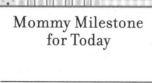

Mommy Milestone
for Today

_____

_____

_____

_____

_____

_____

A Quote for Today

What a comfort to know that God is present there in your life, available to meet every situation with you, that you are never left to face any problem alone.
—Vonette Bright

A Timely Tip

The habit of procrastination is often rooted in the fear of failure, the fear of discomfort, or the fear of embarrassment. Your challenge is to confront these fears and defeat them.

THE REWARDS OF WISDOM

Talk to Wisdom as to a sister. Treat Insight as your companion.
—Proverbs 7:4 MSG

As the mom of a new baby, you make many decisions every day. To make wise decisions, you need at least two things: you need the timeless wisdom that can only be found in God's Holy Word and you need prayer.

The best decisions are made after careful consideration and honest prayer. The worst decisions are made impulsively, without consulting God.

Today, as you make countless decisions about your life, your work, and your baby, don't be in a hurry. Before you make an important decision, talk to God about it. Pray for answers and keep praying until you get them. And, of this you can be sure: the world may lead you astray, but God never will.

A Quote for Today

He teaches us, not just to let us see ourselves correctly, but to help us see Him correctly.
—Kathy Troccoli

A Timely Tip

Absolutely no parental duty is more important than praying for your child.

Mommy Milestone for Today

_____

_____

_____

_____

_____

_____

PLANNING PAYS

Careful planning puts you ahead in the long run;
hurry and scurry puts you further behind.
—Proverbs 21:5 MSG

Because you have so many responsibilities, it's easy to feel swamped. After all, you were a busy woman before your baby was born, and now it seems as though your workload has tripled! How can you find the time to get everything done? Well, it helps to start with a plan.

Dietrich Bonhoeffer observed, "Each morning is a new beginning of our life. Each day is a finished whole. The present day marks the boundary of our cares and concerns. God created day and night for us so we need not wander without boundaries, but may be able to see in every morning the goal of the evening ahead."

Today, as you begin your day, be sure to have a plan. Make a to-do list of the things you want to accomplish, and ask your Heavenly Father to help you accomplish them. And then, you can face your duties with confidence because, with a good plan and with God as your partner, you're destined to have a very good day.

Mommy Milestone for Today

_____

_____

_____

_____

_____

_____

A Quote for Today

A #2 pencil and a dream
can take you anywhere.

—Joyce Meyer

A Family That Serves the Lord

You must choose for yourselves today whom you will serve . . .
as for me and my family, we will serve the Lord.
—Joshua 24:15 NCV

As you consider God's purpose for your own life, you must also consider how your plans will effect the most important people that God has entrusted to your care: your loved ones.

Our families and friends are precious gifts from our Father in heaven. If we are to be worthy disciples of the One from Galilee, we must care for our loved ones and make time for them, even when the demands of the day are great. In a world filled with countless obligations and frequent frustrations, we may be tempted to take our families and friends for granted. But God intends otherwise. God intends that we honor Him by honoring our loved ones—by giving them our support, our time, and our cooperation.

No relationships are perfect, and neither are yours. Yet, imperfect though they may be, your family and friends are God's blessing to you. Give thanks for that blessing . . . and act accordingly.

A Quote for Today

For whatever life holds for you and
your family in the coming days,
weave the unfailing fabric of God's
Word through your heart and mind.
It will hold strong, even if
the rest of life unravels.

—Gigi Graham Tchividjian

Mommy Milestone for Today

_____

_____

_____

_____

_____

_____

HE IS YOUR SHEPHERD

The Lord is my shepherd; I shall not want.
—Psalm 23:1 KJV

Isn't it comforting to know that God is your Shepherd? And, isn't it wonderful that the Creator of the universe is watching over your baby? God's love for you is infinite. His love for your baby is infinite, too. Today, thank Him for His love and for His protection.

God does not exempt us from the valleys of life, but neither does He ask us to walk alone. He is always there. God's heart is faithful. He's faithful to His people; He is faithful to His Word; and He is faithful to you.

Paul writes in 1 Corinthians 1:9, "God is faithful, by whom you were called into the fellowship of His Son Jesus Christ our Lord" (NKJV). God has a faithful heart. Trust Him, and take comfort in the unerring promises and the never-ending faithfulness of your Lord.

A Quote for Today

Our future may look fearfully intimidating, yet we can look up to the Engineer of the Universe, confident that nothing escapes His attention or slips out of the control of those strong hands.

—Elisabeth Elliot

Mommy Milestone for Today

_____

_____

_____

_____

_____

YES, YOU CAN!

You are the God who performs miracles;
you display your power among the peoples.
—Psalm 77:14 NIV

Are you a mom who understands that God can work miracles in the world and within the four walls of your home? Hopefully so. After all, the same God who created the universe out of nothingness can surely work untold miracles in your own life. So whatever you do, please don't try to place limitations on a God who has none.

Sometimes, when we read of God's miraculous works in Biblical times, we tell ourselves, "That was then, but this is now." When we do so, we are mistaken. God is with His children "now" just as He was "then." He is right here, right now, performing miracles. And, He will continue to work miracles in our lives to the extent we are willing to trust in Him and to the extent those miracles fit into the fabric of His divine plan.

A Quote for Today

There is Someone who makes
possible what seems
completely impossible.
—Catherine Marshall

Mommy Milestone
for Today

_____

_____

_____

_____

_____

GETTING ENOUGH REST?

Come to me, all you who are weary and burdened,
and I will give you rest. Take my yoke upon you and learn from me,
for I am gentle and humble in heart, and you will find rest for your souls.
For my yoke is easy and my burden is light.
—Matthew 11:28-30 NIV

Caring for a newborn can be an all-consuming, life-altering, energy-draining task. To do the job properly, you need as much rest as you can get.

Are you determined to get as much sleep as you can, or are you allowing the distractions of everyday life to rob you of the rest you need? Hopefully, you've already learned the wisdom of turning off your TV and powering down your cell phone at an early hour.

Most adults need about eight hours of sleep every night, and you are no exception. But because your baby may be an erratic sleeper, your sleep schedule may be erratic, too. Since you can't be sure how much sleep you'll get on a given night, make it a habit to turn in early. During the day, if your baby takes a nap, consider grabbing a quick nap yourself. And remember that you and your baby are alike in this respect: the more rested you are, the happier you'll be.

Mommy Milestone for Today

_____

_____

_____

_____

_____

_____

A Quote for Today

Life is strenuous.
See that your clock does not
run down.
—Mrs. Charles E. Cowman

LISTENING TO MENTORS

Listen to advice and accept correction, and in the end you will be wise.
—Proverbs 19:20 NCV

No matter how much you already know about raising children, there's always more to learn. And one of the best ways to learn about motherhood is to talk to—and to pick up tips from—experienced, God-fearing moms.

Somewhere, very near you, an experienced "mentor-mom" is waiting for your call. She's ready, willing, and perfectly able to give you advice about the ins and outs, the glories and the setbacks of motherhood.

Have you ever noticed that God manages to place helpful people along your path at the moment when you need them most? Well, that's precisely what God does. So, if you're in need of some expert advice, look around because God probably has an experienced, encouraging mom He wants you to meet today.

A Quote for Today

It takes a wise person to give good advice, but an even wiser person to take it.
—Marie T. Freeman

Mommy Milestone for Today

_____

_____

_____

_____

_____

_____

THE BLESSINGS AND RESPONSIBILITIES OF MOTHERHOOD

The lines of purpose in your lives never grow slack, tightly tied as they are to your future in heaven, kept taut by hope. It's the same all over the world. The Message bears fruit and gets larger and stronger, just as it has in you. From the very first day you heard and recognized the truth of what God is doing, you've been hungry for more.

—Colossians 1:5-6 MSG

Caring for a small baby is incredibly hard work. But it's also incredibly rewarding work. Your challenge, as a faithful, caring mother, is to focus on the rewards, not on the hardships.

A. W. Tozer correctly observed, "With the goodness of God to desire our highest welfare and the wisdom of God to plan it, what do we lack? Surely we are the most favored of all creatures."

Today, remember that you and your baby are the objects of God's favor. The Creator has given you a priceless gift and a profound responsibility: your baby. Congratulations. Because you're a new mom, you're incredibly blessed.

Mommy Milestone for Today

_____

_____

_____

_____

_____

_____

A Quote for Today

The mother is and must be, whether she knows it or not, the greatest, strongest, and most lasting teacher her children have.

—Hannah Whitall Smith

THE DELIGHTS OF MOTHERHOOD

Delight yourself also in the Lord,
and He shall give you the desires of your heart.
—Psalm 37:4 NKJV

Motherhood isn't just the most challenging job on earth, it's also one of the most rewarding ones. So today, slow down, take a deep breath, and carve out a few moments to celebrate the joys of motherhood.

Because you're the mother of a brand new baby, you have your hands full, in more ways than one. Your responsibilities don't really have a beginning or an end; you're on call 24 hours a day, seven days a week.

As you perform your maternal duties, don't forget to celebrate them. And while you're celebrating, don't forget to thank the Creator for all His gifts, especially that precious baby He has entrusted to your care.

A Quote for Today

The highest and most desirable state of the soul is to praise God in celebration for being alive.

—Luci Swindoll

Mommy Milestone for Today

_____

_____

_____

_____

_____

_____

YOUR BABY:
A PRICELESS GIFT FROM GOD

*Teach them to your children, talking about them when you sit in
your house and when you walk along the road, when you lie down
and when you get up. Write them on the doorposts of your house
and on your gates, so that as long as the heavens are above the earth,
your days and those of your children may be many in the land
the Lord swore to give your fathers.*

—Deuteronomy 11:19-21 HCSB

E very child is different, but every child is similar in this respect:
he or she is a priceless gift from the Father above. And, with
the Father's gift comes immense responsibilities for moms and
dads alike.

Even on those difficult days when the baby is crying and your
patience is waning, please don't forget that your infant is God's gift to
you, a blessing of infinite value. Even during those long nights when
your infant is crying and your energy has vanished, don't forget that
your Heavenly Father is a never-ending source of strength. And, if you
become discouraged, remember that the Creator of the universe will never desert you. Because He is always faithful, you can be faithful, too.

Mommy Milestone for Today

_____

_____

_____

_____

_____

_____

A Quote for Today

Trust yourself. As a parent, you
know more than you think you do.

—Dr. Benjamin Spock

MOTHERS CHANGE THE WORLD

You are the light of the world.
—Matthew 5:14 NIV

There's no doubt about it: mothers change the world. And, God intends for you to change the world for the better by raising your child in a home that honors the Father and follows His Son.

Our society needs mothers who love their children and love the Lord. And, our society needs moms (like you) who are willing to share their experiences, their knowledge, and their compassion.

Because you're a mother, you're destined to refashion eternity. It's an enormous responsibility, but with God's help, you can create a lasting legacy for your baby, for your family, and for the world.

A Quote for Today

There is no influence so powerful
as that of a mother.
—Sarah J. Hale

Mommy Milestone
for Today

_____

_____

_____

_____

_____

GOD'S CHILDREN

One day children were brought to Jesus in the hope that he would lay hands on them and pray over them. The disciples shooed them off. But Jesus intervened: "Let the children alone, don't prevent them from coming to me. God's kingdom is made up of people like these."
—Matthew 19:13-14 MSG

Your baby is a gift from above, a priceless treasure loved by the eternal Creator. God's love for your baby is boundless, and it is eternal. In truth, your child is God's child.

Hannah Whitall Smith noted that, "He treats us as sons, and all He asks in return is that we shall treat Him as a Father whom we can trust without anxiety. We must take the son's place of dependence and trust, and we must let Him keep the father's place of care and responsibility."

Today, please find comfort in the certain knowledge that your baby is loved by the Father and protected by the Father . . . now and forever.

Mommy Milestone for Today

_____

_____

_____

_____

_____

A Quote for Today

This child we dedicate to Thee,
O God of grace and purity!
—Traditional German Blessing

A Timely Tip

When all else fails, God's love does not. You can always depend upon God's love . . . and He is always your ultimate protection.

GOD'S GLORIOUS GIFTS

I will make them and the places all around My hill a blessing;
and I will cause showers to come down in their season;
there shall be showers of blessing.
—Ezekiel 34:26 NKJV

God's gifts to you, to your baby, and to your family are simply too numerous to count. But even if you cannot count each and every one of those blessings, you should still thank the Giver.

Praise and thanksgiving are essential elements in the lives of all thoughtful Christians. As Max Lucado correctly observed, "Praise opens the window of our hearts, preparing us to walk more closely with God. Prayer raises the window of our spirit, enabling us to listen more clearly to the Father."

Today, as you fulfill the important duties of motherhood, don't forget to praise your Creator for gifts that are infinite, eternal, and yours for the asking.

A Quote for Today

God wants his people to earnestly seek his will and to pray for it, and thus to become agents of the blessing God brings.

—James Montgomery Boice

Mommy Milestone for Today

_____

_____

_____

_____

_____

_____

NEGATE THE NEGATIVITY

Make me to hear joy and gladness.
—Psalm 51:8 KJV

From experience, we know that it is easier to criticize than to correct. And we know that it is easier to find faults than solutions. Yet the urge to criticize others remains a powerful temptation for most of us. Our task, as obedient believers, is to break the twin habits of negative thinking and critical speech.

Caring for a newborn requires around-the-clock effort. So, even the most energetic new moms can become discouraged. And, discouragement breeds negativity.

Negativity is highly contagious: we give it to others who, in turn, give it back to us. This cycle can be broken by positive thoughts, heartfelt prayers, and encouraging words. As thoughtful servants of a loving God, we can use the transforming power of Christ's love to break the chains of negativity. And we should.

Mommy Milestone for Today

_____

_____

_____

_____

_____

_____

A Quote for Today

Winners see an answer for every problem; losers see a problem in every answer.

—Barbara Johnson

TOO MUCH RED TAPE?

Patience is better than power, and controlling one's temper,
than capturing a city.
—Proverbs 16:32 HCSB

Sorting through the red tape of our modern medical bureaucracy can be frustrating, but it need not be devastating. After all, when compared to the vastness of eternity, today's problems aren't ever as big as they seem.

As long as you live here on earth, you will face countless opportunities to lose your temper over small, relatively insignificant events such as an inconsiderate comment, or an inarticulate doctor, or an incorrect hospital bill. When you are tempted to lose your temper over these things, don't. Turn away from anger and turn, instead, to God. When you do, you'll be following His commandments and giving yourself a priceless gift . . . the gift of peace.

A Quote for Today

When something robs you of your peace of mind, ask yourself if it is worth the energy you are expending on it. If not, then put it out of your mind in an act of discipline. Every time the thought of "it" returns, refuse it.

—Kay Arthur

Mommy Milestone for Today

_____

_____

_____

_____

_____

WHAT'S REALLY IMPORTANT

Anyone trusting in his riches will fall,
but the righteous will flourish like foliage.
—Proverbs 11:28 HCSB

In the demanding world in which we live, financial prosperity can be a good thing, but spiritual prosperity is profoundly more important. Yet our society leads us to believe otherwise. The world glorifies material possessions, personal fame, and physical beauty above all else; these things, of course, are totally unimportant to God. God sees the human heart, and that's what is important to Him.

As you establish your priorities for the coming day, remember this: The world will do everything it can to convince you that "things" are important. The world will tempt you to value fortune above faith and possessions above peace. God, on the other hand, will try to convince you that your relationship with Him is all-important. Trust God.

A Quote for Today

We are made spiritually lethargic
by a steady diet of materialism.
—Mary Morrison Suggs

Mommy Milestone for Today

_____

_____

_____

_____

_____

_____

ENTRUSTING THE FUTURE TO GOD

Those who trust in the LORD are as secure as Mount Zion;
they will not be defeated but will endure forever.
—Psalm 125:1 NLT

Your future may seem uncertain to you, but it is not uncertain to God. God has a glorious plan for you and your loved ones, a plan that only He can see. Today, as you contemplate the uncertainties of life here on earth, don't fall prey to worry or doubt. Instead, entrust the future to the Father.

Corrie ten Boom had simple yet profound advice. She said, "Never be afraid to trust an unknown future to a known God." And, that's advice worth taking today, tomorrow, and every day of your life.

So, whatever this day holds for you and yours, live confidently and trust God. And, remember that He always keeps His promises.

A Quote for Today

As a mother, my job is to take care of the possible and trust God with the impossible.
—Ruth Bell Graham

Mommy Milestone for Today

_____

_____

_____

_____

_____

_____

LEARNING THE LESSONS

Take good counsel and accept correction—
that's the way to live wisely and well.
—Proverbs 19:20 MSG

No matter how much you know about life, love, and motherhood, you still have lots to learn. Every day, God offers you countless opportunities to grow spiritually, emotionally, and intellectually. And the rest is up to you.

When it comes to learning life's lessons, we can either do things the easy way or the hard way. The easy way can be summed up as follows: when God teaches us a lesson, we learn it . . . the first time. Unfortunately, too many of us learn much more slowly than that.

When we resist God's instruction, He continues to teach, whether we like it or not. Our challenge, then, is to discern God's lessons from the experiences of everyday life. Hopefully, we learn those lessons sooner rather than later because the sooner we do, the sooner He can move on to the next lesson, and the next, and the next . . .

Mommy Milestone for Today

_____

_____

_____

_____

_____

A Quote for Today

God is able to take mistakes, when they are committed to Him, and make of them something for our good and for His glory.
—Ruth Bell Graham

OBEYING HIS COMMANDMENTS

*For God is working in you, giving you the desire to obey him
and the power to do what pleases him.*
—Philippians 2:13 NLT

E lisabeth Elliot advised, "Obedience to God is our job. The results of that obedience are God's." These words serve to remind
us that obedience is imperative, but we live in a society that
surrounds us with temptations to disobey God's laws. So if we are to
win the battles against temptations and distractions, we must never
drop our guard.

A righteous life has many components: faith, honesty, generosity,
love, kindness, humility, gratitude, and worship, to name but a few. If
we seek to follow the steps of our Savior, Jesus Christ, we must seek to
live according to His commandments.

When we live in accordance with God's commandments, He
blesses us in ways that we cannot fully understand.

Are you ready, willing, able, and anxious to receive God's blessings? Then obey Him. And rest assured that when you do your part,
He'll do His part.

A Quote for Today

Whoever doesn't have
one Master has many.
—St. Ambrose

Mommy Milestone for Today

_____

_____

_____

_____

_____

INSPIRING YOUR FAMILY

Good people's words will help many others.
—Proverbs 10:21 NCV

Your family needs inspiration, and lots of it. But the world outside the four walls of your home can be a discouraging place, a place where your loved ones may find more cynicism than hope. So, it's up to you to make sure that your home is an island of encouragement and a fortress of faith.

All of us have the power to enrich the lives of our loved ones. Sometimes, when we feel uplifted and secure, we find it easy to speak words of encouragement and hope. Other times, when we are discouraged or tired, we can scarcely summon the energy to uplift ourselves, much less anyone else. But, as loving Christians, our obligation is clear: we must always measure our words carefully as we use them to benefit others and to glorify our Father in heaven.

God intends that we speak words of kindness, wisdom, and truth, no matter our circumstances, no matter our emotions. When we do, we share a priceless gift with our loved ones, and we give glory to the One who gave His life for us. As believers, we must do no less.

Mommy Milestone for Today

_____

_____

_____

_____

_____

A Quote for Today

Who can ever measure the benefit of a mother's inspiration?
—Charles Swindoll

GOD RESPONDS

*Whatever you ask for in prayer, believe that you have received it,
and it will be yours.*

—Mark 11:24 NIV

When we petition God, He responds. God's hand is not absent, and it is not distant. It is responsive.

On his second missionary journey, Paul started a small church in Thessalonica. A short time later, he penned a letter that was intended to encourage the new believers at that church. Today, almost 2,000 years later, 1 Thessalonians remains a powerful, practical guide for Christian living.

In his letter, Paul advises members of the new church to "pray without ceasing." His advice applies to Christians of every generation.

Today, allow the responsive hand of God to guide you and help you. Pray without ceasing, and then rest assured: God is listening . . . and responding!

A Quote for Today

We must leave it to God to answer
our prayers in His own wisest way.
Sometimes, we are so impatient and
think that God does not answer.
God always answers! He never fails!
Be still. Abide in Him.

—Mrs. Charles E. Cowman

Mommy Milestone
for Today

_____

_____

_____

_____

_____

CHEERFUL PARENTING

Do everything readily and cheerfully—no bickering,
no second-guessing allowed!
—Philippians 2:14 MSG

Are you a cheerful mom? Does everyone in your family see far more smiles on your face than frowns? If so, your family is blessed by your cheerfulness, and so are you.

The duties of motherhood can be frustrating at times. And, those duties can be exhausting, too. But please don't allow the occasional headaches and inevitable distractions of family life to rob you of the joy that is rightfully yours.

God has promised that you can experience His peace and His joy, but He will not force you to accept these gifts. You must claim them for yourself. So, today, make up your mind to be a cheerful, upbeat, optimistic mom. It's the right way to think and the right way to live.

A Quote for Today

We may run, walk, stumble, drive,
or fly, but let us never lose sight
of the reason for the journey,
or miss a chance to see a rainbow
on the way.
—Gloria Gaither

Mommy Milestone
for Today

_____

_____

_____

_____

_____

WALK WITH THE WISE

The one who walks with the wise will become wise,
but a companion of fools will suffer harm.
—Proverbs 13:20 HCSB

Here's a simple yet effective way to strengthen your faith: Choose role models whose faith in God is strong.

When you emulate godly people, you become a more godly person yourself. That's why you should seek out mentors who, by their words and their presence, make you a better person, a better Christian, and a better mom.

So, if you haven't already done so, find at least one woman whose judgment you trust, and use her as a sounding board for your questions and concerns. Listen carefully to your mentor's advice and be willing to accept that advice, even if accepting it requires effort, or pain, or both. Consider your mentor to be God's gift to you. Thank God for that gift, and use it for the glory of His kingdom.

A Quote for Today

Yes, the Spirit was sent to be our Counselor. Yes, Jesus speaks to us personally. But often he works through another human being.

—John Eldredge

Mommy Milestone for Today

_____

_____

_____

_____

_____

_____

MAKING A HAPPY HOME

The wise woman builds her house,
but the foolish pulls it down with her hands.
—Proverbs 14:1 NKJV

Are you determined to make your home a happy, peaceful place? Hopefully so, because that's what your family wants, and that's what God wants, too.

For Christian family members, kindness is not an option; it is a commandment. Jesus teaches, "In everything, therefore, treat people the same way you want them to treat you, for this is the Law and the Prophets" (Matthew 7:12 NASB). Jesus did not say, "In some things, treat people as you wish to be treated." And, He did not say, "From time to time, treat others with kindness." Christ said that we should treat others as we wish to be treated in everything. This, of course, isn't always easy, but as Christians, we are commanded to do our best.

Healthy families are built upon the Golden Rule. So, today, as you consider all the things that Christ has done in your life, honor Him by being a little kinder than necessary. It's the right thing to do and the right way to make a happy home.

Mommy Milestone for Today

_____

_____

_____

_____

_____

A Quote for Today

The first essential for a happy home is love.

—Billy Graham

THANKING GOD EVERY DAY

Then I will praise God's name with singing,
and I will honor him with thanksgiving.
—Psalm 69:30 NLT

As the mother of a precious newborn, you have so much to be thankful for. But sometimes, when the responsibility of caring for your baby seems to be overwhelming, you may not have the inclination—or the energy—to slow down long enough to praise God for His incalculable gifts.

Today, as you provide for your family and care for your child, be sure to thank the One who has given you everything. The Lord has given you a life here on earth, a new baby, a family, and the promise of eternal life in heaven. These gifts are beyond comprehension. Be sure to thank the Giver. Now.

A Quote for Today

Why wait until the fourth Thursday in November? Why wait until the morning of December twenty-fifth? Thanksgiving to God should be an everyday affair. The time to be thankful is now!
—Jim Gallery

Mommy Milestone
for Today

_____

_____

_____

_____

_____

ESTABLISHING PRIORITIES

The thing you should want most is God's kingdom and
doing what God wants. Then all these other things
you need will be given to you.
—Matthew 6:33 NCV

Have you fervently asked God to help prioritize your life? If so, then you're continually inviting your Creator to become a full-fledged partner in your endeavors.

When you make God's priorities your priorities, you will receive God's abundance and His peace. When you make God a full partner in every aspect of your life, He will lead you along the proper path: His path. When you allow God to play a role in the organization of your day, He will honor you with spiritual blessings that are simply too numerous to count. So, as you plan for the day ahead, take a few quiet moments to gather your thoughts and consult your Creator. It's the best way to plan your day and your life.

A Quote for Today

The things that matter most
in this world can never be held
in your hand.
—Gloria Gaither

Mommy Milestone for Today

_____

_____

_____

_____

_____

TOUCHED BY THE SAVIOR

*And when the woman saw that she was not hid, she came trembling,
and falling down before him, she declared unto him before all the people
for what cause she had touched him, and how she was healed immediately.
And he said unto her, Daughter, be of good comfort: thy faith
hath made thee whole; go in peace.*

—Luke 8:47-48 KJV

Until we have been touched by the Savior, we can never be completely whole. Until we have placed our hearts and our lives firmly in the hands of the living Christ, we are incomplete. Until we come to know Jesus, we long for a sense of peace that continues to elude us no matter how diligently we search.

It is only through God that we discover genuine peace. We can search far and wide for worldly substitutes, but when we seek peace apart from God, we will find neither peace nor God.

As believers, we are invited to accept the "peace that passes all understanding" (Philippians 4:7 NIV). That peace, of course, is God's peace. Let us accept His peace, and let us share it today, tomorrow, and every day that we live.

A Quote for Today

We will never be happy until
we make God the source
of our fulfillment and the answer
to our longings.

—Stormie Omartian

Mommy Milestone for Today

_____

_____

_____

_____

_____

_____

FORGIVENESS NOW

*Anyone who claims to live in God's light
and hates a brother or sister is still in the dark.*
—1 John 2:9 MSG

Forgiveness is seldom easy, but it is always right. When we forgive those who have hurt us, we honor God by obeying His commandments. But when we harbor bitterness against others, we disobey God—with predictably unhappy results.

Are you easily frustrated by the inevitable shortcomings of others? Are you a prisoner of bitterness or regret? If so, perhaps you need a refresher course in the art of forgiveness.

If there exists even one person, alive or dead, whom you have not forgiven (and that includes yourself), follow God's commandment and His will for your life: forgive that person today. And remember that bitterness, anger, and regret are not part of God's plan for your life. Forgiveness is.

Mommy Milestone for Today

_____

_____

_____

_____

_____

_____

A Quote for Today

Forgiveness is every person's deepest need and the greatest quality of being like Jesus.

—Franklin Graham

LOOKING FOR OPPORTUNITIES TO ENCOURAGE

So encourage each other and give each other strength,
just as you are doing now.
—1 Thessalonians 5:11 NCV

Here's a question only you can answer: During a typical day, how many opportunities will you have to encourage your family and friends? Unless you're living on a deserted island, the answer is "a lot!" And here's a follow-up question: How often do you take advantage of those opportunities? Hopefully, Mom, the answer is "more often than not."

Romans 14:19 advises us to "Pursue what promotes peace and what builds up one another" (HCSB). And whenever we do, God smiles.

Whether you realize it or not, you're surrounded by friends and family members who need an encouraging word, a helping hand, or a pat on the back. And every time you encourage one of these folks, you'll being doing God's will by obeying God's Word. So with no further ado, let the encouragement begin.

A Quote for Today

As you're rushing through life, take time to stop a moment, look into people's eyes, say something kind, and try to make them laugh!
—Barbara Johnson

Mommy Milestone for Today

_____

_____

_____

_____

_____

MOTHERHOOD DAY BY DAY

Keep your eyes on Jesus, who both began and finished this race we're in.
Study how he did it. Because he never lost sight of where he was
headed—that exhilarating finish in and with God—he could put up
with anything along the way: cross, shame, whatever.
And now he's there, in the place of honor, right alongside God.
—Hebrews 12:2 MSG

The job of raising a newborn is an around-the-clock assignment. There are no paid vacations from the responsibilities of motherhood.

If you find yourself becoming discouraged by the inevitable demands of caring for your baby, don't despair. Instead, take your maternal duties one moment, and one day, at a time.

Don't fret too much about tomorrow's responsibilities; entrust tomorrow's worries to God. Don't focus on next week, or next month, or next year. Focus on today. Remember that God is always with you and that He can always provide the strength you need to accomplish His will. God's love for you is infinite. Accept it joyously and be thankful.

Mommy Milestone for Today

_____

_____

_____

_____

_____

A Quote for Today

Raising children is not unlike
a long-distance race in which
the contestants must learn
to pace themselves.
That is the secret of winning.

—James Dobson

INVOLVED IN HIS CHURCH

The church, you see, is not peripheral to the world; the world is
peripheral to the church. The church is Christ's body, in which
he speaks and acts, by which he fills everything with his presence.
—Ephesians 1:23 MSG

In the Book of Acts, Luke reminds us to "feed the church of God" (20:28). As Christians who have been saved by a loving, compassionate Creator, we are compelled not only to worship Him in our hearts but also to worship Him in the presence of fellow believers.

Do you attend church regularly? And when you attend, are you an active participant, or are you just taking up space? The answer to these questions will have a profound impact on the quality and direction of your spiritual journey.

So do yourself and your loved ones a favor: become actively involved in your church. Don't just go to church out of habit. Go to church out of a sincere desire to know and worship God. When you do, you'll be blessed by the One who sent His Son to die so that you might have everlasting life.

A Quote for Today

Be filled with the Holy Spirit; join a church where the members believe the Bible and know the Lord; seek the fellowship of other Christians; learn and be nourished by God's Word and His many promises. Conversion is not the end of your journey— it is only the beginning.

—Corrie ten Boom

Mommy Milestone for Today

_____

_____

_____

_____

_____

_____

LIVING ON BABY STANDARD TIME

*There is an occasion for everything,
and a time for every activity under heaven.*
—Ecclesiastes 3:1 HCSB

With a new baby in the house, your timetable has officially changed. You're no longer living in your old time zone. Now, you're living on Baby Standard Time.

Perhaps your baby is settling into a somewhat normal schedule. Perhaps not. In either case, you'll need plenty of patience, frequent naps (if you get them), and as much optimism as you can muster.

Even during those times when you are exhausted, or discouraged, or both, God stands ready to comfort you. So, the next time you find yourself at the end of your rope, tie a knot, hang on, and say a little prayer for your baby and for yourself. And, please don't forget that with God's help, you can overcome any challenge, including this one.

Mommy Milestone for Today

_____

_____

_____

_____

_____

A Quote for Today

Being a full-time mom is the hardest job I've ever had, but it is also the best job I've ever had. The pay is lousy, but the rewards are eternal.

—Lisa Whelchel

THE IMPORTANCE OF DISCIPLINE

For God has not given us a spirit of fear and timidity,
but of power, love, and self-discipline.
So you must never be ashamed to tell others about our Lord.
—2 Timothy 1:7-8 NLT

Wise mothers teach their children the importance of discipline by using their words and their examples. Disciplined moms understand that God doesn't reward laziness or misbehavior. To the contrary, God expects His believers to lead lives that are above reproach. And, He punishes those who disobey His commandments.

It has been said that there are no shortcuts to any place worth going. Thoughtful mothers agree. In Proverbs 28:19, God's message is clear: "He who works his land will have abundant food, but the one who chases fantasies will have his fill of poverty" (NIV).

When we work diligently and consistently, we can expect a bountiful harvest. But we must never expect the harvest to precede the labor. First, we must lead lives of discipline and obedience; then, we will reap the never-ending rewards that God has promised.

A Quote for Today

I believe the reason so many are failing today is that they have not disciplined themselves to read God's Word consistently, day in and day out, and to apply it to every situation in life.
—Kay Arthur

Mommy Milestone for Today

_____

_____

_____

_____

_____

CELEBRATING HIS GIFTS

Rejoice, and be exceeding glad: for great is your reward in heaven.
—Matthew 5:12 KJV

The 100th Psalm reminds us that the entire earth should "Shout for joy to the Lord" (NIV). As God's children, we are blessed beyond measure, but sometimes, as busy mothers living in a demanding world, we are slow to count our gifts and even slower to give thanks to the Giver.

You probably don't need to be reminded that your blessings include your baby, your family, and your faith—for starters. But it doesn't stop there. As Hannah Whitall Smith observed, "We do not need to beg God to bless us; He simply cannot help it."

The gifts we receive from God are multiplied when we share them. May we always give thanks to the Creator for His blessings, and may we always demonstrate our gratitude by sharing our gifts with others.

The 118th Psalm reminds us that, "This is the day which the LORD has made; let us rejoice and be glad in it" (v. 24 NASB). May we celebrate this day and the One who created it.

Mommy Milestone for Today

_____

_____

_____

_____

_____

A Quote for Today

God has promised us abundance, peace, and eternal life. These treasures are ours for the asking; all we must do is claim them. One of the great mysteries of life is why on earth do so many of us wait so very long to lay claim to God's gifts?

—Marie T. Freeman

TAKING UP HIS CROSS

Then He said to them all, "If anyone desires to come after Me,
let him deny himself, and take up his cross daily, and follow Me.
For whoever desires to save his life will lose it,
but whoever loses his life for My sake will save it."
—Luke 9:23-24 NKJV

When Jesus addressed His disciples, He warned that each one must, "take up his cross and follow Me." The disciples must have known exactly what the Master meant. In Jesus' day, prisoners were forced to carry their own crosses to the location where they would be put to death. Thus, Christ's message was clear: in order to follow Him, Christ's disciples must deny themselves and, instead, trust Him completely. Nothing has changed since then.

If we are to be dutiful disciples of the One from Galilee, we must trust Him and we must follow Him. Jesus never comes "next." He is always first. He shows us the path of life.

Do you seek to be a worthy disciple of Jesus? Then pick up His cross today and follow in His footsteps. When you do, you can walk with confidence: He will never lead you astray.

A Quote for Today

The cross that Jesus commands you and me to carry is the cross of submissive obedience to the will of God, even when His will includes suffering and hardship and things we don't want to do.

—Anne Graham Lotz

Mommy Milestone for Today

_____

_____

_____

_____

_____

_____

PRACTICAL CHRISTIANITY

But prove yourselves doers of the word,
and not merely hearers who delude themselves.
—James 1:22 NASB

As Christians, we must do our best to ensure that our actions are accurate reflections of our beliefs. Our theology must be demonstrated, not only by our words but, more importantly, by our actions. In short, we should be practical believers, quick to act whenever we see an opportunity to serve God.

Are you the kind of practical Christian mom who is willing to dig in and do what needs to be done when it needs to be done? If so, congratulations: God acknowledges your service and blesses it.

God wants believers who are willing to roll up their sleeves and go to work for Him. Count yourself among that number. And then prepare yourself for the countless blessings that the Creator provides for those who serve Him.

Mommy Milestone for Today

_____

_____

_____

_____

_____

_____

A Quote for Today

God has lots of folks who intend
to go to work for him "some day."
What He needs is more people who
are willing to work for Him this day.
—Marie T. Freeman

THE GIFT OF CHEERFULNESS

A miserable heart means a miserable life;
a cheerful heart fills the day with a song.
—Proverbs 15:15 MSG

Cheerfulness is a gift that we give to others and to ourselves. And, as believers who have been saved by a risen Christ, why shouldn't we be cheerful? The answer, of course, is that we have every reason to honor our Savior with joy in our hearts, smiles on our faces, and words of celebration on our lips.

Christ promises us lives of abundance and joy if we accept His love and His grace. Yet sometimes, even the most righteous among us are beset by fits of ill temper and frustration. During these moments, we may not feel like turning our thoughts and prayers to Christ, but if we seek to gain perspective and peace, that's precisely what we must do.

Are you a cheerful Christian? You should be! And what is the best way to attain the joy that is rightfully yours? By giving Christ what is rightfully His: your heart, your soul, and your life.

A Quote for Today

When we bring sunshine into the lives of others, we're warmed by it ourselves. When we spill a little happiness, it splashes on us.

—Barbara Johnson

Mommy Milestone for Today

_____

_____

_____

_____

_____

FAITH AND WHOLENESS

Now the just shall live by faith.
—Hebrews 10:38 NKJV

A suffering woman sought healing in an unusual way: she simply touched the hem of Jesus' garment. When she did, Jesus turned and said, "Daughter, be of good comfort; thy faith hath made thee whole" (Matthew 9:22 KJV). We, too, can be made whole when we place our faith completely and unwaveringly in the person of Jesus Christ.

Concentration camp survivor Corrie ten Boom relied on faith during ten months of imprisonment and torture. Later, despite the fact that four of her family members had died in Nazi death camps, Corrie's faith was unshaken. She wrote, "There is no pit so deep that God's love is not deeper still." Christians take note: Genuine faith in God means faith in all circumstances, happy or sad, joyful or tragic.

When you place your faith, your trust, indeed your life in the hands of Christ Jesus, you'll be amazed at the marvelous things He can do with you and through you. So strengthen your faith through praise, through worship, through Bible study, and through prayer. Then, trust God's plans. If you reach out to Him in faith, He will give you peace and heal your broken spirit. Be content to touch even the smallest fragment of the Master's garment, and He will make you whole.

Mommy Milestone for Today

_____

_____

_____

_____

_____

_____

A Quote for Today

Let me encourage you to continue to wait with faith. God may not perform a miracle, but He is trustworthy to touch you and make you whole.

—Lisa Whelchel

CONSIDERING THE CROSS

Christ did not send me to baptize people but to preach the Good News.
And he sent me to preach the Good News without using words of human
wisdom so that the cross of Christ would not lose its power.
—1 Corinthians 1:17 NCV

As we consider Christ's sacrifice on the cross, we should be profoundly humbled and profoundly grateful. And today, as we come to Christ in prayer, we should do so in a spirit of quiet, heartfelt devotion to the One who gave His life so that we might have life eternal.

He was the Son of God, but He wore a crown of thorns. He was the Savior of mankind, yet He was put to death on a roughhewn cross made of wood. He offered His healing touch to an unsaved world, and yet the same hands that had healed the sick and raised the dead were pierced with nails.

Christ humbled Himself on a cross—for you. He shed His blood—for you. He has offered to walk with you through this life and throughout all eternity. As you approach Him today in prayer, think about His sacrifice and His grace. And be humble.

A Quote for Today

To view ourselves through
our Creator's loving, tear-filled
eyes, we need to climb Calvary's
hill and look down from the cross
of Christ—for that is where God
declared that we are worth the life
of His precious Son.

—Susan Lenzkes

Mommy Milestone for Today

_____

_____

_____

_____

_____

_____

A GLORIOUS OPPORTUNITY

Do your work with enthusiasm. Work as if you were serving the Lord,
not as if you were serving only men and women.

—Ephesians 6:7 NCV

Hey Mom, are you looking forward to the coming day with a mixture of anticipation and excitement? Or are you a little less enthused than that? Hopefully, you're excited about—and thankful for—the coming day.

Nobody (including you) needs to be reminded that some days are filled with sweetness and light, while other days aren't. But even on the darker days of life, you have much to celebrate, including but not limited to your life and your loved ones.

As a mother of a newborn, you have incredibly important work to do and a vitally important message to share with your family. Share that message with gusto. Your children need your enthusiasm, and you deserve the rewards that will be yours when you share your wisdom enthusiastically and often.

Mommy Milestone for Today

_____

_____

_____

_____

_____

_____

A Quote for Today

Enthusiasm, like the flu,
is contagious—we get it
from one another.

—Barbara Johnson

Following Christ

But whoever keeps His word, truly in him the love of God is perfected.
This is how we know we are in Him: the one who says he remains
in Him should walk just as He walked.
—1 John 2:5-6 HCSB

Each day, as we awaken from sleep, we are confronted with countless opportunities to serve God and to follow in the footsteps of His Son. When we do, our Heavenly Father guides our steps and blesses our endeavors.

As the mother of a newborn, you face challenges that may sometimes leave you feeling over-worked, under-appreciated, over-committed, under-staffed, and over-whelmed. But even on the busiest days, you can take comfort in God's promises and God's love.

Today provides yet another glorious opportunity to place yourself in the service of the One who is the Giver of all blessings. May you seek His will, may you trust His Word, and may you walk in the footsteps of His Son.

A Quote for Today

In the work of evangelism we are sent by the same Person, we are sent by the same power, we are sent to the same place, we are sent for the same purpose, as Jesus was.

—Corrie ten Boom

Mommy Milestone for Today

_____

_____

_____

_____

_____

_____

WHOSE EXPECTATIONS?

*The person who knows my commandments and keeps them,
that's who loves me. And the person who loves me will be loved
by my Father, and I will love him and make myself plain to him.*
—John 14:21 MSG

Here's a quick quiz: Whose expectations are you trying to meet?

A. Your friends' expectations

B. Society's expectations

C. God's expectations

If you're a Christian, the correct answer is C., but if you're overly concerned with either A. or B., you're not alone. Plenty of people invest too much energy trying to meet society's expectations and too little energy trying to please God. It's a common behavior, but it's also a very big mistake.

A better strategy, of course, is to try to please God first. To do so, you must prioritize your day according to God's commandments, and you must seek His will and His wisdom in all matters.

Are you having trouble choosing between God's priorities and society's priorities? If so, turn the concerns over to God—prayerfully, earnestly, and often. Then, listen for His answer . . . and trust the answer He gives.

Mommy Milestone for Today

_____

_____

_____

_____

_____

_____

A Quote for Today

You will get untold flak for prioritizing God's revealed and present will for your life over man's . . . but, boy, is it worth it.

—Beth Moore

HE LOVES YOU

*Therefore humble yourselves under the mighty hand of God,
that He may exalt you at the proper time, casting all your anxiety
on Him, because He cares for you.*
—1 Peter 5:6-7 NASB

When we worship God with faith and assurance, when we place Him at the absolute center of our lives, we invite His love into our hearts. In turn, we grow to love Him more deeply as we sense His love for us. St. Augustine wrote, "I love you, Lord, not doubtingly, but with absolute certainty. Your Word beat upon my heart until I fell in love with you, and now the universe and everything in it tells me to love you." Let us pray that we, too, will turn our hearts to our Heavenly Father, knowing with certainty that He loves us and that we love Him.

God is love, and God's love is perfect. When we open ourselves to His perfect love, we are touched by the Creator's hand, and we are transformed, not just for a day but for all eternity.

Today, Mom, as you carve out quiet moments of thanksgiving and praise for your Heavenly Father, open yourself to His presence and to His love. He is here, waiting. His love is here, always. Accept it—now—and be blessed.

A Quote for Today

The unfolding of our friendship
with the Father will be
a never-ending revelation
stretching on into eternity.
—Catherine Marshall

Mommy Milestone
for Today

_____

_____

_____

_____

_____

FORGIVENESS IS A FORM OF WISDOM

People with good sense restrain their anger;
they earn esteem by overlooking wrongs.
—Proverbs 19:11 NLT

Even the most mild-mannered moms will, on occasion, have reasons to become angry with the inevitable shortcomings of babies, family members, and friends. But wise women are quick to forgive others, just as God has forgiven them.

Forgiveness is God's commandment, but oh how difficult a commandment it can be to follow. Being frail, fallible, imperfect human beings, we are quick to anger, quick to blame, slow to forgive, and even slower to forget. No matter. Even when forgiveness is difficult, God's Word is clear.

If, in your heart, you hold bitterness against even a single person, forgive. If there exists even one person, alive or dead, whom you have not forgiven, follow God's commandment and His will for your life: forgive. If you are embittered against yourself for some past mistake or shortcoming, forgive. Then, to the best of your abilities, forget, and move on. Bitterness and regret are not part of God's plan for your life. Forgiveness is.

Mommy Milestone for Today

_____

_____

_____

_____

_____

_____

A Quote for Today

God calls upon the loved, not just to love but to be loving. God calls upon the forgiven, not just to forgive but to be forgiving.
—Beth Moore

HE CARES FOR YOU AND YOUR BABY

And God will generously provide all you need. Then you will always have everything you need and plenty left over to share with others.
—2 Corinthians 9:8 NLT

The Bible makes this promise: God will care for you and protect you. In the 6th chapter of Matthew, Jesus made this point clear when He said,

Do not worry about your life, what you will eat or what you will drink; nor about your body, what you will put on. Is not life more than food and the body more than clothing? Look at the birds of the air, for they neither sow nor reap nor gather into barns; yet your heavenly Father feeds them. Are you not of more value than they? Which of you by worrying can add one cubit to his stature? . . . Therefore do not worry about tomorrow, for tomorrow will worry about its own things. Sufficient for the day is its own trouble (25-27, 34 NKJV).

This beautiful passage reminds you, as the mother of a newborn, that God still sits in His heaven and that He cares for both you and your baby. Simply put, you are protected.

A Quote for Today

It is an act of the will to allow God to be our refuge. Otherwise we live outside of his love and protection, wondering why we feel alone and afraid.

—Mary Morrison Suggs

Mommy Milestone for Today

_____

_____

_____

_____

_____

CELEBRATING OTHERS

*Let us think about each other and help each other
to show love and do good deeds.*
—Hebrews 10:24 NCV

Your loved ones need a regular supply of encouraging words and pats on the back. And you need the rewards that God gives to enthusiastic moms who are a continual source of encouragement to their families.

The 118th Psalm reminds us, "This is the day which the Lord hath made; we will rejoice and be glad in it" (v. 24 KJV). As we rejoice in this day that the Lord has given us, let us remember that an important part of today's celebration is the time we spend celebrating others. Each day provides countless opportunities to encourage others and to praise their good works. When we do, we not only spread seeds of joy and happiness, we also follow the commandments of God's Holy Word.

Today, look for the good in others—starting with your loved ones. And then, celebrate the good that you find. When you do, you'll be a powerful force of encouragement in your corner of the world . . . and a worthy servant to your God.

Mommy Milestone for Today

_____

_____

_____

_____

_____

_____

A Quote for Today

True friends will always lift you higher and challenge you to walk in a manner pleasing to our Lord.

—Lisa Bevere

THE MEDICINE OF LAUGHTER

A cheerful disposition is good for your health;
gloom and doom leave you bone-tired.
—Proverbs 17:22 MSG

Motherhood is no laughing matter; it should be taken very seriously, up to a point. But no mother's responsibilities should be so burdensome that she forgets to laugh. Laughter is medicine for the soul, but sometimes, amid the stresses of the day, we forget to take our medicine. Instead of viewing our world with a mixture of optimism and humor, we allow worries and distractions to rob us of the joy that God intends for our lives.

If your heart is heavy, open the door of your soul to Christ. He will give you peace and joy. And, if you already have the joy of Christ in your heart, share it freely, just as Christ freely shared His joy with you. As you go about your daily activities, approach life with a smile on your lips and hope in your heart. And laugh every chance you get. After all, God created laughter for a reason . . . and Father indeed knows best.

A Quote for Today

Laughter dulls the sharpest pain and flattens out the greatest stress. To share it is to give a gift of health.
—Barbara Johnson

Mommy Milestone for Today

_____

_____

_____

_____

_____

_____

THE PEACE THAT PASSES ALL UNDERSTANDING

*Peace, peace to you, and peace to him who helps you,
for your God helps you.*
—1 Chronicles 12:18 HCSB

Through His Son, God offers a "peace that passes all understanding," but He does not force His peace upon us. God's peace is a blessing that we, as children of a loving Father, must claim for ourselves . . . but sometimes we are slow to do so. Why? Because we are fallible human beings with limited understanding and limited faith.

Have you found the lasting peace that can be yours through Jesus, or are you still rushing after the illusion of "peace and happiness" that the world promises but cannot deliver?

Today, as a gift to yourself, to your family, and to your precious newborn, claim the inner peace that is your spiritual birthright: the peace of Jesus Christ.

Mommy Milestone for Today

_____

_____

_____

_____

_____

A Quote for Today

Where the soul is full of peace and joy, outward surroundings and circumstances are of comparatively little account.
—Hannah Whitall Smith

YOUR MARATHON

See, we count as blessed those who have endured.
You have heard of Job's endurance and have seen the outcome from
the Lord: the Lord is very compassionate and merciful.
—James 5:11 HCSB

By now, nobody needs to tell you that taking care of your baby is a marathon, not a sprint. The responsibility of caring for your newborn doesn't end when the sun goes down. Far from it! Your obligation to your child is a twenty-four-hour-a-day, seven-day-a-week job.

When you become exhausted or discouraged (as you inevitably will from time to time), remember that every marathon has a finish line, and no problem is too big for God. So, ask Him to strengthen you day by day, hour by hour, and moment by moment. God can renew your spirit and restore your strength. He can provide the energy you need to cross each day's finish line. His power is always available to you; all you must do is to ask for it.

A Quote for Today

Perseverance is more than endurance. It is endurance combined with absolute assurance and certainty that what we are looking for is going to happen.
—Oswald Chambers

Mommy Milestone for Today

_____

_____

_____

_____

_____

SHARING THE JOY

Let the hearts of those who seek the Lord rejoice.
Look to the Lord and his strength; seek his face always.
—1 Chronicles 16:10-11 NIV

God's intends that His joy should become our joy. He intends that we, His children, should share His love, His joy, and His peace. Yet sometimes, amid the inevitable hustle and bustle of life here on earth, we don't feel much like sharing. So we forfeit—albeit temporarily—God's joy as we wrestle with the challenges of everyday life.

If, today, your heart is heavy, open the door of your soul to your Heavenly Father. When you do, He will renew your spirit. And, if you already have the joy of Christ in your heart, share it freely. When you discover ways to make "your" joy become "their" joy, you will have discovered a wonderful way to say, "I love you" to your baby, to your family, to your friends, and to your God.

Mommy Milestone for Today

_____

_____

_____

_____

_____

A Quote for Today

When we bring sunshine into the lives of others, we're warmed by it ourselves. When we spill a little happiness, it splashes on us.

—Barbara Johnson

HIS PERSPECTIVE . . . AND YOURS

*Since you have been raised to new life with Christ,
set your sights on the realities of heaven, where Christ sits at
God's right hand in the place of honor and power.*
—Colossians 3:1 NLT

Even if you're the world's most thoughtful mom, you may, from time to time, lose perspective—it happens on those days when life seems out of balance and the pressures of motherhood seem overwhelming. What's needed is a fresh perspective, a restored sense of balance . . . and God.

If a temporary loss of perspective has left you worried, exhausted, or both, it's time to readjust your thought patterns. Negative thoughts are habit-forming; thankfully, so are positive ones. With practice, you can form the habit of focusing on God's priorities and your possibilities. When you do, you'll spend less time fretting about your challenges and more time praising God for His gifts.

So today and every day hereafter, pray for a sense of balance and perspective. And remember: your thoughts are intensely powerful things, so handle them with care.

A Quote for Today

Instead of being frustrated and overwhelmed by all that is going on in our world, go to the Lord and ask Him to give you His eternal perspective.
—Kay Arthur

Mommy Milestone for Today

_____

_____

_____

_____

_____

_____

MEETING THE OBLIGATIONS

In all the work you are doing, work the best you can.
Work as if you were doing it for the Lord, not for people.
—Colossians 3:23 NCV

As the mother of a newborn, your obligations are enormous. So, nobody needs to tell you the obvious: You have lots of responsibilities—obligations to your baby, to yourself, to your family, to your community, and to your God. And which of these duties should take priority? The answer can be found in Matthew 6:33: "But seek first the kingdom of God and His righteousness, and all these things will be provided for you" (HCSB).

When you "seek first the kingdom of God," all your other obligations have a way of falling into place. When you obey God's Word and seek His will, your many responsibilities don't seem quite so burdensome. When you honor God with your time, your talents, and your prayers, you'll be much more likely to count your blessings instead of your troubles.

So do yourself and your loved ones a favor: take all your duties seriously, especially your duties to God. When you do, you'll discover that pleasing your Father in heaven isn't just the right thing to do; it's also the best way to live.

Mommy Milestone for Today

_____
_____
_____
_____
_____

A Quote for Today

For whatever life holds for you and your family in the coming days, weave the unfailing fabric of God's Word through your heart and mind. It will hold strong, even if the rest of life unravels.
—Gigi Graham Tchividjian

REST AND RECHARGE YOUR BATTERIES

Come unto me, all ye that labor and are heavy laden,
and I will give you rest.
—Matthew 11:28 KJV

Even the most inspired Christians can, from time to time, find themselves running on empty. The demands of daily life can drain us of our strength and rob us of the joy that is rightfully ours in Christ. When we find ourselves tired, discouraged, or worse, there is a source from which we can draw the power needed to recharge our spiritual batteries. That source is God.

God expects us to work hard, but He also intends for us to rest. When we fail to take the rest that we need, we do a disservice to ourselves and to our families.

Is your spiritual battery running low? Is your energy on the wane? Are your emotions frayed? If so, it's time to turn your thoughts and your prayers to God. And when you're finished, it's time to rest.

A Timely Tip

It takes energy to care for a baby and
energy to do God's work.
A well-rested mom can do more
for her family, more for herself,
and more for her God. So, if you're
always tired, try this experiment:
turn off the television and go to bed.
You'll be amazed at how good you
feel when you manage
to get enough sleep.

Mommy Milestone for Today

_____

_____

_____

_____

_____

THE HEART OF A SERVANT

The one who blesses others is abundantly blessed;
those who help others are helped.
—Proverbs 11:25 MSG

You are a wondrous creation treasured by God . . . how will you respond? Will you consider each day a glorious opportunity to celebrate life and improve your little corner of the world? Hopefully so, because your corner of the world, like so many other corners of the world, can use all the help it can get.

Nicole Johnson observed, "We only live once, and if we do it well, once is enough." Her words apply to you. You can make a difference, a big difference, in the quality of your own life and lives of your neighbors, your family, and your friends.

You make the world a better place whenever you find a need and fill it. And in these difficult days, the needs are great—but so are your abilities to meet those needs.

Mommy Milestone for Today

_____

_____

_____

_____

_____

_____

A Quote for Today

My heart's desire is to find more opportunities to give myself away and teach my children the joy of service at the same time.

—Liz Curtis Higgs

BEYOND GUILT

*Your beliefs about these things should be kept secret between you
and God. People are happy if they can do what they think
is right without feeling guilty.*
—Romans 14:22 NCV

All of us have made mistakes. Sometimes our failures result from our own shortsightedness. On other occasions, we are swept up in events that are beyond our abilities to control. Under either set of circumstances, we may experience intense feelings of guilt. But God has an answer for the guilt that we feel. That answer, of course, is His forgiveness.

When we ask our Heavenly Father for His forgiveness, He forgives us completely and without reservation. Then, we must do the difficult work of forgiving ourselves in the same way that God has forgiven us: thoroughly and unconditionally.

No mom is perfect, not even you. So, if you're feeling guilty for any reason, it's time for a special kind of housecleaning—a housecleaning of your mind and your heart . . . beginning NOW!

A Quote for Today

Stop blaming yourself and feeling guilty, unworthy, and unloved. Instead begin to say, "If God is for me, who can be against me? God loves me, and I love myself. Praise the Lord, I am free in Jesus' name, amen!"

—Joyce Meyer

Mommy Milestone for Today

_____

_____

_____

_____

_____

HIS WAY

The true children of God are those who let God's Spirit lead them.
—Romans 8:14 NCV

Do you want to experience a life filled with abundance and peace? If so, here's a word of warning: you'll need to resist the temptation to do things "your way" and commit, instead, to do things God's way.

When you make the decision to seek God's will for your life, you will contemplate His Word, and you will be watchful for His signs. You will associate with fellow believers who will encourage your spiritual growth. And, you will listen to that inner voice that speaks to you in the quiet moments of your daily devotionals.

Sometimes, God's plans are crystal clear, but other times, He leads you through the wilderness before He delivers you to the Promised Land. So be patient, keep searching, and keep praying. If you do, then in time God will answer your prayers and make His plans known.

God is right here, and He intends to use you in wonderful, unexpected ways. You'll discover those plans by doing things His way . . . and you'll be eternally grateful that you did.

Mommy Milestone for Today

_____

_____

_____

_____

_____

_____

A Timely Tip

God has a plan for the world, a plan for you, and a plan for your baby. The place where God is leading you is the place where you must go.

A GOD OF INFINITE POSSIBILITIES

We are troubled on every side, yet not distressed;
we are perplexed, but not in despair . . .
—2 Corinthians 4:8 KJV

As we travel the roads of life, all of us are confronted with streets that seem to be dead ends. When we do, we may become discouraged. After all, we live in a society where expectations can be high and demands even higher.

Raising a family is a tough job, especially if one of the family members happens to be a newborn. If you find yourself enduring difficult circumstances, remember that God remains in His heaven. If you become discouraged with the direction of your day or your life, turn your thoughts and prayers to Him. He is a God of possibility, not negativity. He will guide you through your difficulties and beyond them. And then, with a renewed spirit of optimism and hope, you can thank the Giver of all things good for gifts that are simply too profound to fully understand and for treasures that are too numerous to count.

A Quote for Today

When we face an impossible situation, all self-reliance and self-confidence must melt away; we must be totally dependent on Him for the resources.

—Anne Graham Lotz

Mommy Milestone for Today

_____

_____

_____

_____

_____

_____

IF YOU ASK, HE ANSWERS

If you need wisdom—if you want to know what God wants you to do—
ask him, and he will gladly tell you. He will not resent your asking.
—James 1:5 NLT

Is your baby sleeping through the night? Are you getting enough sleep? If so, congratulations. But if not, don't lose hope. This, too, shall pass.

Are you a mother whose batteries need recharging? Ask God to recharge them, and He will. Are you worried? Take your concerns to Him in prayer. Are you discouraged? Seek the comfort of God's promises. Do you feel trapped in circumstances that are disheartening, or confusing, or both? Ask God where He wants you to go, and then go there. In all things great and small, seek the transforming power of God's grace. He hears your prayers. And He answers.

A Quote for Today

By asking in Jesus' name, we're making a request not only in His authority, but also for His interests and His benefit.

—Shirley Dobson

Mommy Milestone for Today

_____

_____

_____

_____

_____

_____

SHARE HIS JOY

The Lord reigns; let the earth rejoice.
—Psalm 97:1 NKJV

Joni Eareckson Tada spoke for Christian women of every generation when she observed, "I wanted the deepest part of me to vibrate with that ancient yet familiar longing—that desire for something that would fill and overflow my soul."

God's plan for our lives includes great joy, but our Heavenly Father will not force His joy upon us. We must accept God's peace by genuinely welcoming His Son into our hearts.

Let us praise the Creator for His priceless gifts, and let us share His Good News with the world. Let us share the Father's promises, His love, and His joy. When we do, we are eternally blessed, and so are our families, our friends, and all whom God has chosen to place along our paths.

A Quote for Today

Joy is the characteristic by which God uses us to re-make the distressing into the desired, the discarded into the creative. Joy is prayer—joy is strength—joy is love—joy is a net of love by which you can catch souls.

—Mother Teresa

Mommy Milestone for Today

_____

_____

_____

_____

_____

CLAIMING CONTENTMENT IN A DISCONTENTED WORLD

But godliness with contentment is a great gain.
—1 Timothy 6:6 HCSB

Everywhere we turn, or so it seems, the world promises us contentment and happiness. We are bombarded by messages offering us the "good life" if only we will purchase products and services that are designed to provide happiness, success, and contentment. But the contentment that the world offers is fleeting and incomplete. Thankfully, the contentment that God offers is all encompassing and everlasting.

Happiness depends less upon our circumstances than upon our thoughts. When we turn our thoughts to God, to His gifts, and to His glorious creation, we experience the joy that God intends for His children. But, when we focus on the negative aspects of life—or when we disobey God's commandments—we create needless hardships for ourselves and our loved ones.

Do you sincerely want to be a contented Christian mom, a woman who, day in and day out, celebrates her family and her life? Then set your mind and your heart upon God's love and His grace. Seek first the salvation that is available through a personal relationship with Jesus Christ, and then claim the joy, the contentment, and the spiritual abundance that God offers His children.

Mommy Milestone for Today

_____

_____

_____

_____

_____

_____

LIVING COURAGEOUSLY

So do not fear, for I am with you; do not be dismayed,
for I am your God. I will strengthen you and help you;
I will uphold you with my righteous right hand.
—Isaiah 41:10 NIV

Christian moms have every reason to live courageously. After all, the final battle has already been won on the cross at Calvary. But even dedicated followers of Christ may find their courage tested by the inevitable disappointments and fears that visit the lives of believers and non-believers alike.

When you find yourself worried about the challenges of today or the uncertainties of tomorrow, you must ask yourself whether or not you are ready to place your concerns and your life in God's all-powerful, all-knowing, all-loving hands. If the answer to that question is yes—as it should be—then you can draw courage today from the source of strength that never fails: your Heavenly Father.

A Quote for Today

If God has you in the palm of his
hand and your real life is secure in
him, then you can venture forth—
into the places and relationships,
the challenges, the very heart
of the storm—and you
will be safe there.

—Paula Rinehart

Mommy Milestone for Today

_____

_____

_____

_____

_____

_____

EMBRACING GOD'S LOVE

We love him, because he first loved us.
—1 John 4:19 KJV

God made you and your baby in His own image. And, He has offered you the priceless gift of eternal life through the person of His Son, Jesus Christ. And now, precisely because you are a wondrous creation treasured by God, a question presents itself: What will you do in response to the Creator's love? Will you ignore it or embrace it? Will you return it or neglect it? That decision, of course, is yours and yours alone.

When you embrace God's love, your life's purpose is forever changed. When you embrace God's love, you feel differently about yourself, your baby, your family, your neighbors, and your world. And, you gladly share His message—and His love—with others.

Your Heavenly Father—a God of infinite love and mercy—is waiting to embrace you with open arms. Accept His love today and forever.

Mommy Milestone for Today

_____

_____

_____

_____

_____

_____

A Quote for Today

The love of God is so vast,
the power of His touch so
invigorating, we could just stay
in His presence for hours,
soaking up His glory,
basking in His blessings.

—Debra Evans

MAKING TIME FOR JESUS

I am the Vine, you are the branches.
When you're joined with me and I with you, the relation intimate
and organic, the harvest is sure to be abundant.
—John 15:5 MSG

I f you're a new mom with too many responsibilities and too few hours in which to fulfill them, you are not alone. Motherhood is so demanding that sometimes you may feel as if you have no time for yourself . . . and no time for God.

Has the busy pace of life robbed you of the peace that might otherwise be yours through Jesus Christ? If so, you are simply too busy for your own good. Through His Son, Jesus, God offers you a peace that passes human understanding, but He won't force His peace upon you; in order to experience it, you must slow down long enough to sense His presence and His love.

Today, as a gift to yourself, to your baby, to your family, and to the world, slow down long enough to claim the inner peace that is your spiritual birthright: the peace of Jesus Christ.

A Quote for Today

The key to my understanding of the Bible is a personal relationship to Jesus Christ.
—Oswald Chambers

Mommy Milestone for Today

_____

_____

_____

_____

_____

_____

SERVING OTHERS

Each one of us needs to look after the good of the people around us,
asking ourselves, "How can I help?" That's exactly what Jesus did.
He didn't make it easy for himself by avoiding people's troubles,
but waded right in and helped out. "I took on the troubles of the troubled,"
is the way Scripture puts it.
—Romans 15:2-3 MSG

We live in a world that glorifies power, prestige, fame, and money. But the words of Jesus teach us that the most esteemed men and women in this world are not the self-congratulatory leaders of society but are instead the humblest of servants.

Today, you may feel the temptation to build yourself up in the eyes of your neighbors. Resist that temptation. Instead, serve your neighbors quietly and without fanfare. Find a need and fill it . . . humbly. Lend a helping hand . . . anonymously. Share a word of kindness . . . with quiet sincerity. As you go about your daily activities, and as you care for the precious baby whom God has entrusted to your care, remember that the Savior of all humanity made Himself a servant. And we, as His followers, must do no less.

Mommy Milestone for Today

_____

_____

_____

_____

_____

_____

A Quote for Today

Jesus never asks us to give Him what we don't have. But He does demand that we give Him all we do have if we want to be a part of what He wishes to do in the lives of those around us!
—Anne Graham Lotz

WHAT KIND OF EXAMPLE?

You are the light that gives light to the world. In the same way, you should be a light for other people. Live so that they will see the good things you do and will praise your Father in heaven.
—Matthew 5:14, 16 NCV

Even if you're a first-time mom, it's not too soon to begin thinking about the role model you are today, and the role model you want to become in the future. Hopefully, the life you lead and the choices you make can serve as an enduring example of the spiritual abundance that is available to all who worship God and obey His commandments.

Are you a woman whose behavior serves as a positive example for others to follow? And, are you determined to become the kind of mother whose life demonstrates the importance of patience, kindness, perseverance, and faith? If so, your child will be blessed, and you will become a powerful force for good in a world that desperately needs positive influences such as yours.

A Quote for Today

Preach the gospel at all times and, if necessary, use words.
—St. Francis of Assisi

Mommy Milestone
for Today

_____

_____

_____

_____

_____

HE IS FAITHFUL

*God is faithful, by whom you were called into the fellowship of His Son,
Jesus Christ our Lord.*

—1 Corinthians 1:9 NKJV

God is faithful to us even when we are not faithful to Him. God keeps His promises to us even when we stray far from His path. God offers us countless blessings, but He does not force His blessings upon us. If we are to experience His love and His grace, we must claim them for ourselves.

God is with you. Listen prayerfully to the quiet voice of your Heavenly Father. Talk with God often; seek His guidance; watch for His signs; listen to the wisdom that He shares through the reliable voice of your own conscience.

God loves you, and you deserve all the best that God has to offer. You can claim His blessings today by being faithful to Him.

Mommy Milestone for Today

_____

_____

_____

_____

_____

_____

A Quote for Today

It is a joy that God never abandons His children. He guides faithfully all who listen to His directions.

—Corrie ten Boom

A Timely Tip

When you have concerns about your future or your family, remember that the Creator of heaven and earth is on your side. He always keeps His promises, now and forever.

BIG DREAMS

With God's power working in us, God can do much, much more
than anything we can ask or imagine.
—Ephesians 3:20 NCV

It takes courage to dream big dreams—dreams for yourself and your family. You'll discover the courage to dream big when you do three things: accept the past, trust God to handle the future, and make the most of the time He has given you today.

Are you excited about the opportunities of today and thrilled by the possibilities of tomorrow? Do you confidently expect God to lead you and yours to a place of abundance, peace, and joy? If you trust God's promises, you should believe that your future is intensely and eternally bright.

Today, promise yourself that you'll do your family (and the world) a king-sized favor by whole-heartedly pursuing your dreams. After all, no dreams are too big for God—not even yours. So start living—and dreaming—accordingly.

A Quote for Today

The future lies all before us.
Shall it only be a slight advance
upon what we usually do? Ought it
not to be a bound, a leap forward
to altitudes of endeavor and success
undreamed of before?

—Annie Armstrong

Mommy Milestone for Today

_____

_____

_____

_____

_____

SHARING THE GIFT OF HOPE

Then you will know that I am the Lord;
those who put their hope in Me will not be put to shame.
—Isaiah 49:23 HCSB

Are you a hopeful, optimistic, encouraging believer? And do you associate with like-minded people? The answer to these questions will determine, to a surprising extent, the direction and the quality of your life.

Hope, like other human emotions, is contagious. When we associate with hope-filled Christians, we are encouraged by their faith and optimism. But, if we spend too much time in the company of naysayers and pessimists, our attitudes, like theirs, tend to be cynical and negative.

As a faithful Christian, you have every reason to be hopeful, and you have every reason to share your hopes with others. So today, look for reasons to celebrate God's endless blessings. And while you're at it, look for people who will join you in the celebration. You'll be better for their company, and they'll be better for yours.

Mommy Milestone
for Today

_____

_____

_____

_____

_____

_____

A Quote for Today

You can't light another's path
without casting light on your own.

—John Maxwell

GUARD YOUR HEART

Guard your heart above all else, for it is the source of life.
—Proverbs 4:23 HCSB

You and your baby are near and dear to God. He loves you more than you can imagine, and He wants the very best for you. And one more thing: God wants you, as the mother of that precious newborn, to guard your heart.

Every day, you are faced with choices . . . lots of them. You can do the right thing, or not. You can tell the truth, or not. You can be kind, and generous, and obedient. Or not.

Today, the world will offer you countless opportunities to let down your guard and, by doing so, let the devil do his worst. Be watchful and obedient. Guard your heart by giving it to your Heavenly Father; it is safe with Him.

A Quote for Today

The fruit of our placing all things in
God's hands is the presence of
His abiding peace in our hearts.
—Hannah Whitall Smith

A Timely Tip

Your world is full of distractions
and temptations. Your challenge
is to live in the world
but not be of the world.

Mommy Milestone for Today

_____

_____

_____

_____

_____

THE ATTITUDE OF GRATITUDE

Everything created by God is good, and nothing is to be rejected,
if it is received with gratitude; for it is sanctified
by means of the word of God and prayer.
—1 Timothy 4:4-5 NASB

As the mother of a newborn, your life is incredibly busy and, at times, completely exhausting. Amid the rush and crush of your maternal responsibilities, it is easy to lose sight of God's love, and it's easy to overlook His countless blessings.

Whenever we forget to slow down and say "thank You" to our Maker, we rob ourselves of His abundance, His peace, and His joy.

Instead of ignoring God, we must praise Him many times each day. Then, with gratitude in our hearts, we can face the day's duties with the perspective and power that only He can provide.

Mommy Milestone for Today

_____

_____

_____

_____

_____

_____

A Quote for Today

A sense of gratitude for God's presence in our lives will help open our eyes to what He has done in the past and what He will do in the future.

—Emilie Barnes

A Timely Tip

Today, challenge your faith by asking yourself if you are sufficiently grateful for the blessings God has given you. And if your attitude could use a little more gratitude, take extra time today, and every day hereafter, to make a more thorough accounting of your blessings.

THE BEST DAY TO CELEBRATE

Celebrate God all day, every day. I mean, revel in him!
—Philippians 4:4 MSG

What is the best day to celebrate life? This one! Today and every day should be a day of prayer and celebration as we consider the Good News of God's free gift: salvation through Jesus Christ.

What do you expect from the day ahead? Are you expecting God to do wonderful things, or are you living beneath a cloud of apprehension and doubt? The familiar words of Psalm 118:24 remind us of a profound yet simple truth: "This is the day which the LORD hath made" (KJV). Our duty, as believers, is to rejoice in God's marvelous creation. Now.

A Quote for Today

Trusting God does not make me less
of a woman. It doesn't compromise
my personality as a strong woman.
Depending on Him celebrates the
wonderful, miraculous gift
He has entrusted to me.
Trusting Him is my strength.
—Suzanne Dale Ezell

Mommy Milestone for Today

_____

_____

_____

_____

_____

_____

ABOVE AND BEYOND THE STRESS

In my distress I called upon the LORD,
and cried unto my God: he heard my voice. . . .
—Psalm 18:6 KJV

Face facts: motherhood can be stressful . . . very stressful. You live in a world that is brimming with demands, distractions, and deadlines (not to mention toils, troubles, and timetables). Whew! No wonder you may be stressed.

What can you do in response to the stressors of everyday life? A wonderful place to start is by turning things over to God.

God's Word reminds us that this day, like every other, is a glorious gift from the Father. How will you use that gift? Will you celebrate it and use it for His purposes? If so, you'll discover that when you turn things over to Him—when you allow God to rule over every corner of your life—He will calm your fears and guide your steps.

So today, make sure that you focus on God and upon His will for your life. Then, ask for His help. And remember: No challenge is too great for Him. Not even yours.

Mommy Milestone for Today

_____

_____

_____

_____

_____

_____

A Quote for Today

The happiest people I know are the ones who have learned how to hold everything loosely and have given the worrisome, stress-filled, fearful details of their lives into God's keeping.
—Charles Swindoll

Day 301 · Today's Date _____

THE SELF-FULFILLING PROPHECY

But as for me, I will hope continually,
and will praise You yet more and more.
—Psalm 71:14 NASB

The self-fulfilling prophecy is alive, well, and living at your house. If you trust God and have faith for the future, your optimistic beliefs will give you direction and motivation. That's one reason that you should never lose hope, but certainly not the only reason. The primary reason that you, as a Christian mom, should never lose hope, is because of God's unfailing promises.

Your thoughts have the power to lift you up or to hold you down. When you acquire the habit of hopeful thinking, you will have acquired a powerful tool for improving your life. So if you find yourself falling into the spiritual traps of worry and discouragement, seek the healing touch of Jesus and the encouraging words of fellow Christians. And if you fall into the terrible habit of negative thinking, think again. After all, God's Word teaches us that Christ can overcome every difficulty (John 16:33). And when God makes a promise, He keeps it.

A Quote for Today

And still today, when you boil it all down, our message to the world—even to the world that comes disguised as our child's schoolteacher, our next-door neighbor, or our personal hair stylist—is hope.
—Becky Tirabassi

Mommy Milestone for Today

_____

_____

_____

_____

_____

HIS PEACE

But now in Christ Jesus you who once were far off have been brought near by the blood of Christ. For He Himself is our peace.
—Ephesians 2:13-14 NKJV

For busy mothers, a moment's peace can be a scare commodity. But no matter how numerous the interruptions and demands of the day, God is ever-present, always ready and willing to offer solace to those who seek "the peace that passes all understanding."

Have you found the genuine peace that can be yours through Jesus Christ? Or are you still rushing after the illusion of "peace and happiness" that the world promises but cannot deliver? Today, as a gift to yourself, to your family, and to your friends, claim the inner peace that is your spiritual birthright: the peace of Jesus Christ. It is offered freely; it has been paid for in full; it is yours for the asking. So ask. And then share.

Mommy Milestone for Today

_____

_____

_____

_____

_____

_____

A Quote for Today

In the center of a hurricane there is absolute quiet and peace.
There is no safer place than in the center of the will of God.

—Corrie ten Boom

DURING DIFFICULT DAYS

In my trouble I called to the Lord; I cried out to my God.
From his temple he heard my voice;
my call for help reached his ears.
—2 Samuel 22:7 NCV

All of us face difficult days. Sometimes even the most optimistic moms can become discouraged, and you are no exception. If you find yourself enduring difficult circumstances, perhaps it's time for an extreme intellectual makeover—perhaps it's time to focus more on your strengths and opportunities, and less on the challenges that confront you And one more thing: perhaps it's time to put a little more faith in God.

Your Heavenly Father will guide you if you let Him. He will lead you through your difficulties—and beyond them—if you let Him. He will share His love and be true to His promises. And, He will renew your strength. Then, with a renewed spirit of optimism and hope, you can thank the Giver of all things good for gifts that are simply too numerous to count.

A Quote for Today

No matter how heavy the burden, daily strength is given, so I expect we need not give ourselves any concern as to what the outcome will be. We must simply go forward.

—Annie Armstrong

Mommy Milestone for Today

_____

_____

_____

_____

_____

HIS ABUNDANCE

I have come that they may have life,
and that they may have it more abundantly.
—John 10:10 NKJV

The Bible gives us hope—as Christians we can enjoy lives filled with abundance.

But what, exactly, did Jesus mean when, in John 10:10, He promised "life . . . more abundantly"? Was He referring to material possessions or financial wealth? Hardly. Jesus offers a different kind of abundance: a spiritual richness that extends beyond the temporal boundaries of this world.

Is material abundance part of God's plan for our lives? Perhaps. But in every circumstance of life, during times of wealth or times of want, God will provide us what we need if we trust Him (Matthew 6). May we, as believers, claim the riches of Christ Jesus every day that we live, and may we share His blessings with all who cross our path.

Mommy Milestone for Today

_____

_____

_____

_____

_____

A Quote for Today

If you want purpose and meaning
and satisfaction and fulfillment
and peace and hope and joy
and abundant life that lasts forever,
look to Jesus.
—Anne Graham Lotz

WHEN YOU ARE TESTED

Blessed be the God and Father of our Lord Jesus Christ, the Father of mercies and the God of all comfort. He comforts us in all our affliction, so that we may be able to comfort those who are in any kind of affliction, through the comfort we ourselves receive from God.

—2 Corinthians 1:3-4 HCSB

When the sun is shining and all is well, it is easy to celebrate your life and your baby. But, when life takes a turn for the worse, as it will from time to time, your faith will be tested.

As the mother of a new baby, you know about hard work, long hours, and occasional bouts of absolute exhaustion. But, even when the job is difficult, the rewards of caring for your baby always outweigh the costs.

Corrie ten Boom observed, "The strength that we claim from God's Word does not depend on circumstances. Circumstances will be difficult, but our strength will be sufficient." So the next time you're exhausted, or frustrated, or both, remind yourself that every difficult day must come to an end . . . and when tough times are tough, tough moms (like you) are even tougher.

A Quote for Today

"But he knows the way that I take; when he has tested me, I will come forth as gold" (Job 23:10 NIV). We will all "come forth as gold" if we understand that God is sovereign and knows what is best, even when we cannot understand what is happening at the time.

—Shirley Dobson

Mommy Milestone
for Today

_____

_____

_____

_____

_____

THE BALANCING ACT

Come to Me, all you who labor and are heavy laden,
and I will give you rest. Take My yoke upon you and learn from Me,
for I am gentle and lowly in heart, and you will find rest for your souls.
For My yoke is easy and My burden is light.
—Matthew 11:28-30 NKJV

Face facts: Caring for a newborn is a responsibility like no other—at times demanding, at times exhausting, at times frustrating, but always rewarding. For first-time moms, the job may become a delicate balancing act.

God's Word promises us that when we ask for His guidance, He will provide it: "In all your ways acknowledge Him, and He shall direct your paths" (Proverbs 3:6 NKJV). So, today, if you're having trouble balancing your life, it's time to have a little chat with God. And, if you listen carefully to His instructions, you will manage your life and your time in a way that's right for you and your baby. When you do, everybody wins.

Mommy Milestone for Today

_____

_____

_____

_____

_____

A Quote for Today

We are all created differently.
We share a common need
to balance the different parts
of our lives.
—Dr. Walt Larimore

Day 307 • Today's Date _____

WHAT'S YOUR ATTITUDE?

Set your minds on what is above, not on what is on the earth.
—Colossians 3:2 HCSB

The Christian life is a cause for celebration, but sometimes we don't feel much like celebrating. In fact, when the weight of the world (and the rigors of motherhood) bear down upon our shoulders, celebration may be the last thing on our minds . . . but it shouldn't be. As God's children—and as the mothers of our own children—we have been blessed beyond measure.

This day is a non-renewable resource—once it's gone, it's gone forever. So celebrate the life that God has given you by thinking optimistically about yourself, your family, and your future. Give thanks to the One who has showered you with blessings, and trust in your heart that He wants to give you so much more.

A Quote for Today

We are either the masters or
the victims of our attitudes.
It is a matter of personal choice.
Who we are today is the result
of choices we made yesterday.
Tomorrow, we will become what
we choose today. To change means
to choose to change.
—John Maxwell

Mommy Milestone for Today

_____

_____

_____

_____

_____

BEYOND BITTERNESS

All bitterness, anger and wrath, insult and slander must be removed from you, along with all wickedness. And be kind and compassionate to one another, forgiving one another, just as God also forgave you in Christ.
—Ephesians 4:31-32 HCSB

Are you mired in the quicksand of bitterness or regret? If so, you are not only disobeying God's Word, you are also wasting your time. The world holds few if any rewards for those who remain angrily focused upon the past. Still, the act of forgiveness is difficult for all but the most saintly men and women.

Being frail, fallible, imperfect human beings, most of us are quick to anger, quick to blame, slow to forgive, and even slower to forget. Yet as Christians, we are commanded to forgive others, just as we, too, have been forgiven.

If there exists even one person—alive or dead—against whom you hold bitter feelings, it's time to forgive. Or, if you are embittered against yourself for some past mistake or shortcoming, it's finally time to forgive yourself and move on. Hatred, bitterness, and regret are not part of God's plan for your life. Forgiveness is.

Mommy Milestone for Today

_____

_____

_____

_____

_____

_____

A Quote for Today

Forgiveness enables you to bury your grudge in icy earth. To put the past behind you. To flush resentment away by being the first to forgive. Forgiveness fashions your future. It is a brave and brash thing to do.

—Barbara Johnson

ACTIONS SPEAK LOUDER

Are there those among you who are truly wise and understanding?
Then they should show it by living right and doing good things
with a gentleness that comes from wisdom.

—James 3:13 NCV

The old saying is both familiar and true: actions speak louder than words. And as believers, we must beware: our actions should always give credence to the changes that Christ can make in the lives of those who walk with Him.

God calls upon each of us to act in accordance with His will and with respect for His commandments. If we are to be responsible believers, we must realize that it is never enough simply to hear the instructions of God; we must also live by them. And it is never enough to wait idly by while others do God's work here on earth; we, too, must act. Doing God's work is a responsibility that each of us must bear, and when we do, our loving Heavenly Father rewards our efforts with a bountiful harvest.

A Quote for Today

Give to us clear vision that we may know where to stand and what to stand for. Let us not be content to wait and see what will happen, but give us the determination to make the right things happen.

—Peter Marshall

Mommy Milestone for Today

_____

_____

_____

_____

_____

HIS WILL AND OURS

Blessed are those servants,
whom the lord when he cometh shall find watching . . .
—Luke 12:37 KJV

God has will, and so do we. He gave us the power to make choices for ourselves, and He created a world in which those choices have consequences. The ultimate choice that we face, of course, is what to do about God. We can cast our lot with Him by choosing Jesus Christ as our personal Savior, or not. The choice is ours alone.

We also face thousands of small choices that make up the fabric of daily life. When we align those choices with God's commandments, and when we align our lives with God's will, we receive His abundance, His peace, and His joy. But when we struggle against God's will for our lives, we reap a bitter harvest indeed.

Today, you'll face thousands of small choices; as you do, use God's Word as your guide. And, as you face the ultimate choice, place God's Son and God's will and God's love at the center of your life. You'll discover that God's plan is far grander than any you could have imagined.

Mommy Milestone for Today

_____

_____

_____

_____

_____

_____

A Quote for Today

To yield to God means to belong to God, and to belong to God means to have all His infinite power. To belong to God means to have all.

—Hannah Whitall Smith

WHEN FAITH SLIPS AWAY

Immediately the father of the child cried out and said with tears,
"Lord, I believe; help my unbelief!"
—Mark 9:24 NKJV

Sometimes we feel threatened by the storms of life. During these moments, when our hearts are flooded with uncertainty, we must remember that God is not simply near, He is here.

Have you ever felt your faith in God slipping away? If so, you are in good company. Even the most faithful Christians are, at times, beset by occasional bouts of discouragement and doubt. But even when you feel far removed from God, God never leaves your side. He is always with you, always willing to calm the storms of life. When you sincerely seek His presence—and when you genuinely seek to establish a deeper, more meaningful relationship with His Son—God will calm your fears, answer your prayers, and restore your soul.

A Quote for Today

We are most vulnerable to
the piercing winds of doubt when
we distance ourselves from the
mission and fellowship to which
Christ has called us.

—Joni Eareckson Tada

Mommy Milestone for Today

_____

_____

_____

_____

_____

_____

BEYOND THE FRUSTRATIONS

But now you must also put away all the following: anger, wrath,
malice, slander, and filthy language from your mouth.
—Colossians 3:8 HCSB

Motherhood is vastly rewarding, but every mother knows that it can be, at times, frustrating. No baby is perfect, and even the most loving mother's patience can, on occasion, wear thin.

Your temper is either your master or your servant. Either you control it, or it controls you. And the extent to which you allow anger to rule your life will determine, to a surprising degree, the quality of your relationships with others and your relationship with God.

If you've allowed anger to become a regular visitor at your house, you should pray for wisdom, for patience, and for a heart that is so filled with forgiveness that it contains no room for bitterness. God will help you terminate your tantrums if you ask Him to—and that's a good thing because anger and peace cannot coexist in the same mind.

So the next time you're tempted to lose your temper over the minor inconveniences of life (or the minor mishaps of your precious baby), don't. Turn away from anger, hatred, bitterness, and regret. Turn instead to God. He's waiting with open arms . . . patiently.

Mommy Milestone for Today

_____

_____

_____

_____

_____

_____

A Quote for Today

Anger breeds remorse in the heart,
discord in the home, bitterness
in the community,
and confusion in the state.
—Billy Graham

PRAYING ABOUT FORGIVENESS

When a believing person prays, great things happen.
—James 5:16 NCV

Have you been unable to forgive someone? Talk to God about it. Do you have questions that you simply can't answer? Ask for the guidance of your Father in heaven. Have you been unable to forgive yourself for something you did long ago? God has forgiven you; now it's your turn to forgive yourself. Do you sincerely seek the gift of peace and wholeness that only God can give? Then obey His commandments and accept the grace of His only begotten Son.

Whatever your needs, God can provide—so ask. Whatever your circumstance, never lose heart. Your Father is faithful. And His promises never fail.

A Quote for Today

Learn to pray to God in such a way that you are trusting Him as your Physician to do what He knows is best. Confess to Him the disease, and let Him choose the remedy.

—St. Augustine

Mommy Milestone for Today

_____

_____

_____

_____

_____

_____

GIVING THANKS TO THE GIVER

Is anyone happy? Let him sing songs of praise.
—James 5:13 NIV

Are you a mom who celebrates life? Hopefully you are! God has richly blessed you, and He wants you to rejoice in His gifts.

God fills each day to the brim with possibilities, and He challenges each of us to use our gifts for the glory of His kingdom. When we honor the Father and place Him at the center of our lives, every day becomes a cause for celebration.

Today is a non-renewable resource—once it's gone, it's gone forever. Our responsibility—both as mothers and as believers—is to use this day in the service of God's will and in the service of His people. When we do so, we enrich our own lives and the lives of those whom we love. And the Father smiles.

A Quote for Today

Our God is the sovereign Creator of the universe! He loves us as His own children and has provided every good thing we have; He is worthy of our praise every moment.

—Shirley Dobson

Mommy Milestone for Today

_____

_____

_____

_____

_____

_____

IN FOCUS

Look straight ahead, and fix your eyes on what lies before you.
Mark out a straight path for your feet; then stick to the path and stay safe.
Don't get sidetracked; keep your feet from following evil.
—Proverbs 4:25-27 NLT

What is your focus today? Are you willing to focus your thoughts and energies on God's blessings and upon His love for your family? Or will you turn your thoughts to other things? This day—and every day hereafter—is a chance to celebrate the life that God has given you. It's also a chance to give thanks to the One who has offered you more blessings than you can possibly count.

Today, why not focus your thoughts on the joy that is rightfully yours in Christ? Why not take time to celebrate God's glorious creation? Why not trust your hopes instead of your fears? When you do, you will think optimistically about yourself and your world . . . and you can then share your optimism with others. They'll be better for it, and so will you. But not necessarily in that order.

A Quote for Today

Whatever we focus on
determines what we become.
—E. Stanley Jones

Mommy Milestone
for Today

_____

_____

_____

_____

_____

_____

BEING GENTLE WITH YOURSELF

Cast thy burden upon the LORD, and he shall sustain thee:
he shall never suffer the righteous to be moved.
—Psalm 55:22 KJV

Proverbs 16:32 teaches us that "Patience is better than strength" (NCV). God's message, then, is clear: we must be patient with all people, beginning with that particular person who stares back at us each time we gaze into the mirror.

Most of us have high expectations and lofty goals. We want to receive God's blessings now, not later. And, of course, we want our lives to unfold according to our own wishes and our own timetables—not God's. Yet throughout the Bible, we are instructed that patience is the companion of wisdom.

God's Word promises that when we genuinely open our hearts to the Lord, He accepts us just as we are. And, if the Creator of the universe loves us, the One who knows us better than we know ourselves, then who are we to believe otherwise?

Mommy Milestone for Today

_____

_____

_____

_____

_____

A Quote for Today

Do not lose courage in considering your own imperfections.
—St. Francis de Sales

ENCOURAGING WORDS FOR FAMILY AND FRIENDS

*Do not let any unwholesome talk come out of your mouths,
but only what is helpful for building others up according to their needs,
that it may benefit those who listen.*
—Ephesians 4:29 NIV

Life is a team sport, and all of us need occasional pep-talks from our teammates. As Christians, we are called upon to spread the Good News of Christ, and we are also called to spread a message of encouragement and hope to the world.

Whether you realize it or not, many people with whom you come in contact every day are in desperate need of a smile or an encouraging word. The world can be a difficult place, and countless friends and family members may be troubled by the challenges of everyday life. Since you don't always know who needs your help, the best strategy is to try to encourage all the people who cross your path. So today, be a world-class source of encouragement to everyone you meet. Never has the need been greater.

A Quote for Today

The mind of Christ is to be learned in the family. Strength of character may be acquired at work, but beauty of character is learned at home.

—Henry Drummond

Mommy Milestone for Today

_____

_____

_____

_____

_____

SEEKING HIS WISDOM

Does not wisdom call out? Does not understanding raise her voice?
On the heights along the way, where the paths meet, she takes her stand.
—Proverbs 8:1-2 NIV

Do you seek wisdom for yourself and for your family? Of course you do. But, as a thoughtful mom living in a society that is filled with temptations and distractions, you know that it's all too easy for parents and children alike to stray far from the source of the ultimate wisdom: God's Holy Word.

When you commit yourself to daily study of God's Word—and when you live according to His commandments—you will become wise . . . in time. But don't expect to open your Bible today and be wise tomorrow. Acquiring wisdom takes time.

Today and every day, as a way of understanding God's plan for your life, you should study His Word and live by it. When you do, you will accumulate a storehouse of wisdom that will enrich your own life and the lives of your family members, your friends, and the world.

Mommy Milestone for Today

A Quote for Today

When you and I are related to Jesus Christ, our strength and wisdom and peace and joy and love and hope may run out, but His life rushes in to keep us filled to the brim. We are showered with blessings, not because of anything we have or have not done, but simply because of Him.

—Anne Graham Lotz

QUIET TIME

In quietness and confidence shall be your strength.
—Isaiah 30:15 NKJV

Face it: We live in a noisy world, a world filled with distractions, frustrations, interruptions, and complications. It's easy to become sidetracked and hard to stay focused. But if we allow the world's distractions to separate us from God's peace, we do ourselves and our loved ones a profound disservice.

Are you one of those busy moms who rush through the day with scarcely a single moment for quiet contemplation and prayer? If so, it's time to reorder your priorities.

Nothing is more important than the time you spend with your Savior. Absolutely nothing. So, make sure that you spend quiet time with Him every day, starting with this day.

A Quote for Today

Faithful prayer warriors and devoted Bible lovers will tell you that their passion for disciplined quiet time with the Lord is not a sign of strength but an admission of weakness—a hard-earned realization that they are nothing on their own compared with who they are after they've been with him.

—Doris Greig

Mommy Milestone for Today

_____

_____

_____

_____

_____

His Promises to You

This is my comfort in my affliction: Your promise has given me life.
—Psalm 119:50 HCSB

God's promises are found in a book like no other: the Holy Bible. The Bible is a road map for life here on earth and for life eternal. As Christians, we are called upon to trust its promises, to follow its commandments, and to share its Good News.

As believers, we must study the Bible daily and meditate upon its meaning for our lives. Otherwise, we deprive ourselves of a priceless gift from our Creator. God's Holy Word is, indeed, a transforming, life-changing, one-of-a-kind treasure. And, a passing acquaintance with the Good Book is insufficient for Christians who seek to obey God's Word and to understand His will.

God has made promises to mankind and to you. God's promises never fail and they never grow old. You must trust those promises and share them with your family, with your friends, and with the world.

Mommy Milestone for Today

_____

_____

_____

_____

_____

_____

A Quote for Today

Fear and doubt are conquered by a faith that rejoices. And faith can rejoice because the promises of God are as certain as God Himself.

—Kay Arthur

WHOM TO PLEASE?

Do you think I am trying to make people accept me?
No, God is the One I am trying to please. Am I trying to please people?
If I still wanted to please people, I would not be a servant of Christ.
—Galatians 1:10 NCV

Rick Warren observed, "Those who follow the crowd usually get lost in it." We know these words to be true, but oftentimes we fail to live by them. Instead of trusting God for guidance, we imitate our neighbors and suffer the consequences. Instead of seeking to please our Father in heaven, we strive to please our peers, with decidedly mixed results.

Whom will you try to please today, Mom? Will you strive to please God first, and will you encourage your family to do likewise? Hopefully so. After all, your obligation is most certainly not to neighbors, to friends, or even to society. Your obligation is to an all-knowing, all-powerful God. You must seek to please Him first and always. No exceptions.

A Quote for Today

Many people never receive God's best for them because they are addicted to the approval of others.
—Joyce Meyer

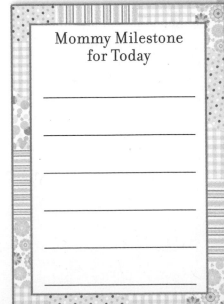

Mommy Milestone
for Today

_____

_____

_____

_____

_____

_____

HE PROVIDES

The Lord is my rock and my fortress and my deliverer;
the God of my strength, in whom I will trust.
—2 Samuel 22:2-3 NKJV

As a busy mom who's been entrusted with the care and feeding of a newborn, you know from firsthand experience that life is not always easy. But as a recipient of God's grace, you also know that you are protected by a loving Heavenly Father.

In times of trouble, God will comfort you; in times of sorrow, He will dry your tears. When you are troubled, or weak, or sorrowful, God is neither distant nor disinterested. To the contrary, God is always present and always vitally engaged in the events of your life. Reach out to Him, and build your future on the rock that cannot be shaken . . . trust in God and rely upon His provisions. He can provide everything you really need . . . and far, far more.

Mommy Milestone for Today

_____

_____

_____

_____

_____

A Quote for Today

God will never let you sink under
your circumstances. He always
provides a safety net and
His love always encircles.

—Barbara Johnson

First Things First

First pay attention to me, and then relax.
Now you can take it easy—you're in good hands.
—Proverbs 1:33 MSG

"First things first." These words are easy to speak but hard to put into practice. For a busy mom living in a demanding world, placing first things first can be difficult indeed. Why? Because so many people are expecting so many things from you.

If you're having trouble prioritizing your day, perhaps you've been trying to organize your life according to your own plans, not God's. A better strategy, of course, is to take your daily obligations and place them in the hands of your Creator. To do so, you must prioritize your day according to God's commandments, and you must seek His will and His wisdom in all matters. Then, you can face the day with the assurance that the same God who created our universe out of nothingness will help you place first things first in your own life.

Do you feel overwhelmed by the challenges of caring for your baby? Turn the concerns of this day over to God—prayerfully, earnestly, and often. Then listen for His answer . . . and trust the answer He gives.

A Quote for Today

Does God care about all the responsibilities we have to juggle in our daily lives? Of course. But he cares more that our lives demonstrate balance, the ability to discern what is essential and give ourselves fully to it.

—Penelope Stokes

Mommy Milestone for Today

_____

_____

_____

_____

_____

_____

REPENTANCE AND PEACE

They should repent, turn to God, and do works befitting repentance.
—Acts 26:20 NKJV

Who among us has sinned? All of us. But, the good news is this: When we ask God's forgiveness and turn our hearts to Him, He forgives us absolutely and completely.

Genuine repentance requires more than simply offering God apologies for our misdeeds. Real repentance may start with feelings of sorrow and remorse, but it ends only when we turn away from the sin that has heretofore distanced us from our Creator. As long as we are still engaged in sin, we may be sorry but we have not fully "repented."

Is there an aspect of your life that is distancing you from your God and robbing you of His peace? If so, ask for His forgiveness, and—just as importantly—stop sinning. Then, wrap yourself in the protection of God's Word. When you do, you will be forgiven, you will be secure, and you will know peace.

Mommy Milestone for Today

_____

_____

_____

_____

_____

_____

A Quote for Today

One of the first things
the Holy Spirit does when
He comes into your life is to give
you a desire to be holy.
—Anne Graham Lotz

YOUR BELIEFS AND YOUR LIFE

For the kingdom of God is not in talk but in power.
—1 Corinthians 4:20 HCSB

Do you weave your beliefs into the very fabric of your day? If you do, God will honor your good works, and your good works will honor God.

If you seek to be a responsible mom and a positive role model, you must realize that it is never enough to hear the instructions of God; you must also live by them. And it is never enough to wait idly by while others do God's work here on earth. You, too, must act.

Doing God's work is a responsibility that every Christian (including you) should bear. And when you do, your loving Heavenly Father will reward your efforts with a bountiful harvest.

A Quote for Today

Jesus taught that the evidence that confirms our leaps of faith comes after we risk believing, not before.
—Gloria Gaither

Mommy Milestone for Today

_____

_____

_____

_____

_____

OUR HOPES AND HIS PEACE

*And as they thus spake, Jesus himself stood in the midst of them,
and saith unto them, Peace be unto you.*
—Luke 24:36 KJV

The beautiful words of John 14:27 give us hope: "Peace I leave with you, my peace I give unto you . . . ." Jesus offers us peace, not as the world gives, but as He alone gives. We, as believers, can accept His peace or ignore it.

When we accept the peace of Jesus Christ into our hearts, our lives are transformed. And then, because we possess the gift of peace, we can share that gift with fellow Christians, family members, friends, and associates. If, on the other hand, we choose to ignore the gift of peace—for whatever reason—we cannot share what we do not possess.

As every mother knows, peace can be a scarce commodity in a demanding, 21st-century world. How, then, can we find the peace that we so desperately desire? By turning our days and our lives over to God. Elisabeth Elliot writes, "If my life is surrendered to God, all is well. Let me not grab it back, as though it were in peril in His hand but would be safer in mine!" May we give our lives, our hopes, and our prayers to the Lord, and, by doing so, accept His will and His peace.

Mommy Milestone for Today

_____

_____

_____

_____

_____

_____

A Quote for Today

Our soul can never have rest in
things that are beneath itself.
—Juliana of Norwich

THE ABUNDANT LIFE

A thief comes to steal and kill and destroy,
but I came to give life—life in all its fullness.
—John 10:10 NCV

When Jesus talks of the abundant life, is He talking about material riches or earthly fame? Hardly. The Son of God came to this world not to give it prosperity but to give it salvation. Thankfully for Christians, our Savior's abundance is both spiritual and eternal; it never falters—even if we do—and it never dies. We need only to open our hearts to Him, and His grace becomes ours.

God's gifts are available to all, but they are not guaranteed; those gifts must be claimed by those who choose to follow Christ. As believers, we are free to accept God's gifts, or not; that choice, and the consequences that result from it, are ours and ours alone.

Today, as you meet the challenges of everyday life—and as you care for your precious baby—accept God's promise of spiritual abundance. Then, share Christ's peace with your family, with your friends, and with the world.

A Quote for Today

Jesus intended for us to be overwhelmed by the blessings of regular days. He said it was the reason he had come: "I am come that they might have life, and that they might have it more abundantly."

—Gloria Gaither

Mommy Milestone for Today

_____

_____

_____

_____

_____

YOU ARE TALENTED

*To acquire wisdom is to love oneself;
people who cherish understanding will prosper.*
—Proverbs 19:8 NLT

Mom, do you place a high value on your talents, your time, your capabilities, and your opportunities? If so, congratulations. But if you've acquired the insidious habit of devaluing your time, your work, or yourself, it's now time for a change. So if you've unintentionally been squandering opportunities or somehow selling yourself short, please do your yourself and your loved ones a favor by rethinking the way that you think about yourself (got that?).

No one can seize opportunities for you, and no one can build up your self-confidence if you're unwilling to believe in yourself. So, if you've been talking disrespectfully to yourself, stop; if you've been underestimating your talents, cease. You deserve better treatment from yourself . . . far better. And if you don't give yourself healthy respect, who will?

Mommy Milestone
for Today

_____

_____

_____

_____

_____

_____

A Quote for Today

Don't wish to be anything
but what you are,
and try to be that perfectly.
—St. Francis of Sales

ACCEPTANCE NOW

People may make plans in their minds,
but the Lord decides what they will do.
—Proverbs 16:9 NCV

Sometimes, we must accept life on its terms, not our own. Life has a way of unfolding, not as we will, but as it will. And sometimes, there is precious little we can do to change things.

When events transpire that are beyond our control, we have a choice: we can either learn the art of acceptance, or we can make ourselves miserable as we struggle to change the unchangeable.

We must entrust the things we cannot change to God. Once we have done so, we can prayerfully and faithfully tackle the important work that He has placed before us: doing something about the things we can change . . . and doing it sooner rather than later.

A Quote for Today

Part of waiting upon the Lord is telling God that you want only what He wants—whatever it is.

—Kay Arthur

Mommy Milestone for Today

_____

_____

_____

_____

_____

_____

SHARING THE GOOD NEWS

I will also make You a light of the nations so that
My salvation may reach to the end of the earth.
—Isaiah 49:6 NASB

Whether you realize it or not, you are on a personal mission for God. As a Christian mother, that mission is straightforward: Honor God, accept Christ as your Savior, raise your children in a loving, Christ-centered home, and be a servant to those who cross your path.

Of course, you will encounter impediments as you attempt to discover the exact nature of God's purpose for your life, but you must never lose sight of the overriding purposes that God has established for all believers. You will encounter these overriding purposes again and again as you worship your Creator and study His Word.

Every day offers countless opportunities to serve God and to worship Him. When you do so, He will bless you in miraculous ways. May you continue to seek God's will, may you trust His Word, and may you place Him where He belongs: at the very center of your life.

Mommy Milestone for Today

_____

_____

_____

_____

_____

_____

A Quote for Today

It never ceases to amaze me the way the Lord creates a bond among believers which reaches across continents, beyond race and color.

—Corrie ten Boom

LOVE WITH NO LIMITS

For I am persuaded that neither death nor life, nor angels nor principalities nor powers, nor things present nor things to come, nor height nor depth, nor any other created thing, shall be able to separate us from the love of God which is in Christ Jesus our Lord.
—Romans 8:38-39 NKJV

Even though we are imperfect, fallible human beings, even though we have fallen far short of God's commandments, Christ loves us still. His love is perfect; it does not waver—it does not change. Our task, as believers, is to accept Christ's love and to encourage others to do likewise.

In today's troubled world, we all need the love and the peace that is found through the Son of God. Thankfully, Christ's love has no limits. We, in turn, should love Him with no limits, beginning now and ending never.

A Quote for Today

No man ever loved like Jesus. He taught the blind to see and the dumb to speak. He died on the cross to save us. He bore our sins. And now God says, "Because He did, I can forgive you."
—Billy Graham

A Timely Tip

Jesus loves you and your baby. His love can—and should— be the cornerstone and the touchstone of your lives.

Mommy Milestone for Today

_____

_____

_____

_____

_____

_____

HE HAS A PLAN FOR YOU

*You will show me the path of life; in Your presence is fullness of joy;
at Your right hand are pleasures forevermore.*
—Psalm 16:11 NKJV

God has a plan for your life. He understands that plan as thoroughly and completely as He knows you. And, if you seek God's will earnestly and prayerfully, He will make His plans known to you in His own time and in His own way.

If you sincerely seek to live in accordance with God's will for your life, you will live in accordance with His commandments. You will study God's Word, and you will be watchful for His signs.

Sometimes, God's plans seem unmistakably clear to you. But other times, He may lead you through the wilderness before He directs you to the Promised Land. So be patient and keep seeking His will for your life. When you do, you'll be amazed at the marvelous things that an all-powerful, all-knowing God can do.

Mommy Milestone for Today

_____

_____

_____

_____

_____

_____

A Quote for Today

I'm convinced that there is nothing
that can happen to me in this life
that is not precisely designed
by a sovereign Lord to give me
the opportunity to learn
to know Him.

—Elisabeth Elliot

Joy Is . . .

*Rejoice evermore. Pray without ceasing. In every thing give thanks:
for this is the will of God in Christ Jesus concerning you.*
—1 Thessalonians 5:16-18 KJV

Are you a mother whose joy is evident for all to see? If so, congratulations: your joyful spirit serves as a powerful example to your family and friends. And because of your attitude, you may be assured that your children will indeed "rise up" and call you blessed (Proverbs 31:28).

Psalm 100 reminds us that, as believers, we have every reason to celebrate: "Shout for joy to the LORD, all the earth. Worship the LORD with gladness" (vv. 1-2 NIV). Yet sometimes, amid the inevitable hustle and bustle of life here on earth, we can forfeit—albeit temporarily—the joy that God intends for our lives.

God's plan for you and your family includes heaping helpings of abundance and joy. Claim them. And remember that Christ offers you and your family priceless gifts: His abundance, His peace, and His joy. Accept those gifts and share them freely, just as Christ has freely shared Himself with you.

A Quote for Today

Joy is a by-product not of happy circumstances, education or talent, but of a healthy relationship with God and a determination to love Him no matter what.

—Barbara Johnson

Mommy Milestone for Today

_____

_____

_____

_____

_____

_____

Day 334 • Today's Date _____

THE POWER OF PRAYER

*Don't worry about anything, but in everything, through prayer and
petition with thanksgiving, let your requests be made known to God.*
—Philippians 4:6 HCSB

"The power of prayer": these words are so familiar, yet sometimes we forget what they mean. Prayer is a powerful tool for communicating with our Creator; it is an opportunity to commune with the Giver of all things good. Prayer helps us find strength for today and hope for the future. Prayer is not a thing to be taken lightly or to be used infrequently.

Do you pray for your family "without ceasing," or do you talk to God less often than that?

The quality of your spiritual life will be in direct proportion to the quality of your prayer life. Prayer changes things, and it changes you. Today, instead of worrying about your next decision, ask God to lead the way. Don't limit your prayers to meals or to bedtime. Pray constantly about things great and small. God is listening, He wants to hear from you now, and the rest is up to you.

Mommy Milestone for Today

_____

_____

_____

_____

_____

A Quote for Today

Whatever may be our circumstances in life, may each one of us really believe that by way of the Throne we have unlimited power.

—Annie Armstrong

HOPE AND HAPPINESS

But happy are those . . . whose hope is in the LORD their God.
—Psalm 146:5 NLT

Hope and happiness are traveling companions. And if you're a Christian, you have every reason to be hopeful. After all, God is good; His love endures; and He has offered you the priceless gift of eternal life. But sometimes, in life's darker moments, you may lose sight of these blessings, and when you do, it's easy to lose hope.

When a suffering woman sought healing by merely touching the hem of His cloak, Jesus replied, "Daughter, be of good comfort; thy faith hath made thee whole" (Matthew 9:22 KJV). The message to believers is clear: if we are to be made whole by God, we must live by faith.

Are you a hope-filled mom? You should be. God has promised you peace, joy, and eternal life. And, of course, God keeps His promises today, tomorrow, and forever, amen!

A Timely Tip

If you want to find lasting
happiness, don't chase it.
Instead, do your duty,
obey your God, and wait for
happiness to find you.

Mommy Milestone
for Today

_____

_____

_____

_____

_____

THE GIFT OF FAMILY

These should learn first of all to put their religion into practice
by caring for their own family.
—1 Timothy 5:4 NIV

As every mother knows, family life is a mixture of conversations, mediations, irritations, deliberations, commiserations, frustrations, negotiations, and celebrations. In other words, the life of the typical mom is incredibly varied.

Certainly, in the life of every family, there are moments of frustration and disappointment. Lots of them. But, for those who are lucky enough to live in the presence of a close-knit, caring clan, the rewards far outweigh the frustrations.

No family is perfect, and neither is yours. But, despite the inevitable challenges and occasional hurt feelings of family life, your clan is God's gift to you. That little band of men, women, kids, and babies is a priceless treasure on temporary loan from the Father above. Give thanks to the Giver for the gift of family . . . and act accordingly.

Mommy Milestone for Today

_____

_____

_____

_____

_____

_____

A Quote for Today

He intended families to be the safe haven where children are born and raised, a place where the tender shoots are nurtured until their roots grow strong and deep.

—Carol Kuykendall

MAKING QUALITY CHOICES

I am offering you life or death, blessings or curses. Now, choose life! . . .
To choose life is to love the Lord your God, obey him,
and stay close to him.
—Deuteronomy 30:19-20 NCV

Every life, including yours, is a tapestry of choices. And the quality of your life depends, to a surprising extent, on the quality of the choices you make.

Would you like to enjoy a life of abundance and significance? If so, you must make choices that are pleasing to God.

From the instant you wake up in the morning until the moment you nod off to sleep at night, you make lots of decisions: decisions about the things you do, decisions about the ways you care for your family, decisions about the words you speak, and decisions about the thoughts you choose to think.

Today and every day, it's up to you (and only you) to make wise choices, choices that enhance your relationship with your God. After all, He deserves no less than your best . . . and so do you.

A Quote for Today

Freedom is not the right to do
what we want but the power
to do what we ought.
—Corrie ten Boom

Mommy Milestone for Today

_____

_____

_____

_____

_____

SERVICE AND LOVE

We know we love God's children if we love God
and obey his commandments.
—1 John 5:2 NLT

Few things in life are as precious or as enduring as a mother's love. Our mothers give us life, and they care for us. They nurture us when we are sick and encourage us when we're brokenhearted. Indeed, a mother's love is both powerful and priceless.

The words of 1 Corinthians 13 remind us that faith is important; so, too, is hope. But love is more important still. Christ showed His love for us on the cross, and, as Christians, we are called upon to return Christ's love by sharing it. Sometimes love is easy (puppies and sleeping children come to mind) and sometimes love is hard (fallible human beings come to mind). But God's Word is clear: We are to love our families and our neighbors without reservation or condition.

As a caring mother, you are not only shaping the lives of your loved ones, you are also, in a very real sense, reshaping eternity. It's a big job, a job so big, in fact, that God saw fit to entrust it to some of the most important people in His kingdom: loving moms like you.

Mommy Milestone for Today

_____

_____

_____

_____

_____

A Quote for Today

Inasmuch as love grows in you,
so beauty grows.
For love is the beauty of the soul.
—St. Augustine

HE CARES FOR YOU

Commit everything you do to the Lord.
Trust him, and he will help you.
—Psalm 37:5 NLT

Open your Bible to its center, and you'll find the Book of Psalms. In it are some of the most beautiful words ever translated into the English language, with none more beautiful than the 23rd Psalm. David describes God as being like a shepherd who cares for His flock. No wonder these verses have provided comfort and hope for generations of believers.

On occasion, Mom, you will confront circumstances that trouble you to the very core of your soul. When you are afraid, trust in God. When you are worried, turn your concerns over to Him. When you are anxious, be still and listen for the quiet assurance of God's promises. And then, place your life in His hands. He is your Shepherd today and throughout eternity. Trust the Shepherd.

A Quote for Today

Are you serious about wanting
God's guidance to become
the person he wants you to be?
The first step is to tell God that you
know you can't manage your own
life, that you need his help.
—Catherine Marshall

Mommy Milestone for Today

_____

_____

_____

_____

_____

_____

THE CORNERSTONE

For the Son of Man has come to save that which was lost.
—Matthew 18:11 NKJV

Mom, here's a very important question: Is Jesus the cornerstone of your family and life? The answer you give will determine the quality, the direction, the tone, and the ultimate destination of your life here on earth and your life throughout eternity.

Thomas Brooks spoke for believers of every generation when he observed, "Christ is the sun, and all the watches of our lives should be set by the dial of his motion." Christ, indeed, is the ultimate Savior of mankind and the personal Savior of those who believe in Him. As His servants, we should place Him at the very center of our lives. And every day that God gives us breath, we should share Christ's love and His message with a world that needs both.

A Quote for Today

A disciple is a follower of Christ. That means you take on His priorities as your own. His agenda becomes your agenda. His mission becomes your mission.
—Charles Stanley

Mommy Milestone for Today

_____

_____

_____

_____

_____

_____

HE IS NEVER DISTANT

Do not be afraid or discouraged.
For the LORD your God is with you wherever you go.
—Joshua 1:9 NLT

If you are a busy mother with a newborn baby and more obligations than you have time to count, you know all too well that the demands of everyday life can, on occasion, seem overwhelming. Thankfully, even on the days when you feel over-burdened, over-worked, over-stressed, and under-appreciated, God is trying to get His message through . . . your job is to listen.

Are you tired, or frustrated, or discouraged? Be comforted because God is with you. Carve out moments of silent solitude to celebrate God's gifts and to experience His presence.

The familiar words of Psalm 46:10 remind us to "Be still, and know that I am God." When we do, we encounter the awesome presence of our loving Heavenly Father, and we are comforted in the knowledge that God is not just near. He is here.

A Quote for Today

When all else is gone, God is left, and nothing changes Him.
—Hannah Whitall Smith

Mommy Milestone for Today

_____

_____

_____

_____

_____

_____

GOD'S SUFFICIENCY

My grace is sufficient for you,
for My strength is made perfect in weakness.
—2 Corinthians 12:9 NKJV

Of this you can be certain: God is sufficient to meet your needs. Period.

Do the demands of motherhood seem overwhelming at times? If so, you must learn to rely not only upon your own resources but also upon the promises of your Father in heaven. God will hold your hand and walk with you and your family if you let Him. So even if your circumstances are difficult, trust the Father.

The Psalmist writes, "Weeping may endure for a night, but joy comes in the morning" (Psalm 30:5 NKJV). But when we are suffering, the morning may seem very far away. It is not. God promises that He is "near to those who have a broken heart" (Psalm 34:18 NKJV). When we are troubled, we must turn to Him, and we must encourage our friends and family members to do likewise.

If you are discouraged by the inevitable demands of life here on earth, be mindful of this fact: the loving heart of God is sufficient to meet any challenge . . . including yours.

Mommy Milestone for Today

_____

_____

_____

_____

_____

_____

A Quote for Today

God is always sufficient in perfect proportion to our need.

—Beth Moore

IF HE RETURNED TODAY

But the Day of the Lord will come like a thief; on that day the heavens will pass away with a loud noise, the elements will burn and be dissolved, and the earth and the works on it will be disclosed . . . .
Therefore, dear friends, while you wait for these things, make every effort to be found in peace without spot or blemish before Him.
—2 Peter 3:10, 14 HCSB

When will our Lord return? The Bible clearly states that the day and the hour of Christ's return is known only to God. Therefore, we must conduct our lives as if He were returning today.

If Jesus were to return this instant, would you be ready? Would you be proud of your actions, your thoughts, your relationships, and your prayers? If not, you must face up to a harsh reality: even if Christ does not return to earth today, He may call you home today! And if He does so, you must be prepared.

Have you given your heart to the resurrected Savior? If the answer to that question is anything other than an unqualified "yes," then accept Him as your personal Savior before you close this book.

A Quote for Today

How important it is for us—young and old—to live as if Jesus would return any day—to set our goals, make our choices, raise our children, and conduct business with the perspective of the imminent return of our Lord.
—Gloria Gaither

Mommy Milestone for Today

_____

_____

_____

_____

_____

_____

Planning (and Working) for the Future

The plans of the diligent certainly lead to profit,
but anyone who is reckless only becomes poor.
—Proverbs 21:5 HCSB

Are you willing to plan for the future—and are you willing to work diligently to accomplish the plans that you've made? The Book of Proverbs teaches that the plans of hardworking people (like you) are rewarded.

If you desire to reap a bountiful harvest for your baby, for your family, and for yourself, you must plan for the future while entrusting the final outcome to God. Then, you must do your part to make the future better (by working dutifully), while acknowledging the sovereignty of God's hands over all affairs, including your own.

Are you in a hurry for success to arrive at your doorstep? Don't be. Instead, work carefully, plan thoughtfully, and wait patiently. Remember that you're not the only one working on your behalf: God, too, is at work. And with Him as your partner, your ultimate success is guaranteed.

Mommy Milestone for Today

_____

_____

_____

_____

_____

_____

A Quote for Today

Allow your dreams a place in your prayers and plans. God-given dreams can help you move into the future He is preparing for you.

—Barbara Johnson

SMILE

Happy are those who fear the Lord.
Yes, happy are those who delight in doing what he commands.
—Psalm 112:1 NLT

Okay, Mom, it's been a typical day. You've cared for your newborn, worked your fingers to the bone, rushed from Point A to Point Z, and taken barely a moment for yourself. But have you taken time to smile? If so, you're a very wise woman. If not, it's time to slow down, take a deep breath, and recount your blessings!

God has promised all of us the opportunity to experience spiritual abundance and peace. But it's up to each of us to claim the spiritual riches that God has in store. God promises us a life of fulfillment and joy, but He does not force His joy upon us.

Would you like to experience the peace and the joy that God intends for you? Then accept His Son and lay claim to His promises. And then, put a smile on your face that stretches all the way down to your heart. When you do, you'll discover that when you smile at God, He smiles back.

A Quote for Today

A joyful heart is like a sunshine of God's love, the hope of eternal happiness, a burning flame of God. And if we pray, we will become that sunshine of God's love—in our own home, the place where we live, and in the world at large.

—Mother Teresa

Mommy Milestone for Today

_____

_____

_____

_____

_____

SEEKING GOD

You will seek me and find me when you seek me with all your heart.
—Jeremiah 29:13 NIV

The familiar words of Matthew 6 remind us that, as believers, we must seek God and His kingdom. And when we seek Him with our hearts open and our prayers lifted, we need not look far: God is with us always.

Sometimes, however, in the crush of our daily duties, God may seem far away, but He is not. God is everywhere we have ever been and everywhere we will ever go. He is with us night and day; He knows our thoughts and our prayers. And, when we earnestly seek Him, we will find Him because He is here, waiting patiently for us to reach out to Him.

Today, let us reach out to the Giver of all blessings. Let us turn to Him for guidance and for strength. Today, may we, who have been given so much, seek God and invite Him into every aspect of our lives. And, let us remember that no matter our circumstances, God never leaves us; He is here . . . always right here.

Mommy Milestone for Today

_____

_____

_____

_____

_____

A Quote for Today

Whatever it takes, fellow seeker after God's heart, do what you must to be alone with God so that He can fine-tune your heart to His.

—Elizabeth George

RESPECTING YOUR TALENTS

Every good gift and every perfect gift is from above,
and cometh down from the Father of lights.
—James 1:17 KJV

Okay, Mom, here's an important question: Do you place a high value on your talents, your time, your capabilities, and your opportunities? If so, congratulations. But if you've acquired the insidious habit of devaluing your time, your work, or yourself, it's now time for a change.

Pearl Bailey correctly observed, "The first and worst of all frauds is to cheat one's self. All sin is easy after that."

If you've been squandering opportunities or selling yourself short, it's time to rethink the way that you think about yourself and your opportunities. No one can seize those opportunities for you, and no one can build up your self-confidence if you're unwilling to believe in yourself. So if you've been talking yourself down, stop. You deserve better. And if you don't give yourself healthy respect, who will?

A Quote for Today

One of Satan's most effective ploys is to make us believe that we are small, insignificant, and worthless.

—Susan Lenzkes

Mommy Milestone for Today

_____

_____

_____

_____

_____

_____

Ask Him

Ask in my name, according to my will, and he'll most certainly give it to you. Your joy will be a river overflowing its banks!
—John 16:24 MSG

God gives the gifts; we, as believers, should accept them—but oftentimes, we don't. Why? Because we fail to trust our Heavenly Father completely, and because we are, at times, surprisingly stubborn. Luke 11 teaches us that God does not withhold spiritual gifts from those who ask. Our obligation, quite simply, is to ask for them.

Are you a woman who asks God to move mountains for your family, or are you expecting Him to stumble over molehills? Whatever the size of your challenges, God is big enough to handle them. Ask for His help today, with faith and with fervor, and then watch in amazement as your mountains begin to move.

Mommy Milestone for Today

_____

_____

_____

_____

_____

A Quote for Today

When will we realize that we're not troubling God with our questions and concerns? His heart is open to hear us—his touch nearer than our next thought—as if no one in the world existed but us. Our very personal God wants to hear from us personally.

—Gigi Graham Tchividjian

TRUSTING HIS TIMING

Therefore humble yourselves under the mighty hand of God,
that He may exalt you in due time.
—1 Peter 5:6 NKJV

If you sincerely seek to be a woman of faith, then you must learn to trust God's timing. You will be sorely tempted, however, to do otherwise. Because you are a fallible human being, you are impatient for things to happen. But, God knows better.

God has created a world that unfolds according to His own timetable, not ours . . . thank goodness! We mortals might make a terrible mess of things. God does not.

God's plan does not always happen in the way that we would like or at the time of our own choosing. Our task—as believing Christians who trust in a benevolent, all-knowing Father—is to wait patiently for God to reveal Himself. And reveal Himself He will. Always. But until God's perfect plan is made known, we must walk in faith and never lose hope. And we must continue to trust Him. Always.

A Quote for Today

When we read of the great Biblical leaders, we see that it was not uncommon for God to ask them to wait, not just a day or two, but for years, until God was ready for them to act.
—Gloria Gaither

Mommy Milestone for Today

_____

_____

_____

_____

_____

_____

PRAISE HIM

And those who have reason to be thankful should
continually sing praises to the Lord.
—James 5:13 NLT

Being a new mom is all-consuming, all-encompassing, and downright exhausting. So, it's understandable that sometimes, in the rush "to get everything done," you simply may not stop long enough to pause and thank your Creator for the countless blessings He has bestowed upon you and your loved ones. But when you slow down and express gratitude to your Father in heaven, you will most certainly enrich your own life and the lives of your family and friends.

Thanksgiving should become a habit, a regular part of your daily routine. After all, God has blessed your family beyond measure. And, He has offered you a priceless gift: your new baby. So take time to thank Him many times each day. He deserves your praise, and you deserve the experience of praising Him.

Mommy Milestone for Today

_____

_____

_____

_____

_____

_____

A Timely Tip

Remember that it always pays
to praise your Creator.
That's why thoughtful moms
(like you) make it a habit to carve
out quiet moments throughout
the day to praise God.

LIVING RIGHTEOUSLY

But now you must be holy in everything you do, just as God—
who chose you to be his children—is holy. For he himself has said,
"You must be holy because I am holy."
—1 Peter 1:15-16 NLT

When we seek righteousness in our own lives—and when we seek the companionship of those who do likewise—we reap the spiritual rewards that God intends for us to enjoy. When we behave ourselves as godly believers, we honor God. When we live righteously and according to God's commandments, He blesses us in ways that we cannot fully understand.

Today, as you fulfill your responsibilities to your baby and to your family, hold fast to that which is good, and associate yourself with believers who do likewise. Then, your good works will serve as a powerful example to others and as a worthy offering to your Creator.

A Quote for Today

Do nothing that you would not like
to be doing when Jesus comes.
Go no place where you
would not like to be found
when He returns.

—Corrie ten Boom

Mommy Milestone for Today

_____

_____

_____

_____

_____

_____

YOUR RESPONSE TO HIS LOVE

This is how much God loved the world: He gave his Son,
his one and only Son. And this is why: so that no one need be destroyed;
by believing in him anyone can have a whole and lasting life.
—John 3:16 MSG

As a mother, you know the profound love that you hold in your heart for your baby. As a child of God, you can only imagine the infinite love that your Heavenly Father holds for you.

God made you in His own image and gave you salvation through the person of His Son, Jesus Christ. And now, precisely because you are a wondrous creation treasured by God, a question presents itself: What will you do in response to the Creator's love? Will you ignore it or embrace it? Will you return it or neglect it? That decision, of course, is yours and yours alone.

When you embrace God's love, you are forever changed. When you embrace God's love, you feel differently about yourself, your neighbors, your family, and your world. More importantly, you share God's message—and His love—with others.

Your Heavenly Father—a God of infinite love and mercy—is waiting to embrace you with open arms. Accept His love today and forever.

Mommy Milestone for Today

_____

_____

_____

_____

_____

_____

A Quote for Today

When you invite the love of God
into your heart, everything in
the world looks different,
including you.
—Marie T. Freeman

HE PERSEVERED AND SO MUST WE

If you do nothing in a difficult time, your strength is limited.
—Proverbs 24:10 HCSB

Someone once said, "Life is a marathon, not a sprint." The same can be said for motherhood. Motherhood requires courage, perseverance, determination, and, of course, an unending supply of motherly love. Are you tired? Ask God for strength. Are you discouraged? Believe in His promises. Are you frustrated or fearful? Pray as if everything depended upon God, and work as if everything depended upon you. With God's help, you will find the strength to be the kind of mom who makes her Heavenly Father beam with pride.

A Quote for Today

Your life is not a boring stretch
of highway. It's a straight line
to heaven. And just look at
the fields ripening along the way.
Look at the tenacity and endurance.
Look at the grains of righteousness.
You'll have quite a crop at
harvest . . . so don't give up!
—Joni Eareckson Tada

Mommy Milestone for Today

_____

_____

_____

_____

_____

_____

DIFFICULT DECISIONS

Now if any of you lacks wisdom, he should ask God, who gives to all
generously and without criticizing, and it will be given to him.
—James 1:5 HCSB

As the mother of a newborn, you have so many choices to make. Some of those choices are straightforward; others are not.

Are you facing a difficult decision? If so, it's time to step back, to stop focusing on the world, and to focus, instead, on the will of your Father in heaven. The world will often lead you astray, but God will not. His counsel leads you to Himself, which, of course, is the path He has always intended for you to take.

Raising a child in today's troubled world requires wisdom. If you're uncertain of your next step, pray about it. When you do, answers will come. And you may rest assured that when God answers prayer, His answers are the right ones for you.

Mommy Milestone for Today

_____

_____

_____

_____

_____

A Quote for Today

The principle of making no decision without prayer keeps me from rushing in and committing myself before I consult God.

—Elizabeth George

God Is at Work

The Lord will work out his plans for my life—for your faithful love,
O Lord, endures forever.
—Psalm 138:8 NLT

Whether you realize it or not, God is busily working in you and through you. He has things He wants you to do and people He wants you to help. Your assignment, should you choose to accept it, is to seek the will of God and to follow it.

Elisabeth Elliot said, "I believe that in every time and place it is within our power to acquiesce in the will of God—and what peace it brings to do so!" And Corrie ten Boom observed, "Surrendering to the Lord is not a tremendous sacrifice, not an agonizing performance. It is the most sensible thing you can do."

So, as you make plans for your baby, for your family, and for your future, make sure that your plans conform to God's plans—that's the safest and best way to live.

A Quote for Today

God has no problems, only plans.
There is never panic in heaven.
—Corrie ten Boom

Mommy Milestone for Today

_____

_____

_____

_____

_____

_____

PASSION FOR LIFE

Never be lacking in zeal, but keep your spiritual fervor,
serving the Lord.

—Romans 12:11 NIV

Are you passionate about your life, your loved ones, your work, and your faith? As a believer who has been saved by a risen Christ, you should be.

As a Christian mom, you have every reason to be enthusiastic about life, but sometimes the struggles of caring for a new baby, and the rigors of everyday living, may cause you to feel decidedly unenthusiastic. If you feel that your zest for life is slowly fading away, it's time to slow down, to rest, to count your blessings, and to pray. When you feel worried or weary, you must pray fervently for God to renew your sense of wonderment and excitement.

Life with God is a glorious adventure; revel in it. When you do, God will most certainly smile upon your work and your life.

Mommy Milestone for Today

_____

_____

_____

_____

_____

_____

A Quote for Today

Gratitude unlocks the fullness of life. It turns what we have into enough, and more. It turns denial into acceptance, chaos to order, confusion to clarity. It can turn a meal into a feast, a house into a home, a stranger into a friend. Gratitude makes sense of our past, brings peace for today, and creates a vision for tomorrow.

—Melody Beattie

TOO MUCH WORK AND TOO LITTLE TIME?

Don't burn out; keep yourselves fueled and aflame.
Be alert servants of the Master, cheerfully expectant.
Don't quit in hard times; pray all the harder.
—Romans 12:11-12 MSG

With a young baby in the house, the work is never completely done. Even if you rush through the day without a moment to spare, even if you work harder than you've ever worked in your life, some tasks remain unfinished.

God gives each of us enough time to do the things He intends for us to do. But sometimes, we want to do more. And because we take on too many opportunities—or because we focus too intently on the wrong opportunities—we suffer. A better strategy, of course, is to do the things that should be done and to leave undone the things that shouldn't.

Today, ask God to help you to prioritize your work and your life. And while you're at it, please remember that the better part of wisdom is often knowing what not to do.

A Quote for Today

Getting things accomplished isn't nearly as important as taking time for love.
—Janette Oke

Mommy Milestone for Today

_____

_____

_____

_____

_____

Prayer Is the Answer

Be cheerful no matter what; pray all the time;
thank God no matter what happens. This is the way God wants you
who belong to Christ Jesus to live.
—1 Thessalonians 5:16-18 MSG

Whatever the question, prayer is the answer. Do you seek a more peaceful life? Then you must lead a prayerful life. Do you seek the serenity for yourself and your loved ones that only God can provide? Ask and you'll receive. Do you sincerely seek the gift of everlasting love and eternal life? Accept the grace of God's only begotten Son.

When you weave the habit of prayer into the very fabric of your day, you invite God to become a partner in every aspect of your life. When you consult God on an constant basis, you avail yourself of His wisdom, His strength, and His love. And, because God answers prayers according to His perfect timetable, your petitions to Him will transform your family, your world, and yourself.

Mommy Milestone for Today

_____

_____

_____

_____

_____

A Quote for Today

The center of power is not to
be found in summit meetings or
in peace conferences. It is not
in Peking or Washington or the
United Nations, but rather where
a child of God prays in the power of
the Spirit for God's will to be
done in her life, in her home,
and in the world around her.

—Ruth Bell Graham

ACCEPTING CHRIST

*We know very well that we are not set right with God
by rule-keeping but only through personal faith in Jesus Christ.*
—Galatians 2:16 MSG

God's love for you is deeper and more profound than you can imagine. God's love for you is so great that He sent His only Son to this earth to die for your sins and to offer you the priceless gift of eternal life. Now, you must decide whether or not to accept God's gift. Will you ignore it or embrace it? Will you return it or neglect it? Will you accept Christ, or will you turn from Him?

Your decision to accept Christ is the pivotal decision of your life. It is a decision that you cannot ignore. And, it is a decision that is yours and yours alone. It is a decision with profound consequences, not just for you, but also for your loved ones. Accept God's gift: Accept Christ today.

A Quote for Today

Surrender to the Lord is not a tremendous sacrifice, not an agonizing performance. It is the most sensible thing you can do.

—Corrie ten Boom

Mommy Milestone for Today

_____

_____

_____

_____

_____

_____

HIS PATH

The LORD says, "I will guide you along the best pathway for your life.
I will advise you and watch over you."
—Psalm 32:8 NLT

How will you respond to Christ's sacrifice? Will you take up His cross and follow Him (Luke 9:23), or will you choose another path? When you place your hopes squarely at the foot of the cross, when you place Jesus squarely at the center of your life, you will be blessed.

The 19th-century writer Hannah Whitall Smith observed, "The crucial question for each of us is this: What do you think of Jesus, and do you yet have a personal acquaintance with Him?" Indeed, the answer to that question determines the quality, the course, and the direction of our lives today and for all eternity.

Let us put down our old ways and pick up His cross. Let us walk the path that He walked.

Mommy Milestone for Today

_____

_____

_____

_____

_____

_____

A Quote for Today

Experience has taught me that the Shepherd is far more willing to show His sheep the path than the sheep are to follow. He is endlessly merciful, patient, tender, and loving. If we, His stupid and wayward sheep, really want to be led, we will without fail be led. Of that I am sure.

—Elisabeth Elliot

LET YOUR CONSCIENCE BE YOUR GUIDE

I will maintain my righteousness and never let go of it;
my conscience will not reproach me as long as I live.
—Job 27:6 NIV

Few things in life provide more comfort than a clear conscience. In fact, a clear conscience is one of the undeniable blessings that you earn whenever you allow God to guide your path through the trials and temptations of everyday life.

Have you formed the habit of listening carefully to that little voice inside your head? And when you hear what your conscience has to say, do you behave yourself accordingly? Hopefully so, because that little voice has much to teach you about the choices you decide to make and the life you decide to live. So today, as you make countless choices about the things you do and the things you say, let your conscience be your guide. When you do, you'll never stay lost for long.

A Quote for Today

There is a balance to be maintained
in situations. That balance is
the Holy Spirit within us to guide
us into the truth of each situation
and circumstance in which we find
ourselves. He will provide us the
wisdom to know when we are to be
adaptable and adjustable and
when we are to take a firm stand
and be immovable.

—Joyce Meyer

Mommy Milestone for Today

_____

_____

_____

_____

_____

_____

NEW BEGINNINGS

Do not remember the former things, nor consider the things of old.
Behold, I will do a new thing.
—Isaiah 43:18-19 NKJV

Each new day offers countless opportunities to serve God, to seek His will, and to obey His teachings. But each day also offers countless opportunities to stray from God's commandments and to wander far from His path.

Sometimes, we wander aimlessly in a wilderness of our own making, but God has better plans for us. And, whenever we ask Him to renew our strength and guide our steps, He does so.

Consider this day a new beginning. Consider it a fresh start, a renewed opportunity to serve your family and your Creator with willing hands and a loving heart. Ask God to renew your sense of purpose as He guides your steps. Today is a glorious opportunity to serve God. Seize that opportunity while you can; tomorrow may indeed be too late.

Mommy Milestone for Today

_____

_____

_____

_____

_____

_____

A Quote for Today

The amazing thing about
Jesus is that He doesn't just
patch up our lives, He gives us
a brand new sheet,
a clean slate to start over,
all new.

—Gloria Gaither

YOUR PRICELESS TREASURES

*He put a child in the middle of the room. Then, cradling the little one
in his arms, he said, "Whoever embraces one of these children as
I do embraces me, and far more than me—God who sent me."*
—Mark 9:36-37 MSG

As a new mom, you are keenly aware that God has entrusted you with a priceless treasure from above: your baby. Every child is different, yet every child is similar in this respect: every child is a glorious gift from above—and with that gift comes immense responsibilities.

Thoughtful mothers (like you) understand the critical importance of raising their children with love, with family, with discipline, and with God. By making God a focus in the home, loving mothers offer a priceless legacy to their children—a legacy of hope, a legacy of love, a legacy of wisdom.

Today, let us pray for our children . . . all of them. Let us pray for our own children and for children around the world. Every child is God's child. May we, as concerned mothers, behave—and pray—accordingly.

A Quote for Today

Kids are great. They are exciting.
Their potential is simply
phenomenal. And in any given
family there is the potential to
change the world for God.
—Maxine Hancock

Mommy Milestone for Today

_____

_____

_____

_____

_____

THE GREAT COMMISSION

*Go, therefore, and make disciples of all nations, baptizing them
in the name of the Father and of the Son and of the Holy Spirit,
teaching them to observe everything I have commanded you.
And remember, I am with you always, to the end of the age.*
—Matthew 28:19-20 HCSB

Are you a bashful Christian, one who is afraid to speak up for your Savior? Do you leave it up to others to share their testimonies while you stand on the sidelines, reluctant to share yours? Too many of us are slow to obey the last commandment of the risen Christ; we don't do our best to "make disciples of all the nations."

Christ's Great Commission applies to Christians of every generation, including our own. As believers, we are commanded to share the Good News with our children, with our families, with our neighbors, and with the world. Jesus invited His disciples to become fishers of men. We, too, must accept the Savior's invitation, and we must do so today. Tomorrow may indeed be too late.

Mommy Milestone for Today

_____

_____

_____

_____

_____

_____

A Quote for Today

Our commission is quite specific.
We are told to be His witness to
all nations. For us, as His disciples,
to refuse any part of this commission
frustrates the love of Jesus Christ,
the Son of God.

—Catherine Marshall

PRAISE FOR MOM

Her children rise up and call her blessed.
—Proverbs 31:28 NKJV

Dear Mom,
　　Thanks for the love, the care, the work, the discipline, the wisdom, the support, and the faith. Thanks for being a concerned parent and a worthy example. Thanks for giving life and for teaching it. Thanks for being patient with me, even when you were tired or frustrated—or both. Thanks for changing diapers and wiping away tears. And thanks for being a godly woman, one worthy of our admiration and our love.

　　You deserve a smile today, Mom, but you deserve so much more. You deserve our family's undying gratitude. And, you deserve God's love, His grace, and His peace. May you enjoy God's blessings always, and may you never, ever forget how much we love you.

Signed,
　　Your New Baby and Your Loving Family

A Quote for Today

The woman is the heart
of the home.
—Mother Teresa

Mommy Milestone
for Today

_____

_____

_____

_____

_____

More from God's Word about Children

Fix these words of mine in your hearts and minds. Teach them to your children, talking about them when you sit at home and when you walk along the road, when you lie down and when you get up.
—Deuteronomy 11:18-19 NIV

Train up a child in the way he should go, and when he is old he will not depart from it.
—Proverbs 22:6 NKJV

Love the Lord your God with all your heart, with all your soul, and with all your strength. These words that I am giving you today are to be in your heart. Repeat them to your children. Talk about them when you sit in your house and when you walk along the road, when you lie down and when you get up.
—Deuteronomy 6:5-7 HCSB

Children's children are the crown of old men; and the glory of children are their fathers.
—Proverbs 17:6 KJV

Even a child is known by his actions, by whether his conduct is pure and right.
—Proverbs 20:11 NIV

Children are a gift from the LORD; they are a reward from him.
—Psalm 127:4 NLT

MORE GREAT IDEAS ABOUT CHILDREN

Let us look upon our children; let us love them and train them
as children of the covenant and children of the promise.
These are the children of God.

—Andrew Murray

Children desperately need to know and hear in ways
they understand and remember that they're loved
and valued by Mom and Dad.

—Gary Smalley & John Trent

Each child is unique, a special creation of God with talents, abilities,
personality, preference, dislikes, potentials, strengths, weaknesses,
and skills that are his or her own. As parents, we must seek
to identify these in each of our children and help them become
the persons God intended.

—Dave Veerman

Children must be valued as our most priceless possession.

—James Dobson

Praying for our children is a noble task. There is nothing more
special, more precious, than time that a parent spends struggling and
pondering with God on behalf of a child.

—Max Lucado

The best thing to spend on your children is "time."

—Anonymous

More from God's Word about Patience

It is better to be patient than powerful;
it is better to have self-control than to conquer a city.
—Proverbs 16:32 NLT

A person's insight gives him patience,
and his virtue is to overlook an offense.
—Proverbs 19:11 HCSB

I wait quietly before God, for my salvation comes from him.
He alone is my rock and my salvation,
my fortress where I will never be shaken.
—Psalm 62:1-2 NLT

Therefore the Lord is waiting to show you mercy,
and is rising up to show you compassion, for the Lord is a just God.
Happy are all who wait patiently for Him.
—Isaiah 30:18 HCSB

God has chosen you and made you his holy people. He loves you.
So always do these things:
Show mercy to others, be kind, humble, gentle, and patient.
—Colossians 3:12 NCV

Be gentle to everyone, able to teach, and patient.
—2 Timothy 2:23 HCSB

MORE GREAT IDEAS ABOUT PATIENCE

Those who have had to wait and work for happiness
seem to enjoy it more, because they never take it for granted.
—Barbara Johnson

When there is perplexity there is always guidance—
not always at the moment we ask, but in good time,
which is God's time. There is no need to fret and stew.
—Elisabeth Elliot

If only we could be as patient with other people as God is with us!
—Jim Gallery

The only person who doesn't need patience is the one who can
control all the people and circumstances in life—
and no such person exists.
—Warren Wiersbe

Patience endurance attains to all things.
The one who possesses God is lacking in nothing;
God alone is enough.
—St. Teresa of Avila

Be patient and understanding.
Life is too short to be vengeful or malicious.
—Phillips Brooks

More from God's Word about Love

Love one another deeply, from the heart.
—1 Peter 1:22 NIV

The one who does not love does not know God, because God is love.
—1 John 4:8 HCSB

Love is patient; love is kind. Love does not envy; is not boastful;
is not conceited; does not act improperly; is not selfish; is not provoked;
does not keep a record of wrongs; finds no joy in unrighteousness,
but rejoices in the truth; bears all things, believes all things,
hopes all things, endures all things.
—1 Corinthians 13:4-7 HCSB

May the Lord cause you to increase and abound in love for one another,
and for all people.
—1 Thessalonians 3:12 NASB

A new commandment I give to you, that you love one another;
as I have loved you, that you also love one another.
—John 13:34 NKJV

Now these three remain: faith, hope, and love.
But the greatest of these is love.
—1 Corinthians 13:13 HCSB

MORE GREAT IDEAS ABOUT LOVE

Love is the laughter of God.
—Beth Moore

Life without love is empty and meaningless no matter
how gifted we are.
—Charles Stanley

You always win a better response with love.
—Helen Hosier

Since love grows within you, so beauty grows.
For love is the beauty of the soul.
—St. Augustine

There is no better or more necessary work than love.
We have been created for love.
—St. John of the Cross

Love seeks one thing only: the good of the one loved.
It leaves all the other secondary effects to take care of themselves.
Love, therefore, is its own reward.
—Thomas Merton

To love another person is to see the face of God.
—Victor Hugo

And whoever welcomes
a little child like this
in my name welcomes me.
—

Matthew 18:5 NIV

Welcome My Baby!

A Mother's Prayer for the New Baby:

_____

_____

_____

_____

_____

_____

_____

_____

_____

_____

_____

_____

_____

Amen

WELCOME MY BABY!

A Father's Prayer for the New Baby:

_____

_____

_____

_____

_____

_____

_____

_____

_____

_____

_____

_____

_____

_____

_____

_____

Amen

Here I Am!

Baby's full name: _____

Weight: _____ Length: _____

Date and Time of birth: _____

Hair color: _____ Eye color: _____

Birthmarks: _____

_____

Special comments about first sounds or moments in the delivery
room:

_____

_____

_____

_____

_____

_____

_____

Who held baby first:

_____

The first time I heard
your cry, the first sound
from your mouth,
it was music to my ears!

*Let every living thing
that has breath
praise the LORD!*
—Psalm 150:6 NKJV

Baby's Family Tree

Baby's name: _____

Mother's name: _____

Father's name: _____

Maternal Grandmother: _____

Maternal Grandfather: _____

Paternal Grandmother: _____

Paternal Grandfather: _____

Brothers and Sisters: _____

_____

_____

For You formed my inward parts;
You covered me in my mother's womb.
I will praise You, for I am fearfully and wonderfully made.
Marvelous are Your works, and That my soul knows very well.

—

Psalm 139:13-14 NKJV